Hippies, Skinheads, Rastas, Punks, and Disco Dancing Bowie Boot Boys

Screening Youth Subcultures 1967-1985

Ian Dobson

FLOWMOTION PRESS

Published by Flowmotion Press 2020

Copyright © Ian Dobson 2020
All rights reserved

Contact: iankeithdobson@gmail.com

ISBN: 978-0-9934314-1-8

CONTENTS

1. UNWASHED AND SOMEWHAT SLIGHTLY DAZED — 13
CHILDREN OF THE REVOLUTION
if... (1968), Melody (1971)
POWER TO THE PEOPLE
The Breaking of Bumbo (1970), What Became of Jack & Jill (1971)
URBAN GUERRILLA
Little Malcomn & His Struggle Against the Eunuchs (1974)
YESTERDAYS PAPERS
The Trials of Oz (1991)

2. IT'S DIFFERENT FOR GIRLS — 59
HELLO DOLLY
Her Private Hell (1968), The Yes Girls (1970), Cool It Carol (1971), Au Pair Girls (1972)
BACKSTAGE PASS
The Touchables (1968), Groupie Girl (1970), Permissive (1970)
DOCTORS OF MADNESS
In Two Minds (1967), Family Life (1971). Equus (1977)
MAXWELL'S SILVER HAMMER
Twisted Nerve (1968), I Start Counting (1979), Goodbye Gemini (1970), Whirlpool (1970), Straight On Til Morning (1972)
MY SWEET LORD
Two A Penny (1967), Made (1972)
SYMPATHY FOR THE DEVIL
Legend Of The Witches (1970), Secret Rites (1971). Dracula AD 1972 (1972)
MOTORBIKIN'
Psychomania (1972), Bank Holiday (1971)

3. SKINHEAD MOONSTOMP — 115
Softly Softly Taskforce (1970-71), Bronco Bullfrog (1970)
LIKE CLOCKWORK
A Clockwork Orange (1971), 16 Years Of Alcohol (2004), Small Faces (1996), Neds (2010), Just A Boys Game (1979)

4. BABYLON'S BURNING — 154
STAND AND DELIVER
TOO MUCH PRESSURE
Pressure (1975), A Hole In Babylon (1979)
BASS CULTURE
Dread Beat & Blood (1979), Babylon (1980)

DI GREAT INSHORECKSHUN
    Handsworth Songs (1986), London's Burning (1986),
    Sammy and Rosie Get Laid (1987)

5. ALL THE YOUNG DUDES   191
    Velvet Goldmine (1998), Flame (1975), Side By Side (1975),
    Never Too Young to Rock (1975), Three For All (1975)

YOU SHOULD BE DANCING
    The Stud (1978), The Bitch (1979), The Music Machine (1979),
    Soulboy (2010), Northern Soul (2014)

ANARCHY IN THE UK
    Young Soul Rebels (1991), The Buddha of Suburbia (1993)

THE QUEEN IS DEAD
    Jubilee (1978)

GOD SAVE THE QUEEN
    The Great Rock n Roll Swindle (1979), Sid & Nancy (1980),
    How To Talk To Girls At Parties (2017), Good Vibrations (2012)

CAREER OPPORTUNITIES
    Rude Boy (1980), London Town (2016)

TRAIN IN VAIN
    The Siege of Golden Hill (1975), Barbarians (1977), Bloody Kids (1979),
    Noah's Castle (1980)

I AM A POSEUR
    Breaking Glass (1980), Worried About the Boy (2010), Hunting Venus (1999),
    Jangles (1982)

6. WHERE HAVE ALL THE BOOTBOYS GONE?   273
AIN'T GONNA TAKE IT
    King of the Ghetto (1986), My Beautiful Launderette (1985)

OI! OI! OI!
    Farming (2018), Oi For England (1982), Made in Britain (1982),
    Treatment (1984)

YOUNG SAVAGE
    Awaydays (2008), The Firm (2009)

STAND DOWN MARGARET
    Johnny Jarvis (1983), This Is England (2006)

Hippies, Skinheads, Rastas, Punks & Disco Dancing Bowie Boot Boys

Whatever Happened to?
(Dial, Shelley)

INTRODUCTION

When it comes to depicting the nation's youth for its cinema screens, UK filmmakers have always been overshadowed by their cousins across the Atlantic. It's not difficult to see why when they could provide not only seemingly endless summers but also open topped sports cars to enjoy them in.

As the teenager came into his rebellious own in the 1950s the Americans quickly gained the upper hand. They had Marlon Brando, James Dean and Elvis to represent their popcorn munching youths, we had Tommy Steele, Melvyn Hayes*, and Cliff. But, unable to generate the required degree of cool and menace from our home-grown movie stars, the youth of London's East End opted to fill that void themselves with the birth of what became known as the Teddy Boy whose combination of outlandish sartorial elegance and menacing swagger put the fear of God into Telegraph readers across the land. However, it wasn't the pupils of the East End's Worrell Street School in *Spare The Rod* (1961) that had them slashing seats and dancing in the aisles; it was those of New York's North Manual High School in *The Blackboard Jungle* (1955).

Both these films were based on best-selling novels by ex-teachers drawing on their own experiences in tough working-class schools, and both were considered hard-hitting and controversial. They nevertheless found their ways into cinemas six years apart, despite producer Ronald Neame having picked up the rights to 'Spare The Rod' as early as the Spring of its year of publication. This says much about the paucity of drape jacketed, drainpipe trousered screen rebels for their similarly attired counterparts in the front stalls to cheer on.

The problem in this case was that in an age when films were vetted by the Censor at script stage, and given that this particular work of fiction had already outraged all the nation's teaching associations, the rather tame film stood no prospect of being awarded anything but a financially restrictive X certificate. And so the project quickly stalled. Already in the can and proving a financial hit in the States, *The Blackboard Jungle* did receive, after cuts, an X certificate, and then only after harnessing the not inconsiderable might of MGM to its cause. In such a climate there was little prospect of any small independent UK producer mimicking the likes of AIP who began their run of low budget JD movies in 1956 with *Hot Rod Girl* and *Runaway Daughters*. This limited the Teddy Boys to a brief and belated appearance in *Flame in the Streets* (1961), director Roy Ward Baker's film of Willis Hall's 1958 Notting Hill set stage play *Hot Summer Night*, that had already been adapted for TVs *Armchair Theatre*.

Despite the odd damaged cinema seat, the success of *The Blackboard Jungle* alerted UK filmmakers to the fact that the nation's cash rich young delinquents would be attracted to films featuring their peers. By this time though, as witnessed in movies like *The Boys* (1962), *Beat Girl* (1960) and *Violent Playground* (1958) a new Italian styling had begun to take hold. The Teddy Boys had already been joined in the nations coffee bars by handfuls of Beatniks but these new 'Modernists', soon to be labelled Mods, position as dedicated followers of fashion placed them more in the mainstream than the delinquent subcultures of their elder siblings.

As well as modern clothes, the Mods were also into modern music, championing the soul of Tamla Motown and Stax, the West Indian sounds of Bluebeat and the emerging R&B influenced homegrown bands like The Roling Stones, the Who and the Animals. When The Beatles arrived almost every youth in the country really was, in answer to the popular question of the time, a Mod or a Rocker, with an imbalance of many thousands to one. It is unsurprising then that a movement that had encompassed both former Teddy Boys and Beatniks should by the close of the decade have spawned both Hippies and Skinheads. It is in 1967 and the birth of the former that this particular glimpse into history begins.

As it had done with the Mods, the mainstream soon embraced much of the Hippie fashion and the long-hairs began to form into two separate camps. There was what Mick Farren called the 'Sloane Square... aristocratic Flower-

---

* I kid you not. The actor best known for his long running role as Gunner 'Gloria' Beaumont in BBC sitcom *It Ain't Half Hot Mum* appeared in both *No Trees in the Street* (1959) and *Violent Playground* (1958) as a tough young deinquent, a role he had also filled in a number of television series now lost in the annals of time.

Power lot' and there were the Freaks who settled around Ladbroke Grove, 'a community of hustlers, rude boys and ne'er-do-wells, both black and white, and we all fitted together rather well in our general dislike of authority.' It is this group with whom the Deviants singer allied himself, adding 'As far as drugs, sex and rock n roll went, there was a rivalry between Chelsea and us lot. And we had them pretty scared.' Along with other staples like drugs and rock n roll there was always a lot more sex and violence than peace and love in the pages of Notting Hill's counter culture papers like Oz and International Times

Many of those former Mods that baulked at all this scruffiness (and the peace and love) became Skinheads. Where the Hippie look lingered well into the next decade, the regimented Skinhead style was fleeting and many of its adherents, to outward appearances at least, soon merged with the 'hairies' as both groups took on a more unkempt, somehow grubby appearance that was more in keeping with the labour strikes, social unrest and slum clearance of the 1970s. This look is captured in *Bronco Bullfrog* (1970), considered for some the only cinematic depiction of the Suedehead, though a glance at the movie's authentically cast main protagonists begs to differ. In what might have seemed an almost impossible act, the Greasers, having looked admiringly across the Atlantic, got even dirtier as they rebranded themselves Hells Angels.

Over the two subsequent decades new youth subcultures were formed at an increasing pace, with the lines between them becoming increasingly blurred. Some said they just wanted to play dress up and party, others like the Punks preached the Hippies loftier ideals of changing the world though most put a more concentrated effort into changing the width of their trousers. Some of these tribes are still very much a part of public consciousness, others much less so, but all in their own way played their part in bringing society to where it is today.

It is now 43 years since peace and love broke out with the sun during that summer of love and whilst the times were indeed a changing it was still a very different world that for those coming of age today must be difficult to comprehend. Forget the internet, if British teenagers wanted to listen to the latest up-to-the-moment sounds they had to tune in to offshore pirate radio stations like Radio Caroline and Radio London where reception, up in the north at least, was at best intermittent. In September the BBC gave the nation Radio 1 and national radio finally made tentative steps into the twentieth century.

Theatre was as ever best placed of all to capture the zeitgeist as it unfolded and there was no shortage of young playwrights making notes, amongst them Doug Lucie, Howard Brenton, Trevor Griffiths, Barrie Keeffe, Hanif Kureishi, Tony Marchant and Nigel Williams. Many of these did occasionally defy the odds by getting thoughtful stories about the new youth preoccupations on long running anthology series like *Play For Today* (1970-84) and *The Wednesday Play* (1964-70) or as episodes of mainstream series like BBC police drama *Softly Softly* and ITVs daytime courtroom set drama *Crown Court* (1972-84), which provided paychecks for Punk playwright and actor Jonathan Moore, and *Babylon*'s Franco Rosso and Martin Stellman.

Television drama appeared to finally catch up in 1982 when it seemed like you couldn't get up out of your armchair to switch between the four available channels without being confronted by a member of the then omnipresent Bonehead fraternity. In the interim the slack had been taken up by a number of current affairs series that hark back to Thames's *This Week* that had first broadcast in the days of Associated-Rediffusion in 1956 and was presented by Richard Dimbleby from 1972 until its close in 1978. ITV could also boast *World In Action* (1963-98) and over at the BBC David Attenborough launched *Man Alive* (1965-1981).

1982 was also the year when Channel 4 came on air with a remit to cater for minority interests and a willingness to court controversy, especially with its adoption of broadcasting X-rated and deliberately provocative, often subtitled, art movies that it preceded with a red triangle 'warning' logo before transmission, much to the annoyance of Mary Whitehouse who said, 'It's not good enough to slap a warning symbol and indulge in sadistic madness of this kind.' Despite these advances, all four channels would still close down soon after midnight following the national anthem and a reminder to turn the TV off. If you had happened to nod off, you would awake to a continuous high-pitched beep and a hot telly, a routine would not be abandoned until ITV reluctantly went 24 hours in 1988.

Though the country's few more commercial minded low-budget producers and directors found the Hippies loosening of sexual morals made them a ripe subject for exploitation, in the world of film, these new youth tribes were most often represented by already dated adaptations of existing works from the worlds of literature and theatre. Occasionally, despite seemingly insurmountable odds, directors like Barney Platts-Mills with *Bronco Bullfrog*, Horace Ove with *Pressure* (1975) and Derek Jarman with *Jubilee* (1978) managed to capture fleeting glimpses into the advancing youth culture before the moment had faded. Occasionally, like Lindsay Anderson with *if...* (1968), a director could capture the zeitgeist by accident or like Stanley Kubrick by repositioning Anthony Burgess's 1962 novel 'A Clockwork Orange' into the beginning of a decade more suited to the story's violent, egomaniac and misogynist hero. The cinema would really come into its own a couple of decades on when some of those kids who were there grew up, such as Peter Mullen, Richard Jobson, Gillies MacKinnon, and especially Shane Meadows, drew on their own experiences when they grew up and became filmmakers.

So, whatever happened to the youth tribes of Britain?

As the eighties progressed, Hip-hop gradually became even more prevalent than Mod had once been as its dress, music and language permeated very aspect of life. Punk like Mod would eventually take on a wide enough brief to adapt to future generations widening tastes and despite the fact that all its biggest names quickly climbed aboard the corporate ladder its most enduring legacy is fittingly that of DIY with which it has become increasingly synonymous.

There were, and still are, attempts at comebacks by neglected old school tribes. The most culturally significant of these came with the second Summer of Love when the nation discovered a new type of psychedelic and everyone hugged for a while. There was also when, after what seemed an eternity of Tory government, Tony Blair smiled his way into power riding the wave of the second, and far more chart friendly, Mod revival. With a cheeky flash of his guitar and the blessing of Noel Gallagher, Blair told the nation's youth there was no longer a need to fight for their right to party, that Britannia was cool and at a post-election victory party he even joked about drugs with his new coke snorting BFF. A few months later his Labour government introduced its Welfare to Work policy and the NME asked: 'Ever had the feeling you've been cheated?'

But no one seemed to notice, and standing out from the crowd no longer seemed so urgent. Dressing up was anyway no longer going to cause much of a stir. These days you're far more likely to hear a member of the House of Lords championing Punk's benefit to the nation's economy than its detrimental affect on youth. As far back as 1980 Punks had appeared on postcards alongside beefeaters and the good old British bobby as an integral part of British heritage and as likely to bring tourists to cities like London and Liverpool as their museums, galleries and historic buildings. Even the government's Visit Britain website sets aside plenty of space for subcultural tourism, be it the *Quadrophenia* walking tour or a similar jaunt though 'Punk Rock Soho'. In the internet age where youths form their identities online, subcultures have, for a while at least, become something that dads did.

Perhaps the post Covid-19 new abnormal will spawn some mutant Disco Dancing Bowie Boot Boys but until then join me on a meandering tour of almost twenty years of Hippies, Skinheads, Rastas and Punks, their music, their preoccupations, and the world they lived in as portrayed on more than 50 years of UK television, film and theatre. Along the way you'll spend time Neil Morrissey as a transgender New Romantic, see Martin Compston strutting his stuff at Wigan Casino, and, after losing out to fellow Oscar winner Gary Oldman for the role of punk icon Sid Vicious, meet Daniel Day Lewis as a gay neo-Nazi skinhead. Then there's Joanna Lumley trying to start a revolution, Paul Nicholas faking one, Olivia Newton John as a student activist and Dennis Waterman held at gunpoint by the Rastafarian Liberation Army.

Hippies, Skinheads, Rastas, Punks & Disco Dancing Bowie Boot Boys

1. Unwashed and Somewhat Slightly Dazed
(Bowie)

In 1982 Ben Elton, Rick Mayall and Lise Mayer wrote a BBC student flat share sitcom, *The Young Ones*, that would redefine the form and herald in a new breed of so-called 'alternative' comedians. With their character Neil as portrayed by Nigel Planer, a clinically depressed, pacifist, vegetarian and environmentalist Hippie working towards a Peace Studies degree, they also drove the final nails into the Hippies coffin that had been constructed a half-dozen years earlier by Punk, which told us never to trust one despite many of its progenitors having been just that a few years earlier.

Despite making an unexpected comeback during 1987s second summer of love as a new generation grew their hair (a bit), and tie-dyed their t-shirts as they discovered their generation's own mildly psychedelic drug and found it made you want to dance in a field until 6 a.m., these new council estate bohemians were down with the peace and love but baulked at being called Hippies.

Unlike these 'ravers' the originals were not begot in a Manchester night club but, like the Beats that begat them, had evolved in the United States amongst middle-class, privileged youths before eventually reaching across all ethnic, social and economic backgrounds. In the UK this coming together never really took place, lacking the one thing that in the States had ensured a generation's lives transcended usual barriers - the prospect of being drafted into the Vietnam War. They regardless left a massive imprint on the nation's history and its future direction before they 'grew up', got jobs and families and took up their place in straight society.

They too baulked at being called Hippies. They preferred Freaks and Freaks is how they must have seemed to the middle England inhabitants whose carefully constructed boundaries of acceptable behaviour were first chipped away at and then as the 60s drew to a close suddenly bulldozed with homosexuality largely decriminalised and abortion partially legalised in Great Britain (but not in Northern Ireland). If that wasn't enough to convince Disgusted of Tunbridge Wells that the country had gone to the dogs, we even tried to join Johnny Foreigner in the EEC, only to rebuffed by de Gaulle who perhaps had visions of a future Brexit.

The term Hippie was common in jazz parlance since at least the 1940s, a derivative of hipster, itself a derivative of hep, as in hep cat, or hip. An early definition exists on the 1959 comedy album 'How To Speak Hip' which calls the Hippie 'a junior member of Hip society, who may know the words but hasn't fully assimilated the proper attitude.' In effect, second generation Beats who their predecessors thought not cool enough to be considered as such.

Around 1964 the name began appearing in the New York press to describe those involved in the underground music and art scene based around the city's Greenwich Village and a year later to the folk and psychedelic rock scenes developing on the opposite coast in Haight-Ashbury where1967 had begun with the Human Be-In, a response to the new California law banning the use of LSD in October of the previous year. There was music by the Grateful Dead, Big Brother and the Holding Company and Jefferson Airplane and speakers such as Alan Ginsberg, Jerry Rubin, and, importantly, Timothy Leary who urged the 20 to 30,000 strong crowd to 'Turn on, tune in, drop out'. They did just that, as 100,000 young people from all across the States descended on Haight-Ashbury, as Beat became Hippie in time for the Summer of Love, many of them making their way via the Monterey International Festival where Joplin, Hendrix, Simon and Garfunkel, the Byrds and The Who had played alongside organisers the Mamas & the Papas.

The 1967 Summer of Love also reached the shores of the United Kingdom where the Guardian introduced it to its readers that June. The paper said: 'Many bystanders believe the London Hippies who flame in the cellars of UFO on Tottenham Court Road or the Roundhouse in Chalk Farm are nothing more than Beats having a second wind. But whereas the Beats, for all their disassociation from mainstream culture, ultimately enriched that culture with their work, the Hippies speciality is not work but "freak-outs" and "raves," ie, elaborate clambakes where the maximum amount of distraction is supposed to create an optimum of personal awareness. At the vortex of the Beats there were mystics and poets, clowns and stylists, but at the centre of the London scene one finds mainly self-aggrandising displaced Americans with an air for

Hippie hijinx at the Camden Roundhouse in *Hammerhead*

publicity and an inexhaustible bonhomie as shallow as it is pervasive.' They were 'not only "drop-outs" but "cop-outs"'.

Despite these put-downs it soon became apparent that a small group of Freaks in London were creating a 'scene' centred around the underground paper International Times (IT) and the UFO Club. Among them was John 'Hoppy' Hopkins who as a young photographer working for the Guardian and Melody Maker, was at the forefront of this emerging underground scene, attending its early happenings and meeting and photographing many of its leading lights, stencil-duplicating their contact details and circulating copies amongst them. In 1966, Hopkins helped found the London Free School whose news-sheet would become the high profile underground newspaper IT. At the end of 1966, with American record producer Joe Boyd, Hopkins held the opening night of the UFO Club held on Friday nights in the basement beneath a Tottenham Court Road cinema where the first two such occasions played host to Soft Machine and Pink Floyd.

By the spring of 1967 the scene had flourished to the extent that Hopkins and his associates staged their most elaborate happening, the 14 Hour Technicolour Dream, held at Alexandra Palace as a benefit for the beleaguered International Times. Those among the 10,000 who gathered to hear the 42 bands who played, sometimes simultaneously from opposite ends of the hall, recount stories of early forms of Skinhead dancing with Hippie chicks whilst off their heads on LSD. As was John Lennon who had seen a news report on television and jumped into his Rolls to join the party and see the dawn welcomed in by Syd Barrett and Pink Floyd. When the original UFO night fell foul of the club's owners in July, the evening was popular enough to move to the much larger Roundhouse in Chalk Farm, but IT was not the only unprofitable Hippie venture and, only breaking even on its most prestigious evenings, the club lasted just a few months longer.

An early attempt to incorporate one of these 'happenings' into a drama appears as an entertaining six-minute opening sequence to *Hammerhead* (1968), one of the better James Bond knock off's from American director David Miller, overseen by producer Irving Allen who had also been responsible for the more successful Dean Martin fronted Matt Helm series. A combination of Judy Geeson's skimpy bra, naked cellists, the dismembering of mannequins and a girl getting covered in tomato ketchup and placed in a bread roll proves too much for the local constabulary who raid the venue, the Roundhouse of course, for 'outraging public decency.'

The 14 Hour Technicolour Dream, partly captured on film by documentarian Peter Whitehead in *Tonite Lets All Make Love in London* (1968), caught the eye of the watching mainstream society who either cashed in or came down hard on the emerging scene. An early insight into the former response was seen in an item in the next issue of IT which named and shamed future Live Aid organiser Harvey Goldsmith for not having paid for the 100 or so tickets he had taken on commission. IT was on the warpath again in July, commenting to the Daily Express on a copy-cat, but purely commercial, International Love-in due to take place at the same venue, calling it 'tasteless, vulgar and not in the least beautiful. How can it be? It is so commercial. You would not get any real Flower People paying money to line a promoter's pocket.'

It wasn't just sour grapes from the underground press. Weekly music paper Melody Maker sent along a reporter who suggested that 'Boot-in' would have been a better name for the event, listing casualties such as 'Who co-manager Kit Lambert, hit in the face and kicked; Arthur Brown... forcibly prevented from getting back into the hall for his second set; Radio Caroline's Rohan O'Rahilly and writer Robin Allen, attacked and beaten by a gang who also stole £500 worth of camera equipment.'

'Hippie uniforms there were - but the large percentage were obviously part-time Hippies who rush home from work on Friday night to swap the working togs for bells and bare feet. One or two seemed to have misread the Smoker's Guide Book and wandered around sucking the ends of sticks of incense... Just to add to the general feeling of love and goodwill, the hot dogs should have been gold-plated at the prices charged.'

The event was successful enough to herald an announcement in the press for a 'Festival of Flower Children', described as a '3-day Non-Stop Happening... to be held in the beautiful grounds of Woburn Abbey'. Amongst the lineup of bands appearing 'By Kind Permission of His Grace the Duke of Bedford' were the Small Faces, the Animals, the Move, and the Bee Gees - all early adopters of the 'flower power' look, but hardly Jefferson Airplane or the Grateful Dead.

By the end of the year, the entrepreneurs had taken a firm hold; UFO had closed because of financial pressures, as the scene became the domain of the forerunners of what would be later, and disparagingly, referred to as Sloane Rangers; young, rich bohemians living in Chelsea and parts of Kensington for whom running the right sort of boutique had suddenly become an 'acceptable to daddy' post-Eton career, allowing them to rub shoulders with the new breed of pop stars and young actors like Terence Stamp who took delight in the fact that he might 'Get into the Saddle Room and dance with the Duchess of Bedford's daughter... and get taken down to Woburn Abbey to hang out for a long weekend and have dinner in the Canaletto Room.' Prominent among Chelsea's boutiques was Hung On You, situated in a basement on Cole Street, whose owner Michael Rainey was the son of a notorious socialite, Joyce Marion Wallace who would become Lady Wrottesley. Rainey, known as the high priest of the peacock style, was himself married to Jane Ormsby-Gore, daughter of Lord Harlech and the subject of The Roling Stones 'Lady Jane'. Those who weren't born quite so high could always take another route to a seat at the top table like Granny Takes a Trip boutique co-owner Nigel Waymouth who married the daughter of the 9th Earl of Hardwicke.

Other movers and shakers included baronet and Old Etonian Mark Palmer, godson of the Queen, who started the English Boy Agency, an early outlet for male models but who also included Anita Pallenberg and Christine Keeler on his books. Another old Etonian, Joey Mellen, ran the World Psychedelic Centre from a flat on Chelsea's Pont Street; gallery owner Robert Fraser, who art-directed the 'Sgt Pepper' album sleeve, was an old Etonian and officer in the Kings African Rifles. Christopher Gibbs, expelled from said school, was the set designer on *Performance* (1970) and helped Mick Jagger to be posh for his role in the film. Both were present at the Jagger and Richards drug bust, with Fraser serving 6 months for possession of 24 heroin tablets.

The second part of straight society's response was also underway and by June 'Hoppy' was biding his time in Wormwood Scrubs, serving a 9-month sentence for possession of a small quantity of cannabis. Also jailed, for 12 months, was Black Power activist Michael X who suffered the indignity of being the first person charged under the Race Relations Act for calling members of the press 'white monkeys'.

Across the Atlantic in Haight Ashbury where it had all begun, a radical community action group calling themselves the Diggers protested the commercialisation of the movement there by holding a 3 day 'Death of the Hippies' celebration in October 1967 which culminated in a funeral procession complete with a symbolic casket. It wasn't quite the death of Hippies but it would mean the end of the Hippie heyday and its original message of peace and love. George Harrison had visited the United States that year with sister-in-law Jenny Boyd who says they were: 'Expecting Haight-Ashbury to be special, a creative and artistic place, filled with Beautiful People but it was horrible - full of ghastly drop-outs, bums and spotty youths, all out of their heads. Everybody looked stoned - even mothers and babies - and they were so close behind us they were treading on the back of our heels... They looked at us expectantly, as if George was some kind of Messiah.' When the Beatle turned down some STP, however: 'the crowd became faintly hostile. We sensed it because when you're that high you're very aware of vibes.' The amphetamine-based psychedelic whose acronym stood for 'Serenity, Tranquillity and Peace' was having quite the opposite effect. Running to their waiting limo, the crowd followed quickly behind and rocked the car. Says Boyd: 'the windows were full of these faces, flattened against the glass, looking at us.' It's purely speculation but amongst them could have been one Charles Manson, a resident of the town between April and November. Harrison had gone in search of Hippies but had discovered the Freaks, and he could have found them a lot nearer home around Ladbroke Grove and Notting Hill.

Harrison might have spared himself this hairy encounter had he waited a while and watched the January 1968 edition of *World in Action: Alas, Poor Hippies, Love is Dead* which crossed the Atlantic to film what the Guardian called 'a grim half hour about American teenagers sunk through drugs to Skid Row level' and 'saw pretty American girls, perhaps a little haggard looking for say 20 or 23, and then learned they were only 16 and 14. Fashion, drummed up on all sides of the media had built up San Francisco and Haight Ashbury into a Mecca of new freedom... But the rot has set in. Thugs and petty thieves abound and young boys and girls are seen walking about in zombie-like drug trances.'

Hippies, Skinheads, Rastas, Punks & Disco Dancing Bowie Boot Boys

In September 1969 the Birmingham Post kindly provided its readers with a guide to 'Finding your way round the underground' which probably only served to confuse the readers in England's second city when it turned out to be 'a guide to the ever changing cults of the young who opt out of "straight" life - from the gentle weekend Hippies who just reject society to the well-educated anarchists who want to overthrow it.'

The writer drew his conclusions from items that 'carpeted the parquet flooring of the London Diocese School in Endell Street, London like the baggage of a routed army.' These included copies of Black Dwarf and IT, Bob Dylan songbooks, erotic pictures, Trotskyist pamphlets, the works of Mao, Ginsberg, Lenin, Che Guevara posters, and a book on learning Japanese, assumed to be 'a Zen Buddhist must.' It gave, he said, 'some indication of the confusion of ideas on which Hippiedom feeds' and 'as with ideas, so with people.'

144 Piccadilly, an empty five-storey disused mansion at Hyde Park corner, was squatted by a group calling themselves the London Street Commune where according to the News of the World they lived in a squalor 'Lit only by the dim light of their drugged cigarettes'. Soon dubbed 'Hippy-Dilly' in the press, The People provided its 'ordinary decent living' readers with 'sordid facts' of 'drug taking, couples making love while others look on, a heavy mob armed with iron bars, filth and stench, foul language, that is the scene inside the Hippies' fortress in London's Piccadilly.'

Before the police raid on the 20th September there had already been a media-incited assault on the premises by air-gun toting Skinheads who the squatters fended off with the buildings unlikely armoury of carpet boules, hundreds of which, ignoring the graffiti underneath declaring 'We Love Peace', they filled with water and pelted down at their would-be-invaders from the building's balconies. Those same boules, and anything else they could lay their hands on, including a solitary petrol bomb, were also used against the police on a Sunday morning at the end of the month, but having being persuaded to lower a makeshift drawbridge to enable an ill occupant to be tended, baton wielding police officers quickly breached the defences. Watched by thousands of onlookers, a Hells Angel's flag was lowered from the flagpole and after three weeks the occupation was over.

Events at the the squat were dramatised as '144 Piccadilly' by American director Sam Fuller, but unfortunately not as a film but as a novel. Fuller inserts himself into the situation as a cigar-smoking American film director (in London for a BFI retrospective of his films) who gets involved with the squatters by accident. Which is partly true. The director had been in London and had witnessed the original break-in whilst enjoying a late night walk. After talking to them he says: 'The dishevelled squatters invited me to stay on,' insisting that if 'I hadn't had prior commitments, a wife, and a flight back to the States the next day, I would have.'

In the novel Fuller extends the director's involvement as he 'tries to bridge the generational gap by becoming the group's mascot and witness. The fictional "me" does what I was tempted to do but couldn't, abandoning his hotel suite for a mattress on the floor with the flower children.'

Sadly, he never made a movie of the book, but according to the internet, there was a thirty-minute film of the same name made by a student at the Royal College of Art who gained access to the squat and filmed inside. When the film ran out of money, Charles H. Schneer, a Hollywood producer best known for his work with Ray Harryhausen, stepped in. Intending to sell it as a support to *Easy Rider* (1969), Schneer got actor Sam Wanamaker involved in the editing, but the film never saw the light of day either here or in the States. It was sold for the Hong

Kong market to Run Run Shaw founder of the Shaw Brothers Studio who popularised the kung fu genre. With the original negatives missing from the lab that handled it, the film remains lost.

The people the Birmingham Post reporter had met at the squats at 144 Piccadilly and Endell Street before the battle was lost ranged from an 18-year-old lad taking a year off from the Clydeside shipyards to spokesperson Dr John, whose aim was 'to take over the streets from the fuzz for the people.' Dr John, actually cultural theorist Phil Cohen, was according to fellow Dilly Dosser Richard Gardner into: 'Agitprop, Tariq Ali, Che and all that stuff. Whereas we were more inclined to skin up and see if we could get the Dilly record shop to play the new Jefferson Airplane on its outdoor speakers'. Cohen wanted to forge: 'an alliance of beats, rockers, student drop-outs, and Hells Angels to accomplish the revolution, oust present society and ring in the Hippie millennium.'

A simpler comparison might have been that one was a Hippie and the other a Freak. The Hippies were sprung from the more middle-class Mods, wanting to look fashionable and have a good time whilst holding down a job or knuckling down to their studies. Hippies experienced the counterculture, but the Freaks, for whom fashion was never a priority, inhabited it. McCartney represented the Hippies, but Lennon, to his regret, was seen as representing the Freaks. On the 1970s 'Plastic Ono Band' track 'I Found Out' John Lennon bemoaned that: 'Freaks on the phone won't leave me alone'. The singer was, amongst other things: 'sick of all these aggressive Hippies or whatever they are... demanding my attention as if I owed them something.'

*

Dr John's manifesto was akin to that offered by John 'Hoppy' Hopkins who continued to be a presence around the alternative society that was taking root around Notting Hill and, specifically Ladbroke Grove, remaining on the editorial board of, and contributing to, IT, and also founding BIT, a free information service that helped hold the scene together. BIT was one of the premises visited by a film crew from the BBC's *New Horizons* TV programme in 1971 which called the 'few square miles around the Portobello Road... the centre of a national network of groups and activities originally called the underground. Sociologist Theodore Roszak calls it the counterculture, its new name is the alternative society. Here the most striking difference is not between black and white, rich or poor, but between long-haired alternative people who call themselves Freaks or heads and the rest, known as straight society. But to be a real Freak is not just a matter of wearing the right uniform or shopping at the right shops on Saturday afternoon. It's more subtle than that.'

It was here that the creators of *Father Ted*, Graham Linehan, credited only as the show's co-deviser, and Arthur Matthews, set their much awaited follow-up situation comedy **HIPPIES (1999)**. The sitcom only lasted one series partly brought down by the heavy sense of expectation after *Father Ted*, the duo's sketch show *Big Train*, and star Simon Pegg's own series *Spaced* that had debuted just a few months earlier.

In *Hippies* Pegg plays Ray Purbbs editor of the counter culture magazine Mouth, so-called he says because it is 'a mouth on the face of young people' and 'also if you change the m in mouth to a y it spells youth' before realising that might have actually been a better name. The magazine is produced on a shoestring from his flat where he is aided by sort-of-girlfriend Jill (Sally Phillips), double-barrelled, in both name and nature, friend Alex Picton-Dinch (Julian Rhind-Tutt) and the slightly befuddled contributor Hugo (Darren Boyd).

As well as the alternative press, over its six episode run the series touched base with a host of other Hippie pursuits. There's the protest movement in the opening episode when, hoping to impress visiting American 'world's biggest Freak' Jerry Gurwitz, he stages an ill-fated protest at a sandpaper convention - the only event being held that day: 'I wish that sandpaper could be as straightforward as

Three Hippies and the world's biggest Freak

Entertaining the straights in Notting Hill Gate

Vietnam.' In the second episode, *Hairy Hippies*, Ray directs a nude Hippie Christian musical in the church hall: 'I'm Jesus and I've come to freak the whole scene.' There's free love in *Sexy Hippies*, and a trip to a festival in *Muddy Hippies* where Ray takes drugs he got 'from a rather nervous Welsh older Hippie who I'd never met before seen in my life so I'm pretty sure they're good stuff.' After necking some, Ray reads the list of side effects on the bottle: 'Nausea? No. Long term depression? Too early to tell. Panic Attacks, excessive urination…'

A selection of real characters can be found in Jo Gannon's documentary on the areas growing significance to the underground, the 25 minute **GETTING IT STRAIGHT IN NOTTING HILL GATE (1970)**. After a two-and-a-half minute roof top sitar solo from Quintessence's Allan Mostert we are told that the area is 'a cultural and racial melting pot' and introduced to Caroline Coon one of the founders of Release, the charity set up to assist the areas many young people regularly being busted, usually on drugs charges, by the police. Coon points out that 'we weren't gonna just cut our hair just cos the fuzz were treating us like shit and we found we had to educate ourselves what best to do in the situation'. The soon-to-be Punk rocker's own haircut looks like it might have resulted from some degree of police brutality but was probably just the fashion.

The camera briefly passes by the premises of the Mangrove restaurant where a sign tells us it's a good place to visit if you're looking for the sort of kicks that were being handed out by the constabulary. 'The interface between public and police,' we are told, is 'complex,' and that 'to live in some parts of Notting Hill is to acquire a second class status instantly, without any reference to age, colour or dress.' In a foreshadowing of times to come, the narration claims that 'the situation was not improved by the recent legislation giving the police open powers to stop and search. There's been no real violence in Notting Hill since the riots in the late 50s but recently after an incident in which a speeding police car crashed, killing a young Jamaican, the area's becoming a little tense.'

After visiting an adventure playground, a poet, and the artist Larry Smart, the film embarks on an aimless wander through Portobello Road market where the Freaks shop alongside the straight population, most of whom seem firmly stuck in the 1950s. It's then back to Quintessence, rehearsing in the local church hall, for a six-minute rendition of the title song before returning to Mostert on the roof as the sun sets.

A better representation of the scene would have been a band like the Pink Fairies who chronicled their world in community anthems like 'Portobello Shuffle', 'Right On Fight On' which tells the story of the police breaking up a free gig with Hawkwind underneath the Westway off Portabello Road, and 'I Went Up, I Went Down' in which Paul Rudolph pops a pill and floats on a cushion over Notting Hill. Or Hawkwind who named their fourth album 'Hall of the Mountain Grill' after a Portobello Road cafe frequented by the band.

Quintessence were far from being the best band active in the area but were probably amongst the most inoffensive which might be why they were also featured heavily a year later in **NEW HORIZONS: THE ALTERNATIVE SOCIETY (1971)**. It could also be for the band's unintentional comedy value such as when flautist Raja Ram declares 'What we try to do is actually raise up the vibrations of the audience and ourselves to a more sort of God-intoxicated state.'

The band also has their own guru, Swami-ji, who 'has visiting hours which are strictly kept, we can go to see him at certain hours of the afternoon and evenings. Other times he'll come and visit us socially or, as tonight, he'll come round and we're gonna have what they call a keertan, which is where the devotees, which are about 20-25 in number, will get together, sit round, read from the scriptures, meditate communally, let Swami-ji talk and discourse about religious things and then afterwards share in what we call prassade, which is food that's been dedicated, and we all sit round and eat and then everyone goes home.'

Asked why so many people are returning to eastern religion, Raja Ram tells us: 'most people like that feeling, that philosophy and enlightenment and all those things... have been set in the east and been tried for thousands of years very successfully and obviously the western way of life being so material and all the other things that go with it, it's very difficult for them over here so they turn towards that. Things are changing and people aren't satisfied anymore with the old routine and doing what they are told to do, and maybe going out and getting a job... People have now got more time to make a choice, and... should really start considering why they are on this planet Earth and what are they gonna do with the time when they're here.'

Oz publisher Richard Neville shares this view of working for the man but rejects Christianity in whatever form it might take, which he suggests, 'makes a promise that in an afterlife somehow it'll all be Pearly Gates and choirs and lots of sugar candy, which will be a big reward for them devoting themselves to this thing called work. Work is good for you. Work is good for the soul, keeps you alive, and that somehow it's ennobling. In previous civilisations it wasn't ennobling... In Greek society [it] was meditation... appreciating music... You cannot fulfil yourself while you're bloody well cleaning up garbage or while you're banging out parts on a Ford motor car.'

Caroline Coon gets another visit, as do the offices of Bit where those seeking advice or information might also have found a crash-pad for the night. As befitting the more practical services these two organisations offered, Coon's take on things is more grounded: 'I don't actually subscribe to the idea that people drop out of society. I think every individual really wants to live and contribute to the society that he's living in. I mean you cannot have any meaning in your life unless you feel that you're doing something, either for yourself or for your own lifetime and that you will leave something to posterity, for your grandchildren.'

*

Where Raja Ram was looking for a 'God-intoxicated state', fellow Ladbroke Grove bands like the Deviants, the Pink Fairies and Hawkwind, whose horn player Nik Turner is seen wandering through the offices of counter culture magazine Friends in *The Alternative Society*, found their intoxication in more traditional forms.

Though an integral part of this new society, drugs, especially the new and very much in vogue hallucinogens such as LSD had a minimal impact on the film and television drama of the time. One reason for this is that such effects were difficult to convey, especially with the limited budgets (and in some cases talent) available to those British directors willing to address the subject. Among these was Donovan Winter, a one-man film industry who after a brief acting career had set up his own production company in the late 1950s, making a series of short films with a

Peter takes a trip in *Come Back Peter*

 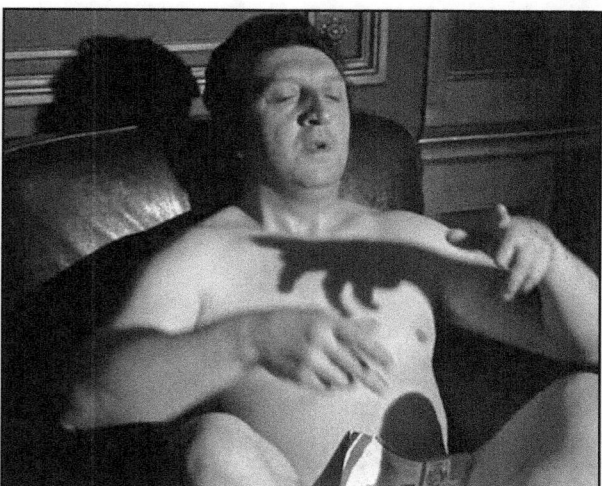

James Fox eats two thirds of the big one in *Performance*

swinging sixties ambience before attempting a feature with **COME BACK PETER (1969)**, a sexed up take on *Alfie* (1966) with none of that film's charm.

Better known now after a re-titling to *Some Like It Sexy*, the film stars Christopher Matthews as he moves through the capital servicing an array of all too willing dolly birds - apart from the Collinson twins, Mary and Madeleine of *Twins Of Evil* fame, who service each other. There's an au pair, a MILF and her daughter (a skinny looking Madeleine Smith), a black singer, and a model but of interest here is hippy stoner Creampuff (Annabel Leventon who was in the original London cast of *Hair* at the Shaftesbury Theatre). Winter may or may not have tried LSD, but hopefully not if his experience is that relayed in the film.

The major exception to the rule comes in *Performance* (1970) when gangster Chas (James Fox), needing to lie low, takes up residence with mushroom-loving former rock star Turner (Mick Jagger), his girlfriend Pherber (Anita Pallenberg) and their lover Lucy (Michele Breton). They give Chas 'two thirds of the big one' and he wonders 'what's wrong with the lights?' 'Artificial energy' explains Pherber, not helpfully adding 'It's pulsating into the voltage.' Chas has already moved on: 'This is a very pretty table... a very pretty table.' He might be high on psychedelic mushrooms but it actually is a very pretty table as directors Donald Cammell and Nic Roeg rely on clever editing, Fox's acting ability and Jagger's music rather than supposedly psychedelic effects. It's a trip that sees Chas and Turner morph into each other in a proto-music video for Jagger's 'Memo From Turner' that concludes with an office full of naked gangsters.

*

When Hippie drug use appeared as a major plot point, it was likely for its criminal cache. Set in 1970, the second episode of the first series of the dramatisation of barrister and author John Mortimer's 'Rumpole of the Bailey' novels, **RUMPOLE AND THE ALTERNATIVE SOCIETY (1978)**, opens with a Hippie walking down a middle-class street as a middle-aged man steps out of his gate and bumps into him. Though it was his fault, the man looks annoyed. 'Hey, hey, no hassle' says the Hippie with a smile as he wanders briskly on, picking up a cat and handing it to another middle-aged 'straight'. 'Hey man, do you wanna cat?', he says as he shoves it into the perplexed man's hands without waiting for a response. 'Peace and love' he adds as he carries on his way.

He is heading to a large detached house called Nirvana where congregated in the front garden are several other Hippie types. They don't seem to know him so he simply knocks and when the door opens he is invited in. From then on, we only see what happens through a small window - the exchange with a young Hippie woman of a huge wad of cash for a suitcase. As he carries it down the street, a police car pulls out and follows him. 'What have we got here then?' he's asked. 'About three years for the girl' he answers with a laugh, as he is revealed that the reason for the OTT performance is that he's an undercover cop.

We next see the girl, Kathy (Jane Asher), after she has recounted those events to her barrister, Rumpole (Leo

Hippies, Skinheads, Rastas, Punks & Disco Dancing Bowie Boot Boys

A dope pushing Jane Asher

McKern), who tells her: '"Cool it man, you're in no trouble with the fuzz." Oh dear me, just from the way the old darling talked didn't you twig that he was from the local drug squad. Nowadays, coppers are issued with beads as well as the book of verbals and size eleven boots.'

Rumpole's defence is to be that the police had coerced her and without their involvement she would never have committed the crime. The undercover officer had asked her to get some cannabis for him and so she had. The prosecutor is no fan of Hippies and has formed his opinion from reading the Sunday papers: 'What a life, eh? Gang bangs on the national assistance.' In fact, they have a 9 year lease on the large property and all have jobs. The judge, in a hurry to get the case over so he can attend a private function, and appalled at the idea of a policeman wearing beads, a wig and a *Viva Zapatta* moustache, favours the defence.

Unfortunately, another of the 'commune', Dave (Nigel Gregory), persuades Kath to use the case to make a point. Kath's brother had recently been arrested and is serving 12 years in a Turkish prison and she tells Rumpole the truth. She got the 20lb of cannabis after her brother was busted and hoped to use the proceeds from selling it to get the £10,000 necessary to grease enough palms to secure his release. Tellingly, *Midnight Express* (1978), Alan Parker and Oliver Stone's account of American Hippie drug smuggler Billy Hayes 1970 arrest and incarceration in a Turkish prison was released the same year. Unfortunately, the imparting of this admission of her guilt brings a conflict with the Bar code of conduct, the real reason for this storyline, and leaves Rumpole's defence is in tatters and Kath looking at the three years the undercover detective had predicted.

The counterculture drug that was making most headlines was LSD and because it was manufactured rather than grown, there was no need for smuggling. Instead, the product was being produced on an industrial scale on a rural Welsh farm near Llanddewi Brefi. When the suppliers were finally busted in 1977, there were enough materials to make 6.5 million tabs with a then street value of £100m and 120 people were arrested in the UK and France with over £800,000 seized.

Directed by Bob Mahoney for Tyne Tees Television and based on the book by Inspector Dick Lee who was in day-to-day charge of the undercover operation, **OPERATION JULIE (1985)**, named for the police operation that led up to the bust, was broadcast as three one-hour (including advertisements) episodes and then combined into a single 105 minute drama for a video release. The story begins in 1974 with the sirens of an approaching police car barely audible above the heavy downpour of rain in which a dishevelled hippy girl sits oblivious of events around her. As she's wrapped in a police officer's overcoat, the soundtrack turns to Lou Reed's 'Oh Jim' from his 'Berlin' album of the previous year, a depressing drug fuelled and themed album that fits the bleak Welsh setting.

In the next scene, a room full of 'Hippies' sit watching as a projector plays movie footage from a rock festival. That these are not ordinary Hippies is clear from the use of the title 'governor' and the presence of a middle-aged man nursing a bottle of light ale at the back. 'I want Hadley, ' he says as the film they are watching ends. Hadley is 'the LSD man... 10,000 tabs a week.' The man who wants him is Inspector Dick Lee (Colin Blakely) and get him he does during a raid on an address in London. But, as he explains to another of the Hippie types picked up and sitting alone in a cell but actually an undercover cop, he's letting him go because he wants 'to see where he runs to'.

Where he runs to is rural Wales, where fast forwarding to 1976 a combined squad from different forces has assembled under the Inspector. Just in case any viewers were tempted to side with the Hippies we are told that the girl from the opening scene was aged just sixteen and had died. The tab was manufactured in Britain and with daughters of a similar age to the dead girl, this makes the dogged Lee even more determined to get his man.

From there onwards it's slow going as the team painstakingly watch and wait for developments; which is almost as dull for the viewer as it would have been for the officers themselves. Seen from a distance through binoculars and rarely heard, there's no attempt to cast any light on the dealers. The drug itself is explained away in tabloid terms. 'What is it about LSD, all this they think they can fly stuff?' asks one senior policeman. 'Claustrophobia' he's told by a man in a white coat. 'They have to get out. LSD is like an expanding valve; it blows the mind.'

Hippies, Skinheads, Rastas, Punks & Disco Dancing Bowie Boot Boys

Ladbroke Grove was no place for superstars and one notable difference between festival documentaries **MESSAGE TO LOVE (1997)** and **GLASTONBURY FAYRE (1971)** is the lack of superstars that take to the stage in the latter. Headliners Traffic had released their acclaimed 'John Barleycorn Must Die' album the previous year, a UK #9, but their subsequent releases stalled on this side of the Atlantic. Pink Floyd who would have headlined had they been able to get their gear through the mud to the stage were still two years away from 'The Dark Side of the Moon'. David Bowie, then just a one-hit wonder after having reached #5 in 1969 with 'Space Oddity', itself thought of as a novelty number, was scheduled for 7.30 but held over when things over-ran didn't appear until 5 a.m. at which point there was no one awake to film him performing 'Memories of a Free Festival' as the sun came up. Many of the rest of the performers, including Edgar Broughton, Quintessence, Hawkwind, and the Pink Fairies were regulars on the free festival and Ladbroke Grove scenes.

The first Isle of Wight festival had taken place in between 1967s Monterey Pop Festival and 1969s Woodstock, at the end of August 1968 where a crowd of 10,000 watched Jefferson Airplane head a line-up that also included Fairport Convention, Arthur Brown, Tyrannosaurus Rex and the Pretty Things. It was successful enough for a second event to be arranged for the following summer and for the promoters to be confident enough to lure Bob Dylan away from home territory in up-state New York where the Woodstock Music & Art Fair was being billed as 'An Aquarian Explosion: 3 Days of Peace & Music' with an offer of £40,000 for a one hour set (think £600,000 today). The troubadour's presence, and to a lesser extent that of The Who, boosted the attendance to 150,000, among them three Beatles and a Rolling Stone who it would be fair to say probably hadn't gone for the Nice, Third Ear Band and the Pretty Things.

In 1971 there was no Dylan, but there was an increased profile, a line-up that included The Doors, The Who, Hendrix, Miles Davis, Joni Mitchell, Emerson, Lake & Palmer, Kris Kristofferson, Donovan, Ten Years After, Jethro Tull, Free and Rory Gallagher's Taste, all of whom were captured on film by Philadelphian documentarian Murray Lerner, whose *Festival* (1967) had compiled performances, interviews and conversation from the Newport Folk Festival between 1963 and 1966. The performances in *Message To Love* are all well shot, though Hendrix and the Doors were both far from at their best, not that this would have mattered too much to those who had witnessed two legends who would both be dead within a year. It is the incidental stuff, however, that makes *Message To Love* special and also the reason the movie never saw the light of day until 1997.

What Lerner also captured on the Isle of Wight was the half a million punters who piled onto ferries to the island to join the 60,000 who had bought tickets. A prospective attendance of 600,000 couldn't have helped but cause pound signs to appear in the eyes of the promoters but unfortunately the Freaks who pitched their tents outside the official perimeter in so-called Canvas City took issue with such capitalist values and good old-fashioned strength-of-numbers meant that flimsy corrugated fences manned by harassed guards with dogs - leading one festival goer to declare it a 'psychedelic concentration camp' - were destined to fail and the organisers were eventually left with no option but to cave in to demands for a free festival, as the bands 'representatives' hustled to secure their particular clients fee. Glastonbury Fayre had charged £1, including free milk, in 1970 and in 1971 attendance was free though farmer-cum-promoter Michael Eavis was eventually forced to adopt the concentration camp look himself in 2002.

In the film Joan Baez neatly sums up the promoters dilemma: 'The question of kids wanting everything free now is very hard to handle. It's hard to talk to those kids... because to them I represent, among other things, somebody who has money. And that makes

Glastonbury Fayre

them angry. So if I charge 15 cents for a concert, that's 15 cents too much. But I am not going to be forced into giving a free concert because they insist.'

The financial fallout may have put paid to a more timely release of Lerner's excellent film but it did provide the inspiration for the directorial debut of exploitation producer Stanley Long with a follow up of sorts to *Groupie Girl* (1970). That film's co-writer Suzanne Mercer was again hired, her involvement bringing her sax playing husband's rock band Juicy Lucy on board.

Says Long: 'I was never very keen on directing... I'm a technician and I'm more interested in technicians, photography and all that. I wasn't greatly interested in directing but I did it because it was something I had to do and felt I could probably do better with my own films than had been done before. There were certain things that I wanted to do, certain standards that I thought were possible with low budget movies and... I directed all the films from then on' (except *Eskimo Nell* (1975) which was, not at all co-incidentally, the best one).

Heralded as 'The King of Sexploitation' in the Sun, Long was one of Britain's most successful independent film producers in the 1960s and 1970s. The ex-RAF man began his life on civvy street photographing nudes for 'glamour' magazine Photo Studio before moving into film, shooting his first striptease movie on a 16mm camera bought for £25. It was a wise investment and by the end of the 1950s his company, Stag Films, had made over 150 under-the-counter shorts. Progressing to more ambitious projects, Long and his partner Arnold Louis Miller shot *Nudist Memories* (1959) at a nudist camp in Herefordshire (beating American Queen of Sexploitation Doris Wishman's *Hideout in the Sun* (1960) though not Charles Saunders' *Nudist Paradise* (1958) as featured in *Carry on Camping* (1969)) and then made newspaper headlines with *West End Jungle* (1961), a documentary looking at prostitution and the sex industry in London's West End, which was notoriously screened to MPs in Parliament and refused a certificate at the time.

Long really hit the big time with *The Wife Swappers* (1970) which was refused an X certificate by the BBFC, leaving the producer wiped out financially until the day was saved when the X certificate, that had previously stated that a film was 'passed for exhibition to persons over the age of sixteen', was effectively split into two by the introduction of the new AA certificate for persons 'over the age of fourteen' and moving the X to 'over the age of eighteen', effective from the beginning of July 1970. A worldwide hit, the film came in at 29 in Variety's top-grossing films of 1970, *2001 A Space Odyssey* managing only 50th position. Grossing over a million in the UK alone, Long decided his follow up to the then topical subject of wife swapping would be the new phenomenon of rock star groupies.

The aptly titled **BREAD (1971)** opens at the Isle of Wight Festival, with glimpses of the real thing seen in stock footage. A group of friends are preparing to make their way home, unhappy at having been ripped off at every turn. Their current gripe is at the thin piece of pink meat and lettuce in equally thin slices of Sunblest they've been charged three bob for: 'You know it really gets me how they put it on for the scene. I mean you pay enough to get in here, and then everything you eat and drink costs a fortune. Cause they know you're stuck here... I mean, the way the straights go on about the young generation. Like if you've got long hair, you're dirty. Then we've all got too much bread. But then if you don't work and you're not a bread scene, they still freak out. Just give them a chance to score off us and they're into it like a shark.'

When hitching home takes longer than expected the friends pitch tent in a field which in the cold light of the following morning turns out to be the grounds of a large country mansion owned by a young aristocrat who after an initial argument, befriends the group. When they suggest staying on to do up the house, which he intends to put on the market, whilst he and his wife are away, he gladly accepts their offer. However, once they have the place to themselves the five Hippies - Jeff (Peter Marinker), Trev (Dick Haydon), Mick (Nigel Anthony), Marty (Liz White) and Cathy (Noelle Rimmington) - have a better idea and decide to hold their own festival. I mean, how hard can it be? Right?

As it happens, not that hard. After a pointless sequence in which the boys convince the two girls that they should make a porn movie to raise funds, clearly sandwiched in by Long to tick boxes that would be required by his distributors, they decide to steal everything they need whilst Jeff heads to London where, posing as an American journalist, he convinces Juicy Lucy's manager to provide the bands services for free: 'I'm interested in this head festival you're into. What I had in mind was a 3 part feature starting with a profile of you and the band. What you're into head-wise, you know, just kind of a heavy rap. Then I do a piece on this festival. Getting into the guys putting it on. Finally tying the two together like "Why you supported it?" And putting the band on free. Whether it's achieved its aims. What effect if any it had on the festival scene as a whole? I want to trip on the fact, you know, of these kids putting it on themselves. You know what I mean? A good caption would read "By heads, for heads, for the benefit of heads." You dig?'

If this really had been Juicy Lucy's manager, it would have gone a long way to explain the band's lack of progress. The festival goes ahead and is a moderate success. Unfortunately, the audience has a similar attitude to that on the Isle of Wight and easily bypass the non-existent security for free entry. There's also the small matter of the owner returning halfway through with a prospective buyer in tow, forcing the friends to flee. Still, having spent nothing they are content in having lost nothing.

This is not as far-fetched as one might think. In 1970, in the months before he was on the Isle of Wight, irritating the festival's promoters by publishing a White Panther newsletter, helping his friends Hawkwind and The Pink Fairies to play in an inflatable tent, and instigating the storming of the 'psychedelic concentration camp', Mick Farren helped organise Phun City alongside cartoonist Edward Barker, a pioneering free pop festival at Ecclesden Common in Worthing, featuring Detroit-based White Panther band the MC5, Edgar Broughton, The Pink Fairies and Mungo Jerry. Backed by International Times the festival did not set out to be free, but a lack of fences or any way of taking admission fees necessitated the fact. Bands who turned up to play were told they would have to give their services for free and all but Free and Matthews Southern Comfort, who both left without playing, did so.

Bread failed to emulate the success of Long's first 'counter culture gimmick movie', falling into a variety of categories from *Carry On* style comedy to sex film to music business drama without providing enough of any one of these to satisfy. On the music front Juicy Lucy had broken into the top twenty with a cover of Bo Diddley's 'Who Do You Love' but subsequently suffered from a near constant turn over of band members which negated the chance of ever recreating this initial success. They did though release four albums of decent heavy blues based rock before calling it a day in 1973. Only guitarist Mick Moody found any subsequent success, recording three albums with Snafu before becoming part of the inaugural line up of Whitesnake in 1978 after having played on and co-written four tacks, including the title song, on the former Deep Purple front man's solo album, 'White Snake'. Since leaving the band in 1983 Moody has been a a member of several bands with the word snake somewhere in their name. Psych blues rockers Crazy Mabel, whose line up includes Henry Cow's Geoff Leigh but whose recording career ran to just one live album released in Germany, also appear.

According to Stanley Long: 'What happened was these independent distributors got into a bit of a twist with all these kind of films. They didn't quite understand the culture. They were really into the sex films per se, and of course we were trying to make films which were sort of more interesting and not just sex. So they got what they deserved in a way, films which were made fairly seriously on the culture that existed at the time but they didn't really get what they wanted because we were very anti this kind of explicit nudity for the sake of it. I always felt that it was very, very difficult show erotica on screen on its own with mediocre artists, most of 'em... it was very difficult to do two things and often we were caught between the two stones.'

'I remember one screening of *Bread*... the distributor was sat there, and he's "Yes, it's very good but there's not enough tits in it." And that kind of remark used to grate on me. And I remember turning round and saying, "Well, how many tits would you like to see? How many tits do you think it needs to make it commercial?" And I think that was the yardstick that they used and I think there was always a bit of a conflict there. And maybe they were right... I don't know. Maybe if they hadn't had that to sell, they wouldn't have been commercial. I don't know.'

When glamping was still a spelling mistake in *Bread*

Hippies, Skinheads, Rastas, Punks & Disco Dancing Bowie Boot Boys

Children of the Revolution
(Bolan)

Trouble had been brewing for France's President de Gaulle since the country's Socialist and Communist parties formed an alliance in February 1968, known as the February Declaration, in which they agreed to attempt to form a joint government to replace the Gaullist Party. At around this time, the hippy movement crossed paths with a revitalised European anarchist movement at Nanterre University on the outskirts of Paris where a dozen or so Situationist students calling themselves Les Enrages (the Angry Ones), the name given to the most radical elements during the French Revolution, stirred up the campus. Situationists create a situation which can be anything as long as it annoys the authorities enough to provoke them into a reaction. That reaction is then used to their advantage. Which seeking educational reform, they did, beginning with the publication of 'On the Poverty of Student Life', written mainly by the Situationist International member Mustapha Khayati. University funds were used to print 10,000 copies which when distributed all over campus on the first day of classes led to a court case in which the judge denounced the anarchistic threat to the University. A less intellectual but certainly effective tactic was to pelt lecturers with rotten fruit.

When students and members of far-left groups occupied the administration building to air grievances about the University's funding and the wider area of class discrimination in the country, the police surrounded the building. Although those inside left peacefully, shortly afterwards the authorities threatened those deemed to be ringleaders with expulsion which only added fuel to the conflict between University and students, as it did when the administration shut down the University on May 2nd. The following day, students at Paris's Sorbonne University met to protest the closure and four days later Nanterre students came together in the centre of Paris and, after continual harassment and over 500 arrests, the gathering erupted into five hours of rioting with police. With over 20,000 students, teachers and supporters marching towards the now sealed off Sorbonne, the police charged, wielding their batons. After initially dispersing, the crowd fought back, creating barricades and throwing missiles, forcing the police to retreat for a time. The police then responded with tear gas, and by the end of the night, hundreds of students were under arrest and 350 gendarmes injured. The following day a 50,000 strong march against police brutality turned into an all-day battle through the Paris Latin Quarter with the protesters now responding to police tear gas with Molotov cocktails. The 10th saw more of the same and soon the police were forced out, allowing the students to take back the Sorbonne University declaring it an autonomous 'People's University', producing leaflets, posters, and graffiti such as 'The most beautiful sculpture is a paving stone thrown at a cop's head!' appeared on the walls of the city.

A one-day general strike and demonstration was called for Monday, 13th May, and over a million people marched through Paris as the police kept a low profile. By the 16th, workers had occupied roughly fifty factories and by the 20th, two-thirds of the French workforce were on strike. This against the wishes of the Unions. Amongst the chaos, protesters seized the National Theatre and made into a permanent assembly for mass debate and set the Stock Exchange on fire. Having retreated to the countryside with his government appearing close to collapse, President de Gaulle announced the dissolution of the National Assembly, with elections to follow on 23 June. Suddenly it was over.

The disturbances of 1968 were not confined to France. In Poland during March, after a march by students from the University of Warsaw was met with police clubs, twenty days of protest ended with the state closing all universities and the arrest of more than a thousand students. In the United States, the assassination of Martin Luther King saw riots break out in the black areas of over 115 cities, some lasting four days. On October 2nd, after a summer of protests against the Mexican government and the occupation of the central campus of the National Autonomous University (UNAM) by the army, a student demonstration in Tlatelolco Plaza in Mexico City ended with police, paratroopers and paramilitary units firing on students, killing over a hundred. There was certainly something in the air.

Director Lindsay Anderson's **IF... (1968)** is sometimes offered as a British response to the revolutionary fervour that was seemingly grasping the world, but its anarchic social satire lies not in the Paris student uprising of 1968 but in the juvenile delinquency furore of the late 1950s. Says Anderson: 'Essentially the heroes of *if...* are without knowing it, old-fashioned boys. They are not anti-heroes, or drop-outs, or Marxist-Leninists or Maoists or readers of Marcuse.'

The first draft of the screenplay by Oxford students David Sherwin and John Howlett, then known as 'Crusaders',

One man can change the world with a bullet in the right place. Malcolm McDowell in *if...*

was penned over three days and nights in 1960 and sent to various, producers, agents, and directors including Nicholas Ray whose *Rebel Without A Cause* (1955) was Sherwin's favourite film. Ray, and all the others, passed and so the script lay dormant until director Seth Holt contacted Sherwin in 1966 with a view to resurrecting the project for Anderson, thinking it best suited to a director with a Public School background. Anderson had also directed the theatrical world premiere of *Billy Liar* in the West End in which Tom Courtenay opens fire with a machine gun at the dullards before him so would not have baulked at the violent ending.

Sherwin and Anderson rewrote the script during the spring of 1967 with Michael Medwin and Albert Finney's Memorial Enterprises attached as producers and financing agreed with CBS. When CBS subsequently pulled out, the project might have been doomed were it not for the sex appeal of one Albert Finney, riding high on the success of *Tom Jones* (1963) and at the time appearing on Broadway.

According to Sherwin: 'Charles Bluhdorn, the billionaire owner of the oil conglomerate Gulf & Western, buys Paramount. Albert Finney is in *Joe Egg* in New York. Mrs Bluhdorn is a great fan of Albert. A word from Mrs Bluhdorn to Mr Bluhdorn. A phone call from Mr Bluhdorn to Paramount in London, *if....* is financed by Paramount and neither of the Bluhdorn's ever read the script.'

The Bluhdorns weren't the only ones not to read the script, or at least not the proper script. With the $600,000 budget now in place, filming could finally begin and as the film's primary location, Anderson was keen to use his old boarding school, Cheltenham College. However, old boy or not, Anderson knew that the film's unflattering portrayal of the institution's traditions and regimes meant gaining the permission of the school would be impossible. To combat this, the production assembled a 'fake' script, removing all references to homosexuality and toning down the violence - the caning scene becoming nothing more than a dressing down. The film's finale became a dream sequence of Mick's during history class. One final change would remain. Worried that the title might also be inflammatory, Anderson thought something 'very old-fashioned, corny and patriotic' might draw the headmaster. With Kipling's poem in mind, Sherwin's secretary Daphne Hunter suggested 'If' and changed by Anderson to *if....* the title stuck.

After an establishing shot of the college, *if....* begins with the chaos of students returning from summer break to resume their place in College House, one of the five houses in a typical English public school. As boys jostle through crowded corridors strewn with suitcases and large chests, Rowntree (Robert Swann), the senior Whip, gleefully adds to the chaos with his barked order to 'Run! Run in the corridors!' As the boys flock around a noticeboard, the camera introduces us to Jute, a junior who can't find his name. A request for help from an older boy is met with the response that he is not to speak to him as he's 'scum' (a junior) and thus the bottom of the school's hierarchy. At the opposite end of this social ladder is Rowntree to whose call the juniors come running, with Jute bringing up the rear. The Whips are the real authority in the school, allowing the masters to concentrate on teaching in return for the privileges that power brings, especially when that power is abused. And abused these 'scum' will be. To fetch and carry, provide tea and crumpets or, as Rowntree informs one such junior, to 'Warm a lavatory seat for me, I'll be ready in three minutes'. For the prettier boys, duties may also involve a certain amount of that popular public school tradition - buggery. It's an elaborately shot and fluid sequence that artfully establishes the hierarchy seen as so essential to the smooth running of the English boarding school system.

As the films hero/anti-hero Mick Travis, Malcolm McDowell's entrance (his first on film) is nothing short of iconic, described by the actor himself as the 'greatest entrance into film that any actor could dream of'. As he sweeps into the school dressed from head to toe in black, the combination of a large fedora with a scarf across the lower part of the face showing just the eyes, this rebel is more Guy Fawkes than James Dean. Retreating to the study room he shares with fellow Crusaders Wallace (Richard Warwick) and Johnny (David Wood), Mick slowly unwraps the scarf to reveal what he has been hiding from the Whips... a neatly trimmed Edwardian moustache which, contrary as it is to the dress code, is swiftly despatched.

Divided into eight Acts, the first six introduce us to the English public school system as a microcosm of a British society still stubbornly clinging to its colonial past, and in particular how its outdated traditions affect the rebellious Travis. Initially feeling as nervous as each other in their new surroundings, the new boy Jute and new teacher Mr Thomas (Ben Aris) throw themselves wholeheartedly, if not always successfully, into proceedings. Like the rest of the adults in this closeted world, Aris' performance is heightened, but not exaggeratedly so. These masters are caricatures because history and tradition demand it of them. When the gown goes on the teacher assumes the role of those who came before him, the 'greats' of his own early years in a similar establishment. When those who upon their release from what writer Sherwin has likened to 'Nazi death camps' return to the bosom of Matron, it is either through institutionalisation or an inability to deal with the real world. A world where Geoffrey Chater's chaplain might be remembered fondly as a 'puff' rather than a paedophile.

The film is best remembered for three remarkable scenes. In the first, the only sequence to take place outside of the school grounds and an occasion in which the cinematography suddenly changes to black and white, Mick and Johnny steal a motorcycle and visit a roadside cafe. When they enter it is empty except for the waitress (Christine Noonan) from whom they order coffee. When Mick asks the waitress for sugar and she leans forward to hand it to him, he grabs her wrist and pulls her forward, kissing her neck. After pulling free, she slaps him firmly across the face. Pouring two heaped spoons of sugar into his cup, Mick moves to the jukebox where moments later, a hand appears on his shoulder. When he turns she just stares, smells, as an animal passion suddenly takes hold and they lunge and claw at each other, rolling violently across the floor. 'Look at me,' she growls, 'look at my eyes, my eyes get bigger and bigger, I'm like a tiger, I'm like a tigress', baring her teeth and sinking them into his arm. In an instant, they are naked and then, as Mick expresses satisfaction they are just as suddenly fully clothed once more. On the DVD commentary, McDowell says he 'was secretly in love with Christine Noonan,' in which he wouldn't have been alone, 'but she was married, so there was no question of any hanky-panky.'

In the second, after they have returned to school, the Whips reprimand them, not for their absconding but for a dislike of the ironic sneer on their lips, and a desire to 'nip unruly elements in the bud'. We do not see Wallace or Johnny receive their canings. The camera cleverly stays outside the gym, hearing but not seeing the blows and allowing the viewer to experience the tension with those anxiously waiting their own turn. When it is Mick's turn and, before they even call him, he throws open the gym doors and strides confidently into the room as the camera follows, capturing for the first time the now-famous McDowell sneer in all its glory. A sneer exploited to even greater effect three years later. He takes further control of the situation by carefully positioning himself across the balance beam, measuredly putting each hand in the optimum place - it's a tactic guaranteed to drive his persecutor mad.

According to Malcolm McDowell: 'I really didn't know how to play the part in *A Clockwork Orange* for Stanley Kubrick and I gave the script to Lindsay Anderson to read and said "can you help me". He read it and... the first thing he said was "Thank God I'm not directing this"; then he said, "Malcolm, there's a scene [in *if...*] where you open the door when you come into the gym, there's a close-up of you, that's how you play Alex. " And that's how I played it and he actually gave me the direction of playing that film, in Mr Kubrick's film. Of course, I never told him that.'

Following his caning, Mick is next seen sitting alone in the sweat room whilst firing darts from an air pistol at a series of magazine images sellotaped to the wall. Audrey Hepburn, Big Ben, a dog, Mel Ferrer, and the breasts of a nude are targeted and dispatched. The final shot of this sequence lines up a picture of Queen Elizabeth seen through the window of the royal carriage. Instead, as we might expect, of shooting the Queen, the dart passes through the facing window and into a man stood on the pavement. It is difficult, given the set-up, to imagine this was anything but intentional and that to Anderson - a man whom everyone reunited on *Cast & Crew*, a BBC programme included with the Criterion DVD, agrees absolutely loved Britain - some things are sacrosanct.

Anderson takes the film in a more surreal direction after Mick makes his 'one man can change the world with a bullet in the right place' proclamation, produces a handful of live rounds and the three Crusaders make a blood pact. In the course of a tea break during the school's war games, the three Crusaders fire a series of live rounds, penetrating the tea urn. When the Chaplain approaches, telling them to stop, Mick fires again and the Chaplain falls. As Mick charges, bayonet fixed, towards the whimpering clergyman, the film cuts to the Headmaster's study where the boys receive a dressing down and are told to apologise to the Chaplain who emerges, literally, from a drawer. In researching the scene, Anderson drew on a recently published book, 'Eton: How It Works', and says: 'It is interesting that a lot of the headmaster's dialogue in that scene was taken from a book written by an ex-housemaster at Eton, so some of the more idiotic things spoken by the headmaster are real.'

This sequence, according to Anderson, 'made the ending possible' because after that anything could happen. What Anderson should have said is that it meant that they could use this surrealism to make everything from this point on, including the film's violent climax, nothing more than a dream. Heavily influenced by Jean Vigo's *Zero de Conduite* (1933), the drawer scene was, according to Sherwin, the first addition of surreal elements to the re-written script and even Anderson would later question its effectiveness, saying: 'Harold Pinter got very upset about that moment. He thought it very out of style. He may well be right.'

Pinter was not the only one to get upset. During September 1968, Paramount's Terence Feeley sent a letter urging Anderson to re-cut scenes such as the cafe sequence and the padre in the drawer. George Ornstein of Paramount UK fought the director's corner: 'Faced with men like Anderson, Kubrick, and a few others... you are obliged to go with them - the whole way. They are in large parts the film that emerges... What's in their minds may be viewable later, but often it can't be written down, or even satisfactorily explained, at the time the money is needed.'

It is the film's bloody finale that proved most controversial and so is best remembered. As punishment for their 'war games' misdemeanour, the boys' are commandeered to clear the chapel basement which, as well as disused chairs, is home to a stuffed crocodile, embalmed foetuses, and, importantly, a cache of weapons, including smoke bombs, mortars, and sub-machine guns. Outside it is Founders' Day, with parents, old boys and various local dignitaries in attendance. This provides an ideal setting for the boys, now joined by The Girl, to exact their revenge on those in authority who have wronged them. As an old General addresses the gathered ranks of the great and good, telling them: 'We still need loyalty; we still need tradition. If we look around the world today, what do we see - we see bloodshed, confusion, decay,' smoke rises from the floor, causing confusion and panic inside and driving people outside into the courtyard. On the rooftops above are Mick, The Girl, Wallace, Johnny and Bobby (Rupert Webster) who meet the fleeing throng with gunfire. As mortars rain down and bodies fall, some below fight back, including an old lady who cries 'Bastard' as she returns fire with a Sten gun. When the headmaster steps forward to appeal for calm, shouting: 'Boys, boys, I understand. Listen to reason and trust me. Trust me,' The Girl simply takes out a handgun and shoots him between the eyes.

Malcolm McDowell and Christine Noonan go on a second date in *if...*

Neither Sherwin nor Anderson went behind the cameras in the Spring of 1968 intending to capture the Zeitgeist; there's sex (a staple), but no drugs and in place of rock n roll is the Missa Luba, a Latin

Mass from the Democratic Republic of Congo - although its use in the film pushed a single release of the 'Sanctus and Benedictus' into the top thirty in March 1969. When French film journal Jeune Cinema pointed out the black and red scarves seen blowing in the wind during Mick and Wallace's motorbike ride resembled the black and red flags that had flown in Paris in May '68, the director had to disappoint. The shooting of the scene having preceded those events, he pointed out in the preface to the published script that: 'Even the coincidence of its making and release with the worldwide phenomenon of student revolt was fortuitous.'

Anderson did, however, add some scenes as the events across Europe unfolded. The scene preceding Mick's beating by Rowntree was already in the can but Anderson felt unhappy and says: 'Just before we were to go into the studio for a week's shooting, I realised what the scene should be. David Sherwin came round to my place, and we made a series of collages which Mick could have on his study wall and fire darts in to', which the director felt 'broadened the impact and stopped the film being just a school story.'

When the film opened in UK cinemas during December 1968 most reviewers praised the realistic depiction of boarding school life but Anderson's vision which they associated with his reputation as something of a Marxist horrified some critics. The BBC thought it 'very close to the borders of fascism,' the Listener called it 'the most hating film I know,' and the Spectator suggested 'Anderson is still lashing out at nanny.' Such criticism forced the director onto the defensive, writing: 'The work is not a propagandist one. It does not preach. It makes no kind of explicit case. It gives you a situation and shows what happens in this particular instance when certain forces on one side are set against certain forces on the other, without any mutual understanding. The aim of the picture is not to incite but to help people understand the resulting conflict.'

'It is about responsibility against irresponsibility, and consequently well within a strong puritan tradition. Its hero, Mick, is a hero in the good honourable, old-fashioned sense of the word. He is someone who arrives at his own beliefs and stands up for those beliefs if necessary against the world. The film is, I think, deeply anarchistic. People persistently misunderstand the term anarchistic and think it just means wildly chucking bombs about, but anarchy is a social and political philosophy which puts the highest possible value on responsibility. The notion of someone who wants to change the world is not the notion of an irresponsible person.'

The film had no problems in attracting an audience when it opened at The Plaza on London's Lower Regent Street as a short-notice replacement for Roger Vadim's under-performing *Barbarella* (1968), taking £40,000 in its first few weeks and guaranteeing itself a national roll-out, where it again did good business. Malcolm McDowell, with an actor's sense for the dramatic, has described the film's impact as 'like an H-bomb had gone off under the British establishment', but it did at least ruffle the feathers of various sections of little England. When the film was entered in the prestigious Cannes Film Festival during May 1969, it was much to the chagrin of the establishment back home. Says Sherwin: 'The British Ambassador arrives foaming with fury. *if...* is an insult to the British nation. It must be withdrawn from the Festival. Lindsay replies it is an insult to a nation that deserves to be insulted and tells the Ambassador to bugger off. Anyway, the film can't be withdrawn; it is the official British entry.'

The filmmakers held little hope of success. Anderson says that at the official screening no one from the Festival had turned up: 'Normally there's a spotlight that comes on and lights up the director. We were left alone. Nothing. No one to introduce us to the audience.' In fact, the film's eventual win was practically pre-ordained. The organisers had abruptly curtailed the previous year's Festival in solidarity with the ongoing protests and as a powerful statement that something far more important was taking place. However unintentional, *if...* had captured that moment and presented it to the judging panel. Says McDowell of the film's conclusion: 'It was amazing; we were shooting on the roof with me firing the gun at the parents, and Lindsay had a copy of The Times and the front page was a student on the roof of a University with an automatic machine gun. It was like a still from our film.'

It was all a fantasy anyway. Much debated over the intervening years, proof positive that the shootings were imaginary can be gleaned from the fact that Anderson and Sherwin had planned an 'if....2', first reported in the Guardian during 1988. In 1993 the project received financing from Paramount for a 'first draft', with all three of the 'rebels' reprising their roles, now respectively a film star (Travis), a priest (Knightley) and a naval officer (Wallace), and reuniting for Founders Day twenty-five years on, at a much-changed Cheltenham where the importance of religion is superseded by media studies and political correctness is the new order. It's quite fitting that two of these would be anarchists are now part of the very same society the school was training them for and that the extent of Travis's rebellion was to become an actor.

if... may not have taken direct inspiration from events in 1968, but another largely school set movie, this time

Not your average revolutionaries - Tracy Hide, Jack Wild and Mark Lester in *Melody*

an inner city grammar, was the unlikely source of an outburst of pre-teen revolution in its final act. At the heart of **MELODY (1971)** is the relationships between middle-class 11-year-old Daniel Latimer (Mark Lester), his rough-around-the-edges friend Jack Ornshaw (Jack Wild) and their pretty schoolmate Melody (Tracy Hyde) whom Daniel spots in a dance class and falls instantly in love with.

The tone is set in a scene during which Daniel and Melody visit an overgrown graveyard, used as an adult-free space by the local kids, and she points out the grave of a couple who had been married for fifty years, observing 'he only lasted two months after she died'. 'He must have loved her very much' responds Daniel. Asked 'Will you love me that long' he smiles and replies 'Of course, I've loved you for a whole week already haven't I?'

Underpinning this is a series of songs from the Bee Gees, acquired by producer David Puttnam along with the finance for a then as yet unscripted movie, on the proviso that the songs featured in the finished film. It was a tactic that Puttnam would use to great effect a few years later with *That'll Be The Day* (1973) and *Stardust* (1974). The Bee Gees songs were then handed to screenwriter Alan Parker with the instruction to write a script based on those seven songs. Hence, the song 'Melody Fair' accompanies a touching sequence in which Melody gets a goldfish from a rag and bone man as well as providing the film's title. The script, says Parker, is 'slightly autobiographical'.

You can probably work out from this that to call the proceedings twee would be something of an understatement. That is until a final act in which the teacher enters his classroom to discover that there is only one child present, Stacey (Ashley Knight). As something of a science geek, Stacey, as we have seen earlier, has been trying to make an explosive but his repeated attempts have all failed with not so much as a whimper. There's even his latest attempt sitting on the desk in front of him, only the teacher is too pre-occupied to notice, especially when he is told that the reason the rest of the class are absent is that they've gone to Daniel and Melody's wedding.

The entire school faculty, and Daniel's mother, head en masse to stop the ceremony and recover their absent charges. Ahead of them though is Stacey, who is able to warn his friends who, outnumbering the adults, fight back, tearing clothes and landing blows. Stacey finally gets his explosive to work, blowing up Daniel's mother's sports car.

Accompanying the action is, not the Bee Gees, but Crosby, Stills, Nash & Young's 'Teach Your Children', a song written by Graham Nash some years earlier whilst still with The Hollies and originally inspired by the difficult relationship he had with his father. The singer songwriter had also begun collecting photographs and one in particular of a young boy in Central Park taken by Diane Arbus 'spoke volumes' to him: 'The kid was only about nine or ten years old, but his expression bristled with intense anger. He had a plastic grenade clenched in a fist, but it seemed to me if it were real the kid would have thrown it. The consequences it implied startled me. I thought, "If we don't start teaching our kids a better way of dealing with each other, humanity will never succeed."'

Says director Waris Hussein: 'Children have a very strong anarchic streak in them and this is very relevant to this particular film because the film is basically about a kind of innocent anarchy - they don't walk about being delinquents or bashing people up - it's a sort of domestic anarchy that takes place in most homes at one point or another.' Of the ending in which Melody and Daniel escape on a railway sleeper he says: 'I think children, at some point in their lives, always wanted to get up and get out. It's a sort of Dick Whittington thing; put your belongings into a handkerchief and get the hell out, but of course they never do. They get as far as the front gate Aunt Fanny's down the road.'

It was all too much for Arlene Kramborg at the New York based Films In Review who said 'In the last few years movies have encouraged so many "minorities" to "revolt" that I'm afraid *Melody*'s plea on behalf of 11-year-olds leaves but one component of the population without a political activist agitating on its behalf; babes at the breast. Who knows? Perhaps the SDS or Weathermen will supply these oppressed creatures with bibs embroidered with slogans that denounce women's lib.'

But there was a real revolutionary feeling in the air in Britain, too. Pakistan born, Oxford-educated Tariq Ali for whom the war in Vietnam 'had become an obsession' says 'I often thought about the possibilities of organising international brigades from Europe, America, and South Asia, which would enable some of us to fight side-by-side with Vietnamese.' Instead, in 1966, he was part of the group that formed the Vietnamese Solidarity Campaign and was behind two major demonstrations in London against the war as well as relaunching the radical 19th-century publication Black Dwarf, numbering the first issue Vol. 13 Number 1 to assert a belated continuity. The front page of that issue, in May 1968, bore a photo from the recent events in Paris and the slogan, WE SHALL FIGHT WE SHALL WIN: PARIS, LONDON, ROME, BERLIN.

Demonstrations against the American invasion of Vietnam, organised by the VSC, began in 1967 with one during July attracting over 5000 protesters and resulting in 31 arrests. By March of the following year, a demonstration outside the American Embassy in Grosvenor Square had tripled in size and resulted in about 300 arrests. The VSC upped the rhetoric as well as the numbers with Ali declaring his attention to invade the Embassy 'for as long as the Vietcong held the American Embassy in Saigon.'

A 1968 editorial in The Times called the demonstration 'bigger and bloodier than any related demonstration in England so far.' 'It was,' the paper added, 'for some of the participants, less a Vietnamese peace rally than a Vietcong war rally, to judge from their banners and chants. The demo was joined by some foreign students who had come over for the occasion – evidence of a degree of the international organisation of the techniques and timing of demonstrative politics. It was also, thought the Home Secretary, 'more aggressive in preparation and mood than any that has gone before.'

He prepared for the worst: 'There is a growing attachment to sub-violence among some of the politically impassioned young. Sub-violent behaviour, (the sit-down, sit-in, pelting with flour or pennies, mobbing, hammering on the body of a car, and so on) dictates the use of physical counter-measures for the preservation of public order or the avoidance of hurt and damage. From that – whether by intent, accident, miscalculation or hysteria – overt violence, very easily springs. There is usually a conflict of evidence on every particular occasion about what ignites the mixture. But the mixture is highly inflammable. The methods have a natural tendency to precipitate violence. Those who organise them know that or if they do not, they are more simple than they would like to be thought.'

In common with Paris and elsewhere, students were at the heart of much of this protest which mainly comprised a series of sit-ins at universities such as Birmingham, Leicester, Leeds (where future Labour Home Secretary Jack Straw was then NUS President and called the sit-ins 'bonkers'), Bristol, Hull, Essex, and Keele. The insurgency was first witnessed at the London School of Economics in 1967 after an announcement that Dr Wallace Adams was to be the University's new director. When protests over Adam's links with Ian Smith's white supremacist government during his previous position as Principal at University College, Rhodesia denigrated into a series of skirmishes, the death of a porter from a heart attack led to the suspension of two Student's Union Presidents, which in turn led to a sit-in of over 200 students, supported by some staff – among them the father of the future Labour leader Ed, Ralph Miliband.

1968 student occupations in the UK began on the 28th of May when, in a dispute over the control of Student Union funds, students at Hornsey College of Art, in imitation of action taken by students in Paris earlier that month, embarked on a 24-hour sit in where staff, students representatives and journalists debated grievances that would then be presented to the Board of Governors. The 24 hours ran until the 4th of July and spread to other art colleges who had similar issues. Not least of these concerns was the Labour government's plans to create polytechnics which, in the case of Hornsey, saw it consumed as part of Middlesex Polytechnic.

As the country's first student protest Hornsey attracted a lot of media attention, but was never seen as any sort of revolutionary threat and so the attention was not as serious as they might have wished. Prue Bramwell Davis, an industrial art student at the time said that they let the Daily Express in for 24 hours only to discover that what the paper really wanted to know was who was sleeping with whom. She says: 'We did pamper the media. In filmed debates, the boys would be at the back looking serious and girls would be on the floor in their miniskirts.' Director John Goldschmidt treated them better in his look at the wider picture of revolting art students in a documentary for Granada Television, *Our Live Experiment Is Worth More Than 3000 Text Books* **(1969)**, visiting Hornsey, Bradford where students burnt their diplomas to protest the respectability of art, and Guildford where faculty who supported the students had been sacked.

Events at Hornsey were recreated by the students themselves for **THE HORNSEY FILM (1970)**, directed by Pat Holland. That's not as exciting as it sounds. 'You must have heard of the Hornsey College of Art' says one disembodied voice fighting to make itself heard over the noise of a double-decker bus as the camera pans across a row of terraced housing. 'Here, wasn't that was where all the trouble was last summer?' 'I wrote to the local paper about it. After all, we're the ones who pay the rates. We're the ones who suffer.' 'Just a load of over-aged brats, that's what I say.' 'Art students, never done a days work in their lives.' 'What are art colleges for, anyway?' 'Layabouts; a dose of National Service would do them good. Load of bohemians. What's the use of learning to paint?' 'They've got too much time on their hands, they do nothing but cause trouble.'

The significance of the bus soon becomes clear when the film explains the 'layout' of the college, with its 'main building at the top of Crouch End Hill; three miles away, one shilling on the 41 bus, Hornsey College of Art, South Grove, Tottenham. I mile down the road, Hornsey College of Art, Page Green. Three miles further north, change at Wood Green, Hornsey College of Art on the North Circular.'

The students at Hornsey clearly had a lot they could have protested about even before the introduction of the Diploma in Art & Design, effectively a degree course that required GCSEs rather than the production of a portfolio and completion of a Foundation Course. The reasoning behind these changes was the lack of prospective associated employment after graduation. Logical enough but missing the point for students the likes of Keith Richard and the Pretty Things Dick Taylor at Sidcup Art College, Ronnie Wood, Pete Townshend and Freddie Mercury at Ealing or Viv Albertine, Ray Davies, Adam Ant and Deep Purple's Roger Glover at Hornsey.

'They call it trouble' says the narrator, 'but for the first time on the 8th of May we began to think for ourselves' as the titles declare 'REVOLUTION HORNSEY 1968'. Well, not quite, but they did hold a lot of meetings and, easily the highlight for one student interviewed, get to use the duplicator in the middle of the night.

As the days passed into weeks, at 6 a.m. one morning Haringey Council sent in a private security firm armed with German Shepherds but found themselves outsmarted by the students feeding the dogs biscuits. Eventually the would-be-revolutionaries faced a dilemma that would face future University occupations. The imminent arrival of end of term meant that if they didn't come to a truce with the authorities, they would find themselves protesting on their own time. As so they agreed that discussions would resume after the summer break only to learn a valuable lesson when the agreement was reneged on and a number of staff and students were expelled. To rub salt into the wounds, the College was integrated into Middlesex Polytechnic soon after.

Art school sit-ins were never the most likely subject to draw a cinema audience but do play an unlikely role in one such venture. **TOOMORROW (1970)** was an attempt by Don Kirshner, the man behind the manufactured pop of the Monkees and the Archies, to do the same on the big screen. Kirshner touted Toomorrow as 'young, with it' and having 'the looks and appeal of "today" and tomorrow. They are undoubtedly the best-looking pop group ever brought together' and that the time was right now The Beatles had 'become big business, leaving behind their image as exciting, real people' and 'the world of pop was facing a tedious and vacuous future.' To bring this to fruition Kirshner assembled a musical team with a track record in this disreputable genre.

With incidental music composed by easy listening maestro Hugo Montenegro, who had provided music for *The Partridge Family*, *Toomorrow*'s songs were composed by Ritchie Adams and Mark Barkan. New York born Adams had a minor hit as a member of the Fireflies in 1959 with 'You Were Mine' before pursuing an unsuccessful solo career. A songwriting career proved more fruitful, providing a #1 hit in the US for Bobby Lewis with, the now rock n roll standard, 'Tossin' and Turnin'. It was not this however that would have got him the Toomorrow gig, but

The happening world of *Toomorrow*

his collaboration with 'Pretty Flamingo' composer Mark Barkan on material for The Archies debut album (but not, tellingly, 'Sugar Sugar') and the duos work on the *Banana Splits* TV show for which they served as music directors and composed the famous 'Tra La La Song' that served as the series theme.

As well as a track record for both spotting and creating new talent, Kirshner had also secured a budget in the region of £1 million to put behind the project via a three-picture deal he had signed with Bond co-producer Harry Saltzman; enough to sign the 20-year-old Olivia Newton John and her equally unknown co-stars to five-year deals with a yearly retainer of £10,000. But... Saltzman was using his interest in the Bond movies as collateral, contrary to the terms of his contract with his Bond co-producer Cubby Broccoli who sued, leaving the film in turmoil and director Val Guest, amongst others, unpaid. Guest had made one the UK's best music biz films in the early Cliff Richard vehicle *Expresso Bongo* (1959) but that was all still a touch Tin Pan Alley and much had happened in the meantime, including a dozen birthdays for the by now 59-year-old director. Guest's first act was to rewrite novelist David Benedictus's script, which he found too 'high-falutin'' - which the director's re-worked version certainly wasn't.

It's probably fair to say that Newton John, whose acting career had been limited to an appearance in an Australian musical comedy *Funny Things Happen Down Under* (1966), wasn't cast for her 'thesping' and she doesn't seem to have been hired for her singing ability either given that the producers paid for singing lessons and she is largely confined to backing vocals. In fact, the non-singer Susan George (who released a couple of singles later in the decade) was also in the running for the role, as well as dating Ben Thomas, one of the film's stars.

The production issued a press release commenting on, among other attributes, Olivia's 'buttery skin' but the actress was mortified to discover she was expected to display more of it than her modesty permitted, refusing to play a scene in her underwear - at which point Guest must have rued not casting George. She did however spend a lot of her screen time in micro-miniskirts, though perhaps not quite the '18 inches above the knee' as also mentioned in the press release, which at barely 5 and a half foot would have ended around her navel.

The story begins as Olivia (Olivia Newton John) gets out of bed in the student accommodation she shares with Benny (Benny Thomas), Vic (Vic Cooper) and Karl (Karl Chambers), puts the kettle on and prepares a tray of tea for the boys (and the girl one of them has hidden in the wardrobe). As well as being students they're also the four members of Toomorrow, which alongside providing the title of the film is also the name for their pop band they come up with: 'I dig it, we're too much, toomorrow.'

Next stop is the fictitious London College of Arts, where the courses have got no more radical than the introduction of nude models, jazz dance and Wagner, though the latter is at least taught by a mini-skirted Tracey Crisp, a Bond girl in *Casino Royale* (1967), with glasses and hair tied back so we know she's also intelligent. Sadly Crisp's career ended with a role in *Percy* (1971) the following year, having had enough of sexual harassment in an industry in which such behaviour was rampant and tolerated.

In the canteen, student leader Matt (Carl Rig) addresses the ranks, fresh from having met the college authorities with his demands: 'I pointed out that the majority of senior staff do no teaching at all, their functions are almost entirely administrative. And yet they control all academic decisions. Following your Committee's decision, we asked the Principal for 20% student and 20% staff participation in the governing body. You now know his answer.'

The students vote to take action but Matt is no Maoist: 'They'll probably try to present this as an attempt to instil anarchy in place of authority, so if we think that we're so smart let's show 'em. Let's keep public sympathy by proving this to be wrong.' This won't be a problem, they're more a mildly irritated mob than an angry one, an attitude evident from their feeble attempts at placards. Olivia is impressed though. 'Isn't he lovely?' she sighs as a sit-in is planned.

The London College of Arts resembles school only with bigger children, especially when we see how the institution's hierarchy in their black suits and gowns deal with the protest, which has suddenly turned into an impromptu performance by Toomorrow until they unceremoniously have the plug pulled on them mid-song. 'How dare you stage an exhibition like this in the curriculum time' barks the principal. 'I haven't stopped any classes young lady' he tells a lone dissenting voice. 'And while this college still has rules i'll not have them flagrantly disobeyed. So kindly take all that out of the building immediately. If the rest of you wish to continue your ill-advised sit-in, henceforth you will do it outside.'

Surely Olivia's bo-hunk Matt will deal with this. 'Let us avoid any misunderstanding about this Mr Matthews', the protest leader is firmly told, 'I want you out of this college by lunchtime and I will be most unhappy Mr Matthews if this has to be accomplished by force.' Matt accedes. The only dissenter is his bearded side-kick who shouts angrily; 'You're not suggesting we do what the man said'. 'I'm suggesting it's the smartest thing to do... it can only put us further in the wrong.' That the kid has a future in politics is confirmed by a radio presenter who says that the return to normality is 'in no small measure down to the persuasiveness of 25-year-old Matt Matthews, leader of the action committee.'

That's it as far as the protest is concerned as there are far more pressing matters for Toomorrow to deal with. There's a band contest being held that evening at the Roundhouse and to complicate matters the band's impromptu canteen jam has caught the attention of a glowing flying saucer orbiting the earth above London. The band have been unwittingly creating 'curative vibrations... a new form of electronic harmony' that have reunited 'two long-discarded intangibles: emotion and heart' that can provide an antidote for this alien race's slow decline. This seems to result from a fusion between Vic's home-made synthesiser and the wholesome appeal of Ms Newton John. It all turns out well but not before the aliens raise the entire Roundhouse up to the mother ship in a beam of light after Olivia has told the aliens that those 'curative vibrations' need to have the emotion of a crowd to reach their full effect.

As a film *Toomorrow* was ultimately always doomed to failure because its songs are nowhere near the standard of 'I'm A Believer,' 'Last Train To Clarkesville,' or, for that matter, 'Sugar Sugar'. When Olivia's then beau, the Shadows rhythm guitarist Bruce Welch, saw a preview he says he knew immediately it would not fly: 'It was reminiscent of so many of the low budget pictures that were made during the early sixties, and the biggest letdown of all was the music. It was all so lightweight. There were no hit songs - the numbers were naïve and instantly forgettable. Instead of going for songwriters with a proven track record as hit makers, Kirshner handed the job to some relatively experienced writers signed to his publishing company.' Welsh was

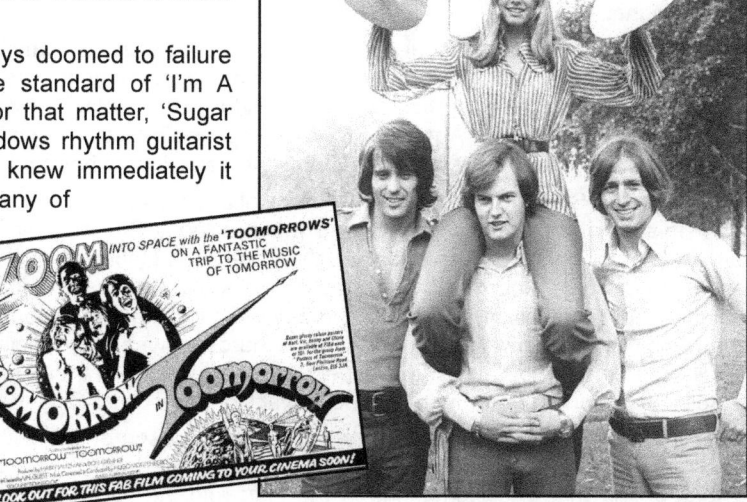

Will you still love them *Toomorrow*?

dismayed enough to approach Roger Cook and Roger Greenaway, Mitch Murray and Les Reed for replacement tunes, though with such changes requiring re-shooting it was always a hopeless quest.

Amiable black drummer Karl Chambers left the band and headed back to Philadelphia to do his own thing before the film was released, leaving the rest of the band to audition new drummers who could also sing. Ben Thomas who sings and plays guitar says that the drummer had left because he 'hated the idea that we were sort of manufactured.' Chambers would go on to work with Teddy Pendergrass, the O Jays and the Three Degrees.

Vic Cooper remained as optimistic as he was naive, believing: 'What's going for us is that the underground people think we're so clean cut, but they'll be surprised at some of the underground sounds that we put over.' However, after a disastrous London opening where it ran for just a week, the film quickly disappeared. Whether or not this was because, as rumour would have it, Kirshner would not allow its release as long as he could still draw breath, *Toomorrow* only turned up on DVD in 2012, a year after the producer's death. Rolling Stone referred to the film's launch as 'the greatest barrage of bullshit in many years' but as a period artefact, and every bit as goofy as it sounds, there's a lot of fun to be had and there's still a chance that publicist Derek Coyte was right when he told the Guardian shortly before its initial release that the film 'could become a cult thing'.

*

After a supporting role in Richard Lester's post-nuclear black comedy *The Bed Sitting Room* (1969), Richard Warwick returned to the subject of the revolutionary counter-culture in his next movie, **THE BREAKING OF BUMBO (1970)**, this time as the film's star. Like *If...,* the source of the film lay in the 1950s, this time with the source novel of the same name, written by the films screenwriter and director Andrew Sinclair, and published against a backdrop of CND and the Suez crisis in 1959.

Old Etonian Sinclair had served his National Service as an ensign in the Coldstream Guards, living in Wellington Barracks alongside Buckingham Palace, which he guarded along with St. James Palace, the Tower of London and the Bank of England. Sinclair's semi-autobiographical novel portrays the young officers as arrogant and childish, spoilt and bored. The assignment to each of his own 'soldier servant', echoes their previous British public school life, and doubtless added to the hours of boredom that were largely filled with drinking to excess and shooting at the ducks in St. James Park. They were, says the novel, 'little scarlet gods, little bowler-hatted gentlemen'. Also part of the Guardsman's duties was attending the succession of debutantes coming-out parties that were an integral part of the London social scene.

With National Service completed, Sinclair took the natural next step and became a Cambridge undergraduate, a position interrupted when the Suez crisis saw him, as an Army Reserve Officer, called back up during his second year. He refused and instead decided to go to Hungary to fight in the revolt against Soviet control there, saying: 'I had been reading political philosophy as well as history at Cambridge, and the intervention at Suez struck me as imperialism and murder, while the Hungarian revolt against Russian control seemed in the just cause of liberty and human rights.'

He never got as far as Hungary, having been met at Victoria Station by his mother threatening to kill herself if he left, and so he returned, 'my heroism between my legs, to Trinity. The Brigade of Guards in its wisdom decided not to court-martial me for desertion and I was told to write a black comedy about a young Brigade of Guards officer who fails to lead a mutiny.' Aged just 22, he completed the novel in just five weeks and it was both a commercial and critical success, though not with the Guards who saw it as a betrayal of the officer class.

The Evening Standard said 'this bitter, ironical and very clever first novel paints a devastating portrait of an upper-class misfit, half clown, half Hamlet' and Tatler called it 'Gruesomely funny... a violent virility that is infectious.' 'The Breaking of Bumbo' found itself placed alongside John Osborne's 'Look Back in Anger', Kingsley Amis's 'Lucky Jim' and John Braine's 'Room At The Top' as the work of a self-styled Angry Young Man - though the author has pointed out that 'they were kicking their way in, while I was kicking my way out. They did, indeed, all move towards the right-wing while I moved towards the left.' Tony Richardson, who had directed both the stage and screen versions of *Look Back in Anger* in 1956 and 1959 respectively, had proposed staging a musical version of Bumbo, to have starred Peter O'Toole and Albert Finney, at the Royal Court but Sinclair instead opted to pursue graduate work in the USA.

Sinclair did eventually work in the theatre, when chosen by the estate of Dylan Thomas to adapt the late Welsh poet's unfinished novel, 'Adventures in the Skin Trade', which was staged at the small Hampstead Theatre with a then-unknown David Hemmings in the lead role. Its success brought cinema work for both writer and actor.

Bird and Lumley in *The Breaking of Bumbo*

Hemmings, having been seen in the play by Antonioni, was cast in *Blow-Up* (1966) and Sinclair 'was offered a serious original screenplay to write for a fortune, and took the offer.' That film was *Before Winter Comes* (1968) starring David Niven, which though no great success, brought him a couple of years working as a script doctor, a trade he describes as 'overpaid, overrated, overseas and under the weather, doing what writers tended to do for the money and knew they should not do.'

Having 'felt the divine spark dying in me', Sinclair began to make films of his own. For this, he returned to 'The Breaking of Bumbo', substituting that novel's Beatniks and Suez crisis for the New Left and the 1968 revolutionary crisis in Europe. After an opening sequence in which Bumbo Bailey (Richard Warwick) is introduced to the rules and regulations of his new regiment, and to the eccentricities of his fellow officers, the film really takes off when he attends a debutante's ball in a Waxworks Museum, where the Graham Bond Initiation provide the entertainment. Also in attendance are a small group of would-be revolutionaries who embark on an impromptu anti-war happening that is part agitprop performance and part protest. It is led by the flak-jacketed tubby University lecturer Jock (John Bird) who uses a blowtorch to melt the faces of various military dignitaries like Churchill and Napoleon, but it is young student Suzie (Joanna Lumley) in, and out of, her tight-fitting red snakeskin trousers that leaves a lasting impression on the young officer. This would be Lumley's first major role following a brief appearance as a Bond girl in *On Her Majesty's Secret Service* (1969), with another of that movie's Bond girls, Anouska Hempel, also turning up here as a convincing debutante. Lumley says the demolition of the Churchill statue left her with 'the uneasy feeling of real wrong doing'.

Accompanying Jock and Susie back to her rather luxurious pad, Bumbo is surprised by her obvious wealth but told 'I don't pretend to be poor, after all, it is only one room, everybody's allowed one room. I'm a dropout from the affluent society. You get just as hung up being rich as being poor.' Susie's appeal to Bumbo is obvious, but while she finds him attractive, his overriding appeal appears to be his position in the Guards and, having sensed his dissatisfaction with everything, how she might subvert that. This is espoused by Jock: 'We could use this guy. He could subvert the entire army. So back to the barracks Bumble boy. Subvert, organise.' And he does, but not before spending the night with the lovely Susie in a scene that, alas, has never been enjoyed in its entirety.

Two further scenes cement Bumbo's conversion to the cause. The first of these takes place in a room in the University where outside, seen via stock footage of the actual event, preparations are being made for the beginning of the March 1968 anti-Vietnam protest march on the American Embassy in Grosvenor Square. There, Jock lays out his ethos for the revolution to his small group of followers. Echoing the non-committal tone of *Toomorrow*'s Matt, he tells them: 'This is a demo, not a riot. We're not ready for a riot yet. We haven't infiltrated. We've got to watch our PR. They've got their PR... Alright, yes, lean on them, but do it gently. After all, we've got to watch the old image you know. TV cameras are going to be there, lots of tourists. Everybody loves a London bobby, so break it up, but softly.' It's not a tactic that finds approval with his younger comrades: 'We can't win that way. It's like a fixed fight; a pre-arranged draw. Nothing ever happens... The trouble with this country is it's so soft. You punch it and you don't hit anything. And people say, "Easy lad, you'll break your fist."'

When an off-duty Bumbo arrives, Jock declares him to be 'living proof that the day is nearer than we thought. We are infiltrating.' 'Or collaborating' suggests a dissenting voice. Jock wants Bumbo to get the men under his charge to lay down their arms as a gesture, despite his protestations that under military law, disobeying an order can get you ten years. 'A political prisoner' offers Susie, 'Is there anything better to be?' It's not an altogether convincing argument to which Bumbo offers an obvious answer: 'In bed with you'. Even less convincing is Jock's assertion that 'the revolution will back you... I put my teaching job on the line every day. I fight for free speech. You don't even dare demonstrate.' But he does dare and lands on the front page of the newspapers, much to the horror of his senior officer who, to pour cold water on his relationship with Susie, sends him off on a regimental rugby tour.

On the way back from one such match, he orders the coach to stop and pick up a dozen student hitchhikers. On their way to a demo in London, they further educate him in the inequalities in the system, and shoehorn into the plot a bit of the counter-culture politics of the time. 'They chucked us out' they tell him, 'We're rebels. They took away our grants. We welded the principal in; he had to pee in his filing cabinet. Tidy bloke. We just wanted a say in what was being done to us. Doesn't everybody?'

They are intending to find an empty office block to occupy, assuring Bumbo that they're not against property per se, 'Just against not sharing it. If young people had somewhere to go in London, there'd be no need to squat.' Compared to the cartoonish politics of Jock and Susie, this is almost social realism - until he adds 'We're gonna have a commune. Share everything. Girls. Ideals. Bread... I suppose one of us will have to work to keep the rest, otherwise, we'll all have to go on a diet, won't we?'

It's after this that, when the coach stops off at a pub, Bumbo broaches the subject to the ranks of them laying down their arms. It's the film's most ideologically coherent moment that addresses why men might blindly follow orders even when it pitches them against their own people. 'Soldiers and students' he tells them, 'they're the scum of the earth. They're pushed around, lousy pay, do this, damn that. The trouble is they hate each other. I mean, can you imagine having a student for a friend? But if soldiers and students got together, they could change the scene; have demos with guns and nothing could stop them.' The Sergeant Major (Derek Newark) points out that as an officer with the benefit of a good education, Bumbo can question such things where, as ordinary guardsmen, they cannot - illustrating this inherent difference by the fact that he alone is holding his pint glass by the handle. Somewhat bemused, they play along.

When, back at the barracks, Bumbo gives the order it is uniformly ignored, leaving him face down on the parade ground floor, as captured on the films intriguing poster, as the squad marches around him. At the film's conclusion Bumbo has settled for his pre-ordained place in upper-class society via marriage to the privileged, and pregnant, Sheila (Natasha Pyne), and the revolutionaries turn their gaze to the Skinheads on their way home from a match between Arsenal and Chelsea. Says Jock: 'Jesus! Skinheads. They'll murder us!' Adds Susie: 'Not if we love them. They can be our shock troops.'

Fans of Joanna Lumley, probably the main reason people might seek the film out today, will be disappointed to learn that, with the film in the can, Sinclair cut the nudity from the love scene between Susie and Bumbo, removing what the BBFCs David Trevelyan described as 'all the running around naked in the naked love-play' in order to receive an AA certificate.- The footage remained missing from the 2013 DVD release despite its claim to be uncut. Those disappointed might like to check out the 1974 sex comedy *The Games That Lovers Play*.

With this version of the film receiving a poor reception at its London premiere, it was removed from EMI's release schedule and the DVD's claim probably refers to the version re-submitted to the BBFC in 1972 when EMI was headed by Nat Cohen, in the hope of receiving an A certificate so that the film might be sent out on a double bill with the *Steptoe and Son* movie. In that version, all scenes of violence, references to mutiny, and dialogue in the scene with the pregnant Sheila, were removed. BBFC records state that 'considerable cuts have been made in the scenes between Bumbo and the constabulary girl, leaving nothing explicit about their love affair except a shot of them lying in bed together (no action) and a talk when it is over. In Reel 4 Sheila tells Bumbo "I'm going to have a..." (sentence not completed) and the argument about abortion has gone.'

The film received an A certificate but the BBFC also pointed out that in the light of the 'Bloody Sunday' massacre two months earlier, 'We think what is left is a pretty sour jest in present circumstances.' EMI, it seemed, concurred, and they placed the film back on the shelf from which it was removed just once for an August 1975 screening on the BBC until resurfacing on Network DVD.

The film ultimately failed because there's no one for the audience to root for, not even Bumbo, whose naivety soon wears thin. The only remotely sympathetic characters are the young ordinary guardsman, among them Warren Clarke as Guardsman Andrews. There would be mileage in Bumbo struggling with the thought that his men might be called upon to turn their weapons on the protesters, and the crisis of conscience that such a situation might bring, if the arguments offered by the films would-be revolutionaries were a little more substantial, especially once Susie has clarified that their relationship will now remain purely platonic. In the words of Sinclair, 'It was slaughtered by the Right for backing the downfall of the Guards and slaughtered by the Left for being an assault on revolutionary chic'. What sits in the middle is not substantial enough to compensate.

Hippies, Skinheads, Rastas, Punks & Disco Dancing Bowie Boot Boys

Power To The People
(Lennon)

Present on the second anti-Vietnam demo, though keeping very much to the periphery, was Mick Jagger who according to writer Barry Miles: 'did have a genuine revulsion against the Vietnam War. But I think much more that it was also the thing to do. That's what everybody in Chelsea was doing that week, going to that demonstration. It was rare for the King's Road people because that end of the underground was very much a hedonistic scene of wealthy aristocrats taking drugs. But there was a political awareness on the King's Road, even if it was transformed into fashion.'

It was the events in Paris several weeks later that would inspire Jagger to put pen to paper and write the lyrics of 'Street Fighting Man', saying, 'There was all this violence going on. I mean they nearly toppled the government in France. De Gaulle went into this complete funk, as he had in the past, and he went and sort of locked himself in his house in the country. And so the government was almost inactive. And the French riot police were amazing. Yeah, it was direct inspiration, because, by comparison, London was very quiet.' Jagger made the comparison explicit in his lyrics:

> Everywhere I hear the sound of marching feet, boy
> Cause summer's here and the time is right
> For rising in the street boy
> But what can a poor boy do?
> Except to sing for a rock 'n' roll band
> Cause in sleepy London town
> There's just no place for street fighting man

At this time, The Beatles were seeking eastern mysticism beside the Ganges in Rishikesh, India where they were disappointed to find their Guru far too interested in the very western delights of actress Mia Farrow. By May they were back in London in time for John Lennon to catch the Parisian students take to the streets on TV. His response was 'Revolution' which took an opposite stance to Jagger, declaring 'If you talk about destruction, don't you know that you can count me out,' and directing 'people with minds that hate' to 'free your mind instead'. It was a message that suited a mainstream publication like Time for whom it was a message to 'radical activists the world over [to] cool it' but a major disappointment to those very radicals.

However, as was usual with Lennon, the full story was rather more complicated. He said, 'I wanted to put out what I felt about revolution. I thought it was about time we spoke about it, the same as I thought it was about time we stopped not answering about the Vietnamese war when we were on tour with Brian Epstein and had to tell him, "We're going to talk about the war this time and we're not going to just waffle"... That's why I did it. I wanted to talk. I wanted to say my piece about revolutions. I wanted to tell you, or whoever listens, to communicate, to say, "What do you say? This is what I say"' Unfortunately, he wasn't entirely sure what his thoughts on the subject were.

There were two very different versions of the song released, and the one that is faster, distorted and was released on the flip side of 'Hey Jude' in August 1968, was the second of the two recorded. The first, appearing on the so-called 'White Album' in November of that year as 'Revolution 1', changes that most contentious line to the ambivalent 'you can count me out-in'. On an earlier demo recorded in May at George Harrison's house, Lennon favoured 'count me out'. In or out, most Beatles fans wouldn't have cared either way.

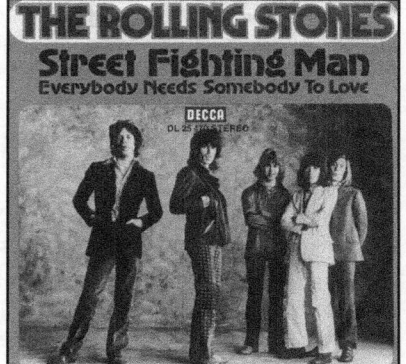

Which is more than could be said of the underground and New Left press who took umbrage at the singer's reluctance to contribute 'money for people with minds that hate' and his mocking reference to people who 'go carrying pictures of Chairman Mao', which would have included a fair chunk of their readership. The release of two musical takes on the subject by the two biggest bands in the world, coming as they did in such close proximity, especially the album versions, meant comparison was inevitable.

In a comparison of both songs under the heading 'Would You Want Your

Sister to Marry a Beatle?', the implication being they'd be better off marrying a Rolling Stone, New Left magazine Ramparts concluded that 'Revolution is a narcissistic little song... that, in these troubled times, preaches counter-revolution... The chorus of the song is, "And you know it's gonna be all right" Well it isn't. You know it's not gonna be all right.' Richard Merton in New Left Review called 'Revolution' 'a lamentable petty bourgeois cry of fear'. In the pages of Black Dwarf, Roland Muldoon said Jagger represented 'the seed of the new cultural revolution' whilst Lennon was declared to be 'safeguarding' The Beatles 'capital investment,' adding 'I hope [they] get so fucked up with their money-making that they become as obscure as Cliff Richard.' (Not the best choice, given Richard's 'Congratulations' picked up an Ivor Novello that year for Most Performed Work).

In their next issue, Black Dwarf reproduced the 'Street Fighting Man' lyrics, handwritten by Jagger with the line, 'I'll kill the king' highlighted. John Hoyland, a regular Black Dwarf contributor, said, 'We took 'Street Fighting Man' very seriously... It seemed to prove that The Roling Stones were a genuinely progressive band in political terms. In retrospect, it's ridiculous because we were so wrong. Jagger was merely dabbling with the image of being a revolutionary. He was actually a Home Counties Tory, and he has been ever since.' Ellen Willis in New Yorker magazine hit the nail on the head when she said that 'Taken together the words of Street Fighting Man are innocuous, but somehow the only line that comes through loud and clear is "Summer's here and the time is right for fighting (sic) in the streets"', with the carefully calculated aura of danger that The Roling Stones had engineered around themselves as a more radical alternative to the Fab Four nullifying Jagger's obvious cop-out that because he's in sleepy old London and all he can do is sing in a band.

Hoyland instead directed his ire at The Beatles in a piece entitled 'Open Letter to John Lennon,' telling the songwriter that 'Love which does not pit itself against suffering, oppression, and humiliation is sloppy and irrelevant.' Lennon responded two months later with 'A Very Open Letter to John Hoyland' telling the author 'I don't worry about what you, the left, the middle, the right or any fucking boys club think,' though from the fact that he responded at all it was obvious he did.

When the VSC organised another march, a poster campaign urged participants to 'follow the lead of the revolutionary students and workers in France: SMASH CAPITALISM'. Lennon and Jagger were both conspicuous by their absence, as one imagines was Speedy Keen who hit pay dirt in July 1969 when 'Something in the Air' by Thunderclap Newman hit the number one spot in the UK. 'We've got to get together sooner or later because the revolution's here' declared the song's writer and vocalist Keen, and 'Hand out the guns and ammo, we're gonna blast our way through here.' Before joining Thunderclap Newman, Keen shared a flat and worked as a chauffeur for Pete Townshend and wrote The Who's 'Armenia City in the Sky'.

'Something in the Air' was essentially a Townsend solo project, having, alongside Keen on drums and vocals, put together Thunderclap Newman by recruiting his former friend from art school, jazz pianist Andy Newman, and a 15-year-old guitar prodigy, and future member of Wings, Jimmy McCulloch. Townsend himself provided the bass lines under the pseudonym Bijou Drains. While probably not particularly heartfelt, the song was clearly a response to the student-based revolutionary fervour in London, but its tenure in the number 1 spot coincided with the death of Francis McCluskey on the 24th of July in Dungiven in Londonderry, found unconscious following a police baton charge on a crowd throwing stones at them outside the town's Orange Hall. It would be considered the first fatality of the Troubles and gave the song a relevance it could not have foreseen.

In 1968 Keen's premonition was a view held by both the police and the press where there was a growing fear that the global Zeitgeist of Sixties political radicalism had finally spread to Britain. Indicative of this growing hysteria, a front-page report in The Times warned, 'A small army of militant extremists plan to seize control of certain highly sensitive installations and buildings in central London next month... This startling plot has been uncovered by a special squad of detectives formed to track down the extremists, who are understood to be manufacturing Molotov cocktail bombs and amassing a small arsenal of weapons they plan to use against police and property in an attempt to dislocate communications and law and order... They plan to take advantage of police preoccupation and hope to face little resistance when storming their selected targets in central London... Militants behind the violence include American draft dodgers and students from the United States, studying in Britain.'

A Special Branch report in September 1968, authored by Chief Inspector Conrad Dixon, identified a shift in the climate of British political activism: 'The climate of opinion among left-wing elements in this country in relation to public political protest has undergone a radical change over the last few years. The emphasis has shifted, first from orderly, peaceful, co-operative meetings and processions to passive resistance and "sit-downs" and now to active confrontation with the authorities to attempt to force social changes and alterations of government policy. Indeed, the more vociferous spokesmen of the left are calling for the complete overthrow of parliamentary democracy and the substitution of various brands of "socialism" and "worker's control". They claim that this can only be achieved by "action on the streets", and although few of them will admit publicly, or in the press, that they desire a state of anarchy, it is nevertheless tacitly accepted that such a condition is a necessary preamble to engineering a breakdown in our present system of government and achieving a revolutionary change in the society in which we live.'

To combat this growing threat, Dixon asked for 'twenty men, half a million pounds and a free hand'. Dixon's wish was granted and saw him head up a unit within the Special Branch, funded directly by the Home Office to maintain its secrecy. At first called the Special Operations Squad and later the Special Demonstration Squad (SDS), the unit used undercover officers to infiltrate political protest groups, becoming intimately involved in the lives of those it sent them to spy on.

The October 1968 demonstration attracted more than 100,000. According to John Rose, a student at the LSE which was being utilised as a base: 'None of us knew what might happen. But we thought the revolution was going to start then.The Times was even predicting the possibility. We would have welcomed a major confrontation which would have raised the stakes and drawn workers into the struggle. Had there been fighting, with serious injuries, possibly even a killing, I'm quite sure a major student rising across the country would have taken place, and the thing would have exploded.'

Instead, the event passed off relatively peacefully with only a couple of hundred breaking away from the main procession in an attempted assault on the American Embassy. A relieved Times declared, 'The festival of angry youth has passed, and what has it shown?' It had shown, the paper said, 'That "the system", which many of the demonstrators are dedicated to break, is sufficiently strong and relaxed to allow them to have their say in their chosen way. That the conditions for insurrectionary violence do not exist in London, and that those who are deluded into believing that the conditions do exist are numerically insignificant.' As if to confirm the Times headline, with troops by then already being withdrawn from Vietnam, a further London demonstration on 16th March of the following year attracted just 4000 protesters.

Nevertheless, in December 1969 when the Stones returned to England from Altamont, it was to newspaper headlines like one declaring 'General Jagger' in the Coventry Evening Telegraph and calling The Roling Stones singer 'the way-out leader of youth's social revolution'. They went on: 'Youth looks for a leader, a hero; someone to look up to. Mick Jagger is one it has chosen... not as it would have done a generation ago - because he was so different, so better than the common herd; someone to hold back from and admire from afar. The young have chosen Jagger because he is one of them - an exaggerated, larger-than-life version of most of them. He has been picked out as a leader in much the same way as revolutionaries elect their general. He is the extremist, the loudest, the fearless fighter. And a revolution is what he is fighting, with all the vigour he and his followers can muster. It is a social revolution, born of youth's frustration and anxiety and nurtured by the new respect for youth's power.' Not bad for a knight of the realm who told the Guardian in 2013 that he was 'surprised by anti-Thatcher sentiment,' and of whom the same paper pointed out that because of his bands pricing policy 'you pretty well need to own a top hat and monocle to get in.'

Jagger wasn't by a long way the only rock star whose politics didn't match up to their stage persona. For the 1970 General Election Melody Maker ran a feature, 'Pop & the Election', which asked musicians where their loyalties lay and found equal parts disappointed socialists like Robert Wyatt (who aligned himself with the Liberals), self-interested Tories like Robin Gibb and those like Robert Plant who pleaded apathy. Eric Clapton rather bizarrely stated, 'I don't see that it matters which government is elected because the country is really run by the youth. Youth is the prophet of the age and they have taken over,' but by this point most of what Clapton said was bizarre and his political affiliation would become clear in a speech made in concert at the Rainbow in 1976, echoing those of Rod Stewart, who told International Times in 1970, 'I think Enoch is the man, I'm all for him. The country is overcrowded. The immigrants should be sent home. That's it.' Aligning himself even further to the right, The Who's Roger Daltrey told a journalist 'We're just not strong enough leaders. You need someone who's gonna make people jump. You need a Hitler figure to just say, "This is what it is". And Hitler was right for Germany at the time, they were really being shit on. He turned out mad at the end, but when he started, he was there, he just did marvellous things for the

German people. You just need a Hitler figure, internationally, for kids.' Daltrey also suggested 'England is full up... They have to stop people from moving in.'

As remains all too common with the left, sectarian splits between Trotskyites, Marxists, Anarchists, and moderate Labourites, those who advocated the raised fist of violent resistance and those who favoured the raised joint of pacifism, were never far from the surface. In February 1970 Black Dwarf disintegrated, splitting into two with Ali starting a new paper, Red Mole. In the election itself, won by the Conservatives, the socialist Marxist vote totalled 0.14 percent, 60% of which was for the Communist Party.

*

In June 1971, Pete Townshend, this time with The Who, released 'Won't Get Fooled Again', a song that he says 'was meant to tell politicians and revolutionaries alike that what lay in the centre of my life was not for sale, and could not be co-opted to any obvious cause.' It was a song, he said, that 'screams defiance at those who feel any cause is better than no cause.' It was a response, he told a 1985 radio special on 'My Generation' to the supposed 'new breed' of politicians that emerged in the 1970s. Some 400,000 punters at Woodstock witnessed another direct response to this when Yippie spokesperson Abbie Hoffman grabbed the microphone as Townsend adjusted his amp between songs, to rail against the jailing of White Panther leader John Sinclair, only to be told to 'Fuck off. Fuck off my fucking stage' and in the words of Country Joe McDonald, 'walked over and bonked Abbie in the head with his guitar.'

Although the song begins with 'revolution' and 'fighting in the streets' by the conclusion it has changed nothing, with the declaration 'Meet the new boss, same as the old boss'. In his biography Townshend is quoted as believing that 'revolution is not going to change anything in the long run, and people are going to get hurt.' In a letter to the Who songwriter, published along with a reply in International Times, Mick Farren and his co-signatories suggested that the songs negativity and the group's defensiveness was 'potentially damaging the consciousness of kids who still strongly identify with the Who as an extension of their lifestyle. In fact, it's calculated to bring down anybody seeking radical change...' Townshend responded that 'I suppose if I wasn't cunt enough to be a rock star I would be round there with you... the fact is... I'm not with you. Neither in your neighbourhood nor frame of mind.' Soon after, Townshend retreated to the safety of the early sixties with 'Quadrophenia'.

The May 2006 issue of National Review published a list of the 50 greatest Conservative rock songs in which 'Won't Get Fooled Again' came in at number 1. Its claim for that, presumably unwanted, title was strengthened when Townshend refused to allow filmmaker Michael Moore use it to highlight a key point in his movie *Fahrenheit 11/9* (2018) in much the same way he had used 'Happiness Is A Warm Gun' in *Bowling For Columbine* (2002). Townshend, who admitted that 'at the beginning of the war in Iraq I was a supporter.' says he was 'unconvinced' by the director's work - but allowed the song to be used to advertise the 2000 Nissan Maxima and to become the *CSI* TV theme. It's hard to imagine Townsend drove many Nissan's and therefore it probably wasn't the Japanese multinational's previous work that clinched the deal so it must have been the ad director's previous work for Aunty Betty's Yorkshire Puddings.

Jagger, meanwhile, continued to play the man of the people. With the Stones Decca contract expiring he told a Danish newspaper, 'I want to earn money off our new records, not for the sake of the money, but to invest in other things, such as the Black Panther breakfast programme for ghetto children. We have already set aside some bread for them, in fact.'

'We found out all the bread we made for Decca was going into little black boxes that go into American Air Force bombers to bomb fucking North Vietnam. They took the bread we made for them and put it into the radar section of their business. When we found that out, it blew our minds. Goddam, you've helped to kill God knows how many thousands of people without even knowing it. I'd rather the Mafia than Decca,' he went on. This excited International Times who envisaged the Stones having 'put themselves into the position of having Worker's Control over their own product.' Instead Jagger, who had attended the London School of Economics, hired, wait for it, Count Rupert Louis Ferdinand Frederick Constantine Lofredo Leopold Herbert Maximilian Hubert John Henry zu Loewenstein-Wertheim-Freudenberg to whom he had been introduced by the art dealer Christopher Gibbs, who reduced the band's tax rate to just 1.6 percent and taught them to cut sponsorship and rights deals with stalwarts like US giants like Anheuser-Busch, Microsoft, and Sprint. After negotiations with all the record corporations for the best deal for the Stones 'independent' label, the band settled on Kinney Corporation who owned Warner & Atlantic.

Vanessa Howard in *What Became of Jack & Jill*

Sink into the mire
Embrace the butcher
But change the world
    Bertoit Brecht 'Die Maßnahme'

'Something In The Air' writer Speedy Keen's first recorded song was 'Club of Lights', released in 1966 by Oscar on Reaction Records. Oscar was the stage name of Paul Nicholas the star of **WHAT BECAME OF JACK & JILL (1971)**, a co-production of the British-based Amicus, best known for their portmanteau horror movies, and the US-based Palomar Pictures International who would presumably have put up much of the money in return for US distribution rights. Based on the little-known 1969 novel, 'The Ruthless Ones' by Laurence Moody, the change of title must have been very much an afterthought, given the two lead characters are John and Jill, most likely a nod to *Whatever Happened to Baby Jane* (1962) as presumably was the same year's less well remembered Shelley Winters melodramatic pot-boiler *What's the Matter with Helen* (1971).

John (Nicholas) is a 22-year-old thoroughly self-centred sociopath who lives with his 78-year-old Gran (Mona Washbourne) and has a theory about the generations. 'The middle-aged are like customers in a restaurant sitting over a slap-up meal. Everything's rosy, so why worry about tomorrow. But the young, they're like hungry people standing in a queue outside. Noses up against the glass, waiting for a table,' he tells his Gran. 'What about the old?' she asks. 'Oh, the old. Well, they've finished their scoff, Gran, and they sit on and on. They just don't know when to get up and go.' And go is what he has in mind for her. Along with girlfriend Jill (Vanessa Howard), he has plans for his inheritance that won't wait: 'Modern medicine, it's too successful, that's the trouble. Old is living longer, eating up more, taking up space, filling houses, hospital beds.' It could have been written yesterday.

Though Gran thinks her grandson dotes on her, behind her back he shows nothing but contempt, at one point casually popping a zit in the mirror whilst she suffers an attack and cries out for her medicine. His girlfriend, whom he sneaks in at night once Gran is tucked up in bed, is even worse with only a heart-of-stone beneath her doll-like beauty. Pushing Jack along in his plan at every opportunity, she would just as soon bludgeon the old dear to death and have done with it.

Rather than push the vulnerable old lady down a flight of stairs, Jack has an altogether grander plan involving the wave of political youth unrest that was causing apoplexy amongst the older generations and would have been especially topical when Moody was writing his novel. He has convinced the house-bound old lady that there's a war brewing on the streets and the youth are taking over. Tired of waiting for their just rewards from the older generation they have taken them by force, with those over eighty having already been targeted and stripped of their homes. Initially, Gran, a veteran of two world wars, isn't too worried. 'Softest generation ever,' she tells him. 'They make their point by sitting down.' But as John and Jill gradually increase the gas-lighting, so too the pressure on grandma's dicky heart.

As John watches a TV news report of police quelling student rioting in the United States, Gran enters the room. 'America?' she asks with contempt. 'You think?' he replies. 'It isn't?' 'Yorkshire. Special anti-riot troops.' 'What are they rioting?' 'Power. Youth power.' 'They're only kids. Why can't they wait?' 'Nobody waits today, there's no guarantee there'll be anything to wait for.'

The climax of the couple's plan comes on the day of a student rag week parade which, by using her obvious charms, Jill has arranged to travel down Gran's usually quiet suburban street. Presented with the news that the

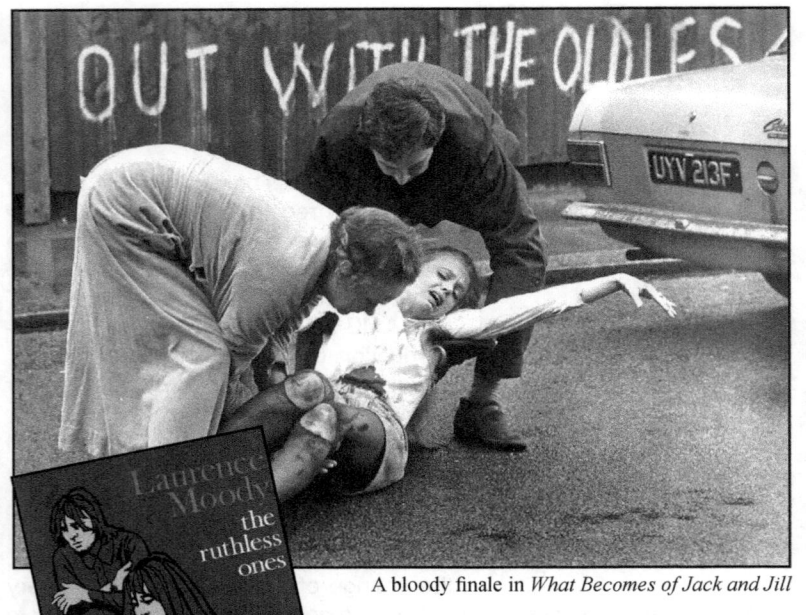

A bloody finale in *What Becomes of Jack and Jill*

age-limit has been reduced to 75 and that the youth are coming for her, and the combined din of Jill hammering at the back door, the front doorbell taped down to ring continuously with the fabricated sound of the extermination squad's jackboots, Gran is left clutching at her heart and beating the walls in terror before collapsing lifeless to the floor.

The couple's elation at the success of their plan comes crashing down when they discover that Gran has left a shock of her own in the form of an amendment to her will that means her grandson can only inherit if he marries – anyone but Jill! Attempts to find a way around Gran's new will see the two scoping out prospective wives in a seedy nightclub but when Johns seems to enjoy himself a little too much, Jill's jealousy – 'Smoke coming out of your pants. Horn on you like a rhino!' she yells at him – brings their relationship crashing to a violent conclusion; she in a pool of blood on the road outside as he whimpers like a child for his Gran by the door.

The film was not well received, with David McGillivray in the BFI's Monthly Film Bulletin pulling no punches, calling it 'An agonisingly slow and uninteresting thriller, which teases one into concentrating on a highly improbable piece of deception by implying that its enfants terrible will at least meet with a suitable surprising retribution. The denouement, a feebly contrived variation on thieves falling out, merely provides the final disenchantment.'

Director Bill Bain was regularly at the helm of some of Britain's most prestigious television drama, including several episodes of *The Avengers* and many of *Armhchair Theatre*. Though he died in 1982 at just 55 he passed his talent on to son Sam, co-writer of situation comedies *Fresh Meat* and *Peep Show* and the film *Four Lions* (2010). Howard, best known for a starring role in *Mumsy, Nanny, Sonny & Girly* (1970), appeared on-screen just once more, in a TV movie adaptation of *The Picture of Dorian Gray* (1972). She retired from acting after marrying film producer Robert Chartoff and moving to California, dying in 2010, aged 62, due to complications resulting from chronic obstructive pulmonary disease (COPD).

Nicholas first embarked on a pop career in the sixties, releasing two singles as Paul Dean and three as Oscar but failed to make an impact, despite the second, 'Join My Gang', being a Pete Townshend composition and the third, 'Over The Wall We Go', being written and produced by David Bowie. Real success came on the London stage, first as Claude in *Hair* and then originating the title role in *Jesus Christ Superstar*. After *What Became of Jack & Jill?* he landed supporting roles in films with a musical backdrop such as *Stardust* (1974), *Tommy* (1975) and *Litzomania* (1975). A third foray into the world of pop was rewarded with three top twenty singles, including 'Grandma's Party', during 1976 and whilst the following year's 'Heaven on the 7th Floor' stalled here at number 40, in America, it reached number 6. Despite this, the peak of his fame came in 1983 in the much-loved sitcom *Just Good Friends* as the loveable rogue Vince Pinner and he remains a regular face on British TV screens.

*

By the end of 1970, John Lennon was 'sick of all these aggressive Hippies or whatever they are – the Now Generation – sort of being very uptight with me... Just either on the street or anywhere, on the phone or demanding my attention, as if I owe them something. I'm not their fucking parents. They frighten me. There's a lot of uptight maniacs going round wearing fucking peace symbols.' A month later the singer had a change of heart, meeting Tariq Ali and his Red Mole co-editor Robin Blackburn, and talking to the duo for several hours with the meeting resulting in not only a magazine article but also in inspiring a change in Lennon's revolutionary priorities, convinced that his part in the revolution would be his songwriting. 'You say you want a revolution' he says in 'Power to the People', written immediately after the meeting. 'We better get it on right away.'

Amongst those from the United Kingdom who had taken part in the Paris uprising was Christopher Bott who would later find himself charged at the Old Bailey alongside seven others as members of the so-called Angry Brigade: 'In the slogan of the times, imagination was seizing power. Over in France... there was a social revolution going on where real forms of liberation were taking place and I was comparing that with the boring, dull stultified atmosphere of Britain at that particular time. Comparing that to France where the revolutionary forces were not small groups of middle-class radicals but ten million people had taken the factories and millions of people were on the streets and over here comparing it to the passive, easy consumption of a life in front of a television screen.'

By the time this revolutionary fervour reached the streets of London for the 100,000 strong anti-Vietnam demo in October 1968, the police were prepared and out in force. Any revolutionaries amongst the crowd swiftly concluded that big demonstrations were no longer the way forward. Elsewhere, radicals were taking their fight in new directions. In Germany, the Baader-Meinhof Group declared war on German society and set the template for how a small yet organised group could terrorise an entire country. Similar groups sprang up throughout Europe - in Holland, Turkey, and even Switzerland. In Italy alone, there were 145 explosions during 1969. In Britain, the Spanish targets of the 1st of May group began to take on a non-Spanish flavour, though the forensics pointed to the same source.

In March 1968, a small bomb was left by the side door of the Spanish Embassy in London. This was the first in a string of twelve bomb attacks on government buildings, which also included the US Officers Club in London, and Italian government offices in London, Birmingham, and Manchester. Though a communique was attributed to the Spanish-based 1st of May group (as was the US Officers Club attack), it was also the first attack deemed to have been the action of the so-called Angry Brigade. Subsequent targets included Spanish banks in London and Liverpool, the offices of the Spanish airline Iberia, the home of the Attorney General Sir Peter Rawlinson, the home of the Commissioner of the Metropolitan Police, Paddington Green police station and the computer room at New Scotland Yard. The latter was the first incident in which the bombers left a communique as The Angry Brigade which read: 'Police Computers Cannot Tell The Truth, They Just Record Our Crime. The Pig Murders Go Unrecorded.' An army recruitment office was targeted, as was the 1970 Miss World Contest, where a BBC outside broadcast van was blown up, offices belonging to the Ford Motor Company as well as the home of its British managing director, the Fulham home of Cabinet Minister John Davies, the Department of Employment and the home of Employment Secretary Robert Carr.

Peter Flannery's **OUR FRIENDS IN THE NORTH (1996)**, a nine-part TV drama spanning 31 years in the lives of a quartet of friends in Newcastle, begins in 1964 where having left school, Nicky Hutchinson (Christopher Eccleston) returns from a summer spent working for the Civil Rights Movement in the USA prior to taking up his place at Manchester University. Despite being the first member of his resolutely working-class family to have such an opportunity, at the last minute he opts instead to work as the right-hand man of a local Labour politician, Austin Donahue (Alun Armstrong).

When Nicky's dreams of doing something positive for his impoverished community, desperate for decent housing, are shattered by the realisation of the depth of corruption in Donahue's involvement with the property developer John Edwards (Geoffrey Hutchings), he heads to London where, by 1970, he has become deeply involved in an armed anarchist commune.

Time for action in *Our Friends in the North*

Flannery based Donahue and Edwards on the real-life T. Dan Smith and John Poulson whose low quality, high rise, high profit, housing projects became a national scandal, and the anarchist cell takes its lead from the exploits of the Angry Brigade. At a group meeting, we see Nicky putting the finishing touches to a communique which he reads aloud to the group: 'You, the politicians, the leaders, the rich, the big bosses are in command. You attempt to control us. We, the people, suffer. You turn us into robots on your production lines; you pollute the world with chemical waste from your factories. You shove mass media garbage down our throats, you turn the law into a pig service; you turn us all, men and women, into sexual caricatures. You kill us; you napalm us; you boil us down into soap, mutilate us, rape us. This has gone on for centuries but it's coming to an end. You cannot control our revolution because it springs from the rank and file. You cannot penetrate our organisation because we have none. The people will smash the system. The people will seize power.'

The cell members have each chosen a target with which they have some personal connection. These include the Spanish Embassy, the Metropolitan Police Commissioner, the Attorney General, the Miss World Contest and, for Nicky, the Ministry of Housing. We see a drive-by shooting at the Spanish Embassy and Nicky photographing the Police Commissioner's house prior to a bomb going off in his hallway but, when Nicky's previous involvement in the Edwards scandal brings the fraud squad knocking, the group gets spooked, and he is despatched back to Newcastle before he carries out his own action. Which is just as well because when he rings his fellow cell member and girlfriend, Helen (Harriet Keevil) from a phone box, the call is interrupted by the sound of a police raid.

A huge success when broadcast, *Our Friends In The North* had a long and problematic journey from its origins at the Other Place in Stratford where directed by John Caird and starring Jim Broadbent and Roger Allam, it was staged by the Royal Shakespeare Company in 1982, before touring Newcastle and ending with a run at The Pit, a studio theatre inside the Barbican. The events in that version of the play ended in 1979 with the election of Margaret Thatcher.

BBC producer Michael Wearing had seen the Newcastle production and approached the writer about adapting it for a 4 part series but the idea was KO'd by the then Director of Programmes, Michael Grade. Having risen to the position of Head of Serials, Wearing tried to get the project off the ground again in 1989 but was stalled by the BBC's concerns about the legal implications of having recognisable real-life characters such as Smith, Poulson and, particularly, the former Home Secretary Reginald Maudling on whom the play's corrupt Cabinet Minister, Claude Seabrook, was based. A third approach, to BBC2 controller Alan Yentob in 1992, also failed but finally, with both Wearing and Yentob having moved on, the young producer Charles Pattinson persuaded Yentob's successor, Michael Jackson, to give the now extended drama the green light.

The subject made an appearance in the ITV daytime drama series *Crown Court*, produced by Granada and broadcast between 1972 and 1984. Each story would follow a case in the fictional Fulchester Crown Court and go out on three consecutive afternoons in 25-minute episodes. The drama was restricted to the Crown Court itself and whilst an array of recognisable actors played the characters, the jury was made up of members of the general public whose independent verdict, with two endings prepared, dictated the outcome. In **CROWN COURT: CONSPIRACY (1972)**, the 27-year-old Trevor Luckhurst (Keith Bell) and Jill Sawyer (Sara Clee), a twenty-year-old student are accused of planting and detonating a homemade bomb at a company called IWS. The two have been witnessed in the act by an elderly night watchman with impaired vision and a grudge against what he calls 'long-haired yobbos... All they want to do is overthrow the country. It's diabolical; they get away with murder these days.'

They are both known to him because they have been part of a picket outside the company's offices, protesting about a magazine it publishes. Aside from that, the evidence consists of two broken alarm clocks, parts from which are alleged to have been used in the bomb timer, glass from the office on a pair of plimsolls, and letters exchanged between the two defendants that express a desire to break in. A prisoner from where Trevor has been held on remand for 6 months says that he had told him he was guilty.

The house from which these items were recovered had been inherited by Trevor and opened up to 'like-minded friends' as a commune where the house rules included the abolition of private ownership, even personal clothing. Trevor won't reveal to whom the clocks and shoes belong because, he says, they're not guilty either. The jury agrees, and they are found not guilty on both charges, yet the judge tells them, 'you are an extremely fortunate young couple'. Based on the actual evidence presented, however, six months already served hardly seems like good fortune.

*

'You bitch about the system. I bitch about the system; Vince isn't like that. He does something about it' says final year sociology student Giles (Peter Settelen). 'Yes,' says his friend Rick (Douglas Heard), 'and God help anyone who gets in his way.' 'Sometimes,' says Giles, 'people get hurt. It's unavoidable.' This conversation takes place in **PUBLIC EYE: THE FATTED CALF (1975)** as two students make their way home from a protest by workers outside a factory due for closure at which Vince (Alun Armstrong) has rallied the redundancy-threatened employees into direct action, breaking through the gates to stage a work-in.

The owner of the factory is Giles's father and the two have a heated argument, Giles calling the closure 'obscene'. When some time later the father calls at the student accommodation where his son should have been staying he is told that he moved out a week ago. Down at heel private eye Frank Marker (Alfred Burke) is subsequently hired to track down the errant son and discovers that, despite his finals being only weeks away, he has also 'dropped out'.

He's lodging with Vince, helping him produce the militant newspaper Workers Arise whilst also working on the night shift at the factory. Vince though is getting fed up with publishing a newspaper that struggles to cover its costs and tells Giles; 'If you want to make a difference, plant a bomb... not a real one, we wouldn't want to hurt anyone, would we? No, I mean a publicity explosion.' This, he suggests, involves sticking a couple of bundles of unsold newspapers in a store and ringing the manager. 'The message should get through loud and clear.' Giles agrees and carries out the plan with Vince's girlfriend Janet (Jan Harvey).

Vince tells Janet he wants to do it again, 'only this time for real' - neglecting however to inform Giles that this second package, left in a boutique, contains more than newsprint. He also neglects to tell him he has paid his father a visit and demanded £5000 not to turn Giles in.

The communique left by the Angry Brigade after the bombing of one of their more unlikely targets, the trendy clothes shop Biba, declared boutiques to be 'modern slave houses. You can't reform profit-capitalism and inhumanity. Just kick it until it breaks. Revolution!' As it turned out, the 'people' never really had their hearts in the revolution beyond taking the single of the same name to number 6 in the charts and it was the trade unions who wanted 'power' as both Conservative and Labour governments would soon learn.

During this period, Lennon would align himself with various revolutionary factions across the Atlantic, but then swiftly abandoned them when his associations began to interfere with his hopes for US citizenship. Referring to the 'Cambridge Graduate School of Revolutionaries', Lennon later said, 'They made us feel so guilty about not hating everyone who wasn't poor that I even wrote and recorded the rather embarrassing 'Power to the People', ten years too late.' Part of this embarrassment might have been related to 'Power to the People' being adopted as the catchphrase for young Marxist urban guerrilla 'Wolfie' Smith (Robert Lindsay), self-proclaimed leader of the Tooting Popular Front in **CITIZEN SMITH**, 1970s revolutionary politics very own BBC sitcom that aired rather belatedly in 1977 and ran until 1980. The series was the first sitcom from acclaimed writer John Sullivan who would strike gold with his follow-up series Only Fools & Horses. Sullivan was working as a scenery shifter at the BBC when he came up with the idea and made an impromptu pitch to legendary comedy producer Dennis Main Wilson, who commissioned a pilot as part of the series Comedy Special, broadcast during April 1977, with a full six episode run following in November.

Robert Lindsay prepares for the glorious day in *Citizen Smith*

At the heart of the series was Citizen 'Wolfie' Smith who would emerge from Tooting underground station at the beginning of each episode to the sound of the international socialist anthem, 'The Red Flag', dressed in his trademark Che Guevara t-shirt, beret and Afghan coat, before raising a fist to declare 'Power to the People.'

Citizen Smith began with an excellent introduction to its two main characters as Ken (Mike Grady) sits cross-legged, quietly meditating while Wolfie paints the graffiti 'THINK AHEA' before running out of space and admonishing the council for not providing a long enough wall. Over subsequent episodes, Wolfie would espouse his Marxist/Trotskyist philosophy and dreams of following in the footsteps of his hero Che Guevara until 'come the Glorious Day' when the downtrodden proletariat rise up and throw off the shackles of their capitalist oppressors.

Despite their inadequacies, Wolfie, Ken, Tucker (Tony Millan) and Speed (George Sweeney) embarked on the occasional piece of extreme direct action. In the sixth episode of the initial series, *The Hostage*, they plan the kidnap of a recently elected Tory MP, after Wolfie's attempt at a legitimate political career results in just 6 votes. They instead mistakenly kidnap local gangster Harry Fenning. More often than not though, Wolfie would simply try to raise the money for his bar tab at the local whilst avoiding the wrath of the aforementioned Fenning and the even more worrying demands, such as engagement, of long-suffering girlfriend Shirley (Cheryl Hall). Occasionally Wolfie's dreams of revolution do temporarily appear to bear fruit, such as when a visiting Spanish revolutionary from the Bilbao Liberation Movement promises 'dinero' and 'one thousand young soldiers' only for the BLM, with its seven members, to turn out to be almost as ineffective and cash-strapped as the TPF.

The show peaked with the third series finale, *The Glorious Day*, in which, following manoeuvres on Salisbury Plain, the TPF liberate an abandoned Scorpion tank which they drive to Parliament in order to seize the reins of power. Only it didn't quite happen that way. With Parliament closed for the summer recess, the foursome are arrested and, even worse, after serving a year in prison, are released for an unnecessary and lacklustre fourth series where, having already run its natural course, the humour becomes strained.

A blacker comedy is at play in **LITTLE MALCOLM AND HIS STRUGGLE AGAINST THE EUNUCHS (1974)** which began life as a stage play, directed and designed by Mike Leigh at the Unity Theatre in 1965, the now celebrated director having met its writer and lead actor, David Halliwell, at RADA in 1960 when the writer was in his mid-20s and the director just 17. The play was not a success. Leigh recalls sitting in a Chinese restaurant one evening and seeing a member of his cast walk past. When he asked what he was doing there, the actor told him, 'There's only four people in, so we're not doing it.' Part of the problem might have been the fact that this version of the play came in at six hours, ensuring it was a case of very sore bums on seats for those who did attend. Leigh says that Halliwell's original script, 191 pages of dense typewritten A4, would have run for 15 hours.

The Leigh production was by most accounts not very good. Leigh found Halliwell, who guarded every word of his text, impossible to direct. Halliwell thought Leigh had not directed it well. There were likewise issues amongst the cast and Philip Martin who was also Halliwell's roommate fell out irreconcilably with his friend, whilst another of the cast was stricken with appendicitis and had to be replaced late into rehearsals. Worst of all thought Halliwell was that the only actress they could find willing to take on the part of Ann was not right for the part. As well as being incredibly posh, he says, 'She was very tall, taller than me and Philip and, needless to say, the director. She was called Julian Bulberry. Her father had dreamt of having a boy but got a girl and called her Julian anyway. We tried to persuade her to drop the "n" and make life easier for herself, but she wouldn't, and one of the reviewers referred to her as "Julian Bulberry (a girl)" so she couldn't be mistaken for a boy in drag. But a bloke in drag would probably have been a better idea. I'm not attacking Julian Bulberry as an actress. But she was huge. And she wasn't right. So she was very unhappy.'

The play nevertheless garnered a review in the satirical magazine Punch that Leigh called 'perceptive and encouraging' and a rave from Alan Brien in the Telegraph, both of which were duly despatched to hot young West End producer Michael Codron who invited the playwright for tea, during which a special performance was arranged for him at the Prince of Wales on the set of another play. Finding it, according to Halliwell, the best first play he had ever seen, Codron agreed to a West End production on the provisos that Halliwell could not act in it and Leigh could not direct. Codron replaced Halliwell in the role of Malcolm with his and Leigh's fellow RADA classmate John Hurt, appearing alongside Rodney Bewes, Kenneth Colley, Tim Preece, and Susan Ashworth. Director Patrick Dromgoole also cut the running time to a more audience-friendly two hours before staging it at the Garrick Theatre at the end of 1965 where despite good reviews and the patronage of the likes of The Beatles and Laurence Olivier, poor attendance meant the show would close within a fortnight. A US production fared even worse, closing after just 6 days and 8 performances at the end of 1966.

As with Leigh's production, the play's subsequent fate lay not with how many but who saw it. Amongst those who had sat through Codron's revised performance was George Harrison, who, nine years later, decided that he would, via Apple Films, produce a film version. It was through his association with another Beatle that another RADA trained actor, Derek Woodward, would come to adapt Halliwell's play for the big screen. Woodward had a supporting role as a werewolf in the rock horror musical film *Son Of Dracula* (1974) which starred Ringo Starr and Harry Nilsson who invited him down to the studio where the two were recording the soundtrack album along with the likes of Peter Frampton and Nicky Hopkins. When he arrived, sitting at the mixing desk was Harrison who, having heard he worked largely on the stage, told Woodward that the only play he

The Party of Dynamic Erection in *Malcolm & His Struggle Against the Eunuchs*

had 'ever enjoyed watching was *Little Malcolm*... He said we should be making that film instead. I told him that putting things together was my game and that I could do the screenplay. He said he'd do it on one condition - that John Hurt played the lead.'

With Hurt on board, the three approached another RADA alumni, American director Stuart Cooper, on the strength of his documentaries on Spanish painter Juan Gerovase, *A Test Of Violence* (1970) and painter Sidney Nolan, *Ned Kelly Country: The Paintings of Sidney Nolan* (1972), made for the BBC's *Omnibus*. The money, says Cooper, came from the company Suba Films, set up specifically to collect profits from the *Yellow Submarine (1968)* animated film, and was somewhere between £1 and 1.5 million: 'He stepped up, wrote the cheque and we made the movie.'

The plot of *Little Malcolm & His Struggle Against The Eunuchs* had its roots in Halliwell's time studying at Huddersfield College of Art in the late 1950s where, like Malcolm Scrawdyke in the play, he was expelled - though in the playwright's case, soon after readmitted. Halliwell denies the story is autobiographical but to Leigh the playwright was Scrawdyke. 'Well, he was, and he wasn't.' He was, adds Leigh, 'in a Scrawdykian way, confrontational and argumentative.' Janet Street-Porter who remained a friend after being cast as a journalist by Halliwell in a television play, calls him 'Totally uncompromising and never interested in fitting in. A one-off.' Codron found him 'a rather grumpy fellow - a real loner, rather scruffy and rather unhappy.' An insight into the man's personality is found in one incident from his childhood, recalled by Leigh, in which after being told to take off his raincoat by a headmaster, he kept it on for a whole year. The choice of titles for his subsequent plays suggests a writer with very little time for the business side of his chosen profession; *A Last Belch For The Great Aulk*; *Janitress Thrilled By Prehensile Penis* and his play about a child killer, *KD Dufford Hears KD Dufford Ask KD Dufford How KD Dufford'll Make KD Dufford* - all of which go some way to explaining why despite Leigh's assertion that 'he could and should have been up there with Beckett and Pinter', he never was.

Shot over six winter weeks on location in Oldham, the play's original setting having been 22 miles across the Pennines in Huddersfield (which appears in a few exterior shots), the film opens in a freezing and suitably squalid student bedsit where Malcolm Scrawdyke (John Hurt) is trying to persuade himself to get out of bed: 'It's no use just theorising about getting up. It's the act that counts'. Once up, he is joined in his squalor by friends and fellow students Wick (John McEnery) and Irwin (Raymond Platt) who bring with them news from a disciplinary meeting of his expulsion. Wick directs his anger towards the two female attendees, whom he describes as 'them two chastity belts on legs... that little Ackroyd's really vicious when she gets going. Nearly clawed my eyes out when I said we should back you. Didn't she Irwin?' 'Aye, she nearly touched you' confirms his placid compadre. 'I'd have touched her!' bites back Wick, with a menace that foreshadows later shocking events.

The expulsion is not unwarranted. Malcolm himself admits it had been the result of 'five years arsin' around. Surprised 'e let me go on so long. Spent 'alf me bloody time down there sittin' in 'is room bein' given a last chance.' Malcolm's ire is aimed at the unseen art college lecturer, Allard, for whom he devises an elaborate revenge involving the theft of a painting by Sir Stanley Spencer from a local art gallery, and the kidnapping of Allard who is to be blackmailed over an extra-marital liaison, into destroying the artwork. To furnish this act with a political significance, Malcolm forms his friends into a revolutionary group called the Party of Dynamic Erection, with himself as the leader - or should that be fuhrer? When Ingham suggests they can't form a Party, being just three strong, Malcolm corrects him that 'Hitler started with seven.' 'Our first goal' he tells them, 'will be to smash Allard. Our ultimate goal'll be t' realise all our dreams, take our proper place in the scheme of things, an' achieve absolute power.' 'Members'll come rollin' in' he assures them. 'You're deceived by appearances... You think because all you can see is three blokes in a drab room, that's all there is. I see the reality. We are the germ. The revolution isn't in this room. It's up 'ere. Will power. The first and last necessity. With it, you can do anything, without it nothin'. An' we've got it.'

While Wick and Irwin are all too happy to adopt the Party's salute and proclaim 'Hail Scrawdyke!', a fourth member, Party Archivist and Minister of Records, Nipple (David Warner) is more questioning - pointedly offering an exaggerated Nazi salute in place of the official 'clawed hand'. With his NHS glasses peering through a permanently hooded duffel coat from the pockets of which his hands seldom stray, Warner's odd physicality steals every scene.

What all four Party members have in common is a fear of the opposite sex - in Malcolm's case of sex itself. Wick expresses this through his open hostility towards women; the childlike Irwin is virtually asexual. Nipple is a delusional fantasist who believes he has power over women through 'a certain inner magnet that pulls them [women] towards me.' Malcolm denies that he even knows the sole female character, Ann (Rosalind Ayers), although he reveals in his opening monologue that he is both panicked and excited because she has asked him out. Ann is actually in awe of Malcolm, attracted to the outwardly rebellious persona he works hard to cultivate, believing him to be a real man. This image is tarnished when, after the date and invited back to her place, his floundering leaves him babbling about her kitchen and wallpaper. It is when later on she challenges him to have sex with her, to confirm her suspicion that he is, in fact, incapable, that propels the second darker half of the film towards its violent conclusion.

Unfortunately, no sooner was the film edited and printed than it was impounded. Says Cooper, 'In the end, we got hung up by The Beatles break-up, when all of the Apple and Beatles assets went into the Official Receiver's hands. So *Little Malcolm...* just basically sat there for a couple of years. Whatever heat and buzz we generated was all lost. It didn't diminish the movie, but it stopped the momentum.' Harrison finally regained control and entered the film into the Berlin Film Festival where it picked up the Silver Bear for the film's direction and they partied with Fassbinder. 'He loved Malcolm,' adds Cooper. 'I think everyone has a pretty clear idea of how Fassbinder looked at that point; scruffy, sunglasses, leather, unkempt beard - watching him drinking with Johnny Hurt with his horrible scruffy beard, and still dressed like Malcolm. Really, they could have been twins. Fassbinder could have played Malcolm.' Despite the award and some positive reviews, the film quickly disappeared.

That would not be the end for Halliwell's play, however. After his run of starring roles in the films of director Danny Boyle, from *Shallow Grave*, through *Trainspotting* to *A Life Less Ordinary*, Ewan McGregor, feeling he had been dumped by his mentor for Leonardo DiCaprio, decided on a return to the stage and, frightened by the prospect, called on his uncle, Denis Lawson, to direct. Lawson chose a production of *Little Malcolm & His Struggle Against the Eunuchs* to be staged at the small, 174-seat, Hampstead Theatre Club, in walking distance from his home, and paying all the cast, including McGregor, the Equity rate of £250 per week. Booked into the theatre for a seven-week run during 1998, there was little chance that this incarnation of the work would struggle to find an audience, having sold out the entire run well before opening night with tickets reaching as much as £300 on the black market. Reviews were mixed, with the Mail on Sunday's assertion that 'McGregor is terrific, a real live wire who bounds all over the stage with a springy cat-like grace. Yet he doesn't quite pin down the dangerous side of Malcolm, nor his sexual inadequacy' being typical. The play nevertheless moved on to a run in the West End.

*

Taking his cue from events in Paris during 1968 was playwright Howard Brenton for whom he says: 'May 1968 was crucial. It was a great watershed that directly affected me.' A lot of the ideas in his 1973 play **MAGNIFICENCE** came straight out of the writing of that time in Paris: 'May 1968 disinherited my generation in two ways. First, it destroyed any remaining affection for official culture. The Situationists showed how all of them, the dead greats are corpses on our backs - Goethe, Beethoven... But it also, secondly, destroyed the notions of personal freedom, freak out and drug culture, anarchist notions of spontaneous freedom, anarchist political action. And it failed. It was defeated. A generation dreaming of a beautiful utopia was kicked - kicked awake and not dead. I've got to believe not kicked dead. May 68 gave me a desperation I still have.'

Magnificence can be categorised alongside other Brenton scripts such as that for the 41-minute film *SkinFlicker* (1972), directed by Tony Bicat for Portable Films and produced by the BFI on a budget of around £3000. The plot, 'a teacher, a nurse, and a garrulous layabout kidnap a public man somewhere in England. They employ a cameraman, a maker of blue films, to record what happens. The story ends with the defecation of the cameraman, the murder of the public man, and the suicide of the kidnappers. At a later date, the material shot for the film is edited by government officials for "training purposes", to instruct public employees in the mores of extremist groups.' Their film ultimately becomes a weapon for the enemy. The high profile Laporte kidnapping inspired the story. Pierre Laporte was the Quebec Minister for Labour and his kidnappers were members of the Front de Liberation du Quebec (FLQ) who demanded the release of 23 'political' prisoners for his freedom. A British diplomat had been kidnapped by the same group 5 days earlier and though he was eventually released Laporte was not so fortunate, found dead 7 days later in the trunk of a car.

In *The Saliva Milkshake* (1975), part of Brenton's Plays for the Poor Theatre, a former student revolutionary socialist who has settled into middle-class academia returns home to find an old comrade has broken in and made herself a coffee after killing the Home Secretary. First performed at the Soho Poly lunchtime theatre in 1975, the BBC broadcast the play later that year as part of its *Centre Play* series.

First performed at the Royal Court, *Magnificence* involves a group of young squatters, Jed, Will, Cliff, Mary, and Veronica, who occupy an empty house in London armed with baked beans and spray paint. As a group they are uniformly middle-class socialist dissenters but as individuals their differences on how to express this dissent are played out from the moment they attempt to enter the house. Jed wishes to enter through the troublesome locked door quietly and unnoticed but the more aggressive Will seeks to 'bash it down', spraying ANARCHY FARM on the inside wall as soon as they enter - by smashing a window and climbing a ladder. Veronica is not fully committed from the off, questioning Mary's hanging of a banner outside the window 'for all the world to see?'

Tensions in the house have worsened considerably by the time they receive a visit from a court bailiff accompanied by the police, with Veronica declaring her contempt with the futility of their stance: 'Liberation City? I loathe us. I loathe all the talks we had... I loathe what we've descended to here. Ten days with fleas and the tin opener lost... for us it's come down to sitting on a stinky lavatory for ten days... mobilise the people? We can't mobilise a tin opener.'

When Will resists arrest, the resultant scuffle leads to the accidental loss of the unborn child that Mary was carrying and the arrest of its father, Jed, who is subsequently sentenced to 9 month's imprisonment. Rather than being an exercise in rehabilitation, in the final act he emerges from his confinement with a revolutionary fervour; intent on revenge on the system and armed with gelignite, the recipient of which is a corrupt MP.

Michael Kitchen & Kenneth Cranham in *Magnificence*

Hippies, Skinheads, Rastas, Punks & Disco Dancing Bowie Boot Boys

Yesterdays Papers
(Jagger, Richards)

As early as September 1966 The People were publishing 'a warning to every parent' about what their impressionable offspring 'may pick up... in a discotheque or record shop. It will look way-out, switched on and hippy. And it will contain precise details of sexual practices that make Fanny Hill seem as depraved as Goldilocks.' They were talking about 'journals that advertisements of the three-in-a-bed type appear.'

'Filth can be swept under the carpet out of sight. But then nobody bothers to get rid of it.' The People had looked under the carpet of issue 19 of Oz and discovered 'a purported interview with a groupie' who it helpfully explained as 'a girl who hangs around pop groups, offering herself to them' and described as 'provocative reading for your pop fan daughter.' There was also an advice column which 'gives advice on grotesque sexual problems' such as 'a horrific amateur surgical experiment to heighten sexual pleasure' which is described as dangerous but, asks the paper, 'how many youngsters will experiment just the same?' An article on how to take LSD is seen as 'perhaps more dangerous' and 'the sort of stuff [that] should not be freely distributed around the country.' The piece finishes by imploring 'shop and discotheque owners: Don't help spread this muck.'

Oz, as we shall see, always made the biggest headlines, but it was International Times (IT) that set the standard for the underground press, publishing original work by established names like Ginsberg, Burroughs and Mailer, introducing the UK to Robert Crumb's Furry Freak Brothers, whilst helping launch original home-grown talent like Germaine Greer, Heathcote Williams and Jeff Nuttall. IT had documented the rise of alternative culture as it happened, from the Black Panthers in the USA, to the uprising in Paris and the UK's anti-Vietnam protests.

As the so-called 'founding father of the London tabloid underground' IT was one of three alternative newspapers visited in December 1972 by Jonathan Dimbleby and the BBC's *Man Alive* team alongside the revolutionary weekly Socialist Worker and the Tuebrook Bugle, a militant community paper published in Liverpool. As well as pursuing revolution in the political sense, the fortnightly IT was also instrumental in promoting the revolution in the music underground that was either ignored or unknown in the mainstream titles. During times of financial trouble, the underground music scene would return the favour via benefit concerts. It was Paul McCartney who suggested to IT that if they wanted to attract advertising from the major record labels, they should run an interview with him. They did, and he was right, with similar pieces with George Harrison, Frank Zappa, and Mick Jagger quickly following.

The financial pressures were not necessarily the result of poor sales, IT was printing some 40,000 copies at its peak but, in common with all the so-called alternative press, the paper had to contend with almost continuous harassment from the police. The IT offices were first raided in March 1967 when 8000 copies were seized on the grounds of obscenity, though no charges resulted. The commonly held belief was that the police's sole intention was to put the paper out of business. In 1972, IT was convicted of corrupting public morals and temporarily closed down as the result of its gay contact ads. After a raid on his flat, co-founder Hoppy Hopkins was jailed for allowing cannabis to be smoked there, serving six months.

IT may have been an irritation but, being primarily a mouthpiece for the various alternative lifestyles - communal living, ecology, vegetarianism and drugs - it was never really considered a serious threat. Unlike Black Dwarf which had strong connections to the Vietnam Solidarity Campaign (VSC), set up by activists from the International Group, a revolutionary socialist organisation, which in 1968 became the International Marxist Group (IMG).

The paper's politics brought it to the attention of Special Branch officers who raided the Black Dwarf offices during September 1968, where they photographed a diagram drawn on the wall and sent it to the Director of Public Prosecutions. It contained instructions on how to make a Molotov cocktail and although it was covered by two posters, the police immediately knew it was there.

With tongue obviously firmly in cheek, Tariq Ali told the Guardian, 'I don't know who did it, it could have been anybody. There are all sorts of people in and out of our offices. Of course, the moment I saw it I gave instructions that it was to be erased immediately but, due to the laziness of the staff here, it wasn't. Actually, they just put two posters over it - they were going to paint over it later.' When the story was picked up by the Evening Standard, the

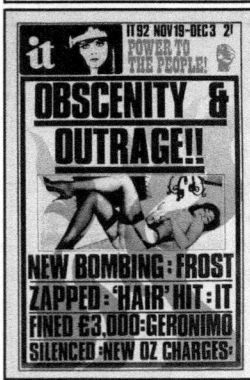

paper expanded on it with the suggestion that Molotov cocktails and bombs were being stored at secret addresses and that small arms were being purchased to use against the police. This was repeated in the Times. According to Ali the Black Dwarf offices had been subject to a number of burglaries during 1968 where nothing had been taken - a not uncommon practice for planting bugs or carrying out illegal searches.

In their May 16th 1969 edition, a 'Special Youth Issue', Black Dwarf complained that 'five free papers have been threatened by the police', listing Oz, IT, Rolling Stone, Black Dimensions and Black Dwarf itself (despite any of them being free). In revenge, Black Dwarf printed their guide to Scotland Yard which gave a detailed layout of the premises and suggested that residents of Notting Hill might want to pay a visit, saying 'Notting Hill to Victoria Street is but a shilling on an 88 bus.'

But it was sex, not revolutionary politics (or drugs and rock n roll) that most frightened the established order and there were three high profile controversies where the topics of sex and school children had dared cross paths. First was the 'Little Red Schoolbook', written by two Danish schoolteachers, which contained information on an array of topics including challenging authority, exams, politics and drugs. But it was the 26 pages on sex, and specifically the part championing the virtues of masturbation, over which Mary Whitehouse successfully campaigned to have it prosecuted under the Obscene Publications Act - and in doing so drove sales of what was a marginal publication to mainstream levels. Now available uncensored, its harm reduction approach to both drug use and sex via the provision of frank technical explanations and information about the dangers is now the standard approach in health education.

Next in the firing line was the 23-minute sex-education film, *Growing Up: A New Approach to Sex Education, No. 1* (1971) which dared to use real people rather than drawings. It's easy to understand why the erect penises and explicit scenes of masturbation would have horrified the moral majority and even its more liberal-minded viewers might have taken offence at Dr Martin Cole's assertions that the role of women was 'giving birth to children', men being 'better at giving birth to ideas'. In the end, such was the outcry that the film was never shown in schools.

Mrs Whitehouse would have been more at home with *Don't Be Like Brenda* (1973), a throwback to the *Reefer Madness* school of 'education', which over its eight-minute running time manages to pile indignity upon indignity on a 17-year-old girl who dares to get pregnant, whilst absolving the boy, Richard Morant who had played Flashman in the BBCs *Tom Brown's Schooldays* (1971), who got her into that state. Written and directed by W. Hugh Baddeley, there's no mention of contraception, no mention of keeping the child, and definitely no mention of abortion.

Brenda falls in love with Gary, goes all the way, and gets pregnant. When she breaks the news to him he says he'll ring her at 8.00 pm but when the phone rings, his mum is on the other end, telling her she's a slut and that if she bothers her son, she'll get the police onto her. So, Brenda has the child and puts it up for adoption because, after all, there's a surplus of loving couples desperate to adopt. But not in Brenda's case because her child turns out to have a defect and is moved from the ever-so-lovely National Children's Home to one where the kids have little chance of ever being adopted as the film concludes that 'Brenda had ruined two lives, her own and her child's'.

These first two controversies paled beside the fallout from Oz magazine's Schoolkids issue. The youth section of Black Dwarf's 'Special Youth Issue' covered schools, apprentice rights, pop and pot; Oz's version, because large parts of it were the offerings of actual school-age kids, was heavily laden with sex. Twenty teenagers were selected from responses to an advertisement in a previous issue and given an almost free hand in producing their own content for the magazine's 28th edition, a special Schoolkids

Issue.

Oz began its life in 1963 as a satirical magazine in Sydney, Australia and based itself on Private Eye. Its coverage of contentious issues such as censorship, abortion, homosexuality, and police brutality quickly brought it into conflict with the authorities and obscenity charges soon followed, first in 1963 where each of its three editors received £20 fines and then again in 1964 over a cover photograph depicting them pretending to urinate into a wall fountain, recently unveiled by Prime Minister Menzies. The magazine was also attracting the attention of Sydney's underworld, and so in 1966, Richard Neville upped sticks for the more enlightened United Kingdom. He had read the 1966 Time magazine story on Swinging London that told of people from all corners of the earth heading to the nation's capital for its music and fashion. What he found was he says: 'more than that… a psychic shift… It was long hair, short skirts, a whiff of pot. You'd walk down Portobello Road and see people dressed up like generals in Gilbert & Sullivan operettas, a satirical dig at warmongers. And yet this great, heaving, British Establishment was still in place. You only had to walk through Hyde Park and read the signs. No dancing, no drinking, no children, no ice cream. There were still so many nos.'

One of those twenty youngsters selected to edit Schoolkids Oz, Peter Popham, speaking to the Independent in 2007, says that, apart from Charles Shaar Murray who arrived 'precociously articulate and already strongly focused on becoming a rock journalist,' they were initially out of their comfort zones but 'slowly emerged from our shells. The most obvious thing we could bring to the Oz mix was schoolkid rage against the education machine and smut. The rage always looked really fake, we were practically all privileged children and it showed, but Viv Berger and one or two others finally came up with some pretty stunning smut.' If the magazine wanted the authentic youth voice, he said, 'Rupert Bear with a vast erection was about as authentic as it got.'

According to journalist and broadcaster Polly Toynbee, Oz used sex as a weapon to frighten the establishment: 'Sex was a metaphor for revolution and rebellion. If it hadn't shocked the establishment, they would have found something else instead. Sex was a kind of Molotov cocktail to throw at the authorities.' The resulting explosion saw Oz publishers Richard Neville, Felix Dennis, and Jim Anderson at the Old Bailey charged with 'conspiring to produce a magazine… containing diverse nude, indecent and sexual perverted articles, cartoons, drawings and illustrations with intent thereby to debauch and corrupt the morals of young persons within the realm and to arouse and implant in their minds, lustful and perverted desires.' This archaic charge, which had lain dormant for more than a century, carried a maximum sentence of life imprisonment.

At the trial, the longest obscenity trial in British legal history up to that point, Oz lost its case. The editors were cleared of the corruption charge; it being clear that the issue was produced by children but not for them, but found guilty under the Obscene Publications Act of two minor, tacked-on charges relating to sending subscription copies of Oz through the Royal Mail. In August 1971, shorn of their long hair after being held in prison for 7 days, the three editors received prison sentences of up to 15 months. Following a public outcry, the verdict was overturned on appeal where it was decided the judge had been so eager to convict that his summing-up became a byword for incompetence and bias and, rather than the knighthood customarily handed out for such incompetence in office, he was sent back to Birmingham where he died penniless and alone in his home as the president of a society dedicated to bringing back hanging.

The trial also raised the question of why you could quite easily find much harder porn in Soho than in the pages of Oz, as thoroughly explored in *Our Friends In The North*. This led to the initiation of a major corruption enquiry into the Metropolitan Police which revealed that there was systemic corruption 'on a scale that beggars description' involving Soho pornographers making weekly payments to senior police officers. As a result, the Detective Chief Inspector of the Obscene Publications Squad was sentenced to 10 years' imprisonment.

Defence barrister Geoffrey Robertson and David Illingworth used the court transcripts to write a play, *The Oz Trial*, which, directed by Buzz Goodbody, was performed three times as a reading by the Royal Shakespeare Company at London's Aldwych Theatre in January 1972 with a cast including Sebastian Shaw, Ben Kingsley, Julian Glover, Paul Hardwick, and John Kane. Goodbody, real name Mary Ann, was the first female director hired by a leading UK theatre, having started out as a personal assistant to the company's co-founder John Barton. In a press statement on her appointment as a director she described herself as 'a Marxist-Socialist revolutionary' and committed to putting socialism on the stage, directing *Occupations*, the Trevor Griffiths penned exploration of the Turin factory strikes during the 1920s, and then *The Oz Trial*. That the RSC should be even staging such a work was a matter for contention when the company, described by Trevor Nunn as 'basically a left-wing organisation', was looked upon by many as being under the control of radicals after Peter Brook and Peter Hall had signed a half page advert in the New York Times calling for an end to the bombing in Vietnam and for the US to recognise Vietnam's National Liberation Front. One newspaper suggested that the RSC had gone 'beyond their terms of reference and their rights by performing something which the public do not want to see performed.' Arthur Goodman, the chair of the Arts Council, questioned whether the state should be subsidising people who sought to overthrow it. The result of all this publicity was that the 300 seat theatre was packed out for its opening night, Richard Neville among them, where the performance was followed by a discussion on the significance of the trial.

A vastly altered production was staged in New York under a new title, The Trials of Oz, at the Anderson Theatre during December 1972. Running for a mere two weeks, the production received only moderate reviews, echoing the New York Times assertion that 'the play as such is not especially immediate' and 'might have more meaning in London.' There was praise for Cliff de Young's performance as Richard Neville, calling it 'exceptionally good' but also the complaint that 'some of the lesser characters were poorly done.'

Australian Jim Sharman who had previously oversaw productions of Hair in Boston, Tokyo and Australia and Jesus Christ Superstar in London directed the play and promised it would be 'Superior to Superstar, Hippier than Hair, Groovier than Godspell'. In common with those the new production added songs; Lennon & Ono's 'God Save Oz', Jagger's 'Schoolboy Blues' (better known as 'Cocksucker Blues') and a selection from Pittsburgh based Buzzy Linhart, written especially for the production. A review of a preview in IT said that next to 'such fine couplets as 'When can I get my cock sucked? Where can I get my arse fucked?', such lukewarm numbers from Buzzy Linhart as 'The Love's Still Growing' sung by the three defendants plus Caroline Coon, as they ostensibly suck on what might well not actually be a joint, are nothing if not soggy.' Although Linhart never achieved commercial success, he was considered a good enough vibraphone player to be credited among the musicians on Jimi Hendrix's 'The Cry of Love' and 'Electric Ladyland' albums.

As well as songs IT also highlighted the production's added fantasy sequences including 'the great and glorious episode of the Fabulous Furry Freak Bros in which Phineas and Frank send Fat Freddie to score a lid in Ripoff Park... enacted in full. The Ripoff Park Werewolves and ROP Pigfuckers appearing with many knives, guns, and other weapons.' Also highlighted was a duet between Richard Dennis and Caroline Coon in blue and pink satin, pompom encrusted costumes and a 'charming rendition of the kiddie's friend, Rupert [that] sported a twelve-inch candy stripe erection, waggling playfully from his green and red fur.' Of these, the reviewer thought, 'If only they had turned up in 1971 to brighten up the real thing.'

In fact, the real thing needed little in the way of brightening up as is seen in the BBC/ABC co-production **THE TRIALS OF OZ (1991)**, which begins with an introduction from David Dimbleby in which, having sat through most of the trial as a reporter, he vouched that as well as using 100% verbatim dialogue, 'it captures the original atmosphere and tone with uncanny precision.' Much of the fun comes from what Felix Dennis calls 'the absurd number of expert defence witnesses' called upon; the reason why the trial went on so long with the prosecution's case being rather more concise. There's John Peel (Nigel Planer), whose early persona always had a touch of the Neil from The Young Ones about it, whom the prosecution tried to discredit because he had previously admitted on air to be suffering from a sexually transmitted disease; George Melly (Alfred Molina) who is called upon to explain the meaning of the word cunnilinctus and helpfully offers: 'Sucking. Blowing. Or going down or gobbling. Or, as we said in my naval days, yodelling in the canyon.' Marty Feldman (Lee Cornes),

A suspiciously handsome Richard Neville

asked to define satire, quotes a producer at the BBC saying he'd 'be allowed two bloodies and one bastard' in a script 'if he took out a tit.'

There are also top-notch performances in the starring roles of legal big wigs Judge Michael Argyle (Leslie Phillips), prosecuting barrister Brian Leary (Nigel Hawthorne) and defence barrister John Mortimer (Simon Callow), whilst the major surprise for many will be the pre-rom-com superstardom Hugh Grant's star turn as Richard Neville, conducting his own defence with an articulate bohemian charm. In fact, if co-producer ABC would have had its way the role would have been filled by Jason Donovan.

In the final episode of *Hippies, Disgusting Hippies*, Ray decides: 'the next issue of the magazine we hand over to a bunch of schoolkids. We give them total editorial control and we don't look at the magazine until it's in the shops.' The resultant issue features a cover photo of Ray with a speech bubble declaring 'I am a cunt' and lands him with an obscenity charge, leaving his barrister to ponder: 'What we've got to ask is this an accurate description of Ray?'

The fourth episode, *Hippy Dippy Hippies*, features an issue of the magazine dedicated to a march against the police and boasting a cover of a pig in a police helmet. In case that was too subtle, there is also a speech bubble saying 'I am a Policeman.' Unfortunately, they need to call in the police when the flat is burgled and the not yet on sale issue is amongst the items stolen. The officers turn out to be really open-minded and when they recover the unopened bundle of magazines, they also bring a celebratory cake. When they see the cover one of them even cries and so there is a reprint of the cover, changed to 'The Police: Doing A Difficult Job in Dangerous Times'.

A more serious dramatisation of similar issues appeared in **CROWN COURT: A DIFFERENCE IN STYLE (1974)**, in which Sophie Mannering (Annabel Leventon), the editor of Tell, described as a community newspaper, faces two counts of seditious libel after publishing an article and a pamphlet said to be likely to incite hostility between her young readers and the police, having urged them to 'Demonstrate against police brutality... the time for talking is over, the time has come for action.' The magazine, a cheaply produced A4 black and white paper, is read by young people who - according to the Police Inspector who purchased a copy 'on information received' - are likely to respond as it is 'practically their Bible.'

It was a subject matter perfectly suited to the episode's writer, Peter Buckman, who was something of a radical himself having explored radical politics in the United States in his 1970 book 'The Limits of Protest, including the Black Panthers, the Yippies, Students for a Democratic Society (SDS) and the commune movement'. Buckman also edited a 1973 collection of articles on the 'deschooling' movement, Education Without Schools.

A protest had taken place against overzealous policing and the violent removal of squatters from a commune. It had begun with chanting which eventually included one of 'Get the Pigs', which is explained to the Jury as inferring 'an act of violence against the police', upon which about 80 protesters were then said to have charged a police cordon and attempted to break into the police station, resulting in 19 injuries (twelve of those police) and 12 arrests.

Apparently Simon pegg is a cunt

Afterwards, the police Inspector claimed to have picked up a leaflet which read 'Get the Pigs! Kill the Bastards Before They Kill Us!' and a flat belonging to the accused was subject to a raid where hundreds more were found in a closet. She had been raided previously, purportedly looking for drugs though none were found, and the police had taken away the paste-ups for the latest copy of the magazine along with its subscriptions list.

The prosecution barrister would have been cheered on by many viewers at home for his attack on one witness for the defence, who had been a member of the commune and helped in the running of Tell, accusing him of 'playing the hippy' because he was public school and Oxford educated yet suggesting he had been hungry. 'Hungry!... when your parents would be all too pleased to give you a hot meal.'

'The whole tone of the publication glorifies what they call the alternative culture, and that means drugs, sex, and anarchic attitudes,' the Court is told by a police officer who the defence soon shows to have been intimidating both the magazine and the squat. Thankfully for the accused, the judge shows a little less bias than seen in the Oz trial and there is an eventual not guilty verdict.

1971 saw the launch of Children's Rights magazine, which declared that 'the first duty of a revolutionary is to build a society geared to children'. The publication boasted an impressive board of editorial advisers including children's author Leila Berg, the former head of the controversial short-lived Risinghill School in Islington, Michael Duane, both of whom would appear as expert witnesses for the defence at the Oz trial, and the Summerhill founder AS Neil.

The magazine's emphasis was on children's political rights, especially in the school setting. Issue 1 featured an article on racism in British education, a discussion on the 'deschooling' movement led by Michael Duane and issue 2 included a feature on setting up a free school, Free Schools & the Law, and items on nursery schools, Summerhill and truancy. However, the publication soon drew controversy over what was seen as an over-emphasis in the magazine of children's sexual rights, doing itself few favours when it described breastfeeding as 'a great erotic exchange' that satisfied a child's 'lust', and which depended on the arousal of the woman for success.

There was also a communique from a supposed Children's Angry Brigade declaring: 'all sabotage is effective in hierarchical systems like schools - unscrew locks, smash tannoys, paint blackboards red, grind all the chalk to dust - you're angry - you know what to do.' The final straw came when issue 5 provided a Children's Bust Book which encouraged children to resist arrest, and Neill and Berg sacked the editor and relaunched as Kids.

The period also saw an abundance of short-lived pamphlets and magazines produced by children themselves. Among them were titles such as Fang, Miscarriage, Blazer, Blackbored, and Braindamage which declared 'schools imprison your mind and control your body... they don't encourage us to develop our potential but rather tame our natural inclinations, causing total apathy in most and rebellion in very few.' Such publications even reached the fictional Fenn Street secondary school in ITVs hit sitcom *Please Sir!* In the series 4 episode *Vive Le Revolution* (1971), one pupil suggests an article on how to make a Molotov cocktail in a science lab. When it is suggested he might have to tone it down a bit, he comes up with '17 Non-violent Ways to Disrupt An English Lesson, Number 1; take your Molotov cocktail...' Later in the series, the revolutionary theme continues in the episode *United We Sit* (1971) where, in protest over new rules about the length of boys' hair and girls' hemlines, the pupils stage a sit-in and demand student representation on staff meetings.

Hippies, Skinheads, Rastas, Punks & Disco Dancing Bowie Boot Boys

2. It's Different For Girls
(Jackson)

One common conclusion of academic texts dealing with juvenile crime during this period is of the underrepresentation of females in crime statistics because of a combination of the public being less willing to report their behaviour and leniency from both the police, seen as more likely to offer a caution, and the judiciary. Whilst this might seem like the system gives girls a fairly good deal, there is one area of 'delinquency' where they have always suffered disproportionately - that of so-called status offences, behaviour that if committed by an adult would not be considered criminal at all. Chief among these are acts were those considered as putting the offender in 'moral danger', be it running away from home, staying out late at night, or the more general being beyond parental control.

At the heart of all these status offences is sex. From the Middle Ages onwards, adolescent girls and young women have been criminalised not for offences against social order so much as for simply the exercising of their sexuality. Much of the concern voiced today over the behaviour of teenage girls is nothing new and can be found in newspaper coverage of almost a century ago during the Great War where, as well as the freedom afforded by men away at war, women also enjoyed a greater disposable income from being called upon to work in areas that was previously the preserve of men - 900,000 in munitions factories, 117,000 in transport and 113,000 on farms.

Though statistics showed juvenile crime had increased by a third for under seventeens in the first two years of the Second World War, this was not considered a serious state of affairs being largely vandalism and small acts of petty theft. What was of greater concern was a 100 percent increase in female juvenile delinquency and a 70 percent rise in the treatment of venereal disease.

This apprehension was being voiced as early as 1939 when, with the war in its infancy, Miss Curwen, general secretary of the Young Women's Christian Association (YMCA) and a National Youth Council (NYC) member, remarked 'we are faced as in the last war (but this time in a more aggravated form due to the blackout), with the urgent problem of how to attract off the streets the young not attached to any juvenile organisation or evening institute. The problem on the girls' side is in some respects more acute than of boys' owing to the fact that 16 and 17-year-old girls, and even younger, walk out with soldiers.' While young lads were expected get up to a bit of 'mischief', boys being boys after all, girls provided an even greater concern in the form of sex delinquency, considered a problem exclusive to that gender. They were told it was their responsibility to maintain the necessary boundaries of sexual conduct as men could not judge the implications of their attentions, nor voluntarily curb their passions.

Calling for, amongst other things, a curfew, a Blackpool Alderman voiced an archetypal belief that women, through Eve, were responsible for the fall and all the subsequent troubles of men: 'if children are allowed to roam the streets at any hour, if after dark painted young women can accost men, how can they or the men be protected against the fruits of their folly and ignorance.'

This pre-occupation with sexual precocity was often legitimised as concern over the girls own well-being, though writers such as the socialist theorist Sheila Rowbotham point out that sexuality has been controlled by the State in almost every culture for economic ends - the institution of marriage, which she saw as closely resembling feudalism, and the continuation of the nuclear family; seen as providing the stability to minimise distraction from the real business of labour. Anne Campbell, in 'Girl Delinquents', published in 1981, says: 'The hinge of this political machinery is the exchange of women, of sex for marriage. To secure such a bargain, sex must not be available by other means, and anyone who attempts to give sex away is severely sanctioned. This is the fate of those teenage girls who come before the courts for their promiscuous behaviour.'

Apart perhaps from brief periods where STD contraction had threatened the war effort or in the 1980s when the AIDs epidemic first hit, the greatest peril attached to promiscuity has been pregnancy. Filmmakers beg to differ. Whereas in earlier decades and in movies as far back as *Hindle Wakes* (1931) through to sixties dramas like *A Taste of Honey* (1961), *Up The Junction* (1968) and *The Yellow Teddybears* (1963), the consequences of a teenage pregnancy form a significant dramatic drive, in recent times the subject has been relegated to the subject of TV movies. Certainly, young girls have continued to fall pregnant in British films from *Rita, Sue & Bob Too* to *Kidulthood*, but these were almost matter-of-fact events against a much wider landscape.

*

Seen as one of the most significant medical advances of the last century, the contraceptive pill was introduced into the UK in 1961 and made available on the NHS. Ostensibly it was up to 'the individual doctor to decide in each case' who it could be prescribed to. In reality, there was a proviso that it should only be made available to married women, seen specifically as an aid to those who already had children and wanted no more. The NHS (Family Planning) Act of 1967 removed this proviso and extended contraceptive services to all women, for any reason – regardless of age or marital status. Despite this, by the end of the decade only 1 in 10 women had ever taken it and the most popular form of contraception remained the condom. A major reason for the slow take-up was that most women, and especially young girls, would not have relished that initial conversation with their family doctor, who would have also been the GP for their husbands, and their parents. In contrast, since 1965, condoms were readily available at high street chemists such as Boots.

This was to change in 1974 when the NHS Reorganisation Act allowed the prescription of contraception by other health professionals, including appropriately trained nurses at newfangled family planning clinics. Even more controversial was advice issued by the Department of Health and Social Security (DHSS) that doctors could provide contraceptive advice to girls under 16 without informing their parents' but stressing that they should always seek the girl's consent to do so. An amendment in 1980 emphasised that doctors should 'seek to persuade the child to involve the parents or guardian'. Ultimately, however, the decision remained with the judgement of the doctor. As a direct result, use of the Pill quadrupled over the next five years, rising from use by 9% of all women to 36%.

Contraception, rather than being seen as a weapon in the battle against unwanted teenage pregnancy, was for many instead considered a leading cause. A letter to the Sheffield Star in 1966, protesting the opening of a family planning clinic in the city, said that 'doctors say that their desire is to prevent the birth of unwanted children, but surely they must realise that by the widespread issue of contraceptives they are removing the only natural barrier to illicit sex - the fear of conception - and encouraging a moral delinquency which is already woefully out of hand.'

This view was tackled in an episode of **CROWN COURT: AN EVIL INFLUENCE (1975)** scripted by Brian Clark, a regular contributor to *Play For Today* and best known for *Whose Life is it Anyway?*, his Tony-nominated play exploring the theme of assisted suicide. Dr Thanet (Stephen Yardley) is a general practitioner who had prescribed a contraceptive pill to Linda Phelps (Victoria Williams), a fifteen-year-old girl, without consulting her mother. Mrs Phelps (Margaret John) found out and after a family row, Linda ran away and hasn't been seen since. Mrs Phelps started a petition about the doctor's actions, attempting to collect signatures of the doctor's patients as they attended the surgery. The doctor has sued for libel at the Crown Court.

Says Dr Thanett: 'Society wants it both ways. They realise there's a very large teenage market and they try to sell it everything. Sometimes using techniques of sexual stimulation tied to specific products; books, records, drink, everything. Adults bombard teenagers with sex and when they've turned them on and the teenager says "yes, I've got the deodorant, the records, the books, where's the sex?", society throws its hand up in horror and denies the teenager the outlet for the energy that adult society has stimulated. Well, that isn't fair.'

In the early 1980s, a real-life Mrs Phelps came to prominence. Victoria Gillick was a mother of ten who took her local health authority and the DHSS to the High Court to prevent them from ever being able to give contraception, or advice on such matters, to her four underage daughters. Although she lost her case, she got the decision overturned at appeal before the Law Lords eventually reinstated it. In recent years, the odd appearance at anti-immigration rallies aside, Mrs Gillick has kept a lower profile, perhaps to concentrate on her 42 grandchildren, leaving the politics to her husband, UKIP Councillor Gordon, who in 2014 caused a stir by telling the Cambridge News that 'the people we describe as obese, thick, badly educated, whichever way you like to phrase it.... they enjoy being 25 stone; they're not discontent; they're just a burden on the state.'

Despite the supposed loosening of morals, sex education in the seventies was still something of an embarrassment. An attempt by ITV to broadcast a special edition of *This Week*, a controversial and influential weekly current affairs television programme broadcast between 1956 and 1979, on the topic in 1975 was moved in the schedule from 8.30 to 9.30 because it was considered by the IBA not to be suitable for family viewing. Called *Sex & the 14-Year-Old* and intended for both adults and children, the film centred on the work of a family planning centre in North London.

Family planning fared little better in the right-wing press who pounced on extreme examples to make their case. As part of a series on 'Sex, Sin & Society', a 1979 Daily Express article began with the tale of a 13-year-old Devon schoolgirl who asked for permission to go to the bathroom and, once there, gave birth to a stillborn baby. The newspaper expressed alarm over estimates of 1300 under 16s having babies and 3000 having an abortion. The number of gymslip pregnancies had doubled in just a decade the paper said because 'girls feel they have to give in to the sexual revolution to prove themselves.'

In true *Reefer Madness* style the Daily Express also illustrated the dangers with the story of a 14-year-old West London girl from a 'happy, working-class background' who had become involved with an older 'known delinquent,' and having been given contraception by a local clinic, was pressured to sleep with him. 'The damage was done,' said the paper. 'The child's character was changed completely and she started to play truant from school. Her first taste of sexual adventure encouraged her to adopt a new personality and she flaunted herself in front of her parents.'

To condemn the work of family planning clinics the paper called upon Valerie Riches, who they described as a former medical social worker: 'The intervention by the family planning clinic undid at one stroke what the parents had been trying to sort out. It was clear the law was being broken but nothing was being done.' Riches was a long-time campaigner against sex education who was Honorary Secretary of an organisation called The Responsible Society at the start of the 1970s, later Family & Youth Concern, then Family Education Trust.

*

As artist Nicola Lane recounted in Jonathan Green's interview book 'Days In The Life: Voices from the English Underground 1961-1971'; 'From a girl's point of view the important thing to remember about the 60s is that it was totally male-dominated. A lot of girls just rolled joints – it was what you did while you sat quietly in the corner, nodding your head. You were not really encouraged to be a thinker. You were really there for fucks and domesticity. The 'old lady' syndrome. 'My Lady'. So Guinevere-y. It was quite a difficult time for a girl.'

In her 1970 best seller 'The Female Eunuch', feminist Germaine Greer called for revolution, not evolution and urged women to know and to accept their own bodies and to abandon celibacy and monogamy which must have sounded manna from heaven for the young male population. The Hippies' interest in revolutionary politics was largely limited to those of the New Left, but the sexual revolution was almost universal in its appeal to long-haired males - for obvious reasons. Free love was the mantra but what it really meant was free sex, a status that, the Pill or not, has always held different consequences for women. Writing in the Huffington Post in 2012, author Liz Mundy summed up women's new found equality thus: 'the right to make love to a man and never see him again; the right to be insulted and demeaned if she refuses a man's advances; the right to catch a sexually transmitted disease that might, as a bonus, leave her infertile; the right to an abortion when things go wrong, or, as it may be, the right to become a single mother.'

According to Caroline Coon: 'In the 60s, the only way you seemed to be desirable as a woman was if you were a dolly bird - a terrible phrase because "dolly" means childish and disposable, while "bird" isn't human. The icons were Twiggy and Brigitte Bardot, but every woman who was young and pretty was a dolly bird. If you weren't, you were invisible. And there was no escape for either kind of woman. If you had a miniskirt on, you provoked rape. If you didn't, you were told only ugly girls get raped. If you said no, you were a frigid bitch; if you said yes, you were a loose slut.'

A male-dominated media's idea of liberation, the dolly bird was expected to be always 'up for it' and soon became a staple in television and at the cinema. On the small screen, cleavage was emphasised whilst for any young actress hoping to make it in movies, nudity became a contractual obligation and a powerful weapon in the battle against televisions growing impact on dwindling cinema admissions. Disrobing became even more difficult to argue against following Glenda Jackson's Best Actress Academy Award for 1969s *Women In Love*, which included just such a display. Even the nation's sweethearts like former child stars Hayley Mills and Jenny Agutter were called upon to disrobe. The 1970s was the decade in which future Academy Award winner Helen Mirren made her name on the big screen, but not one she has fond memories of, saying: 'The decade after the sexual revolution, but before feminism, was perilous for women. Men saw that as a sort of "Oh, fantastic! We can fuck anything, however we like, whenever we like. They're up for grabs boys!"'

This unexpected consequence of the sexual revolution was never more visible than in the world of British film, where the builder's cry of 'Get 'em off,' was adopted by directors. As the sixties drew to a close and swinging

London began to lose much of its sheen, so too did the movies. In 1965 Norman J Warren, best known for his horror output in the 1970s and 80s with the likes of *Satan's Slave* (1976), *Prey* (1977), *Inseminoid* (1981) and *Bloody New Year* (1987), made a short film, *Fragment* (1965) which he says was: 'Out of the frustration of not getting anyone to believe I could direct something.' Warren got the film shown at the Paris Theatre in West London, then known as a porn venue, where it just so happened the owner Richard Schulman along with distributor Bachoo Sen had been considering moving into the production of low budget movies. 'And it just so happened,' says Warren, 'my film was on the screen at the time they were talking about it... So when it came to the subject of needing a director that wouldn't cost much or cause lots of trouble they said, "why don't we give him a call?"' When the call came, Warren gladly accepted, aware that 'the subject matter more or less guaranteed at that time that it would do good box office which is the all-important thing... so if I made a few mistakes, which I did... it wasn't the end of the line for me.'

The film was **HER PRIVATE HELL (1968)** and continued the theme of young girls arriving in Swinging London that had proved successful earlier in the decade with movies like *The Knack (And How To Get It)* (1965), *Smashing Time* (1967), and *Joanna* (1968), only the tone is considerably darker. It is also considered the UK's first narrative sex film despite being decidedly lacking in sex.

Quite simply, says Warren: 'On *Her Private Hell* you couldn't show nipples, no such things, no sir, and when you did do a couple in bed, if the girl was naked they weren't allowed to move, it was quite weird. There was a scene... where the girl strips off and the moment she lies on the bed she no longer moves, so she's just stationary and the actor - you weren't allowed to take the trousers off in these days so he had to keep his trousers on. So you had to make sure the sheet covered the trousers, and all basically he could do was stroke his arm up and down her back and her arms. It was like the Windmill Theatre; the moment they were naked they had to stand still, and they applied it to the film as well.'

Her Private Hell is a cautionary tale of a young Italian girl Marisa (Lucia Modugno who had small roles in Mario Bava's *The Girl Who Knew Too Much* (1963) and *Danger: Diabolik* (1968)) who arrives in England and is met at the airport by Margaret (Pearl Catlin), the representative of the modelling agency employing her. She is driven to a studio where Margaret's partner Hetherington (Robert Crewdson), photographer Bernie (Terence Skelton) and his assistant Matt (Daniel Ollier) await her arrival. That her new agency might not be all she imagined becomes more than clear when, after she comments on his Englishness, Hetherington pulls open the top few buttons of her blouse, remarking, 'Not as British as you thought, am I?' Unsurprisingly she's reluctant to sign a contract but does anyway and part of the deal is that she will stay in Bernie's flat to 'protect her from other photographers.' The wafer-thin plot is padded out by Marisa's relationship with the two photographers and the resultant jealousies before a twist ending that is better than the film deserves.

Warren was right about the prospects for profitability and the film did make a lot of money, playing at the Cameo Royal in Charing Cross Road for over a year, though he says not much of it went his way: 'I signed a contract which... more or less said I'd work for nothing, for two years, seven days a week, 24 hours a day. Well, I think it was 23 hours a day... the contract was a beautiful one because when I finished with him and I tried to get paid, I took it to a solicitor who said the contract was a work of art. He must spend a lot of money on lawyers... even if he doesn't on the film.'

The theme is continued in **THE YES GIRLS (1971)** featuring Sue Bond who began her career in Harrison Marks 1960s 'glamour' shorts and whose cleavage was a regular feature of *The Benny Hill Show*. Her acting career peaked with 13 episodes of ITV sitcom *Mind Your Language* during its final series. All of these require a higher level of dramatic ability than is displayed by anyone in this, her first and only starring role as Maria who is helped to escape from a young offenders institute in Sunderland by an elderly gardener who, after a quick flash of knickers, agrees to leave the gate open in return for more - which a heart attack brought on by the very prospect prevents him from ever getting.

She hitches to London where she is immediately caught shoplifting, though the removal of her top prevents the manager from taking any further action. She meets another girl, Angela (Sally Muggeridge, niece of Malcolm) who says she's an actress and invites her round for a meal that evening, 'My flatmate makes the best spaghetti Bolognese in London.' One tin of Heinz spaghetti later she's invited to stay. Neither of the two flatmates, Carol (Felicity Oliver) being the other, have a job or any intention of getting one and unable to pay the rent, feel a third person might help.

Janet Lynn & Robin Asquith make some dubious friends in *Cool It Carol*

Having been in care most of her life, Maria wants to track down her mum and enlists the help of seedy private eye Sam Hed (Jack Smethurst) - no prizes for guessing what she pays both the fee and the rent with.

All three flat mates end up in a bad porn movie that morphs into a bad art movie and Maria ends up in demand. The producer gets a $500,000 fee for her to do an American movie, putting her on a £25 a week contract. The film in a film's producer inadvertently sums up *The Yes Girls* perfectly when he says; 'I'm not interested in that arty rubbish, we're making a cheap nudie... tits and arses, that's what we're making.' Director Lindsay Shonteff had already tried his hand at comedy with a couple of secret agent spoofs, *Licensed to Kill* (1965) and *The Million Eyes of Sumuru* (1967) but *The Yes Girls* seems simply bleak and grubby. But not as grubby as Peter Walker's **COOL IT CAROL (1970)**.

Director Pete Walker is best known by fans of British genre movies for his mixing of sadistic sex and horror in films like *Die Screaming, Marianne* (1971), *House of Whipcord* (1974), *Frightmare* (1974), *House of Mortal Sin* (1976), *Schizo* (1976), *The Comeback* (1978), and *House of the Long Shadows* (1983); often featuring sadistic authority figures punishing young women who do not live up to their strict personal moral codes. Writer and broadcaster Dr Matthew Sweet perfectly sums up its director's status within the British film industry at the time with his assertion that 'Even when Peter Walker films got nominated for technical BAFTAs, which they did occasionally, they made sure not to invite Pete to the ceremony because they didn't quite like the idea of him being there'. Walker subsequently became known primarily for his horror movies, but like Norman J Warren had started out making 'adult films'.

'I was' says Walker, 'the uninvited guest to the British film industry. Nobody wanted to know me. I knew I wanted to make films, but I would see these serious-looking guys going around with scripts under their arm, spending three or four years trying to get their films made. I couldn't be like that – I had to make a living, and I wanted to get behind a camera and shout action. So I would go out and shoot something like *School for Sex* (1969)– God that was a terrible film – and a few weeks later every cinema in the country would be showing it.'

Of his adult films *Cool It Carol* is easily his best due in no small part to the casting of Robin Asquith who, nineteen at the time of filming, would return to the genre four years later and become a sexploitation superstar with the *Confessions* series of films. Joe Sickles (Asquith) does deliveries for a family butcher, and his seventeen-year-old friend Carol Thatcher (Janet Lynn) works in a garage. She's also a bit of a looker who, having recently won a local beauty contest, has ambitions of making it as a model in the capital. A bit of a Walter Mitty character, Joe tells her he has a job in a car showroom there and is leaving tomorrow. Though they're not really boyfriend and girlfriend, she puts him on the spot by saying that she'll go with him if she can clear it with her parents. 'If I wanted to have it off with Joe, I don't have to go to London for God's sake' she forthrightly tells her mum who says she must ask her dad. 'Is your maidenhead intact?' he asks. 'Well, as a matter of fact, no, No, it's not,' she says. 'Oh, well, it's all right for you to go then.'

On the train down, she changes clothes. Joe is embarrassed as she stands in front of him in just her panties.

She tells him not to be. She doesn't mind people looking at her she says, 'In fact I enjoy it.' On arrival, they book into a hotel and go sightseeing in a taxi; spending £7 on a dress despite having brought only £20 for a fortnight's stay. They also visit an upmarket boozer where Carol attracts the attention of Jonathan (Jess Conrad) and his pal for whom Joe, playing the big shot, buys the drinks.

The next day the pair separate in search of work with little success although Carol, having no portfolio, makes something of an impression at an agency by stripping to her undies and is rewarded with the name of a photographer. That evening they meet up with Jonathan and his pal again who take the couple to a casino where Joe inevitably loses what's left of his money as Jonathan seduces Carol on a snooker table. She has 34 bob left having spent a further £8 on make-up, which means she cannot afford her photographs. Instead, a photographer friend of one of the other models agrees to do them for free on the proviso that she also poses for some nudes that he hopes to sell to Mayfair magazine. The photographer, Tommy Sanders (Derek Aylward), is based on Mayfair magazine's Philip O. Stearns and the scene was filmed at Stearn's own studio. The stills appeared in Mayfair in July 1970.

Joe's idea of finding work involves 'planning' a bank job: 'All I need is a car and you as a decoy'. Desperate for cash he tells Carol 'you should have got £10 off Jonathan... it must be a very sexy thing; a strange man pays you money; you never see him again. Kinky really.' She is surprisingly convinced by this, saying 'It's only a fuck. I just can't believe people would pay good money for it.' She gives it a go and is soon doing the deed in a man's flat whilst Joe makes the tea in the kitchen. Asked how about the same time tomorrow, Carol agrees. The next day, however, when they get there they find there are four new punters waiting - £5 a piece. 'I don't ever want to do that again' says Carol afterwards.

At a party that night, they are offered £60 each to 'appear' in a film. 'What do we have to do?' asks Carol naively. 'It depends how badly they want the money' she's told. They agree. She also receives modelling work at £160 a session and her film appearance leads to an offer of £500 for a night with a sheikh. She's not keen but Joe is and soon the money is rolling in from all over; though Joe still spends it quicker than they can earn it. Rather abruptly they decide they're not happy and go home.

Says the director: '*Cool It Carol* was based on a true story I had read in the News of the World. But I gave it a happy ending, which annoyed everyone because apparently, I was encouraging people to be promiscuous. I just saw it as pragmatic... Strangely enough, *Cool It Carol* did get quite a few good reviews and some critics even called it a serious piece of filmmaking. I think that's going a bit too far, but it was certainly cynical: Swinging London was coming to an end and the film was showing that it wasn't all that it was cracked up to be'. More typical critical responses could be found in the Daily Mirror who thought it 'a depressingly sleazy film, which is as near pornography as makes no odds,' and the Sunday Times who called it 'a patch of untreated effluent... generally repulsive experience'. At the Evening Standard, Alexander Walker called it 'an orgy of trash' which pre John Waters was not a compliment.

Looking back, Sweet begs to differ, 'The heroine of the film... her odd kind of disassociation from everything that goes on around her seems to be at the heart of what the film is. She's not, in the words of the American title of this film, *The Dirtiest Girl I Ever Met*, she's something very different from that. What you'll hear her saying in this film is, "I don't mind," and I think if we're looking back at the history of the Permissive Society at that moment in British culture, "I don't mind" might actually be rather more important than other less convincing exclamations that we might be used to associating it with.'

Asquith is likewise full of praise, saying '*Cool It Carol*... was a film that was a few years ahead of its time. I think that if it had been released in the mid-seventies, it would have the same sort of success the *Confessions* films managed to achieve. Also as enterprising as Miracle Films were, they did not have the same resources as Columbia... Rather like an English *Midnight Cowboy*, it showed how lonely, destructive and dangerous a big city can be. Especially to two naïve young people with innocent hopes and dreams of the big time.'

*

As the 1960s drew to a close British cinema was well and truly in the doldrums. From a historic post-war high of 1.64 billion, UK cinema admissions had gradually declined to just 193 million in 1970 and cinemas across the country began to close their doors as people opted for an evening at home with *Coronation Street* - or a game of bingo, judging by the number of cinemas converted for that purpose. The big American studios fought back against the box in the corner by investing in blockbusters like *Jaws* (1975), *Star Wars* (1977), and the Bond series, whilst in

Britain studios struck gold by transferring popular TV comedies to the big screen. A handful of producers such as Stanley Long and Arnold Miller, who had turned a profit in the 60s by peddling smut (despite what was promised, there was never any sex on offer), combined this proven thirst for comedy with sex and really hit pay-dirt.

With Martin Scorsese's classic *Taxi Driver* being out-grossed at the UK box office by a film like *Adventures of a Taxi Driver*, there's a popular belief that the British sex comedy saved British cinema during this period. Hardly. It made a handful of producers very rich men and enabled the likes of Richard O'Sullivan, Dennis Waterman, Olive from *On The Buses*, and Christopher Biggins to keep up with their mortgage payments, but attendance figures down by almost half to 101 million in 1980 does not reflect an industry in recovery (four years later would see an all-time low of just 54 million admissions).

Judged by any normal standards the films were generally awful, many even worse than that. Some of these films were nevertheless the first step in what would become accomplished directorial careers. Martin Campbell for example would move from *The Sex Thief* (1973) and *Eskimo Nell* (1975) to a couple of Bond movies. Other careers would move in the opposite direction.

Val Guest had directed many highly regarded films across a variety of genres, including *The Quatermass Xperiment* (1955), *The Day the Earth Caught Fire* (1961), *Hell Is A City* (1960) and *Expresso Bongo* (1959) and written several classic comedy films for Will Hay, when, he made his only foray into the genre after having watched the Danish box-office success *Bedroom Mazurka* (1970) on the recommendation of BBFC censor John Trevelyan. With Scandinavia's reputation for permissiveness, Guest thought the subject was ripe for the burgeoning British sex comedy market and set about writing a British variant.

AU PAIR GIRLS (1972) was produced by Tigon, the company founded by Tony Tenser in 1966 after parting ways with Michael Klinger at Compton Films. Beginning with the Boris Karloff mind control chiller *The Sorcerers* (1967), the company was best known for its horror output such as *The Blood Beast Terror* (1968), *Blood on Satan's Claw* (1971), and especially its commercial and critical hit with director Michael Reeves *Witchfinder General* (1968). The company also had a toe in Hollywood, co-producing, with Harry Alan Towers, *Black Beauty* (1971) and the revenge western *Hannie Caulder* (1971), both of which were handled by Paramount.

Guest wrote the screenplay from a storyline provided by the self-proclaimed King of Sexploitation David Grant. While Guest would consider it a career low-point, it is by far Grant's most impressive credit, having begun with a sex education film *Love Variations* (1969) before capitalising on the Eady Levy tax situation by producing several sex comedies such as *Girls Come First* (1975) and *Snow White & the Seven Perverts* (1973), released as opening features to popular European sex films such as *Emmanuelle* (1974). He also issued the film in hardcore versions for the European market. Grant also dabbled with directing for the likes of *The Office Party* (1976) which starred Coronation Street's Johnny Briggs and *Sensations* (1977) which featured 50% of industrial music pioneers Throbbing Gristle, Genesis P Orridge and Cosey Fanni Tutti.

In the early eighties he formed World of Video 2000, launching with a catalogue of soft porn titles before attracting the ire of Universal by releasing an old 1960s 'B' movie called *Night Fright* (1968) under the title *ETN - The Extra-Terrestrial Nastie*, with video artwork that parodied the ET poster before Spielberg's movie had received its official home video release. Whilst Universal only threatened legal action, the DPP pursued a prosecution over the company's release of *Nightmares in a Damaged Brain* (1981) during the video nasty panic, resulting in a 12-month prison sentence for Grant under section two of the Obscene Publications Act.

In *Au Pair Girls*, four young women recently arrived in England, begin their new jobs as Au Pairs. To allow a greater range of stereotypes, there's a Swedish girl, a Danish, a German and a Chinese who all immediately spend more time in bed than on the job. There's Gabrielle Drake, sister of legendary folk singer Nick, who loses her clothes in a barn with the employer's son (Richard O'Sullivan) after they break down in the country and Astrid Frank who gets picked up by a sheikh on her first night. These two plots are played strictly for laughs, though neither could be deemed funny, but from there the proceedings take a downbeat turn as Me Me Lai helps a young piano prodigy lose his virginity, but not the spoilt brat's immaturity, and Nancie Wait squanders her own virginity on a third rate and extremely ungrateful would-be rock god. In the end, all four girls are willingly whisked off by the aforementioned sheikh for a future in the white slave trade. Guest would get the formula right two years later with *Confessions of a Window Cleaner* (1974).

Hippies, Skinheads, Rastas, Punks & Disco Dancing Bowie Boot Boys

Backstage Pass
(Plain)

British television audiences got an early glimpse of the growing phenomena of young girls who 'followed' pop groups in an episode of the ground-breaking current affairs programme *Man Alive*. The series had been commissioned for BBC 2 in 1965 by its then Controller, David Attenborough, who says: 'At BBC2 my policy was we had to try and make programmes that were unlike anything on any other network.' Attenborough wanted 'a new way of looking at human society, British society, and doing so in an uninhibited way... we're talking about ordinary people talking about their own affairs, and in the past it would tend to be, "Oh, we'd better get a child psychiatrist to deal with this matter, or a Justice of the Peace, or a solicitor or somebody". But [producer] Desmond [Wilcox] thought that people could express themselves and their problems and responsibilities themselves if they had the opportunity. All these things were part of a great surge, as it were, of changes across the board, and I would like to think that BBC2 was at the forefront of those changes.'

At the start of the episode **THE RAVERS (1967)**, pop star Mike Dupree talks about how from a simple act of hand-clapping an audience can be brought to mass hysteria. A clip of him performing live and introducing his latest single sees the camera focus on a teenage girl at the front of the crowd who immediately goes into the 'hands on the head and scream' mode familiar from a thousand clips of The Beatles. But this, as the bemused young lad of about 11 or 12 behind her is all too aware is not John, Paul, George or even Ringo, it's Mike Dupree & the Big Sound. A knowing smile by the girl herself as the camera pulls away suggests she's playing a part, doing what is expected of her.

Reporter John Percival sets the scene: 'Girls between 14 and 17, everybody's daughters, everybody's wives to be, out for a bit of excitement, a bit of a thrill, but all of them, most of them innocently, are already familiar with a world their parents know nothing about, a world with its own jargon, its own morality, where the social pattern their parents thought entirely natural has been turned on its head and the girls have become the hunters, the boys the hunted. It is the world of the Ravers.'

The programme, as with much of *Man Alive*'s output, proved both eye-opening and controversial. According to Harry Rainer in the Times: 'BBC2's *Man Alive* is often a disturbing programme on two counts; it goes out into the world and finds depressing things and it has a well-developed technique for persuading people to abandon reticence and openly discuss intimate experiences. Possibly, last night's programme, *The Ravers*, disturbed more

than most and with a more than usual sense of outrage. The ravers are girls aged between 14 and 17 who find fulfilment not so much in pop music as in the frighteningly aggressive pursuit of pop stars. The photography was equally frank; a girl's arms, a girl's leg, and another girl's breast were autographed by their idol. All the interviewees easily identifiable, whatever admissions they made, no attempts were made to disguise them. It was the bravado of the girls' answers made the viewer question the validity of the methods *Man Alive* adopts.'

Re-christened as groupies, these girls came to wider attention in February 1969 via a piece in Rolling Stone and a Time article entitled 'Manners and Morals: The Groupies' where we were told that whilst some girls sought brief sexual encounters, other groupies travelled with musicians for extended periods of time, acting as a surrogate girlfriend often taking care of the musician's domestic and sexual needs when on tour.

Jenny Fabian provided a British perspective in the novel 'Groupie', her first-person insight into the phenomenon, co-authored with Johnny Byrne and published in 1969. Though the book calls itself a fictionalised look at Swinging London's underground music scene, beginning with a detailed account of a one-night stand with Satin Odyssey's singer Ben (based on a mentally damaged Syd Barrett just days before leaving Pink Floyd), the musicians in real-life groupie Fabian's account are barely concealed to anyone with an interest in music of the era. There's the Jacklin H Event for the Jimi Hendrix Experience, The Dream Battery for The Soft Machine, The Elevation for The Nice and The Savage for The Animals. Andy Summers, later of The Police, features heavily as regular boyfriend Davey, a member during this period of Zoot Money's Big Roll Band, the now largely forgotten Dantalian's Chariot, The Soft Machine and The Animals.

As well as Fabian, other groupies could occasionally become famous in their own right, such as the ill-fated Nancy Spungen or Pamela Des Barres who has authored three memoirs, including one, 'I'm With The Band', which spent several weeks in the New York Times Best Sellers list. Des Barres also fronted the GTO's, a groupie based band assembled by Frank Zappa who recorded an album in 1969. The GTO stands for Girls Together Outrageously but togetherness is the last thing on the minds of the girls portrayed in two British movies released to cash in on the trend, *Permissive* (1970) and *Groupie Girl* (1970).

Before those two came **THE TOUCHABLES (1968)** where 'girl power' can be seen in its genesis, and whose four young 'dolly birds' display, for most of the movie at least, a sense of camaraderie and friendship that far exceeds that of Posh, Scary, Sporty, Baby and Ginger in *Spice World* (1997). These girls do really want to have fun and fun they had, according to star Kathy Simmonds, both on and off-screen; 'We had an absolute ball! Shame none of us could act.' More in common with the Spice Girls after all then.

Swedish-born model Monica Ringwald stepped from the pages of early nudie magazine Health & Efficiency into this, her debut acting role, but managed just one more leading part in Derek Ford's 1975 sci-fi comedy *The Sexplorer* (a favourite of Quentin Tarantino), but furthered her 'pop' credentials by appearing on the sleeve of The Kinks 1974 album 'Preservation Act'. Co-star Judy Huxtable continued to turn up in small roles in movies such as *Scream & Scream Again* (1970) and *Die Screaming Marianne* (1971) but was more visible as the face (and body) of Bacardi and Fry's chocolate and is best remembered today as the second wife of Peter Cook.

Kingston born Ester Anderson landed a dramatic role in Ted Kotcheff's *Two Gentlemen Sharing* (1969) alongside Judy Geeson, released in the US by exploitation specialist AIP whose audiences would have been disappointed to discover it was a flat and not Geeson being shared. The film may however have caught the attention of Geeson's *To Sir, With Love* co-star and helped the actress snare a leading role as the love interest of Sidney Poitier in the actors sophomore directorial effort, *A Warm December* (1973). It was as the writer and director of documentaries, including *Bob Marley: The Making of a Legend* (2011), that she finally found her forte.

For Simmonds, knowing her limitations perhaps, this remains her sole screen credit although she extended the part into real-life somewhat by embarking on 'affairs' with Rod Stewart, Harry Nilsson and, famously, George Harrison, moving into a villa in Grenada with the ex-mop top during 1974 after wife Patti had left him for Eric Clapton. Convinced the relationship was the real thing, Simmonds spent several idyllic weeks before George headed off to LA to plan his first solo concert tour and never returned.

In the film's opening the four young girls, Sadie (Huxtable), Melanie (Anderson), Busbee (Ringwald) and Samson (Simmonds) steal a life-size model of Michael Caine from a swinging party in a waxwork museum, perhaps the same one attended by Joanna Lumley in *The Breaking Of Bumbo*. After bundling it into a white 1963 Studebaker Avanti they drive back to their equally swinging pad, stuffed with cool ephemera by art director Peter Hampton, from

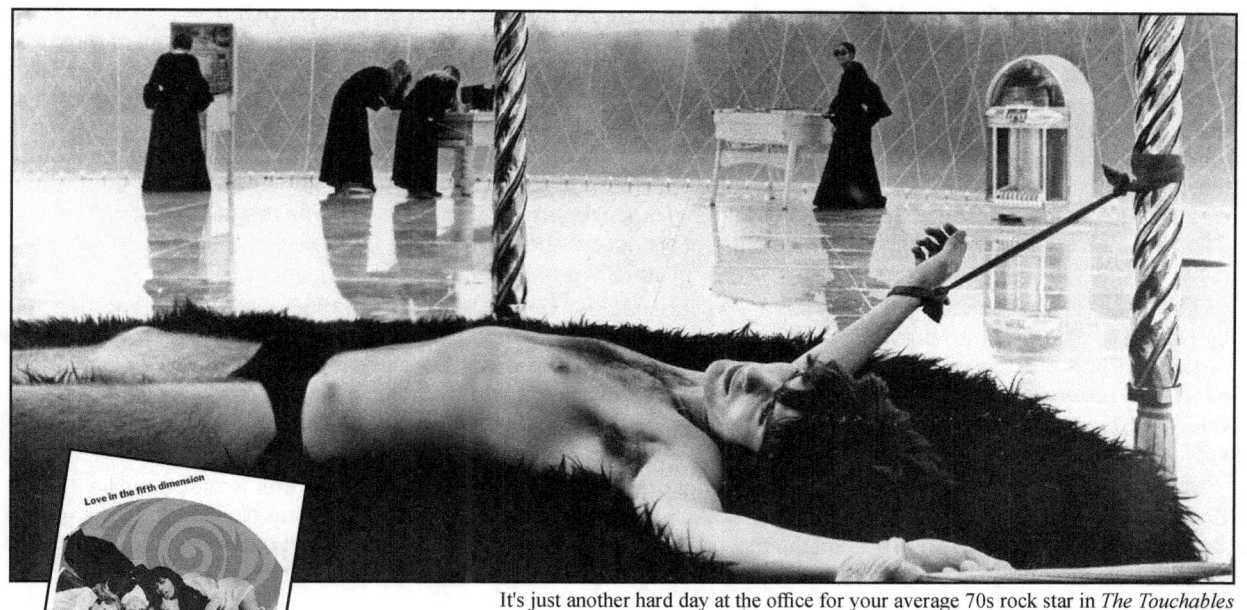

It's just another hard day at the office for your average 70s rock star in *The Touchables*

Spiderman wallpaper, to clockwork robots and Hendrix posters.

This though is just a dry run for their next caper which involves dressing up as nuns to kidnap a vacuous young George Harrison look-a-like pop star, Christian (David Anthony), who they have been watching interviewed on TV by a young Joan Bakewell. Christian is attending a wrestling match that the girl's have wrangled tickets to from their friend Rikki (Rikki Starr, an ex-ballet dancer turned wrestler) who is appearing. Also on the bill at the event is the movie's real villain, Lillywhite (Harry Baird) a masked, gay black wrestler who is in business with upper-class gangster Twyning (James Villiers), and fancies the singer for himself. While wrestling may, to a modern audience, seem at odds with what is considered 'sixties', the 'sport' had recently hit the big time, going out weekly as part of *World of Sport*, which had made up ITV's Saturday afternoon TV schedule since 1964 and rocketed overweight, middle-aged men like Mick McManus and Jackie Pallo to superstardom with audiences of 20 million. Pallo, incidentally, was knocked unconscious by Honor Blackman's Cathy Gale whilst filming a guest appearance on *The Avengers*.

Christian is chloroformed and whisked away to a see-through bell jar dome in the countryside where the girls strip him down to his black speedo's and tie him, spread-eagled, to a round bed that doubles as a merry-go-round. Dressed now in monks' robes, the girls inform him: 'We appropriated you and you're the lucky victim to be played for, the very first prize in our indoor Olympics'. At this, to the accompaniment of Roy Redman's cover of 'Good Day Sunshine' (one of Paul McCartney's favourite interpretations of a Beatles song), each girl takes their turn with him, whilst the non-participants avail themselves of the pinball, table football and pool tables that adorn the dome. Christian, as might be expected, offers little in the way of resistance, before the fun and games are brought to a halt when they are tracked down by a private eye hired by Lillywhite.

Elsewhere the film piles on its hip sixties credentials by scoring a speedboat chase to Pink Floyd's 'Interstellar Overdrive' and hiring Nirvana (the UK psychedelic version) to perform 'All of Us' on the opening and closing credits. Director Robert Freeman came to prominence as a photo-journalist at The Sunday Times but it is for his photographs for the album sleeves of 'With The Beatles', 'Beatles for Sale', 'Help' and 'Rubber Soul' that he will be remembered. Freeman's only foray into film prior to *The Touchables* was in designing the end-credit sequences of Richard Lester's *A Hard Day's Night* (1964), *Help* (1965) and *The Knack... and How to Get It* (1965). He has one subsequent credit as co-director with Paul Feyder on 1969's *Secret World*, a French coming-of-age drama starring Jacqueline Bisset. A further film with Kathy Simmonds, *Greetings Mary Anne*, never saw release.

Based on an idea by the director, brothers David and Donald Cammell worked on a script that was then polished into its final form by *The Likely Lads* co-creator Ian La Frenais. Donald would return to a similar theme of gangster and pop singer in *Performance*, which he co-directed with Nic Roeg and produced in 1968 but was not released until 1970. Despite *Performance*'s bonafide cult credentials, described by critic Mark Cousins as 'if any movie in the whole Story of Film should be compulsory viewing for filmmakers, maybe this is it,' Cammell only directed a further three features, *Demon Seed* (1977), *White of the Eye* (1987) and *Wild Side* (1995). Of that final film, brother David says, 'At one point he was going to go and shoot [producer] Eli Cohen, but I managed to persuade him that it was a negative thing to shoot your producer and then shoot yourself.' When the film was re-cut against his wishes, Cammell took a shotgun and, firing it into the top of his head rather than up through the roof of the mouth, watched himself dying for 45 minutes through a mirror.

Featuring a remarkably similar premise to *The Touchables*, **THE MINI AFFAIR (1968)** was written and directed by Robert Amran who had previously scripted the short film *Mods and Rockers* (1965), notable for its soundtrack of Lennon and McCartney Beatles compositions. After directing a well-received swinging London documentary short, *Dolly Story* (1968), Amram decided to put together his first feature film, and optimistically approached Robert Stigwood for a Beatles song to feature in it. Instead, he had to settle on a Bee Gees song, 'Words', with the stipulation that Hull band The Majority were also featured in the film as part of the deal.

While attending a demonstration of Kendo with her boyfriend Joe (John Clive) and reporter Ronnie, Lucille (Lucille Soong) hatches a plan for her three roommates, Charlotte (Rosemary Nicols), Marianne (Gretchen Regan), and Samantha (Madeline Smith), to abduct the men of their dreams; pop singer Georgie Hart (Georgie Fame), Minister of Popular Culture Sir Basil Grinling (Bernard Archard), and Radio Free Ruritania disc jockey Mike Maroon (Rick Dane).

The film seems to have been scheduled for a UK release around the beginning of 1968, as two singles were issued to tie in. The Bee Gees 'Words' label states it is 'from the film *The Mini Mob*'. The song appears in the film, but not the Bee Gees' version, sung instead by Georgie Fame and also as an instrumental. The label of 'All Our Christmases Came at Once', another Gibb brothers' song, by The Majority carries a similar message, and the band appears in the film performing a shortened version of the song. The film doesn't seem to have even had a premiere or if it had, it's star Georgie Fame wasn't invited. The singer assumes it never received a release, saying 'it may not have been good enough. I don't know if it was edited. I never saw a completed version of it. It was all rather embarrassing - most of it was shot by the river at Maidenhead, I think. We were meant to be kidnapped on a boat.' It did though receive a US premiere in Albany NY in May 1968 but remained unseen thereafter until a screening at the American Cinematheque in Hollywood as part of the Mods and Rockers film festival in July 2002, after which is quietly disappeared again.

GROUPIE GIRL (1970), the directorial debut from *The Yellow Teddybears* writer Derek Ford, was adapted from a screenplay co-written with Suzanne Mercer, for producer Stanley Long, who had decided his follow-up to the then topical subject of wife swapping would be the new phenomenon of rock star groupies. The first of five collaborations from the pair, Mercer based the screenplay on her own experiences, when after dropping out of Oxford University she threw herself into the hippy scene, doing promotional work for Procol Harum and, at the time she met the legendary producer, writing for the New Musical Express.

Says Long, 'We got on superbly and she was full of stories about the music scene, which seemed to me almost as corrupt as the movie business.' Long says Mercer told him that: 'For any groupie, pulling musicians is a career. And my career has been judged on how many rock stars I fucked.' Whilst never quite reaching

Soho stripper Esme Johns displays 'a certain naivete' in *Groupie Girl*

the Premier League of her chosen profession, Mercer did perhaps attain the Second Division Championship by marrying Juicy Lucy and John Mayall's Bluesbreakers saxophonist Chris Mercer.

Continues Long: 'I wanted to give Suzanne a shot at writing a movie script and she didn't disappoint.' Cast in the lead role was Esme Johns, a real-life Soho stripper in her only screen role and of whom Long says, 'Although Esme wasn't the greatest actress in the world, she brought a certain authentic naivete to the role.' Also cast as a groupie was early tabloid newspaper model Maureen Flanagan who went on to be chased by Benny Hill on TV but whose real claim to fame was as the hairdresser to the Kray twins mum. In her autobiography, 'One of the Family: 40 Years with the Krays', Flanagan claims Reggie Kray proposed to her three times and Ronnie tried to steal her toy boy.

As the frontman of the fictional rock band Orange Butterfly, the filmmakers cast Donald Sumpter. Says Long, 'I based his character on Mick Jagger, who I knew at the time,' adding, 'I never found out whether The Rolling Stones actually saw the movie. It was pretty tame compared to their real-life escapades,' which suggests he didn't know the singer that well. Long admits, 'Whilst my contemporaries were listening to The Beatles and The Stones, I was happy to play the beautiful organ music of Reginald Dixon on my record player.'

That might explain why the director brought on board Ashley Kozak, a former jazz pianist who had managed Donovan between 1965 and 1968, as the film's music producer. Interviewed in the Daily Mirror, Kozak attempted to sell what was an exploitation movie as a public service. 'Reading a book about groupies is one thing,' he said, 'but seeing the life visually on screen is another. If there is one way to draw the attention of society to the sick minds of the groupies, then this film is the answer. I think it will deter many young girls from becoming groupies. We kept the sex scenes in the film because we want to get it home to parents that these things usually happen. It's real. The real-life of a groupie isn't milk and honey.' The Mirror's film critic wasn't sold, calling it a 'grimy, catchpenny musical' which 'boringly examines the empty-headed young sluts who insinuate their way into the lives and beds of pop musical groups on one-night stands... after forty minutes I fled silently.'

'Unfortunately, groupies will always exist,' Kovak went on. 'Most of them end up on the slag heap, but one or two make it. They marry their quarry - the pop star - or they become models and maybe it is this incentive that makes the groupie go on and on and suffer it all.' And in *Groupie Girl* suffer they do.

After attending a gig Sally (Esme Johns) climbs in the back of the band's van and hides amongst the speakers. When they get lost on the way back to London, she reveals herself in order to give them directions. 'How old are you?' asks one band member. 'Don't ask her that' interrupts another. When they stop off at the services for a cup of tea, Sally stays behind with the singer, Bob (Jimmie Edwards), who tells her, when she informs him that she's never done it in the back of a van before, that 'you get used to it.' When the rest of the band return to the van she's at the loo so they have to wait. 'I couldn't find it at first' she says, producing giggles from all but Steve.

In London Sally accompanies them to a recording studio they've been booked into by their manager (a pointless cameo by James Beck) where, in a montage sequence set to their song, 'Yesterday's Heroes', they undergo a Dave Clark 5 moment running happily through the streets, holding hands, climbing on walls and spinning around lamp posts. That's where the fun ends. Back on the road, at the next gig, Sally is backstage in the changing room ironing shirts. When she notices another girl sneak in an unconvincing catfight ensues and when the band comes in Bob sends Sally out and takes up with the new girl.

Moving on to the singer of another band, Steve (Donald Sumpter), it isn't long before, following a 'swinging' party where the guests crawl about on all fours doing animal impressions, she's coaxed into a foursome with the Collinson twins of Hammer's *Twins of Evil* fame and offered to the rest of the band before being passed on to another band, Sweaty Betty, through the windows of two moving vans. Unfortunately, the van crashes into a stationary tipper lorry on the hard shoulder resulting in, as a news bulletin tells us, the death of up-and-coming pop star Steve, aged just 22.

Anxious that their involvement in the tragic event should remain secret, their manager secretes both Sally and Sweaty Betty in a country house waiting for things to die down but the place gets raided by the police who have found out there was a girl involved in the crash. They take the occupants of the house in for questioning but Sally, having eaten a large piece of hash and subsequently knocked herself out cold falling head first down the cellar stairs, remains undetected. When a verdict of accidental death is brought at the inquest, Sally is unceremoniously sent packing.

Budgeted at £16,000, the film was sold to America for £50,000 where it was released by AIP under the name *I Am* a *Groupie* with the tagline 'I'm a rock group freak all the way, but what I collect ain't autographs.' In France, it was released in 1973 as *Les Demi-Sels de la Perversion*, which translates as The Pimps of Perversion with sex scenes not in the original cut.

PERMISSIVE (1970) features a real late 1960s and early 1970s band who never quite made the grade, Scottish progressive rockers Forever More who recorded two albums that were met with public and critical indifference. Two of the members would later achieve the level of fame that always seemed to elude *Groupie Girl*'s Jimmy Edwards who skirted the edges of fame in both the Glam era with Flimtlock, and the Punk era via collaborations with both Jimmy Pursey and The Jam's Rick Buckler. Alan Gorrie and Onnie McIntyre would both go on to form the Average White Band and have a series of soul and disco hits between 1974 and 1980 including the million-selling 'Pick Up The Pieces', and have been sampled by various musicians including The Beastie Boys, Ice Cube, Nas and A Tribe Called Quest. The band clearly also enjoyed plenty of drugs with their sex and rock n roll, and when AWB member Robbie McIntosh died of an accidental heroin overdose at a Los Angeles party in 1974, Gorrie also overdosed but Cher kept him conscious until medical help arrived.

The film's Canadian born director Lindsay Shonteff came to England at the behest of fellow countryman Sidney J Furie who, after being offered a more prestigious project, pulled out of directing duties on *Devil Doll* (1964) and recommended his friend. Unlike Furie, though Shonteff maintained a directing career in Britain into the 1990s, he never made it out of low budget exploitation fare. The direction here is pedestrian, but he does, however, imbue scenes with tension and momentum by inserting little flash-forwards in the lives of the characters, silent clips of where they will soon be - whether it's having sex on a toilet or lying dead in a bathtub coloured red with blood. There's none of *Groupie Girl*'s light-hearted moments on show here.

When Suzy (Maggie Stride) turns up in London at the address of her friend Fiona (Gay Singleton) she's pointed towards a room in which she finds her friend in bed with Lee (Gorrie) a long-haired rock musician. She's a groupie but has become a sort of permanent girlfriend. Taken to a gig that night Suzy ends up not with a band member, the competition is fierce, but with an itinerant musician called Pogo who tells her he 'lives under the stars, man, the world's my scene.'

Her friend is going out of town on tour with the band for a few days and suggests that another groupie, Lacey (Debbie Bowen), will put her up so she tracks her down at a gig. All goes well until one of the band members shows interest at which point Lacey immediately tells her to 'fuck off'. With nowhere to stay she ends up sleeping rough with Pogo who gets arrested for preaching in a church – uninvited – and upon release inexplicably steps in front of a car and is killed.

Soon Suzy is sleeping with band members, the road manager, and eventually, in a toilet, Lee. The inevitable catfight ensues when Fiona finds out and the following morning as the band is about to leave for another gig Lee tells her they are over. Suzy puts her bag into the van but realises she's forgotten something. Back in the hotel room, she glimpses a reflection in the mirror. It's Fiona lying in a bathtub full of bloody water. Suzy slams the door shut behind her and we see the van back on the road.

Pop stars weren't the only ones getting in on the action. 'Noone seems to understand what it is to be a disc jockey' says DJ Stevee Daly (Simon Brent) in Norman J Warren's **LOVING FEELING (1968)**, adding 'You get chased by all these birds who think you're some kind of God... these things happen... it doesn't mean a thing.' This also neatly summarises the entire plot of the movie.

The conclusion of Operation Yewtree, a police investigation into sexual abuse allegations against former Radio 1 DJ Jimmy Savile, may have put a more sinister spin of it but there's no doubt that in the late sixties and early seventies DJs were amongst the pin-ups printed in girls pop magazines like Jackie, adorning bedroom walls alongside those of Paul McCartney, Davy Jones and Donny Osmond. Family favourite Savile conjured up a scene more horrifying than anything in Warren's horrror output when he boasted in his 1976 autobiography of his x-rated fun with groupies in which 'the heat of the albeit innocent night had caused the girls to shed the majority of their day clothes. In some cases all. We all resembled some great human octopus.'

Trying to sort out the broken relationship with his wife, Daly is more conflicted over his conquests than Savile, signing one girl's bottom and telling her: 'Now we don't have to go the bother of going to bed. You're an autograph hunter, aren't you? You're more thorough than most, but at least that's all you're interested in, collecting men like signatures.'

Hippies, Skinheads, Rastas, Punks & Disco Dancing Bowie Boot Boys

Doctors of Madness
(Strange)

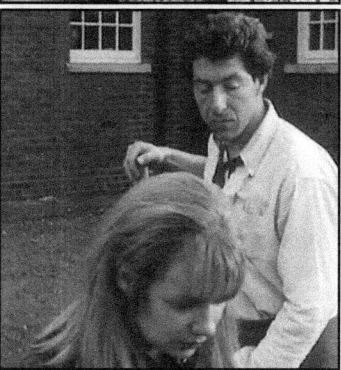

Anna Cropper is *In Two Minds*

Despite all the talk of permissiveness and women's liberation most parents still attempted to organise their own daughters' futures around Victorian stereotypes of the loving mother and dutiful housewife. A society that still expected its women to commit to a long-term relationship with a single partner, after marriage of course, was never going to listen to calls for free love, which got nowhere close to affecting mainstream society.

Despite some advances, in the late sixties and into the 1970s girls and young women were still more likely to be caught up in the legal system because of supposed gender-inappropriate behaviour of which unsanctioned sexual activity was prime and such behaviour could still be a major factor in a girl being taken into psychiatric care.

The story behind director Ken Loach's **IN TWO MINDS (1967)** began in a working-class suburb of 1950s Birmingham where the future BBC producer Tony Garnett was attending the sixth form of his local grammar school and in love with a 15-year-old girl called Topsy Jane. Unlike most schoolboy crushes this one was to last and ten years later, then both actors, the two were living together in the capital as they pursued their respective careers. Garnett was in regular work but Jane was on the brink of stardom having appeared on the cover of the Radio Times for *Time Remembered* (1961), a two hander with Dame Edith Evans, followed by a featured role alongside Tom Courtenay in Tony Richardson's borstal-set drama *The Loneliness of the Long Distance Runner* (1962). Her next role, after turning down a chance to go with Richardson for a season at Stratford, was another role alongside Courtenay in the film version of *Billy Liar* (1963) to be filmed in the northeast. Garnett was filming a Berlin-set David Mercer script for the BBC about CND, in a disused brewery in Watford.

Says Garnett: 'Nearly three weeks later, she returned to London. John Schlesinger had sacked her, saying he was getting nothing. Nothing was coming from her eyes.. Topsy was overweight; personal hygiene had gone out of the window. Her hair was lank, she talked very slowly and what she did say did not make an awful lot of sense.'

With Garnett about to go off on location, Topsy decided she would go home for a few days to stay with her mother, who took one look at her and marched her round to see their GP, who sent her to Highcroft Hall, a mental facility. Says Garnett: 'The psychiatrists there immediately plugged her into the mains, an initial six ECT's, and dosed her with the new drugs that they were very enthusiastic about at the time.' When he discovered what was happening and tried to intervene, as they were not married he was told he had no status.

Both actors final listed credit on imdb is 1965. Garnett left the profession to take care of Topsy until, with no improvement and he 'more or less in a state of depressed incompetence', she went back to live with her mother. He took up a position as an assistant story editor on the BBC's *Wednesday Play*, working on the Ken Loach directed *Up The Junction* (1965) before making the step up to producer and overseeing *Cathy Come Home* (1966).

After reading psychiatrist-come-guru RD Laing's 'The Divided Self', he then commissioned a screenplay from David Mercer with whom, as part of their research, he met Laing, who agreed to be the projects technical consultant, and

Aaron Esterson who alongside Laing and a few others had founded the Philadelphia Association, a controversial UK charity formed to challenge and to widen the discourse around the teaching and practise of psychotherapy. Their work included an alternative mental health community at Kingsley Hall, a community centre in London's East End, which used non-restraining, non-drug therapies for those people affected by schizophrenia.

Says Garnett: 'I did it for Topsy, for her lost life, for the future we didn't have together. Irrational, of course, because the psychiatrists hadn't made her ill. But with no doubt the best of intentions - they had abused her.' Though based on Topsy, it is not her story, and the starting point was a patient called Julie, a case study in Laing's 'The Divided Self'.

RD Laing (Ronnie) was a charismatic Scottish psychiatrist whose belief that schizophrenia was 'a sane reaction to an insane world' found favour amongst the developing Hippie generation who found their evidence to back up such a theory in news bulletins showing children being napalmed for what they saw as little more than a superpower's prestige.

It was Laing's belief that people labelled schizophrenic were the scapegoats of dysfunctional families, despite often being the most sane member of the family. His views influenced health service policy and the day to day psychiatric practice of the time, especially amongst the younger generation of psychiatrists who were more open to his progressive agenda, and he quickly became the country's first celebrity shrink, and a counterculture figure in the mould of Timothy Leary, whose name was regularly dropped by hipsters in the worlds of film, theatre and music, packing out meetings, appearing regularly on TV and even releasing an album. His books were printed as mass-market paperbacks, with 'The Divided Self' racking up sales in the region of 400,000 despite taking three years to reach publication after being turned down by a dozen publishers and, after not even being reviewed by the specialist press, initially selling poorly.

Laing's meteoric rise was relatively short lived and by the early 1970s his theories were being called into question, not helped by a tendency to overplay his hand with statements like 'without exception the experience and behaviour that gets labelled schizophrenia is a special strategy that the patient invents in order to live with an unliveable situation' that were written off as, at best, naïve. However, when production on *In Two Minds* began in the spring of 1966, Laing's standing was at its zenith. It is his 1964 book co-written with Aaron Esterson, 'Sanity, Madness & the Family', which addresses schizophrenia from the perspective of social conditioning, that most influenced David Mercer's scripts for both *In Two Minds* and *Family Life* (1971).

The former opens with Kate (Anna Cropper) in close up speaking about her mother as the title credits roll: 'Well, she... she, she objects to everything I do. She dislikes my friends, she thinks I drink, she criticises me all the time. She doesn't want me to be myself.' As Kate's voice fades, the unnamed researcher (Brian Phelan) introduces himself: 'For some time I have been studying the families of schizophrenic patients. What you will see are extracts from interviews with the family of one of these patients, Kate Winter. When Kate re-entered hospital my research into her case, as necessity, had to cease.' The film then cuts to an interview with her father (George A. Cooper): 'She's sick isn't she. You've only got to look at her... She's killing her mother... We've done all we can.'

Some of the parents' ideas seem to go back to the first half of the 20th century, especially when addressing the topic of girls frequenting public houses. During the Great War, high on the list of worries was that women had taken to visiting pubs, then considered the preserve of men. This lead to calls for measures to to dissuade such behaviour, such as fitting clear windows and, according to the Liverpool Echo, 'removing partitions, snugs and other facilities likely to facilitate secret drinking.' Elsewhere, there were calls for total bans. In the Manchester Evening News one magistrate likened women drinkers to prostitutes and said that unless action was taken, soldiers would return from the battlefields to 'find their wives dishonoured and drunkards.'

Kate's father blames 'her drinking,' for the trouble. Mrs Winter shares her husband's views on drinking but assures the psychiatrist that 'It's not what you'd call drinking...' and is visibly alarmed at a suggestion that she might get drunk. 'Drunk! Our Katie!... I think I can safely say that we brought that girl up to know how to behave. But she does go in pubs. With all sorts, and she talks to them. But it's her illness. She's brought shame on this house, to me and her father, and all we try to do is help her and do what's best for us. But she defies us.'

When asked if Mr Winter goes to the pub, age-old double standards are revealed: 'What are you suggesting young man? Well, he's a man isn't he. He's entitled to a drink isn't he? He has his drink, and that's that... Nobody in this house gets drunk, including Katie. We're respectable people here and we know what's what, and that's how we've brought up our Katie, you don't want to go listening to her.' 'Do you listen?' she's asked.

Going as far back as the Middle Ages, adolescent girls and young women have been criminalised not for offences against social order so much as for the exercising of their sexuality and this is what is really at the forefront of Kate's parents' minds. Especially mum: '... this matter of sex. You have to be careful and obtain a man's respect. You give them what they want and there's no respect and no future. You're no better than a prostitute and one thing leads to another... it's dirty, it's filthy and until you learn some self control... Do you know you're growing into a loose girl. I know what you do when you go out. I know what you all do. But don't you come to me when you've got something inside there.'

It is no surprise then that when Kate gets pregnant matters come to a head. Using her own twisted logic mother blames daughter for having an abortion even though it was the mothers decision and the daughter was all for keeping it. 'What other choice was there?' she points out to the doctor - the implication being that her daughter chose to have an abortion by getting pregnant in the first place. It is this that triggers the initial psychotic crisis, which quickly results in an incident with a bread knife that Kate's mother says her daughter tried to stab her with. We are not shown the incident ourselves but instead are left to build a picture of it through the testimony of others. In doing so the incident of the knife being thrown seems more likely one of it falling near Mrs Winter's feet. It's still enough to have her referred for psychiatric help, at which point the interviewer exits the story, telling us 'When it was decided Kate should go back into hospital, it wasn't possible for me to continue my research into the causes of her unhappiness.'

That it will be all downhill from there becomes apparent when she is shown to her bed and treated like a five-year-old by a nurse administering drugs she will only reveal as 'one of them long chemical names' and considers to be 'not your concern really'.

Kate's thoughts soon become less coherent and her level of self-loathing intensifies; though the play offers faint hope in its final scene in which a dazed looking Kate, drugged up to the eyeballs, is presented to a class of medical students in a hospital lecture theatre. Questions to the lecturer from the class become increasingly challenging, with one asking: 'What, in fact do you know about this family aside from one or two interviews with the mother?', and another: 'with due respect sir you seem to be avoiding any environmental factors. Surely we need to take into account her whole background.' There is no response but the implication is that there is a new generation of practitioners that will place more emphasis on a patient's family life.

This was not enough hope for one early critic, the BBC head of drama, Sydney Newman, who Garnett says: 'did not approve. I showed it in a cutting room at the bottom of the east tower. The basis of his objection was that the film gave no hope and that it was irresponsible with a subject which had caused much distress.' The discussion soon turned into a heated row that continued 'along corridors, up staircases, past offices from which people poked their heads,' and only petered out 'partly because we had both had our say and partly from exhaustion.'

In retrospect Garnett says that they could have given some sense of hope by placing the scene with the sympathetic experience after the one where she receives ECT: 'But David and I knew that wasn't the reality so we chose to rub the audiences nose in it.' In the end no changes were demanded and so none were made.

It would have come as no surprise that there was much criticism from within the medical community. The Head of the Department of Psychological Medicine at St Thomas' Hospital stated that 'the patient portrayed was unrecognisable as a typical schizophrenic. Furthermore, the treatment given in the particular mental hospital shown in the play does not happen these days except in a very limited number of hospitals.'

TV critics were almost universally full of praise, a typical example being the Reading Evening Post's Chris Reynolds who called the play 'devastatingly brilliant'. The inevitable comparisons to *Cathy Come Home* were no doubt daunting and became a focal point of pre-broadcast build-up in the press, but for Reynolds 'It was so much better than *Cathy*... in many ways. From a purely theatrical point-of-view it was more urgent... Oh it was too dreadful. I don't really want to see its like on television again. Even today I still smell nausea at the back of my throat. It moved me as nothing else had done on television.' For the Birmingham Post it was 'a fierce indictment of all self-satisfied parents, who see their children as pretty, clever appendages of themselves... expected to show "due consideration" for being brought into the world for the rest of their lives, and never treated as people in their own right.' He did though feel that 'at the very end... dramatic licence went too far.'

Despite *In Two Minds* commercial - 9 million had tuned in - and critical success, Tony Garnett found he 'couldn't let it go' and proposed re-telling the story for the cinema. David Mercer resisted but was eventually talked around. However, says Garnett, 'his heart wasn't in it. He delivered a perfunctory first draft, didn't want to do any rewrites, and understandably didn't want me to work on it.' Ken Loach was easier to persuade, happy for the chance to work in cinema.

The project, once he had been persuaded to work with a 'bunch of bloody communists', found a backer in Nat Cohen, then managing director of EMI-MGM, a new company formed to make international films, and considered most powerful man in the British film industry.

Now known as **FAMILY LIFE (1971)**, the production was quickly up and running. Says Garnett: 'Doing a film with Nat in those days was different from making a film today. You shook his hand in the morning and could go out and spend his money the same afternoon... He made me put up the whole of my fee as first call on any overage. Considering that represented my total earnings for the year, it concentrated the mind. But when the film was delivered under budget, he always threw in a bonus, although one had not been negotiated. London then was a handshake town, more like a village. Media law virtually didn't exist. There was no demand for film lawyers, except to service Hollywood studios in London.'

In the two key female roles, Loach cast actresses with no experience. As Mrs Baildon the film provided the only screen appearance of Grace Cave, a suburban housewife, cast because Loach felt she would be able to 'unselfconsciously identify with her character'. As daughter Janice, the director cast Sandy Ratcliff, a model who was photographed by Lord Snowden for a Sunday Times cover feature on 'Faces for the 70s' where she appeared alongside Fiona Fullerton, Kiri Te Kanawa and Royal Ballet dancer Diana Vere.

In *Family Life*, Janice Baildon, a 19-year-old unemployed girl living at home with her parents (Bill Dean and Grace Cave), is taken into the Railway Police office by a guard who has noticed her sitting on the edge of the platform for some time and has become worried. The police take her home and her parents decide to get her psychiatrist help.

For *In Two Minds* the story had been presented as a documentary, with the psychiatrist/interviewer only heard as an off screen questioner of a family dealing with a schizophrenic diagnosis, but in the more cinematic *Family Life* he appears on screen as Mike (Mike Riddall), the libertarian head of an experimental community run from a hospital ward. Riddall was a real psychiatrist connected to the therapeutic community movement who, says Loach: 'was fresh from the experience of working in an NHS hospital, where he had to cope with problems on a very large scale... And he made a very real contribution, He could say, "it's not like this - this is how it is." He was one of the touchstones of reality.'

The filmmakers modelled the unit on Villa 21, a residential psychiatric unit for young working-class men at Shenley Hospital in Hertfordshire where, apart from a morning meeting, no treatment was compulsory and prescription drugs were a last resort. David Cooper ran the unit between 1962 and 1966 and it was a forerunner of Laing's better known Kingsley Hall. As research for *In Two Minds*, Garnett and Mercer had visited Villa 21 with Cooper, Garnett calling it 'a most illuminating day'. Cooper also facilitated access to hospital settings for the play's location filming.

Family Life is based more on South Africa born Cooper than on Laing, whom Cooper had met when working at the Seaman's Hospital in South London after moving to the UK to train in psychiatry upon leaving Cape Town University. This is thought to be why Laing declined to be named in the credits. Tony Garnett calls Cooper, who unlike Laing did not train in psychoanalysis, 'a sweaty intellectual, intense and cerebral, lacking the calm of Laing or Esterson.'

In London Cooper threw himself into the emerging counter culture and as a member of the Institute of Phenomenology helped to set up the Dialectics of Liberation conference at the Roundhouse where speakers included Stokely Carmichael, Alan Ginsberg, Herbert Marcuse and himself and Laing. It is in the book of that event that Cooper refers to those therapists attending the conference as 'anti-psychiatrists,' a label that most did not believe they adhered to, including Laing who nevertheless found himself thus labelled thereafter.

Cooper was also involved with the anti-University of London between 1968 and 1971. The anti-University was a short-lived experiment into self-organised education and initially based in Shoreditch from a building owned by the Bertrand Russell Peace Foundation. The establishment offered very cheap courses to anyone who cared to take part from a teaching staff that included social scientist Stuart Hall, feminist Juliet Mitchell, RD Laing, and Cooper himself on aspects of radical politics, existential psychiatry and the artistic avant garde. Other available courses included Black Power with United Coloured People's Association chairman Obi Egbuna, and Dragons with anthropologist Francis Huxley. It opened its doors in February 1968 and by the Spring could boast of 300 students and 50 faculty, but by Autumn it was already in trouble over unpaid bills and forced to leave its premises. Though classes continued in pubs and people's homes, the lack of a campus brought about its gradual decline.

Sandy Ratcliff is a victim of *Family Life*

In *Family Life* Mrs Baildon immediately complains that Mike's secretary had called him by his first name when bringing in tea: 'How much respect should these children show you? I've just noticed now, your assistant just came in here and called you by your Christian name. Now that is the sort of thing that's happening nowadays. I feel with a gentleman in your position a little respect should be shown to you. Come in here and treat you as though you're an equal. The behaviour is just so foreign to me I don't understand it. You see them making love in the middle of the pavement. Is this the right place to do this sort of thing?... Who's making this code of living? Are we going to be dictated to by this generation?'

Historically, there has been very little political or scientific consensus about what constitutes mental illness and how best to treat it and *Family Life* represents schizophrenia, its aetiology and its management in a traditional institution during a decade characterised by transformation, where dissenting views were finding a foothold in the mainstream. Mike and his unit represent those views and so the film initially treats Kate's admission as being a positive step. This changes when Mike falls victim to NHS bureaucracy and biologically oriented psychiatrists at a meeting which he has been told will be a discussion on the renewal of his contract but the outcome of which was decided before he enters the room, condemning Janice to a cocktail of drugs treatment and ECT.

In the play Kate's two boyfriends are an actor and a writer, the former played by a very youthful Peter Ellis, best known as Chief Superintendent Brownlow in *The Bill*. In *Family Life*, Janice's boyfriend is Tim, an art student. When he gives her one of his paintings, she says she can't take it home because her parents could never accept it. He takes her to the loft room's window and points down at the rows of terraced houses that lead to factories in the distance. 'Look at that, out there. That's your mum and dad. Early to bed, early to rise, out to work... and that's what they're going to do to you and that's normal... That's normal, but is it sane? Do you think it's sane because I don't? Punctual, passive, in their place so they can go out there to one of those factories and do a day's work. That's what it's about. That's what it is, and that's what families are. They're like bloody training camps aren't they, to get you to do the same thing.'

'You can't change it' he tells her, 'but you can put your mark on it.' Which they do, courtesy of a couple of cans of blue spray paint, in the movie's only moment of light relief, adding a touch of colour to the bushes, the garden gnomes etc in her parents garden. Naturally, it is not an act greeted with understanding.

There are contentious incidents that in the play are revealed only in snippets of conversation from often dissenting voices. These are dramatised for the film and therefore removed of any lack of certainty. When Janice comes home late on the back of Tim's noisy motorbike, her mother shouts down from the bedroom window and tells her that the door is locked and she 'can stay out!' We can see that she does not mean this and comes downstairs immediately. In the play we did not see this and so are privy to more information that the psychiatrist (who only has the mother's word that her intention was just to 'give her a fright.') From the dreadful weather we also see that Kate/Janice had to make a snap decision before her chance of a lift had gone or she risked being stranded out in the rain. Particularly damning for the parents, is that by showing the alleged knife attack, it is seen to have been nothing of the sort.

Family Life's final lecture theatre scene is no less damning of the psychiatric profession when her current condition, extreme mutism, is described to the class as 'a logical expectation given her case history' and cuts with the request for 'any questions?'

Michael Billington, in Illustrated London News, wrote 'I don't suppose that the film is the kind that will ever cause a stampede at the box office; it's possibly too honest and uncompromising for that. But I sincerely hope that EMI, who had the courage to back it, will also have the courage to see that it gets through to as wide an audience as possible.' The Sunday People called it a 'tense, moving drama'.

The Reading Evening Post carried a complaint from an unnamed Berkshire psychiatrist who said 'the film is produced with such conviction and skill that most people seeing it will believe it to be a statement of truth. That schizophrenia is caused in the way it is portrayed in this film is no more or no less likely than it is due to possession by the devil or sorcery of witches. The film is a statement of belief and not of fact. This film will increase the [pain of] already grievous and sad parents of schizophrenics. Not only will many of them feel intolerable guilt because the film points the finger of blame at them. They may also have to suffer the condemnation of their friends and neighbours.'

Ratcliff would become one of the original cast of long-running soap *Eastenders* as Sue Osman the long-suffering wife of Turkish cafe owner Ali, where her story lines would more than match *Family Life* in their bleakness - cot death, breast cancer, gambling addiction and time on a psychiatric ward. Sadly, her private life was equally complicated, and in 1987 the press revealed that in the past she had been jailed for selling cannabis. Following her departure from the soap two years later she soon found herself in even greater trouble when, in 1990, she provided an alibi for her lover Michael Shorey who would nevertheless become the recipient of two life sentences for the murder of his girlfriend and her flatmate. Ratcliff had claimed the two were making love at the time the killings took place but broke down under cross-examination, admitting she had lied, and to heroin and cocaine use, sharing a spliff with her son and having suicidal thoughts. A descent into heroin addiction soon curbed any hopes she had of continuing with an acting career and led instead to an early death.

Family Life, says Garnett, 'did little business, as Nat had predicted.' A similar prediction might have been made over the commercial chances for the film of Peter Shaffer's stage play **EQUUS (1977)**, which takes some arguments heard in David Mercer's scripts and ups the stakes by making the protagonist the perpetrator of a disturbing act of violence.

While some may commit violent acts, most spurts of violence by alleged schizophrenics are, in fact, produced by individuals with sociopathic or psychopathic tendencies who are taken to be, or pretend to be, mad. Despite what Peter Walker's 1976 low-budget slasher *Schizo* would have you believe in its introductory voice-over which calls schizophrenia 'a mental disorder, sometimes known as multiple or split personality, characterised by loss of touch with the environment and alternation between violent and contrasting behaviour patterns,' the condition does not imply a Jekyll and Hyde split personality being the contrary to a split: fantasy and reality are seen as one, and events happening in the fantasy world of the mind are treated as though they were taking place in the real world.

Equus germinated from a brief conversation playwright Peter Shaffer had with his friend James Mossman, part of the BBC's *Panorama* team. Mossman recounted a story he had been told by a Magistrate of a boy from a repressed and deeply religious family who, after being seduced by a girl on the floor of a stable, blinded 26 horses with a spike not only, the court was told, to erase the memory of his sin but to prevent the horses bearing witness against him to his parents.

That was in 1971 and, says Shaffer, the story 'could barely have lasted a minute but it was enough to arouse in me an intense fascination.' Losing the chance to add meat to the bones of the original story when Mossman committed suicide later that year, the writer nevertheless began to consider crafting a play from this story. A sticking point was the climax which he 'found absolutely impossible to write. There was no way in which a boy's first satisfactory sexual encounter could lead on stage to such horrific violence - unless it had not been satisfactory at all. Unless that is, the presence of the horses had directly prevented that satisfaction. And why would that be unless the horses themselves were the focus of some deep attachment which consummation with the girl would betray? This disturbing thought vitalised the story for me and took hold of my mind.'

Equus made its debut at the Old Vic in 1973 with Alec McCowen as psychologist Martin Dysart and Peter Firth as the seventeen-year-old Alan Strang. The play was, in the words of its writer, 'a play of obsession, possibly unreachable in its nature by very many people and probably shocking to them as well.' There was therefore no one more taken aback by 'the immense surprise which awaited me... that such a private piece could achieve so public a success.' It's first season ran for two years, winning a Drama Desk Award for outstanding foreign play, a Tony for best play, a Tony for best actress, and the New York Drama Critics Circle award for best play.

Transferring to the Plymouth Theatre in 1974 the play made its Broadway debut with Anthony Hopkins as Dysart and Firth reprising his role as Strang, winning a Best Play Tony Award and enjoying a three-year run. Richard Burton succeeded Hopkins in what was considered a comeback role after his troubles with the bottle, and it earned the actor a special honorary Tony in 1976.

Instrumental in the play's success was the innovative staging from director John Dexter in which the actors wore brown track suits and abstractions for horses heads, a style that *The Lion King* would adopt to even greater effect. The cast also stayed seated on stage for the entire duration, watching the play along with the audience.

The director's influence also ran to the script with Dexter, says Shaffer, persuading him to etch the character of Dysart 'with deeper lines of professional self doubt.' This took the form of an agreement between patient and psychiatrist that Alan will answer truthfully if Dysart will do the same. This allows for a series of bitter, self-mocking confessions from the psychiatrist who behind the professional facade is unhappy in his marriage and practising techniques he himself does not believe in.

Given Dysart's own fragile mental state, haunted by a nightmare in which he sacrifices a herd of children all baring Alan's face, the line between doctor and patient is often blurred, echoing Laing's belief that 'schizophrenics have more to teach psychiatrists about the inner world than psychiatrists their patients.'

Dexter also pointed out that Shaffer's Laingian thesis that environment was to explain for Alan's psychosis 'was badly obscured if the boy's parents appeared as blatantly weird. Dysart's perception is that *Equus* finally arises unprovoked by family tensions, even though they are partially instrumental in forming him. I immediately redrew Mr and Mrs Strang to more unassertive proportions.'

A family as an entity where the members should be co-ordinated for the correct development of the individual is a concept Shaffer had already written about in his play *Five Finger Exercise* that had opened at London's Comedy Theatre in 1959, with a young Juliet Mills earning a Tony Award for her role as the teenage daughter. In the play, made into an American film drama in 1962, the Harrington family is at war; husband against wife, daughter against son. The son, Clive, is oedipally drawn to his mother whilst struggling with his repressed homosexuality and an air of something incestuous with, and encouraged by his sister Pamela. In his 1970 play *Shrivings*, the family is referred to as 'a box of boredom for man and wife... a torture chamber for the children.'

American film director Sidney Lumet had seen the stage *Equus* when it was first performed in London and spent over a year adapting it, with Shaffer, for the screen. The film version accurately preserves much of the original dialogue but undergoes a major change because of Lumet's insistence that that the horses had to be real and that the violence had to be depicted: 'A boy who blinds six horses is not your average hero. If you're going to show the boy's magnificence and Dysart's envy of him, you've got to get into the area of his horror, also.' Many viewers would have disagreed with that, including critic Roger Ebert for whom: 'the blinding of horses is something that works a great deal better as stage symbolism than as cinematic fact'

Martin Dysart (Richard Burton), a psychiatrist who works with disturbed teenagers at a hospital in Hampshire, is approached by a magistrate friend and asked to treat a 17-year-old stable boy named Alan Strang (Peter Firth) who has blinded six horses in his care. During an extended psychiatric evaluation, conducted over several days in a provincial hospital, events in Alan's life are uncovered in therapeutic sessions, which reveal that his behaviour stems from internal conflict brought about by the contrasts between a voyeuristic atheist father and a mother who regularly reads her son passages from the Bible. This clashes with his own sexual awakening; sexual desire and religious passion as ever making unsuitable bedfellows.

Alan's initial affection for horses resulted from a combination of his mother's biblical tales, a horse story that she had read to him, cowboy films, and his grandfather's interest in horses and riding. He had first encountered a horse at age six, when a rider had approached him on the beach and took him up on the horse. Though Alan was visibly excited, his parents were angry and pulled him violently off the horse.

After his father insisted on the removal of a painting of Jesus on his way to Cavalry from his son's bedroom wall, Alan replaced the picture with one of a horse, whose large, gaping eyes seemed to stare down. As a result, somewhere along the way Alan has substituted his mother's deity with a horse he refers to as Equus. That image had become the altar in front of which Alan late at night in his room, haltered and flagellating himself, would chant a series of names culminating in the name Equus as he climaxed.

Each parent believes the actions of the other have played a part in their son's transgression which boils over when he forms a relationship with the more worldly Jill (Jenny Agutter) after she visits the electrical goods store in which he is working to purchase blades for horse-clippers. When Alan reveals his own interest in horses Jill proposes that he too should come work at the stables, a suggestion he enthusiastically pursues, becoming what appears on the surface to be a model worker. Digging a little deeper reveals that Alan was erotically fixated on one of the horses which he would secretly take for midnight rides, bareback and naked.

The basis for Alan's sexual development had been his mother's regular declarations that true love and contentment could be found only through religious devotion and marriage, but when Jill insists he takes her to see a soft porn film, they discover Alan's father is also in attendance and flee back to the stables. With his father's apparent hypocrisy having removed one of the barriers that have thus far hindered a normal sexual development, he soon finds himself naked with her. However, having learnt from his mother that God sees everything and punishes transgression, Alan sees his God watching through the eyes of six horses, rendering him unable to act on his desire for Jill. Humiliated, after forcing her away he takes revenge on the earthly incarnations of his all-seeing God.

In 'Politics of Experience' Laing suggests that 'the ordinary person is a shrivelled, desiccated fragment of what a person can be. Humanity is estranged from its authentic possibilities. This basic vision prevents us from taking any unequivocal view of the sanity of common sense, or of the madness of the so-called madman.' This shared belief in the creative possibilities of madness, leads Dysart, who sees Alan's delusional rituals as a fascinating work of art, to conclude that in bringing Alan to whatever society deems normal, he would be destroying the boys authenticity. That without his psychotic rituals he would remain capable of nothing more creative than watching TV.

That psychopathology and the creative imagination are inseparable is an idea at least as old as psychoanalysis with early romantic theories about the relationship between madness and art suggesting that insanity was the price paid by the artist in a kind of Faustian bargain. Acceptable perhaps in the blues of Robert Johnson but a stretch with the delusions of a barely literate stable boy.

Comparisons with the stage version were both inevitable and negative, but the reviewers were generally positive in their appraisals of the film. Oscar nominated duo Burton and Firth picked up Golden Globes but lost out two months later to Richard Dreyfuss and Jason Robards. Shaffer also lost out to Alvin Sargent (for Holocaust drama *Julia*) though the writer picked up a BAFTA.

At the time it was first staged, *Equus* contained the most explicit and prolonged scene of male nudity the British theatre had seen but because it was clinical and in no way erotic, the scene passed barely noticed. Not so the 2007 revival. After having refused all attempts at a West End revival for thirty years, Shaffer finally relented and the nude scene this time caused something of a stir when it was revealed that it would be Harry Potter himself, Daniel Radcliffe, in the flesh as it were. Even amongst the more highbrow press such as the Telegraph who couldn't resist headlines such as 'Radcliffe's naked talent makes *Equus* a hit'.

Richard Burton and Peter Firth in *Equus*

Maxwell's Silver Hammer
(Lennon, McCartney)

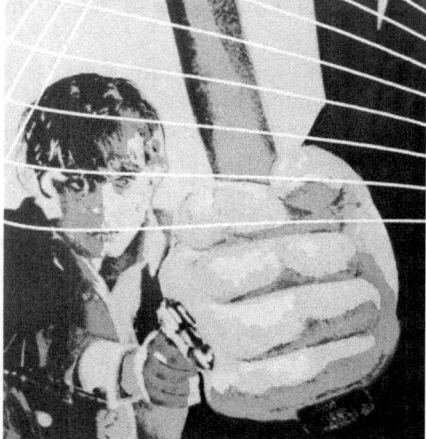

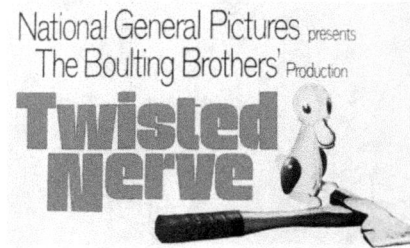

Arguably the country's two greatest directors, Alfred Hitchcock and Michael Powell had worked together twice during the twenties; first when Powell served as the stills photographer on Hitchcock's *Champagne* (1928) and a year later as an uncredited writer on the script of the director's *Blackmail* (1929). Their careers crossed paths again just over thirty years later when each helmed a movie about a psychopath, a character in vogue following the 1957 arrest of Ed Gein, a major influence on the Robert Bloch novel on which Hitchcock's *Psycho* (1960) was based. Three months before *Psycho*'s New York premiere in June, another film with a mild-mannered psychopath at its core opened on this side of the Atlantic. While Hitchcock's movie was immediately hailed as a masterpiece, Michael Powell's *Peeping Tom* (1960) was hounded out-of-town by critics, with those on the left especially scathing in their condemnation. The Tribune said that 'The only really satisfactory way to dispose of *Peeping Tom* would be to shovel it up and flush it swiftly down the nearest sewer. Even then the stench would remain'. This theme was also taken up by the New Statesman who called it 'muck' and said it 'stinks'. Both these reactions were lukewarm when compared to that of Nina Hibbins at the Daily Worker who 'was shocked to the core' at such 'perverted nonsense. It wallows in the diseased urges of a homicidal pervert ... From its lumbering, mildly salacious beginning to its appallingly masochistic and depraved climax, it is wholly evil'.

Eight years after his script for *Peeping Tom* had as good as ended the career of director Michael Powell, writer Leo Marks returned to the subjects of murder and mental health with **TWISTED NERVE (1968)**. Marks crafted the screenplay, along with director Roy Boulting, from a story by Roger Marshall, a regular writer on T*he Avengers* in its Emma Peel period.

That film's director survived to fight another day but the Boulting Brothers were administered a heavy bruising to their reputation. *Peeping Tom* had been branded 'evil and pornographic' on its release; *Twisted Nerve*'s outrage was expressed mainly via the mental health community, who protested strongly about the movies connection of Downs Syndrome, then known as mongolism, with psychopathy.

Peeping Tom was subsequently hailed as a masterpiece by the likes of Martin Scorsese, who cast Marks as the voice of Satan in *The Last Temptation of Christ* (1988). *Twisted Nerve* also found a champion in Quentin Tarantino, who borrowed Bernard Hermann's whistling motif and gave it to Daryl Hannah for *Kill Bill* (2003).

Marks had a more interesting background than the average writer, having been the head of the codes office during the Second World War, supporting resistance fighters in occupied Europe. It is this background that, after the end of hostilities, Marks drew on as an author and a playwright, his two ventures into psychological horror being uncharacteristic.

Roy Boulting, along with his brother John, were household names who would appear prominently on film posters and advertising. Roy's last outing as a director had been *The Family Way* (1966) which, like *Twisted Nerve*, starred Hywel Bennett and Hayley Mills. *The Family Way* was Boulting's foray into the world of kitchen sink, with an adaptation of Bill Naughton's 1963 play *All In A Good Life*, itself an adaptation of the writer's 1961 *Armchair Theatre* episode, *Honeymoon Postponed*. It was also Hayley Mills attempt to leave behind her Disney persona and become accepted as an adult, cementing the point with a brief nude scene.

This clearly worked with Boulting, who embarked on an affair with his leading lady - some thirty-three years his junior. Having been both a financial and critical success, the re-casting of his two leads not only kept together a winning team, it also enabled him to continue his personal relationship with Mills, whom he married in 1971. *Twisted Nerve* would be his take on the psycho thriller genre that, post *Psycho* (1960) and *Peeping Tom*, had continued to provide hits such as *Whatever Happened To Baby Jane* (1962). It was, he considered, his 'silent tribute to Hitchcock'.

Boulting bolstered the film with a raft of top-notch supporting players, including Bille Whitelaw, Frank Finlay and Barry Foster, but at the heart of the film is a fantastic performance from Hywel Bennett in the key role of Martin. Despite being blessed with looks that suggested a traditional leading young man, Bennett avoided such casting for darker material that became all the more so when contrasted with such a doe-eyed picture of innocence. The actor's first major film role had been in *The Family Way* but he had continued to shine with starring roles in two episodes of *The Wednesday Play*, *Where The Buffalo Roam* (1966) and *The Death of A Teddy Bear* (1967). The former, written by Dennis Potter, provided Bennett with an early template for *Twisted Nerve*'s Martin, in the character of Willy Turner who, in the parlance of the day is either 'a bit slow' or 'educationally subnormal' but today would simply have a learning disability.

And this being the 60s, Willly couldn't just have a problem with his reading, he's also both childlike and volatile. The latter we know because we are told that he is on probation for an assault on another youth. The former takes the form of obsessive fantasies in which, in the spirit of *Billy Liar*, he sees himself as a gun-slinger in the Old West. As his fantasies increase in frequency they become more intertwined with a reality that ends with him falling from a warehouse roof to his death in the canal below after being shot by a police marksman.

Martin is a bored and manipulative rich kid with a cloying mother and a step-father whom he despises. He also has a brother with Downs Syndrome who is being 'cared for' in a private psychiatric facility, and it is this, via a suggested genetic mental imbalance, that we are supposed to accept as providing the motivation for his actions.

Billie Whitelaw has confused feekings for Hywel Bennett in *Twisted Nerve*

Visiting his brother at the hospital a doctor tells him that there may be psychopathic tendencies in the siblings of children with Downs Syndrome, even though they themselves do not show symptoms of the condition. It's a statement that causes the startled youth to drop his cup of tea. As did the jaws of the mental health community.

When he is caught shoplifting a toy duck in a department store, to impress college student and fellow shopper Susan Harper (Mills), he reacts to his predicament by adopting the persona of his brother Georgie, leaving the shop manager and Susan to believe he is mentally subnormal. When Susan takes pity on him and pays for the duck, he becomes a rather charming and, being so child like, seemingly harmless stalker who eventually turns up on the doorstep of the house she shares with her mother (Billie Whitelaw) and a couple of lodgers, including the lecherous Gerry (Barry Foster).

Before this we see Martin facing a mirror in his bedroom, seated on a rocking chair and clutching a teddy bear with a childish grin fixed across his face. It's an unnerving image and suggests that Martin may in fact have a split personality. That is until the camera pulls away to reveal that the chair has been strategically placed on a framed photograph of his stepfather and we realise he is more likely preparing for a role.

It is in character that, with a suitcase and a note purporting to be from his 'father', he turns up in the pouring rain at Susan's house. The note asks them to take in 'Georgie' for a week whilst his father is abroad on business. Unable to turn him away that night in the rain, Mrs Harper agrees that he should stay the night, but Martin immediately puts his innocent charm and youthful good looks to seductive effect.

Billie Whitelaw, cast as Hayley Mills mother despite being just 14 years her senior, is sinfully sexy in some jaw dropping scenarios such as when 'Georgie', pretending to having had a bad dream, climbs into bed with her. Vulnerable and frustrated that lover Gerry has come home late and drunk, Whitelaw manages to be both motherly and sexual in the same breath.

There's a reason other than Susan for Martin to have departed the family home. His stepfather, keen to have him as out-of-the-way as possible, has lined him up with a job - in Australia. Worse still his mother has agreed. Martin is not the sort of young man to take such news lying down and the Harper household is the base from which he exacts a bloody revenge.

In the meantime he attempts to get closer to Susan, a process hindered by the fact she has a boyfriend with a sports car as opposed to a teddy bear. This naturally makes Martin jealous, especially when he has to watch him clamp one hand firmly on each of her cheeks. He needn't have worried though, as she immediately informs her very stoned suitor that 'You can either sleep it off or have it off - but not with me' before sending him packing.

With the boyfriend out of the picture, Martin uses an outdoor swimming trip to first 'unwittingly' expose himself before grabbing her, which gets him a slap across the face. He apologises, but it has made her realise that he's a man and that it would be best he should move on. Copies of 'Psychopathia Sexualis' and 'Sex, Culture & Myth' at the bottom of his drawer, raise her eyebrows further. As does a piece of paper with various attempts at a signature matching the man whose brutal murder has been headlines in recent days, and so she sets off to visit his widow.

Unfortunately, that means when Martin returns home and goes into the shed to chop some wood there's no one home but Susan's mother who unwittingly mentions where her daughter has gone, the shock of which causes him to cut his hand. When she reaches into his jeans pocket for a hankie and leaves her hand there much longer and deeper than is necessary, he snaps: 'Take your filthy hands off me.' When Susan returns home, 'Georgie' is gone and she is confronted instead with Martin for the first time and he's not very nice and more than a little scary.

For many, the film is a flawed classic but reviews at the time were savage, the New York Times calling it 'an embarrassing picture, a sour-tasting mess'. Unhappy with the mongolism theme, which was 'a delicate area indeed', it was they said an 'unappetising film, more concerned with effect than understanding and coated over with a detachment approaching blandness.'

Boulting would enjoy one more huge hit with *There's A Girl In My Soup* (1970) before his career went into steady decline as the decade progressed. An attempt to repeat that film's hit formula (Peter Sellers and sex) with *Soft Beds, Hard Battles* (1974) was a flop and cost the director a lot of his own money. By then his marriage to Mills was also in tatters, with the couple officially splitting up the following year.

Twisted Nerve may not have been a success but its adoption of *Peeping Tom*'s template of the blond-haired, blue-eyed young man behind whose boyish good looks lurks a psychopath, would be revisited on numerous

Jenny Agutter and Bryan Marshall in *I Start Counting*

occasions in the next few years. In the first of those, **I START COUNTING (1969)**, the up-and-coming Simon Ward, who had starred on stage in the 1966 production of Joe Orton's *Loot*, followed a walk-on role in *if...* with a small but important role that was a far cry from his breakthrough role as the young Churchill in *Young Winston* (1972).

Sung by Lindsey Moore and composed by the great Basil Kirchin, *I Start Counting*'s opening song provides the perfect juxtaposition of sweet and scary to accompany the opening sequence in which Wynne (Jenny Agutter) is woken by the alarm and readies herself for another day at school, the camera panning through the window and into the distance where two young boys throw stones into a large pond in which, unknowingly, the body of a young girl lies partly hidden by the weeds in shallow water.

Moore vanished from public view after this, her only recording, and remains something of an enigma. She is said to have been either the girlfriend of one of the musicians involved or had been hanging around the studio. It has a twee but haunting vibe that could easily have been attributed to the character or its then sixteen-year-old star - who herself sang backing vocals on Prefab Sprout's 'Wild Horses' in 1990.

Wynne is a hormonal fourteen-year-old schoolgirl living with her adoptive family who has a crush on her 32-year-old foster brother George (Bryan Marshall). Unfortunately, it's not only the familial connection and age gap that makes him an unfortunate choice. She also suspects he may be the local sex killer but still dreams one day of marrying him and he seems to fill her every thought.

The first inkling that all is not as it should be with George are the deep scratches on his back that she sees when spying through a partially opened bathroom door as he washes at the sink. The second is when she sees him surreptitiously disposing of a parcel in a bin when giving her and her friend Corinne (Clare Sutcliffe) a lift to school later that morning. There's also the largely unexplained tale of George's ex, who had been found dead by a much younger Wynne at the foot of the cellar stairs in their old home.

Corinne is more excited that they are to have a sex education lesson: 'Someone's coming from the Catholic Marriage Advisory Council... he's going to answer questions - on sex.' Sadly it's a priest who tells them that 'sin can be regarded as anything that stands in the way of real love, and love, real love, grows only from love and the best sex education we can give to our children is to love them to the end.' To hear her, talk sex education would be wasted on Corinne anyway. 'It hurts the first time you know,' she tells Wynne. 'I've done it seven times so I ought to know. SEVEN!'. It is just bravado, as is her insistence on wearing the hemline on her school uniform a few inches higher than everyone else.

On the way home from school the bus stops by the common, now swarming with police following the discovery of the young girl's body - which isn't the first. Once back home Wynne checks the bin and discovers the package was a sweater she had made for George, and that it is covered in blood. When he says he remembers their brother Len (Gregory Phillips) borrowing it, her suspicions appear confirmed, so she attempts to incinerate the jumper in her former, now derelict, house.

Though he plays a much larger role in the Audrey Erskine Elliot novel on which the film is based, Len's role here seems to be solely to make a half-hearted attempt to deflect the finger of suspicion when he revels a scrapbook of press cuttings of the murders and buys pills from a drug dealer. This latter scene seems particularly pointless unless we are supposed to believe that scoring drugs in the late sixties was a pointer towards psychopathic tendencies.

As a whodunnit? the film falls flat as soon as we see the regular young conductor on the bus who cheerily calls Wynne his 'Coleen', much to the annoyance of Corinne who feels she should get all the attention. There's something decidedly shifty about him that is confirmed when Wynne, travelling alone outside school hours, wears a very short mini and he grabs her wrist and forcefully informs her 'Your skirt's too short.'

When Corinne takes umbrage at George calling her a 'pathetic little mini tart' after she has made a pass at him during a day out she refuses a lift back, effectively going missing. It transpires that she had instead accepted a lift from the off-duty bus conductor and become the next victim. The body is discovered soon after by Wynne, who Corinne had rung to brag about her impending date. Having been told only that the date was with a man they both know and that that she intended to stay out all night, fearing that George would be blamed, Wynne headed to the old house herself.

Ward breaks down into tears and gets to play his big scene: 'She shouldn't have been your friend, she's dirty. They're like that now, you know. They don't seem to know what they're doing... They want you to do it. They make you. And then they laugh. They always laugh. Then I feel this sick in my stomach. I've never had a strong stomach, you can ask my mother. They shouldn't laugh at me.'

Besides this finale, Ward doesn't get much to do with the character but would get to play a similar but larger role in *Deadly Strangers* (1974), on that occasion with Hayley Mills in which the two share a car journey whilst the audience has to decide which of the two is the escaped lunatic that is mentioned, as they invariably are, over the car radio. That film points us toward Ward, who immediately changes stations, especially when we see in a flashback he has trouble getting it up. Also, when two young bikers who lay in wait in a country lay by to terrorise passing motorists, pick on Ward we learn that he has a temper when he drives into the back of them, forcing one bike off the road and into flames. Aspects of Mills character's childhood also raise a few questions but when an hour and fifteen minutes in she reads a newspaper and we see a photograph of Ward alongside the front-page headline's 'Maniac Escapes' and 'Killer Strikes Again' these quaestions seems answered. Or are they?

In **GOODBYE GEMINI (1970)**, the blonde locks belong to Martin Potter who had shot from supporting roles to centre stage the

Judy Geeson aks Agamemnon in *Goodye Gemini*

previous year when Fellini cast him, for his looks rather than his acting ability, as the lead in *Satyricon* (1969), when Terence Stamp was not available. A similar casting decision seems to have been at play here as while his performance is adequate, his look is striking.

Here, Potter plays Julian, one half of twins who arrive in London by coach wearing striking yellow jackets and clutching a small black teddy bear that, we shall learn, never leaves their side. His sister, Jacki, is played by Judy Geeson, the film's real star attraction after roles in *To Sir, With Love* (1967) and *Here We Go Round the Mulberry Bush* (1968). The siblings are according to 'Ask Agamemnon', the experimental novel by Jenni Hall on which the film is based, 'blond, blue-eyed, eighteen' (though Potter was already much older) and are on a break from University. After having spent time with their father in Mexico, they are hoping to take in what's left of Swinging London - the book was published in 1964 but the film did not go in front of the cameras until the decade was coming to a close.

They have use of a house from which to co-ordinate their adventure, and given that it is a regency property on Chelsea's sought-after Cheyne Walk, it seems unlikely money will be a problem. Previous and future residents of the street include Mick Jagger and Marianne Faithfull, Paul McCartney and Jane Asher, Keith Richards, former New York mayor Michael Bloomberg, Prime Minister David Lloyd George, Bram Stoker, Bertrand Russell, Isambard Kingdom Brunel, JMW Turner and Chelsea's billionaire Chairman Roman Abramovich.

Unfortunately the house, their father's, comes with a housekeeper who has no time for their childish antics and comes with a list of rules including which rooms they can and can't enter. Like 'Georgie' in *Twisted Nerve*, the twins are beautiful and childlike, but not innocents, and this hurdle is soon surmounted when they strategically leave their teddy bear, Agamemnon, at the top of the stairs, before breaking the housekeeper's glasses and watching her take a tumble and be carted off in the back of an ambulance.

Free to sample the city's night-life they soon find themselves in the Royal Vauxhall Tavern, the UK's longest running gay bar, where they catch the eye of Clive (Alexis Kanner), a pimp for homosexuals (as opposed to a homosexual pimp). Kanner first came to attention in as Stephen in the war time delinquency drama *Reach for Glory* (1962), and in 1967 had assured his cult status by appearing in TV series *The Prisoner* (1967) as Number Forty-eight, made to stand trial as the representative of rebellious youth in the final episode of the series.

With an eye on the lovely Jacki, but with a libido that swings both ways, Clive introduces the twins to his world of sex, drugs and the sort of upper class houseboat parties that are attended by the likes of Member of Parliament James Harrington Smith (Michael Redgrave) and gangster Rod (Mike Pratt), to whom Clive is in debt to the tune of £400. It's not the sort of swinging London party where you might brush shoulders with Mick Jagger, though if this were 80 years earlier these could have been surroundings where you might have found Oscar Wilde and Lord Alfred Douglas trading pithy put-downs. In their place we get a bitchy gay couple, David (Freddie Jones) and Nigel (Terry Scully), who wears a lurid pink shirt and says 'ducky' a lot. It's also the sort of party where Clive, who David calls 'an ectoplasm with appetites', can further his business as a 'provider of queer boy circuses'.

At the twins house Clive makes a play for Jacki, passing his, is-she-or-isn't-she, girlfriend Denise (Marion Price) off to a disinterested Julian. This lack of enthusiasm is not because he's gay but because he too only has eyes for his sister, struggling to hide his jealousy. Julian sees he and his sister as being the same entity, which he explains as having a hive mind, enabling him to rationalise his incestuous urges. Jacki shares neither her brother's urges or theory, but does herself no favours by being far closer to him than would ever be considered appropriate, in public and in private. They share a connection that does not go unnoticed, even by those they barely know, like the MP who declares that 'they carry their own universe with them.'

When Julian makes his own advances and is rebuffed, he gets his revenge by accepting an offer from Clive, who has just commented on his beauty, of a lads' night out on the town. The evening ends in a seedy hotel room in which Clive often carries out his business. Under the influence of drink and drugs, two drag queens splay Julian across a bed and begin to get intimate with him as Clive snaps away on a camera. When he realises they're men and resists, they beat and rape him. Where *Twisted Nerve* antagonised the mental health community, *Goodbye Gemini* risks a similar response from the gay community, who are painted in a far from positive light.

Under pressure from Rod, Clive intends to use the photographs to solicit money from the twins to pay off his gambling debts but they are no more likely to bow to the demands of a blackmailer than they were to a bossy housekeeper. Instead, Julian suggests he partakes in a challenge to tell the twins apart. Sending Clive out of the room, the twins cover themselves in bedsheets, cutting eye-holes into each with a sword. The sheets, as Clive finds to his horror, also conceal the swords.

This is a beautifully staged almost wordless sequence, lasting over three minutes which is accompanied by a sinister and sparingly used laid-back funk bass line that slowly builds to a crescendo. Under the watchful gaze of Agamemnon the siblings ritualistically go through their preparations, at one point almost like a ballet as they undress in synchronicity.

When the twins re-enter the room in which Clive is tied to a chair, and he removes his blindfold, he is looking at them through a mirror and Jackie is on his left. Though it's easy to miss without repeat viewings, the first blade passes in front of him, whilst the second clearly and bloodily goes through his neck. However, the director's love of mirrors, switching between the two perspectives and only being able to differentiate the two by their eyes, again makes it difficult to pinpoint who dealt which blow.

There is an abrupt cut to Jacki running over a bridge, still draped in a now blood-soaked sheet. For viewers who have ascertained that she did not stab Clive, but was merely going through with what she believed to be the charade of scaring him, as she later tries to explain to a frantic Julian, this makes perfect sense. If not then little matter, with by far the most charismatic character now dead, the film loses its focus.

Jacki is spotted by Herrington Smith who, when she explains that she can't remember what happened or how she got there, puts her up on the sofa. In the middle of the night her memory returns and she rushes back to the house where she, and the taxi driver who has dropped her off, discover Clive's bloody torso before running back to the MP's flat through the darkness. When she awakes the next morning, it is to a newspaper headline that declares the twins are being sought in relation to the 'Cheyne Road Murder'. The MP nevertheless allows her to stay in the flat while she tries to piece together what had happened. This she does during a montage in which she wanders bare-foot through Shepherds Bush market to the folkie 'Goodbye Gemini' sung by Jackie Lee.

When she finally tracks down Julian in the freezing hotel room in which he has been waiting for days, he's packed and ready for them to leave, excitedly talking about catching some rays in the south of France but also ranting that 'it wasn't just us anymore'. It's only now that the intensity of his feelings for her and the murderous jealousy it invokes dawns on Jacki . When she says she can't promise that it will always be just them in the future he attacks her and, during the struggle crushes her windpipe, killing her. In a moment of lucidity, a distraught Jules apologises to the dead Jacki before putting the coins she has given him for the gas in the meter, blocking the bottom of the window frame with towels, extinguishing the pilot light, sitting silently caressing his sister and waiting to die alongside her.

The Daily Mirror said, 'it's stylishly directed and acted. It is also the kind of unpleasant trash that keeps the cinema teetering on the precipice of sudden death. There are a lot of people not anxious to pay out money to wallow in slime... leave a very rancid taste in the mouth.' The People: thought 'you can't say Goodye to it fast enough'. In the provinces, the Kensington Post called it 'glib and tawdry... high camp nonsense that smacks of an Italian B-film director's view of swinging London.' Michael Billington in Illustrated London News said 'we are constantly being titillated with glimpses of a homosexual and a transvestite underground, and the attitude shown towards sex is very much that of filthy postcards on a Cairo street corner... makes sex seem dirty and violence romantic'.

Unsurprisingly given this reception, the film quickly disappeared. In the USA it suffered the ignominy of being re-titled *Twinsanity* for the grindhouse and drive-in market and was released on VHS under that title by Prism in the 1980s complete with a new video-generated title card. The film was given a more deserving presentation in 2010 with a high definition, re-mastered DVD from Scorpion Releasing who should be commended for making the effort of getting the lead actress and producer Peter Snell to sit down together for a moderated commentary track. Unfortunately, neither had seen the movie since its original brief nor seemingly even given it a thought since those days. There's a couple of mis-rememberings that are forgivable given the fact that both they and the moderator are residents of the USA; Geeson mistakes Brian Wilde's taxi driver for Graham Stark before all three acknowledge that they don't have a clue who it was - unthinkable in the UK where the actor has achieved a form of immortality via his sitcom roles as Mr Barrowclough in *Porridge* and Foggy in *Last of the Summer Wine*. Snell writes off Hilda Berry's long television career that had begun in single channel days with a role in the Tod Slaughter TV movie, *Spring Heeled Jack* (1950), and lasted into her 90s, by calling her 'a real market stall lady, it wouldn't have been a cast part.'

Less understandable is both parties remembering the ending as being a suicide pact, Snell saying: 'they move on together so to speak... a suicide pact. For them it was just a matter of moving to the next life together. Which you might expect in a great love story but not necessarily brother and sister.' That both are also under the impression that when Michael Redgrave climbs into bed with Geeson, it is 'in a paternal sense', beggars belief. The moderator, from the Mondo Digital blog, who is clearly a big fan of the genre if not this film in particular, also appears less familiar with the film than might be expected, can only add 'with the subtext in this film, who knows?' Well we do, because we watched the film.

There is nothing in any way subtle on show in the debut feature from the cult Spanish expatriate director Jose Larraz, best known for his later and far superior horror output such as *Vampyres* (1974) and *Symptoms* (1974) which was the official UK entry into Cannes. For years only available from a poor quality time-coded video, this didn't stop Arrow Films following BFI Flipside's lead after their restoration of *Symptoms* by restoring **WHIRLPOOL (1970)** using the film's negative and optical soundtrack found in the UCLA archives for a 2019 DVD and Bluray release.

Listed as a Spanish-Danish co-production but filmed in the UK, *Whirlpool* presents itself as an adult thriller but the real purpose of the film can be gleaned from the casting of Vivian Neves, a former bunny at Raymond's Revue

Bar and Penthouse Pet of the Month as the model, Tulia, who is picked up on a trip into London by creepy middle-aged 'Aunt' Sarah (Pia Andersson) and taken back to the remote country cottage in which she lives with her even creepier photography obsessed 'nephew' Theo (Karl Lanchbury) whose blue-eyed blonde good looks betray the sexual pervert that lies beneath.

Thrown into the mix is the backstory of a previous young model and house guest whose boots are washed up on a river bank at the start of the movie and whose disappearance is now the subject of a police investigation. That and that Theo's idea of a photo op is to have a friend rip Tulia's clothes off in nearby woods and near rape her while he snaps away leaves a sneaking suspicion that foul play may be afoot in a film that makes up for with smut what it lacks in surprises.

Neves would follow the film with numerous appearances as one of the original page 3 girls in the Sun, but her real moment of fame came with her appearance as the first fully nude model to appear in the Times in an advertisement for Fison's Pharmaceuticals. As an actress she would make just two more appearances, as a girlfriend of Tony Curtis in an episode of *The Persuaders* and as a nun in *The Hound of the Baskervilles* (1978), before being struck with MS aged just thirty. Karl Lanchbury would play similar characters in three subsequent Larraz movies before disappearing in the mid-seventies.

In 1972, Hammer entered the blonde psycho market with **STRAIGHT ON TIL MORNING (1972)**, which takes its title from a line in 'Peter Pan', 'second to the right and straight on till morning', referring to its two protagonists refusal to grow up. For the male lead, they turned to Shane Briant who had recently been signed to a two-year contract by producer Michael Carreras, son of Hammer founder James. Briant had recently finished a run playing a damaged youth in *Children of the Wolf* at the Apollo Theatre in the West End, a role for which he had picked up the London Theatre Critics Award for best newcomer - he was 'hot'.

In the director's chair was Peter Collinson, whose life up to the end of the 1960s could be the basis of a film itself. The son of itinerant actors, Collinson was orphaned at 8 and was a self-confessed 'street urchin' by the time he was ten before using the acting experience gained at the Actor's Orphanage in Chertsey, Surrey he trod the boards as a variety act before getting into television as a trainee director with ATV. To make the transition into cinema, Collinson set the ball rolling by using his savings to option Nell Dunn's novel, 'Up The Junction', which enabled him to sell himself as director as part of the package. To prove his worth, Collinson helmed a well received low-budget thriller, *Penthouse* (1967).

More than prepared to take on any genre, as his CV prior to an untimely death in 1980 shows, Collinson followed his cinema version of *Up The Junction* (1967) with *The Long Days' Dying* (1968), a thoughtful anti-war drama starring Tom Bell and David Hemmings, before embarking on the film for which he will always be remembered, caper comedy *The Italian Job* (1969). This was followed by a Tony Curtis and Charles Bronson action comedy set during the Turkish civil war, *You Can't Win 'Em All* (1969) and a reunion with *Up The Junction*'s Dennis Waterman for the Susan George babysitter in peril thriller *Fright* (1970).

Promoted as 'A Love Story from Hammer', on the surface *Straight On Till Morning* is another in a long line of movies in which an innocent young girl heads to London in search of 'swinging London'; a role that Rita Tushingham had already filled in *The Knack... & How To Get It* (1965) and *Smashing Time* (1967). But this is 1972 and those days are long gone, despite the efforts of some to keep the spirit of the 60s going. Like her co-workers at the boutique she gets a job in, boss Jimmy (Tom Bell) and the promiscuous shop assistant Caroline (Katcha Wyeth), whose flat she briefly moves into only to discover her plain looks bar her from acceptance in their world.

Something of an ugly duckling, Brenda (Rita Tushingham) lives with her mother in a Liverpool terrace and spends her spare time writing children's fairy stories whilst dreaming that one day her prince may also come. Now though she is fed up of waiting and at breakfast tells her visibly upset mother: 'Oh mum, nobody's dying… it's gonna be my baby, it's what I want and it's got nothing to do with you.' It seems she has packed in her job as a librarian and is moving to London. When her mother asks 'why?' she is told that 'I'm going to find a father for my baby. Someone who loves both of us.' It's a common enough scenario were it not for the fact that Brenda isn't actually pregnant and, likely, hasn't had sex.

In London she bumps, literally, into Peter (Shane Briant) an androgynous young man who, if a rather sinister flashback is anything to go by, may have done something untoward to a former girlfriend. It is a momentary

Hippies, Skinheads, Rastas, Punks & Disco Dancing Bowie Boot Boys

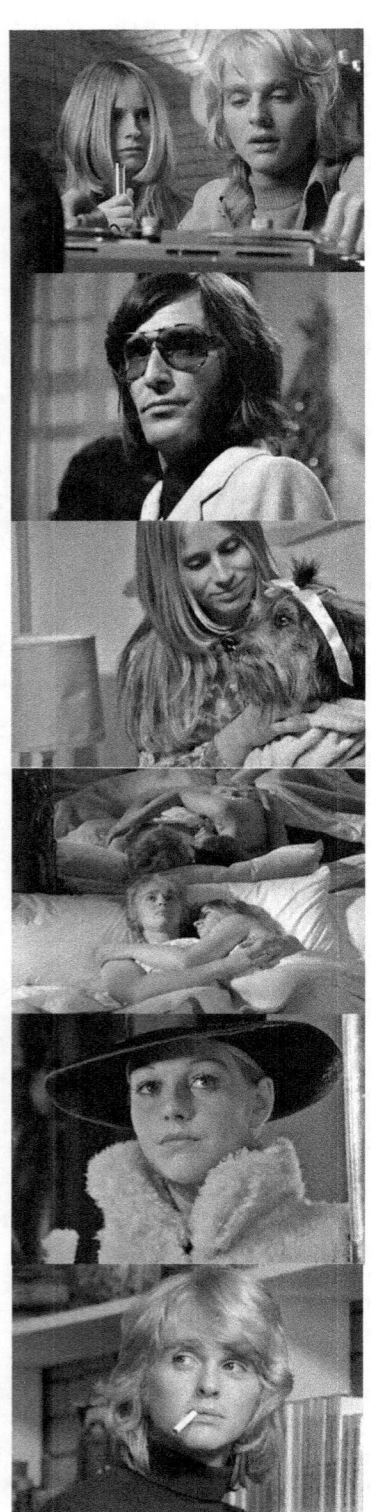

meeting with neither party particularly noticing the other; he heads straight into the shop while she retrieves the items she has dropped all over the floor.

The next time their paths cross is when she's out walking by a pristine-looking Southbank Centre late at night, upset that Caroline has got off with Joey (James Bolam), the only one of the boutique crowd who she felt she might have had a chance with. She is approached by a small dog, Tinker, and notices Peter calling for it but, instead of taking it to him, she instead takes it home where she bathes it and dresses it in a pretty bow before returning to the address on the collar the next morning.

He knows that she had taken the dog and tells her so, stressing that he doesn't mind this, but is curious to know why someone might 'steal someone's dog, wash it, bring it back.' Wondering why she had gone to such lengths to meet him she reluctantly tells him 'I came to ask if you'd give me a baby.' It's an unusual ploy, but then so was her earlier tactic of approaching sundry men in the street, saying 'Hello' and then silently hoping for a reaction.

Peter makes her a proposition. Although he has a nice pad, it's a bit messy because, he says, 'cleaning up's a woman's job; there isn't a woman around so I can't do it.' So, he suggests, 'If you come here and live with me and look after me and mend for me and clean for me, then we shall see.' He also decides she is to be known as Wendy; stacking up the JM Barrie references yet further.

When she returns with her suitcase, Tinker is missing. 'Another Wendy' he tells the dog, 'and she's not pretty at all', before stabbing it to death. Peter does not like pretty things which is why, initially at least, the relationship with Brenda/Wendy goes so well and why a liaison with Carol, who having been contacted by Brenda's concerned mother, finds the broken dog collar and visits the address on the tag to find her friend out shopping but Peter home, doesn't. It's worth pointing out that Peter might not be into cleaning but still manages to leave no trace of his murderous and clearly bloody rampages. His choice of a Stanley knife, a favourite at the time amongst the football fraternity, seems hardly suited to his needs in the murder department.

None of this bodes well for Brenda who, returning with a makeover, is played tape recordings of his crimes. 'She's made you pretty, we don't want you pretty' he tells Tinker before the agonising yelps; to Carol he simply tells her what she has heard a thousand times before.; 'You are beautiful.' Brenda thinks she will be next, but he quickly reassures her that he 'wouldn't hurt you. You don't understand. I wouldn't hurt you.' Her makeover has made her look not beautiful but bizarre - the film's true moment of horror.

The film went out as the top half of a double bill with Hammer's Judy Geeson, Joan Collins and Peter Cushing thriller *Fear In The Night* (1972), but even such added extra value couldn't stop the film's quick slide into obscurity. The Daily Mirror said, 'Whatever merit there is in the story to shock and intrigue is largely wasted by swift cutting from past into present. It is an annoying, distracting, overdone gimmick.' The Sunday People was more complimentary with its summation that 'the film tightens in a gripping climax,' but was a bit premature in its belief that 'Rita Tushingham attempts a comeback'.

Tushingham, for whom the screenplay was especially written, has little fondness for the film but nevertheless starred in another script from its writer John Peacock soon after, *Red Riding Hood* for the BBC's *Armchair Theatre*, where she once again played a repressed librarian.

My Sweet Lord
(Harrison)

Beginning in the mid to late 60s and continuing into the early 70s spirituality had become fashionable amongst the young, championed at first by the Beats and then the Hippies. Initially, and in line with their ongoing rebellion against established tradition, Hippies turned to unconventional beliefs such as Buddhism, Hinduism, and Native American mysticism.

Zen Buddhism, had already been spread throughout the United States by returning soldiers who, many of them damaged by their experiences, had been exposed to the religion while stationed in South-East Asia during that conflict. The works of TD Suzuki, Jack Kerouac, Alan Watts and others in the Beat Movement would give Buddhism a layer of bohemian street cred. Its focus on meditation that centred more on being than thinking, and a lack of the dogma associated with mainstream religion, made it easy to adopt and sit comfortably as a form of spiritual exploration alongside psychedelics such as LSD, Timothy Leary's 'The Psychedelic Experience: A Manual Based on the Tibetan Book of the Dead' having provided a handy connection between the two.

Having already visited India for sitar lessons with Ravi Shankar, Hinduism would soon overtake Buddhism as the go to religion for Hippies when The Beatles visited Maharishi Mahesh Yogi and catapulted the guru's yoga-derived form of transcendental meditation into the mainstream. For most Hippies, the embrace of these eastern philosophies went little further than creating the demand for clothing, jewellery, and other knickknacks that filled the shelves of the emerging 'head shops', but others threw themselves whole heartedly into their new lifestyle.

Rather belatedly, the BBC drama department tackled the attraction of Eastern mysticism in an episode of their long running and by then long-in-the-tooth police drama series, **DIXON OF DOCK GREEN: BAUBLES, BANGLES AND BEADS (1975)**. With the series by then twenty years old and its star, Jack Warner, pushing eighty, *Dixon of Dock Green* was by then never going to be taken seriously and this episode makes no pretence to such.

Being pursued by a panda car, three robbers throw a holdall of jewellery from their car into the backyard of what they believe to be an unoccupied derelict house. It is though the residence of Phil (Peter Denyer, then best known as *Please Sir*'s Dennis Dunstable) and Eric (Leon Vitali), a couple of Hippie squatters.

The robbers (Frank Jarvis, Johnny Shannon, and the inimitable Brian Glover) are arrested but released in the hope that they will lead the police to the loot but when they visit the house, the squatters have moved on, taking the contents of the holdall with them. Followers of the guru Shashti Ap Davies, the boys have moved to a house that is also squatted by three girls, including one, Marion (Kitty Stevenson) a follower of guru Rhum Rhaji, who likes to meditate naked (off screen of course) and tells them 'to deny the body one must first see it in all its gross intransigence'. Smitten, Eric joins Marion at her 'temple' and offers the Guru some of the titular baubles, bangles and beads, a gift he is all too happy to receive.

The Hippie lifestyle is played strictly for laughs and its practitioners as somewhat naïve. At one point Sgt Johnny Wills (Nicholas Donnelly) expresses his belief that many religious cult leaders are little more than con artists, and sure enough Rhum Rhaji and his sidekick are blacked-up East End con men.

Though it's doubtful any real-life would-be spiritual leaders were blacking-up, a section of the Hippie population was susceptible to anyone calling themselves Guru, however self-anointed that title might have been. Many were probably as ridiculously fake as Shashti P Davies but some built up vast followings, and wealth, that would endure for decades. Such as Sogyal Rinpoche whose 'The Tibetan Book Of Living And Dying' sold in excess of three million copies and made him the most famous Buddhist teacher after the Dalai Lama, feted by the likes of John Cleese and Radiohead's Thom Yorke and even co-starring alongside Keanu Reeves in the film *Little Buddha* (1993).

For Rinpoche and his Buddhist organisation Rigpa it was more a case of little acorns. Though it would go on to have centres and groups in 41 countries around the world, Rigpa began with just one run from a hippy squat in Kilburn known as Dzogchen Orgyen Chö Ling. Journalist Mary Finnigan, who helped set up Rinpoche's first British Buddhist centre, has since described him as 'part-tyrant and part-spoiled child'.

Like Shashti P Davies, in 2017 Rinpoche was eventually exposed after using his position to 'gain access to young women' and to 'coerce, intimidate and manipulate' them into giving him 'sexual favours'. With even the Dalai Lama calling him 'disgraced' he had no choice but to quit his position as his organisation's spiritual leader

Christopher Mitchell & Pamela Franklin are bigger than The Beatles in *The Strange Report*

Religious cults were also the topic of an episode of ITC's *The Strange Report*, a short-lived series in which retired criminologist Adam Strange (Anthony Quayle) is called upon by the authorities as a consultant on a variety of their less straightforward cases. Those that are deemed in some way 'strange'. In this he is assisted by an American, Kaz Govas as Ham Gynt, and a dolly bird, model/artist Evelyn Maclean (Anneke Wills).

In **THE STRANGE REPORT: REPORT 5055 - CULT - MURDER SHRIEKS OUT (1969)**, Strange is called upon by pop star Maggie Jones (Pamela Franklin) to look into the death of Jay (Christopher Mitchell), the other half of a pop duo that look like the Carpenters but sound like the Seekers. Despite being as saccharine as both put together, they somehow possess the pulling power of The Beatles and come complete with their very own Norwegian guru, Lars (Ray McAnally) who fronts a secretive organisation called the Cypress Front. Jay had been electrocuted when performing but had earlier hinted to Maggie that he had uncovered something untoward about their spiritual leader.

The writer probably took his cue from the well-publicised electrocution of Keith Richards whilst on stage in California in December 1965. The Stones guitarist was sent flying backwards through the air and was removed from the stage only semi-conscious and aided by oxygen. Richards of course survived but Stone the Crows guitarist Les Harvey, brother of Alex, wasn't so lucky following a similar incident at Swansea's Top Rank in 1972.

The Cypress Front use their recruits to carry out their worldwide 'charitable' work, but it doesn't take a genius to deduce there might be something untoward going on, given that they operate out of a high security compound that, like the organisation itself, would not seem out place in a Bond movie. It's confirmed after half an hour when, after Maggie goes missing, Ham goes undercover as a convert, has a gun pulled on him, and finds himself locked in a basement with her.

Strange discovers their humanitarian work isn't quite as it should be: 'Consider the scale of this organisation, worldwide distribution of goods for the needy and you begin to wonder how much goods the needy are really getting... one tin of cooking oil for the needy, two tins of cooking oil for the boys to cook with.' It is two of the Cypress Fronts most senior disciples, not the organisation itself, that have been on the fiddle and before you can say 'there's a bomb in the helicopter' the episode reaches an explosive conclusion.

Donald Zec in the Daily Mirror said the programme 'showed scant promise' and 'was little more than a glossy attempt to combine all those spy series and American detective series into something which contained the virtues of neither.' Anthony Quayle, he said, 'really ought to know better.' He did like the song 'which sounded as if it ought to make the Top Twenty.'

*

The religious right was also re-inventing itself with what became known as the Jesus movement spreading from California through North America and across the Atlantic into Europe. These Jesus Freaks, as they were disparagingly labelled, had become disillusioned with life in Haight Ashbury after witnessing the negative effects of drug use and promiscuous sex.

By 1968 a shelter, The Soul Inn, had opened in the basement of a Methodist church in nearby Richmond, soon followed by a string of communes throughout the Bay Area. By the following year, similar set-ups were happening throughout other states. The new street ministers kept their long hair and Hippie garb and their 'ministries' attracted all manner of jaded Hippies and runaway youths.

The following year saw the publication of an underground free paper in California, the Hollywood Free Paper, which at first glance could have been any of the many similar papers of that time. Inside however, alongside graphics that would not have seemed out-of-place in International Times, the message was different: 'Well, we're not rapping about positive thinking and playing religious games. Nope. We're rapping about a person - Jesus Christ. And if you can Dig him - that means to depend on him to put your head together - then you're in for some heavy surprises!! He'll turn you on to a spiritual high for the rest of forever.'

Behind headlines like 'Pollution Conspiracy' and 'Free The Prisoners' were calls to combat pollution of the mind and for liberation from bondage and sin. By 1971 the Jesus movement had captured the cover of Time magazine, as news items in which hundreds of American teenagers were plunged beneath the ocean waves in mass baptisms became commonplace.

There were also high profile converts, such as singer Barry McGuire: 'I was the right age at the right time in the wrong place, you might say. And hey, I wanted to be free. Boy, I sang 'Eve of Destruction' lookin' to be free. I went to Broadway. I did a show on Broadway called *Hair*. I played the male lead in the original Broadway cast, lookin' to be free. And the very lifestyle that we were promoting was killing us all. I looked around me and I saw my friends, one, two, three at a time goin' down: drug overdose, suicide, sexually transmitted diseases.'

In 1971 McGuire became a born-again Christian, continuing to release music through various Christian labels but never again seeing anywhere near the sort of commercial success that had knocked The Beatles 'Help' from the number one spot on the Billboard chart. Not that there wasn't a place for Christianity in mainstream rock music, but it was taking on a more theatrical guise.

Jesus Christ Superstar was originally an album by future British musical theatre royalty Andrew Lloyd Webber and Tim Rice, a rock concept album where the concept was the story of the week leading up to the crucifixion as depicted in chapters 37-47 of the book of Genesis. Though it began its life on vinyl, it had been conceived as a stage production and was intended to double up as a demonstration disc for theatrical producers.

Decca released 'Superstar' as a single during November 1969, but it failed to make much impact in the UK, peaking at #47. It did however begin to cause a stir in the USA where it reached #14 on the Billboard chart. Released at the tail end of 1970, the album's credibility took a huge turn for the better when Jesus, Ian Gillan, joined Deep Purple in July 1969 to give the then psychedelic band a more fashionable hard rock sound. In the UK it stalled at #23, but in the USA it erupted, topping the album chart in both February and May 1971, and being ranked number one for the year ahead of Carole King's 'Tapestry'. In August 1972, on the heels of a Broadway production at the end of 1971, a London production opened at the Palace Theatre, directed by Jim Sharman and starring Paul Nicholas as Jesus and Dana Gillespie as Mary.

Jesus Christ Superstar was not the composing duos first foray into Christian rock opera. That was *Joseph & The Technicolour Dreamcoat*, based on the Book of Genesis, and performed in a 15-minute version at Colet Court School in London in March 1968, with a revised and expanded 20-minute version performed at Westminster Central Hall. By its third performance, at St Paul's Cathedral in November, it had expanded to 35 minutes and was recorded by Decca and released on vinyl in 1969.

By this time another Christian rock musical, the American *Godspell*, had enjoyed a successful run off-Broadway and a London production had opened at Hippie mecca the Chalk Farm Roundhouse during November 1971 with a cast that included Julie Covington, David Essex, and Jeremy Irons. Set in contemporary times the show features eight non-Biblical characters, who sing and act out parables from Matthew dressed in the hippy garb of the time.

The 35 minutes *Joseph*... was performed at the Edinburgh Festival and other venues by the Young Vic Theatre Company during 1972 as well as being broadcast that same year by Granada Television. The following year theatre producer Michael White and impresario Robert Stigwood staged a further expanded version at the Albery Theatre in the West End, where it ran for 243 performances. This version included a new section with a book by *Hancock's Half Hour* and *Steptoe & Son* writers Galton & Simpson

Is it a bird? Is is a plane? No, it's David Essex in *Godspell*

The Starshiners take a break from plastering duties in *Shoestring*

but this wordy version was then replaced by the sung-through score that was first performed in 1974 at the Haymarket Theatre in Leicester.

*

In the UK during 1969 the lay pastor of the village of Bugbrooke's Baptist chapel near Northampton founded the Jesus Fellowship Church which through its appeal to a younger generation of worshippers attracted former Hippies, bikers and drug addicts. The Church became better known as the Jesus Army and at its peak in the 2000s could boast 3,500 members in around 24 congregations in various pockets of the UK. There were also UK arms of American organisations like Colorado based The Navigators who were headquartered in Leeds and had gained one very high profile convert in actor James Fox.

SHOESTRING: I'M A BELIEVER (1979) doesn't play its Christian cult for laughs in the way *Dixon of Dock Green* did eastern mysticism but it nevertheless managed to concoct a story almost as ridiculous.

Eddie Shoestring (Trevor Eve) was a down-at-heel private detective working as the self-styled 'private ear' for Bristol radio station Radio West, carrying out investigations on behalf of the stations listeners via a phone-in, whilst seemingly carrying the weight of the world on his shoulders. In *I'm A Believer*, the final episode of the very successful first series, the client was the concerned mother of a 20-year-old girl, Maddy Hopkins (Clare Walker) who has joined a fundamental Christian cult, the Starshiners, whose converts regularly fund raise by selling LP records in the city centre. Maddy is due to inherit £15,000 on her 21st birthday, a sum she will donate to the church.

Eddie confronts Maddy on the street but finds her less than forthcoming about the group's activities and so he purchases a copy of the record and runs it by one of the station's DJs who is able to ascertain it was recorded and pressed by a small studio run from a barge by an American, Jim Huckle. He also visits Maddy and her fellow Starshiners in a house they are living in whilst carrying out renovations and discovers that the 'charitable organisation' is in the process of buying another property.

Shoestring tracks the cult's hierarchy down to a country retreat where he discovers the cults guru, Stephen Steele (Preston Lockwood), supposedly doing charitable work at the South Pole, living a life of luxury from his property portfolio, his followers savings and dole money, and profits from the records they sell. Turning up with a group of the Starshiners and evidence of this skulduggery, Eddie holds an auction, selling off the house's many expensive artefacts for a fiver or so.

For the episode of **MAN ALIVE: THE JESUS TRIP (1971)**, broadcast in July, the current affairs series sent reporter Denis Tuohy and his team to the west coast of the USA to look at the growing phenomenon: 'Fantasy has flourished in these parts from the birth of the movies to the heyday of LSD. Today, a much older message is being newly delivered on Hollywood Boulevard. The messenger is Arthur Blessitt; like his name, the message is straightforward. They call him a Jesus Freak; armed with belief in instantaneous salvation he conducts his mission where he feels it's most needed among the rootless Hippie generation who've tried every other trip and found it wanting...' He was, Tuohy said: 'a pioneer of a radical crusade for the soul of America, a rapid crusade that is rapidly gaining ground.' The message from the permanently smiling Blessitt was that 'if you hit up on Jesus, you'll never have to hit up again.'

It was a programme that Chris Dunkley in his write up for the Times, found 'terrifying' and highlighted what he saw as the similarities between the drug pusher and the pusher of religion: 'Clearly the two cults have similar effects; both induce euphoric fantasies, both alienate their participants from the bulk of society, and both depend on a ringleader who pushes the raw material (someone like Arthur Blessitt in the case of the Jesus People, and the dope pedlar for drug users)'.

In September 1971, the Times declared 'Jesus People Arrive in Britain', reporting on the arrival on these shores of Blessitt 'who wants to bring his gospel to the streets of Britain with a rough wood cross, a guitar and a tambourine, a lot of singing and millions of stickers saying 'Smile. Jesus loves you'. Blessitt himself says: 'We will get some wood from a junkyard and make a rough wood cross weighing 100lb or so and set off from Piccadilly and go to Edinburgh and then across the sea to Belfast and back to London.'

Blissett was a pussycat compared to the organisation who occupied the second part of the *Man Alive* programme, The Children of God, described as evangelists 'for whom the Jesus trip is more like a crusade in the original sense, whose enthusiasm is unleashed with all the force of a military assault... Every week the self-styled Children of God send out their prophet buses from their headquarters in downtown Los Angeles. The nearby Pacific beaches are the hunting grounds they're heading for with a clear idea of their most likely targets... spiritual weaklings.'

Like Blessitt, the Children of God also paid a visit to UK shores but unlike the travelling preacher, they were intending to stay. In November 1972 the Times reported that John Hunt, the MP for Bromley in Kent, had called for a government enquiry into the organisation who had set up a base in his borough. Said to be operating in 42 countries, with 'half a dozen' colonies in Britain, the Children of God had '2300 full-time workers, and is gaining recruits at the rate of 1800 a week.'

If that level of expansion seems a lot, consider the organisation's recruitment method known as 'filthy fishing'. They attributed the practice to Jesus telling fishermen that he will make them 'fishers of men'. The church's leader, David Berg, extrapolated from that that the women members should be the bait, and men the fish. Reminding these 'Gods whores' or 'hookers for Jesus' that their bodies did not really belong to them, he instructed them to use their sex appeal as a recruitment tool. If that meant that sex took place, this was re-branded as 'loving sexually' and they praised the woman for having gone that extra mile for God. The practice continued unabated until 1987 and the AIDS epidemic.

The Times returned to the subject later that month: 'Jesus people, the Children of God, Festival of Light, and the Jesus Liberation Front (of Hemel Hempstead); these and similar groups generically termed as the Jesus Movement are often taken as symptoms of a new interest in religion with the so-called youth culture.' What the reporter wanted to know was 'is it here to stay or has it already begun to go the way of all fads and crazes?'

The paper spoke to Michael Jacobs, described as a friend of Cliff Richard and the author of a pop music column in a religious newspaper, who told them: 'Now it is fashionable to be a Jesus person and church leaders are talking of a worldwide revival, but one can say, without being accused of cynicism, that the Jesus movement is just another craze which will go the way of all flesh (and all trends)... Unfortunately some organisations, and individuals, have felt it necessary to use music, or a freaky appearance, or both, as a means of winning attention or insinuating themselves into positions where they can preach.'

In fact, American style evangelism had been present in the UK since Billy Graham's original London Crusade in 1954, which proved successful enough for the preacher to return the following year. In 1961, Graham held further rallies in Manchester, Glasgow and Birmingham. Amongst his fans was the Queen, who first met Graham in 1955 and invited him to preach at Windsor Chapel the following year - later bestowing upon him an honorary knighthood.

But it was his Earls Court rally in June 1966 that most caught the public's attention - helped in no small part by the fact that another of Graham's fans, pop singer Cliff Richard, took time out from filming *Finders Keepers* (1966) at Pinewood Studios to appear as a speaker. Richard had, so to speak, come out as a Christian to a reporter in that morning's Daily Mirror, ensuring not only a sold-out venue but about 5000, largely Cliff fans, outside unable to get tickets. He had, in the words of the paper, 'joined the Billy Graham Set' which meant not only was he a Christian, but he also believed that it was his duty: 'and the duty of all Christians, to tell as many people as possible about this wonderful thing I have discovered... I want to help the cause of Christianity.' In pursuing this goal, the preacher and his recent convert could also help each other.

As part of its outreach work Graham's organisation, the Billy Graham Evangelist Association (BGEA), had also gone into the film business when the preacher bought up the production company who had filmed his 1950 rally in Portland, Oregan. The revamped company's first film was *Mr Texas* (1951), produced during Graham's 1951 Fort Worth, Texas rally and described by Graham as 'the first Christian western'.

Having previously shown their films in churches, the BGEA took a huge step with the release of *The Restless Ones* (1965) when they began to rent theatres. Screenings were arranged through a committee in the community, whereby in the same way they approached their regular crusades, using what they call 'operation Andrew', Christians buy tickets and bring their friends and pray for their friends. The film was attended by some 4,500,000 during its first

Probably making a dirty phone call, Cliff goes bad in Two A Penny

four years on release, and when an invitation was given to those 'friends' at the end of the screenings to come forward and commit their lives to Christ, it was claimed to have brought forward over 400,000.

Their next picture was to go before the cameras in Britain and would star Cliff Richard. The film, **TWO A PENNY (1967)**, was the organisation's biggest project yet. Producer Jim Collier also had a unique method for casting his movie: 'During production I remember completely committing every moment of the working day to the Lord. And if it sounds presumptuous to say that the casting was "out of my hands," especially Cliff Richard, Dora Bryan and Ann Holloway, those are the facts. I watched the Lord bring these people together and knew that His spirit was at work in their lives.'

With three clear reasons to take the role, for Richard it must have seemed like a win-win scenario. Not only did he get to spread the word, but he also got to stretch his acting range with the role of Jamie Hopkins who is introduced pestering his girlfriend Carol (Ann Holloway) to lend him a couple of quid. Jamie sees himself as something of a jack the lad but that there is nothing particularly loveable about this young rogue. Unless you happen to be his mother Ruby (Dora Bryan) or girlfriend Carol, who hands over the money despite having nothing to spare.

Richard doesn't get off to a promising start with his portrayal of this working class bad lad by making this the first film outing in which he had traded the last remnants of an Elvis quiff for the neat flattened-down fringe he has kept to this day. The choice of a light brown flared corduroy suit makes him look like a Christian. Cast because of their faith rather than any authenticity the pairing might have brought to the role, the mother and son relationship is a hard-sell. Bryan can play this sort of role in her sleep, but Richard struggles to shed his semi-detached upbringing in Carshalton or his innate Cliffness.

Jamie takes the money and heads up west to visit a mens outfitters run by Mr Fitch (Geoffrey Bayldon) in pursuit of a job doing 'deliveries'. He is not, however, offering to deliver the many hats on display in the shop, but is referring instead to the shopkeeper's other, more profitable, sideline in the drugs trade. Jamie is also not content with being a delivery boy and has always intended being his own boss and, seemingly unfamiliar with the concept of consequences, when he approaches bookie Mr Jenkins as ordered it is with the proposal that ripping off Fitch would be to both their benefits.

Instead, it is Jamie who gets double-crossed, finding himself on the receiving end of a vicious beating that's serious enough to make him swear. It may just be 'where's my bleedin' shoe?' but coming from Richard's mouth it's something of a shock. Unfortunately, it doesn't alter Jamie's outlook on life, telling Carol, who witnessed the attack: 'It doesn't matter what you want, there's not enough of it to go around. And if you want it, you've got to get it yourself. And if you've got it you don't want a lot of people pushing in, now do ya?'

Running alongside all this is a subplot in which Carol has been given a couple of tickets for a Billy Graham rally. She wants to go, but he is dismissive, calling the preacher 'a sharp salesman' and religion itself 'all empty promises to line someone else's pockets.' This offers the production the chance to include an eight-minute sequence shot at the actual rally, including five of Graham's sermon, overlain occasionally with Jamie's juvenile and dismissive 'thoughts'. It does, however, include the unforgettable response from Jamie when he sees Carol amongst those going forward to pledge themselves to Christ: 'Oh no, not her an' all. Looks like she's swallowed the whole blooming lot. Ooh, I'll belt 'er one.' He doesn't though and for the remainder of the film interactions between the two leads are limited to her trying to convert him whilst he tries unsuccessfully to seduce her.

Jamie does succeed in getting another chance from Fitch because his mother is the receptionist for a psychiatrist who is experimenting with psychedelic drugs as part of his therapy - 'mind benders!' he excitedly declares. Jamie inveigles his way in to the offices on the pretext of some casual work to 'help his mum out'.

After carefully and meticulously removing the beading from the drugs cabinet so it can be accessed unnoticed, he steals the key from his mother and passes on the key to Fitch, but, still presumably struggling with the concept of consequence, not before stealing the drugs and tipping off the police.

Jamie settles down for the night on a site overlooking the office to see the results of his cunning plan, but as the hours pass he falls asleep to wake once it is daylight to the realisation that something is afoot, and that Fitch has failed to show. With Jamie now in desperate need for the key back in order to return the drugs before they are missed, and the finger gets pointed at him', Fitch dismisses him out of hand: 'There are animals like you on every street corner, hungry little nobodies. The supply always exceeds the demand'.

And so it's up to mum to sort out the mess he has created whilst Jamie takes a stroll in the park with the still loyal Carol still hoping he'll give his life to the Lord, while he would still prefer a career on the telly: 'I've managed to get on without him so far. Even if I wanted to. I don't know how... Suppose we don't get on?' The only hope is offered by a closing song.

> Okay, supposing I were to come to You?
> Not saying I will, just supposing I do?
> Would I have to be, just another guy?
> Two a penny's not for me, it just won't satisfy.
> I'm just confused, by candles and prayers.
> I just need to know, if You are there.

The film did not duplicate the success of *The Restless Ones*. In the UK it premièred at the King Charles in Soho where it ran for a few weeks but did not get a national roll-out, its Christian message scaring away anyone who wasn't devoutly devoted to either God or to Cliff - though those two groups were still significant. 'Two A Penny is dear at the price' said the Daily Mirror's Dick Richards who thought Cliff using his religious convictions 'in an ordinary commercial film seems a dubious idea.'

In the USA, aside from Graham himself, the film lacked a recognisable name above the marquee, and those attracted to its religious content were disappointed in the unresolved nature of the ending. For later showings, Richard added an epilogue telling the audience the story was based on his experiences and adding his testimony.

The film has an unusual source in a 'kitchen sink' novel by Stella Linden, a former lover and muse of *Look Back In Anger* playwright John Osborne, when she was at the time married to gay actor Patrick Desmond. Linden herself adapted the novel for the screen and did not tone down her despicable lead character. The only decent thing Jamie does in the film is turning down Carol's landlady (Avril Angers), a former showgirl who could still turn a head once she scrubs up and loses the scarf, rollers and fag, when she gets all Mrs Robinson on him and offers herself on a plate. Even here though you feel that it might be because any possible sexual gratification is secondary to the pleasure he gets from dismissing her. The trouble is, deep down we all know it's Cliff.

Oh yes, the third reason for Cliff to take the role is that he got to write the three originals numbers used on the soundtrack, 'Two A Penny', 'Love You Forever Today' and 'Questions'. All of which confirm why that on 'Living Doll', 'Move It', 'In The Country', 'The Young Ones' or even 'Devil Woman' and 'We Don't Talk Anymore', the songwriting duties were left to other people.

Religion is at the heart of director John Mackenzie's Hippie kitchen sink drama **MADE (1972)**. The story by Howard Barker began life on the stage of the Royal Court in the guise of his 1970 play *No One Was Saved*, a riposte to Edward Bond's notorious 1965 play *Saved*. Barker's play told the story of young working class single mother Eleanor Rigby (Maureen Lipman) and her relationships with the priest Father Mackenzie (Peter Sproule) and an unnamed John Lennon (Mike D'Abo). It was, as I'm sure is clear by now, influenced by The Beatles 'Eleanor Rigby'.

Commissioned by *Poor Cow* producer Joseph Janni to turn his play into a screenplay, Barker kept the structure of

the story but removed The Beatles references. Eleanor becomes Valerie (Carol White), Father Mackenzie becomes Father Dyson (John Castle) and the Lennon based rocker takes the unexpected form of folk rock Troubador Roy Harper as Mike.

The casting of Harper might have been unexpected but was both deliberate and integral to the development of Mike's character into an anti-religious folk singer. Today best known for the 'Led Zeppelin III' tribute 'Hats off To (Roy) Harper' or his vocal contribution to 'Have A Cigar' on 'Wish You Were Here', when *Made* went in front of the cameras Harper was signed to Colombia and shared a manager with Pink Floyd, Mike Jenner who appears in the film as Mike's musical director. According to Harper 'there was an incredible list of guys auditioned', including Marc Bolan and Americans Tony Joe White and Kris Kristofferson. The producers were looking for, he says, 'something more than just a pop singer.'

That something was the singer's hatred of religion, a consequence of being raised as a Jehovah's Witness despite, he says, being able to see the irrationality of this upbringing by the time he was six. Calling it his 'first and only enemy' he has he says 'taken a stand against religion for as long as I've been able to write and think' - doing this through songs like the 12 and a half minute 'The Same Old Rock' from his four-part-song-cycle 'Stormcock' on which he is accompanied by friend and frequent collaborator Jimmy Page. Or on the 1990 album 'Once' where he showed he was an equal opportunities anti-religion folkster on the controversial 'The Black Cloud of Islam', written by an unapologetic Harper in the wake of the 1988 Lockerbie bombing, saying he 'was absolutely sick of being politically correct.'

In *Made* he gets to express his feelings on the topic during an interview with Bob Harris, where Mike says of God: 'I think we've all been believing in that sort of rubbish for too long and that we've really got to try believe in ourselves for a change. Seeing things as they really are instead of trying to whitewash the whole thing.'

'It pre-supposes that we're all guilty and very dirty with it. Guilt. A newborn child is a relatively clean thing that gets dirtied very quickly by religion.' In its place he recommends love, which he calls 'a great triumph over Christianity.' He seems to be especially fond of the free variety, telling Harris 'I suppose I've had about ten wives and if they've had ten males, that's a hundred of us joined. It just carries on eternally. I think it's the way it's got to be.'

His call to live life 'as it comes. Naturally. Just live and love' is called out by Father Dyson who suggests 'What you really mean is come and go and never mind the consequences'. Mike gets the final word: 'Where would the church be without unhappiness and poverty. You need unhappiness and poverty to survive. You've been running society like that for the last 2000 years. And whose is the biggest congregation now?'

Poor Valerie, as befitting of the kitchen sink genre and of the tragic star of *Cathy Come Home* (1966), *Poor Cow* (1967) and *I'll Never Forget What's 'isname* (1967) herself, suffers the hypocrisy of both men (and others) but, as anyone familiar with Edward Bond's *Saved* will know, these pale besides one particular plot point taken from that work.

Hippies, Skinheads, Rastas, Punks & Disco Dancing Bowie Boot Boys

Sympathy For The Devil
(Richards, Jagger)

According to Dennis Wheatley's biographer, Phil Baker: 'To a great extent Wheatley invented the public image of black magic and Satanism and the weird thing is although it was meant to be terribly evil he made it seem strangely seductive and luxurious. It's all about pentagrams and magic circles on the floor of country house libraries.' That was in the 1930s, but it was over 25 years later that the authors work entered a wider public consciousness. What separated Dennis Wheatley from the likes of Sandra Stellman whose 1960s and 70s novels for New English Library promised to expose 'the evil of Satanism in Britain today' was that he had thoroughly researched his subject, dining with none other than Aleister Crowley and befriending Montague Summers who had translated the 15th century witch hunters manual, 'Malleus Maleficarum'. In contrast, Shulman, whose exploitative quickies were littered with orgies, used a 'shopping list of perversions' despite admitting on *Bookmark*'s *Skinhead Farewell* episode to not knowing what 'shafting' and 'going down' actually meant.

Wheatley was also a believer, the subject scaring him enough to include a warning in his introduction to 'The Devil Rides Out': 'Should any of my readers incline to a serious study of the subject, and thus come into contact with a man or woman of Power, I feel that it is only right to urge them, most strongly, to refrain from being drawn into the practice of the Secret Arts in any way... my own observations have led me to an absolute conviction that to do so would bring them into danger of a very real and concrete nature.'

The sort of witches who would have felt at home settling down in front of the fire with a copy of the latest Dennis Wheatley were on display in **THE POWER OF THE WITCH: REAL OR IMAGINARY (1971)**, a BBC documentary directed and hosted by Michael Bakewell.. First up is Doreen Valiente, who began practising magic as a child and was now High Priest of her own coven and a founder of the Pagan Front (she would later change her allegiance to the National Front), a British pressure group that campaigned for the religious rights of Wiccans and other Pagans. Valiente says, 'The amount of silly dabbling in the occult that goes on today scares me. These people think that they're doing something terribly clever and terribly with it and it's all great fun but what they don't understand is they're invoking forces which they can't fathom and they're making themselves a channel by which those forces can come through into the world.'

The reason for her concern is that: 'On one estimate there are 30,000 people practising in witchcraft in this country alone, a more conservative figure would be 8000 but even so it's enough to make you think. Are there really dangers involved or is it all just a delusion? And if it is just a delusion why do so many really quite intelligent people half believe in it? What just has been going on in this country since the last witchcraft law was repealed in 1951?'

'They don't wear pointed hats and ride broomsticks', the narrator adds helpfully, 'They look very much like the rest of us.' In fact, Valiente, to whom the programme returns, looks very much like Mary Whitehouse. We see her at midnight, deep in the woods and by the light of a full moon where she performs a ritual, 'never before tried out in front of cameras', hoping 'some psychic manifestations might appear on film'. 'Diane of the rounded moon' she chants, 'the Queen of all enchantments here, the wind is crying through the trees, and we invoke thee to appear.' Naturally, no such thing happens, but Cliente assures us that 'Well, it was really difficult to get the spirit of the old ritual, knowing you were surrounded by cameras and technicians and things like that. But when the ritual was almost at an end, I began to feel the atmosphere building up and I think other people did too.'

We next meet another middle-aged witch, this time nude, who informs us that 'without clothes we're all equal', whilst dancing around a fire with a half dozen others, also naked of course, in order to alleviate Mrs Eleanor Bone's friends slipped disc. Mrs Bone tells her coven, 'When you concentrate at the end I want you to picture her cycling around the country lanes on her bicycle, full of energy, full of life, and really fit and well again.' This is beginners' stuff compared to Alex Sanders who informs us he uses his witchcraft to cure cancer, alongside a very famous, but nameless, professor from Munich. 'The result of this cancer experiment,' we're told, 'is yet to be published.'

The programme touches base with the Church of Satan in San Francisco and The Charles Manson murders in Los Angeles before concentrating on young people in the UK being introduced to Satanism at parties. The programme speaks to a Church Army youth councillor in Birmingham who says 'I'm told by a large number... of young people who come to see me that very often the first time they have been taken to a party where witchcraft has been involved they have been initiated, which largely means that they are laid on the alter and the sacred signs are made on their body with animals blood. They do, of course, drink animals blood too as part of the ceremony. But the thing I find most horrifying, are the vows that they're expected to take and these are the things which hold people to the group long afterwards. One of the vows is that you promise to forward the work of our lord Satan... you vow to be loyal to the leader of the coven. Another thing is that you must break the faith of a Christian and this is interesting because a large number of the young people have once been members of the Christian church... the last one, which is even more frightening and horrifying, is that you'll get a man of influence or responsibility in a compromising situation, and this largely means sexual activity where through the taping and photography of what goes on... there is a hold on that person for blackmail and in some sinister way it is possible for certain people to have a hold on some of the decision making of this country through such things as blackmail and witchcraft.'

In the UK Alex Sanders was the undisputed King of the Witches, a largely self-awarded title strengthened by his appearance in two further 'documentary' films, **LEGEND OF THE WITCHES (1970)** and **SECRET RITES (1971)**. Both films are directed by film makers whose best-known works are in the field of sexploitation. Malcolm Leigh followed *Legend of the Witches* with *Games That Lovers Play* (1971), whilst Ford, in partnership with producer Stanley Long, had already made the hugely successful *The Wife Swappers* (1970) and *Groupie Girl* (1970). Leigh's 85-minute effort is by far the more high minded, opening with the story of Dianna, the moon, searching for her soul mate Lucifer, the sun. The film takes in Catholicism and its integration with Paganism, the Pagan symbolism in the Bayeux Tapestry and a trip to a small museum in Cornwall. Of course none of this would hold most viewers' interest (not helped in this by Guy Standeven's monotone voice-over) if it weren't for the recurring footage of naked witches dancing round a camp fire.

The highlight is undoubtedly the Black Mass enacted by Alex Sanders and his wife Maxine, in which a beautiful and very naked woman is laid out on an alter. There's also a nicely shot sequence in which a male initiate is led blindfold across a moon lit pastoral landscape of rocks and gentle streams and caves, that offers little in the way of authenticity but an ample amount of nudity. Derek Long more or less dispenses with any pretence to anything other than titillation and places the Sanders front and centre of his 47 minute film.

The film opens with the staging of what it calls a typical orgy in a witches' coven, all naked breasts, dancing and groping in the ornate grand hall of some equally grand castle. As a sacrificial virgin is laid naked across the alter for a blood sacrifice, a priest bursts in and sends the witches reeling with a splash of holy water.

But hang on, such depictions of his magic art, says Alex Sanders are complete nonsense, bemoaning the fact that when he meets people on the street they become terrified, fearing he will place a curse on them. By way of assurance that such fears are ill-founded, he offers his credentials in the form of a bundle of his fan mail. One such fan is introduced as Penny, a hairdresser who recounts the story of how she met Sanders and his coven - an experience she describes as like having to take 'your exams all over again'. Penny Beeching who is clearly an 'actress' and had appeared as set dressing in all six episodes of the Frankie Howerd 'adult' sitcom *Up Pompeii!* (1970) as a Roman maiden, meets Sanders and fellow witch Wendy in a Notting Hill pub where he again gets all earnest about his craft before initiating her in a scene not unlike that in *Legend of the Witches* but with added nudity, in colour and shot from a far more leering viewpoint.

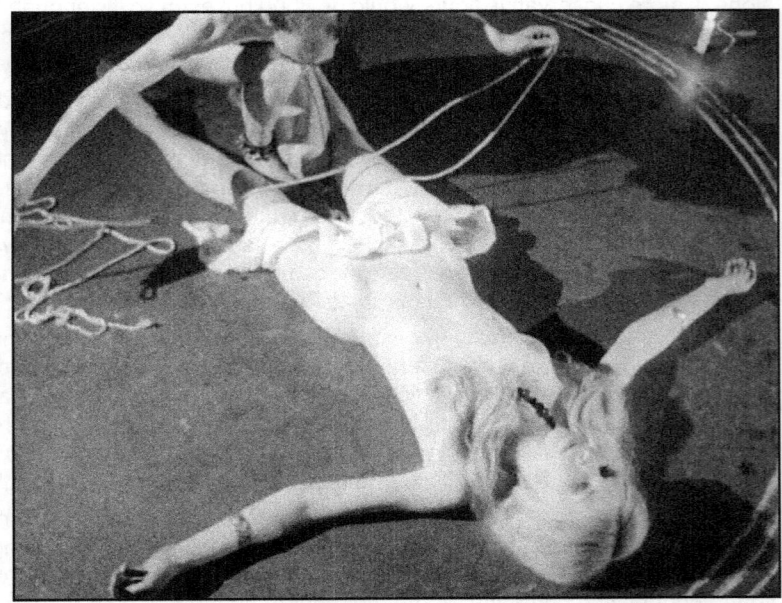

Alex Sanders practices his first aid skills in *Secret Rites*

By 1971 when his non-fiction 'The Devil & All His Works' was published, it was clear that Dennis Wheatley's early warning had not been heeded as the flower power of the love generation had given way to something dark and sinister. Wheatley wrote that 'human behaviour has entered a new phase. It is termed the permissive society; the restraining powers of the church, parental authority and public concern have been overthrown by the younger generation. It is this that has brought about the huge upsurge in the practice of magic. These young people who have become initiates are liable to become pawns of the powers of darkness.' There were however other reasons for the occult explosion of the late sixties and seventies, one of which was surely the Satanic novels of Wheatley himself, described by Professor Ronald Hutton, an English historian with an interest in contemporary Paganism, as being 'for my generation of Essex teenagers... the essential primer in diabolism.'

Such was the occult's appeal to the Hippie generation that in 1970 it provided the inspiration for hit singles by Jethro Tull with 'The Witches Promise' and 'The Witch' by The Rattles, a Hamburg band who had played with on bills with The Beatles, a number 10 at its second time of asking. By the end of the decade Alex and Maxine Sanders had an album of their own released on A&M, at the time the home of The Police, Janet Jackson and Bryan Adams. In effect 'A Witch is Born' is as the sleeve notes by Stewart Farrar tell us 'a recording of the solemn initiation of a new member into the ancient craft.' On this occasion, according to the images with which it was advertised in Rolling Stone, the initiate was Janet Owen who would soon become Janet Farrar. She was obviously a wonderful student because within a couple of years she was the co-author, alongside her new husband, of the book 'Eight Sabbats For Witches' which probably sold a lot more than the album which was largely remaindered.

Wheatley had long since gone out of fashion when, in 1968, Hammer adapted his 1934 novel *The Devil Rides Out* for the big screen, the same year that Roman Polanski's adaptation of Ira Levin's *Rosemary's Baby* (1968) also hit the cinemas. Both films were huge hits and for the rest of that decade and on through the 1970s, Wheatley's occult novels were on display everywhere in a uniform range of black covers depicting a naked woman dancing behind flames, presumably of Hell, each title adorned with its own black magic accoutrements, from candles to goat heads to crystal balls.

In fact, by 1968 the occult had already become hip and begun attracting, let's call them, eccentrics such as the three men who appeared in court accused of nailing a fourth man to a cross on Hampstead Heath that July. A statement read out in court from a witness said the man, Joseph Richard de Havilland, had burned his hands without injury to show his power in black magic and stuck pins and matches behind his finger nails and felt no pain.

Or the 30-year-old man who appeared in court at the beginning of 1970 after having been stopped by police whilst towing a stolen trailer. His defence was that he had been taken to a party in Esher by a girlfriend which was attended by members of a coven who had told him of their fertility rite involving cutting 'off the heads of... cockerels with a dagger. Then the blood was poured into a silver chalice and they both took a sip. Then they had sexual intercourse.' When the coven left the party for just such a ritual on Oxshott Common, he followed 'but did not know why', though he did not go all the way and returned to the house where he passed out. He had no recollection of the trailer he said before receiving a six month suspended sentence.

The Beatles had included Aleister Crowley amongst the collection of 'heroes' that adorned the sleeve of the iconic 'Sgt Peppers' album and arch-rivals The Rolling Stones had ended the year with the release of their 6th studio album, 'Their Satanic Majesties Request', before making their interest more explicit with the opening track, and second single, from their follow-up album 'Beggars Banquet'. On 'Sympathy For The Devil' Jagger adopts a first-person narrative in the role of the Devil, boasting of his role in several historical atrocities, ranging from the death of Christ to the Russian Revolution, World War 2 and the killing of the Kennedy's. Though 'Their Satanic Majesties' contained no direct Satanic references, and 'Sympathy For The Devil' was, in the words of Jagger, 'only one song. After all, it wasn't like it was a whole album', the song - especially coming hot on the heels of previous single 'Street Fighting Man' - cemented the band's reputation as a corrupting influence on youth. Rolling Stone magazine added to the songs infamy by misreporting it as the song that the Stones had been playing during the murder at Altamont.

One song or not, Jagger continued to dabble, providing a Moog synthesiser score for Kenneth Anger's 11 minute film, *Invocation Of My Demon Brother* (1969), with a cast that included, as well as Jagger himself, Church of Satan founder Anton La Vey as His Satanic Majesty, and Manson Family member Bobby Beausoleil as Lucifer. 'Sympathy...' was said to be based on Mikhail Bulgakov's Russian novel, 'The Master & Margarita', a recent translation of which had been given to Jagger by then-girlfriend Marianne Faithfull, who had in turn been introduced to it by Anger.

Jagger also took the occult connection into his feature film acting debut in *Performance* (1970). The film's director, Donald Cammell, as well as being a society portrait painter and a fixture of the party scene around Chelsea, was the son of Aleister Crowley biographer Charles Cammell, who, says Donald, 'filled the house with magicians, spiritualists, and demons' and recalls Crowley bouncing him on his knee as a toddler. According to former Blondie bass guitarist Gary Lachman who has penned a number of books on the occult, *Performance* was 'filmed in 1968 with a real rock star, real sex, real drugs, real gangsters and, so legend has it, real black magic.' Cammell saw the filming process itself as a dark work of art, a ritualistic rather than production process. Marianne Faithfull has called it 'a psycho-sexual lab run by Cammell with actor James Fox the prime experimental animal'. Jagger, Cammell and Anita Pallenberg were said to have played mind games with the actor, with rumours suggesting this included dosing him with LSD, unknown to Fox himself, prior to a scene in which he is fed a magic mushroom.

Fox was so affected by making the film that he underwent something of a personal crisis. It had taken him 'to the door of Hell' where he says he had 'looked in and didn't like what I saw.' Deciding his life had no purpose he dropped out of the film business for fifteen years, moving to Leeds where he worked as a 'telephone sterilising salesman', going door to door on behalf of an obscure Evangelical Christian ministry called The Navigators - which is every bit as mad as it sounds. Not that Fox was the only casualty. By the end of filming both Richards and Pallenberg had become full-blown heroin addicts, as had Michele Breton, whose character enjoys a ménage à trois with Jagger and Pallenberg, and who ended up in a German psychiatric clinic.

It was not Jagger, however, who was said to be the major black magic dabbler in the band. According to Anger, who has expressed his belief that Pallenberg, a girlfriend of both Brian Jones and Keith Richards, was 'for want of a better word, a witch... the Occult unit within the Stones was Keith and Anita... and Brian. You see, Brian was a witch too, I'm convinced. He showed me his witch's tit. He had a supernumerary tit in a very sexy place, on his inner thigh. He said, "In another time, they would have burned me."' A witch's tit, or third nipple, was said by inquisitors to have been a mark of the Devil which was used to feed a witch's familiar, often a black cat. Jones and Pallenberg's Chelsea pad was, according to Marianne Faithfull, 'a veritable witches' coven of decadent Illuminati, rock princelings and hip aristo's.'

Embedded even deeper into the occult was Led Zeppelin guitarist Jimmy Page. The band's public fixation on black magic began when their 'Led Zeppelin III' album included the words 'Do what thou wilt', part of Aleister Crowley's guiding philosophy, etched into the centre of the vinyl, and continued on their fourth album covers use of mystic symbols taken mainly from Rudolf Koch's 'Book of Signs'. A serious collector of occult paraphernalia, Page owned an occult bookstore in Kensington, The Equinox, which specialised in rare, and very expensive, occult texts. His most significant artefact however was Crowley's former home, Boleskine House, on the banks of Loch Ness, telling Disc and Music Echo in a cover story for their April 22, 1972 issue entitled 'Jimmy Page on Magic', 'My house used to belong to Aleister Crowley, I knew that when I moved in. Magic is very important if people can go through it. I think Crowley's completely relevant to today. We're still seeking for truth, the search goes on.' It was here where Page was said to have performed a magical rite with Robert Plant and John Bonham, John Paul Jones declining the invitation, in order to accomplish power and fame.

Page also struck up a friendship with Kenneth Anger when he outbid the director for a Crowley book in an auction at Sotheby's, and agreed to provide a soundtrack for Anger's *Lucifer Rising* (1972) which included a brief glimpse of Page admiring a photo of Crowley in a cast that included Marianne Faithfull and Donald Cammell, and was shot by stills photographer Michael Cooper, best known for his work on the 'Sgt Peppers' cover. The two had a falling out, and the film was re-scored by Bobby Beausoleil, with Anger swearing to put a curse on Page.

The remainder of the decade was not the best of times for the band. Some have been quick to point to curses for the seemingly endless succession of calamities that struck the band, though the hedonistic lifestyle they pursued is obviously not without its own dangers. In 1975 Robert Plant drove his car off a cliff in Greece which forced the cancellation of the remainder of the 'Physical Graffiti' tour and left the singer recording the album 'Presence' from a wheelchair. Two years later, his son Karac died of a stomach infection. The following year, Sandy Denny broke her neck falling downstairs, and in 1980 John Bonham was found dead in bed after choking on his own vomit. All of which made Page's descent into heroin addiction pale into insignificance.

Another person who had a fallout with Page was David Bowie who felt threatened enough by the guitarist's prowess in the dark arts to resort to storing his urine and toenail clippings in the fridge for fear that they might be used in curses against him. This was around 1975 when the Thin White Duke weighed just 80 lbs wet through and was living a vampiric existence behind drawn blinds in a Hollywood mansion, existing on a sort of 'vegetarian vampire' diet of milk, cocaine and 80 Gitane a day. Draw your own conclusions.

Bowie's interest in Kabbala and Crowleyism, what he called 'that whole dark and rather fearsome never-world of the wrong side of the brain', goes back at least as far as 1971s 'Hunky Dory' album where, on 'Quicksand', he sings 'I'm closer to the Golden Dawn / Immersed in Crowley's uniform... I'm not a prophet or a stone-age man / Just a mortal with potential of a Superman.' The peak of Bowie's immersion in magic came with 1975s 'Station To Station' whose title track refers to travel through the Kabbalistic Tree of Life: 'Here We Are / One magical moment / From Kether to Malkuth' - the highest and lowest elements of the Tree of Life, signifying the descent from godhead to the physical realm. The rest of the album is littered with Bowie's preoccupations with all things mystic, though the overriding vibe is one of cocaine.

While it might not have been a true story, the writer of **DRACULA AD 1972 (1972)** had plenty of news material to draw on for the film's premise. In 1971, the Express and News reported that David Farrant had 'performed an exorcism ceremony involving six other young men and two naked girls at a chapel in the cemetery. After the ceremony, one girl claimed she saw a shadowy figure which Mr Farrant said was the cemetery's vampire, 'the King of the Undead'. Farrant had performed the ceremony, he said, because he had found signs the chapel had been desecrated by a black magic sect. The signs were a pentangle marked on the chapel floor with burnt-out candles at each corner, other occult symbols and a lingering smell of methylated spirits: 'The girls were naked as symbols of purity - they were virgins.'

Farrant had begun gaining column inches for his activities of a year earlier, when after having been caught by the police climbing out of Highgate Cemetery, he told Weekend magazine, upon being found not guilty of entering enclosed premises for an unlawful purpose, 'I would have searched through the coffins until I recognised the vampire. Then I would have driven the stake through his heart.' A couple of months earlier he had gone vampire hunting with an Evening News reporter where 'although there are no castles in Highgate, the ivy-covered Victorian vaults and the eerie sound of the wind in the trees helped to make up the atmosphere... clutched under his arm, in a Sainsburys carrier bag, he held the tools of his trade. There was a cross made out of two bits of wood tied together with a shoelace, and a stake to thrust through the heart of the beast.'

He also appeared in a piece on the vandalism in the cemetery for the BBCs *24 Hours* news programme in October 1970 where he re-enacted his original vampire hunt, and described his encounter with a vampire, saying 'It took the form of a tall grey figure about 8 feet tall and it seemed to glide.' Farrant expanded on this for Titbits magazine in 1973: 'I was in Highgate Cemetery in North London late at night. Then I suddenly became aware of something behind me. There was no noise, but it was clear as if somebody had called my name. I turned slowly and saw on the path what I took to be a tree, but as my eyes focused, I saw it was a dark figure. I stood there for what could only have been a few seconds and the figure vanished. That's when I knew I had definitely seen a vampire and that's when I vowed to bring it to bay.'

And so Farrant's quest continued, much to the delight of a tabloid press looking for a fun story to spice up Halloween. The Daily Express reported in 1972 that 'As Halloween witching hour approached in a lonely graveyard a man and a woman danced around chalk circles, a fire and candles. The man stood poised with a wooden knife at her chest... But the sudden appearance of eight policemen soon put an end to the ritual, despite a plea from the man, 25-year-old David Farrant, not to break the circle.' The paper was reporting from Barnet Court where Farrant and a 20-year-old girl were charged with indecent behaviour under the Ecclesiastical Courts Act, and each fined £10. However, when graves started to be broken into and bodies in various states of decay were found lying around, one headless corpse even finding its way into the passenger seat of a parked car, Farrant was arrested. Though he

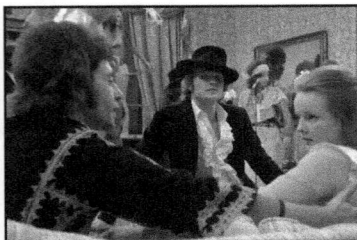

was cleared of the parked car incident, he was unlucky enough to find himself in front of Justice Michael Argyle, the notorious Judge who presided over the Oz trial, and he received two years for interfering with remains, a further two years for sending voodoo effigies to policemen and six months, to be served concurrently, for defacing a memorial.

It is headlines like these that Hammer Studios turned to for inspiration when it found itself in financial trouble due to the gothic horrors that had for years been its bread and butter having run their course. Busty wenches in bursting corsets no longer felt relevant in the wake of the sexual revolution, and so the studio hit on the idea of making the Count contemporary. The result was a project that went in front of the cameras as Dracula Today, was briefly known as Dracula Chelsea 1971 before going on general release as *Dracula AD 1972* (1972).

An opening scene set in 1872, in which a horse-drawn coach chase ends with Van Helsing fatally injured and Dracula impaled on the spokes of a carriage wheel, would have pleased aficionados of Hammer's traditional horror fare no end. Especially so having waited since 1958 to see Christopher Lee's Dracula and Peter Cushing's Van Helsing together, but it is the scene that follows that cements the film as the hippest Hammer horror, despite being met with almost universal derision, not least from star Christopher Lee for whom the role had been a hard sell from the outset: 'At first I honestly thought that the 70s setting wouldn't work for Dracula, that he's strictly a period character. Then, I thought, the novel, written in 1897, was contemporary to its time, and that only in retrospect do we see the character as period.' Hammer would in fact have been well aware that the concept had already been successfully explored in the States by AIP who transplanted *Count Yorga, Vampire* (1970) in a hedonistic present-day Los Angeles, doing well enough to spawn a sequel, *The Return of Count Yorga* (1971).

In present-day London a group of out-of-control youths have crashed the house party of some upper-class young twit whose parents stand around looking aghast as they, if not exactly run amok, behave with less than the required standard of propriety - such as dancing in go-go boots on top of the piano and rolling around under the dining table with your girlfriend. Playing in the background are Bay Area blues-rockers Stoneground, fronted by former Beau Brummels singer Sal Valentino, who perform two tracks, including a 'groovy' updating of the old Jimmy Newman Cajun tune, 'Alligator Man'. The Faces were originally hired for the role but replaced; presumably because Stoneground was under contract to the Kinney Corporation which had recently been acquired by Warner Brothers, the film's backer.

When the gatecrashers become aware that the police have been summoned, the 'kids', out for kicks, rather than flee, instead estimate the police response time. Among them are Greg (Michael Kitchen), Laura (Caroline Munro), Bob (Philip Miller), and Jessica (Stephanie Beacham), a descendent of Van Helsing. Adding a touch of counter-culture credibility is Marsha Hunt as Gaynor. Hunt, who had a minor hit in 1969 with a version of Dr John's 'Walk On Gilded Splinters', had been a girlfriend of Tyrannosaurus Rex era Marc Bolan, was the mother of Mick Jagger's daughter Karis, and said to be the 'Brown Sugar' of the Stones hit. Lurking in the background is Johnny (Christopher Neame), who seems to be channelling Malcolm McDowell's Alex from *A Clockwork Orange*, watching events at what he considers a 'tired scene' from underneath a lowered brow.

The 'kids' reassemble at a cafe come nightclub called The Cavern, more than likely named after Satan's Cavern, a Mayfair cafe run by The Process Church of the Final Judgement, a pseudo-religious organisation formed by former Church of Scientology members Robert and Mary de Grimston, which spread across the Atlantic where it was investigated over alleged links with Charles Manson, and was later a source of inspiration of Genesis P Orridge's Temple ov Psychick Youth, who reprinted the Church's magazine which included interviews with the likes of Jagger and William Burroughs.

In his 'Memoirs of a Dervish', author Robert Irwin describes a black mass held at the cafe where: 'The girls were rather pretty and they looked quite glam in their long cloaks. And they were rather posh. They would have all these fascinating people float in and out. They were all young, very neatly trimmed beards, long golden hair.' Irwin describes the black mas thus: 'A lot of Crowley's terrible poetry was read out early on. We sat on the stairwell looking down on what was acted out down below. The main part of the ritual was like something out of the film version of Dennis Wheatley's *The Devil Rides Out*, and it was aesthetically rather pleasing as it framed black and gold robes, a dark vessel containing a mysterious black potion, a silver mirror, black candles and the Book of the Law... The high point was when the Priestess stripped down to her underwear and made to lay spread-eagled on the alter where she was kissed all over by the Priest. There were no dark manifestations, and I heard someone mutter that the Priestess was not really a virgin. It was not Satanism but merely theatre.'

There's no Black Mass on offer at the cafe, just the usual rather boring evening of dancing fuelled by cigarettes and coca-cola, but Johnny, whose surname is Alucard, suggests that the rest of the group might like to join him for one at midnight in a nearby church for some 'wild kicks', a 'new happening'. What he has in mind is 'Something new yet as old as time... I wonder if you're ready for it my angels. Something way, way out. A date with the Devil, Bacchanal with Beelzebub.' 'Hey, but it sounds wild' says an enthusiastic Laura. Bob is not convinced, calling it 'Sunday supplement stuff' but finally agrees. 'If we do get to summon up the big daddy with the horns and the tail, he gets to bring his own liquor, his own bird and his own pot' he insists, at which point Johnny rushes back to his 'pad' to laugh maniacally and take out his Dracula ring and a vial of ashes from a box.

Also reluctant is Jessica, but a sceptical Bob assures her 'Joe'll turn up with a few bottles of beer, Gaynor will bring something to eat and Greg'll bring his guitar and it'll turn into a bit of singing and maybe a little loving on the side. Then the fuzz'll turn up and we'll be turned out and we'll end up back at the coffee bar.' Her grandfather, who finds her lounging in his office thumbing through a copy of 'Treatise on the Black Mass' for 'a quiet bit of mind-blowing,' tells her it's a serious subject and not to be messed with. 'You can buy that sort of stuff in any shady book shop in Soho' she tells him, 'I think it's kinky, weird man, way out.'

At the mass, the kids form a magic circle and Johnny yells, 'Dig the music kids' as a reel-to-reel tape recorder plays 'Black Mass: An Electric Storm in Hell' by White Noise, a trio comprising David Vorhaus, Brian Hodgson and Delia Derbyshire, best known for her work with the BBC Radiophonic Workshop. Its combination of Gregorian chanting, frantic drumming and piercing electronic shrieks. As the music takes hold, they're told to 'Let it flow into you' - Johnny now seeming to channel Kenneth Williams in *Carry On Screaming* (1966) - as the kids sway from side to side. He calls for Jessica to go up to the altar, but she's still reluctant. Not so Laura who is overcome with it all: 'Me, Johnny, me. I'll do it, me!' When Johnny runs a knife across his wrist to provide a goblet of blood to pour over her cleavage, it proves too much for the rest of the kids who are on their heels before the star of the show is summoned and the Count returns from beyond the grave to sink his teeth into her neck.

Future Bond girl Caroline Munro had already appeared briefly in a few movies, including *Joanna* (1968) and *The Abominable Dr Phibes* (1971) where her presence was purely for, impossibly sexy, set dressing. *Dracula AD 1972* provided her first proper role: 'That was my turning point, when I worked with Christopher Lee, and when I worked with all those young, up-and-coming actors. Suddenly I thought, this is what I want to do, I absolutely know.' It was also her introduction to the thick concoction used for blood that was affectionately known as 'Kensington gore', which was notoriously difficult to remove. So much so that she was still covered in it when she was pulled over for speeding on her way home from the set. She says that it helped get her off, though one suspects other of the actresses attributes might have played their part.

Sadly, that is the last we see of Laura who disappears from the movie, as does the Count's second victim, Gaynor. Instead, we get Hammer's usual plodding policemen, whose only contribution is a throwaway reference to Charles Manson, 'cult murders a few years back in the States', before conceding to Van Helsing's request for one hour alone in the church after sundown where he predictably saves his granddaughter and despatches Dracula via a stake filled coffin. The film could, and should, have had fun with the idea of vampires making their presence felt in modern-day London, but Don Houghton's script restricts such activities to a run-down cemetery. Of his victims, only Laura's boyfriend Bob returns, albeit briefly, and those that manage to avoid this fate, like Michael Kitchen, simply disappear from proceedings.

Horror aficionados drool over the film's prologue and dream of what might have been, but really, the impaling of the Count by the spike of a cartwheel is the cinematic equivalent of sticking a plastic sword under the armpit and pretending to have been run through. They also agree with Christopher Lee who, having talked himself into taking the role, soon realised the error of his judgement: 'The whole idea of 'swinging London' was already dated, and the clothing, mannerisms, and dialogue of the 'teenagers' were all wrong. Some ideas simply look better in the script than they do on the screen,' a view shared by Caroline Munro who thought 'some of the dialogue left a little to be desired... it was quite fun but quite hard to say some of it, really.' The critics ran with the same theme, Monthly Film Bulletin saying 'the trendies... are patently phony' and Marjorie Bilbow in Cinema & TV Today suggesting 'The film would be much more successful if it did not make such an effort to be up-to-date with slang expressions that manifestly do not come naturally to the cast or the characters they are portraying'.

The real problem, however, is not the modern-day settings or the attempted 'groovy' dialogue - that remain the only reasons to watch the film today - but simply that by 1972 the Hammer template could no longer be considered in any way scary, and as 'adult' fare, audiences were looking for something more than Caroline Munro's cleavage and thigh length boots (as pleasant as they are). *Dracula AD 1972* was perhaps a fitting movie for an era that could conjure up the likes of David Farrant and John Pope, who in January 1974 were reported as having appeared in court after 'Police who went to an empty house in Avenue Road, Highgate, London, found two naked men performing what appeared to be some sort of witchcraft ceremony round a two-foot fire in a back room.' They were both committed to trial at the Old Bailey, charged with arson by causing damage to the floorboards. The fire had been burning on silver foil and was obviously not an attempt to set fire to the building but by this time the authorities had had enough, of Farrant in particular.

22-year-old Pope, with Farrant in jail for other offences, went off to Romania the following summer in order to raise the ghost of Dracula, telling Reveille magazine 'I failed', after complaining that the country's authorities would not let him wear his witches robes and brandish his ritual dagger in the streets. 'How could I succeed when I was restricted by this narrow-minded attitude' he said, before warning that 'I am going to form a new coven that will rule the world.'

In 1976 with Farrant out on parole, the duo carried out a 'Battle of the Warlocks' on a Highgate football pitch, attended by the Daily Mirror who said 'They cast evil spells. They called down terrible curses. They mumbled and they gabbled as they celebrated Halloween by trying to eliminate each other. But abracadabra! It was the 'black boots' that won the day. Jock the park keeper in his size thirteen wellies played hell with the pair and even made them... vanish! Pope the magician got weaving, armed with an ornamental dagger, a black staff and a packet of joss sticks. Gravely he announced: "I'm going to call a ball of fire out of the sky which will strike the very ground on which you stand and will render you dead." ...But all he did was conjure up a spellbound crowd and park-keeper Jock, who wanted to know what the devil they were up to. "Out. Out!" he yelled, trampling over the joss sticks and threatening darkly to lock them in for the night unless they 'scarpered'. Hey Presto! It worked like magic.'

Despite *Dracula AD 1972*'s less than enthusiastic reception, Hammer - including Lee and Cushing - returned for one more contemporary Count Dracula outing in *The Satanic Rites of Dracula* (1974), again directed by Alan Gibson and written by Don Houghton. The swinging London idea is reigned in and the film opens in a Wheatley-esque English country home where hooded members of a sinister cult are busy conducting a naked sacrifice involving cockerel blood. Whilst all this is going on a Secret Service agent, being held captive, manages to escape and reveal to his superiors that a number of high-powered officials, including a government minister, a general and a peer are part of a cult intent on world domination. There's also a scientist specialising in blood diseases and, yes, Count Dracula himself - we know this because he has taken photos of the five men but one shows just an empty doorway.

Houghton's script takes no chances by throwing in a bit of everything, from espionage, a Fu Manchu-like villain, a coming apocalypse, corrupt property developers and, in place of the previous films Chelsea set, a group of long-haired bikers who provide the cult's security, uniformly kitted out in polo neck jumpers and Afghan jackets, to add a touch of counter-culture appeal.

Hippies, Skinheads, Rastas, Punks & Disco Dancing Bowie Boot Boys

Motorbikin'
(Spedding)

For undead wannabe British Hells Angels however there is only movie choice, **PSYCHOMANIA (1973)**. By the 1970s, the biker movie had become a staple of the US exploitation circuit, a genre kick-started by AIP's Roger Corman directed *The Wild Angels* (1966), proving such a success, the 16th highest-grossing film of 1966, that the company had three more appearing in drive-in's by the end of the following year with *The Glory Stompers*, *Devil's Angels*, and *The Born Losers*. *The Wild Angels* $5.5 million in domestic box office was dwarfed when the film's star Peter Fonda put on his leathers again three years later for *Easy Rider* (1969), the film grossing $41.7 million domestically in the US ($60 million worldwide) and bringing the genre an unlikely respectability via two Academy Award nominations. There was also countless quickly made cash-ins that tried to provide their own original take on the biker gang such as female bikers in *The Hellcats* (1968), gay bikers in *The Pink Angels* (1971), and the self explanatory *The Black Angels* (1970). There was also an attempt at genre mash-up with *Werewolves on Wheels* (1971) which is the direction taken by Benmar Productions, a company owned by Polish producer Benjamin Fisz and Czech financier Boris Marmor who had a track record of making spaghetti westerns in Spain, like *Captain Apache* (1971) and *A Town Called Bastard* (1971), before moving into horror with *Horror Express* (1972).

Though Hells Angels were an American phenomenon, their notoriety soon travelled across the Atlantic and had already been capitalised on by New English Library in a series of popular pulp novels, encouraging the British rockers to re-brand themselves as outlaw motorcycle gangs. NEL had seen the potential of the Hells Angels as early as 1967 when they optioned the British rights for Jan Hudson's 'The Sex & Savagery of Hells Angels', itself a cheap cash-in on Hunter S. Thompson's 'Hells Angels: The Strange & Terrible Sage of the Outlawed Motorcycle Gangs'. The first British Hells Angels novel came in 1971 with Pete Cave's 'Chopper', whose back cover blurb provided a strong taster of the violence that lay inside: 'Chopper moved into position. The Skinhead was still bent double. Bringing up his knee, Chopper felt with satisfaction the scrunch of broken bone as the kid's nose made contact. The kid went down, while blows from boots rained upon his body. He lay groaning, spitting out gouts of deep red blood and pieces of broken teeth. "Don't ever pull a blade on an Angel," snapped Freaky before they left the kid, "it's not friendly."'

Cave was a science fiction author, doubling as a freelance editor of top shelf men's magazines, who had been contracted by NEL to submit a novel on the subject within six weeks. Three quarters of a million sales ensured it wouldn't be the last. Had he known how popular 'Chopper' would prove he almost certainly wouldn't have killed him off in the final chapter, but the story was nevertheless continued by placing his girlfriend 'Mama' front and centre in a 1972 sequel of the same name which was quickly followed that same year by two more, 'The Run' and 'Rogue Angels'.

When Cave hung up his motorcycle gloves after one more outing in 1973's 'Speed Freaks', NEL editor Laurence James picked up the mantle with 'Angels From Hell', and three sequels, under the pseudonym Mick Norman. Says

James: 'They all did well, they sold about seventy thousand copies each, which was good sales even then.' Such was the demand for biker pulp fiction that, unable to find time to knock out a new title himself, James contacted an old college friend who was teaching English & Drama at a secondary school in Stevenage at the time. Says said friend, John Harvey: 'even though I'd never actually written any fiction, he thought I might just be up to the task. I taught English and I read a lot. Surely I could write? He gave me his Mick Normans to read, explaining they were close to westerns but with bikes instead of horses.' And so Thom Ryder was born and a first novel 'Avenging Angel' was followed by a second, 'Angel Alone'.

Where cinema failed to cash in on NEL's Skinhead titles, Benmar's East European heads hired a couple of American writers, Julian Zimet and Arnaud D'Usseau, in exile in the UK after being blacklisted for their affiliations during the 1950s McCarthy communist witchhunt, to write the quintessentially English script of what would become *Psychomania*, to be directed by the Australian Don Sharp.

Sharp was best-known for his work on the highly rated Hammer horror *Kiss of the Vampire* (1963) but, as part of the second unit, had recently directed the high-octane eight-minute chase boat sequence in *Puppet On A Chain* (1971), the inspiration for *Live & Let Die*'s inclusion of a similar scene two years later. Because of the boom in the industry when the Americans came over to take advantage of Swinging London, Sharp was able to call on some excellent technicians including Oscar winning cinematographer Ted Moore and Oscar nominated art director Maurice Carter.

Psychomania opens on a group of bikers driving slowly around a stone circle as the opening credits roll. We then see them driving in formation down a country lane. A car is coming towards them but there is no effort to disperse into single file, forcing the car to swerve off the road. The bikers come to a rest and the leader, Tom (Nicky Henson) pulls up his visor. 'Well, he's on the hook,' he says, 'Shall we let him go?' 'No, teach him a lesson,' says a girl. 'Blow his mind,' offers another. They are, according to their jackets, The Living Dead and they continue their pursuit, forcing the car to crash and its driver to go through the windscreen.

'We wanna be free! We wanna be free to do what we wanna do! We wanna be free to ride. We wanna be free to ride our machines without being hassled by The Man... and we wanna get loaded... and we wanna have a good time... And that's what we're gonna

do!' says Peter Fonda in T*he Wild Angels*, but if, like Tom you were living in a Walton-on-Thames gated mansion with your clairvoyant mother (Beryl Reid) and butler, Shadwell (George Sanders), that would be just 'dullsville man'. The family has a secret, a locked room that hasn't been opened in eighteen years, ever since Tom's father had died in there. The room holds the secret to eternal life and Tom has plans for him and his gang to cross over to the other side by committing suicide, assuring them 'We'll come back, it'll be better than ever.'

For the members of the Living Dead, Sharp cast a collection of the poshest 'outlaws' ever assembled, headed by the Charterhouse educated Nicky Henson who had trained as a stage manager at RADA, had appeared on stage alongside Laurence Harvey as early as 1964 and would become a member of the Royal Shakespeare Company in 1977. Alongside him was fellow National Theatre and Old Vic regular Roy Holder as Bertram, whose first significant screen performance had been in *Whistle Down The Wind* (1961), and Denis Gilmore as Hatchet, who had replaced Dennis Waterman as the title character of *William* for the second series of the BBC's 1960s adaptation of the 'Just William' books. Also, far from lacking in experience was Mary Larkin as Abby, having made a couple of films the previous year; *Some Kind of Hero* (1972) which had failed to be given a cinema release, and *X, Y and Zee* (1972) alongside Michael Caine, Liz Taylor and Susannah York, which she says is 'possibly one of the worst films ever made'.

In the role of Jane, Anne Michelle had been guaranteed to catch the eye in her only notable previous acting role, spent largely unclothed, in *Virgin Witch* (1971) opposite her sister Vicki. As Hinky, Rocky Taylor was cast for his skill as an experienced stuntman, having taught Cliff Richard judo for *The Young Ones* (1961), and doubled for the stars of ITC action series such as *The Saint*, *The Baron* and *The Champions* as well as the early Bond movies. Even Henson, who considers the film something of an embarrassment that has followed him around ever since, admits 'the stunts are brilliant'. Of the rest, he says it 'just shows the doldrums the British film industry was in at the time, of course there's never been a British film industry, but that was a particularly bad time.'

Henson, a biker himself at the time, says he was attracted to the role after having received a script that 'opens with the line "Eight chop hog Harley Davidson's crest about a hill…" and I said, 'hey I'll do the fucker!' without even reading it. Then I get on the set and they weren't Harley's at all but rather they were these terrible Nortons that were 20 years old at the time. They had four mechanics working full time on set just to keep these things going and that was the biggest expense in the movie, believe it or not.' He adds: 'I remember saying to the producer, "How did you ever raise the finance to make this piece of shit?" And he said, "Listen, I've got a drawer full of wonderful scripts", but I went to my backers and I said "I've got a zombie bikers come back from the dead and ride their motorcycles out of graves" and they handed the money over.'

Having persuaded his mother to let him enter the locked room, once inside Tom is confronted by a mirror and a pair of glasses. Putting them on, his reflection disappears and instead, through a haze of smoke he sees images of himself going back through childhood and culminating as a baby where his mother is seen signing him over to a dark and sinister figure. He collapses and comes round back in the living room. The glasses were his father's who, says Shadwell, had lacked the faith required to come back: 'At the last minute he must have had doubts.' Not so, Tom.

Back out with the gang, he puts into practice his newfound knowledge, telling them they are to do a ton and hold it which, as his girlfriend, Abby, tells him, 'is suicide.' They head into the town centre where they cause havoc amongst the shoppers until a police car arrives and gives chase, during which Tom drives at 100 mph off a bridge and into the river, his body washing up on the bank.

The gang oversee his burial at the stones, known as the Five Witches because they were supposedly witches turned to stone, sitting upright on his bike, to the accompaniment of the song 'Rising Free', sung in its entirety by folk singer Harvey Andrews, though mimed on the screen by an actor because, says Harvey, 'I wasn't a pretty boy'. The song was written by David Whitaker and Johnny Worth who were producing Andrews second album, 'Writer of Songs', on which he was backed by Ralph McTell and Rick Wakeman. Says Andrews: 'Some people think of it as a great biker anthem… others think it's absolute shite. I shall say nothing. I earned my £15.'

It's not long before, much to the gang's surprise, he's back on the saddle and urging his friends to join him in immortality, with the fact that Hatchet (Denis Gilmore) has stabbed him in the back with no discernible ill effect being confirmation enough for Jane. 'Oh man, what are we waiting for?' she asks before she and Hinky drive at full speed into a speeding van - giving her mum a bit of a surprise at the funeral when, seeking a final look at her daughter,

The Living Dead Motorcycle Club in *Psychomania*

she finds the casket empty. No such transformation for Hinky who at the last minute had hesitated, not really wanting to die.

What Tom really wants though is his girlfriend Abby, who along with the rest of the gang is arrested and held at a police station after a series of killings by the pair. He soon frees the gang, killing a couple of policemen in the process, who then set about enacting their own suicides. One jumps from a tower block, another wraps himself in heavy chains and jumps into a river, whilst yet another goes parachuting - without a parachute. Hatchet steps off a motorway flyover into the incoming traffic. Abby though chooses the less messy, but also less certain, route of an overdose of sleeping pills and comes round in a hospital bed with a police officer staring down at her.

Wanting to live, the police persuade her to go to the mortuary and pretend to have died and come back. This she does, returning to the ranks for a drive through a supermarket where, in one of the film's most memorable moments, they deliberately target a baby in a pram. Tom tells Abby that he's 'always fancied driving through a brick wall' and when she fails to do likewise, he realises she is faking and gives her three minutes to commit suicide or instead be murdered. For Mum, it has all gone too far, and she invokes her power to break the spell, creating a half dozen new stones at the Seven Witches.

Almost unbelievably in the time of *A Clockwork Orange*, the BBFC, having vetted the script before shooting began, were concerned about the film's influence on young impressionable minds with BBFC member Stephen Murphy attending the set and even having consultations with the police. Whilst the suicide part of the plot proved uncontroversial, there was a degree of consternation when it came to knocking over traffic cones and pulling off a car's wing mirror. The BBFC it seems took health and safety very seriously, as did the one local licensing committee who insisted on an advance viewing to ease their own concerns about road safety in their town.

Now a bona fide cult classic, given a BFI restoration for release on DVD and Blu-ray as part of their Flipside umbrella, the film was not generally well-received on its initial release, a typical response being that of Philip French in The Times who thought it 'ludicrously unconvincing' and suggested of its appearance as one half of a double-bill with *The Baby*: 'bereft of wit and imagination this double bill is indicative of the moribund state the horror genre has reached after a grand revival in the early sixties. Though all set to go on general release they seem more suited for a post-prandial entertainment at an SS reunion.' He probably wasn't comparing it to the work of Leni Riefenstahl. Writing in Monthly Film Bulletin, David Pirie seemed to grasp what for most only became clear with the passage of time and praised the director's decision to 'treat his material herewith as black comedy rather than horror' and described it as 'both innovatory and humorously macabre'.

Sanders role was completed in a mere six days, and he seems alternately baffled and grimly amused by the proceedings, painfully aware that the film is yet another in a long line of low-budget films he had been obliged to appear in after the collapse of the company he was involved with in 1964. During this time Sanders barely avoided serving jail time (though he was an innocent dupe in the affair) and he was also coping with the death of his wife, Benita Hume (widow of the late British actor Ronald Colman) in 1967. The sixty-five-year-old actor committed suicide shortly after *Psychomania*'s completion, entering a hotel in Spain where he downed five bottles of the barbiturate Nembutal - a short term sedative in small doses but used in the US for lethal injections in death penalty cases and by veterinarians for euthanasia. He famously left a note that read 'Dear World, I am leaving because I am bored. I feel I have lived long enough. I am leaving you with your worries in this sweet cesspool. Good luck.' Perhaps Nicky Henson wasn't the film's harshest critic after all.

In 2007 a drive-by shooting of a motorcyclist on the M40 threw the British Hells Angels into the media spotlight, projecting an image far removed from that offered by onetime spokesperson Ian 'Maz' Harris, PhD, for whom 'The Hells Angels Motorcycle Club is a loosely based organisation of motorcycle enthusiasts who own bikes of 750cc or more. We are primarily and exclusively a motorcycle club. That is all.' Indeed, they are registered at Companies House as Hells Angels Limited with a stated aim 'to foster, encourage and advance the sport and recreation of motorcycling and to promote the acceptance of the ethical code of morality of the Hells Angels Club…' The police saw things somewhat differently, and to them, the Angels were an international criminal organisation with major involvement in the drugs trade.

Following WW2 dozens of biker groups had sprung up across the United States, comprising ex-GI's who had found the serenity of life on civvy street hard to accept and so would meet up at weekends to drink, ride and have the occasional punch-up. In 1947 a drag racing event organised by the American Motorcycle Association was held in the sleepy Californian town of Hollister. A biker gang called the Pissed Off Bastards rode in and created chaos; events which would form the basis of the 1953 Marlon Brando movie *The Wild One*. One Pissed Off Bastard, Otto Friedli, broke away and formed a new club, the Hells Angels, taking the name from fighter pilots and organising his new 'club' along more military lines.

By 1953 and *The Wild One*, a new chapter, formed from members of the San Francisco based Market Street Commandos, was added, the first of many as throughout the sixties a series of high profile incidents increased the Angels notoriety. Legal costs associated with a 1964 rape in Monterey involving four Angels were said to have precipitated the gangs move into the lucrative drugs trade and the decade, and what was left of the Hippie dream, ended at a 1969 Rolling Stones concert in Altamont 'policed' by Angels and resulting in a shooting and a murder. That same year saw the first British chapter who in 1972 made their own headlines when a 14-year-old Girl Guide was abducted in Winchester and subsequently raped at an Angels party.

Skinheads, even the 1960s originals, were never going to be remembered for their high levels of intelligence, but placed alongside the so-called British Hells Angels in an episode of the thirty-minute documentary series **MAN ALIVE: WHAT'S THE TRUTH ABOUT HELLS ANGELS AND Skinheads (1969)** they seem positively cerebral. Narrator Harold Williamson provides an introduction: 'Hells Angels they call themselves; they're known to others as the Grease. If you're not one of them, you're not likely to have much time for them. Certainly, they seem to have no time for anyone but themselves, but they crave attention and they get it by mob action. They roar into town as a mob. As a mob, they'd like to be found more dangerous and frightening than in fact they are.' Williamson hangs out with some 'Angels' from Oldbury, near Birmingham, who operate from a run-down pub, The Odd Fellows Arms, whose regulars deserted when the surrounding houses were demolished for re-generation. 'Here,' we are told 'they can show off what they seem to value most; Nazi insignia, bits and pieces of German military uniforms and as untidy an appearance as it's possible to achieve. Scruffier spells success for Hells Angels. To disgust is to win.'

There's a purported Hells Angels wedding which seems to exist of exchanging rings, saying 'it is done' and slopping beer around as the onlookers offer their congratulations. To Sylvia, an 18-year-old bottle blonde and her 'husband' Hitler, it's a major act of rebellion. In place of the usual text is a motorcycle manual; 'That's a bible to us' says Sylvia, 'in the Hells Angels law.' Her ring is an oil ring from a bike. Asked what this 'marriage' means, and what happens from now? Sylvia's response is 'We've got to get some bread, that means money. We've got to get somewhere to live, we've got to get a job - which will kill us both. Things like that.' She looks livid when Williamson suggests this makes her look less like an Angel and more like the older generation.

Sylvia, believe it or not, is the brains in this unholy union. Hitler's contribution to the proceedings comprises telling us you can beat up a Skinhead to prove yourself; 'If it was legal we'd go around hanging Skinheads.' The Skinheads we meet in the second half of the programme don't see the Hells Angels as an enemy because says one, 'there aren't any… they're just grease, ordinary rockers that used to be in this country, that's all they are.'

In the Evening Chronicle Harry Thompson, calling it 'an irresponsible documentary,' was not impressed: 'The point that is so disturbing is that all these teenagers yearn to be noticed, and paraded in front of the *Man Alive* cameras in a gloating way. It seems both silly and naïve to allow them this when there are so few of them as scarcely constitute a social problem.'

Real or not, 1973 saw the UK's first murder attributed to the Hells Angels. 16-year-old Clive Olive had vanished from his home in St. Aubyn's, Hove, Sussex, on February 28th and almost three weeks later, his trussed and weighted body turned up in Shoreham Harbour. Olive was a member of a gang who called themselves the Sussex Mad Dogs and who, according to the press, 'used to go around with all the gear of a Hell's Angel - except a motorbike'. Despite this, the Mad Dogs initiations aped those of the Angels; including allowing every member, male and female, to urinate over a newcomer's t-shirt and jeans, who must then put the clothes back on and vow never to wash them.

Olive's fascination with outlaw motorcycle gangs had led him to take part-time jobs in the cafes they frequented, hoping to be accepted. Police eventually arrested two men and a woman, Brian Moore, his brother-in-law Albert Dorn, and Christine Dorn. The men were bikers, said to be members of the Hells Angels. 21-year-old Moore believed Olive, who had a reputation as something of a lothario, had raped his 16-year-old girlfriend and so had sworn revenge. In December 1973, both men were convicted of murder and received life sentences. Christine Dorn was sentenced to ten years for manslaughter, though this was later quashed on appeal.

The Sussex Mad Dogs were not officially Hells Angels, as was pointed out by a 1973 BBC documentary which opens by informing viewers that 'there are a million motorbike owners in Britain. Two thousand of them are pretty regular hell raisers but of these, only 32 boast the right to call themselves the Hells Angels Motorcycle Club England, established 1969 by transatlantic decree. Despite their defiant claim to be the only true chapter in England, the 32 fight a running battle with the 2000 odd so-called other bikers from all over the country who deny their exclusive right to the title of Hells Angels.' All this is delivered in an old school BBC voice-over that carries a clear tone of snooty disdain, such as when discussing prospects who, until they are granted full membership, must do whatever a full Angel tells them. 'In public schools, they call it fagging' he adds helpfully.

'As individuals, the Angels are a volatile mix of aggression and instability. When 2 or 3 are gathered together, the combination is explosive. When 3 or more gather, a Hells Angels pack can be described as a riot in search of an incident to set it off,' we're told, which with the chapters annual run on the horizon conjures up visions of imminent anarchy and destruction.

The documentary, made for the BBC's *Midweek*, caused some pre-broadcast publicity and the front page headline 'Gang Bang Shocker Filmed By BBC' when Ormskirk's gullible Conservative MP Harold Soref told the press that the seven stong camera crew had captured in full colour the sexual activities of an 18-year-old blonde and a group of men dressed as Hells Angels. 'I have written to Sir Michael Swan, Chairman of the BBC, saying it should never be put on, and I shall also be writing to Sir John Eden to complain about it.' Though the BBC admitted some footage would be considered offensive and therefore not used, they stressed there was no film shot of the alleged bang bang.

The programme introduces some of those who will take part. There's Mad John, the vice president, his sergeant-at-arms, Karl, whose claim that his cross-eyed appearance results from having his eyes kicked out of their sockets in a fight is likely a self-created myth. There's also Mick, whose mum lends them a portable telly for the occasion. Mad John's dog Hitler will stay at home.

Come the big day the cameras follow the chapter on their outing. The narrator builds them up: 'At garages, nervous

Vice President Mad John & Sergeant at Arms Karl

attendants serve them quickly and hope they'll leave quietly. Mild-mannered dormitory town traffic moves over to let them through; cars pile up behind them in peaceful shopping centres; straights are jeered at.' And then he knocks them down: 'As Hells Angels England ride out of town on their 600cc motorcycles, from a distance it's almost possible to conceive them as sort of ragged glory, this is after all the only glory the chapter will know. A moment of glamour snatched from lives of hollow monotony; close up the illusion of glamour fades.' Fittingly, the annual run ends early on a dilapidated barge just outside Aylesbury, with the Angels drinking cans of warm lager, smoking spliffs and watching *Dr Who* as the rain pours down outside.

One glaring omission from the programme is that of the incarcerated Buttons, the club president, who does not merit a mention apart from in a scene where Mad Dog opens a battered suitcase full of his prized possessions which includes, alongside a hatchet and the Hawkwind logbook, a copy of the biography 'Buttons: The Making of a President'.

In the sixties, there were already countless so-called outlaw motorcycle clubs who adopted approximations of the Hells Angels death head patch, but had no connection with their American counterparts apart from attending flea-pit showings of the AIP movies, among them Hells Angels London. Buttons, real name Peter Welsh, was the president of this 'unofficial' London chapter, and in 1969 he flew to Haight Ashbury to spend several weeks with the real Angels, meeting several of the leading club officers including national president Sonny Barger, joining them on runs whilst his application for the first UK charter was discussed, and eventually granted, bringing home a coveted Hells Angels England patch. With such a 'privilege' came the obligation to bring other, often larger and more powerful, chapters into line by either amalgamating or disbanding.

There was naturally resistance, despite Buttons claiming that, 'They believed they were as tough and as righteous as the American brothers. In time I was to come and show them different.' In fact, despite Buttons bravado, the Hells Angels England membership was limited to about a dozen, whilst others, like Hells Angels Essex and their arch enemy the London based Road Rats, could boast of hundreds. They were also not easily pushed around, as was evident from a notorious incident in October 1970, known as The Battle of Chelsea Bridge in which the two gangs clashed and the Road Rats 19-year-old president was jailed for 12 years for shooting one of his rivals in the stomach. Fifteen others received custodial sentences.

By 1974 when Hells Angels West Coast became the first other chapter to amalgamate under the Hells Angels England colours, the aftermath of the Chelsea Bridge incident had seen the amalgamation of nine of the most prominent unofficial chapters into a powerful alliance. Though these two rival organisations were technically at war, it was the Road Rats who continued to provide problems for both, and, although it would take another ten years, several deaths and countless woundings, all but one of the unofficial clubs would eventually commit to the England patch.

The BBC revisited the outlaw biker lifestyle again in an episode of **40 MINUTES: THE OUTLAWS** (1985), an 'unofficial' gang who seemed like a decent bunch of lads who were in need of some help with health and safety. One of them had even found his forte as an undertaker, specialising in embalming, which was useful as he was soon honing his skills on one of his own: 'I embalmed him, which took a very long time as he had no head left.'

So was the fallen Angel's demise the result of doing a ton on a perilous stretch of road in wet conditions? A particularly violent gang fight? An attempt to meet *Psychomania*'s Tom on the other side after mistaking a late-night TV screening for a documentary? An Outlaw sets the record straight: 'We were up at a party and we got this bulk of timber just standing up in the air, ready to push it on the fire. Somebody lost their footing 'cause by that time everybody would have been on the piss all night... the timber fell back and hit him on the head and from the bridge of his nose to the back of his head was only an inch and a half to two inches wide, man. His brains were just spread all around his head.'

The Sussex Mad Dogs' Clive Olive could have been Tod (Tony Naylor) from the Colin Welland penned **BANK HOLIDAY (1971)**, part of the television series *Scene*, a mainstay of the BBCs school programming from 1968 through to 2007. The episode begins with a motorbike travelling down the road, its rider clad in leather with a large swastika emblazoned on the back of his jacket. Deep Purple's 'Speed King' provides the soundtrack, as long hair waves in the wind from below a crash helmet - though it was still two years until such headwear became compulsory. This is Towzer (Myles Reithermann) and he's on his way to see his friend Tod, whom we meet in his bedroom putting on his 'uniform'. It's 'what I joined them for... to wear it. Some kids join the army, sea cadets, police, for the uniform - just to wear it. Us? We make up our own, summat just ours.'

As he sits at the gate outside the house he's joined by his father who asks 'What do you look like?' 'All I need is the bike' responds Tod. Towzer arrives and Tod takes his place on the pillion, leather jacket covered by sleeveless Levi with a swastika on the back, an iron cross pinned proudly on the chest, and DOGS painted in large white letters across the front of his helmet. They're joined by Tod's mother who kisses her son on the cheeks and tells him 'careful now and no racing for God's sake. Get something to eat; go into a cafe, proper, not just fish and chips.' Waving them away, she says disapprovingly; 'That Towzer, God knows where Tod picked him up. He's not grammar school for certain.'

They're off down the A64, singing happily; 'We're off, we're off, we're off in a motor car. Sixty coppers are after us and they don't know where we are.' But they're on a bike and it's not long before they're pulled over, an easy target for a waiting police car with nothing better to do; 'Well, you're sitting there aren't you, Bank Holiday, hot, sticky, stuck in a car working, and you see these yobbos laughing, out in the open, healthy. Time of their ruddy lives they're having. We're only young uns aren't we? We stop 'em.'

In Scarborough the boys follow Tod's mum's advice and head into a café for a meal but Towzer then insists they leave when another larger group of bikers enter. 'We're all right on our own, separate,' he tells the protesting Tod, 'But in a mob like that we're asking for trouble. Looking for it. But we're not. Are we?' So after a takeaway fish and chips, they set up camp on the cliffs overlooking the coastline.

Come evening they change into suits and ties and head in search of 'birds' but don't get into the disco when a bouncer still takes umbrage with their appearance and tells them, 'No long hair.' Towzer takes it in his stride, as he had with the police en route, but Tod is a bit hot-headed and tries to barge his way in, to no avail. 'You won't change the world by getting your rag out,' Towzer tells him. But the rag is out: 'Systematic it's been, from the word go, from all angles. Diggin' us and pokin' us with looks, heavy sarcasm. It's all so bloody infantile and what for? A scalp full of hair and an odd Gerry badge or two. Morons - they're nowt but flamin' morons.'

This is not the end of the hassle. In the early hours, they're rudely woken by the police and ordered to pack up and leave, which they do, carefully taking down the tent and packing it onto the bike as the police stand silently by. As they mount the bike they're given a few words of advice; 'It's not worth the bother is it, lads, coming down, dressing up and coming. I shouldn't bother next Banky - stay at home where it's safer.'

The boys say nothing and leave quietly with the police car following close behind. When it turns off, Towzer lets out a howl of defiance and speeds towards the municipal gardens, riding recklessly through the extravagant beds of flowers and leaving a trail of destruction behind them as the credits roll. The following episode of *Scene* was a documentary, *The Police and You*, in which police officers give their reactions to the play.

The script for **HELLS ANGEL (1971)** is credited to Jonathan Agnew, the BBCs Alan Smithee pseudonym for writers who do not wish to have their name attached to a work. Here it is the novelist Hugo Charteris. In it a Nazi memorabilia clad Dick Foster (Michael Kitchen) is adopted by a rich aunt after his alcoholic mother is found dead in bed and churns up the croquet lawn by driving his motorcycle across it, being unlicensed to actually take his machine of the public highways. When his behaviour finally results in his marching orders, he is joined by the local Hells Angels chapter.

The critics couldn't have been more polarized. The Times called it 'an engrossing bitch of a play in which Mr Agnew exposed the generation gap, the social divisions of our times and much that was disquieting besides.' The Stage said, 'It is difficult to find anything good to say about this play. It was a totally unnecessary essay in unpleasantness - laden with obtuse innuendo - utterly devoid of wit, charm or interest.'

Tony Naylor and Myles Reithermann in *Bank Holiday*

3. Skinhead Moonstomp
(Naismith, Ellis)

Hippies, Skinheads, Rastas, Punks & Disco Dancing Bowie Boot Boys

Kids in 1965, regardless of background, were largely singing from the same hymn sheet - that of The Beatles and the Stones. But towards the end of the decade, a marked divide began to emerge. With middle-class teenagers increasing their participation in the Mod movement and diluting the initial anger of working class youth, Mod subculture would soon become commercialised beyond all recognition as it blended with the Carnaby Street Hippie style of 'swinging London' - a look adopted by many of their former heroes, like Pete Townshend and Steve Marriott who were dipping their toes in the new 'underground'. Mysticism was a concept that a trendy young executive might feel more at home with than an apprentice bench grinder and as a response, 'certain Mods began to emphasise the more proletarian aspects of the look, cutting their hair shorter and replacing dandified suits and shoes with jeans and heavy boots. These no-frills 'hard Mods' prefigured the first Skinheads.' The Skinheads, said cultural theorist Phil Cohen were 'a systematic inversion of the Mods - whereas the Mods explored the upwardly mobile, the Skinheads explored the lumpen.'

The Skinhead as a fully formed subculture seems to have emerged in the first part of 1968 in London's East End, though a letter from a Skinhead girl to the Daily Mirror in1970 claimed she got the haircut 'about three years ago and I am nowhere near being the original peanut.' It took the press a while to catch up with the trend but once they did, they did so with their usual gusto. Under the heading 'The Age of Identity,' the Daily Mirror used their divergence from the Hippies to introduce the Skinheads to its readership in September 1969 saying 'While 150,000 young fans were peaceably communing with Mr Bob Dylan on the Isle of Wight, eighty miles away in North London a gang of youths were doing their best to kick in the face of a 13-year-old. The youths were peanuts or Skinheads. In contrast to the Hippies vague and shaggy line of peaceful co-existence, they preach an alarming new doctrine of destruction.' The paper quoted a psychiatrist who saw the Skinheads as a natural reaction against the Hippie: 'Adults were accepting of the Hippies. People like Peter Sellers copied their clothes and their slang. We all sat around at the weekend saying how splendidly they were behaving on the Isle of Wight. But the youngsters don't want us to like them or to be like them. Thus the climate was right for a period of reaction.'

The paper profiled what it believed to be a typical Skinhead under the heading 'No Love For Johnny' - a 16-year-old who had lived in the East End all his life and had left school at 15. Since leaving he'd had several jobs, packing in an apprenticeship because 'the money was no good,' then becoming a van boy for a laundry - 'it was boring', selling eels on the market - 'money no good', and presently selling eggs near Upton Park tube station, earning £9 for four days. He had been in court seven times for offences such as stealing lead, having an air pistol, possession of a stolen scooter, a smash and grab at a radio shop and, most recently, assault at the football. He's keen to point out that he 'wouldn't bash an old girl over the head to rob her but a bloke… I don't see what's wrong with that.' He's never read a book or set foot in a church, though the former may well have been about to change.

Though virtually non-existent in the movies of the time, the Skinhead, like the Hells Angel, was instead prominently portrayed in New English Library's series of novels chronicling the exploits of Plaistow Skin Joe Hawkins that began in 1970 with 'Skinhead' ('the savage story of Britain's newest teenage cult of violence' according to the blurb). According to Punk/Skin poet Stephen 'Seething' Wells, 'for any kid attending a comprehensive school between

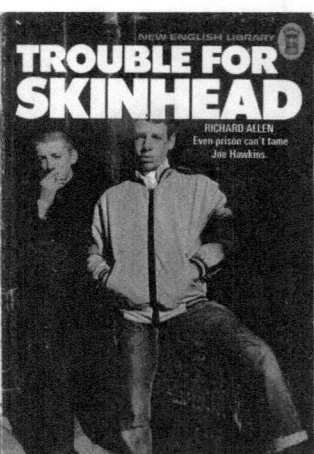

1971 and 1977, Richard Allen's books were required reading… it was New English Library's 'Skinhead' wot provided your sex 'n' violence education.' 'Skinhead' would sell more than a million copies and author Richard Allen would quickly follow it up with 'Suedehead' (71), 'Boot Boys' (72), 'Skinhead Escapes' (72), 'Skinhead Girls' (72), 'Trouble For Skinhead' (73), 'Smoothie' (73), 'Sorts' (73), 'Top Gear Skin' (74), 'Skinhead Farewell' (74), 'Dragon Skins' (75), 'Terrace Terrors' (75), 'Knuckle Girls' (77), 'Punk Rock' (77), 'Mod Rule' (80) – the latter resurrecting Hawkins (killed off six years previous) via his illegitimate offspring (by rape) as its hero.

New English Library, and Allen in particular, was the subject of an episode of the BBC's *Bookmark* programme, **SKINHEAD FAREWELL** (1996), narrated by Tony Blackburn with readings by Ross Kemp and contributions from Bob Tanner, NEL's managing director at the time and editor Peter Haining. At the start of the seventies, despite publishing best-selling authors like Harold Robbins, the company had not made a profit for fifteen years and were looking for something that would appeal beyond the adult mass market to a younger readership. Says Haining: 'There seemed to be this youth market out there who were interested in contemporary things that were happening. Not just about literary far away worlds; what was happening on the streets. We used to have these brain storming sessions… when we would see what was making headlines in the newspapers, what people were discussing, where young people were going, where their interests lay… and use that as the basis for commissioning books on those subjects, which we needed to get out quickly and on sale and catch those markets, because trends, even then, in pop music and whatever were changing very quickly.'

The obvious choice of subject was Skinheads, the selection of a suitable author perhaps less so, certainly to the novels young readership who were convinced the book could only have been written by one of their own. Like those, by then adults, who appear in the programme such as Mick George who was convinced Richard Allen 'must be a Skinhead himself or must be involved in football violence, or had to be in the know how 'cos the way he wrote it was just like real life… he must have been a thug himself, or he must have had friends who were thugs because even if he wasn't, he thought like one in his head, so he was a secret thug.'

On the contrary, the commission was given to the then already middle-aged Canadian James Moffat, a chain-smoking alcoholic living in a cottage by the sea in Sidmouth and for whom the name Richard Allen was one of countless noms de plumes used on his over 290 books. From NEL's purely commercial point of view what Moffat lacked in authenticity was more than compensated by his ability for a fast turnaround - 10,000 words a day when he had a deadline to meet and no going back and re-writing. 'I don't believe in editing. I don't believe in reading more than two pages on the following day,' he says, 'The time given to me for Skinhead's finished manuscript was just over one week. I had to drive to London and venture into a public house seeking those I thought were Skinheads. I found them and said there's a book about the cult being written. Those blokes could not stop telling me everything, they were fantastic… and from them… I had the basic background and Joe Hawkins was born.'

Steve Kelly, interviewed in the programme, was 13 when he picked up his first Richard Allen and speaks for young kids all across the UK when he says: 'They were the only things… apart from Enid Blyton and scrumping in the country, which didn't relate to us in any way. We didn't go to the West Country scrumping apples, we went to the

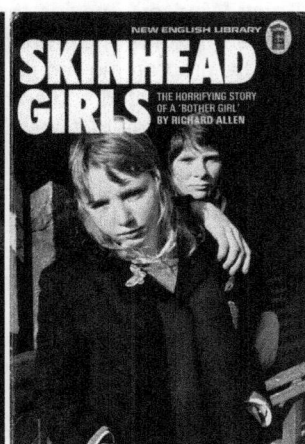

football, we went to Southend on away days on a Bank Holiday. We done those sort of things. That was probably the first book I ever read at school without being bullied into it by a teacher… They were about football, violence and the sex. That's what we wanted as 13-14 year olds. We were right on it.' His eyes visibly light up at this point.

Given the popularity of the NEL titles, while it would be hard to imagine any major film studio dipping a toe into such murky water, such impressive sales figures must have at least piqued the interest of 'exploitation' movie producers. The mix of aggro, sexual violence and extreme racism would probably have been impossible to get past the British censors so the UK industry concentrated instead on 'keeping the British end up' with the *Confessions*… series of sex comedies (themselves based on popular NEL pulp novels) and the many inferior imitations. The only film of the time in which Skinheads made an appearance was *The Breaking of Bumbo* (1970) where a group of football supporters turn up outside Wellington Barracks at the end but are seen off by the Guards. Lacking Skinheads but providing a far more realistic portrayal of football violence was John MacKenzie's *Made* (1972) in which the heroine's young baby is trampled to death by rampaging fans.

Skinheads may not have made much of an impression on the nation's cinema screens but they did begin to crop up in televised drama, thanks largely to a new series from the creator of *Z Cars*, Troy Kennedy Martin. *Softly Softly* was conceived as a replacement for *Z Cars* which was scheduled to be axed following the conclusion of its fifth series in 1965. *Z Cars* received a reprieve of sentence when attempts at a replacement, including twice weekly football soap opera *United!*, failed to live up to expectations and the show ran for a further ten years, initially in a shorter 25 minute format. *Softly Softly* still went ahead however, taking two *Z Cars* characters, DCI Barlow (Stratford Johns) and DI Watt (Frank Windsor), moving them from Newtown, a fictional Merseyside town based on Kirby, to the fictional region of Wyvern, somewhere near Bristol, in a series that concentrated solely on the CID officers of a regional crime squad. The programme ran for 5 series until November 1969 when, coinciding with a switch to colour, Barlow and Watts were promoted and sent to a task force in the southeast in the unimaginatively named *Softly Softly: Taskforce* where the change to 'special operations' would bring them into contact with the then still topical Skinhead subculture.

From the outset, Skinheads became synonymous with football hooliganism, though the phenomena was already well established by this time. On November 11th 1963 a Daily Mirror headline screamed 'This Must Be Stopped,' as the second dart in two weeks was thrown from the crowd, hitting a Northampton player in the back at Leyton Orient, following a similar incident at Everton. 'The Saturday afternoon playing fields of Britain' the paper said, were becoming 'cheap imitations of Dartmoor during a mutiny or riot time at a Borstal. Throwing toilet rolls, orange peel and apple cores at members of the opposition is the sign of a juvenile delinquent - silly little boys who obviously are the worse off for not having been put over some adults knee and spanked until it really hurt… But to aim darts at a member of the opposing team; to hurl an ink bottle, to send a brick crashing through the window of a visiting team's dressing room - THIS IS GANGSTERISM BROUGHT INTO SPORT!'

In the early days much of the concern was centred around the damage being inflicted on the country's railways. Between 1960 and 1966 there were over 25,000 cases of misconduct or damage of train carriages, with much of this put down to the behaviour of travelling football supporters. By 1969 the argument over who should foot the bill for the extra manpower required to keep order had reached Parliament, with the football clubs who were currently footing the bill, keen to stress the illogicality of the situation, and pointing out that 'We do not charge for policing queues outside theatres, the Albert Hall, railway stations or, etc.'

The government agreed and from October the cost was to be borne by the Police Fund, with MP Merlyn Rees declaring 'the standing arrangements for the exchange of information between police forces about football hooligans on trains has been strengthened, a code of practice to encourage good behaviour by supporters is to be circulated by the Football Association to all League clubs; and there is under consideration a scheme to enable stewards, nominated by the League clubs concerned, to travel on football trains as a part of the plan to prevent disorder.'

But the problem was no longer limited to vandalism on trains. 1968 had begun with the publication of 'Soccer Hooliganism: A Preliminary Report', the result of an inquiry into football hooliganism by a multi-disciplinary team led by Birmingham psychiatrist Dr JA Harrington which summed up hooliganisms appeal: 'In the comforting anonymity of the terraces, the young supporter finds relief from trying to be himself. No longer does he have to strive to be somebody... The crowd makes him free of authority and other irksome social pressures that normally oppress him.'

The Harrington report also addressed the lack of resources and technical and communicative aids needed to control large crowds in and around football grounds, stating that 'the knowledge that they will likely get away with their misdeeds encourages hooliganism.' Clubs were resistant to making any significant advances in these areas because of the financial and administrative burden involved. The Lang Report, published in 1969, looked at measures around the detention of offenders at the ground and of getting known hooligans to 'sign in' on match days. One recommendation that was taken up was for the use of 'an official detention room, where persons can be detained prior to removal to a police station.'

The rather basic nature of football crowd surveillance can be seen in an episode from series 2 of **SOFTLY SOFTLY TASK FORCE: KICK OFF (1971)**. Purportedly a match at the fictitious Kingley United but in reality Chelsea's Stamford Bridge, Superintendent Barlow is supervising crowd control which involves a pair of binoculars on a tripod on a gantry under the stand roof and a walkie talkie with which to communicate with the officers below. In one sequence a sergeant deals with two girls by giving them a clip round the ear and sending one of them off to stand somewhere else. Despite these limited resources and old school tactics the day is deemed successful with only seventeen arrests; 'only four people got on the pitch, only seven were thrown out of the ground... there'll be a train torn apart, maybe shop windows broken' - which for Chelsea v Newcastle, if press reports of the time were anything to go by, is a miracle.

For his report on a match at Stamford Bridge in September 1969 a Daily Express reporter 'went to the game with a contingent of Skinheads, sang with them and took their train home. I would like to say I watched the game with them but... they had come with the one intention of starting trouble. The game was of no interest to them.' He went on, 'the first fan was ejected, struggling, at 2.15 p.m... others followed in a steady procession until 3 p.m. Trouble was not long coming. At twelve minutes past three, Birchenall of Chelsea scored. The effect was instantaneous... and alarming. About 50 Skinheads aged between 15 and 18 surged towards the Chelsea supporters chanting 'All together!' It was a pre-arranged lesson in thuggery. The police were temporarily overwhelmed. For the next two minutes, youngsters punched and kicked each other.'

It was not an issue limited to the capital. On March 28th 1970, the Mirror's front-page headline was 'Skinhead Soccer Armoury Seized'. The report concerned an incident five hours before the kickoff of a north-east derby between Sunderland and Newcastle where a passing panda car had noticed a sack being thrown over the wall and into the stadium. It contained 'more than fifty weapons - including bottles, knives, spikes, carving forks, scissors, chisels, hammer heads and lead piping.'

At the end of the following season Labour MP Dennis Howell established a working party on crowd safety and football violence, at one point controversially drawing a football pitch surrounded by land mines with machine gun turrets trained on the terraces. One feels that he might have been only partially joking. Other methods of crowd control being mooted were moats filled with water, wire fencing, and identity cards. The series 1 episode **SOFTLY SOFTLY TASK FORCE: THE AGGRO BOY (1970)** even makes the case for all-seater stadia. Said producer

Hippies, Skinheads, Rastas, Punks & Disco Dancing Bowie Boot Boys

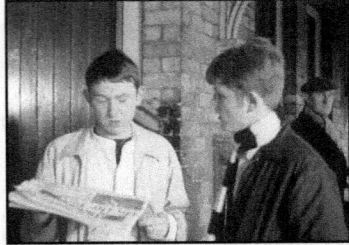

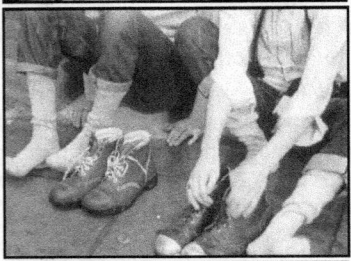

Leonard Lewis 'We make the point that a lot of kids who go to matches aren't the slightest bit interested in the game at all. We don't come up with any conclusions but the point is made that better, more luxurious accommodation might help.'

As the episode begins, it's Saturday morning and preparations are being made for the big match. A groundsman checks the seating, tightening the odd screw where necessary whilst another flattens a clump of turf. The proprietor of Sam's Hot Dog Stall sorts out his buns, a seller prepares his bundles of match day programmes and the local constabulary prepare for this week's hooligan invasion. Likewise preparing for what they bill as an important south east derby is sixteen-year-old Dixie (Charles Bolton). He's invested in some new clobber, much to the amusement of his parents. 'What's the idea of the funny shirt?' asks his mother. His father used to have a shirt like that, she says, 'When he worked on the docks. He used to wear it for work. Union shirt, that's what they call them don't they.' His piece de resistance is hidden in the sideboard - cherry red bovver boots with yellow laces to match his yellow braces. Hidden elsewhere in the kitchen is a cosh.

'Going to work on a building site are you?' asks his dad (Windsor Davies), 'Do a bit of navvying? When I was in the army all I wanted to do was get that stuff off, grow my hair. Why don't you join the army son? Get that lot free.' 'Does he know what he looks like?' he asks his wife who tells him it's fashion. 'Fashion! He looks like a kid from the ruddy school does his hair.' The references to hair don't quite ring true as once cast as Skinheads involved in football hooliganism, actors Charles Bolton and Barry McCarthy, as his friend Ginger, told producer Leonard Lewis that if they had a 'down to the wood' authentic Skinhead cut it might stop them being offered subsequent roles. 'So we did a sort of compromise hairstyle and everyone was happy,' says Lewis. The changes don't seem to have made their way into script revisions by writer Allan Prior.

We catch up with Dixie and Ginger as they exit the railway station having travelled on the football special. Ginger is already bleeding having cut his hand on a mirror whilst vandalising the train. A heavy police presence outside the ground is on the lookout for potential troublemakers, confiscating anything that might be used as a weapon and even making Skinheads remove their boots, but the two boys wait until the final rush for the turnstiles where they can easily pass unnoticed.

It's hard to imagine football fans being sent into the stadium in their socks but such incidents had already been reported in the press. In October 1969 under the headline 'Skinhead Soccer Fans Get the Order of the Boot', the Daily Express said 'The Skinheads of two towns whose teams meet on Saturday were warned by police yesterday: Leave your boots at home.' Ahead of a match against Everton, Wolverhampton police let it be known that 'the hallmark of the Skinheads' or 'any other offensive clothing' would be banned, emphasising heavy industrial boots.

The cosh comes into use during an incident in the gents just before half time, where Ginger has had to go to tend to a wound, leaving an opposition fan needing hospitalisation. Eventually both boys find themselves amongst those arrested inside the ground and taken to a holding area. Chief Superintendent Barlow has a theory why they do it. 'Because you are scared' he tells Dixie. 'You're scared not to. Your mates come and you're scared not to. They say shout at the opposition and you're scared not to. They say fight the opposition and you are scared not to... When it comes to a fight, you are scared. Scared of what your mates say. "He didn't come. He didn't put the boot in. He didn't use one of these."'

Inspector Watt has his own answer: 'It's easy isn't it. It's the only outlet they have. Rotten job; boring. Tension builds up during the week; come out and take it out on each other. It's tribal. Young man's testing time. Red Indians do it. All tribes do it.' He also has a cure: 'Simple. All seating accommodation. It's the contact makes them aggressive. American football has the same youth problems but no trouble. They all sit. Simple.'

'Can't see that happening,' offers Barlow. 'It would halve the attendances. They're scared. Scared not to. Once they start, scared the rest of them will think they're yellow. We have got to scare 'em more. Make 'em see it's not worth it. They're victims. Victims of the permissive society. No discipline at home, none at school, none at work. No National Service, no army, they skive at work. They are seeing how far they can go and society is sitting back letting them.'

In his review for The Observer, George Melly wrote: 'The young have joined sex and money as the most popular dramatic themes' but couldn't think why, given 'the Skinhead verbal range confined... to a series of noises suggesting an intelligent guess at what old-fashioned children's encyclopaedias used to call the birth of language.' Of *The Aggro Boys*, he said 'The documentary side of it was well done, the confiscation of boots and weapons outside the ground, the beer fuelled boasting... dead-end jobs. Barlow's analysis on the traits as to what makes a Skinhead tick was not only accurate but understanding.' He thought the episode had 'a strong storyline... from Alan Prior' but didn't like the fact that the series had lost its sense of locality with the new format covering the whole of the southeast.

The following November Skinheads appeared on *Coronation Street* in the form of four supporters of the fictional Weatherfield County who descended on the Rovers Return on match day and unnerved the pub's regulars. Minnie Caldwell defends their haircuts as having been normal once though her more battle-hardened friend Ena Sharples is quick to point out that in the good old days they weren't wearing those big boots. When a rosette is set alight, they are asked to leave and it looks like they will kick off until regulars Len Fairclough, Ray Langston and Alf Roberts intervene.

All of which is far more believable than **SIX DAYS OF JUSTICE: WE'LL SUPPORT YOU EVERMORE (1973)**. Writer Shane Connaughton, Oscar nominated with Jim Sheridan for the screenplay for *My Left Foot* (1989), was clearly having an off day when he came up with this episode of Thames Television's courtroom set anthology drama series, which looks at three youths who are appearing in the magistrate's court. They are fifteen-year-olds David (Brian Pettifer) and Herbert (Peter Hugo Daley) and their friend Sunday (Ricky Alleyne) who is 14. Herbert doesn't know when he'll be sixteen and neither does his mother. They are all charged with violent conduct at a football match, with David and Sunday also charged with being in possession of an offensive weapon - a broken walking stick - and causing ABH. Herbert is also facing a charge of obstructing an officer in the execution of his duty. Only David has legal representation.

The victim of the suggested violence is another youth, Ronald (Greg Smith), who tells the court that: 'It was in the first half of the match and this bloke turns round in front of me... and he says "Oi, give me my programme back." I didn't know what he was on about. And then he goes and hits me over the head with his stick. I tried to defend myself, but his two mates joined in. One of 'em kicking, the other waving the broken part of the stick about, which broke over my head.'

The stick belonged to David's granddad which the youth had held onto after helping him to his seat, 'To protect myself like, in case the Bristol lot come in, because last time when we went down there we gave 'em a right pasting.' Despite two of the boys having shoulder length hair and the other a huge afro, they are referred to by a witness as 'them Skinheads, they ought to be strung up from the goalposts after the match is over.'

An unlikely trio of 'Skinheads' in *We'll Support You Evermore*

Hippies, Skinheads, Rastas, Punks & Disco Dancing Bowie Boot Boys

According to the Daily Mirror, August Bank Holiday 1967 saw a break in the usual pattern of Mod-Rocker seaside violence, reporting that at Yarmouth rival gangs were 'drowned by sitar music and overwhelmed by Flower Power.' Hardly likely of course, but even if it were true, by 1969 Skinheads had become the new focus for trouble at British resorts, a staple ingredient of the tabloid press looking for a lurid headline on these typically slow news days. In *Man Alive: The Truth About Hells Angels and Skinheads*, a 16-year-old tells of the buzz he gets from being a Skinhead, 'It's like any group or organisation, if you ask an old war veteran, he would tell you about the sort of common cause... you get in the army, a common feeling. And that's what we get between us. We all think the same, roughly, we all act the same. It unites us... when we all go out in really big gangs it's the sort of feeling that gets inside you, sort of feeling of proudness... like a Bank Holiday Monday at Southend as a matter of fact. There was roughly estimated about a thousand of us almost identically dressed and when we grouped up towards the end of the day... as we walked through the Kursal you couldn't see anything but Skinheads. Tears come to your eyes really, cos there were so many of us - looked fantastic. And we just ran wild.'

By the start of the next decade, the authorities were on the lookout for this influx of crop-haired, big-booted youngsters. **SOFTLY SOFTLY TASK FORCE: SUNDAY SWEET SUNDAY (1970)**, written by Alan Plater, opens with the task force receiving a briefing: 'As you know the sea holds an irresistible attraction for that species known as Skinheads... now this attraction is particularly noticeable on Sunday's, especially when the sun shines and, as you can see, the sun is shining today. On the evidence of previous weeks we can expect a sizeable invasion today.'

Superintendent Watt takes over the reins: 'The essence of the scheme is to take out all the fuses. We meet our friends at the station platform as they get off the train, we check them for offensive weapons and we invite them to leave their braces and bootlaces in our safekeeping until the time comes for them to catch their trains home at the end of their happy day.' Broadcast in August 1970 this is a reference to tactics employed by the police at Southend on the Easter Bank Holiday Monday that year where the police removed braces, shoelaces and belts from hundreds of Skinheads with a police spokesman being quoted as saying 'they wouldn't be much use if they had to fight holding their trousers up. It was more or less the equivalent of de-bagging them.'

It may have made an amusing article for the tabloid press but the tactic didn't prove that successful as there were still 46 arrests for breach of the peace and damage to property. In Skegness on the same day the Young Liberals were holding their conference and 'doled out tea and biscuits to roaming bands of Skinheads in a (fairly successful) peace making effort.' Trouble was also reported at Weston-Super-Mare, Rhyl, Brighton and Great Yarmouth. At Rhyl the trouble was largely between Skinheads and greasers, six of whom appeared in court where a Nazi helmet, a motorcycle starter handle and studded leather belts were produced as evidence of weapons. Two were remanded in custody and the others fined £30 to £50.

What the *Softly Softly* writers wouldn't have known when the script went before the cameras is that this practice was illegal and for the Spring Bank Holiday in May the Southend police were told they could not repeat the action with a spokesman forced to admit 'We have no power to take articles of peoples clothing if they have not done anything.' The Skinheads still made the front page headlines, such as the Daily Mirror's 'Skinheads Hit A Bit Of Bovver' which reported that at Southend the Skinheads were met by a strong police presence at the railway station 'and told to behave themselves - or go home.' The resort reported an almost trouble free day due to the police being, according to one youth, 'so thick on the ground that I would never have got within kicking distance of a bit of aggro.' At Brighton, more than a hundred Guilford Skinheads who arrived on the 9.20 train from Victoria, having boarded at Redhill, Surrey, were met by 20 police officers with dogs and 'marched back to the train and sent on their way in locked carriages.' Skinheads arriving in smaller numbers on later trains were allowed into the town but kept under close police scrutiny and prevented from congregating in large groups.

Like the football stadium in *Aggro Boy*, in *Sunday Sweet Sunday* the seaside resort of Torbay is seen in its 'lull before the storm' period - litter being picked from the beach following that morning's tide, deckchairs being uncovered, the shutters on a rock display being rolled up, donkeys sedately making their way towards the beach. The only hint that this atmosphere might soon be broken is a train hurtling its way past a field of gently grazing cows.

The top brass are still wondering 'why those kids move around in their hundreds and kick seven bells out of other people's property?' 'Maybe because it's other peoples,' offers Watt sarcastically. 'Or maybe because they were misunderstood as young children, in love with their grandmothers, that kind of thing.' With the audience primed for the Skinheads arrival and the sight of slowly approaching trains ramping up the tension further, the expected invasion does not materialise and the Task Force are instead left to seek out miscreants wherever they can find them, including Windsor Davies as a bingo caller at the local amusement arcade and Christopher Beeney as a sea front photographer, reducing costs by not bothering to put film in his camera.

The Birmingham Post said, 'Little happened... but I found it necessary to watch every bit because as always with this programme, everything simple thing that happened had some bearing on the overall story. And even though the day was a failure, as far as the police were concerned, the programme was a success.'

*

George Gently began life as a character in a 1955 crime novel, 'Gently Does It', by author Alan Hunter who would follow its success with a further 45 instalments at the rate of approximately one a year until 1998. In 2007, the BBC resurrected the Inspector for a feature length crime series, moving him from Norfolk to Northumberland. The series period setting allowed *Our Friends in the North* playwright Peter Flannery and his team of writers to set a number of their stories against the then new and always troubling concept of the teenager. Having investigated the murder of a black girl at a Northern Soul all-nighter in the 1968 set *Gently Northern Soul* (2012) as part of the fifth series, by series 7 writers Jim Keeble and Dudi Appleton were able to squeeze in a retrospective look at the original Skinheads in **INSPECTOR GEORGE GENTLY: SON OF A GUN (2015)**.

As Gently (Martin Shaw) and his team relax with a few drinks on Christmas Eve 1969, across town a gang of Skinheads in gas masks are entering a bank. The masks are not the only relics of World War 2 at their disposal as we see when one of the gang riddles the ceiling with a warning burst of machine gun fire. As a threat it is certainly effective but as they leave one young lad grabs hold of a robbers leg and the gun clatters to the floor. It is picked up by a security guard who fires down the street as the gang leave in their waiting getaway car, lucky not to take out passing shoppers as the bullets spray everywhere. The gun has been decommissioned but someone has drilled out the plug and fashioned a new firing pin.

When the police arrive, the security guard has a vague description but no car registration: 'I saw his boots, work-wear, no business being in my bank.' He knows where he feels the blame lies: 'Last week we abolish the death penalty, this week we reap the consequences. Violent little toe-rags with no fear of consequences.'

The getaway car is found abandoned and containing the body of the driver, a young girl. 'Interesting haircut' suggests Gently. 'Trying to look like a bloke?' offers newly promoted Detective Sergeant Rachel Coles (Lisa McGrillis). DS John Bacchus (Lee Ingleby), seemingly the only person in the station to have read a newspaper in the past 12 months, puts them straight: 'She was a Boot Boy. She's one of them Skinheads.' Gently is none the wiser: 'What's that? A fashion statement?' 'No, it's one of them innit', Bacchus says flashing a V-sign, 'It's a

bollocks to you statement. I've seen 'em at the football sir; they all wear these boots... and they wear braces... and they cut their hair short and they call themselves Skinheads and they're nothing but trouble sir.'

The dead girl, who had been struck by a bullet from the gun fired by the security guard, is Lexie Dodds (Emma Lundy) and she had been working at a club frequented by Skinheads. Implying that not all Skinheads are this bad, another Skinhead girl who knows her says she was 'hanging round with some scary buggers around Raven Street flats.'

This view is confirmed by the black manager at the care home she had been a resident of: 'They're not all a bad crowd. They were born to slavery; that's how they see it. Working class with no work. Oppressed by the black and the blue - the priests and the police... I grew up on the stuff the Skinheads listen to now; a little bit of soul, rocksteady, ska. The sounds of liberation.' That was how he had got along, formed a connection, with Lexie.

Enquiries point the police toward Jonjo Burdon (Jody Latham), the leader of a group of Skins who put on a music night at a club called the Long Shed. He is by all accounts 'a monster.' He has also done a short stretch for drugs. 'I thought that was Hippies' offers the out-of-touch Gently. Bacchus explains: 'No, it wasn't weed... Dexinol, some form of amphetamine.' The care home manager says he went along to the club once but didn't like it. Jonjo, he says, 'didn't strike me as a lad who cared about the liberation of an oppressed people.'

When Gently pays a visit to the club, Jonjo confirms everything said of him by immediately smashing his own face into a brick wall. When he, along with a handful of others, is held at the station for questioning he starts a chant which begins as a sort of howl before naturally mutating into 'Oi! Oi! Oi!' and back to a howl. Gently is unimpressed: 'These toe-rags John, what if they're the future? What then eh?'

Rachel goes undercover as a Skinhead girl and learns they are to pull another bank job but not the right bank. Taking inspiration from *The Italian Job*, the robbery takes place on match day and by the time Gently and the team set off the traffic is in deadlock. Not that we see this. For budgetary reasons we see the rear of a stationary bus, and another car, from which Baccus exits, walks to the front and returns to say so.

In a contrived denouement, we learn that the meddling kid from the first bank job, Kit (Patrick McNamee) is the son of an ex-police officer who had been killed on duty and that Gently is close to the boy's mother, who tells him: 'A boy needs a dad, George. And if he doesn't get one he finds his own'. But what Kit really wanted was Lexie who he had spent time with in a children's home with when they were both 11. Though his life had gotten back on track, he has had a crush on her ever since. He had recommissioned a machine gun stolen from his school's cadet force and showed it off to Lexie. She had in turn told Jonjo who had taken the lot, the theft of which, with it being out of term, had gone unnoticed. Jonjo gets his just deserts when one of them backfires.

After a steady soundtrack of Skinhead reggae - Desmond Dekker's 'Israelites', Symarip's 'Skinhead Moonstomp', Joe The Boss's 'The Thief', The Upsetters 'Live Injection' and 'Return of Django' - with the bad guy in jail, order is restored as the episode plays out to the sound of Fleetwood Mac's 'Albatross'.

When, amidst the climate of rising youth unemployment during the late 1970s, which would spiral on upwards through the 80s, right wing political parties began targeting disaffected working class youth, Skinhead was already making a comeback amongst a large section of the Punk community disillusioned by that movement's move from the street to the mainstream. Many of these new Skinheads were easy targets for the extreme right and by the early 1980s they had created an image of the Skinheads as inherently racist that has endured ever since, no matter how hard most Skinheads since have tried to distance themselves from it. Two documentary films have since attempted to reclaim the movement to its late sixties origins and at the core of both directors argument is the original Skinheads love of an emerging sound called reggae.

The Skinheads predilection for Jamaican music has its origins with their older siblings adoption of ska, which had appeared in Jamaica around 1961 and was soon adopted by that country's lower class youth before becoming popular with white working class Mods in the UK thanks to labels like Blue Beat who popularised the music on this side of the Atlantic. Blue Beat was founded by Siggy Jackson in 1960 as a subsidiary of Emil Shalli's Melodisc, itself formed in London in 1947 courtesy of a war pension awarded to Shalli for his role in the conflict spying behind enemy lines for the Allies. After a string of Duke Reid produced singles, the Blue Beat template was set by Prince Buster's debut for the label, 'Oh Carolina' by the Folkes Brothers, its heavier guitar courtesy of original Skatalite Jah Jerry helping formulate what would become the standard Blue Beat sound on singles by the likes of Laurel Aitken, Derrick Morgan and Owen Gray, many of which were produced in London using Mod stalwarts like organist Georgie Fame.

In the ghettos of the newly independent Jamaica of the time a section of the island's disgruntled young men christened 'Rude Boys' were making headlines with their violent and antisocial behaviour. The rude boys were quickly immortalised on record, first on Stranger Cole's 'Ruff and Tough', produced by Duke Reid, and subsequently on the Wailers debut single 'Simmer Down'. As well as the music, the Rude Boys sense of style - sharp suits, thin ties, topped by pork pie or Trilby hats - also found favour in the developing Mod scene.

After several years and over 200, now highly collectable, releases Blue Beat called it a day in 1967 as ska began to give way to the new slower and tighter rocksteady beat which evolved out of the Rude Boys desire to look cool whilst dancing. Via 45s such as Alton Ellis's 'Girl I've Got a Date', Hopeton Lewis's 'Take It Easy', Derrick Morgan's 'Tougher Than Tough' and 'Hold Them' by Roy Shirley rocksteady would quickly, albeit briefly, become the dominant force in Jamaican music.

By the spring of 1968 as Skinheads began to appear in London's East End, a new more flexible rhythm had developed via records such as Larry And Alvin's 'Nanny Goat' and the Beltones' 'No More Heartaches' before becoming a bona fide genre with the Pioneers 'Long Shot (Bus' Me Bet) before being given a name check on the Maytals 'Do The Reggay'. In the UK Jamaican music also had an important new home in Trojan Records which was launched in July 1968 by Island's Chris Blackwell and Lee Gopthal of distributor B&C, using the name of a defunct Island subsidiary that had been used for a number of releases from producer Duke Reid. The new label managed a minor hit in July 1969 with Tony Tribe's cover of Neil Diamond's 'Red Red Wine' which reached #46.

Trojan was not the only player in the burgeoning UK market however and the first UK reggae hit was released on Pyramid, a subsidiary of Doctor Bird, a label formed by Australian sound engineer Graeme Goodall who had built Jamaica's first dedicated recording studio and co-founded Island with Leslie Kong and Chris Blackwell before falling out with the latter and moving to the UK. Goodall hit the big time by remixing Desmond Dekker's 'Poor Me, Israelites' which had proved popular in the clubs but did not attract airplay, releasing it in the UK as 'Israelites', where it sold over two million copies and topped the singles chart in March 1969.

Also beating Trojan into the top end of the charts was its major rival during the Skinhead years, the north London based Pama Records, formed in 1967 by brothers Harry, Jeff and Carl Palmer. Pama impacted the British charts, via subsidiary Unity, with their 1968 release of Max Romeo's 'Wet Dream' which made it into the lower regions of the charts in May 1969 and slowly but surely made it all the way to #10 in August on the strength of over a quarter of a million sales, despite its sexually explicit lyrics meaning it was only played twice by the BBC before being banned.

In October 1969 Trojan had its first major hit with Jimmy Cliff's 'Wonderful World Beautiful People' as the Skinheads adoption of the music as its own began to drive up sales and create further chart hits for the label,

'Liquidator' by Harry J's All Stars on Trojan subsidiary Harry J, and the Pioneers 'Long Shot Kick The Bucket' reaching #9 and #21 respectively that same month. A #5 hit for the Upsetters with 'Return of Django' would make it a very healthy month for reggae. Lacking Trojan's distribution, Pama would continue to achieve healthy sales figures through specialist retailers but an inability to reach the chart return shops would mean the label would have no further bona fide hits.

All this chart activity did not go unnoticed by other artists and producers who began to court the Skinhead audience by producing 'Skinhead reggae' - though all reggae released between 1969 and 1971 was essentially Skinhead reggae. The best known of these was Symarip's 'Skinhead Moonstomp', a re-working of Derrick Morgan's now largely forgotten 'Moon Hop' despite it having reached #49 in January 1970 and the Symarip version failing to chart at the time. 'Skinhead Moonstomp' did reach #54 in 1980 during the height of 2 Tone but it was the album of the same name that became an essential accoutrement. Symarip were a London based band who had been around in several guises since the early sixties, and in 1969 were known as the Pyramids and under contract with Eddie Grant. Says 'Mr Symarip' Roy Ellis: 'The album 'Skinhead Moonstomp' was a jam thing. We were just there because we had the studio free. We were just jamming in the 4-tracks studio as we had nothing else to do. Then we tried to put the record out but couldn't because we were still under contract with Eddy Grant. We couldn't use the name to put out our record or they would put us to court. They told us we could never use the name Pyramids to promote the record, so we spelled the name back way without the D.' This much-re-issued album with its cover photo of 5 Skinheads, the band appearing on the reverse, has since sold, according to some sources, over 7 million copies.

Another major player in the Skinhead market was entrepreneur Joe Mansano who had arrived in North London in 1963 intending to sell cosmetics to the growing West Indian population. That Mansano knew little about cosmetics was compensated by a knowledge of Jamaican music which moved from being a sideline to his core business after attending a course in manufacturing and promotion held by EMI and he hit on the idea of paying for 30 minutes studio time to record advertisements for popular DJs - 'Blazing Fire will put fire in your wire... by the flick of my wrist another musical twist' - which he would add to the beginning of existing records and press onto one-off dubplates which, he says, was 'an excellent way of advertising not only the DJ's name, but it also gave this particular record a distinct advantage because it received more airplay than the other records.'

After a spell working with Graeme Goodall at his record shop and label, Mansano was offered his own shop 'Joe's Records' as part of Trojan, from where he also moved into production and was eventually given his own subsidiary label, Joe, where he had a minor success with Rico & the Rudies 'Brixton Cat' featuring legendary Dandy Livingstone and Specials trombonist Rico Rodriguez, after it received airplay on Tony Blackburn's breakfast show. In 1970 Mansano began to concentrate on the Skinhead market with a series of releases, including the popular 'Skinhead Revolt' by Joe the Boss: 'There was a white Skinhead called Shaun who used to help sell records in the shop, and also helped with the sound in the studio. He would say "No, alter that" or "bring that in" to make the record sound right for the Skinheads. I always felt very safe with the Skinheads and shaped the sound for them.'

Eddie Grant may have missed out on the Symarip recordings but along with Brixton based Hot Rod sound system owner Lambert Briscoe in 1970 he formed the Torpedo label to cash in on the craze, issuing instrumental tracks with titles like 'Skinhead Moondust' and 'Skinheads Don't Fear' both by the Hot Rod All Stars. Briscoe also ran a short lived Trojan imprint called Hot Rod which released the Hot Rod All Stars 'Skinhead Speaks His Mind'.

None of these cash-in singles contained anything remotely near the quality needed to trouble the charts but Trojan continued its assault through to 1971 where Dave & Ansell Collins reached the UK top spot with the wonderful 'Double Barrel' after which the original Skinheads had grown up and their younger brothers had grown both their hair and the width of their trousers. They began to instead stomp their boots to the sounds of the burgeoning Glam scene as Trojan began to dilute their recordings by overlaying them with strings. In January 1973 the love affair was over as the NME declared 'Suddenly Reggae Is Up... After Being Almost Bottled To Death By Skins.' With Palma struggling to stay afloat, Harry Palmer bit the hand that had fed him by telling the paper: 'When reggae started to establish itself in the charts, the Skinheads came along and ruined it. We lost half our accounts because shops refused to stock reggae.'

The alliance of white and black working class youth in early 70s Britain would always be a precarious one and

Hippies, Skinheads, Rastas, Punks & Disco Dancing Bowie Boot Boys

1972 proved to be a key year in the end of this honeymoon, when 'Skins' attacked second-generation blacks during rioting in Toxteth, Liverpool. It would be fair to say that Richard Allen's novels probably didn't help. Joe Hawkins racism didn't concern itself solely with 'paki-bashing', for him 'Smashing a few Wog heads open always gave him greater satisfaction than bashing those bleeding Chelsea supporters.'

*

No one has tried harder to redress the balance than director Doug Aubrey does in his documentary **WORLD OF SKINHEAD (1994)** which he saw as 'a way to set things straight about a much maligned and hi-jacked youth sub cult.' Channel 4 commissioned the film, he says, 'Despite the panic from within [their] legal department that they were giving money away to fascists'. Aubrey nevertheless found himself in the enviable position of being 'pretty much left alone to go out on a journey in the world to make our film, even though our production company, Pictorial Heroes, didn't come from the usual North London / BBC / Oxbridge documentary making tradition.'

The film opens with the declaration that 'This is the story of transformation between youth and manhood, a time when a young man must set forth on a voyage into the world. To gain his feathers, become a brave, to adorn arrows in his quest for knowledge and respect' but soon becomes a quest to prove that, as we're informed by a Skinhead in Portland, Oregon, it's the 'most multi-cultural culture in the world,' whilst the director shoehorns in footage of a few black and Asian Skinheads. These are mainly based in the United States but include Barry from High Wycombe who tells us 'If white people have a problem with Skinheads, I think, well, you don't have a clue, mate.' Barry is also the subject of a 1986 photo, Barry's Haircut, which resides in the V&A museum and was taken by fellow 80s High Wycombe Skin Gavin Watson, who also appears in the film. The rest of the opening ten minute mantra includes Symond Lawes, also from High Wycombe and latterly the promoter of the Great Skinhead Reunion, a yearly event in Brighton, who talks about those who become Skinheads for 'the wrong reason' and footage from the BBC's *Man Alive: What's The Truth About Hells Angels and Skinheads?* (1969) programme that shows the solitary black youth amongst those crowded round the ping-pong table - but avoids the racist talk that follows it.

There's a short section on the clothes and on getting that all-important haircut of which Lawes says: 'My dad punched me in the face, my mum quite liked it' and another on the violence of which a member of the infamous Tilbury Skins says: 'In my view being a Skinhead was all about violence, and that's it. Whether it was Paki's, blacks, football supporters, whatever - violence.' When the programme reluctantly gets round to Oi!, it is represented by Roddy Moreno, singer with anti-racist band The Oppressed who assures us: 'The only bad reputation Oi! music has got really, is because of the White Noise bands, the fascist Punk bands, and they don't call themselves Oi!, they call themselves nationalist rock or some crap like that. But real Oi! has never had anything to do with fascist politics or anything like that.' Which is stretching the truth somewhat. The 'nationalist rock' fraternity are represented by Paul Burnley of No Remorse who, even less convincingly, tries to persuade us that white pride doesn't involve hating anyone. The Tilbury Skins likewise fail to convince with their assertion that 'Everyone says all the Skinheads are Nazis and that, and there's no way we're Nazis. My father fought against Nazi's in the war… the anti-Paki League was different, that doesn't make us Nazis.'

The programme ends on a high note when it gets off the defensive, beginning with a photo montage backed by Cock Sparrer's classic teenage anthem 'Because They're Young' from 1994's 'Guilty As Charged' album; a lyric they could never have written in 1977 when they were young. After which Gavin Watson tells us 'I think it should be remembered for the beauty of youth and how people can make

Don Letts finds that Skinheads come in all shapes and sizes

something better out of their environment, out of their selves, even if it's for a couple of years before they go off to drink beer and become a fat slob. It doesn't matter. For those two years they believe in themselves.' 'Just the fun of being a youth' says Roddy Moreno, that's really what being a Skinhead was all about.'

In *World Of Skinhead*, Paul Burnley says: 'People harp on about the old days, in the 60s… with the reggae music and stuff, even back then there were racist Skinheads, but not so much affiliated to political parties.' Moreno, on the other hand says: 'If you ain't got the nerve to stand by your roots, it's time you hung up your boots.' In **SKINHEAD (2018)** legendary director Don Letts, best known for his Punk credentials, does indeed harp on about the 60s as he looks at the history of the subculture from those very roots up to the present with an emphasis on the influence of the Jamaican rude boys and reggae that he feels has been lost among the far more enduring images of football hooliganism and violent racism. Like Aubrey he too wants to rid the cult of its racist reputation and instead paint the early days of the movement as a bastion of multicultural harmony but Letts does mention an early run in he had with a bunch of Skinheads who 'definitely weren't on side' and suggests that in the seventies 'the ugly intolerance common in these years entered the bloodstream of Skinhead' and illustrates the point with the *Man Alive* clip that *World of Skinhead* avoided.

Letts begins his documentary by asking his audience: 'What do you think when you hear the word 'Skinhead'? Violence? Intolerance? Hatred? This image was born in the 1970s, when this youth driven subculture earned a reputation for trouble on the streets and terraces and a toxic association with racism. But that's not how it started, and it's certainly not what it meant to me. There was a time we were united on the dance floor, dressed to kill and, if only for a moment, it felt like colour didn't matter.' To back this up, we have Gary Bushell inform us that: 'Skinhead was always a multicultural thing. Skinhead was born of a mixed marriage between Jamaican culture and white working-class London culture, Cockney culture. That's what it always was. So, for any of these idiots to come along later and say, "No, it's a racist thing," how can it be racist? How can you be so ignorant of the roots of the thing you're trying to be?'

Letts also includes a present day interview with original Skinhead Paul Thompson who became the writer of a short-lived Skinhead column entitled 'Yell' in International Times after he had read an article critical of Skinheads and marched into their offices demanding 'they should help set up a magazine for us instead of slagging us off. God knows why I said that, but their response was, in effect, "Like… far out… like, wow… like, why don't you be editor… like, too much, man …"'

Regardless of what Gary Bushell might want you to believe, nothing was multicultural at the birth of Skinhead. For the vast majority of the white public, not only did they not want black faces in their street, they also didn't want them in the Street. *Coronation Street* executive producer Harry Kershaw, celebrating 8 years of the soap in the Daily Mirror during December 1968, told the paper: 'We made only one big mistake with the Street. We should have had a coloured family in one of the houses right from the start. We couldn't bring a coloured family in now. The viewers wouldn't accept it.' A professor of psychology at Manchester University concurs: 'Peoples feelings are too disturbed - particularly by Enoch Powellism… They would not welcome this disruption in the Street they have grown up with.' True a great number of white kids had, unlike the previous generation, black friends and there was even the odd black Skinhead but for most this tolerance only went so far as any white girl who had sex with him would soon find out, as Steve Thompson the articulate young Skinhead featured in *Man Alive* has pointed out: in an online interview: 'If a white girl went with black boys she was generally thought untouchable. As for South Asians, the problem was that there was no point of contact with the white kids that could have given them obvious common ground.'

On the whole though, like *World Of Skinhead*, the talking heads in *Skinhead* are heavily weighted towards the post Punk era including many of the same faces. The film illustrates the case for the scene's multicultural origins with footage of both black and white youths, including a few Skinheads, sharing the same dancefloor - the implication being that because Skinheads listened to black music, they couldn't be racist. Really? A similar argument to Bushell's is put forward in *This Is England* (2006) by Combo, telling Milky he was an original Skinhead in 1969: 'It was people like your uncle that introduced [black music] to me. The soul of that music just resonated with us, you know. It was unity. It was black and white together. You know what I mean'. That of course did not end at all well. Sure, Skinhead wasn't 'born' as a racist thing but to say that most so-called 'original' Skinheads weren't racist doesn't ring true in a society in which racist was the default setting, not least amongst the working class.

Despite Don Letts assertion that 'I'm guessing some of the white kids parents were a little racist', if their offspring weren't, the heads of most white working-class homes were racist, even those that would be quick to point out they weren't, though God forbid their daughters should bring home a black boyfriend where a typical defence for any objection would not be because they were racist but that the rest of society was. 'It wouldn't be fair on your children' was a well-worn remark.

While most kids at the time would have heard casual racism from the adults in their home environment, at school, though racist teachers existed, such views were scarcer. And at school age anyway, the perceived wisdom of parents and teachers has always carried a lot less weight than that with which they hoped it was laden. In the nation's factories and shop floors, for those school leavers lucky to find themselves a place from the shrinking opportunities, adults would suddenly become their peers and their views more eagerly taken on board. Cliff Cummings, a shopkeeper in Liverpool 8 at the time of the 1980s riots, sums this up in *Voices From The Ghetto*, an edition of the BBC's *Panorama* broadcast in 1985: 'Black children and white children, they go to school together from form 1, day one. They leave school together and as soon as they get to 18, 17, they part company. Why? The

system has driven them apart.' It's a process we see neatly laid out in Horace Ove's *Pressure* (1975) where black British recent school leaver Tony realises he faces a different future to his white school mates because the adult world, from landladies to personnel officers, was determined to keep them apart.

In his book 'The Way We Wore', Robert Elms, old enough in 1969 to wear the clothes but not old enough for them to fit, says 'The relationship between Skinheads and West Indians was bizarre and complex. On the one hand, there is no doubt that some Skinheads were racist. All right, let's be horribly honest, most all Skinheads were racist, in the way that sadly most British people were racist at the time, when the language of 'Paki' and 'Wog' was commonplace amongst the supremacist verbiage of a dying empire.' This is backed up by Benjamin Bowling's book, 'Violent Racism: Victimisation, Policing and Social Context', which points out that in London's East End over a three-month period in 1970 there were 150 people seriously injured in 'Paki bashing' incidents.

*

The Sex Pistols last-minute appearance on the show in 1976 wasn't the first time that Thames TV's *Today* programme had resulted in newspaper outrage. An episode featuring Skinheads, broadcast during April 1970 resulted in the Daily Mirror banner headline, 'Yard Hunts 3 Paki Bashers', after Labour MP for Paddington North, Arthur Latham, saw the programme and contacted the Director of Public Prosecutions, resulting in the programmes producer, Nicholas Mellersh, being interviewed by the police. 'There's a new word around - Paki bashing. The beating up of Pakistanis by Skinheads just for the hell of it. It is the growing 'bloodsport' of the streets. A vicious, cowardly kind of sport which must be stamped out,' said the paper, its outrage brought on by a trio of 'East End bovver boys' describing 'in sickening detail how they go about their work.' First jostling the victim, then 'As they go down you give them a good kicking, bash them with an iron bar…'

Richard Allen's 'Skinhead' came under fire at Lincolnshire Assizes in January 1971 when the book, found by police at the home of a defendant, was used as mitigation by the defence barrister in the trial of a gang of ten teenagers who had been on a Paki bashing spree. The book was said to have encouraged, or at the very least given examples of, how young people could conduct themselves. Eight of the ten were nevertheless sent to Borstal or detention centres.

'Paki kicking' had in fact already featured in two BBC documentaries, first in BBC1's *Free For All: Truce*, some 5 months earlier in November 1969, and then in BBC2's *Man Alive: What's The Truth About Skinheads and Hells Angels?*, broadcast the following month. In the first programme, Skinheads, Hells Angels,

Hippies and Greasers were collected together in the studio and interviewed by presenters Amanda Theunissen and Paddy Feeny. *Free For All Truce* was not aiming to be highbrow. What programme in which a Greaser and a Skinhead each eat a raw egg off the floor could be? 'People sitting in armchairs at home seeing this are going to blow their minds,' it was suggested. There was a consensus among the subjects that the press and television were guilty of over emphasising the violence but, Hippies aside, all present showed a propensity for aggro - 'Violence? You name it, we do it' boasted an Angel; 'Paki kicking is their favourite sport' offered a girl member of the Skinheads. Shocking stuff but that said, these early Skinheads were probably far more tolerant than their parents and older siblings.

Most Skinheads distinguished between West Indians and Asians, the former seen as less of a threat to their supposed sense of identity because the two cultures were not that removed from each other, whereas the emphasis on family and achievement of the Asians placed them closer to the middle classes. Black youths were also far more likely to be just as tough as the Skinheads were and willing to stand up for themselves.

One characteristic that distinguished the Skinheads of '68 and '69 from their later incarnations was their age, generally not much older than the mid-teens. At this age there was more tolerance, especially for the young West Indian kids with whom most had grown up and who, according to one young Skin in the *Man Alive* programme, 'don't like Paki's either.' This is confirmed by Dotun Adebayo of X-Press Books and Radio 5 Live who as a youngster was 'adopted' by his local Skins and lapped up Richard Allen's novels: 'I hate to say this today but I think, in fact, because a lot of racism was focussed on people of Asian origin, as a twelve-year-old Afro-Caribbean in London, I didn't feel as uncomfortable with it - as politically incorrect as that sounds today - as if it was perhaps an NF book and straight out against blacks from Africa & Caribbean.'

Two-thirds of the *Man Alive* programme is dedicated to the so-called Hells Angels but the Skinhead section begins with footage of Chelsea Skinheads away at Newcastle United which is followed by an interview with some of the young Skinheads. The highlight is the 16-year-old printer's assistant Steve Thompson who is interviewed at home with his mum and dad, himself a former Teddy Boy, who realises from his own experiences that his son will soon move on. Despite not having a problem with racism, Steve is a bright and articulate young man, with an IQ which is probably greater than all the bikers shown beforehand combined, who knows "It'll die out I suppose. All cults, they don't last very long. The Teddy Boys, the Mods and the Rockers, now you've got us. We'll last for a little bit longer I suppose, then summat new will come along but until then there's us.'

This sense of inevitability seems to have seeped into the rest of his life and is depressing in one so young and seemingly capable of more. It's class, not race, that seems to be his overriding bugbear. 'Really, I just go to work to earn some money to go out at weekends. That's as far as it goes now. I used to really think about work, 'cos when I was at school I always wanted to be a journalist but that sort of fell through. I went for an interview once... and the interviewer had all the information about me in front of him and as soon as he realised I come from the East End... it sort of put a barrier between us. Sat there and said, "Oh, you come from the East End do you? Oh, that's very nice." That sort of tone. I thought to hell with it if they're going to stick up snobbery in front of you. I just didn't bother any more, so I got the first job that came along... There's just no breaking away from this area. People put you in classes, like middle and upper, and if you're stuck in one you'll be like that all your life. I thought I could get out of it but I've come to my senses and seen that I can't, so why try? I'd rather be with people like me.' Being a Skinhead, he asserts, brings him 'security, something you wouldn't get anywhere else.'

*

In December 1970, the Observer declared, 'Skinheads hang up their boots. London Skinheads have disbanded. When we weren't looking, the Bovver Boys slipped out of their braces, grew their hair long and quietly de-mobbed. Football club secretaries, policemen... and hairdressers have all known about it for some time. Mr Gordon Borland, Secretary of Millwall Football Club, once the home of the Lion's Den Mob, was happy to admit last week he had not seen a Skinhead around the place for months, "I think they're a dying breed."' By way of confirmation the broadsheet asked 'Paddy behind the bar at the Upland Tavern in Crystal Palace Road, South London,' who told them, 'Skinheads, they were a flash in the pan, weren't they?' and 'Chris, who is 16, and works as a furniture porter,' who said 'there was a possibility that we might see some Skinheads lingering in out-of-the-way places like Kent.' Though in serious decline, the Skinheads, of course, never really went away but instead took a pace or two backwards, growing their hair and becoming Suedeheads, Smoothies and Boot Boys.

Barney Platts-Mills may have left school on his fifteenth birthday, but a background befitting of his double-barrelled moniker would buffer him from the realities of life that would have faced the young cast, and characters, of his debut feature film **BRONCO BULLFROG (1969)**. Platts-Mills was the public school educated son of a former Labour MP, who, likewise, also felt at home rubbing shoulders with the lower orders in his career as a celebrated defence council for the likes of the Great Train Robbers and the Kray twins. When chatting to director Lewis Gilbert at the cricket, the father mentioned his son was talking of becoming an actor. Gilbert suggested a better career might be had on the other side of the camera and fixed the boy up with a third assistant editor's job at Shepperton Studios, working on movies including *Spartacus* (1960) and *A Kind of Loving* (1962).

From there he became an editor at Granada, working on current affairs series *World In Action*, and at Anglia where he edited nature series *Survival* before forming his own production company with the financial support of the Premier Viscount of Ireland - another benefit of a privileged upbringing. 'All my business partners were millionaires,' he admits, 'which helped in getting bank loans.' The company produced a number of documentaries, including *St. Christopher* (1967) on the 'special' school of the same name and, importantly, *Everybody's An Actor Shakespeare Said* (1968), both directed by Platts-Mills. The latter film looked at the Play Barn and some of its attendees. Housed in a factory warehouse on Martin Street, the Play Barn was a drama workshop started at Joan Littlewood's Theatre Workshop to occupy the local teenagers who would hang around during her tenure at the Theatre Royal in Stratford and be a constant source of minor vandalism. At the workshop Littlewood taught them all about acting and Platts-Mills about directing actors, telling him 'Don't let the buggers sit down or they'll go to sleep on you.'

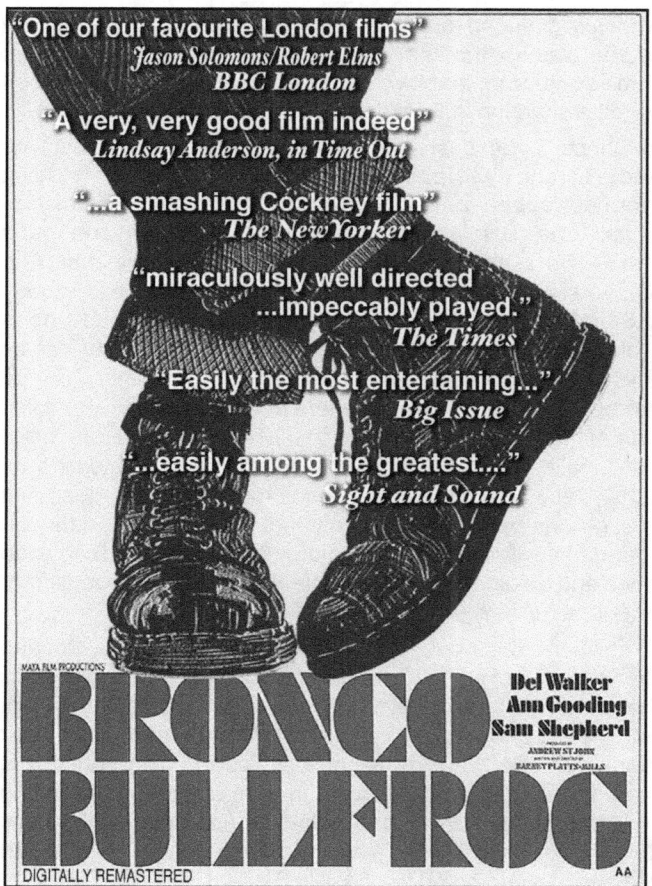

Among the youngsters interviewed in the film was 16-year-old apprentice plumber Del Walker, whose enthusiasm for the project runs only as far as 'it's better than hanging about the streets.' Despite its success, the Play Barn closed the following year, and the boys approached Platts-Mills with the idea of making what they called 'a proper film.' Initially daunted by the prospect, Platts-Mills convinced himself to go ahead: 'What did I know about film theory? Very little, but I knew what neo-realism was. As I understood it, Rossellini proposed that one take a neighbourhood and make a film to represent or reflect that place by using the stories that emerged from people's experience, and by getting the people themselves to act them out in their natural locations. I thought I could manage that.'

Such a project would require a commitment from the young cast and so, says Platts-Mills: 'To film Bronco we got them 6 weeks off work – because they all had apprenticeships – got them holidays and gave them twice their normal pay. So they were well looked after. But the kids had no aspirations to be an actor. The whole thing was an end in itself – very little consciousness of going anywhere with it, which I can't help feeling would not be the case today. There was no *Eastenders* then, or indeed very little other opportunities for young actors.'

Bronco Bullfrog opens with four lads breaking into a café. It's hardly the crime of the century as the till contents amount to a meagre 9d and the jukebox is empty. But at least there are some cakes and after

The East End stars of the film without stars

pooling their money there's enough for seventeen-year-old Del (Del Walker) to pay into the cinema and let the others in through the fire exit. Following an altercation in which they trip another youth and tell him to stay out of their area, the evening ends at their 'gang hut' in a derelict building where the conversation revolves around the news that Jo (Sam Shepherd), also known as Bronco Bullfrog, is out of prison.

Del works as an apprentice welder and has an eye for the opposite sex but is far from a smooth talker as we see when an encounter with two girls in the local café results in an awkward silence. When his father wins £400 and contributes the outstanding balance on the BSA motorcycle Del has been saving for, the youngster finds the bravado to call at the home of the girl, fifteen-year-old Irene (Anne Gooding), from the encounter in the café. 'Is your daughter in?' he asks. 'Which one?' 'About that high, slim, long hair.' It again may not be the smoothest of patter but a date is arranged for the next evening.

This relationship provides the story's foundation and, says the director, came from 'a youth who came to my house... in London, several years before. A sixteen-year-old boy painting the house came with his girlfriend and they were on the run from the law because she was six months younger than him. Fifteen, and that was a crime apparently, and I was quite shocked by that... I imposed that story on a situation in East London.'

The romance flourishes, though neither set of parents are impressed. His can't see past the fact that Irene's father is doing time for armed robbery and if that wasn't bad enough he's also of Italian stock. 'She's just like her mother, too good for anyone round this street... The sooner you get rid of her the bloody better. And her father, you know where he came from, bloody I-tie he is, bloody Ricardo Spaghetti. You know where you'll finish up. Where he is now. In bloody nick if you don't watch yourself. Get rid of her as soon as you can.' This advice is echoed by Irene's mother, 'You go out with a boy like that, you know where you'll finish up?' she asks, 'You wanna finish up with a boy like that? He'll never be any good to you. He'll never amount to anything.' Mum's concern stems from the fact that Del wears boots and doesn't have a job. He does, but she's having none of it. The concern is not unjustified as, although neither parent knows it, Del and his mates have recently done a job with Bronco and an older accomplice, stealing electronic goods from a container in a railway yard.

Having nowhere to conduct their blossoming relationship, Del and Irene hit on the idea of going to stay with his uncle in the country. It is a plan that, consistent with what we have learnt about the youngsters previously, hasn't been thought through. When they arrive at their destination, well after dark, he's not even sure which house it is so they are forced to spend the night in a café. The next morning they're told they are welcome for the day but no longer, so it's back to London and round to Bronco's where the couple are given a bed but have Bronco sleeping on the floor at the foot of it.

Knowing that his girlfriend is the under age of consent, Del seeks the advice of his employer on what he should do. That he should take her home and be in work by lunchtime is the older man's not unexpected reply. Unfortunately, the police have tracked them to Bronco's flat and now all three are on the run; except there's nowhere to run to.

Some critics lauded the film, with the Evening Standard's Alexander Walker saying 'It sets your heart leaping,' and The Times calling it 'a piece of neo-realism far more rigorous and effective than anything the Italians attempted even in the movement's heyday. One can only hope it is given a chance to reach the audience it deserves.' In the United States, where it was released with subtitles, The New Yorker declared it 'a smashing and pretty sobering cockney film.'

Despite this positive press coverage, the film was unceremoniously pulled from its Cameo Poly showcase 18 days later to accommodate *Three Sisters* (1969). In response, Sam Shepherd organised a demo involving about 200 young East Enders, chanting and jeering as the then 20-year-old Princess Anne arrived to see the premiere of the Laurence Olivier film. The incident was picked up by the press with a Daily Telegraph headline announcing 'Princess Anne Met by Skinhead Mob at Film Premiere.' The Princess Royal would later accept Sam's invitation to see *Bronco Bullfrog* at the Mile End ABC where according to the young actor (while Irene's mother was railing at her daughter's taste in boys): 'She turned to me and said, "My mum was like that". It took me a minute to twig that she was talking about the Queen.'

The director followed *Bronco Bullfrog* with another feature, *Private Road* (1971) which picked up the top award, the Golden Leopard, at the Locarno International Film Festival in Switzerland but then gave up producing despite being offered the money to do so, feeling it 'irrational if we couldn't make them work financially.' Independent cinema, he decided 'was a lie then, and it's a lie now. Film is just a way of showing off Tom Cruise's underpants.'

The cast were even less prolific than their director, with none of them going on to other drama projects, because suggests Platts-Mills: 'Their style of acting was Joan's style of acting. There's no place for that in the RSC. And Sir Peter Hall doesn't like it either, the cunt.' Sam went to work in pubs and on the barrows at Spitalfields market whilst Anne flirted with a modelling career that quickly faltered, sadly dying of a brain haemorrhage, on a dance floor, at 50. Del continued with his trade, working as a plumber, latterly on the Isle of Wight.

For years, the film was forgotten until its unique setting struck a chord with students of Mods, Skinheads, and other youth sub-cultures. *Bronco Bullfrog*, might have been made in 1969, but Stratford, E15, was both culturally and geographically a long way from Carnaby Street, the King's Road, Chelsea, and other so-called centres of swinging London and as such the film is a unique time capsule of the transition of Skinheads into Suedeheads and Smoothies. In the mid-1980s, however, it was almost lost forever when the master negative was thrown on a processing rubbish tip. 'Fortunately one of the graders saw it there, and picked it up and sent it to the archive,' recalls Platts-Mills. 'Otherwise the negative would have gone forever. Film is a very ephemeral business. Here today, gone tomorrow.' Now it's deemed worthy of restoration and screenings at the BFI who packaged it alongside a booklet and the directors Play Barn documentary on DVD and Blu-Ray where it was again lauded by a new generation of critics.

More measured appraisals were offered by members of the cast when contacted by the Guardian at the time of the BFI release. Sam Shepherd found the film's growing cult status baffling: 'I look at the old streets, the motors, the clothes. But that's about it. I remember at the time, this film critic, Alexander Walker, he said, "This is a film that will be talked about in years to come." And I thought, "You're mad" What do people get out of it today? They're mad. I mean, does it say anything to you at all?' What it was, he says, was 'An honest film with dodgy acting, dodgy actors. We were all like that in those days. Turn your back and we'd have nicked the camera,' and in doing so unwittingly describes why the film is so good.

By the end of 1970 Skinhead had become a catch-all term for young, delinquent, white working-class boys, most of whom were by this time trying to get their hair to reach their shoulders. It is one such gang of 'Skinheads' who was the subject of an edition of Thames Television's *This Week*, presented by David Dimbleby in 1972. The programme visits the Falkner estate in Liverpool 8 where, over four consecutive August nights, said gang clashed with black and mixed race youths from nearby Granby who had been called to the neighbourhood by the under siege residents. Though both sets of youths talk about petrol bombs, the disturbance seemed largely limited to the breaking of windows.

For the adults on the estate, the tension centres on housing. The newly built Faulkner estate had become home to former residents of nearby Granby who were moved from the dilapidated terraced housing that had been targeted for slum clearance. The new estate's nearest neighbours on the predominantly white Windsor Gardens estate were unhappy with this, especially those who had spent years on the waiting list for a move. The tenement blocks of the Windsor Gardens were hardly palaces themselves.

Though widely reported as race riots, the impression given from the interviews with the young lads themselves is that the trouble stems more from two neighbouring gangs from segregated neighbourhoods with little else to do with their time. Asked about their 'coloured' neighbours, the consensus amongst the so-called Skinheads is that 'they're alright' and blame three or four trouble makers, whilst one black youth says the Skinheads were 'beating up any person in sight, black or white.' Just one of the white youths, the only one bearing any resemblance to an actual Skinhead, frames his response in clearly racist language, referring to 'coons'.

As one white youth says: 'They've got less than us. Most of them coloured fellas have got a bum steer. They have, I don't care what anybody says. They haven't got jobs, they've got no club or nothing... they've got nowhere to go. You can't blame them really for fighting... looking for trouble, because they've got nothing else to do, really.'

It's a point of view echoed in the voice over by Dimbleby: 'When unemployment becomes a national problem, here it becomes a national disaster. There are no exact figures, but with 15% of Liverpool's youths out of work, over 30% of the city's young blacks are likely to have no jobs. But many of them are no longer prepared to accept the lot forced on their parents and grandparents.'

In a forewarning of more volatile times ahead, police aggression comes in for criticism from both sides, heard mainly on this occasion from the white community, one such youth claiming they're arrested 9 to 1 because the police are frightened of being accused of discrimination, though the programme says both communities have made similar complaints. As soon as it was established in 1970, the Liverpool Community Relations Commission was said to be overwhelmed by complaints of harassment by the police with a programme on Radio Merseyside claiming that 'in certain police stations, particularly in the city centre, brutality and drug planting and the harassing of minority groups takes place regularly'.

In the late 1960s singer Frankie Vaughan had fronted a well-meaning anti-gang campaign in the Easterhouse area of Glasgow which ended in a half-hearted weapons amnesty. If his relevance to young hoodlums was questionable then, it was perplexing when removed from mothballs in 1971 to open **ALL DRESSED UP & GOING NOWHERE (1971)**, a new take on the conflict between Skinheads and Hells Angels, this time in the north-east. He tells the viewers: 'Any young people today who are causing problems and causing vandalism and hooliganism; they're doing it because they want to be noticed... They'll create gangs, they'll create murders to be noticed, to show the public, to tell the public "Look, you're not providing the things we want. We want to have a bit of fun, we want a bit of danger, we want the hazards of life."'

To the sound of The Who's 'Won't Get Fooled Again,' we are told that violent crime has soared by 17% in the past year and it 'is there, round the corner... Gangs of youths, some of them 100 strong, roam the city. To them, violence means survival. It's excitement, and it's become instinctive. Street battles flourish as young people flock to one or the other - Skinheads against Hairies.'

The programme concentrates on a group of lads calling themselves the Scotswood Aggro Boys who unsurprisingly revel in the attention. Elsewhere, the programme offers little in the way of insight apart from the fact that boys, as the saying goes, will be boys. A police spokesman says: 'We find the hooliganism is taking place in the main for no apparent reason. It seems to be a form of amusement or pleasure.' Both groups exaggerate wildly, blame each other, with each claiming they are being singled out by the police. Sociologist Stanley Cohen, best known for his work on the Mods and Rockers of the previous decade, pops up to blame the bad design of council housing that offers little for the youths before the programme plays out to The Who's 'Behind Blue Eyes'.

A follow-up programme, broadcast on regional TV news programme *Inside Out* some four decades later, re-united some of the Scotswood boys, by then well into middle-age and with teenagers of their own. In the original programme, gang leader Geordie's dad believes the answer to the gang problem is to meet violence with violence and threatens to 'slot him off the four walls' if the police come to the door. Geordie has no such problems as his grandson, now the age he was when the original programme went out, reassuringly wouldn't dream of such behaviour so perhaps the veteran North East presenter Mike Neville was right when in his introduction to the original broadcast he said the city was being 'reshaped, remodelled for the future', and giving 'the young the flavour of a new life.'

In **SOFTLY SOFTLY: TASK FORCE: SAFE IN THE STREETS (1970)**, an Asian man leaves his house after dark where a few girls are playing on the street corner as he passes. One of the girls runs off and is seen talking to a group of young Skinheads. Before he can do anything about it, the Asian man finds himself halfway down an alley with one half of the gang of Skinheads at each end. 'Go on, put the boot in' eggs on a girl to her boyfriend who dutifully obliges.

'They say they attack us to make us go back home' says a doctor at the hospital where the victim is subsequently treated for three broken ribs and fifteen stitches to the face, 'In that case why do they take our money?' Not long after this the same gang hurl a brick through the window of an Asian-owned shop. Like the previous victim, the shopkeeper is reluctant to involve the police.

'Rough young devils' suggests Watt. 'Country's full of them... Bunged up to their eyes on welfare state milk; orange juice. Have the best food the working class ever had. All that mad young masculine energy and nothing to spend it on,' offers Barlow. 'Nothing? We've heard all this before. When I was their age...' 'You were at school, John.' 'Like heck I was.' 'Oh, well you were clever.' 'I had to work.' 'Yeah, well they don't believe in that... not the way we did. I mean they'll graft some dead-end job, they're not fit for anything better.' 'They could get better if they shaped.' 'They can't shape John. They're victims of their environment they are. They are the Ds and Es of our society. Advertising jargon... the people who buy the least expect the least. They're the dregs. The sort of people Hitler recruited.' 'And there's no Hitler round here for them to join.' 'Just as well. They've got this street terrorised.'

The talk again reverts to why? 'All these young men' says Barlow, 'All this energy. Maybe not enough of the right sort of youth clubs to wear it off?' Watt is unconvinced: 'They wouldn't even join a strip club this lot, let alone a youth club.' 'With the right sort of propaganda they might.' 'You'd have to tear the street down first.' 'The streets aren't so bad. You wanna see New York.' 'Our streets are gonna get bad if we don't do something about it.' 'Like what? Huh? You know there's a climate, has been a climate for a long time that says, "Take it easy on the sods on the path". Fines of ten and twelve quid even in serious cases.' 'There's only one thing you can do with yobs like that once you get the bit between the teeth, that's bloody clobber them.' 'So let's bloody clobber them,' concludes Barlow as the two finally agree.

In the Observer, George Melly found 'nothing easy or sentimental' about the episode, and praised its 'subtle ironies', saying writer Allan Prior had 'managed to present the giggling psychopath as repulsive and yet pitiful... There was no attempt to soften anything, but the violence was used absolutely justifiably to force us to ask why... it was a remarkable programme.'

Like Clockwork
(Geldof, Briquette, Crowe)

Although the original 1969 Skinheads have had no movie made specifically about them, their presence on the streets of Britain and across the headlines of its newspapers would influence Bonar Canonero, the costume designer of a planned adaptation of Anthony Burgess' cult novel 'A Clockwork Orange'. Looking at the country's many youth gangs for inspiration he concluded, 'the notorious Skinheads [...] were the most dangerous of all. Their striking, conspicuous look, which used grotesque elements, was very frightening. Their freakish ways inspired my idea of the Droogs.'

Whether, as Stephen Spielberg stated, Stanley Kubrick's 1971 masterpiece was 'the first Punk rock movie' is open to debate, but it's certainly the first Skinhead movie. The Skinheads, who by the time of the movie's release had already mutated into various splinter groups, reciprocated by attending the cinemas in droves. Some suedeheads would also pay tribute by wearing bowler hats, but also accessorising this City Gent look with the addition of an umbrella which says George Martin, author of 'Spirit of 69 – A Skinhead Bible', served 'to aid and abet a few rounds of fisticuffs.' In the words of author Tony Parsons, then a Skinhead himself, 'Someone had been paying attention, and we were flattered beyond belief.'

'A Clockwork Orange' was one of a quartet of novels hurriedly written during what has been called author Anthony Burgess's 'pseudo terminal year', 1960, after he had been mis-diagnosed with a brain tumour and given a year to live. The writer was influenced by the Teddy Boys who he had seen congregating in coffee bars during his leave from an overseas British Colonial Services posting at the tail end of the 1950s when, due to their high profile involvement in the rioting around Notting Hill, their reputation for violence peaked. He first considered setting a proposed novel in the past. Said Burgess, 'I at first thought of making my new novel a historical one dealing with a particular apprentice's riot in 1590s, when young thugs beat up women who sold eggs and butter at prices considered too high, with perhaps William Shakespeare breaking his hip when slithering on a pavement greasy with blood and eggyyolk.'

The book, which turned out very different, was finished in 1960 but was a hard sell in getting it published. Speaking in 1974, Burgess said, 'In those days people were very squeamish, in 1960, in England, only then for the first time was it possible to buy a copy of 'Lady Chatterley's Lover' in its unabridged form, it's only just over ten years ago. The climate has changed fundamentally in ten years, that it's very hard for us now to believe what life was really like in the 1960s.' Indeed, publishing house Heinemann would still have been reeling from their 1954 prosecution under the Obscene Publications Act 1857 over the publication of Walter Baxter's homosexual themed novel, 'The Image and the Search'. In that case, when the jury could not agree after two trials, the defendants were acquitted, but this prosecution would most certainly have been behind the publisher's decision in 1959 to reject Nabokov's 'Lolita', despite having published all of his earlier novels. Two of Burgess's books had already attracted expensive libel actions, and one of them, 1961s 'The Worm and the Ring', was pulled from circulation.

When 'A Clockwork Orange' finally appeared in 1962 the British critics were lukewarm, and occasionally scathing, like the Times Literary Supplement who called it 'A vicious verbiage... which is the swag-bellied offspring of decay.' Maire Lynd, the in-house fiction reader for Heinemann, writing before publication, thought the book 'fascinating but rather hard work to read and... only indirectly funny.' She concluded that 'With luck the book will be a big success and give the teenagers a new language. But it might be an enormous flop. Certainly nothing in-between.' It managed both, thanks largely to a film by Stanley Kubrick.

The novel was first dramatised in 1962 by the BBC's *Tonight* programme, using excerpts from the first three chapters. With a good nine million people watching *Tonight*, the author supposed, rather optimistically, that at least one percent of those would buy his book. Says Burgess, 'I would become moderately rich; I had the accolade of a television appearance and would now be a sort of public personality.' But the book sold worse than his previous novels.

Andy Warhol also used parts of the novel for *Vinyl* (1965) which renames Alex as Victor but is barely recognisable as Burgess's work. There were other attempts to transfer the novel to the big screen. Says the author: 'A clothing store tycoon in America, movie struck since he was a kid, was establishing a production company... he had read all the books I had written and found them cinematic... he would begin by setting up *A Clockwork Orange*... my four delinquents were variously to be turned into mini-skirted girls and violent old aged pensioners. The serious music crap was to be eliminated and hard rock substituted.'

A screenplay by Michael Cooper and Terry Southern was rumoured to be considering casting Mick Jagger as Alex and his fellow Rolling Stones at the droogs. The Beatles even sent a petition and addressed it to Terry Southern. Signed by all the fab four as well as Marianne Faithfull and Peter Blake, it read, 'We the undersigned, Do Hereby Protest With Extreme Vehemence As Well As Shattered Illusions (In You) The Preference of David Hemmings Above Mick Jagger For The Role Of Alex In *A Clockwork Orange*.' Burgess himself had also penned a script and Nic Roeg was at one point provisionally pencilled in to direct that version.

In May 1967, London International acting on behalf of Paramount presented the BBFC with the Cooper & Southern script. The reception from the censor was damning with reader Audrey Field concluding: 'The script does of course contain a moral message which I take to be an indictment of a world in which violence is the only law and human beings are programmed like computers. But I think it presents an insuperable obstacle from our point of view if we still hold... that an unrelieved diet of vicious violence and hooliganism by teenagers is not fit for other teenagers to see. The dialogue is a specialised sort of slang... but the general intention (crude violence and obscenity) is always plain and the visuals, however restrained, could not possibly get even into the 'X' category, unless we are willing to turn our existing standards upside down for the sake of this one film. In my opinion, this would be ill-advised.'

In a Britain of the near future – 'just as soon as you could imagine it, but not too far ahead – it's just not today, that's all' – teenage Alex (Malcolm McDowell) and the three members of his gang. Dim (Warren Clarke), Georgie (James Marcus) and Pete (Michael Tarn) are one among several street gangs who rule the night. On the evening that the film opens, the foursome down their drug-laced milk in the Korova Milk Bar. Upon leaving they beat up a drunken old tramp in a pedestrian underpass simply because Alex abhors the idea of 'a drunk old man'. They then fight a rival gang in a derelict casino and go on a wild high-speed joyride into the countryside where they viciously beat an upper-middle-class writer and gang rape his wife. They conclude their evening's entertainment back in their favourite milk bar where, much to Alex's delight, a woman is singing a selection form 'Beethoven's 9th'. Dim, who does not share his leader's love of the classics, is admonished for showing disrespect with a rap across the knees from Alex's cane.

After a day spent bunking off school, having sex with two young girls he meets in a record store (one of them played by *Beat Girl*'s Gillian Hills), when the gang meet up again, Dim and Georgie challenge Alex's authority, calling for a 'new way,' abandoning their usual itinerary of mindless violence and petty thievery for bigger crimes. When Alex violently reasserts his authority, his droogs avenge themselves by hitting him over the head with a milk bottle and leaving him unconscious at the scene of a robbery in which the householder has died, to face the police and a fourteen year prison sentence.

After serving two years, and with the promise of an early release, Alex volunteers himself as a guinea pig for an experimental rehabilitation programme known as the Ludovico Technique. Via a combination of drugs and a series of films depicting rape, violence, and fascism, he becomes averse to any aggressive or libidinous urges. The treatment brainwashes him so effectively that he becomes a helpless victim, incapable of defending himself and nauseated by all his former passions including, inadvertently, his love of Beethoven, whose music has been used to soundtrack the films.

Out of prison, Alex is confronted and punished by those he has wronged in the past, including the tramp, and his former friends who by now are using their violent tendencies for the 'good' of society as police officers. Finally, trapped in the house of the writer whose previous attack by Alex has left him somewhat deranged and intent on revenge, Alex is driven to throw himself out of an upstairs window in a failed attempt at suicide. With the former poster boy for the Ludoviko Technique now threatening to become a publicity nightmare for the government-sponsored treatment, Alex is deprogrammed and given a cushy job in the civil service. 'I was cured all right' he says, the smirk spread across his face leaving the sentence dripping with a bitter irony as, cured, the removal of his physical castration leaves him free to partake in ultra-violence and in the old in-out once more.

This was not the way Burgess intended the story to end, and the British editions of the novel feature a final chapter omitted from American imprints in which Alex grows up, grows bored with violence and opts instead for a more conventional future with a wife and son, whom he does not want to turn out like himself. Kubrick did not read this version until nearing the end of his draft of the screenplay, having been previously unaware of its existence. He anyway says he found it, 'unconvincing and inconsistent with the style and intent of the book. I wouldn't be surprised to learn that the publisher had somehow prevailed upon Burgess to tack on the extra chapter against his better judgement, so the book would end on a more positive note. I certainly never gave any serious consideration to using it.'

McDowell, who has called the missing last chapter 'a rip off,' was perhaps getting his conversations mixed up in the passing of time when he suggested that Burgess was 'told to do it by the publisher who said "Look this is going to make it very difficult if you don't make him acceptable." So he told me he just banged it out in two hours. So it's not the original story at all.' This seems unlikely as the publisher's house reader Maire Lynd, writing before publication called the ending 'a little soggy.. but the rest of the book is pretty cynical. No one escapes.'

This opinion is in keeping with that of the novel's American publisher, who, says Burgess in a new introduction, 'A Clockwork Orange Resucked', 'believed that my twenty-first chapter was a sell-out,' and insisted on leaving it out of American editions, a compromise the author, in need of an advance, reluctantly accepted. Burgess suggests, 'Such a book would be sensational and so it is. But I do not think it is a fair picture of human life.'

For Burgess, as a Catholic concerned with sin and free will, *A Clockwork Orange* was intended as a morality tale about the dangers of attempting to eliminate evil by robbing people of free will. Behavioural psychology, as propounded by psychologists John B Watson and BF Skinner, who believed that the experiments conducted by Pavlov in the behaviour modification of animals could be applied to human beings, was a hot topic at the time. Burgess was not a fan, calling Skinner's best-known work, 'Beyond Freedom & Dignity', which argued that behavioural modification was the key to an ideal society, 'one of the most dangerous books ever written.' This sociological argument is best expounded in TS Elliot's essay on Baudelaire: 'So far as we are human, what we must do must be either evil or good; So far as we do evil or good, we are human; and it is better, in a paradoxical way, to do evil than to do nothing; at least we exist. It is true to say that the glory of man is his capacity for salvation; it is also true to say that his glory is his capacity for damnation.'

For Kubrick, this aspect was secondary. The question of the morality of the Government's compliance in trying to change Alex's nature through brainwashing was, he thought, 'an interesting level, it serves to provide the structure of the plot, but I don't think that it's actually from this aspect that the story derives its uniqueness of power.' The real power of the story, he suggested 'is in the character of Alex, who wins you over somehow like Richard III despite his wickedness, because of his intelligence and wit and total honesty. He represents the id, the savage repressed side of our nature which guiltlessly enjoys the same pleasures of rape.'

At the heart of the character of Alex is violence and Kubrick, who had found there was a hypocrisy shown towards the subject, is not afraid to revel in it. 'Everyone is fascinated by violence,' he said. 'After all, man is the most remorseless killer who ever stalked the earth. Our interest in violence in part reflects the fact that on the subconscious level we're very little different from our prehistoric ancestors.' Skids frontman Richard Jobson, whose own *16 Years of Alcohol* (2004) is heavily influenced by Kubrick's film, agrees. 'There's a mechanism in the male dynamic that's drawn towards that stuff,' he says. 'I find it really odd when people deny that. It seems almost unreal now but for a young guy living in a completely grey world, it was an incredibly liberating experience in many ways and one that translated beautifully for me into rock n roll.'

Stanley Kubrick's approach to the casting process is simple: 'I try to hire the best actors in the world,' he says. 'The problem is one a conductor might face. There's little joy in trying to get a magnificent performance from a student orchestra. It's difficult enough to get one with all the subtleties and nuances you might want out of the greatest orchestra in the world. You want to have great virtuoso soloists, and so with actors... You can make a mediocre actor less mediocre, you can make a terrible actor mediocre, but you cannot go very far without the magic.' It seems impossible to picture *A Clockwork Orange* without the magic that Malcolm McDowell brings to the role of Alex, in a performance that, in the almost fifty years since his face filled the screen in the opening shot, has inflated the character to become bigger than the movie itself.

For some critics, the director's pleasure in the wickedness of his leading character and his self-proclaimed desire 'to show that it was great fun for him, the happiest part of his life,' stepped over the line. Pauline Kael at the New Yorker was perhaps the loudest in her condemnation. 'Kubrick,' she said, 'has assumed the deformed, self-righteous perspective of a vicious young punk who says, "Everything's rotten. Why shouldn't I do what I want? They're worse than I am"... I can't accept that Kubrick is merely reflecting this post-assassinations, post-Manson mood; I think he wants to dig it.'

With Kubrick feeling: 'It was necessary to find a way of stylising the violence, just as Burgess does by his writing style,' the result is often exhilarating in its grace and beauty such as the sequence where Alex responds to his droogs rebelling against his domination of them. In slow motion Alex first beats two of his friends with a cane, tosses them into a river, then kneels to offer a helping hand to Dim whilst surreptitiously unsheathing a blade and running it across his friend's hand. The music of Rossini adds to the ballet of the carefully choreographed sequence as the screen fills with a close-up of McDowell's leering face.

It is Kubrick's artistic interpretation of the novel's sexual violence that many found especially troubling. Part of the film's most famous sequence, during the home invasion of the writer and his wife, just after Alex had done his 'Singing in the Rain' sequence and prepares to rape the wife, is described in the book as:

'So he did the strong-man on the devotchka, who was still creech creech creeching away in a very horrorshow four-in-a-bar locking her rookers from the back, while I ripped away at this and that and the other, the others going haw haw haw still, and real good horrorshow grrodies they were that then exhibited their pink glazzies, O my brothers, while I untrussed and got ready for the plunge.'

Kubrick composes the scene from floor level, with Alex kneeling in the right foreground of the frame speaking directly to the camera with the phallic nose of his mask jutting out towards it. On the left, deep in the background before a large painting of a garden, the writer's nude wife stands, held from behind by one of the droogs.

Burgess got an early insight into how audiences would react when he attended a public screening in New York and discovered 'The violence of the action moved them deeply, especially the blacks who stood up to shout, "Right on, man" but the theology passed over their coiffures.' McDowell meanwhile found himself 'driving around in Hammersmith and seeing half a dozen kids in white with the codpieces and the bowlers and the eyelashes. I went, "Wow, people are really taking it seriously." I was horrified.'

Vincent Canby's assessment in the New York Times that *A Clockwork Orange* 'makes real and important the kind

of fears simply exploited by other, much lesser films,' was typical, the film winning the New York Times Critics Circle Award for best picture and also an Academy Award nomination in the same category - losing out to *The French Connection*.

Dissenting voices like that of Kael were in a small minority but were loud and pulled no punches. Roger Ebert called it 'talky and boring... an ideological mess, a paranoid right-wing fantasy masquerading as an Orwellian warning.' Leslie Halliwell hit harder than most, calling *A Clockwork Orange* 'a repulsive film in which intellectuals have found acres of social and political meaning, the average judgement is likely to remain that it is pretentious and nasty rubbish for sick minds who do not mind jazzed up images and incoherent sound.'

That *A Clockwork Orange*, a movie essentially about juvenile delinquency, would cause consternation amongst the nation's moral guardians was not too surprising given that the comparatively tame Marlon Brando biker movie *The Wild One*, banned outright by the BBFC in 1954, had only finally been passed fit for public consumption as recently as 1968. The controversy began immediately with, Labour MP Maurice Edelman saying, 'I believe when *A Clockwork Orange* is generally released, it will lead to a clockwork cult which will magnify teenage violence. The phallic dress of the droogs with their codpieces will no doubt become as widespread as the sub-Western gear in the high street imitated from Western films.'

It was left to Anthony Burgess to come to the work's defence, saying: 'Mr Edelman is assuming that man is a sort of naked ape whose imitative faculty is such that it cannot resist copying what it sees. I doubt it... I had to show that God made man free to choose either good or evil, and that it is an astonishing gift. It would pay viewers of the film better to ponder the real sin, that of taking away this divine bestowal of human freedom of choice.'

Burgess's words would fall on deaf ears and before long the anti-Porn campaigner Raymond Blackburn was announcing his intention to sue the BBFC. Lord Longford said the rape rate was increasing in London and claimed the film should never have been released. Both views were confirmed by Mary Whitehouse who said, the 'sick and violent film is indeed showing signs of affecting human behaviour.'

The film's cause wasn't helped when reports started appearing on the crime pages of the press, such as that of 15-year-old ex-Grammar School boy Richard Palmer who had followed sixty-year-old tramp David McManus from the Swan public house in Fenny, Stratford. Palmer had been in the pub discussing the film, which he had not seen, with friends, when the tramp had been cadging cigarettes from the drinkers. Once outside Palmer beat McManus to death in the porch of a nearby church.

When arrested the next day, Palmer told police that friends had told him about the film 'and the beating up of an old boy like this one.' At trial it was suggested by the prosecution that the act 'may have been carried out for excitement as a result of the film,' an angle the defence lawyers were also eager to pursue, saying 'the link between this crime and sensational literature, particularly *A Clockwork Orange*, is established beyond any reasonable doubt.' Three months earlier the Sunday Times had reported on a group of clergymen who had spent time living rough with drop-outs in London and been witness to the violence being inflicted on down and outs by youths, with one calling it 'straight out of *A Clockwork Orange*... the down and outs around me said this sort of thing never happened before *A Clockwork Orange* was shown.'

Some reported incidents did have links with Kubrick's movie, such as in the case of the group of British youths who sang 'Singing in the Rain' while raping a seventeen-year-old Dutch girl on a camping trip in Lancashire. Others though stretched credibility way beyond breaking point, with even the police occasionally getting caught up in the hysteria. When Frank Boulton, a 50-year-old wood seller, was murdered in Newton-le-Williams in May 1973, despite no evidence to support their rationale, detectives started a search for a 'Clockwork Orange gang'. The Daily Mail quoted a police spokesman as saying: 'Teenagers in Newton-le-Williams have been buying similar make-up and dress to that used in the film. Special squads have been detailed to check out fancy dress shops in the area... The comparison with facts in the film are being followed up as a strong line of inquiry.' An excuse for an afternoon at the cinema and a chance to buy a pair of plastic boobs to wear at the Inspector's leaving do perhaps.

Causation was never proved, despite the remarks of some, including those who should know better. Sentencing a 16-year-old youth to Borstal for savagely beating a younger boy whilst wearing white overalls, black bowler hat and combat boots, Judge Desmond Bailey said, 'We must stamp out this horrible trend which has been inspired by this wretched film. We appreciate what you did was inspired by that wicked film, but that does not mean that you are not blameworthy.' Writing in the journal Human Communication, David Stewart summed up the ridiculousness of Bailey's statement: 'If this was the logic of the court system of the Seventies, then The Beatles might well have been on trial for the song 'Helter Skelter' being linked to the crimes of Charles Manson or Kool-Aid being the culprit of mass-murder rather than Jim Jones.'

By October 1976 the Times reported of an advocate, Mr AH Kerrigan, in Edinburgh as saying: 'I have been instructed in three separate murder trials of relevance to this point, and having studied the brief prepared for my solicitors at the subsequent consultation with each of the three accused it became clear that the accused had committed the crime of murder and in considering the possibility of the accused's fitness to plead I explored the reasons for their action... I discovered in each of these cases that there was a direct link between viewing of the film and the imitation of the action of the main character within that film... On one occasion the individuals were actually wearing the distinctive clothing which was part of the fantasy of the film.' By this time however, Mr Kerrigan's worries were unfounded, the film had not been shown in the United Kingdom for three years and would remain largely unseen for some time to come.

In April 1972, Stanley Kubrick wrote to the Detroit News complaining about censorship after the newspaper had refused to review or advertise the film because of its X rating. An editorial in the paper, but not singling out Kubrick, declared: 'In our view, a sick motion picture industry is using pornography and appeal to prurience to bolster theatre attendance: quite simply, we do not want to assist them in the process.' The director told them: 'There is no power, legal or otherwise, which should be exercised against the rights of adults to select their own entertainment. High standards of moral behaviour can only be achieved by the coercive effect of the law.'

A year later *A Clockwork Orange* would face censorship, not from the press or the BBFC but from a much more unlikely direction. The director himself quietly withdrew the movie in the UK once its 61 week run had ended; the ban only coming to light after the National Film Theatre requested a copy to show in a retrospective of the director's work six years later. It was originally thought that the movie had been removed due to the aforementioned spate of supposed copycat or 'inspired' incidents and the resultant negative publicity. This was never realistic when similar occurrences had also been a feature of the movie's after life across the Atlantic, including the very high profile failed assassination attempt of Alabama Governor George Wallace by the supposedly *A Clockwork Orange* fixated, and future inspiration for *Taxi Driver*, Arthur Bremer, with the would be assassin saying that after seeing the movie he imagined himself as McDowell's Alex.

Says Kubrick's wife Christine: 'Suddenly Stanley was blamed for every crime ever. So, it became frightening, because we had Mary Whitehouse, and all these other religious moral groups write to us and write in a way that wasn't so religious or moral. And finally, somebody really threatened us and the police came. I always had my head in the sand about the whole thing, but suddenly it was really scary. There were people in front of the house and asking the children questions.' The right of violent youths to exercise free will did not extend to the point where it threatened the Kubrick family safety.

Following the death of its director in 1999, the film was given a limited UK cinema run and a DVD release to great fanfare and zero controversy, though certain tabloid reporters have continued to try shoehorn the movie onto their crime pages. The Sun, in November 2005, claimed 'Clockwork Orange Nut Killed Lovers' in its report on 47-year-old Peter Foster in Bridlington who had battered two of his live-in lovers to death thirteen years apart. The paper said he had an 'unnatural interest' in the movie and recited the Lord's Prayer backwards whilst dressed as the film's villain.

Alex takes a selfie in *A Clockwork Orange*

In 2006, the Daily Mail were really clutching at straws when their headline called 14-year-old Chelsea O'Mahoney 'A Clockwork Orange Killer'. And the tenuous connection? 'Like the fictional droogs in Stanley Kubrick's 1971 film... Chelsea and her male accomplices carried out sadistic attacks purely 'for kicks' on random, defenceless victims. Like the film, their stomping ground was a warren of dusky passageways, this time on London's South Bank, and like the film, their assaults were triggered by code words. One of the gang, sometimes Chelsea, would say "You know what time it is."'

By now though the film was more at home in advertisements for products like Stella Artois, who depicted a gang of droogs slurping milk in a sleepy Korova milk bar in sleepy middle England. Or in family friendly cartoon series on tea-time television. It's a turnaround Malcolm McDowell finds in no way surprising; 'When we made the film 40 years ago, we made it as a comedy, albeit a very black one. There was a lot of humour, but when it came out, because it was so startling and shocking, people just sat there dead silent... Now audiences take it how we meant it. They have a really good time and laugh. They have caught up with it.'

Whether it's the Blur video for 'The Universal', Bowie's 'say droogie don't crash here!' line in 'Suffragete City' or the Nadsat used in the lyrics of 'Girl Loves Me' from his last album, 'Blackstar', Heaven 17's use of Burgess's name for a fictional pop group, likewise Moloko's appropriation of the droogs beverage of choice, or Brazilian metalheads Sepultra's 2009 *A Clockwork Orange* themed concept album 'A-Lex', both the film and novel have provided inspiration for artists from all corners of the musical spectrum. Ziggy-era Bowie's use of 'Beethoven's Ninth Symphony', may have been the first to incorporate *A Clockwork Orange* into a live setting, but Madonna wore an all-black ensemble involving a cage vest, the longline bra, skin-tight shorts, knee pads and a bowler hat for a 'Bob Fosse-meets-Clockwork Orange' rendition of 'Keep It Together' on her 1990 Blond Ambition Tour and in a case of 'anything you can do', Kylie Minogue, accompanied by truncheon-wielding droogs in red codpieces, donned a bowler hat and white jumpsuit for 'Spinning Around' in her 2002 live shows.

On television, *The Simpsons* would turn to *A Clockwork Orange* time and again, with Homer, thinking it would help teach him to tell the time, buying Bart the *A Clockwork Orange* video for his fifth birthday. Bart poses as Alex in the 1992 episode *Treehouse of Horror III*; likewise Maggie in *Treehouse of Horror XXI*. There's a shot-for-shot recreation of Alex's press conference escapade with a naked woman in 1993s *Duffless*; as well as numerous Ludoviko references in episodes such as *Homer Goes to College* and *Dog of Death*. The list goes on. Not to be outdone, to an accompaniment of Rossini's 'The Thieving Magpie', *South Park*'s Cartman's alter-ego, in season 14s *The Coon*, hands out a vicious beating to his superhero friends Mosquito and Mint Berry Crunch in order to consolidate his influence over his band of crime fighters.

On the big screen, Danny Boyle paid homage to the Moloko milk bar in *Trainspotting*'s Volcano Club, Heath Ledger channelled McDowell's Alex to Oscar glory for his portrayal of the Joker in *The Dark Knight*, whilst even Quentin Tarantino's juxtaposition of Stealers Wheel and a severed ear in *Reservoir Dogs* was inspired by McDowell's Gene Kelly moment. Richard E Grant saw the movie as a 14-year-old growing up in the colonial outpost of Swaziland and recreated the incident in his directorial debut *Wah Wah* (2006), having gained admission by flattering the cinema manageress that she looked like Elizabeth Taylor, 'Although she was actually an extremely grotesque, toad-like version of her.'

As the young Grant watches from the stalls, his face is dissolved into that of McDowell's Alex. Later, the youngster adopts the single eyelash. Says Grant; 'Putting on that eyelash in a town as conservative as the one I grew up in was a fairly bold thing to do. It annoyed people, but I never went round beating up tramps. I suppose it was the feeling that Alex takes on the system. When you're an adolescent, you feel as though you've got to confront the world in some way.'

Grant may have felt emboldened, but nearly 9000 miles away in some parts of Scotland, in the 1970s, just the act of growing up involved a certain amount of bravery. 'Rebus' writer Ian Rankin was too young to see the film when it reached his local cinema in Cardenden, Fife and only donned a droog outfit some years later for a fancy dress party whilst at University. He does though remember the film's impact north of the border: 'Back in 1972 as I progressed from primary school to secondary, my male school friends seemed to undergo a metamorphosis. They lost their short trousers and got their Doc's and skinners, their penchant for square go's and spray paint. I'd spent that transitional summer writing lyrics for the pop group that I kept locked in my head. My contemporaries had, obviously, been engaged in different pursuits. The initiation at Auchterderran Junior High involved being dragged into the toilets by the fourth year and given a half-hearted kicking...'

'The boys – now entering their teens – were passing round dog-eared paperbacks with titles like 'Skinhead', 'Suedehead' and 'Boot Boys'. Tribes gathered at football matches. Neighbouring towns arranged pitched battles to a soundtrack of The Sensational Alex Harvey Band, whose slogan – Vambo Rules OK – started appearing on bus shelter walls throughout Scotland. It was a strange new world order, and Kubrick's film seemed to be its figurehead.'

When Rankin finally got round to seeing the film he was, 'after all the hype, the terror, the controversy... decidedly disappointed. I didn't feel like kicking a tramp as I slouched out of the picture house. But came pretty close to kicking myself for not walking out half way and hitting a bar.' Not so fellow aspiring pop star and Scot Richard Jobson, coming-of-age in an Irish Catholic family fourteen miles to the south on the hardcore Presbyterian Abbeyview housing estate in Dunfermline: 'A Clockwork Orange was seminal for me – both as a book and as a film. I was far too young to see the film at the cinema, but I got in anyway. It captured something that a film hasn't captured so successfully since; the sheer exuberance and excitement of being young.' The sectarian environment he was brought up in, says Jobson, 'toughens you up. I was a tough, violent kid because I had to be to protect myself and survive. It was a very strange upbringing, to grow up in a community where you're made to feel you've got six fingers and three eyes and that you should go back to the hole you came from.'

Adds Jobson; 'From the mid-1970s I was a Suedehead, which was the second generation of Skinheads. It was a big deal in young male gang culture in the east of Scotland. I was into a special look, influenced by my older brothers. We used to go to Glasgow and get our shirts from a tailor called Arthur Black in St. Enoch Square, Fair Isle jumpers from Argyll House on Buchanan Street, and beautiful Crombie overcoats. But it was very regimented, and already I was getting more interested in individual style.' He ran with, and led, a gang called the AV Toi (after the housing estate) who traded in alcohol, football and, especially violence. 'There's an element of fun in violence when you're that age' he says. It was 'an exhilarating, exciting experience,' which he 'prosecuted with great venom.' In his directorial debut, **16 YEARS OF ALCOHOL (2004)** there is a stabbing and an assault with a hammer, both of which the real Jobson had first-hand experience of.

The former Skids and Armoury Show frontman, actor, performance poet, model, television presenter, and film critic adapted a screenplay from his semi-autobiographical novel of the same name. Filmed over four weeks in Edinburgh on HD for just £400,000, the influence of *A Clockwork Orange* becomes clear after twenty minutes in a recreation of Kubrick's similar set-piece, when a now teenaged Frankie (Kevin McKidd) is seen larking about with three fellow Skinheads inside a small underpass, skanking to the ska playing on the soundtrack, the days of playing cowboys with his adulterous father long over. We see their less playful side when they enter a local pub. When the barman momentarily continues with his ongoing conversation, one of them slips around the edge of the bar and helps himself to a couple of bottles. This gets the barman's attention and as he makes his way from behind the bar, one of them tosses a handful of coins to the floor in payment. Ordered to leave, the response from Miller (Stuart Sinclair Blyth) is to break a bottle on the corner of a table, but Frankie, clearly the leader, intervenes. He tells his friend to drop the makeshift weapon and holds out his hand as an act of, supposed, conciliation, but when the barman stretches forward to take it Frankie's forehead shoots forward to meet his with devastating effect.

We soon discover that Frankie's relationship to Miller is closely akin to that of Alex and Dim in Kubrick's film. The next scene takes place in a record shop where the gang object to what is being played on the store's turntable. Budgie (Michael Moreland) asks for Desmond Dekker, Kill (Russell Anderson) requests Alex Harvey. Both choices meet with Frankie's approval, but Miller's suggestion of Mott The Hoople is met with derision. 'Stand in the corner,'

he's told, 'for being a fucking idiot who likes idiot music made by big poncey bastards.' When the girl behind the counter, Helen (Laura Fraser), instead plays the Velvet Underground's 'Pale Blue Eyes', Miller becomes threatening and she orders him from the shop. 'Or what?' she's asked, 'You'll call the police?' 'No, I'll put Mott The Hoople on,' is her somewhat unexpected answer, which is met with hilarity from all but Miller who attempts to jump over the counter but is pulled back. Frankie is clearly smitten with the girl but Miller is seething and tells the other two: 'Next time he fucks with me, that's it.' The next time, at a local disco where Miler is holding a knife inside his victims mouth, is not long coming.

It's a dynamic that is colourfully explained by Terry, one of the youngsters interviewed for Dave Robbins and Philip Cohen's 1970s study of a working class youth on a North London estate. 'You usually find it's a dim bitch that's got all the bottle. If you look at *Clockwork Orange*, the one in there, he was dim, he had all the bottle there. You usually get that in crews... like we've got this kid, he's called Willy, he's as dim as they come and every time there's a fight he don't care what the odds are, he just steams in..' Not so the leader who, when the fight starts off is 'usually at the back, he may be the best fighter there, but he's clever like. So it's the poor mugs blind at the front that gets the first chunk of lead and all their faces just going splat all over the place and all you hear is chop chop and little grunts and groans, and little kids crawling out with half their jaw missing.'

Like in Kubrick's film, the leaders authority is eventually challenged. Miller pulls a knife on his former friend and although Frankie easily overpowers him, he is unwilling to finish the job and attempts to walk away. Miller though won't give up and after insulting Frankie's family he receives a vicious kicking. When it goes on a little too long, Kill intervenes, kicking Frankie whilst Budgie attempts to pull Miller away. But with Frankie now on the ground, Miller breaks free and returns to plunge his blade, though not fatally, into his grounded leader's stomach.

In reality, Frankie had already reached Anthony Burgess's 21st chapter and decided to move on after his initial encounter with Helen. As his voice over narration tells us, 'You don't wake up one day a new person, but you might wake up one day and hear things in a different way, see things in a different way. Start to behave in a different way.'

The Guardian's Peter Bradshaw, somewhat bemoaned the 'glacially slow pace' but was impressed by 'the director's aesthetic concern for visual texture and light.' The Independent on Sunday said 'It's a change from the chatty mundaneness we usually expect from British realism' and though 'uneven and requires a certain leap of faith... It looks as if Jobson has found his true forte.'

Hippies, Skinheads, Rastas, Punks & Disco Dancing Bowie Boot Boys

At the beginning of the 20th Century, Glasgow could proudly call itself the Second City of the Empire, having cemented its position as the shipbuilding capital of the world. This attracted migrants from Ireland and the Scottish Highlands, pushing the city's population past the million mark by 1911, 70% of whom were crammed into an area of just three square miles. The Depression would hit early and hard, reducing shipbuilding output by three quarters in just three years between 1920 and 1923, and the following year the city would attract a less flattering moniker as The Cancer of Empire, from the title of journalist William Bolitho's book about Glasgow's housing conditions.

Glasgow's gang warfare dates back to the 1920s and 30s where in the slums of the city's east end the Billy Boys from Bridgeton Cross could call on up to 400 men to fight their catholic enemy the Sally Boys from Salamanca Street. Across the Clyde in the Gorbals, the Beehive Gang, named for a drapery store on Cumberland Street, mixed their street fighting with safe cracking and burglary. The city's reputation as a home for crime and violence that could rival prohibition era Chicago was cemented for a global audience by the 1935 publication of Alexander McArthur and Kingsley Long's Gorbals set novel, 'No Mean Streets: A Story of Glasgow Slums', which the Evening Citizen declared 'positively... harmful' and the areas libraries resolutely refused to stock.

In 1954 the housing problem was confronted head on by the government's Housing (Repairs & Rents) (Scotland) Act which set out the requirement of local authorities to begin the process of slum clearance, leading to the demolition of 32,000 homes over the next ten years. Whilst some of those who were displaced settled in new towns like East Kilbride and Cumbernauld, many families moved onto the new housing estates that were built on the greenbelt on the edge of the city. These were Castlemilk, Drumchapel and, the most notorious, Easterhouse.

For families moving from cramped conditions in areas of the city where population densities could rival Calcutta, their new accommodation which provided indoor bathrooms and toilets, separate living room and kitchen, and individual bedrooms, initially seemed manna from heaven yet by the mid-1960s there were queues each morning outside the housing offices of people looking to transfer out of the area. With an emphasis on the provision of as many houses as possible, planners had ignored other factors essential in creating a successful community. For a population that by the 1960s had reached 40,000, Greater Easterhouse had 3 doctors, 1 dental surgery, no swimming pool or cinema, no banks and a lack of shops that left residents reliant on vans providing mobile grocers with less than competitive pricing. There were also insufficient local employment opportunities and inadequate schooling, necessitating long and expensive commutes back into the city. To rub salt into residents' wounds, flaws in the housing's construction would also soon become clear.

Seven miles from the city centre and the furthest point to which one could travel and still be said to be in Glasgow, it was Easterhouse in particular that became synonymous with the resurgence of the gang activity that began to make headlines around 1966. In January of that year, the Glasgow Herald carried a front-page story about a gang of 150 Easterhouse youths carrying weapons in an altercation with a residents group that was formed to combat the areas gang problem. The press coverage picked up pace following the publication of the Chief Constable's Report in July 1966 which spoke of 'new difficulties to the Police in the shape of juvenile group disorders.' With half of the Easterhouse population under the age of 21, the lack of facilities was thought to be instrumental in this, leaving little for the younger inhabitants to do other than congregate on street corners and other public spaces. With little reason to travel beyond their own specific areas, there was a tendency for youngsters to identify solely with their immediate 'territory' which they would champion and defend. Not that Easterhouse was alone in this. Where in the majority of the country the arrival of the Skinhead cult would signify an alarming increase in street violence, in Glasgow it was business as usual only with shorter hair.

The situation came to a head during the Indian summer of 1968 where senior police officers, and the Scottish Under-Secretary of State, asked Easterhouse residents to keep clear of a local stretch of vacant ground for an hour on a Saturday evening in July 'to give disarmament a chance.' The proposed arms amnesty had been the idea of singer Frankie Vaughan who had visited the area three days earlier to meet gang leaders, having told the Evening Times that 'I feel I can do some good because the boys like and respect me and know I am not just a do-gooder.'

Though the Liverpool born singer had no direct connection to Glasgow, he developed an affinity with the city when he had lost his voice during a concert in the city's Barrowlands Ballroom and rather than complain (or worse in a venue in which local folklore said that bouncers would search youngsters for weapons and if they did not find a knife would supply one) the audience sang the rest of the set for him. The cynics view of the amnesty was

A message of respect to Frankie from *Glasgow Razor Gangs*

that the whole thing had been a publicity stunt and that most of the knives handed in came straight from the youngster's mother's kitchen drawers. TV and radio comedy writer Rikki Brown who grew up in Easterhouse during the 1960s can be counted among those who viewed the supposed success of Vaughan's amnesty with a heavy dose of cynicism: 'A metal bin was provided as the receptacle for the weapons, but it was just one bin. By local reckoning, Frankie was about 99 bins short of what was needed to disarm the gangs. Many gang members did turn up carrying an assortment of weapons, some dangerous, but mostly just odd bits and pieces they'd found en route to the photo opportunity. A pal said: "Aye Frankie, this is ma chibbing brick which I did nae just find. Honest man."'

Vaughan had played a juvenile delinquent over ten years earlier in *These Dangerous Years* (1957) when he was already a good ten years to old for the role but it is debatable how much relevance, by then pushing 40, he would have had to the wayward youth of Easterhouse. By 1968, his pop career had long since been exchanged for a career on the cabaret circuit and the singer actually flew in to Glasgow from a summer season in Blackpool. He did reach #29 with 'Nevertheless', his last hit, in 1968. What wasn't open to question was Vaughan's sincerity, having, in the words of his son David who carried on his father's altruistic outlook on life, 'grew up in Liverpool and always felt it was a similar port to Glasgow, a real melting pot. He was a bad boy and got into street gangs, but the boys' clubs helped him have some sort of structure.'

Vaughan's interest in boys' clubs led to him donating the royalties from three of his hits, 'Seventeen', 'The Green Door' and 'Something In The Bank Frank', to the movement. As payback for handing in their chibs, Vaughan promised the youths of Easterhouse he would donate the profits from a concert at Glasgow Pavilion, some £3,500, towards the setting up of a youth centre, with the city Council doubling his donation to make it £10,500. The result was the opening, in January 1969, of the Easterhouse Project on Westerhouse Road, comprising two disused Nissen army huts erected with the help of the Royal Engineers.

Said Vaughan: 'I'm very critical of youth clubs. I'm very critical of authorities who think that by just sticking up a youth club and saying 'here's a magnificent youth club now get on with it' and that's it. That isn't it at all... Family units are more important than boys clubs and girls clubs and youth clubs put together but it's not possible for families today to provide all the good things in life and at the same time provide love and affection for their own. I'm afraid it's a mess, society at the moment. We have to study our own home, and then study our leisure time and study opportunities for kids to let off their inhibitions in a proper atmosphere.'

An episode of *This Week* on the subject of **GLASGOW RAZOR GANGS (1968)** opens with an optimistic Vaughan declaring, 'No more gangs!' He is followed on the screen by a young lad who seems to suggest otherwise. This was the leader of the Shamrock, sixteen-year-old Joe Devlin: 'I do things other people don't do. I'm always at the front of a crowd if there's a fight. I'm always right at the front if there's any damage.... [not fists though]... hatchets, other kinds of weapons. Anything, you know.' Told that he might kill someone, he responds 'You don't think about it, killing... if six of you plunge him at the same time there's a good chance but you don't think about you're gonna kill him until maybe after. Maybe seriously, seriously ill or something like that... you don't think you're gonna do him in. A bloke's lying there screaming and long as he still screams it's okay, you know.' A career in medicine clearly does not await.

A voice-over paints a similar picture of a beleaguered city: 'Saturday night at the Locarno dancehall and Glasgow belongs to its youth. Burly men watch warily for the known troublemakers. Glasgow sprawls over 62 miles, but the entertainment spots are crammed into a few streets in the city centre. On Saturday, all roads lead to Sockihall Street. For most, the Locarno is the place for an evenings innocent enjoyment, for a few it is a disputed no-man's-land. Everything is planned to nip trouble in the bud. The front door is heavily guarded and each male must submit to a frisking. Some are known to the doormen and are asked firmly to go elsewhere.but the weapons are not easily found. Only the boys are frisked, and a sharpened steel comb slips easily into a handbag. Most experienced gang members take great care not to be caught in possession of an offensive weapon.' This is a practice that has gone on long before the reputation for violence grew - down to the common practice of youngsters taking a 'carry out' into venues to save money. It now serves a double purpose.

The city has a special task force to deal with young gangs, known colloquially as the Untouchables - the police themselves call them Group Disorder Vehicles and Officers and do not refer to gangs. 'In 1966 there were numerous outbreaks of group disorders in the housing schemes of the city and in January 1967 the Chief Constable formed in each division a Group Disorder Vehicle. Composed of a sergeant and a number of constables... brought in in the event of a call being received and dispatched to the scene to deal with it.'

The BBC's flagship current affairs programme, *Nationwide*, also covered the Glasgow gangs and caused a stir over a £5 payment, to be split eight ways between a group of youths who had appeared proudly showing off their weapons. According to the programme makers no fee had been mentioned to the youths prior to filming and the practice, known as a field payment, where small sums are paid to extras on location was not unusual. That did not prevent those concerned about the negative image being portrayed of the city from crying foul!

In the Glasgow Herald, political analyst Murray Ritchie wrote: 'Glasgow is a violent, vandalised slum city. That is a fact. But to say so nowadays is, it appears, to be guilty of heresy. The BBC programme *Nationwide* have become the latest heretic. Their sin was to contravene the unwritten but apparently inviolable law which has become established in the last few years. It may not even be a law: more a state of mind... The City Chambers promote it, the police support it, and the establishment in general abides by it. Simply interpreted it is this: "Thou shalt not tell the truth about Glasgow" and its existence betrays a rather worrying reluctance by some to come to terms with reality.'

Glasgow's Razor Gangs ends, in Easterhouse at least, with a truce between the various gangs in exchange for the building of a Frankie Vaughan youth centre. The area provided the working title of **SMALL FACES (1996)**, but being set in a past that the estate's current residents had no wish to be resurrected, the title was changed. Says director Gillies MacKinnon: 'They pointed out that it had taken a long time to get rid of that image so please don't do this, and I felt we had to respect that... It is a reference to an idea no longer in the film; nothing in the film resembles the real Easterhouse area, and we have promised the people who live there that we won't use the name of their community.'

The housing of the period was, to the cities credit, hard to reproduce and much of the film was shot in Darnley to the southwest of the city. Says Gillies: 'In 1968 the Glasgow tenements were black from decades of soot and industrial smoke. Since then they have been cleaned, which causes us real problems. Some dark tenements exist, often between cleaned walls – a strip of black in a shiny yellow sandstone terrace. This limits camera angles and restricts the actors' movements to useable spaces.'

Shot on super 16mm with a budget of £1.2 million, *Small Faces* tells the story of three teenage brothers of a single-parent Scottish family crammed into a tiny flat in a downtrodden section of Glasgow circa 1968. Bobby (Stephen Duffy), the oldest, is introduced feeding a goldfish an entire tub of food. He's next seen crying out in the dark from a nightmare and is clearly a troubled young man. Not that youngest brother Lex (Iain Robertson), whose goldfish has had to be flushed to a premature watery grave, is an angel, as we see when he is caned at school. He reluctantly takes one blow, having pulled away his hand at the last second on the first attempt. When the teacher tells him to put out his hand for a second strike he says 'no, that's enough,' and he means it. Middle brother Alan (Joe McFadden), who has a passion for art, is in the sixth form and is planning to enrol in art college. Lex shares both his talent and passion. Bobby runs with a gang.

In crafting their screenplay, Gillies says he and his co-writer brother, Billy, drew on their own childhood: 'Billy and I had never really talked about it before because you just take where you grew up for granted until you stop and see this was really something quite exceptional which hasn't really been recorded. And, incidentally, it was a great time to grow up, this isn't a film about victims and social deprivation. It's a kind of celebration, but in the middle of that some violent events come together.' Lex is loosely based on Billy, Alan on Gilles, who attended the Glasgow School of Art in 1969 and 1970; Bobby however does not have a real life parallel though Gilles, who also directs the film, suggests that 'Maybe the older brother represents the dark forces which were around us at the time.'

Gillies pinpoints the source of those dark forces to 1963: 'That's when the weapons started appearing – by 1970 it was all over. All the sixties influence was there, music and flower power and Czechoslovakia… and here in this corner of northern Britain you had this strange situation. They had got rid of a lot of the old tenement housing, whole communities had been uprooted and dispersed and that's when the gangs really came into their own. They would pour into town from all these new housing estates. There were hundreds of these gangs all over Glasgow.'

Gillies was himself in a gang until his early teens: 'We used to fight with other guys, but when all the weapons started it wasn't for me. That doesn't mean I wasn't interested in it or didn't have contact with it. Friends of mine who were apprentices knew all the boys in gangs. Whenever we went for a drink, we would meet these guys and they'd invite us to come down and fight against some other gang, but I always had somewhere else to go. I remember one night talking for hours and hours to the leader of this gang about George Orwell, and at the end of it he showed me his bayonet and invited me to join them. About 30 of them all piled out of the pub, and I went to the art school dance. There was no obligation; it was an invitation.'

Still smarting over the loss of his goldfish, when Lex gets pissed by sneaking drinks at a family party, he attacks Bobby. The next day Bobby gives the youngster an air pistol as a peace offering. Unfortunately, out walking with Alan past a local football match, Lex shoots a participant in the eye. This is not the best way to keep the peace given that the victim is Malky Johnson (Kevin McKidd) leader of the notorious Garrowside Tongs. The incident also brings the two brothers to the attention of Charlie Sloane (Garry Sweeney) leader of Tong's rivals the Glen, the gang that Bobby runs with. In return for the Glen's protection, Charlie gets them to break into an art gallery and add his likeness into a painting on display.

It's not the behaviour one naturally associates with gangs but, says Billy MacKinnon: 'It's a different kind of working class culture in Glasgow. In some respects it's a very rough one, but it's also an intelligent culture and it quite cherishes things of the mind. 1968 was a very restless year. It was the same year as the TET Offensive, Paris, the Prague Spring. You'd have these boys with sideburns, carrying razors, but they knew all about Ho Chi Minh.' Not that the film shies away from those tougher aspects of life. Tooled up with flick-knives, lead pipe, bricks and broken bottles the skirmishes in *Small Faces* are brief but always full-blooded;

Bobby shattering Malky's nose with a half-brick in one encounter.

Things become even more complicated when Alan dates Joanna (Laura Fraser) who Malky Johnson is in love with. 'He'll do anything for me except leave me alone' she tells him. Charlie Sloane also has an eye for her and the two of them have a regular date ice skating together on Saturday mornings.

When the Tongs girls set upon an artistic friend of Alan and Lex's, Fabio (David Walker), he refuses to fight back, humiliation turning to horror when the boys arrive and brutally finish the job, hospitalising the youngster for no other reason than his being in the wrong place at the wrong time. Lex, acting with all the characteristic impulsiveness and naivete of the child he still is, vows to do whatever it takes to take revenge on Sloane. His plan is to take the bus to Tongland, intending to offer his services to Sloane's rivals. There he meets a young kid called Gorbals (Mark McConnochie) who takes him home to meet his stepbrother, a member of the Tongs who turns out to be none other than Malki Johnson himself. Initially laughed at, Lex offers the useful information that they can find Charlie with only a couple of girls for company at the ice skating rink every Saturday morning.

Tragically, this information is not 100% accurate as also present is Bobby, and when he soon lies bleeding from a knife wound he's most definitely not alright. Says Gillies MacKinnon: 'If we were going to make a film about youth violence, and kids carrying knives, it was inevitable for us that we had to carry it through. We had to show the excitement of it, but had to show the consequences. It's not a film about hard men and all that crap; it's really a film about innocence. This little boy loses that innocence. He crosses that wasteland into hell and becomes culpable.'

Lex's thirst for revenge now moves to Malky and having been given a switchblade by Gorbals for his own protection, he returns to Tongland with the sole intention of using it on the Tongs leader. Losing his nerve at the last minute, Lex drops the knife outside his would-be-victim's front door in his hurry to escape. It is a weapon Malky instantly recognises and the young Gorbals receives a harsh kicking. When his step-brother falls asleep drunk later that evening, Gorbals turns on the gas fire, but doesn't light it and leaves. Malky wakes up coughing and manages to switch the fire off, then immediately lights a cigarette.

Though filmed before, *Small Faces* was released in the immediate slipstream of the phenomenal success of *Trainspotting*, which would prove to be both a blessing and a curse. Danny Boyle's film would have whetted the appetite for a youth-orientated movie that was both set in Scotland and shared a cast member in Kevin McKidd, but comparison was inevitable and always likely to be unfavourable. These comparisons would have annoyed Gillies MacKinnon: 'This was the late Mod period, fashion was important. It was also the Harold Wilson period, and most working-class kids were actually encouraged by the education system. What people forget is that there was almost full employment at the time; the gangs didn't really come out of poverty, it was almost an ebullient thing.' Adds the director: 'I don't think they're comparable at all. This is not a film about deprivation – these kids had money. But years later, the apprenticeships weren't there anymore. You've got unemployment, you've got drugs, so *Trainspotting* describes a very different time.'

Despite having since largely vanished from public consciousness, *Small Faces* was at the time critically very well received, winning at both Edinburgh and Rotterdam international film festivals and receiving a nomination for a Scottish BAFTA, though *Trainspotting* won the award. In 1999 the British Film Institute surveyed 1000 people from the world of British film and television to produce the BFI 100 list of the greatest British films of the 20th century, Danny Boyle's film not surprisingly managed the #10 spot but also there at #90 is *Small Faces*.

Another future director who fell under the spell of *A Clockwork Orange* as a teenager growing up in Scotland was actor Peter Mullen, who says 'I joined a gang when I was 14 and loved it. I had my Skinhead, my Crombie coat, my boots and my umbrella, my Clockwork Orange bowler hat and my one false eyelash, the whole bit. At that time my ambition was to end up in jail as a murderer and do my time.' Mullen drew on these experiences for his semi-autobiographical film **NEDS (2010)** which takes place in the early seventies.

Despite Frankie Vaughan's best efforts, in 1973, the Times wrote: 'The graffiti bear witness. The gangs are still alive in Glasgow, painting their names on the walls of their areas, marking out their territory to remind anyone who has forgotten them. They are also capable of leaving more permanent epitaphs with casual violence against the unwary individual, the innocent bystander.' Gangs such as the Carlton Tongs and the Derry Boys with their roots in the depression were still active, joined by newcomers like the Wee Men, the Bar L, the Drummie and the Toi. The reason for the paper's renewed interest in an image that the city had been hoping to shake itself free of, that of

the most violent city in Britain, was the publication of a new book, 'A Glasgow Gang Observed', by an educational psychologist using the pseudonym James Patrick, for fear of reprisals against members of his family still living in the city.

According to the then Assistant Chief Constable of Glasgow Police: 'There are still gangs here, but they are not as bad as they were.' Patrick begged to differ. There were differences certainly; the gangs were no longer based around religious differences, and the age range had dropped: 'The gangs then were made up of men between the ages of 18 and 30. Now they are made up of young people between 10 and 18.' But not as bad? Patrick believes that although 'in the thirties they would fight each other with almost any weapon,' the younger gangs were less concerned with harming innocent bystanders. A fight reported in the press in March 1972 highlighted evidence relayed in court of a gang of about 50 boys armed with weapons, including bayonets and swords, who fought another gang, one of whom had fired above their heads with a shotgun.

The city's housing is taken to task in the book which points out that 'for 100 years Glasgow has suffered from appalling housing conditions. For the same length of time gangs have been known in the city. The inhabitants, I fear, have become inured to both evils, to cramped verminous houses and to brutal, barbarous violence.' The city's Lord Provost is quoted as saying: 'There are places in Glasgow that I would not let my family grow up in, they are appalling. But we have to put up with it. You cannot evacuate the city, plough it into the ground and come back in 100 years. You have to keep on trying.'

Neds begins during the end-of-term school presentation day, where the conscientious 11-year-old John McGill (Gregg Forrest) goes up to collect an award, much to the delight of his grown up elder sister. As the rest of his family leave the building, John dawdles behind, his head buried in a book. He is confronted by an older boy, Packer, on whom poor John had left a quite different impression to that of his sister: 'Going to big school after this summer, aye? That's my fucking school... see when you're in my school you're gonna get your cunt kicked in, every fucking day. First day I'm gonna break all your fucking legs, fucking demolish you, rip your head off. I swear to God you're dead wee man. First day, you're fucking dead.' Welcome to big school.

John, who is also an altar boy, has an older brother, Benny (Joe Szula), who seems his exact opposite. Benny, who had assaulted two teachers and been expelled indefinitely from school, is a hard nut who runs with a gang. Director Peter Mullen keeps this older brother very much in the background, feeling that: 'Benny was as much a myth to John as a reality and I wanted that to be the case for the audience. So you only see little bits of him and you should ask yourself, "Well is he as tough as everybody tells you he is?" because normally there's so much self-mythologising amongst kids within a gang. You create your own heroes, your own villains, your own sense of order. And mythology plays a big part in that. Within the original script more stories were told, and I had to cut them sadly, because the film was just too long. What I liked about the storytelling aspect was that it gave you that sense of these people simply perpetuating a myth. And the myth is to be that really bad guy in that other gang, or the really bad things that your gang members had done. Nine times out of ten it's bullshit.'

Because of his elder siblings reputation, John is placed in a class lower than his abilities warrant, 1A2 instead of 1A1, and told if he finishes in the top two he can move up at the end of term – Mullan himself was put down a class because his older brother (Lenny Mullen, now Peter's casting director) was a tearaway. This he duly does and continues to excel through the rest of the school year. During the summer break, John (now played by Conor McCarron) attends summer school in order to stay out of trouble but when he's treated badly by the parents of his new middle class friend he decides to hang with his own kind.

Mullen fell in with his own juvenile street gang, the Young Car-Ds, in much the same way as in the film, after a middle-class friend's mother told him never to come round to their house again. Walking home he strayed into the Moss Heights housing scheme, where a gang of lads started on him, before realising who his older brother, who had a serious rep back then, was. Suddenly scared, they invited Peter to join the crew there and then. 'And,' says Mullan, 'that was me for a year, I dodged school. I hung around in places like this. Moped round all day. And occasionally got into fights... you completely jump into it because it's so exciting... And I was happy to lose the "good boy" tag because it hadn't done me any good.'

There is more than enough going on at school to get John into trouble and the next year sees him involved in a gang fight at the youth club, robbing a bus driver, sniffing glue and carrying out a particularly nasty assault on Canta (Gary Milligan), who he drops a concrete slab on. Though not based on an event in Mullan's life, this act of extreme violence was based on a real incident. Says the director, 'I read this story about these two wee lads who battered the shit out of a guy and left him on the floor in a state of semi-consciousness. But they came back an hour later with a concrete slab and dropped it on his head. Now that was about twenty years ago, but you just think why did they go back? They'd proved their point, like don't mess with us or don't come back into this area, but why did they go back and kill this fella?' John even gets into a fight with Jesus, enacted somewhat bizarrely to the sound of The New Seekers 'You Won't Find Another Love Like Me', who he shanks.

Speaking on BBC4's *The Film Programme*, Mullen says: 'The idea that you can only make a film according to a certain dogma drives me crazy... the idea that the only image you can pursue truthfully, particularly when looking at a working class subject is through the prism of social realism, then for me it's just too limiting. Irvine Welsh was great for that. Irvine broke all those boundaries because suddenly it was almost sexy to be Scottish and working class. And one of the main taboos that Irvine broke, whether consciously or otherwise, was that the working class were suddenly allowed an exotic sex life. And it's the same when you look at, if you like, violence in a working class context, there's a pre-conceived notion that if you're gonna look at, really look at it you can only use this one means of interpretation which is called social realism and I just find that too debilitating.'

*

Director John Mackenzie began his career as an assistant to Ken Loach at the BBC, working on classic slices of social realism for episodes of *Play For Today* like *Up The Junction* (1965) and *Cathy Come Home* (1966). He made his debut feature film in 1971 with the disturbing boarding school drama *Unman, Wittering & Zigo* and ended the decade with his best known work *The Long Good Friday* (1980). In between he left an indelible mark on a generation of schoolboys with his public safety film *Apaches* (1977) by gruesomely picking off seven young lads on an extremely hazardous farm. There was also a trilogy of episodes of *Play For Today*, all set in Glasgow and written by Peter MacDougall.

Affectionately known as the Bard of Hard, MacDougall was raised on Greenock's Larkfield estate and started work as a fourteen-year-old in the Clydebank shipyards, both of which feature in **JUST A BOY'S GAME (1979)**, the third and final part of his trilogy. Unlike Jake McQuillen, *Just A Boy's Game*'s hero, MacDougall - like his friend and fellow workmate Billy Connolly - escaped the docks, heading to London where he became a house painter. Legend has it that that it was whilst painting the house of Colin Welland, MacDougall's tales of marching

Frankie Miller stares his victim to submission in *Just A Boys Game*

and mace throwing as a drum major on an Orange Parade led the Oscar winning writer and actor to encourage him to put his story down on paper for *Just Another Saturday* (1975). In fact, when he wrote his first play, *Just Your Luck*, aged 20, he was on probation for breaking and entering - burgling rather than painting houses.

One Scottish journalist could have been summarising *Just A Boys Game* when he said: '...from the poverty and unemployment of the 19th Century and the first part of this century has emerged the idea of the "hard man", a tough, fighting, drinking man who is respected and admired. Glasgow admires aggressiveness and when adult law-abiding society generally puts such high values on these qualities, it is hardly surprising that young people get drunk and stick knives in each other.'

Greenock docker Jake McQuillen (Frankie Miller) works hard and plays hard, spending his evenings drinking and larking about with best mates Dancer (Ken Hutchinson) and Tanza (Gregor Fisher). Jake is a hard man, and something of a local legend in this tough, working class community, which is why up-and-coming youth gang members see him as a quick way to earn a reputation. He's been there and done that and has no desire for trouble but, if looking for a quiet night out, he's certainly not chosen the ideal venue for an evening; propping up the bar with Dancer, where across the crowded room, the Cuban Heels, a regular fixture of Glasgow's early Punk scene alongside The Jolt and Johnny & the Self Abusers (later Simple Minds), bash out a Punked-up version of 'Paint It Black'.

It doesn't take long for the venue to break into violence as, led by Dunky McCafferty (*That Sinking Feeling*'s Billy Greenlees), the Young Team Boys make their presence felt by slashing their chibs across the faces of anyone who crosses their paths. The barman urges Jake to keep his cool, telling him, 'I thought you'd given up the games,' but as the brawls overtakes the entire venue he is forced to stand his ground. It's a scene that impressed Martin Scorsese enough, the most realistic he'd seen, to ask after how it was choreographed. That this is an average occurrence in the city's bar rooms on a Thursday evening is signified by the police patrol car parked outside, its occupants happy to let the fracas run its violent course before making their belated presence felt. 'Yer too late' yells one passer-by, 'Custer's deid!'

The following day, walking on his own at the back of a housing estate, Jake is stopped by 4 or 5 youths and asked about the previous night's incident and whether the Young Team Boys were involved. When the leader of the group become threatening Jake simply slaps him hard across the face, leaving the humiliated youth on the verge of tears and his friends open-mouthed in shock. When some of the Young Team see Jake, Dancer and Tanza entering a snooker hall, a couple follow them in whilst, unknown to Jake, the others go for re-enforcements. Recognising one lad, Jake bundles him into the toilets - 'step into my office' - and reduces him to tears with nothing more than a prolonged, silent stare. That blues singer Miller so convincingly captures the Glasgow stare might in some way be attributed to the fact that he is a cousin of former Gorbals villain Jimmy Boyle, the subject of McDougall's *A Sense Of Freedom* (1979) for which the musician also provided the soundtrack.

When three more youths enter, Jake and his mates slip out of a back door only to bump straight into half a dozen more. Dancer and Tanza are all for doing a runner, but Jake doesn't go backwards. In the ensuing battle Dancer doesn't make it, losing an eye and running blindly into throat high mooring cable which catapults him into the dock, but, says Jake, 'That's how it goes. That's the game.'

4. Babylon's Burning
(Ruffy, Jennings, Owen, Fox)

Stand And Deliver
(Pirroni, Ant)

On the 17th of August 1972, the Daily Mirror introduced its readers to something most of them had thought was confined to American Police series like the Streets of San Francisco or the Dirty Harry movies. The newspaper reported on the violent robbery of pensioner Arthur Hills as 'a mugging gone wrong'. 'As crimes of violence escalate,' the report said, 'a word common in the United States enters the British headlines: mugging. To our police, it's a frightening new strain of crime.' The term, said the paper, derived from phrases such as 'a mug' meaning 'an easy victim' and the act was described as 'an assault by crushing the victim's head or throat in an armlock or to rob with any degree of force, with or without weapons'.

A month later, mugging was again headline news as the Evening Standard proclaimed 'London Mugging? Judge Talks Of City In Fear'. The paper quoted Judge Alexander Karmel, QC: 'Mugging is becoming more and more prevalent, certainly in London. As a result, decent citizens are afraid to use the underground late at night, and indeed are afraid to use the underpasses for fear of mugging.' Not that mugging was in any way new. The London Transport Police had already set up a special patrol on the underground which came to be known as the 'Anti-Mugging' Squad. Violence on the underground was a high-profile public concern at the time and attitudes towards minorities, even at the highest level, were less than enlightened.

Because mugging, like 'gangs', had no definition - there being no such offence with that name. Depending on who it was doing the reporting, mugging could refer to bag snatching, pick-pocketing and a myriad of other street crimes (the more recent trend for snatching mobile phones from motorcycles is often referred to in the press as mugging). The terms mugging and black soon became synonymous; hardly surprising given Enoch Powell's statement to a Police Federation seminar that 'mugging is a criminal phenomenon associated with the changing composition of the population of some of Britain's larger cities.'

Powell was not the only person in authority to fan the flames of racial hatred; Albert Sherman, a close advisor of Margaret Thatcher who co-founded the Centre for Policy Studies alongside her and Sir Keith Joseph, would have welcomed the new police initiative having told the Soviet newspaper Pravda, in 1974: 'As for the lumpen-proletariat, coloured people and the Irish, let's face it, the only way to hold them in check is to have enough well-armed and properly trained police.' The blacks were, of course, easier to spot. In 1979 Sherman suggested, 'The imposition of mass immigration from backward alien cultures is just one symptom of this self-destructive urge reflected in the assault on... in short, all that is English and wholesome.' Once in office, Margaret Thatcher wasted little time in rewarding his views with the bestowal of a knighthood in 1983.

In February 1972, the 'Anti-Mugging' Squad made their mark at Stockwell Station when 6 black teenagers were arrested and charged with offences ranging from 'attempting to rob' to 'assault with intent to rob'. Accord to police testimony, shortly before 11 p.m. a plain-clothed officer was followed into an empty carriage and threatened with a knife to hand over his money at which point he signalled to other undercover officers waiting in the next carriage. There were no other witnesses to the event. At the trial, the Judge spoke of 'decent citizens [afraid to] use the underground late at night ... for fear of mugging' and handed out sentences ranging from six months' detention to three years' imprisonment.

A month after this incident there was another high profile case in which four black youths, members of the Fasimbas, a South London black political organisation, who were on their way home from a meeting in Harringay, were arrested and charged when, in the words of the prosecuting counsel and corroborated by police statements; 'On March 16th this year, London Transport Police were keeping observation at the Oval station when they saw the four accused hanging around and it was clear that they intended to pick the pockets of passengers.'

At Kennington police station they were separated and beaten until they signed false confessions to scores of local unsolved crimes, but one of them had the foresight to only 'confess' to crimes committed on Thursday morning at 10.00 a.m. when he was signing on at Peckham Labour Exchange. This ensured they could not be convicted for offences in their confessions, but by a majority verdict a jury found all four guilty of 'attempted theft' and 'assault on the police'. The youngest was sentenced to Borstal, the other three to two years' imprisonment each.

The officer in charge of both actions, as well as similar instances including arrests at Tottenham Court Road and Waterloo, was DS Derek Ridgewell who had previously served in the South Rhodesian police force. It was the incident at Tottenham Court Road in May 1973, where two black men were arrested and charged with robbery, that a clearer insight into the Squad's activities came to light. At the trial, it emerged that the two men were both Jesuits studying at Plater College, Oxford University, with no previous convictions.

As trials began to collapse, there were several demands to the Home Secretary for a Home Office enquiry into the Squad's activities, including from the Labour spokesman on race, John Fraser, MP, but the robbery squad was instead disbanded and Detective Sergeant Ridgewell quietly moved to a new post, without loss of rank, where he duly teamed with a couple of career criminals and began to split the proceeds from stolen parcels. During his 15 months in his new position, around 11 van-loads of parcels had disappeared at an estimated cost of £367,000 and he was sentenced to seven years in prison in 1980. 47 years too late, the Oval 4 members finally had their sentences quashed in 2019.

Sadly, in the early 70s at least, this sort of police practice was not widely known outside of black circles, but it would have been to Jamaican born writer Paul Wheeler who tackled the subject for *Crown Court*. In the episode, **THE MUGGING OF ARTHUR SIMMONS (1973)**, 58-year-old Arthur Simmons has been mugged by two youths on his way back from the pub. Adhering strictly to the Daily Mirror definition of mugging, he was grabbed from behind and held in a full nelson by one of his attackers whilst an accomplice went through his pockets, taking £2 and some loose change. Fleeing the scene the youths almost bump into a pensioner, Winifred Palmer, who goes to Arthur's aid, before seeking the local beat bobby who takes them to a youth club that is populated largely by black youths. After an impromptu line up two youths, John Dempsey (Gregory Munroe) and Colin Langham (Christopher Assante) are arrested and charged.

The prosecution's case rests on the eyewitness evidence of Mrs Palmer, for whom an earlier incident involving black youths letting off fireworks in the flats has clearly prejudiced her, if she weren't already. This can be easily deduced from her use of the word 'they' when referring to blacks, as in 'since they moved in.' The police officer refers to the 'coloured fraternity' as opposed to community, fraternity being a word the police reserve for the criminal classes. The youth club itself had been the target for police raids six times over the preceding two years, one of which had turned into either a 'riot' or a 'minor disturbance' depending on whose evidence is believed.

Dempsey, a 19-year-old well-spoken University student, was already on the police officer's radar for his involvement in a local 'black power' group, and the prosecution made much of an article he had authored for a student publication in which he had suggested a state of war existed between the black population and the white majority. The article stated that: 'Members should be prepared to fight such a war on every level. Not only with polemic and invective but also with fists and weapons... take the war into the streets, we need money, we need support, we need weapons. Get them, don't bother about the ethics. Go out and get them. Take them from the people who hold us down, disarm them. Remember Spartacus.' Langham is more of a street hustler, and there is no previous connection between the two. Though the defence point to the incompatibility of the two men in the dock,

Gregory Munroe and Christopher Assante in *The Mugging Of Arthur Simmons*

comparisons can be made with the well-educated middle-class Bonsu Monroe for whom frustration with society's white-bias led him towards radical black politics, and his accomplice in the 1975 Spaghetti House Siege, the petty criminal Franklin Davis.

The drama highlights an obvious flaw in the way the authorities handled such cases. Prior to the formation of the Crown Prosecution Service in 1986, a few particularly difficult or 'important' cases were referred to the Director of Public Prosecutions, for the remainder it would not be unusual for the same police officers to both investigate and prosecute cases. This was despite a Royal Commission in 1962 recommending separate prosecution departments to stop this very practice. In the programme, the judge is fair in his summing up and the jury finds both men not guilty. Others would not have been so lucky.

This inherent racism was also examined in **SOFTLY SOFTLY TASK FORCE: TROUBLE MAKER (1973)** in which a police raid on an address containing flats occupied by black residents, part of an operation under the name Weedkiller, results in just two youths being arrested for possession of small amounts of cannabis, but the heavy handedness of one police constable in particular leads to complaints from the other residents. What the police hadn't counted on was the white middle-class wife of one of those residents contacting a high profile black solicitor whose involvement means Supt. Watt has to carry out an investigation.

Says the solicitor: 'Yes there are people smoking pot in the Brighton Road area but there are probably more people smoking it in the fashionable parts of Chelsea and Hampstead, in our ancient and well-loved University towns and other places of that kind, where rich people live. It can be an expensive habit. Somehow, the police prefer to carry out their investigations where the poor people live. That is to say the poor black people.'

When the main culprit is given a dressing down by Superintendent Watt and admits that were the roles reversed he would have 'punched him on the nose,' he is told '...and whatever happened you'd have got away with it in court because you're a policeman and he's black and a court will always believe a policeman rather than a black man.'

Subtle in its portrayal, the officer in question is never seen to be overtly racist, simply heavy handed, leaving at least a modicum of doubt even when in a final scene where, as 20 illegal immigrants embark a boat onto a beach, he breaks the silence with 'I can't wait to see their faces.'

In the documentary *Britain's Black Legacy* (1991), defence lawyer Ian MacDonald called the 1971 trial and acquittal of the Mangrove Nine, a group of black activists arrested and charged with inciting a riot when they protested police targeting of a black community space in Notting Hill, a watershed 'because after that there was a very big change in the attitude of judges in trials of this kind. It was the beginning of a realisation that the police didn't behave like gentlemen... by the establishment in this country.' It certainly allowed the space for the previous two dramas to be made and broadcast but perhaps overly optimistic when it came to the judiciary.

Most definitely, according to a youth interviewed in **BLACKS BRITTANICA (1978)**, a documentary illustrating racism in Britain from the black perspective, made by WGBH (Boston) in the USA and never broadcast in the UK. The youth, who had found himself arrested on SUS after venturing to Ladbroke Grove for a job interview at Boots, says: 'The magistrate just didn't look interested... when it came to giving us a sentence... said... I don't believe a police officer would come to court and commit perjury.' The truth was that at that time if a barrister was to even suggest in court to a policeman he was telling lies, it would guarantee a hostile judicial reaction as Dennis Bovell, whose story we shall get to soon, would find to his chagrin.

What chance would they have if presented before Judge Gwyn Morris who, despite having been the judge who had halted the trial of the two Jesuit students, saying 'I find it terrible that here in London people using public transport should be pounced on police officers without a word,' sentenced five West Indian youths to five years in May 1975. In his summing up he observed, with reference to Brixton and Clapham: 'Within memory, these areas were peaceful, safe and agreeable to live in. But the immigrant resettlement which has occurred over the past 25 years has radically transformed that environment. Those concerned with the maintenance of law and order are confronted with immense difficulties. This case has highlighted and underlined the perils which confront honest, innocent and hard-working, unaccompanied women who are in the street after nightfall. I notice that not a single West Indian woman was attacked.' A year later, the same judge suggested white Londoners should create 'some form or other of vigilante corps' to stop black men from preying on white women.

How little police attitudes would really change over the following decade can be gleaned from an episode of **THE GENTLE TOUCH: FOX & HOUNDS (1984)**. *The Gentle Touch* was the first British series to feature a female police detective as its leading character, reaching the nation's TV screens ahead of the similarly themed BBC series *Juliet Bravo* by four months. Made by London Weekend Television and broadcast on ITV between 1980 and 1984. The series dealt an array of social issues, though Detective Inspector Maggie Forbes (Jill Gascoine) 'gentle touch' never went so far as to properly admonish the racist officers under her command. The depiction of racism and its associated low-level corruption in the police had by now become just another accepted facet of police procedure and as such needed no commenting on.

In this series 5 episode, an elderly man making his way home through a housing block is mugged when a light bulb is removed and he is coshed and robbed in the ensuing blackout. The description of the assailants is 'young and black' and Inspector Forbes wants every car in the area on the case - 'I want those bastards,' she exclaims and as if to prove the point she's out of the office and on the scene even before the ambulance. Her officers respond with vigour, chasing down the first black youth they come across, an eighteen-year-old called Winston Leroy Jones (Victor Romeo Evans). He runs but when cornered insists he has done nothing wrong. His protestations naturally fall on deaf ears. 'Kicking an old man half to death, you call that nothing you black bastard,' he's told before being roughed up.

Victor Romero Evans recieves *The Gentle Touch*

One detective assigned to the case is equally racist. 'That's the spades for you,' he says, 'Personally, I'd pull the lever on scum like that.' Winston has amongst his possessions a small amount of Lebanese black, a wristwatch, a cigarette lighter and case and is on the dole - all of which is immediately taken as evidence of his guilt. His record however comprises nothing more than a shoplifting charge when fifteen, though he has been arrested a couple of times on SUS. 'When you're black and my age and two anaemic coppers jump out of a car at you, you'd be flippin' stupid not to run. Because this is what happens if you hang around' he says, pointing out the injuries he has sustained during his arrest. Even though a youth worker (Oscar James) signs a statement saying that Winston was in a youth centre at the time of the assault, and that there at least 20 other witnesses, Inspector Forbes insists that he is guilty and they all must be lying. It is in spite of the police rather than because of them that the two real culprits are eventually arrested and charged with what is now murder.

Hippies, Skinheads, Rastas, Punks & Disco Dancing Bowie Boot Boys

Too Much Pressure
(Davies)

Broadcast a couple of years earlier than the rest of this book, but providing an important insight on what lay ahead, was an episode of the ITV weekly current affairs programme **THIS WEEK: COLOURED SCHOOL LEAVERS (1965)**. It begins with several 16-year-old black schoolchildren asked what they would like to do when they leave school. Their aspirations are all white collar, ranging from a would-be typist to careers in teaching, commercial art, journalism and the Women's Royal Air Force. Whilst in school, the narrator says, they have been able to get to the top. Their number includes prefects and the head boy. But what does the future hold?

They're next asked if they think there would be jobs that they couldn't do because they wouldn't be allowed to. A girl doesn't think 'coloureds' will be given office jobs. The head boy who says it has never occurred to him before, says 'I shouldn't think so' before refining his answer with 'there shouldn't be anyway.' The next boy questioned is certain that 'if you have the qualifications, you can easily get in.' The others agree. What all the girls are unanimous on is that they will not work in a factory or take jobs of that nature. Their parents, themselves factory workers, agree that it is not for their children and likewise believe that with better education and qualifications come better jobs. A boy who had left and failed to find a good job has returned to school, but he too believes that if he achieves the right qualifications he will. He does, however, believe that if he became, say, a clerk, he would not be promoted above white employees with similar qualifications.

The head teacher rather naively suggests 'they haven't actually come up against much prejudice of any kind themselves,' and says of the school: 'we are completely unconscious of race.' A discussion between a mixed group of children in the library paints a more realistic picture. The head boy says he is accused by his own race as being a 'pinkie lover', whilst a white boy says it's difficult to not go along with his prejudiced mates: 'It's hard to say to a group of friends, "I like coloureds, what's wrong with them", if they're all saying "throw them out of the country, they're ignorant. Out of the trees."'

Despite working in an area where there are three vacancies for every school leaver, this rather depressing picture is also described by a youth employment officer who equates black children with 'handicapped' people or how women 'used to be', saying there are certain firms who would not take them on, and there are 'some classes of occupation for which they're not acceptable. We also find variations of acceptability... some employers say we will take them if they're not too dark.'

The programme closes by sending out two similarly educated and presentable 17-year-olds, one black and one white, to apply for a series of posts. When the black boy gets there in the morning, he finds the vacancies are already filled, but when the white boy turns up in the afternoon, the jobs miraculously become available.

During September of the following year both the Observer and the Telegraph reported on similar outcomes to separate experiments that had been carried out by the Campaign Against Racial Discrimination. The matter, and the programme itself, was raised in parliament during December 1966 by Labour MP for Croydon South, David Winnick. In response to the question, Shirley Williams, then Labour MP for Hitchin, tried to place at least some blame not with racist employers but with the children themselves, saying: 'it takes longer, and is more difficult, for youth employment officers to place an immigrant

Optimism abounds in ITVs *Coloured School Leavers*

boy or girl because of, in some cases, an inadequate understanding of the standards demanded in this country for jobs... We will all know, not this year or next year but in about ten years' time, because we will then have boys and girls whose whole school experience has been in the British educational system, just how great a part prejudice plays in this.'

By the time of Menelik Shabazz's half-hour documentary **STEP FORWARD YOUTH (1977),** the perception of the easy-going 'don't rock the boat' West Indian as portrayed by Earl Cameron in films like *Pool of London* (1951), *Sapphire* (1959) and *Flame In The Streets* (1961) had well and truly died, worn down by the 1976 Notting Hill riots and a society that had increasingly less to offer. Unemployment prospects for youths of all colours were bleak, but it is clear from the interviews in the film that the ten years that Mrs Williams said the government needed in order to determine what was already obvious to the rest of the nation had bred a sense of discontent that was no longer under the surface.

Barbados-born Shabazz, a pioneer of independent black British cinema best known for the 1981 feature film *Burning an Illusion*, would go on to found Ceddo Film and Video Workshop, publish Black Filmmakers Magazine and create the BFM International Film Festival. This, his first film, begins with a black girl of perhaps 18 talking about her time at school where, she says, the teachers were racist and the only one who could get work out of them was a black supply teacher who the head brought in but was let go after a month 'because they didn't like the idea that he was getting work from us that they couldn't get.' She believes that all-black schools with only black teachers would be a good idea. Her views are shared by the next interviewee who tells us that black pupils can

Step Forward Youth

'relate to a black teacher better than they can relate to a white teacher, just like a white kid can relate more to a white teacher than he can relate to a black teacher.'

The youths in a group interview are also in favour of segregation. 'There's more conflict when you try to integrate... very occasionally you'll find black people and white people that can mix,' says one girl. Footage at a dance in what seems like a large working men's club reveals no white faces. 'We've got more pride in ourselves than the white people have... we might steal, they say black people are criminals... but there's always a streak of good somewhere where they believe in religion because of [our] parents... white people haven't got that strong background to fall back on.' The consensus is that white families don't look after their kids or their elderly. Using a term usually heard as the afterthought when a white racist is caught out in a generalisation, one black British boy defends a statement he has just made with, a somewhat familiar, plea that 'I'm not saying all of them are the same.'

Both the two main interviewees are British born but say they would rather be West Indian and refer to themselves as such. 'British means white to me,' says the girl. There's also little in the way of hope for the future. 'I see things getting worse because racial prejudice is never gonna end no matter what you do... In our school the black boys are beginning to get on with their work, worrying about how they'll do in their exams But that won't help them because the unemployment's getting so bad in this country that they won't get a job anyway.' Asked what will happen, the same boy says, 'Well, if they can't get a job and get money the legal way, they'll get it the illegal way.'

Made by a group of left wing filmmakers working under the banner of the Newsreel Collective, and intended to be shown in schools and youth clubs to help stimulate discussion on racism, *Divide & Rule - Never* (1978) thankfully offers a more harmonious picture of black, white and Asian youth but retains the hatred for the police. The soundtrack to the documentary is heavy on the Punk and makes much of the Rock Against Racism movement as well as visiting the first Anti-Nazi League Carnival.

The feeling of hopelessness over the lack of prospects facing school leavers is also very apparent in **TUNDE'S FILM (1973)**, as is the antagonism with the police. The film was an unusual change of direction for producer and co-director Maggie Pinhorn who had previously worked as an anonymous member of the art department on two huge movies, *Chitty Chitty Bang Bang* (1968) and *You Only Live Twice* (1967), before becoming art director on the exploitation classic *Mumsy, Nanny, Sonny & Girly* (1970). She then produced Stephen Dwoskin's *Dyn Amo* (1972), an art film in which films four striptease acts performed for an imaginary audience in a seedy club, including *Jubilee*'s Jenny Runacre, Catherine Kessler from *Groupie Girl* (1970) and *That Kind of Girl*'s (1963) Linda Marlowe.

Tunde's Film came about when a youth worker, aware of her background in film, approached Pinhorn and asked if she might be interested in making a film with a group of East London youths who had indicated that was what they wanted to do. 'What he didn't tell me' she says, was that they 'were a group of young people who were chronic habitual truants'. She nevertheless found the group, a 'real East End mix' of mixed race, black, white and Irish, 'interesting' and took on the project. Also exciting was that they wanted to film a story based on their real lives: 'They wanted to make a narrative film, not a documentary. For me, that was: Hooray!'

The youth worker was Dan Jones who ran the Kwango Dance Club for the kids in the old Seamen's Mission Hall in Tower Hamlets and rented his home from an estate agency run by Maggie's father. Though approached because she was the only person working in film that Dan knew, her belief that if something is worth doing, it is worth doing well made her the perfect choice. Says Pinhorn: 'A lot of people, when they make things for the community, they think the community has to do everything. I, as an artist, didn't view it that way at all. I felt that they had this idea that they wanted to make a film and they would, therefore, deserve to make it in the best possible way they could. So we engaged a cameraman and a sound engineer and a lighting guy... good technicians.' And if the acting from the amateur cast was a bit wooden, it certainly wouldn't have phased cinematographer Paddy Seale whose previous credits included *Stingray*, *Fireball XL5*, *Thunderbirds*, and *Joe 90*. Shot on about four streets over a week in April, Pinhorn kept the set professional enough to even have call sheets but admits 'I made the call for 10 a.m. but nobody turned up before 12, so the technicians and I had a very long breakfast most mornings.'

The film was originated by its co-director, 17-year-old Tunde Ikoli who was born in London's East End to a Cornish mother and Nigerian father, had left school at 15 and spent two years as a trainee tailor's cutter. It was then rewritten into script form by Pinhorn: 'basically like a synopsis because... people weren't going to be able to learn lines... They were given a situation and [told to] talk, improvise... also, not everyone in the group could read, so it was important we read everything out loud and everyone felt part of the process.' With a script in place, Pinhorn set about raising funds, coming up trumps with a request to the Rowntree Trust, who were interested in the idea and had already supported another filmmaker working in the community on a documentary about an adventure playground in Islington.

The 43 minute film opens in the aforementioned youth club where the kids dance to Prince Buster's 'One Step Beyond' until the youth worker, Dan Jones playing himself, signals that time is up and the crowd spills out into the darkened street. They do so under the watchful eye of a police meat wagon driving slowly along before stopping by a group of them, black and white, who are chatting by a low wall. One youth reaches over the low wall and grabs an empty bottle, smashing it on the wall. Two are bundled into the back of the van and the rest make their escape.

The next day, with those arrested now on bail after a morning appearance at the Magistrate's Court, the group reconvene in a cafe where they discuss their lack of job prospects. The black youths claim to be discriminated against in their search for work, but the white boys say it's the same for them. Tunde and Colin, one of the white youths, go in search of work but are constantly knocked back. Stopping by a car to light a cigarette, they are immediately approached by a police car and searched. One officer pulls out a key ring with two keys, declaring 'What's this? You're nicked!' but the two youths immediately have it on their toes. In another scene, one boy, having been on a date, is rudely interrupted when saying goodnight by the girl's racist mother from a balcony above.

After covering many of the issues that would have affected the lives of the young filmmakers, the finale is more indicative of their age. With no prospects, and a couple of them looking at a probable custodial sentence for the earlier fracas, the boys carry out a bank robbery. A shotgun and pistol are bought, a car is stolen but as they pull up outside their target, they are immediately boxed in by two police cars. As the group scatters, the film closes on a freeze frame and a closing theme written by Joan Armatrading.

The film screened at the London, Edinburgh, Mannheim and San Francisco film festivals, and led to a job at the Royal Court Theatre as Assistant Director where his productions included Mustapha Matura's *Play Mas*. Ikoli's first play *Short Sleeves in Summer* was produced at the Royal Court Theatre in 1974 and subsequent plays were produced at Bush Theatre, Riverside Studios, Theatre Royal Stratford East, and the Tricycle Theatre. In 1991, Ikoli wrote and directed a 90-minute heroin infused love story, *Smack and Thistle*, produced by Working Title and broadcast on Channel 4.

Many of the issues raised in *Tunde's Film* are also explored in Horace Ové's **PRESSURE (1975),** the first British feature from a black director. *Pressure* began its long journey to the cinema screens with one of the few non-black major contributors to the film. Producer Robert Buckley was born in Camberwell Green to a working-class family and spent much of his childhood in the 1950s and early 60s in Peckham, a time when many people were settling in the area from the West Indies. Some years later he worked as a script editor on *Play For Today* at the BBC but was finding that the output was not reflecting the London he had grown up in and in which he continued to live and work. 'It was doing fantastic things,' he says, 'there were all these wonderful northern working-class playwrights. Hundreds of them it seemed at the time; an unstoppable flow but nothing being done really about London now.'

Deciding that what was needed was a series of plays by black writers, Buckley first set about educating himself who those writers were, taking in lots of lunchtime theatre and theatre groups in church halls, where he met people like Alfie Fagon and Mustapha Matura to try to encourage them to do something for the BBC. 'Somewhere along the line, someone said "yeah, well isn't that a bit racist, because you'll do the season, then you'll have done your black stuff and then that's it. It's over."' It was an argument he found persuasive, but an even greater problem was the realisation that the writers all wanted to write about the West Indies while he 'became obsessed with this idea that we should be doing something 'now'. About a black Englishman, because that was where the dramatic conflict was as far as I could see.'

Having drawn up a list of people who might participate in such a project, one important part of any possible production was proving elusive for Buckley. 'I was sitting in the BBC club talking to Mustapha Matura and I said "This is all very well but who on earth is going to direct this" and he said, "Well, of course, my mate Horace Ové."' An introduction was then made that Buckley calls 'a total breakthrough.'

Ové teamed with author Samuel Selvon and they came up with a script, then called 'The Immigrant', that Buckley took the BBC where it was put into development. Soon after however Buckley moved from *Play For Today* to *30 Minute Theatre* and with no one around to fight the production's corner 'The Immigrant' was put into turnaround. A chance meeting with Ové whilst walking along Westbourne Park Road one afternoon put Buckley back in charge. Ové had got the BFI interested and, after providing him with an initial £150 to improve on the script, were now willing to put up the rest of money. The project needed a producer and having just left the BBC, the producer needed a job.

A voluntary committee within the BFI, The British Film Institute Production Board was formed in 1972 to make films that could not raise finance by other means. With funds of £125,000 a year, profitability was not a consideration. The Board received £95,000 from the Department of Education and Science and £30,000 from the Department of Trade, known as Eady money.

With an upper-cost limit of £20,000, for budgetary reasons the films were shot on 16mm and exempted from normal union manning levels. The more experimental films received a grant to cover the cost of materials alone whilst documentaries and features used professionals and also paid a wage during the filming and editing process. Because the filmmakers were usually very inexperienced, test sequences were originally commissioned, but these were eventually discontinued when, never being raised with inflation, the value of the fund decreased.

With a budget of £11,000, eventually raised to £14,909, the film, now called *Pressure*, was shot on 16mm in October 1974. It was, says Buckley, money that 'forty years ago could buy you a house, but it couldn't buy you a film,' and the cost of clearing music for the soundtrack sent it further into the red.

Pressure tells the story of black sixteen-year-old school leaver Tony Watson (Herbert Norville) and his struggle to find a place in the world. In terms of the two documentaries mentioned earlier, Tony begins the story very much in the camp of the Head Boy and Prefects of 1966's *Coloured School Leavers*, but by the end, he has aligned himself with the rest of the Notting Hill black youths who have far more in common with those of Shabazz's film.

Living with mum, dad, and (when it suits him) much older black power activist brother Colin (Oscar James), Tony is immediately marked as different from his family. Ové illustrates this with the films opening scene in which breakfast is prepared prior to Tony leaving for a job interview with an accountancy firm – eggs and bacon for Tony, avocados for Colin, only to Colin they're not avocado but zoboca, their name in Trinidadian patois. 'Don't forget, he's not like us. He's born here' offers mum (Lucita Lijertwood) after Colin chides his brother over his taste in food and music. Yes, there's even a poster of, God forbid, Gary Glitter hanging on the wall and it doesn't get any whiter than that. Well educated, polite and well-spoken, Tony ticks all the boxes in his search for suitable employment – except one. In July 1969 The Observer reported that it had been estimated that white youngsters from equivalent backgrounds were approximately five times more likely to find skilled work, in the meantime youth unemployment was undergoing a sharp rise. In September 1973, figures showed 14,000 school leavers under 18 were without employment, by the end of the decade the figure was well over 350,000 despite the higher numbers entering further education.

All of this is lost on mum who is keen he doesn't mess up his interview. 'I don't mess up any of them' complains Tony. 'Well, you didn't get the last one,' she responds. His father (Frank Singuineau) is more realistic but no more encouraging: 'It's months now since you left school and after all them interviews you still aren't working. You can't go on like this, you know. Sooner or later you've got to take anything.' It's an attitude based on his own circumstances that had taken him 'from an accountant in Trinidad to a kiss ass labourer in this country for sixteen years.'

While Tony might appear markedly 'white' in his own manor, his blackness is all too apparent when he steps into the all-white environs of the British office and an interviewer who struggles to disguise his surprise at his applicant's skin colour, place of birth and love of football as opposed to cricket. No snarling racist, the interviewer is shown as simply ill-informed and awkward in his institutional racism but despite mums assertion that he might get lucky this time, this (or the next and the next) job won't be going Tony's way. 'This is the tenth job I've been for, and I know I'm not going to get it. Lucky?' he protests, 'this is nothing to do with luck. They've been "letting me know" for a long time and I'm starting to get the message.' What 'the message' is requires no explanation. 'Oh God,' exclaims mum, 'you're starting to sound like your brother.'

Ové based this on an incident from his own life, attending his first interview for a job on the TV series *The World About Us*. Upon entering the office he was confronted by a red-faced producer demanding to know who he was and what he wanted. When giving his name rang no bells, Ové then told him he was the film director who has come to be interviewed for a job. 'He started to look down at his books very nervously' says Ové, 'Then I started to laugh [and said] "If you go in the sun next summer and take all your clothes off and lie in it, you will get a tan and you will look as good as me".' This broke the ice, and Ové was hired.

No such luck for Tony, for whom worse is to come when a night out with his former (white) school mate David (Ray Burdis) ends first with a tirade of abuse from the racist landlady of a girl he has walked home (the girl stands up for him but Tony is keen to avoid confrontation) and then the witnessing of a black youth being arrested for carrying an offensive weapon – his afro comb. When shown hanging out with a group of local black youths, he seems even more alien, especially when mistaking patty and pate. When the youths stop by a hypermarket for a spot of shoplifting, Tony, oblivious to what is going on, inadvertently messes up, which results in the arrest of one youth. Though the rest get away and, having enjoyed the exhilaration, take events in their stride, it leaves Tony practically in tears. After the group sells some 'black power' newspapers on behalf of Colin, a reluctant Tony is taken to a blues party with the proceeds. 'I'm really gonna get the blues when Colin asks me for that money' pleads Tony who has been told he is responsible for it, 'We just can't take this money and spend it, can we? I thought it was for a good cause.' His plea falls on deaf ears. 'Every day we live in the blues,' they tell him, 'we're the people that the cause is all about.'

Elsewhere Ové uses black militant meetings organised by Colin to address very real topics of the time such as the placing of black kids into 'subnormal' schools, contrasting this against the religion of his parents where a black pastor tells his flock, without the slightest trace to irony, to 'drive all black thoughts from your heart and replace them with good white holy thoughts.' This is even more alarming when one considers the fact that they filmed this with a real and un-prepped congregation who offer not a hint of dissent. One particular speech takes on an added significance given what was to happen a year or so later at the 1976 Notting Hill Carnival. 'Hatred, violence, bitterness and anger will inevitably result from this system, from the frustration of our expectations and aspirations.' Samuel Selvon similarly lampooned the transposition of American-style black nationalism to the United Kingdom in his 1975 novel 'Moses Ascending'.

At a subsequent interview, the racism is more in your face. 'You people got it easy ain't you' he is told by the owner of a garage where he has been sent for a non-existent clerical post. 'You come over here; get an education. I had to leave school when I was 14 and two years' national service. Another job you people wouldn't know about.' Finally biting the bullet, Tony takes a job below his skill set as a hospital porter and with money in his pocket to upgrade his wardrobe he opts for a more 'black' look and, encouraged by one of the black activist group's leaders, the attractive American Sister Louise (Sheila Scott-Wilkensen), attends a 'black power' meeting. The meeting comes to an abrupt end when it is interrupted by the Met, supposedly in search of drugs, who drag people out indiscriminately, including both Colin and Tony, and pile them into police vans. Tony is questioned at the police station while we hear his brother being beaten in a side room.

Though Colin is held in custody, Tony is released to find they have also turned the family home over, which means he finds little in the way of sympathy. 'You must respect the white people laws' says mum, 'they know best. They own the place. They is the lord and masters. They have all the bombs. All the guns. All the police force. We is only poor black people who have to work hard and hope they accept we, and leave we alone.' Kicked out by mum, Tony takes up residence in the 'black power' house where the occupants are busy making placards for a demonstration. He also smokes his first joint, resulting in an out of place dream sequence in which, after waking up in bed with Sister Louise, he takes a knife from a drawer, walks to a big house in a park and, now naked, repeatedly stabs the occupant of a bed which, when the bloodied covers are pulled back, is seen to be a pig.

The return to reality provides a much more depressing outlook when the demo is seen to involve a dozen or so people marching in circles around a small roundabout opposite the police station whilst being totally ignored. When the heavens open up and a heavy downpour begins their placards, one of which reads 'Death to White People', are destroyed along with their spirits.

Says Ové: 'I didn't make the film sitting in my room: I went out with Samuel Selvon and researched it. I was aware of the political situation, I know what's going down. So when it was made, and people started saying, "That's not true," I knew that either they didn't know what they were talking about, or they didn't want to admit to things. *Pressure* has had a lot of pressure. It's a touchy film, about something that's happening here.'

The film was completed in time to screen at the 1975 London Film Festival and then seemed to hit a brick

Life's a struggle in *Pressure*

wall. 'You know what this country's like' says Buckley, 'No one would ever use the word and say we've 'banned' it, but we were wading through treacle and we heard all sorts of things; that MPs had seen it [at] private screenings in the House of Commons somewhere.' He believes the film's cause was not helped by the 1976 Notting Hill Carnival riot which 'frightened the life out of the powers that be and they didn't want this film adding to it.' Immediately after the Carnival, he and Ové were interviewed by the BBC but it was never broadcast.

Whilst there were views expressed in *Pressure* that sections of the state would have been happy to see repressed, there were other non-political factors at play. The main criticism from those who had been beneficiaries of the fund that financed *Pressure*, was that completed films were never seen by an audience. In fact, they were in most cases never even viewed by the Board. Once completed, the film-makers were left with the nigh on impossible task of finding a distributor If not they would be distributed by the BFI distribution service. In these circumstances the BFI retained copyright, undertaking to share any profits with the film-makers on a 50/50 basis, but no film had ever made a profit because the BFI had no mechanism for promoting them.

Art-film distributors had taken some earlier films, such as those by Bill Douglas, but large commercial distributors were not interested and smaller operators could not afford the £10,000 needed to blow up the 16 mm negatives to 35 mm. This is the position that the makers of *Pressure* found themselves in after their festival premiere. According to the director, the at-the-time Production Board head Barrie Gavin had assured him the film would be blown up to 35mm at a later date. However, nothing was put down on paper and when Gavin was replaced by Peter Sainsbury, the new man said 'all our films are made on 16mm and they are made essentially, for a non-theatrical market... While one might well get one's money back if *Pressure* is distributed... if we'd paid for a blow-up it would have meant taking the money away from this year's applicants.'

Help was at hand in the form of Philip Oakes at the Observer who championed the film in several articles and attacked the BFI for sitting on it and roughly four years after the cameras stopped rolling it opened at the Coronet, Notting Hill Gate in February 1978 where there were queues outside the cinema every night. Says Buckley: 'I used to go up there and look at the queues because I couldn't believe that we'd made something that would draw all these people... I was completely in awe at what we'd done.' Sadly, he concedes that 'It didn't really play like that outside London, it was a very specific sort of London event.'

Reviews were largely positive and played up the film's authenticity. Marjorie Bilbow reviewing the film in Screen International, said: 'Although the pressure on Tony is all the greater because he is black, the scene has changed so much since Horace Ové and Richard Buckler made the film in 1974 that many white school-leavers will identify with the young hero as his hopes fade and he is forced into the life of a layabout on the fringes of crime and violent protest.' Race Today said: 'Ové is a pioneer, in that he is attempting for the first time, to use the medium of film to reveal the inner soul of the black condition in Britain... Perhaps the greatest pleasure of the film was being able to watch black actors allowed the freedom to interpret their roles with authenticity and accuracy.'

Coming so close to *Pressure*'s early days in production, and there being a paucity of television looking at the black experience in Britain, it is unthinkable that John Pilger's 1974 documentary, **JOHN PILGER: ONE BRITISH FAMILY (1974)**, had not been watched by Ové. There are clear parallels between Errol and his father Gus and Tony and his father in *Pressure*, despite 1970s Gateshead being so far removed from Notting Hill Gate that it might be mistaken for a different country.

'Where Gus has struggled and is grateful,' we are told, 'Errol is the opposite. Errol was a bonus clerk in a firm making beer kegs. Unlike Gus he has no need to crave acceptance because he's grown up here; he regards himself as no different from any other young Geordie... Errol is a black who's grown up white and there are now the first signs that he's having to choose. Until recently he drew his heroes straight from the white telly world, James Bond and white sharpies like that, and now that's changed, now in his fantasy he's Shaft, the all black hero.'

There's a marked lack of communication between father and son which a family friend suggests is down to Gus wanting to better himself by moving from the West End where most of the city's black population reside, to Gateshead. 'Errol then had to grow up completely in a white society. All his friends are white even from his time going to school.' The friend believes that his removal from the influence and stories of his father's grown-up friends has meant that his ideologies have been Europeanised.

This, what Pilger calls 'growing up with a mental white skin', it is suggested puts Errol in danger of the problems he will inevitably run into because of his colour hitting him even harder. As it happens, Errol's problems come sooner and from a less expected source when, halfway through the programme, we learn that he is having to marry his pregnant, white and middle-class girlfriend.

*

A term first used by Stokely Carmichael and Willie Ricks, organisers and spokesmen for a non-violent student civil rights organisation, black power grew out of the US civil rights movement and was actively involved in promoting the concept of self-empowerment in the black community via projects such as black-owned book shops, food co-ops, media, schools, and clinics.

By the late 1960s, and following rioting and the 1956 assassination of Malcolm X, black power had become almost exclusively connected to armed struggle despite in October 1966, Huey P Newton and Bobby Seale founding the Black Panther Party - their case not helped by the party's adoption of open-carry gun laws to allow members to display guns in public.

The Black Power movement hit Britain in 1967 when Stokely Carmichael arrived to speak at what was essentially a hippy counter-culture conference, the Dialectics of Liberation, organised by the Scottish psychiatrist and LSD advocate RD Laing.. Attendees included radical feminist Angela Davis, who a few years later would be on the FBI's Most Wanted list after having purchased guns used in freeing George Jackson from a California courtroom, including one used to shoot the Judge in the head. Davis said Carmichael's words cut 'like a switchblade, accusing the enemy as I had never heard him accused before. I felt the cathartic power of his speech.' It was a power that did not go unnoticed by Special Branch, who 'advised' he should leave the country and the Home Secretary who, once he had left, banned him from returning. The lid, however, was already off the bottle.

Considering Carmichael's words 'manna from heaven', Nigerian born novelist and playwright Obi B Egbuna quit his position as Chairman of the Universal Coloured Persons Association to form a British Black Power movement. The new climate also emboldened the country's most potent voice for black radicalism, Michael X, who had acted as a guide for Malcolm X during his 1965 visit to Britain and had subsequently converted to Islam, setting up the Racial Adjustment Action Society (RAAS). Within days he had, somewhat ironically, found himself charged under the 1965 Race Relations Act for inciting racial hatred.

A similar fate would befall Egbuna who, alongside Guyanese-born Roy Sawh, wrote the manifesto 'Black Power In Britain' and intended his new group to be a secret, tightly knit organisation that would use guerrilla tactics against the British state. When a copy of an essay he had written was passed on to police, he found himself charged with conspiracy to murder police officers (albeit in self-defence) and given a three year suspended sentence, but not before having already undergone several months of incarceration.

John Ridley, as a child of the 70s, grew up amongst the black power iconography of Davis, George Jackson, and Bobby Seale who he regarded as 'badasses and very cool', and in 2007 he conceived the story that would eventually become the six-part Sky TV series **GUERRILLA (2017)**. It was, he thought, 'a very American story'. That opinion changed in 2013 when he was in London for post-production work on the Hendrix movie *Jimi: All Is By My Side* (2014) where, asked by a producer if the story might translate to the UK, though sceptical, he contacted activists in London who had been involved in the struggle there and discovered that, though aspects of each struggle were unique to their locality, 'ultimately, the struggles are the same, and the people who are fighting for recognition or fighting for franchisement or fighting for equal representation - those fights, passions, human imperfections do translate.'

Here and in the United States as the peace and love of the sixties gave way to the stark reality of the seventies, those involved in these struggles began to contemplate employing more extreme methods that were already being turned to by other revolutionary factions. Howard Brenton considers *Magnificence* 'a tragi-comedy of perhaps naïve but enlightened young people who want to make a better world' who, when events turn against them, descend upon a path that leads to an act of terrorism. 'It came out of a debate that was raging... amongst young left-wing activists in the early 1970s. It was as if each carried a smoke-filled room in our heads with Lenin, Mao and the great anarchist leader Bakunin shouting at us personally. The debate was about 'direct action': you say you are for revolutionary change but that's just words, what are you prepared to do? Direct action could mean going on a demonstration, occupying a building... all fine and civilised but, the voices shouted, totally ineffective. Would you fight? Would you take up the gun? The Baader Meinhof Red Army Faction in Germany and the Red Brigade in Italy crossed that line. So activists were getting caught in a vicious kind of political psychodrama. I felt the pressure of it myself... "deeds, not words, do ends justify means". A tightening spiral.' In *Guerrilla*, this internal debate is raging in the character of Jas (Freida Pinto).

Lovers Jas and Marcus (Babou Ceesay) have been on the fringes of black activism which has largely meant talking the talk until the police murder a friend at a march against the anti-Immigration Act brought in during 1971 by the then Tory government. The murder was overseen by Pence (Rory Kinnear), the head of Special Branch's Black Power Desk, a Rhodesian who has brought over not only his country's racist beliefs but also its methods of policing. Using an agent provocateur, Pence stokes the peaceful protest into violence after first showing his squad a photograph of their intended target who is delivered countless blows to the head with heavy truncheons; murdered in plain sight. It is an act that pushes Jas and Marcus to walk the walk and become real revolutionaries, the first act of which is to break out imprisoned black radical Dhari (Nathaniel Martello-White) whilst on a hospital visit, during which Marcus panics and shoots an ambulance worker.

The opening episode ends with the contrite Marcus asking 'Are we cool?' to which Jas responds 'We are so fucking cool.' She then ups the ante by shooting up a party at Rhodesia House, which forces them to go underground and, with the help of a German Marxist revolutionary group, begin a major terror campaign played out against a game of cat and mouse with the Black Power Desk, leading to a powerful and wholly unexpected outcome in a thrilling finale.

Though the backdrop against which the story plays out was all too real, the story is fictional, and black radicalism in the UK never resorted to armed conflict. The activists who Ridley turned to to ground his story, Darcus Howe, Farrukh Dhondy, Neil Kenlock, never thought of themselves as 'so fucking cool', leaving that to Michael X and Egbuna, who Howe dismissed as a 'Hyde Park revolutionary'. Their legacy, says Paul Reid of the Black Cultural Archives, was a story of 'constant community activism and social responsibility... a quieter story perhaps but one that still needs to be told.'

Early in 1979, Horace Ové was contacted by Graham Benson, a producer at the BBC working on *Play For Today*, who had seen *Pressure* and was looking to collaborate on a project that might similarly look at the plight of young second-generation black British. Ové had researched the 1975 Spaghetti House siege soon after its resolution and had completed a screenplay as early as 1976 but could not raise the financing. Feeling Ové lacked experience as a scriptwriter, Benson brought in Hull-based writer Jim Hawkins, much to the chagrin of the director who feared this would lead to a whitewashing of his work. Despite this, the pair worked well together and Ové subsequently compared the collaboration favourably to that with Samuel Selvon on his debut feature. The result was **A HOLE**

A Hole In Babylon

IN BABYLON (1979) and Ové carried several of *Pressure*'s themes into the project, with black political activism again at front and centre of the film, this time proving even more problematic.

On Saturday 28th September 1975, as the weekly takings were being prepared for the bank, three armed men held up a branch of the Spaghetti House restaurant chain. The men were led by 28-year-old Franklyn Davies, a Nigerian who had already served time for armed robbery. His accomplices were 24-year-old Wesley Dick who had previously attended meetings held by the Black Panthers, the Black Liberation Front, the Black Unity & Freedom Party, and was currently volunteering at the Institute of Race Relations Kings Cross offices, helping on the switchboard; and 22-year-old Bonsu Monroe who also had links with the black power movement and had set up a supplementary school in the front room of a derelict house in Hammersmith.

A member of the restaurant staff escaped and alerted the police who were on the scene in numbers within a matter of minutes, forcing the three gunmen to bundle the remaining members of staff into a storeroom and turning the would-be robbery into a five-day siege as the police negotiated for the release of hostages. The three men issued a statement declaring themselves to be representatives of the Black Liberation Army though the police continued to treat the ongoing incident as a robbery gone wrong; a decision which in the case of Davies at least, it was difficult to argue against. However, in the words of Ambalavaner Sivanandan, director of the Institute of Race Relations, 'the line between politics and crime is a thin one in a structurally racist society.'

The mainstream press positioned the protagonists as either bungling amateurs or hardened gangsters and in their briefings to journalists says Ové, 'the police deliberately played down the political overtones' with much of the subsequent press coverage completely ignoring any underlying political motivation for the robbery. It was this perceived bias in the press coverage that attracted Ové to the project: 'I get very annoyed with the media coverage. It is so superficial. They don't do proper research. That is why I made *Pressure*. I was tired of reading in the papers about young blacks hanging around on street corners, mugging old ladies. Nobody tried to find out why they were doing it. The same with *A Hole in Babylon*; the men on the siege were represented as a bunch of hooligans. Nobody looked at their background.'

In a 1979 interview for the Evening Standard, Ové said he considered the film to be a sequel of sorts to *Pressure* and that film's Tony could be seen as a younger Wesley Dick or Bonsu Monroe, where in each case 'a black kid is not given a chance and ends up on the wrong streets with the wrong people. Then he fights back for his rights.'

Ové's film dramatised the unfolding siege situation, interspersing events with flashbacks showing the backstories of the three main characters and the planning of the robbery from which they hoped to emerge £40,000 the richer. With budgetary restrictions making the reconstruction of events outside the Spaghetti House impractical, the filmmakers hit on the idea of using archival news footage of the event which would fit easily alongside Ové's handheld 16mm footage, all of which was filmed on locations around Ladbroke Grove and Notting Hill. This included the actual Spaghetti House storeroom after Ové charmed the owners by speaking to them in Italian, having previously lived there. Further authenticity came in the casting of actress Carmen Munroe, who was the aunt of the real Bonsu Monroe. Ové's persuasive personality also enabled the production to have a first-class reggae-infused soundtrack, persuading Sammy Abu to come to London at his own expense, bringing to the Lime Grove recording studios a host of musicians willing to work for free.

As *A Hole in Babylon*'s transmission date neared controversy around the production began to rear its head with the Daily Mail suggesting 'Viewers may be shocked, outraged that controversial criminals – now serving a total of 56 years in prison – are depicted... as heroes.' They said that the film was 'blurring the edges between fact and fiction... but they are not the events. They are not history. The audience needs to be warned that they are merely make-believe.' The criticism was enough for the BBC's Director of Television Programmes, Alasdair Milne, who had withdrawn *Brimstone & Treacle* (1976) and *Scum* (1977), to summon the director to a meeting three days before the programme was due to be broadcast. Benson convinced Milne, who did not even know a film was being made about the siege until he read about it in the press, that although the play was bound to attract criticism, the story had been handled responsibly. On the morning following the broadcast, the producer says he received a call from Milne calling it 'a marvellous piece of work' and 'a bit controversial but that's fine, that's what we are here for.'

Ové's film was not the first drama based on the Spaghetti House siege to reach the small screen, beaten by the first episode of a new ITV comedy-drama series *Minder*, broadcast exactly a month previous. The episode, *Gunfight at the OK Launderette*, changed the location of the robbery to an Italian-owned launderette with Trevor Thomas, Bonsu in *A Hole in Babylon*, again turning up as one of a trio of calamitous robbers who on this occasion were claiming affiliation of the Independent Rastafarian Army (IRA – geddit?)

Following *A Hole in Babylon*, Ové secured intermittent employment on TV, for the BBC with a few episodes of black soap *Empire Road* and another *Play For Today* with *The Garland* (1981), with ITV for six-part children's series *The Latchkey Children* (1980 and starring Ové's daughter Indre), and then Channel 4 with *Playing Away* (1987) and the four-part dramatisation of Phyllis Shand Allfrey's 1950s island of Dominica set novel *The Orchid House* (1991). Most of his subsequent work has been in theatre and documentary.

A lack of further opportunities might be partly down to the director's reluctance to be pigeon-holed, having told Sight & Sound in 2005: 'I believe I'm an artist and want to go beyond my blackness as a filmmaker, a painter, and a photographer. But every time I try to do something they put me in a corner.' Adds Ové: 'I wanted to break away. A filmmaker like me gets typecast as a black filmmaker. People seem to think you are not qualified to do anything else, but a director is a director, regardless of colour. Some regarded me as a kind of father of black filmmaking in England, but that is a terrible load. Just being a black filmmaker is a heavy load anyway because somehow you have to answer to everybody every time you make a film. People meet you in the street or ring you up and say, "Why didn't you do this or that?" Sometimes it can be a drag. People want you to make films for them but you can't.'

The Independent Rastafarian Army in *Minder at the OK Launderette*

Hippies, Skinheads, Rastas, Punks & Disco Dancing Bowie Boot Boys

Bass Culture
(Johnson)

The Jamaican sound system with its custom-built speakers and massive specialised speaker cabinets, deejays, selector, operator, engineer, and sundry other crew members can be traced back to the 1940s with such now legendary names as Tom the Great Sebastian and Count Nick the Champ, then playing R&B and jazz records imported from the USA, outside on lawns and street corners, and who were the participants of the first known 'clash' in 1952.

It was the next wave of systems who would elevate their art form to the next level, particularly those of former policeman Duke Reid the Trojan, named after the flatbed truck he used to transport his equipment, and Clement Dodd whose Sir Coxsone Downbeat began producing music from local artists for exclusive use on his own system, such as Clue J and His Blues Blasters, led by double bassist Cluett Johnson and featuring future legends Ernest Ranglin, 'Rico' Rodriguez and Skatalites founder member Roland Alphonso. Coxsone's studio would become the famous Studio One. It was during this period that competition for an edge over rivals led to outbreaks of violence, more often than not attributed to Reid whose previous employment had fostered links with gangland. Among the Sir Coxsone deejays was Cecil Bustamere Campbell, aka Prince Buster, who had his head split open by a stone wielded by one of Reid's thugs.

Writing in 2003, *Babymother* (1998) director Julian Henriques said; 'Over the last 40 years, reggae sound systems in Jamaica have become institutions on a par with the local churches and football teams. Sound systems also inspire loyalty and fervour in equal measure. They employ large numbers of people and directly influence the lives of so many others from the peanut vendors to the politicians who employ them to draw the crowds to their meetings.'

When the first wave of emigrants from the West Indies arrived in the UK, they quickly discovered that rather than the welcome acceptance into British social life they had expected they would instead face cultural and social exclusion from a xenophobic public. This exclusion did not just apply to housing but also to leisure pursuits with many pubs and clubs operating a strict colour bar. In response, the new arrivals set up their own 'shebeens' or 'blues' dances in private houses where the entertainment would be provided by sound systems, one of the first of which was set up by Duke Vin who, back in Kingston, had been the selector for Tom the Great Sebastian.

From their origin in basement flats, nights began to be held in church halls and by 1955 an event was held at Brixton Town Hall as the systems began to find regular homes in legal, above-ground clubs. Duke Vin had arrived in Britain in 1954, not on the HMS Windrush but as a stowaway on a banana boat. With him were two friends, one of whom, Wilbert Campbell, would run a rival system as Count Suckle, competing with Vin regularly at sound clashes. Suckle's sound system won a booking at the Flamingo Club in Wardour Street where his access to early Caribbean imports was a huge influence on the likes of Georgie Fame. As the sixties began to swing, Suckle became resident deejay at the hip Roaring Twenties on Carnaby Street, where the regular clientele included members of The Rolling Stones and The Who. As the decade came to a close, he opened his own club in Paddington, The Cue, where his sound system played ska, reggae, funk, and soul until its closure in the eighties.

The visit of Haile Selassie to Jamaica during 1966 had begun to influence that country's reggae scene, with spiritual themes becoming increasingly common, which, combined with the political unrest that had, in 1972, led to the election of Michael Manley. Manley had run for office with the slogans

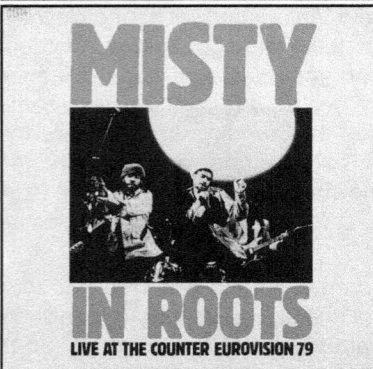

'Better Must Come' and 'Giving Power To The People', which had struck a chord with the country's ghetto communities. Out of this came a new sub-genre of reggae that combined spirituality with black pride and resistance to government and became known as 'roots', spawning artists like Burning Spear, Culture and The Abyssinians.

By the middle of the seventies, numerous roots bands had formed in England including Black Slate, whose anti-mugging anthem Sticks Man was a minor hit; Birmingham's Steel Pulse whose first single, 'Ku Klux Clan', and album, 'Handsworth Revolution', were landmark moments in British reggae; and Misty in Roots who were involved in setting up People Unite, a community centre in Southall which was used at the anti-fascist HQ for the April 1979 protest over a National Front election meeting. The centre was stormed by the SPG and a sound system and other equipment were smashed, with those inside badly beaten, including Misty's manager Clarence Baker who was left in a coma. The event was immortalised in The Ruts 'Jah War'.

> Hotheads came in uniform
> Thunder and lightning in a violent form
> Clarence Baker, no trouble maker
> Said the truncheon came down
> Knocked him to the ground
> Said the blood on the street that day

Also 'strictly roots' at this time were Aswad whose early songs such as 'Three Babylon', before going on to conquer the charts with an R&B and soul fused reggae, dealt with the issues surrounding the experience of growing up black in the UK. Most militant of all was Linton Kwesi Johnson for whom 'writing was a political act and poetry was a cultural weapon', and whose work, performed over Dennis Bovell's dub reggae, pulled no punches.

This period of black British history can be traced in the work of Chapelton, Jamaica-born, Brixton-raised dub poet Johnson, who had been a thorn in the side of the authorities since his teens when he became involved with the British Black Panthers, for whom he organised a poetry workshop, after meeting Althea Jones, one of the Mangrove 9 defendants, at a sixth form debating society. It was an association that gave him his first experience of being thrown into the back of a police van, given a thorough beating and a subsequent charge of assault. His crime had been to take down the numbers of two policemen involved in the arrest of a black man.

Later, he would become a part of the Race Today Collective led by his friend Darcus Howe. Twenty-five years on, Johnson was an emissary of the overseas cultural exchange initiative, the British Council, but unlike many, he has never watered down his message since his first collection of poetry, 'Voices of the Living and the Dead', was published by Race Today in 1974. This was followed a year later by a second collection, 'Dread Beat An' Blood'.

Johnson had been writing copy and advertisements for Virgin Records reggae imprint Front Line and whist at a recording studio it was suggested that he record a reading of some of his poetry. After recording three demo's, Front Line agreed to put up £2000 to record an album. In 1978, Johnson took eight poems from this second collection and teamed up with reggae musicians led by Dennis Bovell under the name Poet and the Roots.

The struggle of black youths in Britain's inner cities of the time is a theme that runs through most of the tracks on the album. One track in particular, 'All Wi Doin' Is Defendin', predicts in no uncertain terms the riots that were still a few years away.

> ...oppressin man
> hear what I say if yu can
> wi have
> a grievous blow fi blow
>
> wi will fite yu in di street wid we han
> wi have a plan
> soh lissen man
> get ready fi tek some blows
> [...]
> all wi need is bakkles an bricks an sticks
> wi hav fist
> wi fav feet
> wi carry dandamite in wi teeth
>
> sen fi di riot squad
> quick!
> cause wi runin wild
> wi bittah like bile...

Unhappy with his spelling as well as his politics, an April 1982 edition of The Spectator (for six years edited by Johnson's namesake Boris) in a page long rant, accused Johnson of helping 'to create a generation of rioters and illiterates.' These were the days before he became only the second living poet to have his work published by Penguin Modern Classics, and was awarded a Golden PEN Award for distinguished service to literature.

Despite these accolades, any sighting of Johnson continued to rile certain sections of the media. After an appearance on the *Today* radio programme in 2007, the Sun complained of being 'subjected for nearly five minutes to the thoughts of the 'reggae poet', as his publishers call him, Linton Kwesi Johnson, whose most famous words are: 'England is a bitch.' Johnson came out with a rant about racism then proclaimed that, in his view, England was still 'a bitch'.'

And England was a bitch as documented over the next decade on Johnson's subsequent albums. The self explanatory 'New Craas Massakhah', 'Di Great Insohreckshan' about the 1981 Brixton riots, 'Sonny's Lettah (Anti-Sus Poem)', the wrongful arrest and conviction of George Lindo in Bradford on 'Dread Inna Inglan' and fighting the National Front, in protest, on 'Reggae fi Peach' and in the streets on 'Fit Dem Back'.

*

Writer and director Franco Rosso was born in Turin, moving to Streatham in south west London with his parents when he was eight. As an outsider, Franco initially had to fight his way through school: 'I had an accent and I was picked on heavily so I had to learn to defend myself. They called me names and beat me up because I was an 'eye-tie', and the 'eye-ties' had lost the war.' The pressure was erased he says, when the 'blacks came along and we moved up the ladder if you like'.

Work as a crew member on Ken Loach's *Kes* (1968) led to editing work for John Lennon on his and Yoko's short film *Bed Peace* (1969) and the film for the 'Give Peace A Chance' single. His next editing job was on *Reggae* (1971), Horace Ové's documentary of the 1970 reggae concert held at Wembley Stadium. Next was a further look at London's West Indian culture in his own documentary on the targeting by police of the Notting Hill Caribbean restaurant The Mangrove which was raided 12 times between January 1960 and July 1970. A month after that last raid, a protest march against these events ended in violence and the arrest of nine protesters on charges that included conspiracy to incite a riot. Rosso's film, *The Mangrove Nine* (1973), was associate produced by Ové and includes interviews with the defendants before they were eventually acquitted. Rosso continued his working relationship with Ove by editing and operating the sound camera on the director's own 1973 BBC documentary *King Carnival*.

Rosso followed this with a documentary on Linton Kwesi Johnson, **DREAD BEAT & BLOOD (1979)**. Made for the BBC's *Omnibus* series, the corporation held back broadcast until after the 1979 General Election, feeling the film to be politically biased – it included an uncomplimentary reference to the then leader of the opposition.

> Maggi Tatcha on di go
> Wid a racist show
> But she a haffa go

Rosso cites his own immigrant status for his interest in the plight of minorities, but concedes: 'it was a lot easier for us than West Indians or Indians or any people of colour because we were white so you could, in fact, hide and disappear into the background. If you kept quiet, nobody knew. Whereas, of course, when West Indians came along they were very easily picked off because of their colour.'

Included on the DVD release of the director's *Babylon*, in the documentary Johnson speaks about his method and form of writing; 'The words usually come to me with a beat, the words come simultaneously with music, usually a bass line'. He speaks of the 'urgency of expression, the need to articulate, the need to say something 'cause of what was happening at the particular time' and how he 'couldn't communicate fluently that experience within the English language' which he found 'too dead, too sterile to communicate the violence of that experience' and so 'naturally reverted to.. the language of the group to which I belong, about whose experience I wanted to write.'

He takes us on a tour around Brixton market where he says the vibe is very much like Kingston and describes the importance of the sound systems which, 'the whole lifestyle of young blacks revolves around.' It is from attending sound systems he 'learned from the DJs that poetry isn't what you read in books... that there was a thing called aural poetry, where the emphasis is on the spoken word... [which] has a greater immediacy [and] reaches more people than written poetry could ever dream of doing.'

Johnson is seen working alongside Darcus Howe at the Race Today offices and performing a reading and Q&A at a school, explaining in voice-over how black boys coming from Jamaica are put into the bottom stream because it assumed they belong there, having himself had to fight for the education he received. He also performs '5 Nights of Bleeding' with a band in the recording studio (or is it a 70s living room?) and then, to even greater effect, at a spoken word gig at Railton Road Community Centre.

With footage from the 1976 *Carnival* and extracts from 'All Wi Doin Is Defendin', he tells us 'For the first time in the history of the British police force they underwent a major defeat, and it was just young blacks on the streets of Notting Hill. They were a force, and they knew they were a force, who unlike their parents, a demoralised people from the Caribbean... a new generation who were born in this country, who knew exactly who they are and what they're about, were not willing to take anything from anybody, who couldn't give a fuck about nobody and nothing. The state has realised that young blacks have come to assert themselves as a force in this society and that we've made some progress and they're trying to take those gains away from us. We're gonna be in for some very dread time in Inglan'

In interviews, Rosso has suggested that the idea to base his feature debut on sound system culture came after he visited them whilst making his documentary with Linton Kwesi Johnson and meeting Jah Shaka. In the same interview he suggested the project took 5 or 6 years to come to fruition, which places the film's origins sometime earlier and gives credence to screenwriter Martin Stellman's assertion that 'I took Franco with me to Sound Systems – he wasn't going before, but, funnily enough, he knew about them because this church where he lived in Lewisham had a blues party every Friday... literally at the back of his garden.'

Rosso initially contacted Martin Stellman, who had scripts written later – *Quadrophenia* (1979) and *McVicar* (1980) – opening in the cinemas before what would become *Babylon*. Says Stellman: '*Babylon* was a long haul, as you can imagine because we were doing a fairly marginalised subject.' After reading a piece he had written for Time Out on Native Americans, Rosso suggested they might collaborate on a script. By a stroke of luck, initially unknown to the director, Stellman not only lived locally but was working as a youth and community worker in Deptford where part of his remit was overseeing a sound system.

Hippies, Skinheads, Rastas, Punks & Disco Dancing Bowie Boot Boys

Don Warrington is in the dock in *Black & Blue*

In the meantime Stellman and Rosso co-wrote an episode of **CROWN COURT: BLACK AND BLUE (1978)**. After arresting three black youths for an attempted robbery, the police had called at the home of Mrs Wilbur Conway and her son Delroy (*Rising Damp*'s Don Warrington with a Geordie accent). During the visit, a serious fight had broken out between the investigating officers and the Conway's. As a result, Wilbur and Delroy were arrested and charged with assaulting police officers in the execution of their duty. Delroy faces an additional and more serious count of wounding.

A vehicle registered in Delroy's name had been used in a robbery, and a fourth youth had evaded capture. According to the police officer, when asked to accompany him to the station in order to identify the vehicle, Delroy 'lunged forward and punched me in the face with his fist' and his mother had stepped in to try to prevent him making an arrest. 'She took hold of my hair and at the same time she pulled, she kicked me,' he continued. Delroy was then said to have struck him with a heavy object. At one point, they remove Delroy from the court for contempt: 'Immigrant this, immigrant that. I'm not an immigrant. I was born in this country.'

Delroy claims to have been 'done over' at the police station but his barrister has agreed with the prosecution not to bring it up if they do not bring up a previous conviction, as it is purely his word against theirs. The defence suggests the glass 'heavy object' toppled from a bar during the scuffle when both men grappled on the floor after the police had barged into the house aggressively without producing their warrant cards. In a scene echoing one in *Pressure*, it is a rude awkening for Delroy's mother who hadn't previously believed her son's stories of unwarranted police attention and aggression.

Delroy demands to defend himself and has much to say about the racist society he lives in: 'I never walk anywhere after 11 p.m at night, nor does any other young black kid who lives round here 'cos if you're on the street walking home you get picked up on suspicion. In fact, it's got so bad, the other night I was walking the last half mile from the station to home when I got stopped three times by three different coppers. They're falling over themselves to try arrest us. So here I am, unemployed, having to take a taxi to go out at night and the way things are going I think I'm gonna have to use 'em during the day cos it's getting out of hand with the buses and all. Couple of weeks ago I was standing at a bus stop, going to the pictures with some mates. There were a lot of shoppers and a lot of young kids, just going to the pictures cos it's midday Saturday, then this police van and a panda car screeches to a halt. All these coppers leap out, separate the black kids from the white kids and so it's just black kids. They've got the idea fixed in their minds, every time they see a black he's a mugger or a pickpocket. So every time they see a black face they're gonna look twice at him.'

Despite numerous knock backs Rosso and Stellman did not give up on **BABYLON (1980)**. Slated at one point to become a *Play For Today*, Rosso says, 'the BBC got scared and gave it back to us,' and so the two writers began the search for backers who might fund their script as a feature. Things began to fall into place when the script was read by Gavrik Losey, the son of blacklisted American director Joseph Losey, who had previously worked in various positions on high-profile projects for companies such as Apple for *Magical Mystery Tour* (1967)), Woodfall for *If...* (1968)) and EMI for *That'll Be the Day* (1973) and *Stardust* (1974).

Having been part of the Board at the BFI that had green-lit *Pressure*, Mahmoud Hassan next joined the grandly titled National Film Finance Corporation. The NFFC was started in 1951 by Harold Wilson, then at the Board of Trade, as a response by the Labour government to counter the monopoly of American movies that were being distributed. It was in effect a bank that provided 30% of the budget, with the producer having to raise the other 70% from the distributors. It was investing in 50 films a year and was profitable because in those days there were 1500 million admissions to the cinema.

By the time Mamoun Hassan came on board as Managing Director, he was joining an organisation that had almost

Hippies, Skinheads, Rastas, Punks & Disco Dancing Bowie Boot Boys

The country's gone to the dogs in *Babylon*

no money from a government that was not interested in backing even the handful of features a year it was then helping. Neither it seemed were major outside investors, with Losey, who had presented the script to Hassan after joining the *Babylon* team as producer, finding only two minor interested parties, including, no doubt utilising experience gained on *That'll Be the Day*, one from Chrysalis Records as an advance for the rights to a soundtrack album.

Says Hassan: 'In the extreme situation that I found myself when co-investors were thin on the ground or non-existent for the films that I wanted to back (this was before Film Four) I decided early on that we would invest whatever was necessary to get a film made.' With *Babylon* that would involve persuading the rest of the Board to allow him to invest 83% - almost £300,000 of the films eventual £375,000 budget. 'I was breaking all the rules at one go,' he says, 'I backed a first-time director to film a subject that was considered a no-goer and took nearly all the financial risk.'

This proved easier than might be expected: 'I didn't have any problems. The thing is, if you're willing to be sacked you don't have any problems.' The appointment taught him that 'Boards will let you have your way at the beginning and end of your tenure. At the start, they think it is just possible that you may be right but if you're wrong, then you'll have shot yourself in the head and that's that. At the end, they just want to see the back of you and will agree out of weariness. It's the middle period that's sticky.'

Just as England's white youth had found a voice for their discontent at the country's growing economic inequality in the Punk movement, so too did the country's black youth in Britain's burgeoning reggae scene. One further important addition to the complement of *Babylon*'s immigrant creative team was Matumbi keyboard player Dennis Bovell. Bovell, who had arrived in the country from Barbados as a pre-teen in 1965, was not Franco Rosso's first choice to provide the film's soundtrack, having initially approached Linton Kwesi Johnson. Johnson, says Bovell, 'graciously said no, you want Dennis for that.' Bovell, who had been the sound engineer on *Dread Beat and Blood*, gratefully accepted, noting that the script had echoes of his own recent past.

The involvement of Bovell, whose father had run a sound system playing at blues parties, weddings and christenings, often just for 'some beer or some weed,' gave the project a real authenticity. Soon after leaving school Bovell himself had a reggae band, Matumbi, supplying the backing to visiting reggae artists such as

Ken Boothe and I-Roy, and, after a friend heard the dubplates he had recorded in the school studio and sold to the likes of Duke Reid and Coxsone, became part of a system called Sufferer's Hi-Fi, consisting of four 600-watt amplifiers and 40 18 inch speakers. Sufferer's started playing in a club called the Lansdowne in Stockwell and were soon appearing at prestigious venues, first playing The Four Aces in Hackney in 1972, and soon after had managed to secure a residency at the Metro youth club on the corner of Tavistock Road, where on New Year's Eve 1975 they staged their first sound clash with Jah Shaka, who appears in *Babylon* and whose system provides the rivalry for the fictional Ital Lion crew who comprise the film's major characters. One incident from Bovell's real-life sound system career resounds heavily on the film's final scene.

Bovell had written music for the TV series *Empire Road* with his band Matumbi, but this was the first time he had attempted a film soundtrack, working from rushes that he would play on a video recorder provided for him by the production, an expensive piece of kit at the time, as the filming took place, creating a tune for each character.

Bovell thought it would be improper to just write new music because of the movie's ties to Jamaica and also his awareness that the Shaka Sound System 'wouldn't be playing any kind of British productions unless they was his own.' One track that Shaka submitted was his friend Johnny Clarke's 'Babylon,' which was suggested as a probable theme tune but Bovell says 'I had to override that because Brinsley Forde was the protagonist and the frontman of Aswad and it seemed... if I didn't allow him to get a peep in, Aswad-wise, it would have been seen as selfish of me. When it came to the writing of the piece of music Brinsley was gonna do in the move I was like, "Brins, you can do that yourself, you don't need me."'

The Aswad connection to the film was anyway stronger than just the inclusion of Forde in the cast, Bovell having brought band members Angus 'Drummie Zeb' Kaye and Tony 'Gad' Robinson on board for the soundtrack, because, he says, 'I suspected it was aiming to be a showdown sound clash of sorts on film between Aswad and Matumbi and I was anxious to nip that in the bud.' It was not an unfamiliar set up for any of those involved as Bovell, Kaye and Robinson had already worked as a team on Janet Kay's 'Silly Games', which was riding high in the charts. Bovell also provided the films Punk credentials in the form of Pop Group, Slits and PIL drummer Bruce Smith who appears on the music that plays when they are in the West End. Bovell recorded the music twice, first with reggae musicians and then with Smith replacing the drummer, mixing the reggae version into the Punk version halfway through.

Babylon spends a few days in the company of a group of young friends in South London whose lives revolve around their reggae sound system, Ital Lion, as they prepare for a sound clash with the long-established Jah Shaka. They are, leader Dreadhead (Archie Pool), toaster Blue (Brinsley Forde), roadie Beefy (Trevor Laird), electrician Spark (Brian Bovell), hustler and fixer Errol (David N Haynes), ladies man Lover (Victor Romero Evans) and Blue's pork-pie hat-wearing white friend Ronnie (Karl Howman).

It's a world where everything is a hustle, be it getting the right dubplates from local record shop owner Fat Larry (Stefan Kalipha), replacing broken equipment by stealing the local secondary school's tannoy system, or securing a cannabis deal – where we learn loyalty to the group goes only so far when Ronnie gets royally ripped off by Errol (as does Beefy over a stolen video camera).

Racism is a constant presence, from the white nationalist slogans that seem to occupy every wall in pre-gentrification Brixton, to the neighbour who suggests the boys should return to their own country, told by an aggrieved Beefy that 'This is my fucking country lady and it's never been lovely, it's always been a fucking tip for as long as I remember, so don't fucking tell me, right!' In fact, it's so prevalent to the group's everyday existence that Beefy apart, it barely registers. There's more of the same, this time from the woman's husband and son, when they return from an engagement party and a bottle from the balcony is hurled as they chat by the van. It's Beefy again who is quick to react, this time pulling a knife, intent on taking them on, but restrained and eventually calmed down.

The worst offenders are the police, presumably the SPG, who drive slowly alongside Blue in an unmarked Hillman Hunter during the wee small hours, causing the scared youth to make a run for it. When he's caught he's roughed up, racially abused and arrested. Says Franco: 'A black kid is going to be used to having a certain kind of treatment. If it's late at night and a car with a load of white guys in it follows him, he'll either panic and run, or stop and hope. If he runs, the cops in the car will have triggered off within them an automatic response. They'll assume they're seeing guilt.' One kid quoted in a New Standard review suggests the director's opinion

Brinsley Forde is under heavy manners in *Babylon*

of the police might be somewhat naïve, saying Blue 'was lucky they didn't plant anything on him. If you run from a policeman, you've got to make sure you're not caught.'

Though he's bailed by his mother, events for Blue go from bad to worse. When his stepfather voices his disgust at having footed the bail money, he packs a bag and heads over to his girlfriends only to find her out. He instead hooks up with two friends who are heading into central London but once there discovers they are there to mug gay men, one pretending to be a male prostitute and leading the prospective punter into an alley where he is robbed and brutally beaten. Back on the estate, when his girl does finally arrive home at 6 a.m. from a soul club, his attitude leads her to blow him out. He instead goes to the lock-up where more bad news awaits.

In one of the most disturbing moments, more so in current times where British kids of all races have incorporated a form of Creole into their everyday language, the rest of the lads return to the lock-up to discover their equipment has been vandalised and the walls dubbed with NF slogans. 'Them a deal in pure wickedness' says Ronnie in his best faux Jamaican accent only to be rewarded with a bloody nose by Beefy, who retorts firmly, 'don't talk black.' It's the final straw for Blue who, when the other have left in search of a replacement system for that evening's sound clash, marches up to the racist family's flat and stabs the father.

A final sequence echoes events from Dennis Bovell's recent past. In October 1974 Sufferer's Hi-Fi appeared at the Carib Club in Cricklewood Broadway, one of three sound systems appearing that night. According to the police, they had arrested someone outside who had subsequently run into the club to escape but was apprehended in the toilets. When they emerged with their prisoner, members of the audience assaulted them and set him free. After returning with reinforcements the police, says Bovell, 'Came back and kicked everybody else's heads in.'

In 'Bass Culture', Lloyd Bradley's book chronicling the history of the sound system, Bovell says: 'They arrested forty-two people, and all those who didn't have visible bruises they let go.' Bovell was not amongst those initial arrests but afterward, in Ladbroke Grove, he was told that the police were looking for him and so voluntarily went to the police station 'and they went, "Yeah, come here, we want to talk to you." And then they accused me of starting the fight which I deny to this day. Basically, a policeman just went in court, put their hands on the Bible and lied.'

When the police raided, Lord Koos was at the mic geeing up the crowd and Junior Byles' 'Beat Down Babylon' was on the turntable. Says Bovell: 'That was all attributed to me. What I didn't do was go and say, "No no no no no, that wasn't me that was him!" My point was, "It wasn't me and I'm not saying who it was." Because if I'd had said, "It was him," I'd have had to go to court and stood in the witness box and said, "It was you, you did it." Right? Where I am I gonna go after that, in the community of sound systems.'

Charges were brought against twelve people, nine of whom were acquitted following a nine-month trial. Bovell was one of three on whom the jury could not reach a decision and so faced a retrial at which he was found guilty on a majority verdict and sentenced to three years, serving six months in Wormwood Scrubs before the conviction was overturned on appeal. Bovell says he was supposed to have urged the crowd to 'Get the boys in blue!' 'Get the boys in blue? There were a load of black people in that hall. Black people don't call the cops the boys in blue, that's an English term... a cockney term... The police further perjured themselves by saying they saw me on the stage with a microphone in my hand geeing up the crowd... I wanted to have a lie detector test; the judge was like "You can't expect police officers to take a lie detector test". I'm going, "Well why not? They're lying." It cost me dearly that.'

Franco Rosso had indeed read about the incident in the paper and based the final scene in *Babylon* on it. At the sound clash in the film, the atmosphere is tense because of the earlier violence involving Beefy. With Jah Shaka having finished his set, Ital Lion is on stage with Blue on the mic. Outside though, the police have arrived, pile out of their vans, and are soon up the stairs of the concert hall, hammering on the doors that are barricaded against them as Blue defiantly plays on.

Not everyone was happy that the film's main creative forces were not from the black community. Molara Ogundipe-Leslie, in the Guardian, suggested this whiteness negated the film's authenticity; 'If there are funds for the making of such films as *Babylon*, should they not be awarded to black filmmakers? Or, could non-black filmmakers work more closely at the conceptual level with black artists and intellectuals who know their people better and who can define their own reality more truthfully? This is not to argue that culture runs in genes but to say that it is necessary to know a people's emotional life from within to produce authentic works of art about such people. And the barriers are not racial: they are cultural, psychological and emotional.' Audiences, including the three youths who attended a preview screening with the New Standard's Guy Pierce, disagreed, finding the film 'very true to life. That's exactly how it happens' as did Brinsley Forde who said '*Babylon* is as accurate as you can go in a film.'

The Guardian also accused the film of negative stereotyping when one of its journalists went on a tour of Brixton public houses to gauge reactions to the film, and found 'a holding back, a lack of outright enthusiasm.' It was an attitude he felt was summed up by a young cook of a similar age to the film's main characters: 'People seeing the film seem to think it's about West Indians, not a few individuals. So we get all the clichés of behaviour. Blacks are into drugs, casual sex, loud music, violence. It confirms all the prejudices. Me, if that group playing their loud reggae music under my house, I'd protest like the white people in the film did.' He preferred, he said, rock or classical music, 'Only that doesn't fit the stereotype, does it?... When will we see a film in which English people of West Indian descent are not into drugs, casual sex or violence, but are living ordinary lives like white characters in English films?' It's an early example of a question that is still asked after the release of nearly every film featuring black youths.

The film was largely positively reviewed. The Guardian's Derek Malcolm called it a 'genuinely good film in a year when we are in need of something that isn't put together simply and solely to make a box-office killing.,' and the Times' David Robinson thought 'it gives a wholly believable, unsentimentalised, unglamorised feeling of what it is like to belong to a black community in London.' Time Out featured Trevor Laird and Brinsley Forde on their front cover with the headline 'Great Black Hope'. The film was also favourably received in the United States where Variety called it 'rich, rough and real... threatening, touching, violent and funny,' and said it was 'a British film with more heart and soul than any home-produced feature of the last twenty years.' Their reviewer praised the film's 'lack of an overt social or political message' and the filmmaker's decision to allow 'the chain of events to develop its own momentum, rather than one imposed by script or direction.'

Dissenting voices included the Monthly Film Bulletin who called it 'merely another depressing, but easily consumable slice of life' and Sounds who, flexing their supposed music credentials, suggested that no decent sound system would ever play 'Warrior Charge'. In fact, Jah Shaka had already played 'Warrior Charge' in the 1980 Gold Cup at Acton Town Hall where the line-up was Soprano B vs Sir Coxsone vs Jah Shaka.

Unfortunately, the box office never matched the reviews, a situation perhaps not helped by the BBFC's imposition of an X certificate on a film that had a clear appeal for a youthful audience who would have been comfortable with the patois dialogue, but were at a stroke, banned from seeing it. This combined with distribution problems, original distributor Osris going out of business, to mean the film had only recovered a little over £90,000 of its budget by 1986.

Hassan puts the film's financial difficulties down to the distribution system itself. 'It's a system which really only favours the very successful... it's not an even way of dealing with the money coming in. The producer of the film is the last person to get the money back. The first person is the exhibitor who holds on to anything up to 60 or 70% of the take. Then the cinema owner passes on a small amount to the distributor, and then they pass a small amount of that on to the producers... the ones who took the greatest risk. That means the system favours the big companies, the majors... who are both distributors and makers.'

Di Great Insohreckshan
(Johnson)

In 1980 the Black and White cafe on Grosvenor Road, in the largely black St. Paul's area of Bristol's 'frontline', was simply the ground floor of a terraced house but nevertheless an important part of the community - a place where the areas unemployed youth might gather to play pinball or dominoes and smoke a little weed. It had also been a place to have a few beers until it had its licence to sell alcohol removed.

With racial tensions in the area already running high, in April twenty or so police officers raided the premises and arrested a customer and the café's owner, Bertram Wilks, for possession of cannabis and allowing it to be smoked on his premises. The police also confiscated a large quantity of alcohol, including brandy, vodka, and 132 crates of beer. In the time it took for the police to load up such a large haul, an angry crowd had begun to accumulate outside. The result was hours of violent clashes that left 33 people injured and 21 arrested, though no one was ever convicted of any crime. In an event that would foreshadow the riots of 2011, at one point the police withdrew and by the time enough back up had arrived to force the rioters back, a branch of Lloyds Bank, a post office, a row of shops and a warehouse in Brighton Street were all attacked and robbed.

Though not resident in the area, the events left an impression on the 26-year-old Diane Abbott. Writing in Leveller magazine, the future Labour MP for Hackney North and Shadow Home Secretary under Jeremy Corbyn said: 'My mother is a black working-class lady nearing 60. Eminently respectable and conservative-minded, she was pleased and excited by the ITN film of policemen running away from black youth and said firmly: "It shows they can't push us around anymore". The riots politicised my mother and others like her and the state is well aware they posed a direct threat to its power — the more so because they were entirely spontaneous. But those on the white left who won't learn the lessons of Bristol and insist on incorporating what happened into their own world-view may well find that the revolution happens without them'.

The next day, a Daily Telegraph headline declared '19 Police Hurt in Black Riot' and blamed a lack of parental care. Though barely reported outside of the area, the ink had barely dried on the Telegraph article when copycat riots broke out four miles down the A38 in Southmead. The difference was that this was a White Riot, the rioters being residents of a predominately white working-class council estate. With no 'spark' in evidence, the youth of Southmead who shared many of the grievances of their black neighbours, had obviously pricked up their ears and decided they would have 'a riot of our own'.

Speaking to the Guardian, Franco Rosso said: 'What we were trying to do [with *Babylon*] was tell a good story that was also a warning. That was a year ago. But now that warning seems even more necessary. We are sitting on a powder keg where racial trouble is concerned. Bristol proved that. It also proved that we were totally unprepared for what happened there, and what could occur again and again as unemployment rises and the economic squeeze tightens. What was happening to young blacks when we made the film is now happening to young whites too. Yet we are doing nothing coherent about it. We're just hoping it will all go away. The thrust of our film is that it won't.'

'But I don't think we've made a film that suggests there's no hope either. If *Babylon* angers some blacks of the older generation because it suggests that their children are trying to organise themselves politically, then it has done its job. They are indeed trying to organise because they know that, if they don't, no change will be forthcoming. They should be encouraged, not discouraged. It isn't just a matter of 'black is beautiful' but of 'black is powerful'. People must begin to listen before it's too late.' But they didn't.

Also predicting a riot was Barrie Keeffe's 1979 play *SUS*. Filmed in 2010, that version closes with the reminder that although the riots of the eighties caused the Thatcher government to scrap SUS, under current legislation black people are 7 times more likely than white people to be stopped and searched. The rioting that would break out across London just 15 months on from the film's opening inspired a host of new playwrights to put pen to paper. Many, like Alecky Blythe and Gillian Slovo, would document events of 2011, but it would inspire some to revisit the eighties.

Calls for a post-Bristol public enquiry were dismissed by Home Secretary William Whitelaw who felt the inevitable criticism of the police could serve no good purpose. Some subsequently believed that an enquiry might have prevented the widespread violence that took place the following year, though this assumes, the highly unlikely scenario of any findings of such an enquiry being properly implemented. What the authorities should have noted was the way the young people of Bristol had been emboldened by the events, especially when, of the 12 'rioters' hauled in front of the court, eight defendants were acquitted and the jury found itself deadlocked on the other four. It would not have gone unnoticed in similar areas across the country. 'We took on the police and beat them. They will never again treat us with contempt.... They will respect us now' said one youth, quoted in the Sun. The local parish priest reminded the media of Martin Luther King's assertion that riots are the voices of the unheard, telling the Telegraph, 'the community has stood up to say, very loudly, "I am"'.

Failing this, the writing was certainly on the wall - in South London at least where graffiti read: 'Bristol now, Brixton next?' and 'Bristol yesterday, Brixton today'. In the Spring of 1981, just two weeks before the streets of Brixton erupted in violence, a half dozen journalists met with the Commander, Deputy Commissioner, and other Met top brass to discuss race relations. Among them were two black radio journalists who told of young blacks 'picked on and roughed up in the back of police cars.' They also warned that 'the fire was coming.' One journalist, Syd Burke from LBC, had tested the atmosphere in Brixton by driving around the area with three youths in his car one evening. They were stopped three times. 'When the police stop you, they tell you to go stand under the light,' he said, 'The obvious implication being that they won't be able to see your face unless you do.'

That little note would be taken is clear from the response to such accusations from Eldon Griffiths MP, Parliamentary consultant to the Police Federation, who said: 'Enoch Powell was right when he warned that the concentration of large numbers of black and brown immigrants into urban ghettos, sooner or later would lead to racial confrontation and bloodshed.' He also told the newspapers that 'the accusation... that the Metropolitan Police is racially biased' was 'a damnable lie'. On the contrary, he suggested that, 'Day by day, the police offer far more practical help to the coloured community than any other single group.' Griffiths had served for four years as Sports Minister under Ted Heath, an appointment it is said was made because of his support for sporting links with South Africa, having famously walked out of a service in Bury St Edmunds' abbey ruins when the anti-apartheid activist Bishop Dr Trevor Huddleston attacked arms sales to South Africa. His denunciation of the legislation which would become the Race Relations Act as 'a wretched little bill' would, therefore, seem to have made him an ideal candidate for appointment to the Police Federation - and his subsequent knighthood.

*

With *Babylon* having taken several years to make the transition from an idea to the nation's cinema screens, the events across the country that followed it were never likely to be depicted in a feature film anytime soon, and so it was left to documentary makers and playwrights. Menelik Shabazz had just completed his feature film *Burning An Illusion* (1981) when he heard the news about a fire in New Cross and became involved in the coming together of various organisations to express their anger at the way the police and the authorities were handling the case. One outcome of this was the Black People's Day of Action March, the first time black people in the UK had demonstrated publicly in such large numbers. Calling it a compulsion as opposed to a project, Shabazz borrowed old film stock from cinematographers, who used to keep film cans in their fridges, known to be sympathetic

On the march in *Blood Ah Go Run*

to the cause and organised two film crews to capture the events. The film, **BLOOD AH GO RUN (1981)**, was edited after hours by a BBC editor, without the corporation's knowledge of course. It also contains footage of the rioting in Brixton a few months later.

The fire broke out at a house in New Cross Road where a joint birthday party was being held for Yvonne Ruddock (who died) and Angela Jackson (who survived). The party had begun on Saturday evening and continued into the small hours of Sunday morning when at 5.40 a fire broke out in the living room. There had been complaints about the level of noise and it was widely believed in the community to have been a deliberate attack, a theory also initially favoured by the police who suspected it may have been the result of a firebomb through the living room window.

This theory was ruled out at the inquest where the coroner's summary for the jury, who reached an open verdict, was heavily directed towards suggesting the fire was accidental. A judicial challenge brought by the victims' families to the High Court agreed that the summing-up was inaccurate but did not overturn the verdict. A second inquest was held in 2004. Ruling out the possibility 'that a petrol bomb or incendiary device was introduced from outside or inside the house', the deputy coroner concluded that 'on the totality of the evidence that while I think it is probable, more likely than not, that this fire was started by the deliberate application of a flame to an armchair near the television or curtains, I cannot be sure of this.' But because there was still a possibility that the fire was started accidentally, this second inquest also resulted in an open verdict.

Shot as deliberate agit-prop and in newsreel style which harked back to the propaganda films of World War 2, Shabazz's documentary makes no attempt at partiality and was intended to be circulated in the black community, though in reality few people ever saw the film because it was only available as a 16mm print.

There's a moment in *Blood Ah Go Run* where the camera lingers on a black police officer in a very white police force where I wondered how he might have survived his life in the black community once he was out of uniform. I was reminded of him when watching an episode of *Law & Order: I Predict A Riot* (2014) in which a car pulled from the river iis found to contain the body of a black undercover police officer who had gone missing during rioting in Brixton some decades earlier. When the murder weapon turns out to be a police truncheon, the investigation leads the investigating officers to the still serving and still racist DS Darren Grady (Ralph Brown), who tells black officer Joe (Ben Bailey Smith) that it was too dark to see the victim who was also black.

Close your eyes and you can smell the petrol and taste the tear gas in Rex Obano's 90-minute radio play **LOVER'S ROCK (2012)**, broadcast on BBC Radio 3 during November 2012, bringing alive the events in Shabazz's documentary. To the accompaniment of Dennis Brown's 'Revolution,' the play opens with a voice-over by Benoit Boateng (Kobna Holdbrook-Smith) a 23-year-old black youth who tells us that Brixton has gone up in flames. To some, he says, it is lawlessness and criminality but 'to others, this is a festival of the oppressed. Taking Brixton back from the police who have swamped the area with a vengeance.'

It is the afternoon of the 10th April 1981 and he is joined by his white friend Ginger (Will Howard) and the two of them pour petrol into bottles before stuffing the necks with rags. 'This is Thatcher's Britain and it couldn't be defeated with pacifism. This is our revolution. The end of being pushed around. The end to standing by.' As the riot goes into overdrive, we learn of the events that led the largely apolitical Benoit to the front line.

The action moves back ten weeks to the early hours of the 18th January where Benoit and Ginger are making their way home from the Cats Whisker's nightclub where the soundtrack was 'D.I.S.C.O' by Ottawan and the décor had comprised a glitter-ball. Their car is pulled over and Benoit is searched by two police officers, one of whom, Sergeant Fraser, refers to Benoit as a 'monkey' and says of Ginger, it 'looks like they've shaved this one.' Ginger, steeped in radical politics, is mouthy but Benoit is quietly accepting of his treatment.

According to Fraser: 'Prejudice comes with the job. We can't do our job without it. How else are we supposed to single the wrong un's out?... they came here with nothing and they want something we have.' The evening takes an unexpected twist when the other officer, Ray, turns up at Benoit's flat for the night as his lover.

This is also, and not co-incidentally, the night of the New Cross Fire. Though the play is top and tailed by the outbreak of rioting, it is events that immediately preceded this that provides the heart of Lovers Rock. Events that would create a seminal moment in black British history, politicising people nationwide who had hitherto been reluctant to rock the boat, it was said Obano 'a line in the sand'.

The story takes in the meeting on the 25th of January at the Moonshot Club in New Cross which was attended by over 1000 and the Black People's Day of Action in which 20,000 marched for eight hours from Fordham Park to Hyde Park, despite the police cutting the march in two by blocking off Blackfriar's Bridge, part of the agreed route. Though this, seen as a deliberate act of provocation, caused anger and confusion, the event passed relatively peacefully enough for it to receive only a cursory mention in the newspapers, apart from The Sun who went with a headline of 'Day The Blacks Ran Riot in London'.

At the time of the events depicted in the play, its author was a second-year pupil at his comprehensive situated between Brixton and Hackney; a Soul Boy who was being introduced to lovers rock by his sister. It is a genre that never really left the underground but has remained a staple of Obano's playlists - evident from the play's title and in the majority of its music with tracks from the likes of Jean Adebambo, Victor Romero Evans, Louisa Marks, Janet Kay, and Carroll Thompson.

The anchor for this music is 18-year-old Derek Monroe (Tobi Bakare) who assists on his brother's sound system and after hearing 15-year-old Angela (Eleanor Crooks) singing in a sasparilla shop, uses the tragedy to persuade her to skip her homework and lay down some vocals in his brothers studio: 'C'mon girl, those kids died before they had a chance to live - it's up to us to live - yeah?' Derek believes that in Angela he 'has found the real deal' that can provide lover's rock with a crossover into the mainstream. She is, he tells a producer 'pretty too - pretty like money.' The producer is interested, saying the scene needs a star with a commercial look that can break into the mainstream. Derek is too naïve to know that commercial means white.

Derek is arrested (and given a going over in the interview room) on the day of the march, despite not attending, for being 'outside Dickie Dirts with some Hi-Fi equipment in the back of a van. He didn't look like he could afford it... When I turned him upside down fresh air fell out of his pocket so that's why he was kind enough to accompany me here.' When he is stopped again by Sgt. Monroe on the way to the cinema to meet Angela he too is drawn into the rioting that will break out that day.

An early response to the 1981 riots was Doug Lucie's **HARD FEELINGS** which was first staged at the Oxford Playhouse in 1982 before transferring to London's Bush Theatre the following year, then becoming a BBC Play For Today in 1984. The rioting provides a backdrop to the events that take place inside a shared house in Brixton occupied by a group of white upper-middle class Oxford graduates, using the tensions outside in much the same way as Trevor Griffiths had used the same years Moss Side riots in Oi For England.

The play examines the tensions amongst a bunch of housemates living in a house ruled over by Viv (Frances Barber) on account of her parents. with an eye on the future, having bought it as an investment. There's the anti-Semitic model Annie (Diana Katis), her New Romantic boyfriend Rusty (Ian Reddington - soon to be Eastenders Tricky Dicky), fence-sitter Baz, trainee solicitor Jane and her working-class boyfriend, left-wing agitator Tone (Stephen Tiller), the only one of the group who gets involved in the trouble outside, and whose inability to hide his contempt for Viv sets in motion a vendetta against Jane that reaches its peak with the unveiling of a montage of Hitler in the living room.

The events were covered retrospectively in two BBC programmes, one for television and one for radio. Helen Littleboy's **THE BATTLE FOR BRIXTON (2006)** was broadcast on BBC2 for the 25th anniversary of the time when 'a thousand Londoner's declared war on the police' and who Alex Wheatle, whose novel 'East of Acre Lane' is set in 1981 Brixton, reminds us, 'were the enemy, simple as that.'

The distance between the two sides of this war is clear from their descriptions of Railton Road, the frontline. To Wheatle it was a place that 'from this cruel world we could just go... and be with our kin. We thought it belonged to the West Indian community… It was the place to be, the place to be seen, where DJ's practised their rhymes, the place where we scored weed.' To Brian Fairbairn, Brixton Police Commander at the time, it 'was the place where young blacks, muggers or thieves or whatever congregated. A place where the blacks and the police were staring at each other.'

The Conservative government of the time are not well served by the inclusion of a clip from *Newsnight* of MP Nicholas Winterton saying 'if any people wish to return to their country of ethnic origin they should be encouraged to do so.' Winterton's wife and fellow Conservative MP, Ann, became Shadow Rural Affairs Minister in 2001 and was sacked the next year for telling a racist joke at a rugby club dinner. Both stood down in 2009 after being found to have misused their MPs' expenses to pay rent for a flat they had already bought outright. Not to worry, Winterton had already picked up his knighthood back in 2002.

The police, most senior officer aside, admit mistakes were made and one, Peter Bleksley, confirms the racism and the brutality amongst officers. For the community, even after a quarter of a century, there's a sense of regret at some of the destruction but of pride at the confrontations with law and order from the rioters, represented by Wheatle, Blacker Dread (now the subject of Molly Dineen's 2017 documentary, *Being Blacker*), and his friend Brian Beckford, a former armed robber.

Described by the Telegraph as 'an unilluminating and biased perspective on the Brixton riots', **THE REUNION BRIXTON RIOTS**, was broadcast on BBC Radio 4 in 2011 in time for the 30th anniversary. Alongside the leader of Lambeth Borough Council, Ted Knight and journalist and broadcaster Darcus Howe, the discussion also reunited three alumni of Helen Littleboy's documentary, former policemen Brian Paddick and Peter Bleksley and Alex Wheatle. Their comments are largely the same, but the format allows for expansion of the earlier TV programme's sound-bites.

Wheatle, now an MBE and just 18 when the riots took place says: 'I arrived in Brixton at 14 after spending some time away in a Surrey children's home and my view of the police was not a very good one. When I came out to Brixton… I was told by the new friends that I made that they were the enemy and slowly but surely I found out why they were the enemy. At 16 I had a party and we were asked to turn the music down by officers. I have to admit we didn't, but the response… I could not quite believe. There were two SPG vans that came in, they busted down the door, busted down the furniture, ripped up the floorboards, arrested about thirty of us. Some of my Rasta friends had locks torn out their scalps. Beat us in our cells, had their feet down on our necks and faces.'

Author and reality TV presenter Peter Bleksley was then a young PC, brought in as backup, and recalls: 'Young black men in Brixton and Peckham were routinely fitted up, beaten up, tortured and worse' and that three years in the force had turned him from 'a pretty sort of decent 18-year-old boy from Bexley Heath' into a 'violent, racist, very unpleasant thug.' His stories of what went on in the confines of the police station make the horror of Wheatle's experience fade somewhat. 'We used to have skirting boards in some of the offices and the interview rooms and the technique would be to get a prisoner to go onto their knees and then their toes would be rested on the skirting board and then pressure would be applied on the heels. As the heels were forced downwards this would cause excruciating pain. This was carried on until the prisoner would say "Okay I'll admit to the burglary or attempted robbery", whatever it is the cops are alleging that person has done.' Lord Scarman's report found that though there

was racism in the police, it was not institutional. Blecksley agrees: 'It was compulsory, it wasn't institutional... and where the dreads were ripped off Rastafarians, they were proudly pinned to the notice board and displayed as some sort of trophy.'

*

Just two days after the 1981 rioting in Brixton came to a close, the then Home Secretary William Whitelaw appointed Lord Scarman to hold an enquiry that as well as looking at the 'spark' that ignited the disorder might also identify the underlying conditions in Britain's cities that had led to the rioting and suggest a remedy that would prevent future recurrence. Published during November 1981, Scarman concluded that the riot was 'essentially an outburst of anger and resentment by young black people against the police'. This resentment was blamed on 'complex political, social and economic factors' that included racial disadvantage, inner city decline, and the disproportionate and indiscriminate use of 'stop and search' powers by the police against the black community.

Though Scarman recommended changes in training and law enforcement, and the recruitment of more ethnic minorities into the police force, with positive discrimination being 'a price worth paying', his report fell short of apportioning direct blame to the police. The report acknowledged that some officers had been guilty of 'ill considered, immature and racially prejudiced actions', but suggested that any discrimination against black people was 'unwitting'. The Met was not 'institutionally racist'. Accepting that hard policing such as stop and search would always be necessary in areas with severe social breakdown, the report pointed to the benefits of better community-police consultation and addressing the problems, both criminal and socioeconomic, at their root.

In 1982, in direct response to the previous autumn's disturbances, Sir Kenneth Newman was appointed as Commissioner of the Met, bringing with him to his new role a familiarity with public order policing gained as the head of the Royal Ulster Constabulary (RUC). Newman 'put the people of London on notice' that he would not shrink from... a decision [to use plastic bullets].' Plastic bullets had already killed 12 people, 6 of them children, in Northern Ireland and on the mainland police were holding 20,000 rounds, mainly in London. If certain people inside government had their way stocks would have soon been dwindling.

Newman's idea of better police-community consultation was to continue the high profile targeting by means of intense surveillance and military-style raids of trouble spots that included Broadwater Farm, the Notting Hill Carnival, and Railton Road. This time they were given a name, 'symbolic locations', and were areas where large numbers of black youths might congregate.

Said Newman: 'This brand of destruction and hostility is at its height in certain parts of ethnic areas which have become a focal point for congregation and association by black youths. In these locations confrontations with the police are deliberately engineered either to make a political point or to create a diversion in order to facilitate organised crime in relation to drugs or stolen property. If allowed to continue, locations with these characteristics assume a symbolic importance, a negative symbolism of the inability of the police to maintain order... The youths take a proprietorial posture in this location; they regard it as their territory. In general, they will regard the police as intruders.' In the meantime, high profile incidents involving negative police treatment for members of the black community continued unabated. What could possibly go wrong?

Some of these events were revisited in **WINDRUSH SQUARE** which, presented by the Monument Theatre Company in 2018, spans the years from 1981 to 1985. Beginning with the New Cross fire, the play visits the riots of 81 and 85, and also a death in custody. All these events are all seen through the eyes of three generations of one family, Granma Johnson, who came to England in the late 40s; her son Elijah; and his three children, Naomi, Ruby, and Isaac. They discuss each of these events at a community meeting chaired by Elijah.

The least revisited of *Windrush Square*'s events, was the death of 21-year-old Colin Roach inside the foyer of Stoke Newington police station in January 1983 from a single gunshot wound through the mouth. Recorded as a suicide, discrepancies in the police version of events from the outset led to suspicions of a cover-up. This included the fact that Colin's father was interviewed at the police station for two-and-a-half hours before he was told of his son's death. In court and on oath, the police claimed this period to be 15 minutes, a claim that was proved to the jury to be false. This was just part of what the leading barrister Lord Gifford, who subsequently chaired the Broadwater Farm inquiry, called an official version of events 'tainted by lies and conflicting evidence'. Other problems with the police version of events included the police surgeons conclusion that the position of the body contradicted suicide, the bag that the youth was said to have concealed the gun in not being big enough to do so, and an absence of any forensic evidence to show any connection between him and the gun. Despite this, the verdict of the inquest was that Colin had committed suicide.

This was also the subject of a documentary **WHO KILLED COLIN ROACH? (1983)** from director Isaac Julien who, then a student at St. Martin's School of Art, knew nothing about Colin Roach until, coming out of a jumble sale on a Saturday afternoon, he stepped straight into a protest march. Says Julien: 'It turned out that Colin Roach... had lived quite near my home. Which meant, of course, that Mrs Roach could have been my mother, that his family could easily have been my own.'

Harking back to the radical film workshops he had attended in his teens and the 'idea of the camera as a street weapon,' Julien decided to 'document on video, from a black point of view, a black family's and people's struggle against the state.' Shot on Super 8 and then transferred to tape, the 34-minute film features interviews with the Roach family, local campaigners and poet Benjamin Zephaniah, who had been just down the road when the killing happened and was amongst the first group of people to gather outside the police station. Zephania also performs his poem of the same name, 'a rather simple poem... written for chanting at demonstrations rather than reading in the comfort of your own home.'

The killing was also name-checked in 'We've Had Enough' by Birmingham reggae artist Macka B, a protest song which named the growing list of black people who had died in police custody, released on Mad Professor's south London based Ariwa label. Further name-checks can be found on 'Bright Lights', the b side of The Special AKA's 1983 'Racist Friend' single, and Demon Rockers' 'Iron Lady' from 1985.

But it was Sinead O'Connor who took Colin Roach into seven million homes across the world, on her second album, 1990's 'I Do Not Want What I Haven't Got'. On the track 'Black Boys on Mopeds', O'Connor addresses Colin's death alongside that of Nicholas Bramble, who in 1989 was chased by police on a moped they had wrongly suspected him of stealing and crashed. Though the song does not mention Roach by name, the album was dedicated to him and the record sleeve includes a photo of Colin and his family in the artwork.

Pointing the finger of blame in *Who KIlled Colin Roach*

In November 1982 a fourth channel made its debut on British television with a remit to 'ensure that the programmes contain a suitable proportion of matter calculated to appeal to tastes and interests not generally catered for by ITV' and to 'encourage innovation and experiment in the form and content of programmes'. The newly created Channel 4 was controlled by the IBA but funded by the ITV companies. Each had to pay an annual subscription from their net advertising revenue, freeing the channel from the usual commercial pressures. Unlike the other channels, Channel 4 did not produce the vast majority of its own programming. Instead, it hired independent producers. The voice of black Britain was provided by collectives and workshops such as Black Audio Film Collective, Sankofa Film and Video Collective, and Ceddo Film and Video Workshop. The government response, or lack thereof, to the recommendations in the Scarman Report meant they would have no shortage of subject matter. To fulfil this part of its remit, Channel 4, along with several other funders such as the BFI and the GLC, helped to establish workshops and made available production funds for these communities.

The best known of these 'workshop' programmes was **HANDSWORTH SONGS (1986)** produced by the Black Audio Film Collective. The collective was co-founded in 1982 by a group of black artists and filmmakers who had attended Portsmouth Polytechnic and subsequently relocated to Hackney where, says John Akomfrah, for whom *Handsworth Songs* was his directorial debut: 'we made film essays rather than YouTube shorts.' Born in Accra, Ghana, Akomfrah moved to London with his mother, his late father having been a cabinet member in the government of former revolutionary, Kwame Nkrumah, who became the country's first Prime Minister after having lead the country to independence from Britain in 1957.

That little of Scarman's advice would be acted on had been apparent as early as the 13th April 1981, when Margaret Thatcher categorically dismissed the suggestion that either unemployment or racism were responsible for the Brixton disturbances', a point-of-view finally laid to rest in 1999 when, in the wake of the Stephen Lawrence murder, the Macpherson Report pointed out that contrary to Scarman, the Metropolitan Police had been and was still 'institutionally racist'. Little surprise then when on the 9th September 1985, in the Handsworth district of Birmingham, a yellow and orange glow once again lit up the night sky. Once again the spark that set the years of simmering discontent alight was the arrest, for a minor traffic infraction, of a black man who fled into a nearby cafe. Police back-up was sought but by the time it arrived, the officers were met by a crowd who pelted them with stones and bottles. Following a subsequent police raid on the Villa Cross public house, rioting broke out that would last until the 11th, with 45 shops looted and burnt, one of which, a post office, led to the deaths of its two Pakistani occupants.

Premiering on Channel 4 in 1986, as part of the series *Britain: The Lie of the Land*, *Handsworth Songs* was the Black Audio Film Collective's attempt to document the rioting. The film originally had the wider brief of the country's underclass until a friend asked him to film in Handsworth on the third day of the riots. Says Akomfrah: 'Essentially most of the events that you see in the film happened in three afternoons and two evenings. We were shooting

with 16mm equipment, magazines that last for ten minutes max. So we were having to make choices there and then about what we could capture in that ten minutes that might be of value...' Akomfrah and editor Anna Liebschner then placed this footage within a wider historical context by interspersing it with photographs and archival footage including that of black immigrants in the 1950s. The documentary contradicts the existing news coverage's focus on young black males as 'criminals' and instead of community elders condemning the violence, Akromah filmed older black residents sympathising with the plight of young people in the community.

Handsworth Songs was never an attempt to explain why the riot happened, much to the annoyance of Salman Rushdie who attacked the film in the Guardian, calling it 'no good... we don't hear about their lives or the lives of their born-British children. We don't hear Handsworth's Songs.' Says Akomfrah: 'We didn't claim to be political theorists with all the answers. Because in some ways it was the very idea that there was an answer that the film was trying to problematise. Because all the "answers" seemed to suggest that someone was at fault. And invariably the category that was at fault was the "rioters". So it was a more complicated attempt to look at why people do what they do. Why does anybody do what they do?'

And so the film offers no voice-over interpreting events, instead relying on the audience to draw their own conclusions; in its place is an exceptional piece of sound design from Trevor Matheson which draws on dub but is equally reminiscent of bastions of the era's post-Punk movement like Cabaret Voltaire, or Mark Stewart and the Mafia whose dub cut-up of 'Jerusalem' features.

The film was well-received, winning several awards, including the prestigious John Grierson Award. City Limits said its 'overview of Black Britain, past and present... alone merits its widespread viewing' and to the Guardian, it was 'one of the very few examples of a political film also capable of poetry,' and called the film 'the most forceful and persuasive black film to be produced here since Horace Ove's *Pressure*.'

The Handsworth riot also featured in **BOMBIN' (1988)**, a Channel 4 documentary produced by Central and directed by Dick Fontaine. Previously responsible for the BBC's early look at the then-emerging musical genre with *Beat This: A Hip-Hop History* (1984), in *Bombin'* the director and his crew follow Bronx graffiti artist Brim Fuentes to the UK where he appears on TV-AM, delivers workshops in London, talks to students at the Oxford

University School of Drawing and does some graffiti, commissioned on the set of Michael Winner's *Death Wish 3* which was shooting in London. A case of right time right place means he also visits Handsworth the day after the riots where he talks to locals in the area and one raps about the riots. Again the documentary puts forward views that contest those heard in local news footage, where some Indian shop owners argued that they were deliberately targeted. Here, local rapper Cash Money argues: 'If it was black people that owned them shops they'd still get robbed... It doesn't matter who owns them, right.' The film is notable today for featuring early appearance of, then graffiti artists themselves, Goldie and 3D, the latter joining fellow future Massive Attackers in performance as The Wild Bunch.

As in 1981, the disturbances in Handsworth would prove just the beginning.

London based Ceddo also made a documentary film about the 1985 riots, **THE PEOPLE'S ACCOUNT (1986)**. Ceddo was a black collective set up by Menelik Shabazz and included people like Milton Bryan, Imruh Bakari Caesar, Glenn Ujebe Masokoane, Lazell Daily and cinematographer Roy Cornwall. Focusing mainly on the Broadwater Farm riot, like *Handsworth Songs*, *The People's Account* also tried to respond to how mainstream media had reported events, focusing on police mistreatment of Tottenham's black community, before, during and after the riots.

The programme was initially scheduled to be broadcast in July 1986 as part of *Eleventh Hour*, Channel 4's outlet for experimental filmmaking. This was then moved to November, re-scheduled first for reasons of 'balance', then because lawyers said it might interfere with ongoing criminal cases. When this fell through a third slot was scheduled for March 1987, but the Independent Broadcasting Authority (IBA) demanded changes. The film also commented on events in Brixton and it was its coverage of the police shooting of Cherry Groce, calling her 'a victim of police racism', that would mean it would never be shown.

According to the then Channel 4 Commissioning Editor Alan Fountain, Chief Executive Jeremy Isaacs made it clear his role was not that of a producer and to let the people who make films make the film they want: 'What we'd do was argue if we didn't like something or thought that something should be changed, or end, differently or whatever. We might spend a lot of time arguing about it, but in the end the decision would be left to them.' Ceddo's decision was no. Says Shabazz, 'we stuck with our guns because we said there was no legal reason why that cannot be said.' The IBA had also objected to a reference to the riots as 'a classic example of self-defence by a community' and insisted that the broadcast be followed by a discussion programme over which the producers would have no control.

Writer Cecil Gutzmore suggests the problems with the programme were of a broader nature: 'What made it go too far was precisely that it had ordinary black people describing what their experience of policing had been and it was in the kind of context where it asserted boldly and, as it happens, truthfully that our experience of policing is racist. That the police operate in relation to black people in a lawless and racist way.'

Shabazz's next piece to be broadcast on Channel 4, *Time and Judgement* (1988), was an 88 minute sci-fi/documentary which, with music from Bob Marley, Steel Pulse and Aswad, combined biblical prophecy with events across the African diaspora - wars, famine, riots, celebrations - ranging from Haile Selassie to Bernie Grant, but also Nation of Islam leader Louis Farrakhan and former Black Panther leader Kwame Ture, both banned from Britain. Shabazz thinks it 'may have triggered the movement to start to close down the workshops' but in reality, the writing was already on the wall. Preparations were being made for the 1990 Broadcasting Act, which would usher in an era of further commercialisation and spurring on the development of satellite broadcasting. With the new Chief Executive Michael Grade preparing for this changing market by introducing a higher level of 'professionalism' to the channel, by 1993 Channel 4 was selling its own advertising. The days of programmes like *Eleventh Hour*, which Alan Fountain says considered Grade to be 'ghetto rubbish', were quickly numbered.

*

When three times BAFTA winning television writer Jack Rosenthal became friends with Les Murphy, a London-based firefighter, the stories about life in the fire service his friend recounted inspired the writer to pen something about the men and women, of which he says, 'Unlike soldiers or policemen to whom danger and possible death are a virtual raison d'être, they are civilians. They don't face flick knives, guns, or bombs. They live at home with their families and go off to work like the rest of us. And there the similarity stops. At any moment in the next eight hours, they could be fighting for people's lives in a literal hell of pitch-black smoke and searing infernos.' Having considered writing both a documentary and a sitcom, a real-life incident that unfolded in Tottenham on the 6th October 1985 provided a focus for a story that would take the form of a one-off TV movie, *London's Burning* (1986).

The events of that night had their roots in an incident just over a week earlier, on the 28th September, that had resulted in the shooting by police and subsequent paralysis of a mother of eight, Cherry Groce, in Brixton, causing an increase in tensions between the city's black population, especially its youth, and law enforcement.

The Broadwater Farm housing estate in Tottenham was built on open land that had previously been allotments under a recently elected Labour government that was encouraging local authorities to build 1000 new units a year as part of a slum clearance programme. Construction began in 1967 and was completed in 1973, and given the slums conditions most of the estate's new residents had moved from, the new flats were enthusiastically received, being warm, dry and spacious. In total there were 1063 properties arranged into 12 blocks connected by raised walkways. Of these, 34 were made available to people on the housing waiting list, drawn by lots, with recipients described in the local press as the 'lucky 34'. Lucky they were if that includes bad luck.

In 1980, just seven years after completion, the estate featured in a Department of the Environment report into difficult-to-let housing which concluded that 'the possibility of demolition is one that will have to be considered.' Structural defects and disrepair began to take hold almost immediately, as did negative reports in the press, the first of which (with blatantly racist undertones), in the Hornsey Journal, talked of 'Problem families - many of them single-parent families - were seen to be placed together… The sight of unmarried West Indian mothers walking about the estate aggravated racial tension.'

But the problems had begun to emerge much earlier than that. As early as 1976 the Tottenham Weekly Herald claimed that tenants were living 'in the shadow of violence', and by 6th October 1978 'living in a subculture of violence' in 'terror flats'. Such reports were dismissed by both the residents association and the police, who said crime on the estate was no worse than anywhere else and better than some parts of the borough. Despite this, transfer requests were 20% above the average with a reluctance for housing applicants to move there, meaning empty properties were increasingly filled by those whose needs were most desperate; the homeless and single parents.

The Broadwater Farm Youth Association was formed when, at a residents' meeting to discuss the increase in burglaries on the estate, it was suggested that the police should open a mini police station on the estate - an idea quickly dismissed by the police as unlikely to prove helpful, but strongly supported by the tenants. Instead, a group of mainly black youths decided to do something about the problems on the estate themselves and formed a youth association which, based out of an unoccupied former fish and chip shop, began serving meals and organising trips out for the elderly residents of the estate. Other initiatives included a community launderette, food Co-operative, hairdressing salon, and photography and sewing workshops. This good work and positive effect on the area had been recognised by Sir George Young, Minister of State at the Department of the Environment and they had received a visit from the Princess of Wales in February 1985.

The police held an entirely different view, which was outlined in a November 1985 issue of Police, the magazine of the Police Federation, which said: 'The official picture of Broadwater Farm Estate as a beehive of flourishing rehabilitation and positive community involvement which was fostered by skilful propaganda from the Department of the Environment (and swallowed by TV and the press) cloaked the ugly reality of criminal gangs ruling the estate, robbing and terrorising the inhabitants and making daily war on any police officer who dared to venture near.'

That same evening Cherry Groce was shot, saw the violent arrest, south of the river in Tottenham, of Roger Scott, a member of the Broadwater Farm Youth Association, for allegedly breaking into Broadwater Farm Social Club - itself run by the youth association. As Scott had, at the time the alleged offence was committed, been in a meeting where the association's chair had also been present, it sent a delegation to Tottenham Police Station to voice their concerns that the arrest was a case of mistaken identity. When their concerns were dismissed, the police forcibly removed the youths from the lobby of the station and four youths and one young woman were arrested and charged with obstruction and assaulting police officers. They included the youth association's vice-chair and the daughter of the chair - all of whom were subsequently acquitted.

A week later on the 5th of October, the police stopped a BMW being driven by Youth Association member Floyd Jarrett, supposedly because his tax disc was out of date. He was subsequently arrested for the suspected theft of a motor vehicle and charged with obstructing and assaulting the police who claimed he had thrown two punches. He too was later acquitted of all charges. With Jarrett in custody, a search was carried out at the home of his mother Cynthia and sister Patricia, despite their protestation that Winston did not live there and the attending officers had no warrant. During the search it was alleged that Cynthia was pushed to the floor and then stepped over by the officers, who denied Patricia's plea that they call an ambulance, saying she was 'play-acting'. When the police left the scene, they reported to the station that the search had passed 'without incident'. In fact, Mrs Jarrett had suffered a heart attack and when an ambulance was eventually called, it was too late and by the time it reached the North Middlesex Hospital she was declared dead on arrival.

The following day, a small group gathered at the police station to demand the suspension of DC Mike Randall, the officer said to be responsible for the death. Randall already had a reputation among the areas black youths as something of a racist with a declared mission to 'clean up' Tottenham, a demeanour that had earned him the nickname 'Sweeney'. Their demands were dismissed and Randall's appearance smiling at a window triggered the throwing of several missiles and subsequent clashes, but the incident was calmed down and the Youth Association gathered for a meeting later that afternoon.

The meeting was attended by about 150 mainly young people, who concluded that they should return to the station and reiterate their demands. When they left the meeting, however, they found several riot vans filled with officers of the SPG already in place on the estate. When the disgruntled youths began banging on the side of the vans, officers were said to enter the estate from every direction - banging shields with their truncheons, making monkey noises and chanting 'Nigger, Nigger, Nigger, Oi!, Oi!, Oi!'

The subsequent violence began at 19.05 and ended at 1.00 the following morning, during which 243 police officers were injured. Two of those and three members of the media received shotgun wounds and one officer, PC Keith Blakelock, was killed. In the words of the then leader of Haringey Council and future member of Parliament for Tottenham, Bernie Grant, 'What the police got was a bloody good hiding.'

PC Blakelock, who was hacked to death with a machete, was protecting firefighters who had found themselves under attack. Says Rosenthal: 'To the small core of hard men from the ghetto, a fireman's uniform presented the same badge of authority as a policeman's and provoked the same hatred.' The fire service had been finding themselves under occasional attack on the Broadwater Farm estate for a long time before the riot unfolded, lured by hoax 999 calls, only to find themselves bombarded with missiles, thrown from the balconies.

This attitude is highlighted in the story of Ethnic (Gary McDonald) in **LONDON'S BURNING (1986)**. The watch's sole black firefighter; he lives on the estate with his family, but is careful to keep the nature of his employment secret from the local youths. When he leaves a rehearsal with his band and heads off to his full-time job, the carrier

London's burning in *Sami & Rosie Get Laid*

bag in his hand contains a change of clothes. He has not gone more than a few yards before he's stopped by three youths, two Rastafarian, the other white, and asked what's in the bag. He explains and, asked what work he does, he tells them he's a cleaner. As he heads around the corner, he is confronted by two policemen. 'In a hurry, Sambo?' asks one. 'What's in the bag?' demands the other, 'Heroin? Ganja?' When one officer opens the bag and recognises the shirt as that of the fire service their demeanour changes. 'Sorry about that, mate. Just doing our job.'

Back on the estate, a black man delivers a television set to a flat containing five others. 'Time for *Gardener's World*,' says one. It's packed with cannabis, the unusual packaging no doubt due to the estate's very visible police presence. The poverty level of the estate is highlighted by the fact that Ethnic's mother feels unable to buy all the family's shopping in one go. 'Mrs Green was in, and Mrs Mead and old Mr Winston. I can't go flash money on red salmon and jam and stuff in front of them. Maryland cookies. They have their pride.' Crime is signified by the excessive number of locks visible on the inside of the front door, their necessity revealed when a lit rag is pushed through the letterbox.

There's no explanation to any one event that sparks the riot that eventually breaks out, but Ethnic suspects something is afoot when he realises the estate is eerily quiet. Preparations are witnessed in the breaking of concrete paving slabs on a balcony into more manageable sized missiles. A car is set alight just as two policemen on foot patrol pass by. A cry of 'Come on you pigs' goes up and when the officers investigate they are ambushed. A patrol car that turns up to assist is quickly overrun and overturned, and by the time the fire crew arrives there is a full-scale riot in process. Ethnic is not on duty, instead, he watches events unfold from the balcony outside the family's flat. When he sees a firefighter come under attack, he runs down to help but, witnessed from above, a yell of 'Oi! Traitor!' is followed by a slab on concrete that hits him on the head.

Costing a then massive £1 million to produce, a record for London Weekend Television who had taken on the project when producer Linda Agran, known for hits like *Minder* and *Widows*, moved from Thames, *London's Burning* was broadcast in early December 1986 and was a huge success, attracting an audience of 12.5 million and gaining three BAFTA nominations, including Best Single Drama. The success led to the commissioning of a full series which, despite Rosenthal declining to write any episodes, attracted an average of over 12 million viewers. By the fourth series it had peaked at 18.5 million and the show continued to be one of ITV's highest-rated programmes until drastic cuts to the budget for series 11 meant the show became more of a soap opera with stories concentrating on the private lives of the firefighters rather than the major incidents viewers had become accustomed to. With figures down to below 5 million for series 14, the show was finally axed in 2002.

Of **SAMMY AND ROSIE GET LAID (1987)**, screenwriter Hanif Kureishi says: 'I suppose, in the sense that I'd worked in the theatre before, and if there were riots down the road, then you'd put on a play about it, I thought, well, why can't we make a film about it? There was the shooting of Cherry Groce in Brixton, there were riots and all that, and I thought, well let's put that in a film.'

Kureishi could also draw from his own life for the screenplay: 'I was fascinated by the story of one of my uncles, who came to England from Pakistan after being away for years, and he arrived during those riots. He was a very sedate, middle-aged man. The streets were on fire, and every time he turned on the telly there were riots and so on, and he said, "I can't believe this is England. I've worshipped England. England occupied my country for years, now the place is burning down."'

Stephen Frears film of Hanif Kureishi's screenplay sets the scene with a quote from Margaret Thatcher, speaking inside Conservative Central Office in June 1987 following her election to a third term in office: 'We have a great deal of work to do, so no one must slack... You can have a marvellous party tonight, you can clear up tomorrow but on Monday, you know, we've got a big job to do in those inner cities.'

Danny (Roland Gift) disembarks a tube train and arrives back home just as a police van pulls up and armed officers rush out as another begins sealing off the area with tape. In the house that the police are about to enter, a middle-aged black mother is seen frying chips on the stove whilst her son sits at the kitchen table blowing on his trumpet. As the sound of a policeman's boot on the door is heard, we see the son have it on his toes and out the back. When the police burst in the contents of the chip pan goes flying into the air and all over one officer, whilst an instant later, amid all the chaos a shot is heard and the mother falls. Also arriving in the street is Sammy's father, Rafi (Shashi Kapoor), who is told: 'The police shot a woman by mistake, they were looking for her son. It's easy enough to mistake a 50-year-old office cleaner for a 20-year-old jazz trumpeter.'

When Rosie (Frances Barber) goes out that evening, a riot is in full swing. A fire engine pulls up and the officers are immediately under attack from youths hurling bricks, forced to return to the relative safety of their engine. The following morning things are quieter but the 'uprising' is still going on and, whilst helping Rafi who has been caught up in it, Danny overhears a snippet of a private conversation: 'It might surprise you but there's a lot of money to be made out of this.' Money from the land under the motorway that Danny and his caravan consider home.

A more recent use of the 1985 riots as the background to a drama came from playwright Roy Williams who was in his late teens in 1985 and says: 'Those riots came from a sense of real anger – a whole generation who felt they were being shat on by the establishment and were made to feel they don't belong here. Their parents, our parents, the Windrush generation, they had to put up with a lot of racism, a lot of, you know, "go back where you've come from, you don't belong here", but they stuck through it, they stuck at it, had the children – us – then I think we kind of grew up thinking, "OK, well, bad for our parents, but we were born here". But growing up it was still the same, as bad as it had been for our parents, so there was a raw anger. It was like "You're not gonna get away with this, you're not gonna attack us, you're not gonna hurt us the way you hurt our mums and dads, we're gonna fight back."'

He revisited the night of the Broadwater Farm riot in 2010 for its 25th anniversary with the play **SUCKER PUNCH** which was staged at the Royal Court. Williams decided to visit the topics covered by the play, the race riots and the SUS laws that formed the backdrop to his youth, when from working with today's school kids he realised they hadn't a clue what he was on about, being 'so swamped with American culture, American music, American clothes, the whole gangsta rap thing' that they knew nothing about the Britain he had grown up in. It's a Britain where for young black boys the only path they can see that might take them out of the estates is through sport, primarily football and boxing, the choice of *Sucker Punch*'s two protagonists, Leon (Daniel Kaluuya) and Troy (Anthony Welsh). It's not exactly a choice though as the two 16-year-old schoolboys had already embarked on a different career trajectory, that of breaking into the premises of white gym owner and trainer Charlie Maggs, who takes them on as boxing hopefuls rather than handing them over to the police. Racism (some of it casual and some of it not so), the SUS laws, police brutality and a doomed interracial romance combine with the boxing in a play that, following an extended sell-out run, was nominated for the Evening Standard Theatre Award for Best Play of 2010 and the Olivier Award for Best New Play of the same year, winning the prize for Best Theatre Play at the 2011 Writers' Guild of Great Britain Awards and rave reviews for future Oscar nominee Daniel Kaluuya.

Hippies, Skinheads, Rastas, Punks & Disco Dancing Bowie Boot Boys

5. All The Young Dudes
(Bowie)

KING OF ROCK AND ROUGE

WORDS: DEBORAH THOMAS
PICTURE: RICHARD IMRIE

A GIANT new star shines over the pop scene. His name is David Bowie. His music is bizarre and bitchy and his song "Jean Genie" is the No. 1 disc.

As you can see, the gentleman with the make-up and the hair do reminiscent of a bright orange lavatory brush is very fond of feathers.

The 25-year-old singer composer designs most of his clothes—if you can call them that—and he's leaning towards lurex and other shimmering [...]

There's a common misconception that until Punk arrived, 1970s teenagers eager to avoid the mainstream approved diet of chart-friendly fodder were reduced to sitting in their bedrooms admiring the Roger Dean artwork on the gatefold sleeve for 'Tales From Topographic Oceans'. While music historians like to cite Iggy Pop, Lou Reed, The New York Dolls and 'Nuggets', the ground-breaking 1972 compilation of largely obscure garage rock singles from the sixties assembled by soon-to-be Patti Smith guitarist Lenny Kaye, as the major influences on the teenagers who would become the harbingers of the Punk revolution, in Britain the major influences were largely home-grown and glittery. Says Andy Scott of The Sweet: '... it was noticeable in the Olympic Opening Ceremony, music from the early seventies was virtually ignored. It does seem sometimes that music history tends to jump from the end of the sixties straight to Punk.' What was prominent in the intervening years was Glam, beginning with Marc Bolan's appearance during March 1971 on *Top of the Pops* in glitter and satin for 'Hot Love' and quickly followed by 'Ziggy Stardust' era David Bowie and Roxy Music.

Bowie's influence was unparalleled, from the Banshees Siouxsie Sioux and Steve Severin to the Wire's Colin Newman, who called himself 'a big, big Bowie fan' to Poly Styrene for whom Bowie was a staple in her DJ set. Adam & the Ants guitarist Marco Pirroni described Sid Vicious as 'a tall, geeky kind of bloke into Roxy and Bowie... I think Sid would have wanted to be Bowie - but without the talent to pull it off.' Eater included a cover of 'Queen Bitch' on their debut album and also covered T. Rex's 'Jeepster'. The Damned, who covered The Sweet's 'Ballroom Blitz', supported T. Rex on tour, and Marc Bolan included Punk bands such as Generation X on his teatime TV show *Marc* (1977). John Lydon has name-checked Bolan and Bowie, 'but not too much', as influences and both he and Mick Jones have cited Mott the Hoople. Jones and his school pal Robin Banks (of 'Stay Free' fame) followed Mott wherever they could from Liverpool in the north to Plymouth in the south, as part of a group of friends who became friendly with Mott's road manager who would get them in for free through the stage door where they would rub shoulders with the band, who were always open to their fans.

It's not unusual these days to see Mott The Hoople called 'proto-Punk', with their early album 'Brain Capers' especially singled out as birthing Punk (despite sounding like Dylan and the Stones). Mott frontman Ian Hunter produced Generation X's 'Valley of the Dolls' album, following a début overseen by Phil Wainman, chosen for his work on the Sweet's 'Ballroom Blitz'. The Clash played on Hunter's 'Short Back & Sides' and Manchester's Slaughter and the Dogs were named after a combo of Mick Ronson's 'Slaughter On 10th Avenue' and Bowie's 'Diamond Dogs' and were still in their original Glam phase when they supported The Sex Pistols at their second Manchester Free Trade Hall gig. Ronson would guest on their 'Quick Joey Small' single for Decca and ex-Mott the Hoople drummer Dale Griffin was enlisted to produce their 1979 album 'Bite Back', recorded after front-man Wayne Barrett had left.

Glam had its roots in the horror rock of Screaming Lord Sutch whose 'Jack the Ripper' has been covered by the White Stripes. Sutch, with his self-confessed lack of vocal abilities, might even claim his place amongst the originators of Punk. His 1969 album 'Lord Sutch and Heavy Friends' was named in a 1998 BBC poll as the worst album of all time, despite having called on Jimmy Page, John Bonham, Jeff Beck, Noel Redding, and Nicky Hopkins. Malcolm McLaren incorporated an image of the singer into a T-shirt during his Let It Rock years and Sutch even helped McLaren paste the pink letters onto the Let It Rock shop facade. Says Sutch: 'I'd known Malcolm McLaren for years because he used to make my Teddy Boy suits before he got into Punk. He and Vivienne Westwood both made my stage clothes. They were very arty and very wild, so we suited each other' Sutch's single 'My Monster In Black Tights' was a fixture on the Sex jukebox as well as being name-checked on the 1974 t-shirt design You're Gonna Wake Up One Morning And Know What Side Of The Bed You've Been Lying On! Two years later The Sex Pistols supported Sutch at a 1976 Valentine's dance, trashing his equipment for good measure.

For the cover of their 1966 single 'Have You Seen Your Mother, Baby (Standing in the Shadows)' The Rolling

Stones slipped into WW2 nurses uniforms a good five years before Bowie adorned the sleeve of his 'The Man Who Sold The World' album in a 'man's dress' or The New York Dolls complemented their tousled hairdo's with lipstick and blouses on the sleeve of their 1973 debut.

Marc Bolan had already had a couple of stabs at stardom, first as the guitarist in Mod band John's Children, having been - as plain 15-year-old Mark Feld - one of the 'faces' in the famous early Mod article in a 1962 issue of Town magazine, and then as a Hippie folk troubadour in the acoustic duo Tyrannosaurus Rex, sitting cross-legged on stage alongside the Ladbroke Grove bongo-playing Steve 'Peregrine' Took. The photogenic Mickey Finn replaced Took for their final album as the band went electric. In 1971 Bolan sat down with the deliberate intent to write a song that could impact the singles chart and, with the band's name shortened to the more manageable T Rex, unleashed 'Ride A White Swan' on the world, riding it all the way to #2.

The change of direction may have alienated many of Bolan's small but dedicated Hippie following but brought in its wake an army of new teenage, and largely female fans. Now a bona fide 4 piece band, T Rex cut a follow-up single, 'Hot Love' which went all the way to the top. Bolan was calling his unique new sound 'cosmic rock' but an appearance on Top of the Pops would forever mark the band as 'Glam'. An important role in this is credited to Bolan's publicist, Chelita Secunda, who hit on the idea of dressing the petite singer in women's clothes on a shopping trip around World's End. For the *Top of the Pops* appearance, Secunda augmented this new look with the application of a pencil line and mascara to Bolan's eyes and, as a last-minute inspiration, glitter stuck to his cheeks. The rest was, as they say, history though no one was more surprised by the impact of this than Bolan himself: 'Elvis Presley wore eye make-up for years. People thought he had dark, sultry eyes. Jagger has wonderful skin embellishment. People are really works of art, and if you have a nice face, you might as well play about with it. It gets boring otherwise. Two hundred years ago, men covered themselves with something scented or wore powdered wigs and faces. If someone is prudish enough not to realise it's all been done before, they're very stupid. Anyway, I don't believe chicks like really butch guys... Valentino was proof of that.'

Bowie had been thinking along the same lines for some time, or at least his wife Angie had when she dressed the band in silver lame with dyed hair and glitter for a support slot to Country Joe & the Fish in 1970. It went down like a lead balloon, and much to the rest of the band's relief, the look was quickly dropped. It was however just the wrong audience at the right time. What works on *Top of the Pops* doesn't necessarily play well to a room full of Hippies at the Roundhouse. Tony Visconti, who produced both artists, believes Glam was born that night. If it was, then it was stillborn, but his claim is strengthened by the fact that taking notes in the audience that night was Marc Bolan.

Both men saw glamour as the antithesis of Hippiedom in much the same way that Punk did; itself essentially a more street level continuation of Glam. The UK had Alternative Miss World founder Andrew Logan and mime artist Lindsay Kemp but Bowie wanted the real thing - Warhol - and he had made friends with the cast of *Pork* during its London run, including Cherry Vanilla, Lee Black Childers and Wayne County, all of whom would have an impact on Bowie's look. When his management company MainMan set up an office in New York, Bowie met his musical heroes, Lou Reed, and Iggy Pop, and when he returned, it was with a new sense of purpose, and a new persona, undergoing 'a wild mutation as a rock and roll star'.

And if the skin-tight PVC jumpsuit and orange mullet didn't get him noticed, he made doubly sure by telling Melody Maker that he was 'gay and always had been,' though the journalist was far from convinced. The new image wasn't an immediate success, with the initial response, according to the singer, being 'Aw, a bunch of bloody poofters.' It was the music that would seal it, and with the release of 'Starman' during April 1972 and then the album 'Ziggy Stardust' in June suddenly Bowie was a superstar, and not just in the Warhol sense. At a press conference in June at the Dorchester Hotel, Bowie introduced Iggy Pop, dressed in a T. Rex shirt, and a platform heeled Lou Reed, over here to record 'Transformer'. Reed greeted Bowie with a kiss on the lips and the less glittery US branch of Glam was officially declared open for business.

Also on the list for a Bowie make-over was Mott the Hoople who, after four only moderately successful albums, had called it a day until they were made an offer they couldn't refuse in the form of the Glam anthem 'All the Young Dudes', which duly took the band to #3 during June 1972. In August, as well as supporting David Bowie on two nights of his 'Ziggy Stardust' tour at the Rainbow, Roxy Music reached the # 4 spot with their debut single 'Virginia Plain'. With producers like Mike Leander and Nicky Chinn taking notes the bandwagon was soon well and truly rolling with bubblegum band Sweet and Gary Glitter adopting the new look. Glitter had managed an accidental monster hit when a DJ mistakenly played the B side, 'Rock n Roll Part 2', a version of the song minus the lead

Jonathan Rhys Myers is Brian Slade in *Velvet Goldmine*

vocal track used to cut down on recording costs, meaning the singer had to appear on *Top of the Pops* to 'sing' a song that lacked his vocals.

Meanwhile, as befitting bona fide mainstream pop sensations both Bolan and Bowie were soon to capture their magic on celluloid, via the filming of important live performances. With what the tabloids had now dubbed 'T-Rextasy' at the height of its powers, former Beatle Ringo Starr filmed the band playing two concerts at the Empire Pool, Wembley in March 1972, each attended by 10,000, largely female, screaming fans. These were edited into one as part of the movie **BORN TO BOOGIE (1972)**, interspersed with a couple of studio performances in which the band were joined by Elton John and Starr himself, some acoustic numbers, and a series of 'Alice Through The Looking Glass' inspired (but not inspiring) skits filmed in the grounds of John Lennon's mansion. The film was produced and released into UK cinemas by the Apple Corps film division. Bowie was filmed by the *Don't Look Back* (1967) and *Monterey Pop* (1968) director DA Pennebaker during the Spiders 'farewell' concert at the Hammersmith Odeon in July 1973 although in its complete 90 minute format, **ZIGGY STARDUST AND THE SPIDERS FROM MARS (1973)** did not receive its premiere until 1979 when it screened at the Edinburgh Film Festival.

For the ultimate 'Bowie' movie fans would have to wait another 25 years for the Ziggy-era biopic that wasn't, with the US/UK co-production, **VELVET GOLDMINE (1998)**, helmed by American director Todd Haynes. Jonathan Rhys Meyers plays Brian Slade, a Glam rock icon who, at the height of his fame, stages him own assassination much the same way as Bowie had killed off his 'Ziggy Stardust' character at the Hammersmith Odeon. Unlike Bowie, for Brian Slade, once the truth of his demise is revealed, there is no way back, and the singer disappears from public view.

Velvet Goldmine began life as an artistic take on the early career of David Bowie that ran into problems when the man himself objected and refused to allow the use of his songs. That should have spelled disaster for the project but Haynes put aside his disappointment and restructured the film to make this set back a positive. The changes meant that instead of playing a Bowie-esque character, Rhys Myers found himself with 'ten days to sort of readjust to not playing Bowie but playing a mixture of Bowie, Marc Bolan, Brian Eno, basically a general idea of Glam rock.'

Opening with the message that: 'Although what you are about to see is a work of fiction, it should nevertheless be played at maximum volume,' both these points become clear from the opening blasts of Brian Eno's 'Needle in the Camel's Eye' and an opening scene in which the infant Oscar Wilde is dropped on a doorstep from a UFO. For Haynes, as an American trying to understand the English element of Glam that clearly didn't derive from American culture, 'all roads led back to Oscar… That particular tradition of effeminacy in English culture, the androgynous dandy, the camp aesthete who can fully articulate his relationship to society… goes right back to Oscar Wilde. And the ways in which Oscar Wilde was attacking the Romantics that preceded him... were very similar to what the Glam rockers, particularly Bowie and Bryan Ferry, were attacking; the earnestness of 60s culture. Trying to shock, but with wit, cleverness and homosexuality.'

Through interviews with Brian Slade's original manager Cecil (Michael Feast), ex-wife Mandy (Toni Collette), and fellow Glam rocker Curt Wild (Ewan McGregor), the film covers Slade's (and Bowie's) rise to stardom, and liberally adds to the mythology that Haynes called 'the stories that these real-life people wove around themselves in their stage persona's.' That was always far more interesting to the director who says: 'The idea of doing a gritty, naturalistic film about Glam rock is absurd. My challenge to myself was to try and apply a lot of the language that I identified in my favourite Glam rock music to a narrative context, which basically meant doing away with a naturalistic approach and elevating this notion of fiction and artifice.'

Thanks largely to Bowie's non-cooperation, the music, overseen by producer Michael Stipe of REM fame, is nigh on perfect. Instead of the 'Ziggy Stardust' cuts that the production had requested, Brian Slade instead gets to perform tracks by Roxy Music (vocals by Radiohead's Thom Yorke), Cockney Rebel, Brian Eno and an original by Shudder To Think (vocals by Meyer himself). Ewan McGregor gets to perform several Stooges songs backed by the likes of Thurston Moore, original Stooge Ron Asheton, Mudhoney's Mark Arm and producer Don Fleming. Fleming and Moore had been brought on to the project on the strength of their input to The Beatles biopic *Backbeat* (1994) in which they formed part of a supergroup that also included the Afghan Whigs Greg Dulli and Soul Asylum's Dave Pirner, recreating the early days of the fab four. Elsewhere, the film utilises the so-called Britpop scene with Elastica's Donna Matthews fronting Teenage Fanclub on a rousing version of the New York Dolls 'Personality Crisis', a Placebo cover of T Rex's '20th Century Boy' and a Pulp original.

The official reason for Bowie's non-participation is that he was developing a similarly themed project, which never materialised, and the unofficial reason is that he was uncomfortable with the relationship between Wild and Slade. It's also not too much of a stretch to see that he might have been troubled by the implication that when he was a teenage Mod he was also buggering young schoolboys. In a scene where Slade snogs an equally androgynous girl, she asks him if he is a Mod or a Rocker to which he responds in a faux Ringo accent that he's, 'six of one, half a dozen of the other, really.' He then leans against a wall with a couple of mates as a group of young, uniformed schoolboys troop past to the sounds of Gary Glitter's 'Do You Wanna Touch?' In the next scene his watch denotes its 3.40 and school's out, and we see one of the said young boys face down and trousers down in front of him on a bed.

The film makes much of the relationship between Slade and Wild, who looks and dresses like Iggy Pop but whose background in 'the aluminium trailer parks of Michigan' owes much to the early life of Lou Reed who had been 'sent off for 18 months of electric shock treatment' which 'was guaranteed to fry the fairy clean out of his mind', when his parents tried to cure him of his bisexuality. The kiss between Slade and Wild at a press conference was likewise based on the previously mentioned incident between Bowie and Reed. It's a theme that Haynes runs and runs with as the two take a romantic fairground car ride through a laser light show to the strains of Reed's 'Satellite of Love'. There's also a drug-fuelled orgy at a party where in the morning the two are seen spooned together naked in bed. This was based on an incident involving Bowie and Mick Jagger which is recounted in Angie Bowie's unauthorised biography 'Backstage Passes', the reliability of which is alluded to elsewhere in the script. Angie is represented in the film as Mandy (Toni Collette) of whom Cecil, in recounting his own version of events, tells Arthur 'every story needs a contrary opinion and with Mandy, you're ensured excesses of both.'

The heart of the story is Arthur (Christian Bale), at the time of Brian Slade's 'murder' himself a young Glam fan and now, ten years on, a journalist working in the USA who is tasked with doing the tenth anniversary 'Where is he now?' piece on the singer. Arthur begins his journey through the film wearing the same cap-sleeved t-shirts, flared jeans and leather jackets as the rest of his schoolmates but when he discovers Brian Slade he quickly adopts his new heroes style.

There's a beautifully drawn sequence that begins with Arthur in a record shop begging his older brother to borrow him the money to buy an album. It's one on which Brian Slade's semi-naked pose for the gatefold sleeve resembles both 'Aladdin Sane' and the Jobriath album, eliciting a not unexpected homophobic comment from one of his brother's friends. When he gets home to his bedroom with the album and a copy of that weeks NME, the process takes the form of a ritual that will be familiar to many thousands of teenagers of the time as he lovingly and delicately places the record on the turntable, the cover spread out on the floor in front of him as he slowly turns the pages of the music paper.

When he leaves the house soon after he is still hiding his changing appearance from his parents, covering himself in a heavy coat that he stashes in a hiding place once outside. The newfound sense of freedom this gives him is visible in his every movement as he struts down the street. His sense of elation is only temporarily dulled when he passes a small group of similarly attired youths who ought to ally with him but from their assumed, socially superior position, respond to his smile with indifference.

When later on he watches an interview with his hero on a TV programme, as his parents sit disapprovingly at the edge of the room, he finds himself unable to contain himself any longer. The interviewer asks Slade if he is concerned that the way he presents himself might give people the wrong idea, to which he replies that if that's what they assume they probably wouldn't be wrong. When it's pointed out that he is married, Slade replies, 'I am married, quite happily in fact. I just happen to like boys as much as I like girls, and since my wife feels pretty much the same about such things, I think we've been able to make a fairly decent go of it so far.' 'That's me!' exclaims Arthur as he jumps up and down excitedly, pointing at the TV. When some time later his father goes upstairs to complain about the noise of the music and discovers his son masturbating to a picture of Slade and Wild's kiss, he is accused of bringing shame to the family and told to leave.

That there's no happy ending for Arthur is immediately apparent from his early scenes in New York where he makes it clear that this episode in his life is not something he would choose to revisit. He looks, like Cecil, Mandy, and Kurt, worn down. Somehow washed out and grey seems to have become the new look as he makes his way from the newspaper offices to the tube where he passes a giant screen on which the current pop idol, Tommy Stone (Alastair Cumming), can be seen to bear a very deliberate resemblance to the 'Serious Moonlight' era David Bowie, repackaged with bouffant hair and shoulder pads for mainstream America and MTV. It was a period when, says Haynes, 'everything went back into little categories… in the 80s for all sorts of reasons [there was] a lot of fallout of 60s excesses: the drug culture and AIDS, and all the sort of cost of that period. People got scared again and went back to the old-fashioned definitions… Almost every artist in the period, except Gary Glitter, drastically changed, or drew back, or reverted to something very different, or went into hibernation.'

So, recouping just $1 million from a $7 million budget, it begs the question, what went wrong? The reaction of Miramax head Harvey Weinstein didn't help. Feeling the film was too long (it isn't) he adopted his 'Harvey Scissorhands' persona. Says Haynes, 'He made suggestions that I didn't follow, and then he just buried it.' For many, the resulting film wasn't the Bowie bio-pic that they had wanted but *Velvet Goldmine* had its fans. The New

Noddy Holder and Jim Lea in *Flame*

York Times. despite finding the film 'has at least one more major character than it needs', was full of praise, calling it 'dazzlingly surreal' and 'blazing with exquisite yet abstract passions'. It went on, 'without addressing Mr Bowie directly, it appropriates his shimmering, protean aura in virtuoso ways that put ordinary period film-making or time-capsule musicology to shame.'

Unfortunately, the vast majority of critics at the time were either lukewarm, like Roger Ebert who said the film 'wants to be a movie in search of a truth, but it's more of a movie in search of itself', or scathing, like CNN's Paul Tatora who said the film 'sinks like a Glam rock' and that 'if you bother to scratch through the silver glitter eye shadow, there's absolutely no movie left.' The pattern continued on this side of the Atlantic with the Guardian's Rob Mudie calling it 'the most unhinged music biz film since *The Doors* (1991) and nearly as formless' and concluding, correctly, 'your degree of interest is likely to be in proportion to your interest in the musical era it represents.' Empire magazine said 'its sole triumph is to replace *Absolute Beginners* as the most derided British music movie of all time.'

In the intervening years, the films reputation has grown exponentially, where repeat viewings have allowed fans to delve deeper into this pop culture treasure trove to find that amongst all the glitter is a seam of pure gold. Glam itself has also gone through something of a re-appraisal, having for decades been dismissed by writers and historians of both youth culture and music for not fitting the fashionable trope of working-class authenticity that could be attached to the Skinheads before it and after, with less conviction, the Punks. Glam was classless, placed image ahead of authenticity and, most troubling of all was largely followed by young girls.

*

No prizes for guessing where Brian got his surname from. Most successful of all the subsequent converts to Glam rock were ex-Skinhead band Slade who in the decade up to 1973 sold in excess of 6.5 million records in the UK alone, including six number 1's, three of which debuted in the top spot in their week of release, a feat not achieved since The Beatles heyday. According to Paul Weller, 'the whole Punk rock thing really happened because of bands such as Slade and the like; rock bands that wouldn't back off.' Another fan of Noddy Holder's boys was Sex Pistol Steve Jones who says 'Slade never compromised. We always had the feeling that they were on our side'

Though they ostensibly set it during the late 1960s, albeit one that looked remarkably like the seventies, Slade was also responsible for the Glam era's best movie with **FLAME (1975)**. The period setting is signified by things like the offshore pirate radio station, Radio City, that the band visit, with most such operations having fallen away when the BBC restructured in 1967 and introduced Radio 1, though Radio Caroline battled on for many years. Radio City broadcast from a WW2 marine fort off the Kent coast and a dispute with Radio Caroline ended with its owner, and Screaming Lord Sutch manager, Reginald Calvert being shot dead. In the film. Stoker's (Noddy Holder) initial band, The Undertakers, are based on Sutch's The Savages.

After having abandoned their manager Chas Chandler's plan to film a *Quatermass* spoof penned by the drummer of the Animals with Noddy Holder playing a mad professor called 'Quite-a-Mess', Slade opted instead for a gritty tale of the rise and fall of a rock band, the fictional Flame (who of course bore an uncanny resemblance to Slade). Though the plot is the standard cliché of a band struggling to make it in the cut-throat music business it is lifted above the norm via some first-rate and understated performances by Tom Conti, in just his second film role, as the advertising executive turned Machiavellian music mogul Robert Seymour, and Kenneth Colley as his assistant, Tony Devlin. There's also a far too believable turn from Johnny Shannon as the band's original manager, Ron Harding, and a wonderfully self-deprecating one from Alan Lake, best remembered as Mr Diana Dors, as the bloated former Teddy Boy Jack Daniels, who fronts Jim Lea and Dave Hill's pre-Flame outfit. The band also hold their own.

Soon the floodgates were open and over the next few years it seemed as if everyone had gone Glam from minor 60s pop stars Paul Gadd and Shane Fenton, who both found a level of success that had previously proved elusive as Gary Glitter and Alvin Stardust, to rock 'n' roll revivalists like Mud and Showaddywaddy. If Slade made the best foray onto the silver screen, then Gary Glitter has to be a contender for the worst. His hour-long **REMEMBER ME THIS WAY (1974)** was released into cinemas as the second feature 'for all the family to come and see', as support to the Canadian children's film *Brother of the Wind* (1973). It was produced by GTO Films and directed by Ron Inkpen who had previously produced several low-budget films that were most definitely not for family viewing, including *Sinderella* (1972), *Karma Sutra Rides Again* (1972) and *Snow White & the Seven Perverts* (1973).

The documentary offers a fly-on-the-wall, though clearly staged, look into the day-to-day life of its star who is seen doing the rounds of publicity, recording, rehearsing and throwing a party while his manager wheels and deals on the telephone. He also gets to try out his karate moves on some pretend bad guys. Its one saving grace is the fifteen minutes of footage of Glitter performing at the Rainbow, the setting in which he most excelled and could always be relied on to put on a good show. The film most recently caused something of a stir in the nation's tabloid press when it was added to Amazon Prime's streaming service, who were quick to point out that at one point the convicted paedophile is seen pinching a girl fan's bottom. *Remember Me This Way*? Hardly.

By 1975 and the release of two further movies by GTO Films, the scene's leading lights had moved on with both Bowie and Bolan, through wife Gloria Jones, exploring more soulful territories. By 1973 Bolan was already bemoaning the 'Glam' tag, having found himself increasingly bundled in with the second wave of Glam acts, telling the press, 'I don't put anyone down who is involved in it, but once the vision takes over from the music, they're in bad shape.' Unfortunately, unlike Bowie, Bolan had nowhere to go. Bowie had no such reservations and said the Glam tag had become 'a sense of embarrassment... I certainly didn't wanna be associated with the likes of Gary Glitter.' The arrival of Glitter on the scene also provoked Bryan Ferry to rethink his image: 'I remember there was this great jacket of Anthony's with black sequins and a green chevron that I wore on *Top of the Pops*. But shortly after that you saw Gary Glitter wearing the same kind of things, and that's where the tuxedo came in.'

And so **SIDE BY SIDE (1975)** has to make do with a selection of even lower rent artists. Club owner Gary (Billy Boyle) tells Max Nugget (Terry-Thomas), his old-school rival next door, that 'the kids today don't want to know about your lot, they want the top groups. Have you never heard of the Stones, Mud, Hello, the Cream, the Rubettes.' Guess which two of these don't put in an appearance here.

Standing in both clubs way is Mr Crumb (Frank Thornton), a representative of the court which has decided that only one venue will have its licence renewed, and who wants 'to see the country saved from the moral turpitude that's overwhelming it. If there's one thing worse than strip shows and variety turns, it's pop music.' To Max Nuggett, pop musicians are 'prancing poofters' and in an even more un-PC moment Barry Humphries even blacks up.

Gary travels down to London in search of some quality acts to give his club a better chance of securing the licence and meets Stephanie de Sykes who performs her hit single 'Born With A Smile On My Face' and puts them on to Mud, Hello, Kenny and the Rubettes. There's also an unexpected but always welcome Desmond Dekker performing 'Israelites' but the best performance is at Max's place where leather-underwear clad, whip-wielding 70s sitcom regular Jennifer Guy does a striptease to 'I Love You Love'.

None of *Side By Side*'s saving graces are present in GTO's follow up of sorts **NEVER TOO YOUNG TO ROCK (1975)** where in the near future, with pop music banned from TV, *Please Sir*'s Peter Denyer and his driver Mr Rockbottom (Freddie Jones) travel the countryside in an ice-cream van that has been converted into a pop group detector van in search of pop acts to perform at a concert for the kids. They 'detect' Glam motorcycle gang Mud, complete with plumes on their crash helmets, at a transport cafe where they are performing 'The Cat Crept In' to a crowd of football supporters, both red and blue, then accompanying a food fight with a rendition of 'Tiger Feet'. They also track down the Rubettes performing on a flatbed truck on Borehamwood High Street, the Glitter Band on a boat and a pre-fame Slik featuring an embarrassed-looking Midge Ure. They are all assembled for a concert that seems to go on forever.

Side By Side's Australian director Bruce Beresford would soon direct the superior Aussie coming-of-age drama *Puberty Blues* (1981) and receive Oscar nominations for both writing, *Breaker Morant* (1981) and directing, *Tender Mercies* (1984) and win a BAFTA for *Driving Miss Daisy* (1989). *Never Too Young to Rock*'s Dennis Abey would be limited to the occasional TV work. GTO Films was, like GTO Records, part of the Gem Toby Organisation, founded by Laurence Myers. The record label had hits with Fox and Dana but really hit the big time by snagging the UK rights to Donna Summer's early output, as well as that of Billy Ocean and

Heatwave. Not to be outdone, fellow UK minnow label Dick James Music (DJM) threw its hat into the Glam movie marketplace with **THREE FOR ALL (1975)**.

Brian Epstein had contacted Dick James in early 1963 when looking for a publisher for 'Please Please Me', an association that would lead to the formation of Northern Songs who published subsequent Lennon and McCartney songs. James sold Northern Songs in 1969, profiting handsomely and using the proceeds to set up DJM which was run by his son Stephen.

For *Three For All*, the company engaged the services of director Martin Campbell and screenwriter Tudor Gates who wrote the script from a story by Howard Shapman, a friend of Gates who had recently sold his small music publishing company to James. Tudor Gates best work appeared on the stage where he had a degree of West End success in the mid to late 70s with *Who Saw Him Die?* starring Stratford Johns, *Who Killed Agatha Christie* with James Bolam, and *The Kidnap Game* with Richard Todd and Hayley Mills. His best remembered work is the three screenplays he wrote for Hammer, *The Vampire Lovers* (1968), *Lust For A Vampire* (1971) and *Twins of Evil* (1971), though largely for the lesbian sex and nude Collinson twins than for the complexity of the story. Director Jimmy Slaughter called the *Lust For a Vampire* script 'an embarrassment'.

Shapman was a plugger at Pall Mall Music during the 1960s and this is the last entry of a film cv that comprised two 'ideas' and two 'stories', all involving the music business. *Band of Thieves* (1962) was a starring vehicle for Acker Bilk who had appeared as himself and performed three songs in Richard Lester's *It's Trad Dad* (1962). *Live It Up* (1963) starred David Hemmings as a member of a pop group, the Smart Alecs, that also includes singer Heinz Burt and a young Steve Marriott on guitar, and is largely a showcase for the songs and production of the legendary Joe Meek, performed in the film by Sounds Incorporated, Andy Cavell, Gene Vincent and the Outlaws, whose line up includes Richie Blackmore and Chas Hodges, of Chas & Dave fame. *Dateline Diamonds* (1965) with a screenplay by Gates stars the Small Faces whose manager is an ex-con with an eye on stealing the titular diamonds. The band's role is minimal in proportion to their billing but they do provide 5 songs including the classic 'Watcha Gonna Do?'

Perhaps Shampan had run out of ideas because it would be ten years until his next one. In the meantime, Tudor Gates had dipped his toes into the British sex comedy market with his script for *The Sex Thief* (1972) which was the feature debut of director Martin Campbell, whose *Eskimo Nell* (1975) released the same year as *Three For All* is generally considered one of the much-maligned genre's high points. Campbell would go on to exceed all expectations by directing two Bond movies, including the 2006 Daniel Craig reboot *Casino Royale*.

Three For All begins with three friends, Diane (Adrienne Posta), Pet (Cheryl Hall) and Shelley (Leslie North) making their way through the streets to their local Top Rank, where Showaddywaddy are appearing. The girls are there to see support act Billy Beethoven, three of whom are their boyfriends. All this is to the accompaniment of an awful theme song performed by The Marionettes and written by Chris Arnold, David Martin and Geoff Morrow, a song writing trio best known for Barry Manilow's 'Can't Smile Without You,' who also provide an even worse song for Posta.

Billy Beethoven then performs a number from the stage, making it five and a half minutes before a single word of dialogue is uttered. The band comprises drummer Tom (Robert Lindsay), guitarist Gary (Paul Nicholas), fellow guitarist Ricky (Christopher Neil) and vocalist Kook (Graham Bonnet). Lindsay was then a recent RADA graduate whose only notable screen credit had been as David Essex's school pal in *That'll Be The Day* (1973) though was on the cusp of becoming a household name through roles in the sitcoms *Get Some In* (1975-1977) and *Citizen Smith* (1977-1980). Perhaps Lindsay attended auditions carrying a set of drums because he would appear behind a kit again in an episode of a bizarre drama-panel show amalgam, in which a panel of celebrities had to deduce *Whodunnit?*, in this case the electrocution of one of his bandmates. It was the band's manager, Mike from *Bless This House*, in case you wondered.

Neil, like Nicholas, had started out pursuing a pop career, turning to acting when that career path stalled. He had sung with Manchester band The Chuckles who were signed to Polydor and released a few singles in the sixties and he also released a solo album for RAK in 1972, 'Where I Belong', which quickly made its way to the discount bins. Having trod the boards as the titular character in a Manchester production of *Jesus Christ Superstar*, he took further acting roles in the aforementioned *The Sex Thief* and *Eskimo Nell*. Unlike his two co-stars, Neil's acting career never really took off, though he had a recurring role in *Rock Follies*, and ended after roles in two more sex

comedies, *Adventures of a Private Eye* (1976) and *Adventures of a Plumber's Mate* (1978), though he got to also write and perform their respective theme songs.

Three For All may have done little to further Neil's acting career, but it did inadvertently revitalise his music career via the pairing with Paul Nicholas, whose three hit singles he produced, leading to a career providing hits for Dollar, Shaking Stevens, Mike + the Mechanics, Celine Dion and, Mr 'Sing the theme tune' himself, Dennis Waterman.

Graham Bonnet had achieved the pop hits that had eluded his costars in the early stages of their careers as far back as 1968 when as The Marbles, a duo he formed with his Australian cousin, he had a #5 hit with 'Only One Woman' and a #28 with its follow up single 'Walls Fall Down'. This success was due in no small part to the fact that both songs were written by the Gibb brothers, Maurice, Robin and Barry. By 1975 though he was working as a songwriter at DJM and also on songs for a solo album which was released in 1977 and sold well in Australia but not elsewhere. In 1979 Bonnet was offered the opportunity to replace Brian Connelly in Glam rockers The Sweet but instead took over the spot vacated by Ronnie James Dio in hard rockers Rainbow with whom he achieved two more top ten singles in 'Since You've Been Gone', a #6, and 'All Night Long', a #5.

Billy Beethoven, whose songs are written by Bonnet, are managed by Jet Bone (Richard Beckinsale) who fixes the band up with Svengali and estate agent Eddie Boys (George Baker) and, after rebranding them as glitter cowboys, sets the band up with some gigs at tourist hotels in Spain. With the management feeling the presence of girlfriends might dilute their teenybopper appeal, the girls are banned from going with them but instead book a cheap package holiday to Torremolinos, where mainly through Diane's dizziness they get into various comic, but not funny, scrapes.

These are interspersed with glimpses of the band on tour, performing a few more of Bonnet's numbers, the best thing in the film, and an endless stream of guest appearances from the likes of Anna Quayle, Dandy Nichols, Diana Dors, Ian Lavender, Roy Kinnear, Hattie Jacques, Arthur Mullard and Edward Woodward.

According to Gates it was the wrong film at the wrong time: 'Howard Champan, before the war, had been a very successful cinema manager and he felt he wanted to get back to the family film and his idea of the ideal family film was Deana Durban's *Three Smart Girls* (1936)... And I tried to say to him, you know, honestly we need to make some money to make Dick feel confident and you make money by making films that contain sex and violence, that's what the public wants. Anyway, he was adamant about this and he talked Dick round, and of course he had the musical input because they had artists they wanted to push... young artists.' And so in the end Gates wrote 'a perfectly nice little film with some quite good songs in it' which 'came out and one can only say it died.'

The release was accompanied by a soundtrack album that nobody would have wanted, though Glam fans might consider Billy Beethoven's tracks - two of which were also issued on a single -

worthwhile additions to their collection. The album also includes DJM's one big hit that wasn't by Elton John, Mr Bloe's 'Groovin' With Mr Bloe' which is heard briefly in the background.

*

Although according to Todd Haynes Glam rock is implicitly and inextricably linked to a gay or bisexual awakening, as it most certainly is for Arthur in *Velvet Goldmine*, and undoubtedly many others, in reality for most Glam rock fans, and seemingly 99% of its performers, it was either an irrelevance or an artifice. Those who were gay, such as Freddie Mercury and Elton John, were still firmly in the closet. Indeed, in the 1970s there was, according to the Irish Times, a gang in Dundalk called the Bowie Boot Boys who wore Crombie's and brothel creepers, combed oxblood polish through their hair to achieve the Ziggy look and had a BBB logo with a cross through the centre. 'When you have men in a Republican town', said the paper, 'more interested in eye-liner or where they might source some Oxford bags or size 11 heels or the latest Bowie/T Rex LP than in any kind of political ideology, you arguably have a safer populace.'

Glam took a step closer to what would become Punk via the more 'street' end of the look, which would have been the music of choice for many of what author Richard Allen would have called Smoothies and Bovver Boys. These were by 1972 the latest incarnation of what would once have been called Skinheads and a description that would have fitted future Sex Pistols Paul Cook and Steve Jones who, says Jones: 'became Skinheads when that movement first started. It was great, soccer matches, dressing up and looking better than the other guy. I stole all my clothes, so I always had a good wardrobe... After the soccer matches, you could loot stores. That's what I enjoyed - total chaos and anarchy. Football hooliganism was a great outlet if you're a frustrated kid. I wouldn't call myself a tough guy, but I was definitely a street person... We supported Queens Park Rangers, Chelsea, Fulham; but it wasn't as much the game as the whole scene. We didn't really watch the matches. We just walked around the ground trying to look good.'

One band who managed to break into the mainstream were Newcastle boot stompers Geordie, fronted by future AC/CD singer Brian Johnson, who, after touring with Slade, managed four top 40 singles in a twelve-month period during 1972-73. Another Slade support act who made it into the charts was The Sensational Alex Harvey Band. In the retrospective documentary broadcast as part of BBC Scotland's *ex-s* programme, *Vambo Rools: The Sensational Alex Harvey* (2001), journalist Billy Sloan's description of Alex Harvey's approach to stage craft is pure Johnny Rotten: 'Alex walked on stage... walked straight up to the microphone, didn't say a word, just stared straight at the audience. And that was like a red rag to a bull because simultaneously three and a half thousand people hated him.' Noddy Holder takes up the mantle: 'He'd insult the audience, especially the English audiences, he'd insult 'em and insult 'em, and they'd love it. And by the end of the set, the audience used to warm to him.' Rotten confirmed the influence by including the band's 'Faith Healer' in a collection of songs that inspired him during a stint standing in for Jarvis Cocker on his BBC 6 radio programme. Another singer influenced by Harvey's stage presence was Madness frontman Suggs who saw the band supporting The Who in 1976, and told the Scotsman in an interview plugging his book: 'I didn't put this in the book 'cos the publishers said it was controversial and too outrageous, and it's not funny, but Alex Harvey came on dressed as Adolf Hitler and did 'Framed' with a German accent. It was fucking outrageous.'

Equally outrageous, and sharing Harvey's love of theatrics but not his level of success was The Heavy Metal Kids and their enigmatic front man Gary Holton, who found themselves too early for mainstream recognition and a few years too long in the tooth when Punk broke. During these years the key buzz words being bandied around as part of the tabloid newspapers continuing obsession with the country's delinquent youth were 'bovver', 'aggro', 'hooliganism' and 'vandalism' in an urban landscape where it was becoming increasingly difficult to find an inner-city high street that wasn't covered in graffiti, with a working phone box or a bus shelter that didn't stink of piss. It was against this background that the BBC's *Panorama: Younger Every Day* (1974) introduced the nation's mums and dads to Holton, who told them 'in the sixties, it was all beads, peace, and pop. What the kids want now is Boots, Bovver & Booze.'

In the programme, the Heavy Metal Kids appeared on stage at the Fulham Greyhound performing 'The Cops Are Coming'. Adopting the persona of a Mod hating rocker about to do a smash and grab on a chemist's shop, Holton sings 'As I approached a freeway on this hot and sweaty day / I saw a young pig fresh from the farm / Now I did not wish him any harm / But to my alarm he spat at my bike, I no like / So he on his Triumph and me on my Harley / Started to have a little rondula / I took his right flank with my machine-like tank / And gave him a cheesecake grin /

I took a chain and felt it wrap around his chin / And his head fell off'. It's all clearly tongue in cheek but not everyone seemed to realise and the band subsequently found themselves banned from many venues, a situation that, unlike The Sex Pistols two years later, didn't catapult them into the big time.

Most of these edgier bands quickly fell by the wayside. The most likely to succeed was Jook whose line-up contained two members of former Mod band John's Children who had been fired from a tour of Germany as the support to The Who for being 'too loud and violent'. At the first gig, in Düsseldorf, the guitarist took to thrashing his instrument with a chain, drummer Chris Townson smashed his kit and Andy Ellison and John Hewlett had a fight before the latter flung feathers around and dived into the crowd. They were literally a hard act to follow, with Roger Daltrey complaining that he couldn't sing because of the feathers still floating around in the air. Turning his hand to management Hewlett formed Jook with Townson, guitarist Trevor White, bass player Ian Hampton and songwriter Ian Kimmett who had been working as a producer with the then-unknown Mud. Through Hewlett's connections (he would later successfully manage Sparks) the new band secured a contract with RCA.

Adopting a Suedehead look that would in time morph into a more terrace/smoothie style, the band took a monthly residency at The Sundown in Edmonton, North London, and quickly began to build a following, which led to support slots with Wizzard and The Faces. Yet four mediocre singles later the breakthrough hit failed to materialise. The fifth, however, 'Bish Bash Bosh', could have been a contender; a foot-stomping, hand-clapping Glam anthem that had the added benefit of a spot on the Sweet tour to promote it. Unfortunately, whilst recording their 'Sweet Fanny Adams' album, Sweet vocalist Brian Connolly got in a fight on Staines High Street and was punched in the throat and although they completed the album the tour was cancelled and Jook soon after called it a day with White and Hampton joining Sparks.

Hammersmith Gorillas frontman Jesse Hector told the press 'Wot we're about is violence, we're the most violent band in Britain' whilst Edinburgh's Iron Virgin would take the stage to the music from *A Clockwork Orange*, adopting elements of the movies iconic look with drummer John going the full droog, wearing a bowler hat, fake eyelash and cane. Signed to Decca offshoot Deram, the band went into the studio with Thin Lizzy producer Nick Tauber but failed to make an impact. Nevertheless, their Glam foot-stomper 'Rebel Rules' was retrospectively deemed worthy of a place in Jon Savage's top twenty Glam tunes. Other bands like Portsmouth's Hector cultivated a more comic book aggressive pose, supplementing their platform boots with Dennis the Menace style hooped t-shirts, dungarees with catapults placed strategically in the back pockets, and even painted on freckles. Signed to Elton John's DJM the band would have been more at home in Gary Glitter's gang than Alex DeLarge's.

Two American bands often cited as having been hugely influential on their British counterparts were the New York Dolls and The Ramones. The New York Dolls were as Glam as they come and Joey Ramone says: 'I spent most of the early seventies listening to 'Slade Alive'... A couple of years later I found myself at CBGB's doing my best Noddy Holder.' Then plain Jeffrey Hyman, Joey fronted Glam rockers Sniper: 'I used to wear this custom made black jumpsuit, these like pink, knee-high platform boots.' Closer to home, TV Smith fronted his own Glam band, Sleaze, influenced by 'Rebel Rebel' era Bowie, and whose song 'Listen Don't Think', recorded as a demo, was reworked into 'Newsboys' for The Adverts. Casino Steel of The Boys was a member of The Hollywood Brats, a snotty Glam band whose career ran parallel to The New York Dolls without achieving the same level of fame despite, or perhaps because of, Keith Moon's assertion that they were 'the greatest band I've ever seen.' When Steel formed The Boys, he carried over several songs, such as 'Sick On You' and 'Tumble With Me', which his new band duly speeded up - the former track coming in at half the length of its original incarnation.

  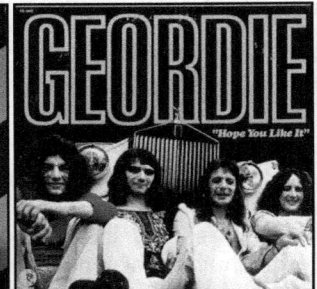 

Hippies, Skinheads, Rastas, Punks & Disco Dancing Bowie Boot Boys

You Should Be Dancing
(Gibb, Gibb, Gibb)

As Glam began its inevitable decline, another scene, 'Disco', was stamping its authority on the British charts where in July 1974 George McCrae hit the number one spot with 'Rock Your Baby', the first 'soul' related record to do so since The Tams 'Hey Girl Don't Bother Me' in 1971. That black music was again becoming a force to reckon with was soon cemented by two of the subsequent three chart-toppers, The Three Degrees 'When Will I See You Again' and the Brit Carl Douglas's 'Kung Fu Fighting', both having made the step into the mainstream after building up a steady following on the nation's dancefloors.

These would soon be followed to the top by records from Barry White and The Tymes. By the end of the year, the weekly music paper, Record Mirror had introduced both a Disco column and a Disco chart. The hits continued over the next couple of years with records like Van McCoy's 'The Hustle' and the Giorgio Moroder productions for Donna Summer such as 'Could It Be Magic?' but it was the release of the movie *Saturday Night Fever* (1977) that cemented the music's position amongst a white heterosexual audience and took Disco to unprecedented heights - a process begun with the re-invention of The Bee Gees from successful 60s pop act to Disco superstars via singles like 'Jive Talkin',' a UK #5 in 1975, and 'You Should Be Dancing' which hit the same spot the following year.

In New York, high profile clubs began to appear, amongst them Le Jardin, which had opened in 1973 as a gay club across two floors of the Diplomat Hotel, and the Loft where their respective DJs Bobby Guttadoro and David Mancuso became the burgeoning scene's taste-makers. In 1974 the Discos pushed three records to the Billboard #1 spot, Love Unlimited Orchestra's 'Love's Theme', The Hues Corporation's 'Rock Your Boat' and George McCrae's 'Rock Your Baby'. Then came KC and the Sunshine Band and The Bee Gees, who added a pop polish to the music that would help shift 30 million copies of the *Saturday Night Fever* soundtrack album.

By 1977 there was just one set of velvet ropes that New York clubbers hoped to find their way past, those of Studio 54 on West-Fifty-Fourth Street where the club's co-owner Steve Rubell said he 'would let in anyone who looks like they'll make things fun' but where being rich and famous was an advantage. And there was no shortage of those, attracted by a restrictive door policy that ensured the celebrities of the day could indulge in the era's excesses, protected from the outside world. And rich and famous is what the clubs owners quickly became, as the IRS discovered when in 1978, acting on a tip-off, they discovered almost $1 million in cash hidden away in the buildings crawlspaces and amongst the plumbing pipes earning Rubell and his partner three and a half years each in prison.

In the UK Disco was big but its club scene was lacking, the plastic palm trees and sunken dance floors of London's best-known clubs such as Annabel's in Berkeley Square, the Embassy in Old Bond Street and the members-only Tramp in Mayfair were little match for their Big Apple counterparts. DJs in the UK were still considered as the enemy by the Musicians Union and the best like Chris Hill, Gary Edwards and Robbie Vincent preferred to spin soul boy funk to the more populist Disco.

It was amongst the London elite rather than its teenage ne'r do wells that provided the setting for the UK's first glimpse into the world of the discotheque with **THE STUD (1978)**. The screenplay by Jackie Collins, Dave Humphries, and Christopher Stagg was based on a novel of the same name by Collins that had been a best seller in 1969. Collins sister Joan was given the movie rights to the novel for free, and both sisters' husbands were credited as producers. The finance for the film was provided by Brent Walker, a company founded by boxer Billy Walker and his Billingsgate fish market porter brother George, who had bought the Hendon Greyhound Stadium and developed it into the Brent Cross Shopping Centre. In the movie business, the company also produced *Quadrophenia* and in 1987 acquired Goldcrest. Other ventures, before the company collapsed in 1991 with £1.2 billion in debts, were the Pubmaster chain and William Hill bookies.

Collins had met George Walker whilst at Cannes promoting *Empire of the Ants* (1977), an all too visible signifier of just how low the former starlet's career had sunk, and pushed the prospective film as a British *Saturday Night Fever*, which it certainly wasn't. The film is set in an upmarket London discotheque, The Hobo, managed by Tony (Oliver Tobias) but it is the owner, Fontaine Khaled (Joan Collins), the trophy wife of wealthy businessman Ben

Oliver Tobias is *The Stud*

(Walter Gotell), who rules the roost. The club is her personal playground, her reward for the fact that 'Old Ben gets his cock sucked once a month, in the dark', and Tony's primary duty is to be sexually available for her at all times. And that's pretty much it really.

Studio 54 was frequented by the likes of Mick & Bianca Jagger, Andy Warhol, Liz Taylor, and Salvador Dali whilst across the pond, Tramp, where *The Stud* is filmed, could boast Roger Moore, George Best, Rod Stewart and Michael Caine (or 'Disco Mike' as he was known). Hobo can only muster a guest appearance from ex-boxer John Conteh.

In between people dancing to a string of the latest pop and Disco tunes, Collins gets to show off the fact that the passage of time had done little to diminish her assets as she frolics with Tony in a mirrored elevator as the act is filmed on early VCR technology; and with her best friend Vanessa's (Sue Lloyd) husband Leonard (Mark Burns) on a giant swing as it passes to and fro over a pool at a party to celebrate her birthday; a drug-fuelled orgy that comes to an abrupt end when an out-of-it Tony realises it is Leonard who is giving him head.

Meanwhile, Fontaine's barely legal step-daughter (Emma Jacobs) is exacting revenge for the treatment of her father by sleeping with Tony who is also plotting with an investment broker to finance a club of his own. There's no place for the likes of *Saturday Night Fever*'s young delinquents at Hobo, though there's no shortage of underage girls to accompany the clubs middle-aged male clientele, who make no bones about their predilections.

Though almost universally panned, *The Stud* recouped its budget almost tenfold, helped in no small measure by the level of coverage in a tabloid press that was obsessed by the fact that Collins was baring all at the ripe old age of, gasp, 45. The soundtrack album also added to the film's profitability with its combination of Disco hits like Heatwave's 'Boogie Nights', Odyssey's 'Native New Yorker' and The Biddu orchestra's title music, alongside pop hits like 10cc's 'I'm Not In Love', Roxy Music's 'Love Is the Drug' and Sweets 'Love Is Like Oxygen'.

All of which made a sequel, **THE BITCH (1979)**, inevitable. With no novel on which to base the film and *The Stud*'s director Quentin Masters passing on the project, both duties were handed to Gerry O'Hara whose career as a second-unit and assistant director went all the way back to the 1940s and prestige movies like *Richard III* (1955) and *Cleopatra* (1963), before he helmed sexploitation dramas *That Kind of Girl* (1963) and *The Pleasure Girls* (1965) in the sixties. To put him on the right track he was handed a twelve-page outline from Jackie Collins and a VHS copy of *The Stud*.

Like *The Stud*, *The Bitch* was universally panned by the critics but proved profitable at the box office, spawning a second hit soundtrack album. The film also found an additional critic in the form of Collins herself: 'I hate, hate, hate the film! It was a cheap imitation of *The Stud*. I did not like the script, which was half-written; furthermore, I did not like the director. They also gave it a damn awful exploitative title, which stuck to me like flypaper through the popular press for years. I begged Brent Walker not to use that title.'

By then, relations between the Collins sisters and their producers were already strained over the fact that *The Stud*'s profits were not making their way into their bank accounts (years of court proceedings would follow), hitting rock bottom when a banner trailing from a light aircraft flew over her on a yacht in Cannes declaring 'Joan Collins is *The Bitch*'. Nevertheless, the persona would be the making of her when TV producer Aaron Spelling, who had seen both films, cast her as Alexis Carrington in *Dynasty* and turned her into a television icon. Jackie meanwhile would have two more films released that year, with each including the inevitable Disco scene. *The World Is Full Of Married Men* (1979) featured Paul Nicholas as Disco star Gem Gemini who begins a relationship with the newly single Carroll Baker much to the annoyance of her former husband Anthony Steel. *Yesterday's Hero* (1979) stars Ian McShane as an alcoholic football player who is saved from the abyss by Disco singer Suzanne Somers and gives McShane the opportunity to shake his booty to the Dooleys.

Disco owes much to a dance craze that had been around for a couple of years in the Latino section of the Bronx and was taking off in the more upmarket Manhattan nightspots by the beginning of 1975 where clubbers danced to records like Barry White's 'Can't Get Enough Of Your Love, Babe'. When, on a night out, Van McCoy's business partner witnessed it he immediately took two of the dancers straight to the studio where McCoy was working on an album of instrumentals with his 'Soul City Symphony'. What McCoy saw was 'something completely different from the you-do-your-thing-and-I-do mine dances; it was people dancing together again.' The dance was known as the hustle, and by the following day, it had its own tune. Soon after McCoy would have his sole hit single whilst Disco would leave the underground for world conquest.

It is this form of couples dancing that was at the forefront when four months before *The Bitch*; the UK had finally got its own *Saturday Night Fever* in the form of **THE MUSIC MACHINE (1979)**. Based around a Disco dancing contest, it wasn't worth the wait. Such contests were by this time big news and the previous year had seen the staging of a so-called World Disco Dancing Championship which had begun life as part of the LWT programme *Bruce Forsyth's Big Night*, with the 1978 final presented by Radio 1 DJ David Hamilton and produced by Thames Television. From 1979 to 1982, Thames again produced the programme with each of the regional ITV franchises airing their own heats. The winner of the final went through to the world event which included entrants from 32 countries and the format continued on Channel 4 in 1983 and 1984.

Among the judges for 1978's inaugural final was Patti Boulaye, who had recently won the TV talent programme *New Faces* with a record score. The first World Disco Dancing Champion was Japanese entrant Tadaaki Dan who won a new car and £2000 prize money. The following year, this rose to £6000. In 1980 the event was parodied in an episode of *The Goodies*, *Saturday Night Grease*, in which a strategically placed carrot in Tim Brooke Taylor's underpants brought complaints from sensitive viewers - well one sensitive viewer, a certain Mrs Mary Whitehouse.

The World Disco Dancing Championship was promoted in a bizarre 24-minute short produced by Arundel Films. Providing the sole credit of writer Mark Cockle and director Oscar Riesel, **DISCOMANIA (1979)** opens with a sequence which shows various dancers, including the 1978 UK champion whom a voice-over tells us is now 'quite a celebrity in the national Disco scene' which 'is now a multi-million pound business; the Disco boom is all around us providing Disco music, specialist Disco lighting, ultra high powered music systems'. It is then revealed that this is actually a film within a film, part of a double bill with *Grease* (1978) that is being watched enthusiastically in the cinema by the dorky David (Stuart MacKenzie) who is straight out for some Disco dance lessons where he quickly discovers his abilities lie far short of his daydreams - in which his spots also miraculously fall off. In the end, he dons a pair of roller boots for a shot at an even more recent fad, Roller Disco, which we can only assume will not end well.

The Music Machine opens with a visit to Camden's Music Machine night club by a film producer looking to make a disco movie. He wants the club to hold a heat for a disco dancing competition, with another being held at the rival Disco Palace. The eventual competition winners will become the film's stars, and one club will form its backdrop.

Sure to be entering is Gerry (Gerry Sundquist) who is at the club with his friends when the announcement is

Like much of the nation Stuart MaKenzie is just a few dance lessons and a white suit away from Travolta stength pulling power in *Discomania*

made. He's a big disco fan and we know this because it blasts out from a portable cassette player he carries wherever he goes - including during his appointment in the Job Centre, which seems to single him out as also being a bit simple. Gerry has the hots for Candy (Mandy Perryment) but she's the girlfriend of the clubs best dancer, Howard - we know this because he wears a white suit. This means the only way Gerry gets to dance with her is in a dream sequence where he also gets to wear a white suit and stick one hand in the air ala John Travolta.

The role of Howard was filled by David Easter. To his then girlfriend and future Rovers Return landlady, actress Denise Welch, the actor was perfect for the showy role of Howard Tefler, the club's Travolta wannabe. She described their meeting in her autobiography: 'There in front of me was the man of my dreams, a dead ringer for John Travolta. He had Travolta's slicked back hair, the twinkle, the whole package. The only difference was John Travolta isn't classically good looking and David undoubtedly was. I took one look at him and thought, Oh my God! I was smitten from the word go. It was an immediate physical reaction for both of us and we were together from that night onwards... Even if you didn't fancy David Easter, you couldn't say he wasn't strikingly handsome.'

When Easter was cast in *The Music Machine*, it didn't matter to the actress that the film turned out to be a disappointment. 'None of that mattered to me because one night at the flat, David walked into my bedroom wearing his white suit, and struck the iconic pose from the *Saturday Night Fever* poster... "Well if I can't have John Travolta, I'll have Howard Tefler" I thought, "it's the next best thing."'

Following the film Easter signed a short-lived recording contract with EMI, releasing the single 'Lady Soul' in 1979. He returned in 1987 with a duet with Hazel O'Connor of *Blackadder* theme composer Howard Goodall's stage musical about the Woman's Auxiliary Air Force (WAAF). Recorded and released in part to gain airplay to promote the production, it was subsequently sold in the theatre.

With Candy off limits, Gerry instead teams up with his friend's girlfriend and the pair make it through to the next stage, though only because of the intervention of the clubs DJ Laurie (Clarke Peters) who, although it's glaringly obvious that neither Gerry the actor or Gerry the character can dance, sees something in him that suggests if he would stop doing 'that honky hustle' and do his own thing he 'might just have a chance.' Well, that and some out-of-hours lessons from the DJ himself, who turns out to be a bit of a mover. Unfortunately, when the couple improves, his partner's boyfriend gets the hump, not wanting a girlfriend who's a film star. Enter Patti Boulaye as Claire.

To ensure things don't run too smoothly the film introduces an arch-villain in the form of the Music Machine's manager Nick (Michael Feast) and his Punk henchman Aldo (Gary Shail). Nick stands to make £10,000 if Candy and her beau win, having signed the pair to a management contract. When Gerry and Claire look like they might interrupt his plans, Nick first sets Aldo the task of nobbling Gerry and when that fails he directs Claire to the wrong venue on the evening of the final. Will she make it in time? What do you think?

The Music Machine uses *Saturday Night Fever* as its template, from the disco tunes to the dance contest to its blue-collar social-realist setting but gets none of the elements right. These failings begin with the casting of

Gerry Sundquist, a good-looking lad and a decent enough actor whose career had begun promisingly with lead roles in two much-loved children's television series, *Soldier & Me* (1974) and *The Siege of Golden Hill* (1975), but thereafter had stalled, resulting in a depression that would in 1992 lead him to commit suicide by jumping in front of a train, aged just 37. His casting here probably didn't help. As a dancer, he's obviously a non-starter and given that the acting side of the role isn't particularly taxing, a better idea might have been to plunder the film's plot and cast the winner of a dance competition.

The actors were trained by Cathy Lewis and Anthony van Laast of the London Contemporary Dance Theatre who also provided the choreography. To make Jerry Lundquist into a dancer good enough to win a contest they had four weeks which van Laast says was 'a bit of a rush job... Jerry wasn't actually stiff and self conscious as a person; only when he knew he was going to dance he became like that. But if you take any actor who has never danced and tell him is going to star in a disco movie he is bound to have total paranoia on the spot.' The fist hurdle any non-dancer must overcome is to shed inhibition and physical stiffness. Here they clearly failed. Boulaye is better but her late arrival to the proceedings means the film doesn't even have the option of a romance to fall back on.

Where *Saturday Night Fever* was low budget, *The Music Machine* is simply cheap. That this should be so can be gleaned from its producer Brian Smedley Aston's previous credits which included two starring vehicles for porn actress Fiona Richmond, the comedy *Let's Get Laid* (1978) and the biopic *Hardcore* (1977), both of which were directed by *The Music Machine*'s co-producer and screenwriter James Kenelm Clarke, who also supplied the script of *Hardcore*. The budgetary failings are most evident in its low rent soundtrack that even Travolta might have found trouble strutting his stuff to. There are no dancefloor-filling hits here, just a series of insipid disco-lite tunes from a bunch of session players, credited as Music Machine, with vocals from Tony Jackson and Boulaye herself.

As a subculture, one thing that is not usually associated with disco is violence; that was the domain of Punk right? Not quite. During 1979 there had been eight violent deaths in London's discos, including one at the Music Machine. The GLC even introduced a new code of practice for such venues, issued with the title 'Disco Rules OK?' Just how out of touch the GLC were, one aspect of the code was to ensure a 50-50 gender split, the not entirely unreasonable logic being that if there weren't enough girls to go round, the men would fight over them. However, this showed little knowledge of a scene that had a large gay clientele who would have found themselves excluded. Rightly annoyed, they would have been even more so given that the Music Machine murder had been committed by a 35-year-old at a Troggs nostalgia gig!

Never matter, disco was already on the wane - largely a victim of its own success. There were by this point disco versions of everything, from *Sesame Street* (2 albums' worth) to *Star Wars* and ill-advised attempts to cash in by everyone from Rod Stewart and Mick Jagger to Frank Sinatra and Ethel Merman. In the USA this had led to the formation of an anti-disco movement that culminated in the infamous Disco Demolition Derby at Chicago's Comiskey Park during July 1997 where anyone attending a baseball double-header could gain admittance for just $0.98 if they brought a disco record along to be destroyed. It was a 50,000 sell-out with a further 15,000 stuck outside in what had become as much an anti-black, anti-gay event as it was anti-disco. In fact, black music had already moved on by 1979 as hip hop entered the public consciousness via the Sugarhill Gang's 'Rapper's Delight' and in the UK Disco and Punk began to merge via Spandau Ballet and Duran Duran, as well as less chart-friendly acts like Pigbag and Shriekback.

A s well as Glam and disco, there were several other 'scenes' bubbling just below the surface. The counter-culture were still represented by the likes of Hawkwind, Edgar Broughton, and the Pink Fairies, whilst up north the kids were popping pills and dancing till dawn to obscure sixties soul at venues like Wigan Casino.

Growing up in the industrial town of Bury on the outskirts of Manchester, future director and screenwriter Elaine Constantine attended a large youth club in the town hall where the usual sight of lads dancing to Status Quo 'with a denim waistcoat on and doing air guitar' was interrupted by a 'weird record' coming on. It was, she says, 'quite strange-sounding – a bit old-fashioned, with lots of reverb and just really heartfelt.' Even more startling was the reaction of a small group of lads who 'came out on the floor and cleared it. They were doing fast spins and high kicks and drops and this amazing footwork, but they were each dancing on their own and locked into the track.' The 'weird' music was 'Northern Soul' and the surrounding scene would, as it did for thousands of others, become the focus of her life.

It was a time, says playwright Mick Martin whose 2003 play, *Once Upon a Time In Wigan*, was set against a Northern Soul backdrop: 'when too many teenagers were destined to become factory fodder, checkout girls or shelf stackers. People were married by 21 and faced a life of mind-numbing tedium. Then in the face of this came the Northern Soul scene that offered up a dream, a step outside of their lives, of real excitement, once a week that didn't involve hurting anyone.'

Some years earlier, Roger Eagle walked into Manchester's Left Wing Coffee Bar, where people could take in their own records to play, clutching a pile of Chuck Berry and Bo Diddley imports on Chess & Checker. In the cafe at the time were the Abadi brothers, who were buying the place and turning it into a nightclub and Roger was asked if he knew anything about rhythm and blues. Replying in the affirmative, he was asked if he wanted to DJ. Despite never having done it before he thought 'why not' and in doing so became a fixture at the legendary Twisted Wheel.

This was 1963 and Northern Soul was not yet a thing, but Mod was coming into its heyday. The playlist bore little resemblance to what would be heard at the Wigan Casino several years later. Says Eagle: 'The favourite record of all time at the Wheel was 'It Keeps Raining' – Fats Domino... then you would go to something like 'Walking the Dog' – Rufus Thomas. Then you could go to any one of a dozen Muddy Waters records... The next on the list would be 'That's What I Want To Know' – James Carr, then one of Bobby Blue Bland's, 'Turn on Your Lovelight'. Then would come 'Amen' by Reverend Robinson and 'Long Distance' by Garnell Cooper and the Kinfolks. You could pick up any one of a dozen records by Booker T and the MGs... There was always plenty of records from the Stax label... but there was not quite so much Tamla Motown as people like to think.'

The Twisted Wheel was never a Northern Soul club per se, but in its last couple of years of operation it played a major role in laying the foundations, as fewer and fewer 60s style soul records were being released in the UK and DJs were forced to dig deeper in the import bins for new sounds that would get people on their feet. By the time the club ended in 1971, a good 50% of the records would have fitted the 'northern' criteria. A burgeoning Northern Soul scene made the pages of the Times as early as May 1971 in a small news item headed, 'Teenagers on drugs may go to Torquay', which stated that the resort could 'expect an invasion of drug-taking teenagers - calling themselves the soul sect - searching for places where they can dance and listen to 'soul' records throughout the night, kept awake by pep pills.' They based the feared invasion on the testimony of a 16-year-old Blackburn girl who was among 64 people arrested and charged with possession after a raid on a venue in Wakefield.

When the Twisted Wheel shut its doors for the last time, the Northern torch was carried on elsewhere. In Manchester, it was at the Pendulum, a basement club across from Victoria Station that had been a jazz cellar, whilst in Crewe, there was Up The Junction and in Blackpool, the Highland Room of the Mecca (though not for all-nighters). But it was the Golden Torch, in Turston on the outskirts of Stoke-on-Trent, that became the place to be. Originally a Mod club, the venue started holding soul nights in 1969 and, following the closure of the Twisted Wheel, began hosting all-nighters in March 1972. These were an immediate success. So much so that the 680 capacity venue found itself packed out by up to 1400 revellers, and it was this and a reputation for drug-taking that led to the withdrawal of its licence, after just one memorable year, in March 1973.

When DJ Russ Winstanley and the Wigan Casino manager Mike Walker persuaded the club's owner to let them hold all-nighters in September 1973, they thought that 'if it lasts until Christmas we'll have cracked it.' And crack it they did, continuing for another eight years. There were other clubs playing Northern Soul but for dancing there was nowhere that could touch it. What the venue lacked in location and décor was more than made up for by its acoustics and the huge and immaculately kept maple-sprung dancefloor of the main room, which could easily accommodate the 1200 who would strut their stuff during the Casino's heyday (to say nothing of the further 800 that could be accommodated in the 'oldies' room), with balconies on three sides for those who preferred to watch the acrobatics below.

Dave Grodin, a Covent Garden record shop proprietor, is credited with having first coined the phrase 'Northern Soul,' to differentiate for his employees the difference between the tastes of their regular soul seeking customers and those visiting the capital from up north. He would become a regular spokesman for the scene via his column in Blues & Soul magazine, where he became 'the sole champion of the right of northerners to make their own choices and dissent from what the mainstream establishment would have preferred them to have listened to… the establishment didn't like Northern soul at all, to begin with, and was often overtly hostile towards it and me in particular for being its libertarian champion… They saw it as a threatening phenomenon that was getting way beyond their ability to control and manipulate, and this really riled them.'

One distinct aspect that made the Northern Soul scene both unique and truly revolutionary was that it was based around music but eschewed current, commercially available records. It is hardly surprising then that the subculture won no favour with an establishment that had a vested interest in such things. It provided a threat to the record industry that Punk initially tried to claim for itself before it was quickly seen to be little more than a pose. Unfortunately, and much to the horror of most of the scenes die-hards, there were attempts during 1975, abetted by the Casino, to cash in on the club's growing popularity resulting in successful assaults on the pop charts. The first of these was 'Footsie' by Wigan's Chosen Few, which spent nine weeks in the top 40, peaking at #9 in January. Not a real group, the recording was by an obscure Canadian band from 1967 which was speeded up to fit the Northern Soul template and augmented with hand claps and chants. The original was a novelty record released to cash in on the popularity of a children's hoola hoop toy, the footsie, a ring worn over the foot with a weighted ball attached to a piece of string over which the user would hop when the leg was rotated. The one saving grace for many was that for the discs inevitable *Top of the Pops* outing, the programme used a selection of dancers from the club.

Lee Ingleby and Lenora Crichlow in *George Gently: Gently Northern Soul*

No such luck with the second release, 'Skiing in the Snow' which was credited to Wigan's Ovation, but who were in fact a pop group from the town called Sparkle who had been persuaded by Winstanley to record a cover of a soul single released in 1965 by the Invitations. The record reached #12 in March and the band appeared on *Top of the Pops* in baggy trousers decorated with Northern Soul patches with the performance being described, rather melodramatically and with little substance, in Stuart Cosgrove's 'Young Soul Rebels: A Personal History of Northern Soul' as 'the night that Wigan Casino died'. What was more reasoned was that same book's description of the record itself as 'a fucking travesty'..

Another controversial move was granting Granada Television permission to take their cameras into the club for an episode of it's *This England* programme. **THIS ENGLAND: WIGAN CASINO (1977)** opens on a bubbling cauldron of iron ore and intersperses footage from the Casino of eager punters pushing their way through the crowds outside, showing off their moves on the floor and flicking through their boxes of obscure ex-jukebox 45s, contrasting such with the town's run-down city centre, and its crumbling factories. Interviews with clubbers for whom their Saturday night and Sunday morning means everything, sits alongside the town's pensioners recounting tales of life down the pit and the price of a packet of fags. There's also a look at how difficult it was to explain this strange new culture to those on the outside of its tight-knit community; from their peers for whom the concept a club with no beer was unfathomable, to the parents of young girls for whom staying out all night is intrinsically linked to promiscuity.

'I think there's something wrong with the world really,' says one endearingly naïve clubber, Dave Withers, 'to get enjoyment out of their life during the teens and twenties, people do have to build more or less an alternative society, just to enjoy themselves because they can't within the normal channels. They can't go to the normal Mecca, Tiffanys circuit and enjoy themselves because it's... just not an enjoyable experience.'

'If you're working in some very tedious job, you don't wanna look forward to something that could go wrong anyway. That's like your week falling through… but every week if you're going somewhere where there's a certain good time, just from the community sense, it brightens up the people's lives who go. I'm okay with mine really, but if you've got a very boring job, I don't think there's anything to fill your mind except stupid little things people think about at work.'

Director Tony Palmer was commissioned to helm the episode at the request of the Casino all-nighter's organisers; his seventeen part history of popular music, *All You Need Is Love* (1977), having been aired earlier in the year to great acclaim. He was, he says, 'auditioned by the committee that ran it. This was their private world - they didn't really want it publicised. Yet they also wanted to show a joyful celebration of a kind of music and dancing.' The production was also made aware of the need for the Casino to be seen in a positive light. So it is no surprise that the one subject that the documentary gave a wide berth was that of the drug use that had led to the downfall of the Golden Torch. The sheer size of the dancefloor at Wigan Casino would play its part in the growth of amphetamine use which led to a demand for faster, stomping beats which again boosted the 'need for speed'.

Up to 1954 and the Pharmacy & Poisons Act, anyone deemed a 'fit and proper person' by a pharmacist could buy drugs over the counter. The new legislation required prescriptions which soon became a major source of forgery. Whilst it was illegal to sell amphetamines it was not an offence to possess them and a grey market soon emerged that meant they could be easily obtained under-the-counter in coffee houses and via dealers at dances.

It was the increased recreational use of amphetamines in the emerging Mod subculture in the early part of the 1960s that eventually led the government to introduce regulation to criminalise possession of the drug. A forceful voice that brought the situation to the forefront was that of Anne Sharpley, a reporter for the London Evening Standard who published two articles on Mod amphetamine use, the first of which appeared on the 3rd of February 1964 under the headline 'Purple Heart Trip in Soho: Super teenagers are the prey for pushers'. This was followed the next day by 'The non-stop world of Pills Paradise'.

Both reports show a high degree of perception for the reasons for the drug's popularity but still managed a touch of *Reefer Madness* sensationalism, evident in a belief that the Mods were 'prey to pushers' and 'addicted'. Sharpley said: 'They are looking for, and getting, stimulation not intoxication. They want greater awareness, not escape. And the confidence and articulacy that the drugs of the amphetamine group give them are quite different from the drunken rowdiness of previous generations on a night out.' A number of other stories on the subject were covered by the paper over the rest of the month.

During February 1964 the Home Affairs Committee authorised the preparation of a Bill to control amphetamines which would become the 1964 Drugs (Prevention & Misuse) Act and criminalise possession. A number of further measures were introduced the following year that tightened the security around the production process and stemmed the flow of tablets into the wrong hands. Although the use of forged prescriptions continued unabated, a new and more worrying method of misappropriating the drugs was by breaking into chemists, where they were not required by law to be kept under lock and key and sat in alphabetical order on the shelves. In extreme cases, there was also the hi-jacking of lorries carrying supplies.

At the burglary of a pharmacy in Kings Norton in 1966, 50,000 tablets were stolen, whilst in Salford that year, 16 of the town's 47 pharmacies were burgled. Government regulation then turned to the safekeeping of drugs inside chemist shops and in 1973 new legislation was passed requiring that pharmacists should ensure controlled drugs were kept in a 'locked receptacle as at present required for Dangerous Drugs.' Class B drugs were therefore now stored alongside Class A drugs in locked steel cabinets that were bolted to either a wall or the floor. These were however not safes, and burglars going suitably equipped could still gain access, or even remove the entire cabinet, an unintended consequence of which was the sweeping up of 'unwanted' Class A drugs. The measures reduced the number of pharmaceutically manufactured amphetamine tablets coming to the grey market and so illicitly manufactured 'backstreet' blues and dexy's in blue and yellow pill form helped to plug the shortfall, but not fill it.

This inadvertently provided the pharmacy burglars with a way to offload those unwanted Class A drugs, rather than flushing them. Dealers on the Northern Soul circuit found they could exchange them for illegally manufactured amphetamine powder. Whilst this was at odds with the scene's 'Pillhead' culture, a combination of diminishing supplies and an increasing user base made its eventual take up a necessity. The better buzz that can be obtained from powder by injecting led to 'cranking' and the introduction onto the scene of needle culture.

The Debbie Horsfield penned **OUT ON THE FLOOR (1983)**, a half-hour BBC drama, began life on the stage, performed in 1981 at the Theatre Royal, Stratford East. It opens with two girls sorting out the cash for a drugs deal. 'Get me some of those bombers; stop me getting bored,' says Nadine (Natalie Ford) to her friend Donna (Amanda Noar) whilst stuffing bank notes in her hand. 'Okay, okay,' she is told, 'I'm not flogging you an overdose.' Nadine is a newcomer to Wigan Casino and is next seen being put through her paces by Donna and Lally (Sally Baxter) on the dance floor.

From the balcony above, they are watched by two lads, Nico (Pete Howitt) and Ton (Reece Dinsdale). Nico tries chatting up Gem (Julie Shipley). He's far from charming. 'You know what you are darling,' he says when he realises he's getting nowhere, 'There's a name for girls like you. Prick teaser.' She gives and good as she gets: 'We've got a name for blokes like you, and all, Pricks.' He instead turns his attention to Lally. It's not clear whether or not they're officially a couple, but she clearly has feelings for him. Any reciprocation from Nico originates purely from below the waist, because he quickly turns his attentions to Nadine, taking her out onto the dance floor, and then outside, before she returns with her skirt unfastened, which doesn't go unnoticed. The charming Nico brushes any protests aside: 'What am I supposed to do? She's a mate of yours, isn't she? I was only trying to be polite.'

An already emotional Lally gets even more upset when she disapprovingly spots Gem popping a couple of tablets from a bottle concealed in her bag. 'So what's the point, Gem?' she asks, 'What's your excuse?' 'You know. You get tired. You get narked. You get pissed off with the little things. It's not much... a quick blast to stop you going under. Honest, there's no kicks, it just gets you by,' says Gem to assure her it's not a problem. 'No problem, I've heard that one before,' an unimpressed Lally tells her. 'They all know what they're doing, don't they? Smashed out in corners, stretchered off to casualty.' 'The idiots,' says Gem, 'Yes... I've seen what happens. Don't you think I've got more sense.'

It quickly transpires that she doesn't, and when Nico, annoyed that Gem has interfered in an attempt to stop him taking advantage of Lally, takes his revenge by telling her that her absent-because-of-a-hangover-from-a-stag-do boyfriend was instead with another girl the previous evening, she responds by necking a load more tablets and passing out cold. Taking an upset Lally out to 'comfort' her, Nico then gets all rapey until a swift knee in the groin softens his ardour. In the production's finest moment, after walking away, leaving the wounded sex pest kneeling on the floor, she swiftly retraces her steps and follows up with another forceful kick before returning to the dancefloor for the closing credits.

Horsfield, who went on to greater small screen success, has returned to Northern Soul in subsequent works such as hairdressing drama *Cutting It* (2002-2004), where one character was said to have been conceived in the Wigan Casino car park, and *Clocking Off* (2000-2003) where another character was pissed off that her boyfriend was always away attending all-nighters at weekends and includes a northern scene at the Ritz, Manchester. Which is surprising because if *Out On The Floor* represents her Northern Soul experiences, they must have been bleak times.

In 2010, almost thirty years on from Wigan Casino's closing night, Northern Soul had resolutely refused to go away with music lovers with itchy feet from Aberdeen to Brighton attending all-nighters and the longest-running regular night, 6Ts at the 100 Club, itself passing the thirty-year mark. Labels like Kent, run by 6Ts Andy Croadsell, were committing the era's classic tunes to CD for the first time to be enjoyed by a new generation, Casino legends like Nolan Porter were flying into the country to perform sell-out concerts and, nearer home, artists like Moloko and Duffy, whose 2008 single 'Mercy' used 6Ts regulars for its video, were mining the northern scene for inspiration. There were also two feature films in production.

SOULBOY (2010) is set in Stoke-on-Trent during 1974, where Joe McCain's (Martin Compston) head is turned when he spots blonde hairdresser Jane (Nichola Burley) and follows her into a record shop where he discovers her love of obscure 1960s American soul. It is a genre that has previously passed him by on his nights down at the local boozer, The Onion, strutting his stuff to the likes of Mud's 'Tiger Feet' with best pal Russ (Alfie Allen) whose favourite dance move is the 'dying fly', which is every bit as embarrassing as it sounds.

Visiting Jane's salon for a haircut, he feigns interest in the Northern Soul scene and is handed a flyer for an all-nighter at Wigan Casino, to which he persuades an initially reluctant Russ to accompany him. That the pair are fish out of water is immediately obvious from their awful seventies suits and ties, and Russ's distress at the discovery that there is no bar. To make matters worse, Joe's hopes of impressing Jane are unceremoniously quashed when his attempts to emulate some of the clubs best movers leave him on his arse. An even greater obstacle to his romantic allusions manifests in the shape of 'boyfriend' and Casino face Alan (Craig Parkinson), who also holds the venue's drugs franchise. Complicating matters further is Mandy (Felicity Jones), the younger sister of Dexie (Brennan Reece), a former classmate of Joe who carries a torch for him but is relegated to soul-mate as she teaches him the moves that will eventually impress Jane.

Martin Compston has the vest but not the moves in *Soulboy*

Alan finally gets his comeuppance in a 'dance-off' with Joe that resembles Justin McArdle's excellent 2002 14 minute short, *Function at the Junction*, where a bloodied Jake 'the Manc' Bancroft (Robert Tannion) takes to the floor to win the Northern Soul dance contest despite having taken a beating from the club's bouncers at the behest of a crooked club manager played by the excellent John McArdle (despite a lengthy career still best known for his role as *Brookside*'s Billy Corkhill). Joe's cuts and bruises are from an altercation in the bus station on his way but not only does Alan, in a reversal of the earlier scenes, end up on his arse but the dozens of pills stuffed in his pockets spill out across the floor with the drug squad on the premises. To complete the clichés, Jane now makes a play for Joe but is rejected for Mandy as the two drive off into the sunset, on a coach to Nottingham where she is due to attend art school.

The Independent called it 'Film of the week, by a distance' but elsewhere the film was generally labelled too simplistic and hackneyed. The Guardian praised Compston's performance but concluded that 'in the end, there is something just a little too formulaic about the film,' and the Telegraph suggested it 'feels oddly detached from the compelling genre of music it claims to advocate.' The Radio Times meanwhile said 'It's more than a little clichéd, with a disco-floor bully who's straight out of panto, but the music and period detail will help take your mind off such deficiencies.' The Daily Express was a little kinder, saying that 'Everything about *Soulboy* is predictable and yet it manages to deliver a passably entertaining little slice of British entertainment,' which is just about right.

The producers of *George Gently* were jumping the gun somewhat when they decided to include an episode of the 1968 set fifth series against the backdrop of the Northern Soul scene before Dave Godin even had time to give it a name. But despite much of the action being set in and around Durham's Carlton ballroom, home of a popular all-nighter, it is the specific time period within which screenwriter David Kane sets the story that provides the real backdrop. In particular three key events in the period between the 4th of April when Martin Luther King was assassinated and the 23rd of the month when the Race Relations Act had its second reading. Whilst these two events are referenced, neither takes place within the time frame of the story but a third event does.

In **GEORGE GENTLY: GENTLY NORTHERN SOUL (2012)** a young black girl, Delores Kenny (Pippa Bennett-Warner), is found dead on a piece of waste ground by the side of a road with her head caved in. DS Baccus is quick to assume that the dead girl must have been a prostitute likely killed by a disgruntled punter, but this theory is immediately thrown into doubt by the £20 she was still in possession of and the fact that there was no recent sign of sexual activity.

Further investigation reveals she had spent the night at a Northern Soul all-nighter at the Carlton ballroom, which is an alien concept to the policemen. The promoter Gary Watts (Craig Conway), who is not in it for the music, explains: 'We give them a kind of soul music they don't play anywhere else. They come from all over the place. London. Scotland. They're obsessed by it. I don't know why though, it's all jigaboo to me. But there you go, they love it and it makes me some money.'

Following his primer on the scene, where he also learns there are other substances available to keep one's energy levels up than alcohol, DS Baccus immediately concludes she must have been a dealer. He is taken to task by Gently: 'She's coloured so she must be on the game? She's got money so she must be selling drugs?' This pegs Baccus as something of a racist but the truth, as with the murder itself, is far more complex.

Not that the programme is short of racists queuing up to be suspects. There's a landlady who displays the 'No Blacks, No Irish, No Dogs' poster in her window and who has 8 English budgies, 3 American, a pair of love birds, a parakeet and a cockateel. When Gently questions her keeping the latter two in the same cage she tells him brusquely: 'Birds don't cross breed. Not like people. They're only attracted to their own species.'

There's also local gangster Bernie Watts (John Bowler), father of the promoter and the clubs DJ, Charlie (Philip Correia), who as well as supplying the Carlton's amphetamines is also involved in running the campaign against the upcoming Race Relations Act. The Act seems to be one area in which the police and the criminal fraternity can agree. We see a group of police officers gather to listen to Enoch Powell's 'Rivers of blood' speech, to which one remarks, 'Bout time somebody said it.' 'We have lift off' says Bernie also tuning in at his scrap yard. He wouldn't have been too happy then to learn that Charlie was seeing Dolores who we learn was pregnant.

Feeling that the murder is connected to the ballroom Baccus practices his dance moves in the station, much to the amusement of his colleagues, before he is sent undercover to the Carlton toting a box of 45s where he slips up immediately by accepting an offer of ten bob from Dolores best friend Carol (Lenora Crichlow) for 'Born A Loser' when it's worth £15, but redeems himself when he says he prefers Frank Wilson. 'Do I Love You?' she asks. 'Deed I do' he responds having seen a copy of the single in the dead girl's bedroom.

Gently's fears about his sergeant being a racist appear unfounded when he becomes romantically entangled with the mixed race Carol. Baccus is also proved right about Delores being involved in dealing and without his enquiries amongst the local working girls the murderer may have never been found. It is Gently himself, after catching the pair in a passionate embrace, who is shown to be in need of diversity training: 'How serious is it? Well, I hope you're prepared for the stick you'll get. It would be career suicide. Now I'm not saying it's right, it's just a fact.'

Northern soul fans will be disappointed at the lack of decent dancing in the few brief scenes on the dance floor where the clubbers seem content to shuffle along like they were in their local Tiffanys. Prior to going in front of the cameras the production visited northern nights within travelling distance of the episodes Hartlepool filming location in the hope of attracting talent as extras. One reveller in Gateshead gives an indication of why the search was unsuccessful: 'It was so funny as we were nearly all in our 50s and we were all measured up for costumes, our names and mobile taken and we were all told if we received a call we would be in the show, needless to say I know no one from that night that is in the episode.'

NORTHERN SOUL (2014) was a long time in production, during which a buzz had begun that this might be 'the' film the scene deserved following the comedown of *Soulboy*. This optimism was helped by the director's credentials as a long time face on the scene, and a primer in the form of the video for Moloko's single 'Familiar Feeling' in which a flared up Paddy Considine showed off his moves on the dance floor. Despite *Soulboy* taking a disappointing £101,000 at the box office, director Elaine Constantine was confident that her film would find its audience – or the audience would find her film: 'Northern soul is not a passive audience. People travel across the whole country to experience an all-nighter. Going to the cinema does not present a challenge.' The director's faith was vindicated when *Northern Soul* enjoyed an opening weekend of £279,000 from 83 screens, many of which were limited showings, grossing close to £800,000.

Elliot James Langridge in *Northern Soul*

Growing up in Burnsworth, representative of the many Lancashire industrial towns that in 1974 were undergoing a steady decline in fortunes, for teenage misfit John (Elliot James Langridge) life isn't easy. That he's the butt of his classmates' jokes is not helped by the fact that much of it is initiated by his teacher (a memorable turn from Steve Coogan). He paints his displeasure in foot-high letters on the wall at the bottom of his street – BURNSWORTH IS SHITE!

Retreating into his own company, his parents badger him into a reluctant visit to the local youth club where a lacklustre crowd shuffle along to the likes of Leo Sayer, Cliff Richard and Melanie's 'Brand New Key' – Constantine knows how to stack the deck in her favour. The tedium is broken by fellow misfit

Matt (Joshua Whitehouse), whose street cred is signified by a wispy moustache and the Northern Soul record he persuades the youth worker/DJ Terry (John Thomson) to spin. Whilst the song immediately clears the dancefloor, Matt dances enthusiastically and acrobatically alone which captivates the watching John who tells him, 'You were like Bruce Lee'. High praise in an era when every young man wanted to be just like the *Enter the Dragon* star and an intense friendship is formed.

Soon after, John walks out in the middle of an exam, and moves in with Matt, taking a dead-end job in the same factory. Before long, after letting Terry's tyres down, the two aspiring DJs are spinning discs at the youth club and winning new converts, whilst dreaming of a trip across the Atlantic in search of the rare grooves that will help make their name on the scene. At the factory, John meets the heavily tattooed Sean (Jack Gordon), a few years older and a regular at Wigan Casino who has the transport to get them there, and a regular supply of stolen tablets to keep them dancing. Says Sean: 'Word of advice, don't go on the needle, once you're into that there's no coming back... it's for fucking divs.' Matt, needless to say, is a fucking div.

Like in *Soulboy*, Constantine provides a love interest in the shape of Angela (Antonia Thomas), a nurse who John regularly sees on the bus but, her being older, is too shy to approach. Angela is clearly based on Fran Franklin, one of the star dancers from the Casino's heyday who appears in the BBC's *Culture Show* episode *Northern Soul: Keeping the Faith* (2003) and who, like the film character, is the mixed-race daughter of a black American serviceman. Franklin worked on the project for three years, putting the dancers through their paces but sadly passed away before the film's release, though she lived long enough to see it in its completed form. A closing credit dedicates the film to her.

Constantine first thought of doing something on Northern Soul in the early nineties and began documenting the then-current scene on film but felt 'it didn't have the vibrancy and urgency that we had when we were teenagers.' Realising that the only way to capture what she wanted to get across was by recreating the scene in its heyday, a much harder and costly thing to put on film, she abandoned the idea of a documentary, 'because,' she says, 'all I wanted to do was say Northern Soul is brilliant.'

That *Northern Soul* doesn't quite achieve that is down to Constantine's decision to depict the scene 'warts and all', rather than concentrating on the highs, or compromising for the sake of attracting a bigger audience. 'Anyone who has only dipped their toes into the scene,' she says, 'will try and tell you that it wasn't like that, but it really was and there were elements to the scene that were dark and scary.'

Also like *Soulboy*, *Northern Soul* is light on plot but makes up for it with authenticity. Says Constantine: 'Nearly every scene, every word of dialogue and every character represents people I knew or things that happened to me and my friends. It's literally straight out of the real world I lived in, in Lancashire in the 70s, but not necessarily in the same order it happened in the film.'

There were some dissenting voices, such as The Spectator who pulled no punches in its assertion that: 'It also isn't a film of light and dark. It's dark and then darker again, with no humour or sense of joy', and the Irish Times, who said it was, 'In short, a roaring, chaotic, often unintelligible mess.' Overall, though the response from the critics was favourable. The Times concluded that the director's love for the scene 'shows in every frame of her directorial debut, a buzzing love letter to the enduring, exclusive underground movement.' And for the Guardian 'every other scene showcases a northern treasure (Coogan, Thomson, Tomlinson, Stansfield) and looks, feels and - crucially – sounds true to its sweaty-hazy, slightly cramped corner of history.' The Radio Times said 'Like a British *Saturday Night Fever*, it captures the look and energy and exuberance of a youth culture, while not shying away from the more violent and amphetamine-fuelled darker sides.'

The film also found favour with critics across the Atlantic, with the New York Times saying 'Funny and feisty, gritty and sometimes grim, this first feature film from the photographer Elaine Constantine delivers a sweaty snapshot of a very specific time and place,' whilst the Los Angeles Times suggested, 'the film has a ferocious, shaggy energy that mirrors that of the testosterone-amphetamine-and adrenaline-pumped boys.'

Former soul boy, *Channel 4 News* economics editor Paul Mason told the Observer, 'Northern soul's legacy was to give birth to the modern dance club. When the rave scene started in the 1980s, ex-northern DJs (and drug dealers) saw it as a kind of second coming. And today if you want to experience some of the mania, working classness and speed-enhanced goodwill, a Gabber night might come close, although there's a deathly absence of humanity inside the music.'

Hippies, Skinheads, Rastas, Punks & Disco Dancing Bowie Boot Boys

Anarchy In The UK
(Matlock, Rotten, Cook, Jones)

Further south a soul scene was also developing in tandem with its northern counterpart but, where in Wigan the emphasis was on dancing hard, in the nightclubs of Essex there was an added emphasis on looking good. For clubbers in South East England, in venues such as The Goldmine in Canvey Island, the Greyhound, Chaguaramas, Spats, Crackers, Gossips and Lacy Lady, the emphasis was similarly on DJ's rather than bands; the music more contemporary but similarly obscure via rare and expensive imports by the likes of Roy Ayers and Lonnie Liston Smith. Looking the part was essential; Hawaiian or bowling shirts, mohair jumpers, jelly sandals, brightly coloured peg-topped trousers, and string vests topped by wedge haircuts were popular choices. Faces who might be seen strutting their stuff at the time included Danny John-Jules, later to become The Cat in *Red Dwarf*, 80s rapper Dizzi Heights and Peter Francis, the black daddy who falls foul of Ray Winstone's 'tool' in *Scum*.

Much of the soul boys wardrobe would be found on the Worlds End part of the Kings Road, in shops like Paradise Garage at number 140 where they could pick up Hawaiian shirts and dungarees, and where a couple of owner Trevor Miles acquaintances rented a corner from which they sold second-hand records and clothes before, in 1972, taking over the shop and renaming it Let It Rock as essentially an outlet for the Teddy Boy scene which was undergoing something of a revival. Other venues for the sartorially concerned would be Johnson's - The Modern Outfitters, Alka Seura, Mr Freedom and City Lights where you might hope to bump into the likes of David Bowie. By 1974

Another kind of soul boy. Valentine Nonyela and Mo Sesay in *Young Soul Rebels*

McLaren and Westwood's Let It Rock had become Too Fast To Live Too Young To Die and was widening its clientele and its range, attracting kids from the funk and soul scenes, much to the disdain of the Teds who were unhappy at seeing parts of their heritage twinned with children's bright plastic sandals. The shop's next incarnation, as Sex, would give them apoplexy.

By then, McLaren had serious competition for the title of Kings Road's coolest and most intimidating (but not most expensive) boutique from Acme Attractions, situated in the basement of the covered antiques market Antiquarius and selling clothes from the 40s, 50s, and 60s, as well their own items like electric blue zoot suits and fluorescent pink peg leg trousers. The shop was overseen by Don Letts who would pump out dub reggae and, if you were lucky, share a spliff. Both shops were regular haunts of the Soul Boys, amongst them some of those who would soon become Punks original movers and shakers. As rare groove DJ Norman Jay remembers: 'To my mind, the first Punks – not the music ones, the fashionistas – I saw at Crackers. You know the Punk thing didn't blow up until the summer of 76, but I can remember seeing Punks around Christmas '75 in the club. I first saw bondage trousers in Crackers before I saw them on the Kings Road.'

Another witness to this transformation from Soul Boy to Punk was Acid Jazz artist, DJ, and Duffer of St. George co-founder Barrie K Sharpe who says: 'For me, Punk started in the Lacy Lady. The whole Punk style was fashioned there. Punk music was none existent back then. I thought that 'Play That Funky Music White Boy' was a Punk record. The music didn't exist 'cause it was a style. I remember Zubbis where they had partings shaved in their heads. Plastic trousers. I dressed a bit like that. We all touched on it.' There can't have been many of them though as a Clash gig at Lacy Lady during November 1976 attracted just 20 punters, though this was somewhat better than in Guildford the previous month where, in an *NBC Live at 5* interview, in early 1982, the band refer to the fact there was only one person in the audience.

Where back in the day Mod and Skinhead clubs might have attracted a few black faces, the Soul Boys were truly the first fully integrated British youth subculture and their clubs were (where racist door policies would allow it) initially populated by a fairly even mix of black and white kids. However, whereas the black kids were drawn by what was considered 'their' music, many of their white counterparts had arrived at the scene via their ongoing love affair with Bryan Ferry and, especially, David Bowie who, having hinted at things to come by covering the Ohio Players 'Here Today, Gone Tomorrow' on his 'Diamond Dogs' tour and releasing a live cover of Eddie Floyd's 'Knock On Wood' as a single in 1974, had gone full blue-eyed soul boy with the March 1975 release of the 'Young Americans' album. Spandau Ballet's Gary Kemp told the Face in 1981: 'I think the idea of going out every night to see a band as a form of entertainment never really appealed to a lot of those people. They are people who like being looked at; that's why dancing is so important... it's also why clothes are so important.' When Punk arrived it took a large chunk of what he calls those 'white kids with two left feet' with it and Chaguaramas became the Roxy and Crackers became the Vortex.

Amongst those not-yet-named Punks would have been several members of the group of friends who would become infamous as the so-called Bromley Contingent, amongst them future Banshee Steve Severin: 'By the time we'd hit our mid to late teens, we were mainly going around as a group. This was even before The Sex Pistols came along. By definition, and out of need, we were into making our own fun. Because of the way we looked and the kind of music we liked, there weren't that many places we could go in and around Bromley - even London for that matter. Now there's a club or a part of town for every music cult or gang you can imagine. Then it was either the Bee Gees or gay discos, so we gravitated to the gay discos because they were much more tolerant... Everything sprang from that gay scene.' In those days there was a fine line between what constituted a soul and a gay club which, despite billing themselves as 'New York gay discos' were held in dingy basements with postage-stamp-sized dancefloors, and seemed a million miles away from the superclub scene that arrived in 1976 with the 1000+ capacity Bang, held at the Sundowner on Charing Cross Road. What they provided was a haven in a time when gay or straight, dressing different was rife with danger.

Amongst the black Soul Boys who stayed with the scene was East End born Isaac Julien who studied film and painting at St. Martin's School of Art where his student film, *Who Killed Colin Roach?*, signalled him as a talent to watch. During 1984 he co-founded Sankofa Film and Video, a production company for black and Asian British filmmakers, and over the next five years, he made *Territories* (1985), *This Is Not An Aids Advert* (1987), *The Passion of Remembrance* (1987) and *Looking For Langston* (1987), an homage to Harlem poet Langston Hughes

Hippies, Skinheads, Rastas, Punks & Disco Dancing Bowie Boot Boys

The tribes take to the streets in *Young Soul Rebels*

which made him the darling of New York and a favourite of film festivals worldwide.

For Julien, 1977 was a significant year, combining as it did 'the incredible chauvinism of the Queen's Silver Jubilee' and 'very powerful narratives that outlined new kinds of national possibilities.' The most obvious of these was Punk but equally important to Julien, who felt 'divided between politics and pleasure', was disco/funk/soul. 'All the left had to say was that disco music was part of the capitalist music industry and that one should adopt the Punk ethic of dismantling it,' he says, 'But what the left didn't realise was that their formulaic slogan 'Black & White, Unite & Fight' actually had some reality in this black popular culture… Reggae is part of the mythology of 1977… but reggae really relates back to the Caribbean whereas soul takes one into the wider black diaspora.'

Black politics at the time was dominated by far-left publications such as Race Today, which followed a rigid discourse that Julien found at odds with cultural and political reality, and he suggests that even the National Front's youth magazine, Bulldog, was more clued in, quoting a 1979 article: 'The record and cassette is more powerful than television or newspapers where youth is concerned. Disco and its melting pot pseudo-philosophy must be fought or Britain's streets will be full of black worshipping Soul Boys.'

When the time came to make his debut feature, **YOUNG SOUL REBELS (1991)**, the director decided to return to those times to put the record straight and, along with producer Nadine Marsh-Edwards, set about finding a story 'which would highlight being seventeen in London in 1977 and which would [feature] this subculture that was as exciting as Punk and which people still didn't know much about.'

Set during the week of the Queen's Silver Jubilee in June 1977, *Young Soul Rebels* follows two childhood friends, straight mixed-race Chris (Valentine Nonyela) and gay black Caz (Mo Sesay), who run Soul Patrol, a pirate radio station and DJ at a small club, the Crypt. As the show is being broadcast live from the back of an East End garage owned by Caz's older brother Carlton (Eamonn Walker), TJ (Shyro Chung), ghetto blaster in hand, is attending a liaison in nearby Dalston Park which doubles as a gay pickup point. When it turns violent and TJ is stabbed and killed, what the killer doesn't know is that the cassette player had been knocked into record mode, and neither does Chris whose little sister had subsequently found the ghetto blaster abandoned elsewhere in the park.

Chris dreams of making it big and visits Metro Radio hoping to get a slot on the legitimate station during which the script squeezes in a comment on a common problem in many of the clubs of the time when the station's only soul DJ tells him, 'a few weeks ago I was booked at some god-damn club in Essex, they started giving me this 10% black entry crap otherwise their regulars were gonna cause some trouble'. While Chris does not get beyond reception, he does manage to catch the eye of production assistant Tracey (Sophie Okonedo, in her film debut), who accepts his invitation to come and see his set at the Crypt that evening where she encourages him to make a mix tape which she promises to get into the right hands at the station. She's as good as her word but when he is faced with one of the station's executives who says he enjoyed the selections, if 'a bit obscure', and presentation, but that should the station take him on, they would be looking for a 'more recognisable style, something a bit more..' 'English', suggests Chris, who then becomes angry, mocking his interviewer in patois. This turns out to be the least of his problems when, soon after, he is arrested on suspicion of the park murder on the strength of an anonymous tip-off.

The film culminates in a somewhat contrived ending at a Stuff The Jubilee (would they have really been so polite?) concert in the park which is invaded by a large gang of Skinheads and turned into a riot during which Chris plays the tape over the PA on the petrol-bombed stage. Before then though, the film introduces the various youth movements vying for attention. There's a neighbourhood trio of Skinheads led by Sparky (James Bowers), one of whom, Kelly (Billy Braham), is mixed-race. The Skinheads, old schoolmates of Caz and Chris, are shown to be all pose and their half-hearted attempts at menace easily deflected. Far more racist and homophobic are Carlton and his mechanic Davis, the former begrudgingly accepting of Caz's homosexuality 'as long as you do it to them.' There is also a love interest for Caz in the form of white Punk activist Billibub (Jason Durr) whose dismissal of Metro radio as 'capitalist crap' is quickly shot down by Tracey pointing out the twenty pounds price tag of his Westwood designed Cowboys T-shirt. His defence that 'it has to do with homo-erotica, nicked homo-erotica actually' cuts no ice. 'It's like anarchy courtesy of EMI, so rebellious, so St. Martin's School of Art.'

Though it's good to see the integration between the various factions which, contrary to popular opinion did exist, it's sometimes a little overdone and the club scene which goes from kids pogoing to 'Oh Bondage Up Yours', the largely black soul boys standing patiently in the wings, and then straight into the Soul Patrol set is stretching things more than a touch. Compared with Punk there is very little documentation of the Soul Boy scene, and especially what black kids were wearing and so the production had to rely on the memory of costume advisor Joey Attawia and a few snapshots. Its authenticity would require someone closely connected to that scene but the Punk look is sometimes slightly out of sync with the time, such as the inclusion of the band English Dogs, whose name is emblazoned on the back of Billibud's heavily studded leather jacket, itself more of an 80s look, and who didn't form until 1981.

Despite taking the Critic's prize at Cannes, the film found a more subdued reception elsewhere and failed to attract a black British audience that even today still doesn't seem ready for gay-themed movies and at the time of the film's release were still dancing to Buju Banton's 'Boom Bi Bi' which urged 'And some men still no want the panty red / Bare bottom business them love... / Send the Uzi instead / Shoot them now / Come let me shoot them.' The director got an early glimpse of this attitude when Soul II Soul's Nellee Hooper turned down a request to provide the film's soundtrack, Julien commenting: 'They refused to do the 'Red Hot & Blue' AIDS music programme... so I doubt if they like some of the themes in *Young Soul Rebels*, i.e. gay stuff. Too bad, maybe they're not so cool after all.'

Young Soul Rebels was compared to Spike Lee's *Do The Right Thing*, but it's ethnically and culturally diverse setting is more reminiscent of Hanif Kureishi. Ultimately, though its script comes nowhere near the standard of either of those. The problems seem to stem from an inexperienced director bowing to the pressures of a producer for whom 're-writing is absolutely essential' and who clearly had no interest in making a film of Julien and co-writer Derrick Saldaan McClintock's original vision. Executive Producer Colin MacCabe thought the first draft 'read more like a sociological tract than a drama' and after the first script meeting called for 'something much more dramatic'. When McClintock told him he had spent a day in police custody because he was the right colour and age to match the identikit picture of the murderer of Altab Ali, a young textile worker attacked by three youths in East London, MacCabe said 'the minute I heard that I was convinced we had a film.' And so, after five drafts and the introduction of another writer, Paul Hallam, Julien's 'sociological tract' became a forgettable and almost immediately deducible murder mystery.

Just how much influence on the script the producers wielded can be ascertained from the knowledge that in May 1989, because of increased responsibilities at the BFI, McCabe's role became more administrative and the role of Head of Production was handed to Ben Gibson who, says McCabe, 'was tireless in his detailed comments and criticisms of the script... and the last couple of drafts were written largely in response to his queries and concerns.' This despite it being Gibson's first major production.

Punk in Britain could not have existed without The Sex Pistols. It is equally certain that The Sex Pistols could not have existed without Malcolm McLaren. Sure, something would have come along eventually to shake things up, but whatever form that would have taken, it wouldn't have been Punk. There would have been some Bowie fans who liked to turn heads by dressing provocatively in McLaren and Westwood's creations; there'd have been fast, gutsy rock n roll with an attitude from the likes of Dr Feelgood, Eddie and the Hot Rods and the 101ers. There would have even been a visit from the Ramones, but no 'Punk', in the UK sense at least.

A Sex Pistols gig at Ravensbourne College on the 9th of December 1975 would mark the birth of what would become known as the Bromley Contingent, the title coined for the early Pistols crowd by the then Melody Maker journalist Caroline Coon. Says Simon Barker: 'It was a Saturday night and there was nothing to do... we had this group of people. Steve Bailey and I went to school together, the Bromley Technical High. Billy Broad went to another school in Bromley: I met him through college. Siouxsie, we met going to a Roxy Music concert. We liked to be noticed: We were influenced by Bowie, Roxy, and 'A Clockwork Orange' but we were doing it in our own way. Bowie had dyed his hair red, but we went into a hairdresser and saw all these tubes of crazy colour and went mad.'

NME's 'hip young gunslingers' Tony Parsons and Julie Burchill, described them as a 'posse of unrepentant poseurs, committed to attaining fame despite the paucity of talent other than being noticed; achieving their aim in a manner meticulously calculated to kill.' The Contingent themselves were keen to point out that in fact only three commonly labelled as such were actually from Bromley - Simon Barker, Steve 'Severin' Bailey, and Bertie 'Berlin' Marshall (who lived 3 doors from Bowie's mum). Another two however lived close enough for all but the most pedantic cartographer; Billy 'Idol' Broad lived one tube stop on in Bickley, and Susan 'Siouxsie' Ballion came from Chislehurst, about three quarters of a mile further. Jordan came all the way from Seaford and Soo Catwoman was from Ealing.

The effect of The Sex Pistols on the middle-class teenagers of suburban Bromley plays a significant role in Hanif Kureishi's part-autobiographical 1990 novel and its subsequent TV adaptation, **THE BUDDHA OF SUBURBIA (1993)**. The novel and series are centred around the 17-year-old mixed-race Karim Amir (Naveen Andrews), living with his English mother and unconventional Pakistani father in the south London suburb during the 1970s.

Kureishi came to public attention first as a playwright and then as a screenwriter, scoring considerable hits with his collaborations with director Stephen Frears, *My Beautiful Launderette* (1985) and *Sammy & Rosie Get Laid* (1987) but a chance remark from a renowned author spurred him to write a novel. He says, 'I'd written novels all through my teenage years. I've written actually three or four novels, complete novels, which were really early versions of The Buddha. About being at school, race, about being called a Paki, about having an Indian father and an English mother. And the youth culture - dressing up, drugs, parties and all that.'

'But I also remember [Salman] Rushdie saying this really cutting thing to me. "We take you seriously as a writer, Hanif," he said, "but you only write screenplays." I remember being really hurt by this and provoked by it, and I thought, well, I'll write a novel, and then I'll be a proper writer; that somehow that's what being a proper writer was. Perhaps it is, in the sense that what you write goes to the reader unmediated: there are no actors, directors or anybody else involved.'

A smash hit and winner of the Whitbread Award for best first novel, 'The Buddha of Suburbia' was dramatised for a 1993 television series of the same name. Says Kureishi: 'The BBC wanted to do it and I thought the BBC were exactly the right people to do it because they do all the costume dramas. And the Buddha, really it's a costume drama. All the clothes and the furniture and the wallpaper and the carpets are brilliant. As my mum said when she watched it, "it's just like being at home, isn't it?" And that's true, the BBC are very good at all that kind of detail. Also, the BBC gives you a really long time. It would be four hours long. You can really stretch out and enjoy all the details.' Kureishi also found an ally on the project in the choice of director Roger Michell, later of *Notting Hill* (1999), with whom he had worked previously at the RSC.

Kureishi, whose father was a civil servant at the Pakistani embassy, had a privileged middle class and extremely liberal upbringing, allowed to have girls sleep over at 15. Muslim by birth rather than inclination, he was educated as the only non-white pupil in a Jesuit secondary modern where racism was ever-present. Kureishi found escape in literature and music, particularly that of David Bowie, who was especially inspirational, having attended the same school and escaped the boredom of the suburbs: 'It was really the introduction of this idea you could make yourself up, that identities weren't fixed. That you weren't born a white working-class boy, or you weren't born a Paki, or a Scotsman or whatever. And Bowie blew all that up. He said you can do that, you can pretend to be that; identity is just a masquerade.'

Many of the characters who pass through *The Buddha of Suburbia* have their basis in real people. Some are obvious - the band playing the Nashville, for example, are clearly The Sex Pistols - others more ambiguous. Says Kureishi: 'There are two basic reactions. There are those who hate you because they think you put them in the book, and there are those who hate you because they think you didn't put them in the book.' One famous member of the Bromley Contingent who Kureishi admits is included is Billy Broad, better known as Billy Idol, on whom Charlie is partly based: 'although I haven't seen him since I was 16. But with all these characters, you create them by taking one person's nose and adding it to another person's hands and another one's feet, and you mix them all up.'

Karim (Naveen Andrews), like Kureishi, lives and breathes pop music, and he has a crush on Charlie (Steven Mackintosh), a boy a year older from school whose band, Mustn't Grumble, had appeared on the front page of the local paper after playing at an open-air concert on a sports ground. This has given Charlie a 'rock star' status amongst his peers, a persona he is more than happy to milk for all it's worth. Charlie, naturally, styles himself on David Bowie. The two boys become friends and, briefly, lovers when Karim's father begins a relationship with Charlie's mother, Eva - though it is a friendship that is one-sided due to Charlie's good looks and charm being matched only by his cruelty and vanity.

Having dropped out of school to pursue his rock star dreams, a lack of success temporarily brings Charlie back down to earth. Then one night the two boys go to the Nashville in London where the audience's clothes: 'were full of safety pins. Their hair was uniformly black, and cut short, seriously short, or if long it was spiky and rigid, sticking up and out and sideways, like a handful of needles, rather than hanging down. A hurricane would not have dislodged those styles. The girls were in rubber and leather and wore skin-tight skirts and holed black stockings, with white face slap and bright red lipstick.'

Initially apprehensive of what was to come and planning to leave, the band ambles onto the stage: 'This was no peace and love, there were no drum solos or effeminate synthesisers. Not a squeeze of anything 'progressive' or 'experimental' came from those pallid, vicious little council estate kids with hedgehog hair, howling about anarchy and hatred. No song lasted more than three minutes, and after each, the carrot-haired kid cursed us to death.'

Despite Karim's belief that: 'We're not like them. We don't hate the way they do. We've got no reason to. We're not from the estates. We haven't been through what they have', Charlie becomes Charlie Hero, adopting a working-class persona to go with his new name; declaring that the 'sixties have been given notice tonight. Those kids we saw have assassinated all hope. They're the fucking future'. His new Punk band The Condemned are described in the press as 'a phenomenon' and he is soon enjoying a rock n roll lifestyle as a solo artist in the States.

Whilst for the Bromley Contingent Punk began at early gigs by The Sex Pistols, most of the country's youth had to make do with reports in the nation's handful of weekly music papers which would leave them able to do little other than wonder, with no 100 Club on the doorstep and no records in the shops until the October 1976 release of the Damned's 'New Rose'. Come November they could pick up 'Anarchy in the UK' and look forward to a nationwide tour from The Sex Pistols, The Clash and the Damned by which time the new scene had attracted the attention of the tabloid press.

For a six-month period between the release of the first two Sex Pistols singles, 'Anarchy in the UK' in November 1976 and 'God Save The Queen' in the summer of 1977, the Sunday People's assertion that Punk's aim to 'smash the system, depose the monarchy, throw convention out of the window' seemed to be more than mere rhetoric. For Punk's young chroniclers, like Mark P at Sniffing Glue, 'Anarchy in the UK' 'destroys all the rock n roll laws… the Pistols have kicked the establishment right in the balls… no question about it, this is the real thing… Gatecrash disco's and shove 'Anarchy…' on the turntable… Don't anybody understand that anarchy's the only thing left to happen? You see, the Pistols have smashed 'em all.'

The more established writers, having been witness in their time to other would be calls to arms from the rock world, remained more cautious. To Caroline Coon, it was 'a threat, a malediction' but essentially, knowing the real purpose for its release, 'an instant hit'. At Sounds, Alan Lewis made it Single of the Week but, calling himself 'an old fart who loved the early Who', thought it 'makes nonsense of any claims that the Pistols are revolutionaries: they may want to push the old farts aside, but they've borrowed a lot from 'em… it's really a simple basic record, so simple in fact that even fans of Hawkwind would feel at home.'

It wasn't the record itself however that 'kicked the establishment right in the balls' but a last-minute slot on Thames Television's *Today* programme to promote it, arranged by their record label EMI, when label-mates Queen were forced to pull out due to Freddie Mercury's illness. At the beginning of December, the Daily Mirror had run a two-page spread saying 'Watch Out Parents! It's The Punk Rock Horror Show! - A new teenage craze is rearing its head. And it's not a pretty sight. This is the Punk rock scene. And Punk rock people don't want to be pretty. They reckon they are appealing only if they seem appalling. The Punks despise "establishment" pop stars. Instead, they dance to songs that preach destruction. They spurn conventional ideas of how teenagers should look and dress. Instead, they do their own horrific thing.'

Devotion to the cult, the paper said, 'means wearing safety pins through their nostrils… other Punk hallmarks include swastikas and hairstyles that look as though they have been created with carving knives. Punk rock girls, with lips painted black, are just as startling. Their outfits include coloured tights with just a G-string over them and T-shirts with zips over the boobs.' 'Tomorrow' they promised, 'the truth behind this disturbing new cult.' Instead, they got 'The Filth And The Fury,' the band having that evening been interviewed by one Bill Grundy. It was probably the most important moment in televised music history since Elvis Presley appeared on the *Ed Sullivan Show* in September 1956.

The incident was dramatised for an episode of the Sky Arts comedy series **URBAN MYTHS: THE SEX PISTOLS VS BILL GRUNDY (2018)**, written by Simon Nye and starring Steve Pemberton as Grundy, Frankie Fox as Rotten, Charlie Wernham as Jones, Matt Whitchurch as Matlock and William Kettle as Cook.

The funniest part is when after the interview has concluded the band return to the green room and, such is the level of complaints, find the BBC has had to divert some complaints there - answered of course in a less than professional manner by the band: 'No, you listen, you twatty whingebag.' Whilst much of the drama is a more or less verbatim copy of actual events, this is clearly all artistic licence as confirmed by Glen Matlock's version of events: 'When we finished I wanted to go have another drink in the green room. Malcolm just grabbed me and threw me into the limo EMI had provided. As we pulled off, half a dozen cops turned up with their truncheons hanging out. We waved at them nicely as we drove off.'

*

Adapted for television by *The Likely Lads* and *Auf Wiedersehen Pet* writers Ian LeFrenais and Dick Clement and broadcast as a three-part mini-series on BBC2 in 2005, the protagonists of Jonathan Coe's 1970s set and autobiographical 2001 novel **THE ROTTER'S CLUB (2005)**, are as far from the council estates as Karim and Charlie, attending Birmingham's King William's College, the best school in town, which seems a million miles from the comprehensives of Handsworth.

The would-be grammar school progressive rock band, Maws of Doom, want to 'push back the boundaries of the three-chord song.' But change is afoot and as one lad writes in the school paper, 'On a rainy night last November, The Sex Pistols walked on stage at St Martin's Art School in London and triggered a musical revolution. There's a new kid in town and his name is Punk. He's not a pretty sight. He has bad skin, bad hair, and bad teeth. He snarls and spits…' The transition from prog' to Punk, for two of author Jonathan Coe's four main characters at least, is cemented when the band takes an unexpected change of direction when a rehearsal of the first movement of a rock symphony, Apotheosis of the Necromancer, breaks down. 'Shall we try again from the top?' 'There's no top, there's no bottom, it's all bloody middle' is the response, 'Dole queue rock's the thing now, it means the country's more polarised than ever before, it means you've got your haves and have nots and your never will haves. They're the people we should be playing for.'

In his book on Coe Philip Tew says 'In my experience of growing up on a council estate in Stoke in the mid to late seventies it was the working-class kids who followed the prog-rock bands, Genesis, Yes, Pink Floyd Gentle Giant and their North American prog' counterparts Rush, Styx and Kansas, and the kids from the private housing estates nearby that were rebelling against their middle-class parents by latching on to Punk'.

In the documentary *Divide & Rule - Never* (1978), the lad who is seen putting his Clash LP on the turntable and settling back with his packet of Player's No. 6, is tellingly sitting beside a Roger Dean poster. This route into Punk will presumably be closer to that of Danny Baker, TV personality and former Sniffin' Glue writer, whose teenage years were captured in his autobiographical comedy-drama series *Cradle To The Grave* (2015), the second series of which was to have moved onto his Punk years before the 'family commitments' of, his screen characters father, Peter Kay, put filming on a lengthy hiatus.

Baker and fellow Sniffin' Glue writer Mark P have never been shy of airing their prog-rock formative years, with Baker saying: 'People said "What crap King Crimson turn out" but we knew every word of it and it was entirely what brought us there and gave us the desire to have a band to follow of your own when you're young. Sniffin' Glue used to feature Camel!' He believes other Punk luminaries had trodden a similar path but 'they were all too scared to admit it: 'Plainly Mick Jones and Joe Strummer had ELP albums and were having fun with it back then - we all loved rock music.' Neither writer fully bought into Punk as a year zero, where everything that arrived before it had to be rejected. Perry believes 'There was real snobbery. You could like old guys but they had to be touching on Punk. The Velvets, Iggy Pop, MC5, Flamin' Groovies… but Emerson, Lake & Palmer?' According to *Rude Boy*'s Ray Gange when he first visited Strummer's place and spotted a Bob Dylan record lying on the floor it seemed so alien that he had to pretend he hadn't seen it.

The Maws of Doom go Punk in *The Rotters Club*

Hippies, Skinheads, Rastas, Punks & Disco Dancing Bowie Boot Boys

The Queen Is Dead
(Morrissey, Marr)

The best early Punk movies were either American or like *Babylon*, *Made in Britain*, *Scum* and even *Quadrophenia* (despite being set a decade and a half earlier), contain no actual Punks, at least not in the accepted sense. Trevor in *Made in Britain* perhaps qualifies as by 1982 (and in fact by the tail end of the seventies) Skinhead had become a sub-genre of Punk. What's left from Punks heyday then are dramas that already seemed dated when first released such as *Breaking Glass* (1980), the drama/documentary/biopics *The Great Rock n Roll Swindle* (1979) and *Rude Boy* (1980), and documentaries like German director Wolfgang Buld's *Punk in London* (1978), shot during a two-week visit to London in September 1977, and Don Letts' *The Punk Rock Movie* (1978).

And then there's **JUBILEE (1978)**. Though never a Punk, being already 35 in 1976, Derek Jarman had worked as a set designer on Ken Russell's *The Devils* (1971) and *Mahler* (1972), directed his first feature film, *Sebastiane* (1976), and was very much a part of the underground art elite that sat on the fringes of the movement. He had, along with Jenny Runacre who appears in *Jubilee* in the dual roles of Queen Elizabeth I and Bod, been present at one of The Sex Pistols earliest gigs on Valentine's Day 1976 at a party thrown by artist Andrew Logan. Says Jarman: 'The Sex Pistols were playing on Andrew's stage for a slightly bemused audience of glitterati while Jordan and [Vivienne] threw themselves about with bacchic abandon, hurling insults at the band and the audience. John Rotten turned his back on us and sang to the Roman frescoes, while the drummer, Paul, picked his nose. Christopher [Hobbs] who had guarded me and the camera from the pushing and shoving, said when it was all over - "Thank God that's finished and we'll never hear of them again"' The footage ended up, uncredited, in *The Great Rock n Roll Swindle* (1980).

Jarman's debut feature film had featured Punk icon Jordan, real name Pamela Rooke, in a small role as Mamea Morgana, a prostitute who 'has slept her way from Bath to Rome'. The director had first set eyes on Jordan at Victoria Station and she made enough of an impression to warrant an entry in his diary: 'White patent boots clattering down the platform, transparent plastic mini-skirt revealing hazy pudenda. Venus t-shirt. Smudged black eye-paint, covered with a flaming blonde beehive... the face that launched a thousand tabloids.. art history as make-up.'

In fact, Jarman had originally wanted to make a Super 8 film of Jordan but was encouraged by *Sebastiane*'s producers Howard Malin and James Whaley to instead capitalise on his contacts in the burgeoning Punk movement by making a Punk feature. Whaley used what little money remained in production company Megalovision's bank account on a flight to Tehran to put the squeeze on an old school friend whilst Jarman, script in place, began to assemble his stars.

With the non-actor Jordan a shoo-in for the role of Amyl Nitrate, other early casting decisions went in favour of more accomplished professional Thespians like friend and star of Jarman's Super 8 movies Runacre, already an art-house fixture via roles in Pier Paolo Pasolini's *The Canterbury Tales* (1972) and Michelangelo Antonioni's *The Passenger* (1975), with Ian Charleson, then at the National Theatre, and Welsh actor Karl Johnson, cast as incestuous brothers Sphinx and Angel.

The role of Crabs went to Australian Little Nell who had played Columbia in the original stage production of *The Rocky Horror Show* and the subsequent movie as well as having a minor pop career. The character was said to be based on Debbie Juvenile, a seventeen-year-old member of the Bromley Contingent and Seditionaries shop assistant who can be seen singing backing vocals with Steve Jones and Sid Vicious during their rendition of 'The Great Rock 'n' Roll Swindle' in the film of the same name. When the Pistols folded Debbie, who said 'I had my first punter when I was 14,' worked the streets around Shepherds Bush Market. Her memoirs were featured in Men Only for whom she often did soft porn shoots well into the eighties.

Toyah Wilcox's big break came when she was cast in the thirty-minute BBC play *Glitter* (1975), part of the *Second City First* series, as Sue, a girl who sang with a band called Bilbo Baggins and who dreamt of appearing on *Top of the Pops*. Wilcox performed two songs she had co-written, one with the band and one accompanied by none other than Phil Daniels on acoustic guitar. By 1979 she was, like Charleson, at the National. According to Wilcox she was in effect 'a 19-year-old public schoolgirl from Birmingham' who 'didn't know that men could have sex,' so it must have come as quite a shock when having arrived at the Jarman's flat, she was confronted by 'a beautiful French boy called Yves... wandering around naked'. She adds, 'I had to hide all this to a certain extent because I was afraid of people discovering how little experience I had in life in case they thought I had little to offer the film.' Audition passed, she was asked what remaining role she would like, counted the pages allocated to each character and chose pyromaniac Mad.

According to John Maybury, who worked on the film as assistant production designer, in the retrospective documentary *Jubilee: A Time Less Golden* (2004), Toyah turned up in a Laura Ashley floral print dress with a brown bob, and she herself says 'I had never heard of Jordan, I had never heard of Seditionaries... I didn't know who Vivienne Westwood was, I didn't know who Malcolm McLaren was... I was completely innocent of everything that was going on around me.' Wilcox's assumed innocence is open to question and it is likely that the actresses sober appearance was down to her having been cast in the part of Emma in the National's production of *Tales from the Vienna Woods*.

In a somewhat contradictory 2001 piece in the Guardian, she recalls, 'In September 1976 I saw The Sex Pistols play Bogart's in Birmingham and it was fantastic. I'd already dyed my hair bright pink and was wearing bin-liners,' and in her autobiography, she says that 'Already by then I was known in Birmingham for being the oddball that walked around with dyed hair. And you've got to remember that this is pre-Punk, this was about 1973–74.' In fact, after moving to London to join the National Theatre, Wilcox was soon fronting her own Punk band, When The Streets Were Dark With More Than Night, playing youth clubs and pubs and even the Ford Youth Club at the company's Dagenham plant. A photograph of Toyah, complete with the word 'lesbian' painted on her bondage top, was photographed during an early 1977 shopping trip to the Kings Road and is included in the book 'In The Gutter' by Val Hennessy. In April 1977, she appeared as a Punkette called Buzz in an episode of Diana Rigg's BBC2 comedy sketch series, *Three Piece Suite*.

The casting of another role was, in part, down to Jordan. Jarman had seen Adam Ant making his way down the Kings Road to Seditionaries in a dirty white shirt which had been purposely ripped to show the word 'Fuck' that Jordan had carved on his back with a razor blade. This is referenced in *Jubilee* when Bod tattoos Amyl with a carving knife before sealing the wounds with salt. Says Ant: 'I had been looking at a lot of tribal books when the idea came to me - particularly 'People of Kau' by Leni Riefenstahl. This was a rite of passage for the warrior and I had decided that I wanted to be one... A few hundred yards down the road, a very bubbly character ran up to me. He had short-cropped black hair, piercing eyes, and a cut-glass upper-class accent. He said he was a director and would I like to be in his film *Jubilee*, all the while beaming a cheeky smile at me. This became bigger when I told him I was in a band and that he should talk to Jordan too. He told me he had already cast her in the leading role.' At the time in the early stages of his Adam & the Ants career, Adam's Punk pedigree went right back to the very first Sex Pistols gig where, as plain Stuart Goddard he was in the band, Bazooka Joe, that the Pistols had been booked to support. Despite the Pistols having the power pulled on them, Ant says: 'I just knew this was the way to go... I left Bazooka Joe that night.'

The film opens during the late 16th century in the court of Queen Elizabeth I who with the aid of her magician and advisor John Dee (Richard O'Brien) is given a glimpse into, for cinema-goers of the time, the near future, a desolate landscape that looks a lot like the declining Britain of the 1970s. Jarman's bleak vision of the near future wasn't

A lesson in Punk from Jordan in *Jubilee*

difficult to recreate says Runacre: 'Derek had a large studio in Butler's Wharf which was at the Shad Thames (now full of office buildings)... All along the river the property developers were active and throughout 1977 the warehouses, mostly inhabited by struggling artists, continued to mysteriously go up in flames... but the very desolation of the area, fringed with rotting estates and closed shops mirrored to perfection the desolation Derek was portraying.'

In this future where Amyl Nitrate tells us 'on my fifteenth birthday law and order were abolished... the crime rate dropped to zero,' bands of nihilistic, mainly female, Punks rule the lawless streets. *Jubilee* features one gang in particular consisting of former ballet dancer Amyl Nitrate (Jordan), bull-dykish pyromaniac with a bad temper Mad (Toyah Wilcox), Chaos (Hermine Demoriane), an androgynous goth who barely speaks, and incestuous boy-candy brothers Sphinx (Karl Johnson) and Angel (Ian Charleson), Crabs (Little Nell), an actress between jobs who prefers to wear as little as possible and Bod (Jenny Runacre) the leader of the group.

The first of these we meet is Mad, toting a bright orange buzz cut and a machine gun as she rounds up a gang of female Punks who are beating up a curly-haired woman, who is presumably the owner of the pram we see on fire as the camera pulls back. Mad takes the girls back home for a 'lesson' with Amyl. In between committing various, some random and some not so, acts of violence the gang engage in philosophical musings and Mad informs her captive audience that 'the world is no longer interested in heroes. So sad. We now know too much about them, don't we,' but introduces Amyl as 'our heroine.'

Amyl tells them: 'Our school motto is faites vos desirs realite. Make your desires reality. I myself prefer the song 'Don't Dream It, Be It'. In those days, desires weren't allowed to become reality, so fantasy was substituted for them - films, books, pictures. They called it art. But when your desires become reality, you don't need fantasy any longer, or art... As a child, my heroine was Myra Hindley. Do you remember her? Myra's crimes were, they say, beyond belief. That was because no one had any imagination then. They really didn't know how to make their desires reality. They were not artists like Myra. One can smile now at their naivete.'

The idea for the Myra Hindley reference was culled from Jordan's own fascination with the killer and also provided the controversy that went hand-in-hand with Punk. Seditionaries was already flogging T-shirts featuring the Cambridge Rapist, so Hindley fitted nicely into that category of shock value. Jordan wasn't the only Seditionaries regular with an interest in Hindley and another Punk icon, Soo Catwoman, suggested The Moors Murderers to a friend of Glen Matlock, Steve Harrington (soon to be Strange), as a good name for a Punk band. It was, she says, 'a big joke to be honest. I was joking about getting a band together called the Moors Murderers and doing sleazy love songs. I had no idea he would actually go out and do it.' Strange roped in Chrissie Hynde and members of the band The Photons, formed around recently sacked Adam and the Ants guitarist Mark Ryan (who appears in *Jubilee*) and a gig was played supporting The Slits at Ari Up's Holland Park comprehensive school at the end of 1977, with door money reportedly going to the NSPCC. Steve Treatment who appears alongside Jordan in *Jubilee*'s bonfire scene suggests he was approached on set by Strange, who was an extra, about being in the band.

A press shoot was organised in which the band wore pillowcases over their faces and the in January 1978 the Sunday Mirror took the bait, publishing an article under the headline 'Why Must They Be So Cruel'. Later that month Sounds ran a full-page article on the band and their supposedly upcoming single, 'Free Hindley', which only appeared in cassette form as the project was quickly forgotten, though not the band members. Hynde would form The Pretenders and Strange would kick-start the New Romantic movement via his club nights at Blitz and eventually find a less controversial route to pop stardom with Visage.

In an early hint at the violence to come, we see Bod laughing maniacally as she goes in pursuit of an unidentifiable woman who is eventually caught and killed. Filmed in a long shot, the sequence is not significant until she returns to the squat wearing on her head Queen Elizabeth II's crown and declaring, 'I captured it. It's high fashion.' In a scene at a cafe where Crabs is on a date with the Kid (Adam Ant), Bod attacks the waitress, covering her in tomato sauce while Mad steals her Shirley Temple wig, declaring, 'For a moment I thought you would kill her.' It is, Bod tells her, 'Just a dress rehearsal.' Later Crabs and Bod suffocate a sexual partner, Happy Days (Chelsea frontman Gene October, who had been seen on a TV set performing 'Right To Work'), before wrapping his body in the bedsheets and dumping it from a bridge onto the muddy banks of the Thames.

Other monologues, mainly from Amyl, conjure up Punks preoccupations. As part of his research Jarman listened to a plethora of 45s and read as many Punk fanzines as he could and would have found many such rants inside their pages. Amongst these are Amyl's take on materialism: 'Human beings have no rights but some dumb fuck told them they have them. First political rights - freedom of speech and things like that. And if that wasn't enough they had material rights too. They forgot about the political rights soon enough, but they got hooked on the material ones. One desolate suburban acre and a car, then a TV, fridge and then another car. That was by right, mind you, but the habit demanded more and more. The day came when expectations couldn't be fulfilled any longer and everyone felt cheated. So here we are in the present... with civilization destroyed by resentment. But since civilization itself was always fucking awfully boring for everyone, who gives a shit?'

Sometimes the film is camp: 'You clammy slag, you've sat in the KY with your fat arse.' On other occasions, it's hilarious, such as Sphinx's treatise on high rise living as told straight-faced to Kid/Adam Ant who struggles to suppress his laughter: 'I never lived below the fourteenth floor till I was old enough to run away. Never saw the ground till I was four. Just locked in alone with the telly all day. First time I saw flowers I freaked. I was frightened of dandelions. My old gran picked one once, I had hysterics. Everything in that tower block was regulated. Planned by the social planners to the lowest common denominator. Sight: concrete. Sound: the telly. Touch: plastic. Taste: plastic. Seasons regulated by thermostat. Once a year me mum and dad dusted down the plastic Christmas tree and exchanged pathetic presents. Didn't know I was dead till I was fifteen. Never experienced love or hate. My generation's the blank generation.'

The chief target of Jarman's satire is capitalism's insatiable desire to own and profit from everything, represented in the impresario-figure of Borgia Ginz (Jack Birkett) who, eating live goldfish from a bowl, says: 'This is the generation that grew up and forgot to live their lives. They were so busy watching my endless movie. It's power, babe, power. I don't create it. I own it. I sucked and sucked and I sucked. The media became their only reality and I own their world of flickering shadows.' The character of Ginz evokes the speech by former news anchorman Howard Beale in Sidney Lumet's *Network* (1976): 'We'll tell you any shit you want to hear! We deal in illusion man! None of it's true. But you people sit there – all of you – day after day, night after night, all ages, colours, creeds. We're all you know. You're beginning to believe this illusion we're spinning here. You're beginning to think the tube is reality and your own lives are unreal. You do whatever the tube tells you. You dress like the tube, you eat like the tube, you raise your children like the tube.' Such sentiments were also expressed in Punk records such as the Kursaal Flyers 'Television Generation'.

In *Network*, the station's president tells Beale: 'There is no America. There is no democracy. There is only IBM and ITT and AT and T and Dupont, Dow, Union Carbide and Exxon. Those are the nations of the world today... The world is a business.' Ginz is a megalomaniac who has merged the businesses: 'BBC, TUC, ITV, ABC, MGM, KGB, C of E. You name it, I bought them all.. and rearranged the alphabet.'

Another target is Punk itself. According to Runacre, in the beginning at least, 'Everybody thought the Punk movement was like the most exciting thing that had happened in this country since the time of flower power. Nothing had happened, it was all absolutely dead and then suddenly all this new music comes up and all these kids out there doing all this kind of stuff... And it was all so original.' Yet Jarman had his reservations about Punk from the beginning, putting these down in a diary entry during August 1976: 'The music business has conspired with [the Punks] to create another working-class myth as the dole queues grow longer to fuel the flames. But in reality, the instigators of Punk are the same petit-bourgeois art students, who a few months ago were David Bowie and Brian Ferry lookalikes - who've read a little art history and adopted some Dadaist typography and bad manners, and who are now in the business of reproducing a fake street credibility.' It's a view shared by John Maybury: 'British Punk was made up almost entirely of upper middle class [kids] and aristo's pretending to be commoners.'

Ginz has also turned Buckingham Palace into a recording studio and Westminster Abbey into a discotheque, not as strange as it seems given that seven years later Canadian promoter Peter Gatien opened the Limelight Club in the once the former Welsh Presbyterian Church in Shaftesbury Avenue. He also decides who makes it in the pop world, which despite Punk's supposed values, the youths of the movie all desire. Amyl, miming to Suzie Pinns 'Rule Britannia', in the movie's best musical moment, is England's entry in the Eurovision Song Contest; Kid is dating Crabs on the promise of an audition with Ginz. We see Mad fronting a female Punk band (in reality, Adam's Ants). Punk is seen as yet another product to distract the masses from pursuing any worthwhile rebellion. As a cackling Ginz says, 'As long the music's loud enough we won't hear the world falling apart.'

If life at the top of the pop world is a fleeting thing, this can be partly attributed to Bod and her gang who not

Jordan, Jenny Runacre and Toyah lead the gang in *Jubilee*

only kill Happy Days but also the new 'next big thing' Lounge Lizard (Wayne County). Seeing him on TV at home on TV, Bod decrees the singer a good target for elimination, stating 'the world won't miss his missing chromosome' and the gang strangles him to death in his front room with a microphone chord as he sings along to himself on TV. Another of Jordan's interests taken on by Jarman, and studied as part of his research for the movie, was Valerie Solanas' radical feminist tract published in 1967 as the 'SCUM Manifesto' (an acronym for Society For Cutting Up Men) which begins as it means to go on: "Life' in this 'society' being, at best, an utter bore and no aspect of 'society' being at all relevant to women, there remains to civic-minded, responsible, thrill-seeking females only to overthrow the government, eliminate the money system, institute complete automation and eliminate the male sex.'

Solanas' theory is that the male is an 'incomplete female' who is genetically deficient because of the Y chromosome, rendering them emotionally limited, egocentric, and incapable of mental passion or genuine interaction - unable to relate to anything apart from his own physical sensations. Accusing men of turning the world into a 'shitpile' she then presents a long list of grievances for which they are culpable which is pretty much everything wrong in the world, concluding that the elimination of the male sex is a moral imperative.

The female-driven violence proved unsettling for some. Time Out thought 'the determined sexual inversion (whereby most women become freakish characters, and men loose-limbed sex objects) comes to look disconcertingly like a misogynist binge.' Jenny Runacre suggests the director was 'fairly critical of women but I don't think he was really misogynistic, but... those are really castrating women in the film... I mean literally, aren't they? So there's a lot of undercurrents in that film. He was a very complex man, a very intellectual man... and he had all those views.'

Angel, Sphinx and Kid become victims of something many 1970s cinemagoers, and Jarman himself, would have been familiar with - homophobic police officers. When they and Viv go to a bingo parlour proceedings are interrupted by two officers of the 'law' who, when Sphinx playfully suggests 'come on, give us a kiss', shoot he and his brother dead. Kid escapes but is tracked down in an alley and beaten to death. According to Ant's autobiography, his fate as originally scripted was to have been raped in a photo booth by the two policemen. Ant had already been in a fight scene at a party involving the actor who was to play one officer, Donny Dunham. Says Ant: '"I don't care if you break his leg," Jarman told Donny before we started, "It's got to go on celluloid." Jarman decided not to tell me about it though, so Donny took a swing at my head and I ducked what was a hard right hook. I grabbed him, caught him off balance and knocked him over. Jarman loved it and screamed: "Again! do it again!" Donny jumped up and lunged at me, trying to break my jaw. If you look at my face, you can tell how pissed off I am. No way was I going to be stuck in a small space with a possibly pissed Don Dunham 'pretending' to beat me up, so I refused.'

The deaths send Mad and Amyl Nitrate off on a vendetta against two of the fascistic police officers. They find one alone, taking a pee, and Mad whips out her knife, as she and Amyl jump him, wrestle him to the ground, kicking and screaming. Then Mad castrates him. Bod, with a cry of 'No Future!' throws a fire-bomb into the house of the other policeman - inadvertently killing her friend Crabs who was in bed with him.

For a movie that provided plenty of ammunition for the 'moral majority' the cinema release of *Jubilee* provoked little in the way of furore, though some extras, who were apparently Christians, walked out of the premiere. Most of the complaints occurred not when the film came out but when it was screened by Channel Four, with a briskly typed letter from Mary Whitehouse declaring it a 'new low in television viewing.' Jarman imagined the disappointment of anyone, therefore, tuning in for the sex and violence: 'An Oscar for sex and violence for that!... It's a fucking con, wot we want is... films... with all American boys bashing the brains out of wogs so you can leave the cinema cheering. None of this grim stuff that leaves you feeling sick and puts you off.' The most criticism however was not over the full-frontal male and female nudity, bad language or even the demise of HRH, but centred on the murder of the policemen. An accident of timing over which Jarman had no jurisdiction meant that in the month prior to transmission PC Keith Blakelock had been murdered by a mob during the Broadwater Farm riot.

The films loudest critic, if condemnation by t-shirt can be classed as loud, was Vivienne Westwood, who, claiming the film misrepresented Punk, took to her then preferred medium with the 'Open T-shirt to Derek Jarman' which called *Jubilee* 'the most boring, and therefore disgusting film.' She seemed particularly offended by the director's use of Elizabeth I as a framing device: 'I'm a PUNK man! And as you use the values you give to Punks as a warning, am I supposed to see the old Elizabethan England [sic] as some state of grace?' Whilst Queen Elizabeth I's horror and concern at the desolation does seem a little bit rich given that she had seen and practised similar barbarity in her own lifetime, the references to John Dee and Ariel add a spiritual and romantic dimension rather than any genuine royalism. Jenny Runacre got a t-shirt and 'wore it with pride.'

The fashionista's other comments hint at the presence of less than pure motives for her attack. As well as calling the director a 'dull little middle class wanker,' Westwood also seemed to have issues with the director's sexuality, referring to Jarman's 'gay (which you are) boys love of dressing up and playing at charades' and calling him 'a gay boy jerking off through the titillation of his masochistic tendencies.' In 'Derek Jarman's Angelic Conversations' author Jim Ellis suggests 'in the presentation of Amyl Nitrate as a verbose, schoolmarmy autodidact, it is hard not to see a satire of Westwood, who was originally a teacher.'

The movie also threatened McLaren and Westwood's 'ownership' of Punk. Not only did Jordan work for Westwood, Helen Wellington Lloyd, who is the first character seen, accompanied by some huge hunting dogs, was a close friend of McLaren and has a larger role in *The Great Rock n Roll Swindle*, a film that the Pistols manager was in Hollywood in search of finance for whilst Jarman, stealing his thunder, got on with the job of shooting his film on a tiny budget of £50,000. Wanting the film released in Jubilee year (but ultimately missing that deadline) and having seen a street he wanted to use and hearing that it was about to be demolished Jarman had shot guerilla-style on the back streets of London over a Whit weekend with the financing not yet even in place.

Opinions closer to the film were barely kinder; Siouxsie Sioux reportedly thought it was 'hippy trash', and Adam Ant says he 'was embarrassed by the film, to be honest; it seemed like a complete mess' though he has subsequently grown to appreciate it, saying, 'Today I think it's an amazing achievement and testament to Derek Jarman's persistence and ingenuity.' Not even the music press could get on side with Melody Maker's film critic, Chris Brazier, detecting 'the pervasive reek of perverse and esoteric artiness, the delight in degradation and decay simply for its beauty when stylised. An irresponsible movie – don't remember Punk this way.' At the time good reviews were the exception, Variety called *Jubilee* 'one of the most original, bold, and exciting features to have come out of Britain this decade' and Time Out said 'in conception the film remains highly original, and it does deliver enough of the goods to sail effortlessly away with the title of Britain's first official Punk movie.'

History has been kinder and for Jon Savage, it is 'the best film about Punk, for all its failings,' and Julian Upton has called it 'the most important British film of the late '70s. Okay, it faced little competition at the time - just a weak trickle of ill-conceived co-productions, third-rate soft-core, and the usual heritage and nostalgia. Next to those, *Jubilee*, then as now, stand out like a sore thumb.'

Like their characters, most of the Punk actors in the film were soon absorbed into the much-reviled mainstream, from Toyah Wilcox presenting holiday programmes and *Songs of Praise* on the BBC to Adam Ant becoming a pop star pin-up who, say Jarman, 'signed up with Margaret Thatcher to sing at the Falkland's Ball'. Borrowing a line from Ginz, 'They all sign up one way or another'. Vivienne Westwood's own designs moved further into English heritage status and she accepted an OBE. A 1992 diary entry by Jarman reads 'Vivienne Westwood accepts an OBE, dipsy bitch. The silly season's with us: our Punk friends accept their little medals of betrayal, sit in their vacuous salons and destroy the creative - like the woodworm in my dresser, which I will paint with insecticide tomorrow. I would like to place a man-sized 'insectocutor', lit with royal-blue, to burn up this clothes moth and her like.' In 2006, Westwood accepted the role of Dame Commander of the Most Excellent Order of the British Empire (DBE). Ironically, as the Punks were selling out, Jarman continued to get more subversive as time went on.

Hippies, Skinheads, Rastas, Punks & Disco Dancing Bowie Boot Boys

God Save The Queen
(Matlock, Rotten, Cook, Jones)

If 'Anarchy in the UK' could be dismissed, in the words of Andrew Marr, as a 'juvenile political attack', The Sex Pistols' follow up was to prove far more incendiary, and in the words of John Lydon, 'there are not many songs written over baked beans at the breakfast table, that went on to divide a nation and force a change in popular culture.' Immediately banned by the BBC for being in 'gross bad taste', the tabloids went into overdrive in condemning the band as the nation's public enemy number one.

Malcolm McLaren had stoked up 'God Save The Queen's already formidable level of controversy by organising for the band to promote the record by performing on a boat, causing an outcry in the tabloid press. The Sunday Mirror's 'Punish the Punks' story was taken literally by some its readers, leading to subsequent headline's like 'Punk Star Rotten Razored,' which reported the singer 'was ambushed by a gang outside a London pub' and 'taken to hospital where stitches were put in his wounds... Last night there were fears that the attack was part of a backlash against the Pistols... seen as possible targets because of their anti-royal record.' The attack was, the Daily Mirror said, 'the second aimed at the group within days' after the record's sleeve designer Jamie Reed 'was beaten up in the street and left unconscious with a broken nose and a broken leg'. Lydon's attackers 'were not teenage thugs, but men in their thirties.' The paper didn't mention that it was the day after its Sunday sister paper had run its 'Punish the Punks' story.

The best, and most realistic, filmed document of what Punks were like during the movement's 1977 heyday is an episode of the BBC series **BRASS TACKS: PUNK**, filmed away from its Kings Road media epicentre in Manchester and presented by Brian Truman who tells us that 'for many people it is a bigger threat to our way of life than Russian Communism or hyperinflation.'

The programme opens with a clipping from the Daily Mirror, dated August 2nd 1977, in which under the heading of 'Showdown Date For Punks' the paper 'reported' that 'the Punks and Teds have arranged the date for a showdown.' The venue was to be Margate beach on the forthcoming Bank Holiday Monday. It would not have escaped the paper's attention that the piece, a follow up to the paper's OTT coverage of weekend activities on the Kings Road, was likely to send a message out to anyone who fancies a punch-up, and many always were in what had become something of a holiday tradition, that the resort was the place to go and the rest of Fleet Street doubtless had their photographers out in force on the off chance.

The programme begins with a 20 minute pre-recorded film that looks into the lives of a handful of Manchester Punks, initially seen at a Drones gig at the Electric Circus. Prominent among them is a 20-year-old office worker called Denise from 'a comfortable north Manchester family and by no means the dead end kid of Punk rock legend. Tellingly, though you can tell she is a Punk from the bleached hairdo, the jeans she leaves work in contain enough material to sail a yacht across the Atlantic. Her mums runs up her Punk gear on the sewing machine at home and is seen taking in some leather pants. At the opposite end of the social ladder is 16-year-old Paul, described as a 'refugee from London' who leaves the Department of Employment looking like a New York street hustler on his way to meet either a trick or a dealer.

There's lots of naivety, such as one girl who, dressed the same as those around her, without a hint of irony talks of 'all these horrible people you've got walking round, they just follow each other in fashion, really. One goes out and buys a flared skirt so they all buy a flared skirt.' Then there's Allan Deaves who is handy with a monkey wrench, married with a four-year-old son and who is a member of a band called The Worst with fellow interviewee Ian (Odjie) Hodges. Alan tells us 'The Sex Pistols should have the right to free speech. If somebody produces a pornographic magazine, even though it might be absolute trash, he has the right of free speech to produce that magazine and say something.' Mrs Deaves looks far from impressed with this logic.

The Worst were a regular fixture on the Manchester Punk scene but never courted success because of an ambition to live up to their name. The band were however immortalised by Joe Strummer who said: 'It only takes three or four weeks to learn to play guitar, but apparently for The Worst, this was too long to wait.' John Peel said 'the Worst's aural minimalism - a sandpapered hybrid of bleached Hawkwind and 'case history' Kevin Coyne - and a total lack of orthodox technique provoke immediate alienation and scorn. But it works because it's so totally unpretentious and spontaneous, possessing absolutely no pose...'

There then follows a studio discussion with Councillors from up and down the country who had 'banned' Punk, including representatives from the GLC, Birmingham, Glasgow and Newcastle. There is also the pastor who took his congregation to prey outside The Sex Pistols Anarchy Tour gig in Caerphilly who says Punk is 'degenerate and evil' and that it is 'the payoff of a Punk society. I feel that we have Punk parents. We have Punk politicians. We have Punk clergymen and we have Punk sportsmen.'

The Councillors are to a man stuck in the 1950s and clueless, summed up by a remark from one that 'we have had Punk rock in Birmingham. Unfortunately... and now they're bringing out these Freak Punk rock groups' or his Newcastle counterpart who suggested that the audiences are between 10 and 13 years old. Cheering on the good guys are the Buzzcocks Pete Shelley, John Peel and a man from Virgin.

Joe Public's attitude to Punks, and the part played by the baiting of the tabloid press, is at play in **CROWN COURT: SUGAR AND SPICE (1979)**, which, written by Frances Gallymore, opens with a middle-aged road worker giving evidence of his run in with two girls that has placed them in the dock. He had called out at them from in the hole he was digging. '"Mind you don't scare the sunshine away" and another little joke like "Going to a fancy dress party?" seeing as they were dressed up so funny' he says, 'with chains and dangly safety pins and they had bright pink socks on'.

The two Punkettes are Beryl Betts (Sylvestra Le Touzel) and Deanna Fine (Lynsey Baxter), though only one of them fits that description today. Deanna is neatly dressed in her catholic school uniform and pigtails. Beryl was residing in hostel, having moved out of the children's home in which she had resided since being a toddler just a year ago. Though she had received two convictions for shoplifting during that time she had on both occasions pleaded guilty, explaining that she was having a hard time at the prospect of having to leave her home: 'I'm all alone see.'

Having realised that he had left his jacket, containing a wallet, hanging on the fence nearby he climbed out and approached them and says 'They were like a pack of bitches they were. I was terrified. You don't expect girls to behave like they was. They were like perverted maniacs. Wrong in the head. You expect girls to act proper, look nice... It's not safe to be on the street with

Never trust a part time Punk in *Crown Court: Sugar & Spice*

girls like them rampaging.'

In fact, as he admitted, his first reaction had been to grab Beryl by the collar, shaking her 'just to frighten her a little bit'. When she pushed him away, Deanna had tripped him. He says that she had punched him and that it had put him out like a light. What is not in dispute is that when he came round, he had a pair of nail scissors sticking in his back. He says this was Beryl but an elderly independent witness watching from a flat across the road says it was Deanna.

Both men share a similar opinion of Punks. The 'victim' says 'You get 'em down the town. Drunks and perverts. Nasty little kids'. Referring solely to their appearance he says: 'They were asking for trouble weren't they.' The witness says: 'I'm no expert but you've only got to look at the papers to see what a rotten lot they are... They're all twisted inside, the things they get up to, inside and out.'

Deanna says she only dressed in Punk clothes because she was afraid of Beryl but puts it on a little thick and her claim that she's not the sort of person who would carry a pair of scissors to use as a weapon allows her previous convictions to be brought up. 'Look, I go to school. To a convent school. Do you honestly go around with axes, bicycle chains and broken bottles in my gym slip?'

With two convictions, one for unlawful wounding and another for carrying an offensive weapon the game is up, and she shows her true character: 'They were wrong and so are you, you bitch. Just so they'll all be prejudiced. Just cos you feel sorry for that drippy cow. I bet you take on all the useless sodding cases don't you? I know your sort. I bet you defend drunks and blacks don't you you bitch?'

Despite Paul Cook's bizarre statement that 'God Save The Queen', 'wasn't written specifically for the Queen's Jubilee. We weren't aware of it at the time,' it wasn't so much the message that packed a defiant political punch but the timing of its release and the establishment's fear that the Pistols really did 'mean it, maaan.' Whether the powers that be really did get together to stop the record embarrassing Her Majesty by being the official number one of Jubilee week is best left to the conspiracy theorists.

Contrary to a ridiculous claim in the press release for John Lydon's autobiography, 'Anger Is An Energy', that 'So revolutionary was [Lydon's] influence, he was even discussed in the Houses of Parliament under the Traitors and Treasons Act, which still carries the death penalty,' in truth, whilst the Pistols caused a degree of consternation for the man in the street - egged on by the tabloid press - they were met with what can only be called indifference by the system that the Sunday People seemed to believe it intended to 'smash'.

There were exceptions from the government 'back benches' such as the Conservative MP for Christchurch and Lymington, Robert Adley, who in 1976 had written to EMI chairman Sir John Read. Adley insisted that the company should neither be 'financing' nor 'sponsoring' a group of 'ill-mannered louts'. Labour MP Marcus Lipton was 76-years-old when 'God Save The Queen' was released and had already had a go at the unhealthy influence of Bay City Rollers so his argument in the Daily Mirror that 'if pop music is going to be used to destroy our established institutions, then it must be destroyed first' would never be taken seriously, though he came close to achieving this goal by releasing a single himself, 'Hand In Hand'/'Friends In Need', on the Butterfly record label and every bit as awful as you would rightly expect it to be. Lipton joined forces with Neville Trotter, Tory member for Tynemouth, in a half-hearted campaign to get the Pistols single banned.

Of the members of government whose diaries have since been published, neither Punk nor The Sex Pistols warrant any mention at all apart from in those of those of Tony Benn who bemoans the fact that the Labour Party could not deploy the 'tens of thousands of young people [...] banners and badges and Punk rockers' he had witnessed at a Rock Against Racism concert. Mentions in parliament were limited to Kenneth Marks, Under-Secretary of State for the Environment, who cited the lyrics of The Clash in expressing concern about what Punk symbolised, and Bruce George, Labour MP for Walsall South, who after reading a Sunday People article that even he considered was likely exaggerated, raised concerns about Punk in a debate on health and safety at concerts.

In 1977, with The Sex Pistols banned from playing live and their second recording contract, with A&M, in tatters, Malcolm McLaren had an idea: 'If you have four rock stars who can't play, why not make a film with four actors who can't act?' Though definitely not amongst his better ideas, there was a certain logic to his thinking. Says Julien Temple: 'The idea was if they couldn't be seen playing, that they could be seen in a film.' In the summer of

1977, following the releases of 'God Save The Queen' and 'Pretty Vacant' the Pistols went global and McLaren headed to Hollywood to set the ball rolling. It would be a long and chaotic process and for the band, it was all downhill thereafter.

By Christmas of 1977, and with the band by then seeming about as threatening as Kenneth Williams, a Daily Mirror article under the heading 'Never mind the filth, here's The Sex Pistols' glimpsed into a crystal ball and anticipated the cartoon-like persona that the band would adopt post-Rotten, and was captured by Julien Temple in **THE GREAT ROCK N ROLL SWINDLE (1979)**. The article could just as easily have been titled Carry On Sex Pistols and opens with 'Steve Jones, the only handsome member of The Sex Pistols band, resplendent in tight black trousers, a beautiful pink-patterned shirt, and an immaculate matching leather jacket, stands up, thumbs his nose and blows a raspberry. Sid Vicious orders the first of a series of beefsteaks, belching loudly. Across the hotel dining room, a large party of middle-aged Dutch people are celebrating a silver wedding...'

Having joined the Pistols on a four-day tour of Holland, the reporter's 'first encounter with the band was at the reception desk. "Buy me some sweets, Malcolm," said a gangly lad, wearing a battered leather jacket... "I want some sweets". The chorus continued until Malcolm brought a large tin of pear drops. Sid... crammed them into his mouth six at a time... Gaps in the conversation were punctuated by Sid's belching. Rotten: "Shurrup! Sid you are an animal, disgusting." Sid: "Share a room with me tonight John?" Rotten: "Not likely. You're insanitary. You haven't washed for weeks. And I'VE just had a bath."'

TV spoofs by this time didn't seem that removed from the real thing. Broadcast on 29th November 1977 on BBC 2, *The Goodies* formed a group called the Little Laddies but changed their image with the arrival of Punk, much to the disgust of Tim Brooke Taylor who decided that Punk was not for him and instead joined the Keep Britain's Shoes Shiny League. The country goes Punk crazy with MPs, and newsreaders adopting the look. There's even a Punk Patrick Moore. Also appearing was *Are You Being Served*'s Frank Thornton as the Punk Master of Ceremonies, complete with a safety pin and green hair. By Christmas of 1977 Punk had even made its way into pantomime in a production, at Covent Garden's Freemason's Arms of *Cinderella - The Truth!*, staged by the Covent Garden Community Theatre with a cast including Keith Allen, where the title character is a Peckham Punk adept at snatching bags from old ladies.

In February 1978 the youth movement of the moment entered the middle-class world of musical theatre via a production of Doug Lucie's *We Love You*, a play about, and featuring three songs by, a Punk band staged at the Roundhouse downstairs. Described in the programme notes as 'using the microcosm of the music business to study the ethos of success and exploitation in society' it looks at the disintegration of a Punk band called The Filth, brought about by lead singer Rikki Kult's solo success. As well as including the playwright in an acting role (and as co-director and composer) as the band's guitarist, this long-forgotten and largely improvised piece is most notable for having featured Tim McInnerny as Flick Knife, The Filth's bass player and lyricist.

The Goodies do Punk

Punk, in its original incarnation, was over by the end of 1977 anyway and the Daily Mirror started the New Year with its rundown of what to expect in the coming year, announcing 'Punk will go pop this year. Songs will be shorter and snappier... the cult which has taken over a generation will calm down and become respectable.' An easy prediction to make as it already had. The article quotes a spokesman from WEA who said: 'Punk will become poppier. It won't go any further in notoriety but will become more acceptable and reach a far wider audience.'

In an article running alongside headed 'No One Will Kill Off The Safety Pin Set,' written by the paper's fashion writer, Punk was heralded as legitimate fashion as represented by a Punk model wearing a £250 Zandra Rhodes top. Said the paper: 'The brave tried it and now, the beautiful like Jerry Hall, top model and girlfriend of Bryan Ferry AND Mick Jagger, are wearing black leather and pins and handcuffs.'

Two weeks later under the heading 'Sex Pistol In Drugs Scare,' the Mirror reported that 'only hours after lead singer Johnny Rotten revealed that the controversial Punk rock group had split up', Vicious had passed out on a flight and been rushed to hospital where 'he was put on a drip machine and heart monitor as doctors gave him oxygen and a drugs antidote.' And the drugs? A bottle of scotch and 'two or three valium pills' according to their road manager. No need for concern then, eh?

Meanwhile, Malcolm McLaren's first port of call in his quest to put the Pistols on the silver screen was Peter Cook; a meeting was arranged, but the comedian decided to pass. Next on the list was the then 26-year-old producer Don Boyd who Variety had called the 'Whizz Kid in Brit pix Biz' following the release of the John Hurt vehicle *East Of Elephant Rock* (1978). Unlike Cook, Boyd was interested and having already made a £100,000 budgeted movie said he would have no problem bringing it home financially but also clarified that he would want to direct as well as produce. The two agreed that the film should be a cross between *The Girl Can't Help It* (1956) and the Carry On movies, and at the suggestion of Boyd, a meeting was arranged with Alf Garnett creator Johnny Speight who agreed - for a £25,000 fee - to write the script. Boyd got on with both the band and their manager and says that after a screening of *East of Elephant Rock* they were complimentary of what he had achieved with the budget. Negotiations, however, stumbled and eventually ground to a halt over the question of how much control they would allow him. It would become a common stumbling block.

McLaren next approached American Sandy Lieberson who was the then head of 20th Century Fox's London based production and marketing. Lieberson knew of the Pistols and thought: 'if we were going to make a film in England, this was the kind of thing we should do. It was fun, stimulating, exciting, and I found Malcolm very engaging, clever and ambitious.' He set up meetings with Ken Loach and Stephen Frears, neither of which went anywhere, Loach concluding 'there were, quite simply, more differences than similarities between us.'

Instead, McLaren suggested cult exploitation director Russ Meyer, who Lieberson immediately enthused over: 'As soon as I heard Malcolm mention Russ Meyer I knew it smelled of the perfect combination. Meyer was a guy who was not going to make something pretentious or add some unnecessary artistic element to the story. I thought it was... a match made in heaven.' Meyer also had a connection with Fox who had produced the director's big studio hit *Beyond The Valley of the Dolls* (1970), about a fictitious all-girl rock band.

On his arrival in Hollywood McLaren was met by the 31-year-old Dutch writer and director Rene Daalder who Meyer correctly deduced would have much more in common with an English Punk band manager than would the ageing ex-WW2 veteran. The two immediately hit it off and put together a 60-page treatment which Daalder called 'quite inspired'. Meyer disagreed, finding its tale of dole queues and angry young rock stars too depressing and called in *Beyond the Valley of the Dolls* writer Roger Ebert, to turn the script into something more Russ Meyer-esque. This meant various sexual adventures for the ever-willing Steve Jones in the Cambridge Rapist Hotel, the notorious 'Who Killed Bambi' scene of the killing of a young fawn and a scene where Sid Vicious rapes his mother while she was shooting up. According to Meyer 'Sid didn't object to fucking his mother, he objected to shooting up on screen.' Temple suggests the choice of writer was at least partly down to the fact that he was cheap: 'Meyer actually pays him with the women that he has. He doesn't pay him money. He offers him Mary Ann and Cherie for the night.'

Says Daalder: 'As far as Malcolm was concerned this movie was going to be a Sex Pistols movie and since, as it happened, The Sex Pistols liked Russ Meyer's movies, Malcolm hoped that Russ would respect them.' There was one Pistol, however, who didn't hold the director in esteem, with Rotten saying: 'I hated Russ Meyer from the first second I saw him - an overbearing senile old git.'. Says Temple: 'By then Rotten was actively sabotaging the film, mostly by not turning up for meetings and being aggressive to Meyer. But once... he showed me a sack full of the most ridiculous clothes - platform shoes and flared floral trousers and bright blonde wigs. He'd obviously gone to all these jumble sales, buying up all these early seventies clothes, and he was determined he was going to play a Hippie in this ultimate Punk film. He kept saying, "This film is not going to happen, not going to happen," and that was an accurate reflection of his power because by then he hated Malcolm and he knew he could make it not happen.'

Although four days were shot, matters came to a head at a 20th Century Fox board meeting in Monte Carlo. Says Lieberson: 'There was no arguing, no discussion, no reasoning. It was. "Pay them off, get rid of that thing. If you have to, give them the money, but tell them to go away. We don't want Fox to have anything further to do with them."' The London Standard ran the headline 'Pistols Sexy Film Has Princess In A Rage,' - Princess Grace being a board member.

With Meyer off the picture, McLaren contacted Daalder who, after first putting his own name forward for the job, pointed him toward Jonathan Kaplan and his writer Danny Opatoshu. Kaplan had directed exploitation films for Roger Corman like *Night Call Nurses* (1972), *The Student Teachers* (1973), the Isaac Hayes vehicle *Truck Turner* (1974) and *White Line Fever* (1975) with Jan Michael Vincent. Opatoshu would write the screenplay for Allan Arkush's sixties set rock comedy *Get Crazy* (1983). The duo duly arrived in London where McLaren gave them a potted history of Punk, which Opatoshu sums up as being 'it was all, and I mean absolutely all, Malcolm,' and offered them total creative control. After checking out the sets left over by Meyer - a Dickensian London street that had originally been built for *Oliver* (1968), and a replica of the inside of the Nashville - they set about writing an 11 page treatment in which a glimpse of swinging London would dissolve into The Sex Pistols in a run-down part of the capital called Dead End, all broken down buildings and children running around dressed in rags. Into the area arrives rock superstar Rod Bollocks, back from tax exile to find his home had been burgled by Jones and Cook and squatted by Vicious. When Bollocks complains to his record company, rather than helping, the company try to sign the Pistols but are told to 'fuck off' and they become successful on their own terms.

Rotten is kidnapped because in the words of the Chairman: 'The Punk movement has become too big to be left to Punks. Trained experts are now taking control.' When the singer hurls himself through a high window to escape, a montage of the future of Punk flashes before his eyes - adverts for Sex Pistols Punk Kits, middle-aged Punks singing 'Anarchy in the UK' in a Holiday Inn, an ordinary family all dressed in bondage trousers and safety pins and the band themselves knighted. Rather than falling to his death Rotten's plummet is halted when he becomes suspended on the flagpole of a Union Jack from where he drops gently to the ground, somehow back in Dead End where he discovers that it has all been a dream, and Her Majesty the Queen is shortly to be unveiling a statue of the band in the newly christened Pistols Park. The film ends with the band commandeering an open-topped double-decker bus from which, to the sound of 'Anarchy in the UK', they spray the opening ceremony with machine-gun fire and hand grenades.

It was a treatment that Kaplan says seemed to please everybody until he asked to be paid. Julian Temple suggests the script was always a none starter for a much simpler reason: 'Johnny Rotten really liked it, so they stood no chance with Malcolm.' Summoned to a meeting at the Glitterbest offices, McLaren declared that he had decided a narrative film was not right for the band and he now wanted a concert film, suggesting they should set up a Punk Woodstock and call the police ahead of time so that there would be a riot. 'At that point' says Kaplan,

'I had to leave because I did not want to be part of a bloodbath.'

This idea, if ever seriously considered, was quickly abandoned and an attempt to revitalise the project was next made with British low budget sex and horror director Peter Walker who says: 'It was a terrific script called A Star Is Dead and every other word was a four-letter word beginning with an F or a C... the script was set up, we were going into Bray. The script had been very cleverly constructed in the sense that none of The Sex Pistols, in the movie, never worked together unless they were doing their numbers... together they were problems and separately they were frightened little boys, really.' Temple says the script was: 'a diluted version of Who Killed Bambi, only it didn't have any of the guts.' Once again though the project was abandoned.

What McLaren had wanted all along was to create the gospel according to Malcolm, and to this end the directing duties eventually went to Julian Temple, who had been working for some years by then as the bands unofficial film archivist; McLaren presumably thinking an inexperienced and familiar face would be more compliant with his own vision of *The Great Rock n Roll Swindle*. Temple had been trying to do a film on Mods in 1976 when a student at the National Film School and had heard about a band who did crazy versions of a couple of Small Faces songs and went to see if they would be any good for the film. The band was The Sex Pistols and, says the director: 'There was no need to make a film about Mods anymore. I was really fascinated by it and I just started to make a documentary about the Punk thing.'

Says Temple: 'We finally wrote it so that there were swindles within swindles... there's the basic rock n roll swindle of the kids going into a record shop and buying a record with their hard-earned cash and getting two hit singles and a mountain of crud, buying a worthless piece of plastic because they've been fed this bullshit about some larger-than-life demigod who's going to instil them with a bit of wisdom. There's the second swindle of The Sex Pistols stealing the money they'd got. There's the swindle of Steve Jones as the ex-Pistol trying to get his share of the swindled money back from McLaren. And then probably the most interesting swindle of all is the way in which the film was designed to swindle an avid fan of his expectations, destroying the fans illusions about The Sex Pistols.'

In the edit, McLaren once again tried to take total control but lacked the technical ability and so he and Temple fought into the wee small hours for weeks on end until, in February and just five days after Sid's death, Lydon v Glitterbest hit the High Court, where a receiver was placed in control of the Pistols assets which, with the money gone, was *The Great Rock n Roll Swindle*. The court appointed McLaren sub-manger for the completion of the film but his attitude soon rubbed the receiver up the wrong way leaving the door open for Temple to take control.

Lydon, who had left the band and played no part in the filming, appearing only in animation and archive footage, naturally hated it. Sid was dead before its completion. Steve Jones says: 'I just thought it was funny, the whole thing, the whole idea, me being a detective in it. It was like one of these old Carry On movies... it was all tongue in cheek to me. Probably Malcolm was taking it all a bit more serious. This is how he wanted everyone to see him. The big genius. Whatever. I was just going along for the ride.'

Temple returned to the topic two decades later with **THE FILTH AND THE FURY (2000)**, supposedly to redress the balance in favour of the band's version of events but in reality substituting McLaren's overblown sense of self-importance for Lydon's. The film adopts *Swindle*'s jokey tone but where the former is an obvious mockumentary and not intended to be taken as entirely factual, *The Filth And The Fury* is a more straightforward documentary. In his introduction of the film for its broadcast on Film Four, Lydon says 'the total message of this movie is honesty, total full-on, take no prisoners, tell no lies.' Temple knew different and says: 'It wasn't meant to be objective, there are many truths to everything, and particularly to a process like The Sex Pistols, this was their version.'

One notable piece of revisionism in the film is the omission of the latter-day recording history of the band as depicted in *The Great Rock n Roll Swindle*'s final section after the departure of Rotten, a brief clip of Sid shooting up the 'My Way' audience aside. So there's no 'Silly Thing' and 'Friggin In The Riggin', no cavorting with Ronnie Biggs for 'No One Is Innocent', and neither of the Sid fronted Eddie Cochran covers, 'Something Else' and 'C'Mon Everybody', both #3 singles with the former also being the bands biggest seller. None of these are likely the way rational people, and Lydon, would like The Sex Pistols to be remembered but however uncomfortable they might be to some they are part of the whole truth.

A more balanced picture had already been achieved in **PUNK AND THE PISTOLS (1995)**, directed by Paul

Tickell for BBC's arts strand *Arena*. In the late seventies following the explosion of Punk Tickell gave rock stardom a go with a stint as a 'pathetic' drummer before settling for what he calls a 'failed entrepreneurial career' as the manager of Kirk Brandon's pre-Theatre of Hate Punk band The Pack. After a spell as a freelance journalist working for the NME, Time Out, and The Face, he began working as a researcher on youth-related television series such as London Weekend television's *South of Watford*, gradually working his way into roles as associate producer, producer and finally director.

Most of the original footage seen in *Punk And The Pistols* was shot in 1991. Interviews with all four surviving band members and their manager being a stipulation of the film ever being broadcast, Tickell then spent the next few years massaging the ego of John Lydon until the singer finally agreed to go in front of the camera. The film also provided some hitherto unseen footage such that shot by the Buzzcocks of The Sex Pistols at the Lesser Free Trade Hall in Manchester, and Adam Ant's Super-8 footage of the Pistols gig at the Screen on the Green in Islington. Footage from John Samson's National Film School fetish film, *Dressing For Pleasure* (1977), later used in *The Filth & The Fury*, was also first seen here.

Alex Cox's **SID & NANCY (1986)** has at its heart a love story between a musician and a groupie. Whilst Sid Vicious (Gary Oldman) was no ordinary musician, Nancy Spungen (Chloe Webb), says photographer Eileen Polk, who hung out with Nancy at clubs and parties, was equally a different form of groupie who used drugs to make up for her other shortcomings. 'She was blatantly honest about it. She bought drugs for the bands. She was honest about being a prostitute as well, which I thought was refreshing… There were groupies that had been around for a long time because of their looks. In order to be a groupie you had to be tall and skinny and have fashionable clothes. There were a bunch of girls like that on the scene. And then comes Nancy. She's not trying to be cute or charming. She wasn't telling people she was a model or a dancer. She had mousey brown hair and she was a bit overweight. She basically said, "Yeah, I'm a prostitute, and I don't care."'

Nancy, born into a Philadelphian middle-class Jewish family in 1958, entered the world as she meant to go on. This meant, in the words of her mother: 'kicking and screaming at some unseen enemy.' From there her behaviour only got worse, frequently threatening and verbally abusing her siblings, and on one occasion attempting to stab the babysitter with a pair of scissors. Though she excelled academically, Nancy suffered from recurrent violent nightmares and her depression expressed itself in self harm. At fifteen they diagnosed her as schizophrenic.

Expelled from college (and supposedly the entire state of Colorado) during her freshman year, Nancy left home at seventeen and moved to New York where, in the developing music scene around clubs like CBGB's and Max's, her behavioural problems were considered nothing out of the ordinary. Quickly developing a taste for drugs, Nancy funded her habits through stripping and, occasionally, prostitution. For kicks, she threw herself into the groupie scene, initially with Aerosmith. 'I was concentrating on big rock 'n' roll stars,' she says, '…One of the first nights I was with them… we drove out in the limousine. I was sitting in the back seat with Tom Hamilton on one side of me and Brad Whitfield on the other. I had one hand on one prick and one hand on the other… I had a good time, and I got treated nice.'

Her spiritual home was in the city's burgeoning Punk scene where she worked her way through all four New York Dolls, Richard Hell and Iggy Pop who says 'She wasn't a beauty, but I liked her. There was something really spunky here, but I was a big boy then. So my thought was, Trouble.' Following The Heartbreakers over to the UK, she quickly entered the UK Punk scene and after being rebuffed by Johnny Rotten, she met Sid and, far from being a big boy, the liaison set in motion the tragic chain of events that was to follow.

Cox's production was kick-started when the *Repo Man* (1984) director met a producer who told him he was planning to film the story with Rupert Everett and Madonna. 'That could not be allowed,' says Cox. 'So really our inspiration was to stop that happening by getting our own version into production first.' Cox had already written a script inspired by Vicious and Spungen back in 1980, 'Too Kool To Die', about a blind detective hired to rescue the daughter of a wealthy American family from the clutches of an English bass player. Says Cox, 'the script depicted the flooding of London, the Shah of Iran's heroin dealing and the Jeremy Thorpe scandal, as well as many other things that guaranteed it would never be made into a film. So I put it aside.'

Having learned of the rival production, he immediately set about researching his subjects, talking to people who had worked in the boutique Sex, members of the Bromley Contingent, as well as Johnny Thunders, Malcolm

McLaren and the surviving Sex Pistols. The director brought in Abbe Wool as co-writer and the two worked on a screenplay from adjoining rooms at the Chelsea Hotel. With the script quickly completed, Cox headed back to London in search of financing. He found Eric Fellner who had made countless pop videos using 'glossy images to sell faux bands like Duran Duran... nailing shut, in the process, the coffin lid of Punk.' Half of the film's £4 million budget came from legendary producer Margaret Matheson, then working at Zenith Productions, who were bankrolled by Central Television, the holder of the ITV Midlands television franchise. Matheson shopped the project around the States and secured the other half of the money from Embassy Home Entertainment.

Cox next embarked on the lengthy process of assembling the cast with the help of the casting director Lucy Boulting. Suggestions for a Sid included Peter Lee Wilson, Lee Drysdale, and even Sandra Bernhard, whilst amongst those passed over for the role of Malcolm McLaren, which eventually went to David Hayman, was Ian Dury, which Cox calls 'A great idea of Lucy's that I perhaps should have pursued.' The part of Sid eventually came down to a straight choice between Gary Oldman and Daniel Day-Lewis. Says the director, 'I realised Dan could easily play the dashing leading man, Oldman was less credible as a lover, less debonair, but he knew where Sid was coming from. Gary, like Sid, had the misfortune to grow up south of the river. So I was classist in my decision making. Instead of the Poet Laureate's son, I picked the Bermondsey boy.'

For the role of Nancy, Cox considered Patti Tippo and Courtney Love, who Cox thought, 'had tremendous drive and potential' but looked too young alongside Oldman. All other readings were eclipsed by the stage actress Chloe Webb who, says Cox, immediately 'got' the character and was hired without delay, with Love securing a secondary role as Gretchen, one of Nancy's New York friends (and a starring role in Cox's next venture).

The movie opens with an NYPD dispatcher sending a unit to the Chelsea Hotel in response to what is believed to be a domestic violence incident. As Nancy's body is zipped into a plastic bag, a police officer hands Sid a cigarette and asks, 'Where did you meet her?' Taking a deep drag on the now bloodstained cigarette, Sid replies, 'I met her at Linda's'.

The film then crosses the Atlantic to a time a year earlier where with The Sex Pistols on the verge of a US tour, Paul Cook and Steve Jones voice their concerns with Sid's musical ability to McLaren. 'We have to turn his amp off half the time. We'd be playing one thing, and he'd be playing a fucking 'nother,' complains Jones. 'Look, I sympathise,' says McLaren, 'but Sidney is more than a mere bass player. He's a symbol, a metaphor who embodies the dementia of a nihilistic generation.' He is, he adds, 'a fabulous disaster.'

The rest of the action portrays the doomed love story between this one 'disaster' and another in the form of Spungen, who, the movie suggests, introduces him to heroin. Vicious himself has said otherwise telling the NME: 'I've been doing every-fuckin'-thing they reckon she turned me on to two years before I met 'er.' The film plays out in a dingy New York hotel room where, with The Sex Pistols having acrimoniously imploded and any, albeit slim, hopes of a solo career in tatters because of Sid's insistence on not just singing 'No Future' but living it, an argument between the heavily addicted couple leaves a blood-soaked Nancy splayed out across the bathroom's white tiles.

Tonight Matthew, Chloe Webb and Gary Oldman are going to be *Sid & Nancy*

Though there were some dissenting

voices, such as Sight & Sound's assertion that 'Relentlessly whingeing performances and a lengthy slide into drugs, degradation, and death make this a solemnly off-putting moral tract,' Sid & Nancy was generally well-received in the press on both sides of the pond. Roger Ebert gave it full marks in his review for the Chicago Sun-Times and told a Late Show audience that Oldman 'definitely won't be [Oscar] nominated – and should be', because 'Hollywood will not nominate an actor for portraying a creep, no matter how good the performance is.' Despite this, the film failed to recoup its budget at the box office but soon went into healthy profit via its subsequent life on video and DVD. The movie's standing has only increased in the intervening years with an approval rating on reviews aggregator Rotten Tomatoes of 88% and Rolling Stone, in 2003, ranking it third-best rock movie ever made, and ShortList in 2014, naming it the 9th greatest music biopic of all time.

The film's biggest critic was John Lydon. Asked what the script got right, the ex-Pistol deadpanned, 'The name Sid'. Lydon was particularly vociferous in his distaste for the films first half, saying 'The squalid New York hotel scenes were fine, except they needed to be even more squalid. All the scenes in London with the Pistols were nonsense. The chap who played Sid, Gary Oldman, I thought was quite good. But even he only played the stage persona as opposed to the real person. If only he had the opportunity to speak to someone who knew the man. I don't think they ever had the intent to research properly in order to make a seriously accurate movie. It was all just for money, wasn't it? To humiliate somebody's life like that – and very successfully – was very annoying to me... It was all someone else's fucking fantasy, some Oxford graduate who missed the Punk rock era. The bastard.'

It was never Cox's intention to create a historically accurate snapshot of late seventies London. 'Memory,' he says, 'plays tricks, makes good things great. It was these memory tricks that I was emulating in a recreation of London Punk, a scene I'd never seen. Real London Punk in 1976 or 1977 was a couple of skinny, spotty boys bouncing up and down. Ours was a mob of tattooed Skinheads and Mohicans slam dancing in a mosh pit. It looked like California Punk, circa 1984, because that was what I knew, and it was visually more exciting.'

Not everything rings untrue. One scene recreating the 100 Club Punk Festival, says film director and ex-Skids frontman Richard Jobson, who was there: 'captures that very evening when [Sid] brutally assaults music journalist Nick Kent, a soft hippy-like writer who was an easy target. Not the act of a tough guy.' Jobson is less convinced by some of the casting, 'most of the key players were still alive and still young. Therefore, it was easy to compare and contrast the screen performances with people I knew very well. The cartoon-like behaviour and dialogue in the film is nothing like how the real-life Johnny Rotten... and manager Malcolm McLaren expressed themselves. What I remember is a combination of humour, irreverence and, most importantly, intelligence.'

Calling the movie, 'the lowest form of life,' Lydon says he 'cannot understand why anyone would want to put out a movie like Sid & Nancy and not bother to speak to me; Alex Cox, the director, didn't. He used as his point of reference – of all the people on earth – Joe Strummer! That guttural singer from The Clash? What the fuck did he know about Sid & Nancy? That's probably all he could find, which was really scraping the bottom of the barrel.' This outburst seems particularly unreliable, having more to do with Lydon's long-held dislike of Strummer, whose only involvement in the film was in the provision of music.

Cox, on the contrary, says he met with Lydon, having previously sent the singer a copy of the script, in the bar of The Mayflower Hotel in September 1985. 'John was on time and most agreeable' he says. 'In the course of 90 minutes we each consumed eight sea breezes' which he suggests left his notes, 'made right after the meeting... a little confused... I think there was some talk of the script; Lydon was very kind about it.' Acknowledging that Lydon's hatred of the movie was 'understandable, given that it was based on incidents from his life and centred around one of his friends,' it was unlikely that the two would ever see eye-to-eye on the portrayal of Vicious. Cox cited one reason for making the film in the first place was that he was afraid that if someone else made it, it would portray its subjects as 'real exemplars of Punk like I am; rather than sold-out traitors to it', saying Vicious had 'contributed nothing of value, died an idiot.'

Of his own portrayal, Lydon says: 'It was so off and ridiculous. It was absurd. Champagne and baked beans for breakfast? Sorry. I don't drink champagne. He didn't even speak like me. He had a Scouse accent. Worse, there's a slur implied in the movie that I was jealous of Nancy, which I find particularly loathsome. There is that implication that I feel was deliberately put there. I guess that's Alex Cox showing his middle class twittery. It's all too glib, it's all too easy.' It's easier to sympathise with the singer here, Andrew Schofield comes nowhere near to capturing Lydon's persona which, whatever the casting, would always be a challenge. Paul Simonon of The

Clash has called the portrayal, 'some sort of fat, bean-slurping idiot.,' and whilst ranking it at number one in their '10 Worst actors in rockin' roles' feature, Uncut magazine likened it to a 'short-arse Scouse Bleasdale regular never once looking like he means it.'

The Pistols heyday, but not the band themselves, was revisited in **HOW TO TALK TO GIRLS AT PARTIES (2017)**, the fourth feature from *Hedwig and the Angry Inch* creator John Cameron Mitchell. The film opens with The Damned's 'New Rose' but that's the only classic of the time you'll hear because they were beyond the film's budget. Mitchell is not the only one who finds it somewhat ironic for songs that 'are anti establishment and for the people.'

The film concerns three fanzine producing friends, Enn (Alex Sharp), Vic (Abraham Lewis) and John (Ethan Lawrence) on the day of the Silver Jubilee celebrations. As Enn's parents and their friends and neighbours begin their street party, the three youths bid their farewell and head for a night at the local Punk club.

This is 11 miles south of the legendary Roxy in Croydon where the real Punk local hero was Johnny Moped, through whose ranks Chrissie Hynde and Captain Sensible at one time passed, and whose 'Incendiary Device' made number 15 in John Peel's Festive Fifty of 1977. In the film the local heroes are The Dyschords whose attention seeking singer Slap is played by Martin Tomlinson, formerly of attention-seeking art Punk band Selfish Cunt whose 'Britain Is Shit/Fuck The Poor' single made it to number 66 in 2003 on the back of an aggressive stage show but who are probably best remembered for getting into a brawl with Pete Doherty after throwing manure at the Babyshambles frontman during a photo-shoot outside of Buckingham Palace the following year.

How To Talk To Girls At Parties began life as a short story by Neil Gaiman in which Punk gets just a cursory mention: 'This was during the early days of Punk. On our own record players we would play The Adverts and The Jam, The Stranglers and The Clash and The Sex Pistols. At other people's parties you'd hear ELO or 10cc or even Roxy Music. Maybe some Bowie, if you were lucky.' It was *Shortbus* producer Howard Gertler who read and loved the story he came across in Gaiman's 'Fragile Things' collection, saying: 'It was a Punk alien love story in 10 pages. There was mystery to it, there was fun, there are scary moments - it was all there.' Well, not quite. Gaiman's story ends at the film's 25 minute mark, leaving quite a lot to do.

It was when writer Philippa Goslett interviewed Gaiman about his youth and discovered he had been a teenage Punk with both a band and a fanzine that the initially reluctant director was persuaded to get on board. Says Mitchell: 'we made Enn into Neil and this is really an alternative history of Neil Gaiman.'

The Punk club, and the Dyschords, are run by fashion designer Queen Boadicea (Nicole Kidman), a low-rent Vivienne Westwood who even has her own cut price Don Letts played by Jermayn Hunter. Says Boadicea: 'I knew them all back in the day, which was only a few months ago... sell-outs now, of course. I worked for Vivienne Westwood until she fired me for improving on one of her designs... They pose as mentors but they suck your blood because they know their days are numbered.'

The gig is great, despite Enn's ritual humiliation by the opposite sex, but it's getting in to the after party that they've set their hearts on. Instead, the trio of youths stumble upon a brightly lit townhouse populated by a colony of aliens in shapely human form and skin tight pvc to accentuate that form.

Nicole Kidman channels Vivienne Westwood in *How To Talk To Girls At Parties*

There's a backstory to the aliens that involves the seven chakras, parents devouring their young and a dying race but what really matters is that they're colour coordinated, into kinky sex (as Vic discovers to his almost regret) and one of them, Zan (Elle Fanning), takes a pair of scissors to her dress and tells Enn to 'Do Punk to me.' Which he does during an allotted 48 hour romance, the payoff of which we get in the 1992 denouement.

In between we get another trip to Boadicea's club where, referring to a previous physical manifestation, Zan tells the smitten hostess that she used to be a star and 'once harmonised with a brown dwarf' who in turn says 'A Brown Dwarf? Didn't they open for The Shit?' before pushing her on stage and announcing her as The Dyschords new singer.

Just the director's fourth film since the 2001 film adaptation of his 1998 off-Broadway Glam musical *Hedwig And The Angry Inch*, *How To Talk To Girls At Parties* is not held in the same level of esteem as his previous movies with most critics finding it either side of hit and miss. Much of the criticism from the cult director's existing audience was that the film did not go far enough but with Fanning's name above the marquee it was never going to be another Shortbus. From a commercial point of view it's debatable how much of the audience drawn by the high profile casting of Fanning, who is excellent in the role, would have been into latex fetish wear, 70s Punk and kinky sex. But everyone involved look like they're having so much fun, and there's indeed much to be had.

To see a recreation of the 70s emerging Punk scene somewhere close to how it really was then you have to cross the Irish Sea to Lisa Barros D'Sa and Glenn Layburn's Belfast set **GOOD VIBRATIONS (2012)** where the perils of growing up a Punk were a little more perilous than a few middle-aged Teds. This extra threat is heightened by skilfully inserted archive footage that shows Belfast as it was and fits organically into the action. There are also a couple of Skinheads who carry an extra menace in that they 'know people'.

Despite this, in the words of Joe Strummer chosen to close the film: 'When Punk rock ruled over Ulster, nobody ever had more excitement and fun. Between the bombings and shootings, the religious hatred and the settling of old scores, Punk gave everybody a chance to LIVE for one glorious moment.'

Good Vibrations is as different to John Cameron Mitchell's film as you can get, being essentially a standard biopic of Terri Hooley (Richard Dormer) who in the mid-1970s opened a record shop in the most bombed street in Belfast, naming it after the tremors that all too often struck the city's so-called Bomb Alley. He also discovered local band Rudi performing at the Pound bar and discovered kindred spirits in a scene that had originated in the East Belfast Protestant heartland but whose adherents adopted no religious divide.

Bringing Hooley's story to the screen was a long haul, taking fifteen years from screenwriters Colin Carberry and Glenn Patterson initial idea to its premiere at the Belfast Film Festival with James Nesbitt and Michael Fassbender both at one time set for the starring role. It was just before Christmas 2007 that the project went into development thanks in part to the deep-pockets of some well-heeled Northern Irish music lovers including producer David Holmes and Snow Patrol's Gary Lightbody and Nathan Connolly, who are amongst the 12 producers. Holmes also provides music whilst Snow Patrol provided an otherwise unaffordable 2000 extras for a key scene by playing an acoustic gig for any of their fans going suitably attired.

The film begins with the young Terry becoming 'Terri with an I' as he is hit in the eye with a toy arrow for being a 'Fenien lover' and a 'Commie bastard', an act that leaves him with a glass eye which is casually dismissed as 'he's just gonna see things differently.' Which he certainly did.

Having been born in 1948, Terri's youth had been during the hippy heyday where he had been drawn to CND and the anti-Vietnam movement, combining the two into the grandly titled Northern Ireland Youth Campaign for Peace and Nuclear Disarmament. Post the opening titles it is the mid-seventies and Terri is still wearing the CND badge but, as the almost zero turn out at the disco he is running is testament to, the movement has shrunk somewhat in the intervening years.

The one person present is the woman who will soon become his wife, Ruth (Jodie Whittaker). 'Truth is' he tells her, 'I used to have lots of friends. Lots of anarchist friends, lots of Marxist friends and socialist friends and pacifist, feminist friends and friends who were fuck all. Then the first shot was fired, the first bomb exploded and suddenly... I just had Catholic friends and Protestant friends.' As he didn't consider himself either he soon found he had no friends.

Well he has one, Eric (David Wilmot), but he soon has to leave town for London after having been 'lifted' for selling drugs by some of their old anti-war pals: 'Except of course they're all a bit more pro-war these days.' He believes it wasn't really for selling a bit of blow; that had just provided the excuse: 'It's me. It's you Terri. They let on like they're rebels but we show them up to be just cops in balaclavas.'

It's 23 minutes before, having opened the Good Vibrations record shop, a young kid with safety pins in his school uniform comes in and asks for 'Orgasm Addict' and 'If You Don't Wanna Fuck Me, Fuck Off" by the Electric Chairs and hands over a poster advertising a gig to display in the shop, significantly placed over one for The Roling Stones at the Unity Hall in 1966.

The gig is at the Pound, which Terri is told was used 'as a morgue on Bloody Friday', and it is a revelation, telling his wife afterwards: 'You'll never believe what I've just seen. These kids. They don't give a shit. You have to hear them. Everybody has to hear them.' When he discovers he can't get Rudi's record for the shop, because they've never made one, he decides to do it himself. Other releases follow including Rudi's support band that fateful night, The Outcasts, and promotion of a regular Punk night in a struggling pub.

Eventually he records a couple of numbers by a band who wander into the shop, though it's unlikely that by the time John Peel's needle had dropped on the single for the second time he would have been, as he is in the film, dancing in the street with half a dozen young Punks, bathed in light from a helicopter hovering above, with Seymour Stein on hold on the phone.

Though Hooley was key to The Undertones breakthrough, the bigger Irish Punk bands are not dwelled upon, the script concentrating instead on those bands who, like Hooley himself who sold the 'Teenage Kicks' rights to Sire for £500, remained independent. Whether they wanted to or not. As The Undertones make their debut on *Top of the Pops*, Terri aside, faces are gloomy. None more so than Rudi's guitarist who says 'Look at the state of those trousers. How come they're on TV and we're not.'

Though the film ends on a high note with Hooley staging a Good Vibrations night at the 2000 capacity Ulster Hall as a benefit for the failing shop, which loses money despite being full, by the time the Undertones hit the charts it was already October 1978, the Punks in London, two of whom we meet at a gig, had a new look and the scene would never again recreate that initial excitement.

As befitting of its subject matter the film has a fabulous soundtrack that includes Shangri-Las, The Animals, The Small Faces, Lee Scratch Perry, Bowie, Aussie Punks The Saints and Stiff Little Fingers as well as the Good Vibrations roster. As a biopic there are doubtless many occasions in the film where a mythical Hooley steps into frame, but as a choice of subject for a true representation of what the movement should have been all about, Hooley, beard and all, and his bunch of safety pinned revolutionaries are about as Punk as it gets.

The film's success hinges on Richard Dormer's ability to capture Hooley's wide-eyed enthusiasm for life and overwhelming conversion to Punk, which he does without words in two key scenes. In the first, when he first comes across the Punks seeing off an RUC officer with a united cry of 'SS RUC', Rudi break into 'Big Time' and his face moves from bewilderment to an all-encompassing exuberance, taking you unquestioningly with him in his belief that music can change the world. In the second he listens to 'Teenage Kicks' in the studio for the first time, but being on headphones we get only silence and an expression that must have been the one John Peel (and the less said about Kieron Forsyth's brief appearance here as the DJ the better) pulled when he first heard it.

Punks as they really looked in *Good Vibrations*

Hippies, Skinheads, Rastas, Punks & Disco Dancing Bowie Boot Boys

Career Opportunities
(Strummer, Jones, Headon, Simonon)

Though mass youth unemployment is generally associated with the Thatcher years, the warning signs were in place long before. ATV had broadcast a documentary about unemployed teenagers in Liverpool, **THE DEAD END LADS (1972)**, early in the decade. The programme was directed by John Goldschmidt and researched and narrated by Ashley Bruce whose pronounced regional accent set it apart from similar efforts from the BBC, offering a voice that was sympathetic to the plight of the programme's sixteen-year-olds facing a future of cafes and dole queues. Though documentary in form, the programme includes boys at a school dramatising their future, part of a growing army of unemployed youth, condemned to not only the dole office but also persecution by the police and eventually jail. Less sympathetic was the Reading Evening Telegraph who simply described it as 'about idle teenagers.'

The programme received high praise from Chris Dunkley in the Times who expressed his delight at the unbalanced nature of the content: 'The BBC would never have made a programme on unemployed teenagers in quite this way or that if it did, then it would never be transmitted.' Bruce suggests that the city's spiralling youth crime rate was part of a vicious cycle that began on street corners where arrest for petty misdemeanours, committed largely out of boredom, led to their education being completed by their peers in the Borstal system. Added Dunkley: 'There is not much doubt that somewhere in the BBCs version somebody would have been found willing to face the camera and demand why these layabouts did not join the army, or become dustmen, or move to London and work on the underground. That would have represented 'balance."

With the number of unemployed school leavers rising from 28,000 in 1968 to 58,000 in 1971, the first step in reducing the number of young people finding themselves on the dole had already been taken in the raising, from 15 to 16, of the school leaving age. This wasn't a universally popular move, and not just amongst disgruntled fifteen-year-olds school kids. In the Times during May, future Chancellor under Thatcher, Nigel Lawson penned 'a plea to the Government to abandon while there is still time, its regrettable insistence on raising the school leaving age to 16 in September 1972.'

He suggested that as well as costing £40 million a year for the extra 220,000 places in education, the loss of even one percent of the nation's workforce for a year would add a heavy burden of the country's finances: 'The dull jobs will still exist: they will simply be filled by the same people one year later.' They should have been so lucky; only weeks on from Lawson's plea, the Times raised doubts over the availability of those 'dull jobs' he was so keen to see filled. The paper predicted that there was 'a bleak future facing the 500,000 children due to leave school this summer. It is now certain that many who had hoped to get jobs will find all doors closed.'

This pessimism, based on figures from the Institute of Careers Officers, was not unfounded and a spokesperson from the Department of Employment was quoted as being 'very concerned about this, but there is very little that we can do. There is a general lack of vacancies, and until there is a great deal more expansion in the economy it is going to be a hard time for youngsters leaving school.' In fact, though it had taken longer than was usual to absorb the 460,000 1971 school leavers into the workforce, at the close of the year there were just 10,000 still seeking work. Problems were on the horizon however, as the number of 15 to 17-year-olds was due to increase from a low of 2.2 million at the close of the 1960s to 2.8 million at the end of the 1970s, with the increase in the school leaving age providing only a temporary respite.

A Manpower Services Commission report, 'Young People and Work', pointed out that between 1971 and 1977 youth unemployment had increased three times as fast as unemployment as a whole, rising from 5.4% to 9%. The recession, which had begun in 1972 coincided with the baby boomers leaving school. Across the EEC, in 1973 3.7 million children had reached the age of 16 and entered the job market. By 1977 that figure was 4.2 million, with figures not predicted to drop to pre-1977 levels for a good ten years.

With the number of unemployed school leavers up to 209,000 in 1976, with 19% of those under 20 already out of work, right-wing politicians were touting early, hard-line versions of the youth training schemes that would become synonymous with the next decade. Anthony Steen, Conservative MP for Wavertree, Liverpool was quick off the mark, saying it was 'a golden opportunity to launch a long term imaginative scheme changing the slogan from

Trouble at the youth club from Billy Hamon and Gerry Sundquist in *The Siege of Golden Hill*

'the right to work' to 'the right to create work" The aim he said would be 'to smash the cycle of unemployment by giving every school leaver the chance to create his own work experience, either through personal social service or undertaking practical community work.' For those who did not comply, he was adamant that: 'If he gives nothing to the community, why should he demand something from it?' Steen's own imaginative use of parliamentary expenses - claiming over £87,000 on the constituency mansion designated as his second home for tree surgery – saw him abruptly give up his seat in 2009.

Despite worsening figures and declining prospects for any sort of employment for many school leavers, it was youth employment rather than youth unemployment that was of concern in

THE SIEGE OF GOLDEN HILL (1975), a twelve-part series from writer Nick McCarty, directed for ATV Television by John Sichel, and broadcast at 5.35pm. Along the way the programme took unlikely topics for teen drama such as gentrification and council corruption, and wound them into a story of a tough teenage gang, the Anvil, from the areas council housing and their run-ins with the middle-class kids who attend the Golden Hill Youth Club, allowing for a *Romeo & Juliet* sub-plot between the daughter of council planning officer, Sarah Small (Sara Clee), and gang member Billy Adams (Gerry Sundquist).

The series opens in the youth club where rehearsals for a play are in progress as outside we see the group of teenagers who call themselves the Anvil, clearly up to no good in the woods outside. When they make their entrance it is by throwing a brick through a glass panel in the door and the kicking over of a table, much to the annoyance of Sarah's father, a youth club committee member, whose threat to call the police is given short shrift by gang leader Jacky (Billy Hamon), as is a suggestion by the new Club leader Des Johnson (Peter Dudley) that they should join the club: 'We're not the posh kids, we're the estate kids... it's not our scene mate all this. Ping pong and acting. We're real, we're not pretending like them.'

When Jacky's girlfriend, Mary (Karen Berlinski), tries to pick a fight with Sarah, it is one of the Anvil that steps to her defence. This is Billy and despite the company he keeps he is a nice lad, which we know because he looks after his elderly grandad. His actions nevertheless see him expelled from the gang. Billy is not the only member of his family with problems; his grandad is the last remaining resident of a block of houses that are part of a proposed re-development and the landlord, Mr Allen (John Malcolm) and his henchman Franks (Chris Sanders) wants the stubborn pensioner out, hiring the Anvil to give him a hard time. Billy's grandad wins the day however with the help of some youth club members, a few converts from the Anvil, and a load of rotting fruit and veg. In one of the series few missteps we're meant to believe that the hurling of this is enough to see off some hardened thugs.

The responsibility for all this teenage delinquency is put squarely at the feet of lack of worthwhile opportunities. 'Remember, I once told you that I had a dream, that I looked down a dark tunnel with no ending? Have you ever looked round a steel works? You should, really you should,' Billy tells Mary. 'Its noise and dirt, and heat, and, well, nothing. Not really. Old men in their thirties with no hair, or their nails gone in the acid plant. Their teeth stained black because every time they take a drag... they get acid in their teeth. There's showers all along the plant to chuck a man in if he falls in the acid bath. Not much use. Not really. And maybe you get a pension at the end of 40 years clocking in and clocking out, and when you're an old man, a handshake and a clock.'

It's a theme that is carried on into follow-up series, *Golden Hill* (1976), which centres around Jacky who tells Mary: 'Golden Hill! The works are closing down, everything's changing. What have I got that anyone wants to buy? Working in an assembly line for the rest of my life... I'm better than that. I'm not gonna jump when a gaffer says jump. I've got me own thoughts for me own life. Look at 'em, they just put a bit into a machine, they pull a lever and out comes something else. So what! All you've done is shove something into a machine and pulled a lever. Seven hours a day and overtime, you think I wanna do that? You've seen 'em, all around Golden Hill; men waiting for the pubs to open, sitting on their own back steps and saying nothing. Well I've watched 'em, and it's not for me. There's men, old men, deaf from working in the steam hammer shed... with hardly any eyesight because they stared at the forges to see when the metal was ready to pour... You're a number. Clock in, clock out. Well I'm not a number, I'm me, Jackie and I'm not going to be a punch card to a clock. Not me.'

These views were very much in keeping with the feelings of a nation on the verge of Punk. Despite Chelsea's popular anthem of the time, 'The Right To Work', the Punks were coming round to the idea of not accepting shitty jobs as espoused by the like of The Clash's 'Career Opportunities', Elvis Costello's 'Goon Squad', The Sex Pistols 'I'm A Lazy Sod' or XTC's 'Making Plans For Nigel' - as was Chelsea front man Gene October whose rant was not about unemployment but the occasional gay porno actor's inability to get an Equity Card.

Both Billy and Jacky needn't have worried because the jobs they didn't want would soon no longer exist. Set in an unnamed midlands town which, given the number of Wolverhampton scarves on display, *Golden Hill* is likely Dudley, six miles down the A4123, or more specifically Brierley Hill a further four miles south where the Round Oak Steelworks had provided employment for 3000 locals at its peak before Margaret Thatcher's appointment of Ian MacGregor as the head of the by then nationalised British Steel in 1980 saw the industry workforce reduced by almost 60% in just three years, leading to an inevitable closure in 1982, and 25% unemployment, amongst the worst in the country.

Indeed, that same year, the subject of youth unemployment was deemed topical enough to be the basis for a sitcom targeting teens. In **4 IDLE HANDS (1976)**, Phil Daniels and Ray Burdis teamed up as 16-year-old school leavers Mike Dudds and Pete Sutton who have big ideas but little in the way of qualifications. Through the series the two hapless youths chance their arm at 'careers' ranging from selling antiques, factory work assembling pamphlets, a home cleaning business to helping out a local gangster. Despite Phil Daniels' assertion that 'it was the first of it all, really. The first programme for youngsters that was anything more than middle-class kids running up and down a railway track and waving...' the series, written by John Kane as a follow up to his work, alongside other up-and-coming writers such as Lynda La Plante and Phil Redmond, on the fondly remembered *The Kids From 47A* (1973), *4 Idle Hands* was short on laughs and ended after just 6 episodes.

In the week that the government launched a £150 million programme intended to relieve youth unemployment, the BBC's **WORLD IN ACTION: STARTING ON THE DOLE (1977)** looked at the plight of the 600,000 teenagers who would leave school that summer, and predicted that a third of them would still be looking for work in three months time. Indeed, a government report was suggesting there could be no real improvement expected over the coming few years.

The programme makers again visited Merseyside, soon to become synonymous with unemployment through the works of dramatists like Willy Russell, Carla Lane, Alan Bleasdale and Phil Redmond. But what was presented was a far cry from the soon-to-be stereotypical Scouse scrounger. Both of the two opening interviewees, a boy and a girl, were desperate to get a job. Karen says she would be okay with a wage of just £13 or £14 (the dole at the time being £9). Eddie had left school at Easter and was still looking for work. Presentable and well spoken, his story is made all the more sad because of how he keeps trying. 'It makes me feel downhearted and depressed,' he says. 'Going to three interviews a day and you come back and you've been out in your suit all day in the hot weather and you just come in, throw your jacket off, your dad's got a cup of tea ready for you and you're out the next day... and go after another couple of jobs.'

Karen however has given up on the job centre altogether, finding it a waste of time. Her opinion is shared by an unlikely source, Manchester United Chairman Louis Edwards, who tells the interviewer: 'They give up trying, and frankly I don't blame them. What's the use of going to the Career's Office and the Job Centre day after day and then, if they can afford it, a bus ride to an interview where they'll probably find 30 other people waiting and they know they've got no chance of getting the job.'

An interview with the head of the Liverpool Careers Advisory Service offers no hope whatsoever: 'In the city as a whole, at its peak in August, they will be looking for jobs for 7000 youngsters... how many vacancies there will be, it's impossible to say. When I went to check the other day, with a register probably in the region of 4000 at the moment, there were 51 vacancies.'

The Chairman of the Merseyside Job Creation Programme spells it out: 'We're now aware that youth unemployment is not a temporary crisis issue, but growingly people realise that youth unemployment, 16 to 18-year-old unemployment, will be with us even if we have an economic revival. Even if industry booms, very few firms will be taking on large numbers of, particularly educationally disadvantaged, youngsters. Productivity will come by slimming down labour forces, not by taking on more.'

He quoted a report from The Holland Committee which looked at problems of youth employment and concluded that the problem was probably structural, which suggested it wouldn't go away with rising productivity or with a revived economy. For ten years, the report said, youth unemployment would not be reduced to acceptable levels: 'It's a bit like the old days of the Luddites when machinery was invented and workers thought they would be unemployed and they smashed the machines. Youngsters are going to see the same sort of thing I think. And sooner or later we will have to rethink our working patterns.' He said there was already talk of a shorter working week, with no overtime so that work could be spread around. A second suggestion, that 'We may have to rethink about married women being employed', sounds shocking under today's, supposed, workplace equality, although a third idea offered a glimpse of the future. 'We may have to think about youngsters not going into normal employment for a while; until much later than the present. Doing other useful things.'

In the final years of Jim Callaghan's Labour government, the country had been hit by an economic downturn that had seen the unemployment figure reach 1.4 million, some 5.3% of the workforce. Margaret Thatcher used this statistic to great effect for the Conservative Party's Labour Isn't Working campaign, famously captured on the nations hoardings alongside a picture of a lengthy dole queue. When she took office during 1979 the official unemployment total stood at 1,299,300; by January 1982 the advertisement could have read 'Nobody Is Working' as the new government's policies pushed the figure to 3 million.

Nowhere was hit harder than Liverpool, where the docks closed and the manufacturing sector shrunk 50% between 1972 and 1982, with the loss of 80,000 jobs. The situation is summed up by writer Jimmy McGovern who had been tasked with writing a CV for his brother: 'From 1976 it was this litany - Birds Eye, Bendix, Leyland, every one of them - reason for leaving - factory closed, factory closed, factory closed.' Fellow Liverpudlian Alan Bleasdale's seminal series *The Boys From The Blackstuff* (1982), a sequel to his *Play For Today*, would forever cement the city's battle against diminishing prospects, a theme continued in sitcoms like *Help* (1986) which followed the fortunes of a trio of nineteen-year-olds, whose view of life on the dole was significantly more upbeat, as was that of the Boswell family in Carla Lane's *Bread* (1986-1991) in which eldest brother Joey made claiming an art form and gave the city a reputation it has yet to shake off.

Liverpool writer Willy Russell's first play, *Keep Your Eyes Down*, was performed in December 1971 by the drama society of St. Catherine's College in Childwall where he was training to be a teacher. It looked at the problems facing a school leaver and was taken to Edinburgh during August of the following year where it was staged alongside two other Russell plays, *Playground* in which a group of school kids kidnap and eventually kill a teacher, and *Sam O'Shanker* – as a trio under the title *Blind Scouse*. *Keep Your Eyes Down* would later be re-worked to form the basis of **THE BOY WITH THE TRANSISTOR RADIO (1980)**, a 25-minute adaptation of which was broadcast by ITV at the beginning of 1980 as part of the channel's *The English Programme* series of wide-ranging dramas and documentaries intended as support materials for use in schools. In it, 16-year-old Terry (Simon Driver) appears as a music-obsessed youth on the cusp of leaving school who takes his careers advice from a fantastically optimistic local radio DJ, Float Jones, an optimism that is heavily at odds with the challenges that face him.

Comparatively, by this time he's one of the 'lucky ones' in that his father is lining him up a job at the warehouse in which he works. Terry though has other ideas: 'Warehouse? I'm not gonna work in a warehouse, am I Float? I'm gonna do somethin' like you. I'm gonna do somethin' good, somethin' that makes y' feel as good as the music does.' But, because like most of his class he's 'gonna walk out them gates as thick as when we came in', it's the warehouse where he finds himself. It's as mind-numbingly boring as he imagined, and to rub salt in his wounds, Float Jones constant optimism follows him across the warehouse floor from a large speaker. Two weeks in and he snaps, takes a hammer to the speaker and is 'let go'. Paid-up, less deductions for his act of vandalism, he buys a guitar tutorial and settles back on his bed and attempts his first chord, which he just about manages as the scene is superimposed with Sid Vicious performing 'My Way' from *The Great Rock n Roll Swindle* as the final credits roll.

However much John Lydon disliked *The Great Rock n Roll Swindle* and *Sid & Nancy*, he could at least take solace in the fact that they're not **RUDE BOY (1980)**, of which the first thing that comes to mind is how The Clash ever got involved in the project in the first place, with seemingly no one, including both directors, having a clue what they were making. On paper though the concept is promising; a document of The Clash in the studio and on tour with a fictional element exploring the socio-political climate of the time.

If as already determined, Punk in the UK would not have existed without The Sex Pistols, without the Pistols there also wouldn't have been The Clash, The Damned or Chelsea/Generation X. There was though London SS who, despite never quite getting beyond the rehearsal stage, would provide the basis of the bands whose existence would make Punk a 'scene'. The nucleus of that band was Mick Jones, Brian James, and Tony James. The trio first came across The Sex Pistols when Malcolm McLaren was touting for more bands to manage and they visited the band's Denmark Street rehearsal studio where, says Tony James, 'there were these guys there with really short hair. It was quite a shock. We thought the Dolls were revolutionary because they had long hair. We didn't realise that short hair could be used as a reaction to the excesses of rock n roll.' Glen Matlock recalls 'a bunch of guys with hair down their backs. They looked ridiculous. We were all laughing.'

McLaren never managed the band but a chance meeting at a gig brought them to the attention of Bernie Rhodes, an old friend of McLaren whose t-shirt designs, including 'You're Gonna Wake Up One Morning and Know Which Side of the Bed You've Been Lying On' were sold in SEX. In fact, Rhodes has been cited by Lydon as being instrumental in the final piece of the jigsaw without which the Pistols themselves would likely be as unknown now as they were when they first crossed paths with the soon-to-be Mr Rotten. It was 'Bernie Rhodes got me in the band' he told the Face in 1980, 'Malcolm hated my guts because of the way me and Sid used to take the piss out of him.' Then again, given the singer's antagonism towards his former manager, one might conclude that 'he would say that wouldn't he'.

Rhodes set London SS up with a rehearsal space under a cafe in Praed Street and a PA, which Steve Jones had stolen from backstage at the Mick Ronson/Ian Hunter gigs. Says Brian James: 'We rehearsed and rehearsed for about a year... but it never really got off the ground. We couldn't find a singer or drummer. When we did find a drummer [Rat Scabies], the others didn't want him so me and Rat went and formed The Damned.' When London SS folded Mick Jones went on to form The Clash with Paul Simonon, who, on the strength of his looks alone, had once been asked to try out as a singer. Tony James joined Chelsea, a band being put together by John Krevine of Acme Attractions, where he met Billy Idol and went on to form Generation X.

There may have been in place the beginnings of a burgeoning scene but it was one which presented a far from united front. A review of The Clash in August 1976 by Giovanni Dadoma in Sounds was a rave one, but it was one line in particular, that got up the nose of some in the opposite camp: 'I think they're the first band to come along who'll really frighten The Sex Pistols shitless.' Caroline Coon had also written that 'the atmosphere amongst the Punk bands on the circuit at the moment is positively cutthroat. Not only are they vying with each other, but they all secretly aspire to take Johnny Rotten down a peg or two.'

In fact, it was the Pistols who instead set about taking The Clash down a peg or two when the band was added to the Screen on the Green gig along with The Buzzcocks, of which Matlock says: 'It didn't do us any harm to have other bands of our sort supporting us.' The sound for The Clash that night was so bad that it earned them their famous Charles Shaar Murray review that suggested, 'they are the kind of garage band who should be speedily returned to their garage, preferably with the motor running.' When the Pistols took to the stage, the sound problems mysteriously vanished and the same writer remarked: 'the first 30 seconds of their set blew out all the boring amateurish, artsy-fartsy, mock-decadence that preceded it purely by virtue of its tautness, directness, and utter realism.' According to The Only Ones John Perry, such an attitude was par for the course: 'In England, the primary dynamic in Punk was exclusion. Sneer at everything that isn't in your gang. Scared little boys mostly. England has always been more competitive, less cooperative - a line back through the Stones of bands loving themselves and thinking everyone else shit. I don't mind that, to some extent I'm guilty.'

There's not a hint of middle-class Bromley about Brixton-born Ray Gange, the titular *Rude Boy*, who when cast was working in a record shop on Bond Street, regularly blasting 'Anarchy In The UK' from a loudspeaker out front, much to the disdain of the blue rinse brigade who would pass by. Which was very much the point. Through having friends in the Punk scene, he became a regular at the Roxy, the Vortex and other Punk haunts. It was at one such venue, a pub on Putney High Street where the Lurkers were playing (or maybe it was Wayne County - Gange's Special Brew consumption was not a device created solely for the film), that he spotted a familiar face sitting alone at a table and struck up a conversation. The face belonged to Joe Strummer who, living in nearby Regent's Park, became a regular visitor to the record shop. Another visitor to the shop was filmmaker David Mingay who told Gange that, with his partner Jack Hazan, he was making a film about The Clash. Gange told Mingay he knew the band and a couple of weeks later the director returned to the shop offering him a part in the film. Initially reluctant, with the encouragement of Strummer he eventually accepted and, he says, 'then it all became a little strange.'

The 'plot' of the film meant that Gange would become a roadie for the band on their 'On Parole' and 'Sort It Out' tours and to gain experience he spent two weeks on tour with the Subway Sect, also looked after by Bernie Rhodes. This experience taught him he'd have never made it as a roadie: 'Too much hard work for me... all that lifting and stuff' which would have meant putting down the ever-present can of Special Brew, and so, mostly, he didn't bother. Accepting the role also meant that he would have to leave the record shop, taking occasional shifts in a sex shop opposite to make ends meet - duly incorporated into the film.

Says Gange: 'Most of the people I knew at the time were like me, you know? That was the vibe then, it seemed to me at the time that nobody had a career plan or any motivation. The music was our world. There wasn't a world beyond that, and if there was we were just not interested. Kind of like a flat earth society! It was kind of like, "this is shit, that is shit, but we like this shit."' Which would explain why when in scenes where he was expected to improvise dialogue, usually with Strummer, it was a situation he was far from comfortable with. This was never more obvious than when the subject turned to politics, something he had no opinion on and so took the contrary view to whoever he was talking to: 'When the person opposite says something, what are you supposed to do? Just go "Oh yeah... I think you're absolutely right da de dah de dah kiss my arse?" We had to create dialogue and there are four geezers standing around you with expensive equipment so it's well ok, so what's obvious? Just create a counterpoint.' In one scene he refers to political Punk bands as 'left-wing wankers' but when asked to expand on this all he can offer is because 'it annoys me.' The directors were out of their depth when it came to drama, with all aspects of what little passes for a plot under-developed and far too much of the films running time spent on people doing absolutely nothing; driving, walking to and from buildings and cars (but not in the dynamic Alan Clarke sense).

As the only lead role apart from the band, Gange was right to be apprehensive and it should have been clear from the start that he was out of his depth. Had it been shot earlier the film would have had a ready-made roadie who would have fitted the role to a tee had he not fallen out with Mick Jones by telling him 'he needed a valet rather than a roadie' and began working exclusively with The Sex Pistols. The said roadie, Roadent, as is clear from his inability to remember much of those heady days, shared Gange's love of excess but, as seen from his appearance in *Punk In London* owned the personality and quick wit that would have served him well In Buld's documentary he says he was in prison 'for insurrectionary activities, expropriation of substances from other people, richer people. Stealing. Political activities (laughs). That's what the Angry Brigade man said in court.' According to Tony Parsons, Roadent: 'went along to see The Clash soon after his release from prison. At the time he was carrying a copy of 'Mein Kampf' around with him. Prison can mess with your head. Strummer in his usual manner of abrasive honesty straightened him out.'

Mythology aside, the prison sentence was actually just two weeks for non-payment of a fine, barely time to mess with your hair. Fellow Clash roadie and poster designer Sebastian Conran, son of the Habitat millionaire, says Roadent was 'intelligent. He probably had as much to do with the political background as anybody else.' In fact, about as far from Ray Gange, the film version at least, as you could get, which is why when some suggest that he inspired the *Rude Boy* character, he dismisses the rumour out of hand: 'definitely not. Ray Gange was his own person in that film. That's the real Ray Gange... The characterisation is pathetic and Ray Gange as a character is sorely in need of psychiatric help, rehabilitation and education.'

One for the road for Ray Gange in *Rude Boy*

The fifty minutes allotted to the band on stage are electrifying, but then how could they not be? The band was such a live presence that not even Mingay and Kazan could fuck that up. As for the rest; When the band was presented with the rough cut, they instructed the directors to cut it down to a simple 50-minute concert film. When their request was refused, the band removed any support.

Hazan had used similar techniques to those he uses in *Rude Boy* on his only previous outing, *A Bigger Splash* (1975), having filmed artist David Hockney for three years and mixing in fictionalised drama. The result sent the artist into a two-week clinical depression, and he tried to buy the negatives for £20,000 to destroy them. Mingay refused and the artist later came round. These days the film is revered for its candid look at a homosexual relationship but, like *Rude Boy*, remains best viewed with a remote control in hand in order to fast forward through its many tedious passages. Looking back, Hazan believes his form of not-quite-documentary 'reached a dead end' with *Rude Boy*. Adding 'I think it might have reached a dead-end before with *A Bigger Splash*. We shouldn't really have carried on in this way, and we did, and *Rude Boy* was the consequence.'

The film has its fans. When the film premiered in Berlin, as an official entry into the Berlin Film festival in February 1980, the band refused to attend, so road manager Johnny Green went along with fellow crew member Barry 'The Baker' Auguste. Says Green: 'I loved the film. I loved being able to sit back and watch The Clash perform without wondering what could go wrong. It overwhelmed me and it did the audience too. I couldn't understand why The Clash objected to the film. Mingay said, "I think Mick realises his film image is at contrast with his self-image." After the film, I walked down the aisle of the two thousand seater cinema with Mingay and the Baker and the audience burst into applause.'

In the NME, Neil Norman called it 'an innovative piece of cinematic art... a genuine cri de cœur for a generation already on the retreat.' The consensus though was that the band was right and that as a live document it is up there with the best - shame about the rest. Typical was Phil Sutcliffe in Sounds who said: 'it hovers uncomfortably between fiction and documentary in its narrative sections and it still feels flabby in parts despite the editing marathon it took to reduce it to its present dimensions. But the simple fact is it's a must for Clash lovers,' and The Guardian's Derek Malcolm who said 'musically, at least, the film is extraordinary... there could not be a better advertisement for them or their records.' The band's point of view finally saw fruition with the 2015 Collectors Edition DVD release and it's 'Just Play The Clash' option.

There's a sequence in *Rude Boy* of the fans lined up outside the Apollo in Glasgow that sums up the difference between the fans associated with The Clash and those we think of as following the Pistols - it's also largely a difference between those in the capital and those in the provinces. It shows the sort of kids that can be found in Jon King's 2000 novel 'Human Punk' which, says its author, 'presents Punk as social practice, deeply rooted in the "ordinary life" of "ordinary people." These kids don't - can't - dress in Vivienne Westwood's latest creations, in fact says one "We're not dressing much different to how we've always dressed, just shorter hair and straight legs. Suppose there's kids with safety pins, but that's more fashion."' These kids were ordinary people and needed a 'people's band', and The Clash seemed to fit the bill.

Beginning in the summer of 1977, 'Human Punk' tells the story of a fifteen-year-old Slough schoolboy, Joe Martin, and his friends, Dave, Chris, and Smiles, for whom there's a full year of school still to get through before they can 'earn decent money... and go to the sort of places we've only read about in the NME and Sounds. London venues like the Vortex and the Roxy, treat the girls to a film and a drink instead of shinning up the Odeon drainpipe the whole time.' The boys regularly skip lessons, swear at and taunt teachers and pupils alike, breaking rules wherever they can. Outside of school, they like to party - drinking, experimenting with drugs, fighting, joyriding and attending Punk gigs. 'They're putting into words what we're thinking' says Joe, 'It's like The Clash album. The songs on there sum up our lives. That LP was already inside us, waiting for someone to write it down.'

Another young Clash fan, actress Kathy Burke, used a chance meeting with her heroes as the basis for her episode of Sky's **LITTLE CRACKERS: BETTER THAN CHRISTMAS (2010)**. It's Kath's (Ami Metcalf) last day of school and in her Punk poster adorned bedroom she laces up her monkey boots and applies Germoline to the letters - THE CLASH - that she has carved into her arm; having one last dance to 'Oh Bondage Up Yours' before she leaves. Post exam, which she is not going to pass, it's off to the local shop for a packet of fags (which they won't sell her) and a copy of that weeks NME, the cover of which carries a tribute to the late Ian Curtis who she declares 'is nice looking' and 'he's from Manchester but I don't think that's why he killed himself because I've been to Manchester and it's a lot better than London. Posher.'

Hippies, Skinheads, Rastas, Punks & Disco Dancing Bowie Boot Boys

Ami Metcalf & Sam Palladio as the young Kathy Burke and Joe Strummer in *Kathy Burke's Little Cracker*

Upon leaving the shop, she has an OMG moment. There sat by the side of the road is The Clash. She knows she has to go over but doesn't know what to say. Her friend suggests asking for an autograph but 'that's not cool, they're Punks. They might tell me to F off or they might gob at me.' They don't of course, they're terribly nice and happily sign her NME, despite her intimating that she could sell it and make a few bob, with Joe also offering her some life changing advice. She didn't sell it. Says Burke: 'It's in a frame now, but it does piss me off when people come round and ask, "Oh, what auction did you get that from?"' Burke would leave her own unique mark on Punk cinema with roles in *Sid & Nancy* and the same director's spaghetti western parody *Straight To Hell* (1987) where she starred alongside Strummer himself.

The Farm's Peter Hooton was a young fan of The Clash who got backstage at gigs in Paris and found himself 'welcomed... like a long-lost brother. Mick Jones told me in later years that he had followed Mott The Hoople around in his youth and they had always treated him well so The Clash adopted the same philosophy. On the last night of the tour they wanted to go to a nightclub, so with 50 or more in the entourage, they wandered the streets of Paris until a club would let the whole lot of us in. A couple of the clubs said the band only, but the group insisted it was everyone or no one.'

Another who saw Joe Strummer's boys as the people's band, saying 'I almost feel like Punk was smaller than The Clash', was director Derrick Borte whose dream project was to film the story of a young kid discovering the band and finding his life changed, 'which' he says 'really happened to me.' Borte was in high school in America when he was handed a cassette of the band by a friend of which he says, 'within the first few minutes I had a realisation that was the music I was supposed to listen to.'

Borte made his dream come true in **LONDON TOWN (2016)**, a project which began way back in 2007 with producer Sofia Sondervan who was working at Sony (she gets a minor credit on Julian Temple's *Joe Strummer: The Future Is Unwritten* (2007)) with a remit to make films that incorporated the company's vast music catalogue. Following a Jennifer Lopez project and *Cadillac Records* (2008) with Beyonce, with the company owning the rights to The Clash back catalogue a film that could exploit that was an obvious port of call. They sought a screenplay from *Disco Pigs* (2001) director Kirsten Sheridan and her writing partner Sonya Gildea, though Sondervan called that 'a different script' to the one they went with, ostensibly a re-write by Matt Brown. The film eventually surfaced via Sondervan's own production company, Dutch Tilt.

The film begins with Willi Williams version of 'Armagideon Time', played over a background of turbulent images of the time, from riots, to National Front marches, to the Ayatollah and bin strikes, following which we see 14-year-old Shay Baker (Daniel Huttlestone) being picked on by a group of older lads. The Brutus flares, tank top, and gaudy shirt probably don't help. His day gets better when he receives a package from his absent mum, in London trying to make it as a singer, which contains a cassette of The Clash and the message that he should play it loud. He does, much to the annoyance of his part-time black cab driving and piano shop owning dad.

When he gets the chance to go to London to pick something up for his dad (oddly choosing to do so in his school uniform) he sits opposite a young Punkette, Vivian (Nell Williams), on the train who is playing the band on her Walkman and lets him listen. She's going to get tickets for a Clash gig and she suggests he goes too. When they pass a poster of the band, she tells him they're sexy. 'No wonder I can't get a girlfriend' he tells her. 'I thought it was my spots.' When they pass a group of National Front Skinheads as they head for Camden, he tells her he had assumed Punks were right wing. She puts him right: 'All you've got to do is listen to one of Strummer's lyrics, like 'white youth, black youth, better find another solution / Why don't you phone up Robin Hood and ask him for some wealth distribution'. It's about us all getting along. It's the rich that are killing us.' She also tells him he'd look good with black hair, 'like Strummer', a look he quickly adopts. In fact, though he soon has the bands debut album and a poster on his wall (which are recreations using the film version of the band), when Vivian played him the band on the train he didn't recognise them as the same band his mother had sent him a tape of and it is the girl rather than the music that appears the most life-changing.

On the day of the gig, his dad has an accident moving a piano and finds himself hospitalised for a few weeks meaning Shay is left looking after his young sister. Going to the gig once she's asleep, it erupts into violence when it is invaded by a gang of right-wing boneheads and Shay gets bashed by a copper, eventually returning home to find the house empty. Fortunately, his wandering sister has been taken in by a neighbour. With his dad still hospitalised, Vivian teaches him to drive and, on his 15th birthday, takes out his dad's cab to earn some money. So he will look old enough, Vivian dresses him as a woman when they realise that a fake moustache will not fool anyone. The final passenger of the night is none other than Joe Strummer (Jonathan Rhys Meyers) whom he impresses when he has to lose a police car that asks him to pull over, handing him a wad of cash. The night is rounded off nicely when Vivian sleeps with him.

Lightning strikes twice on the day of the Victoria Park Anti Nazi League Carnival when, after another run-in with Nazi boneheads, he finds himself arrested and sharing a cell with Strummer, giving the singer a lift home when they are released in the morning and getting to watch the band rehearse 'Clampdown'. With debts piling up and the cab getting repossessed, Shay hits on the idea of turning the failing piano shop into a rock shop, trading the stock for guitars and amps. To launch the new business, he hatches an ill-thought-out plan to have The Clash play at the launch - without telling them, though he does leave a flyer at their rehearsal room. Will Mr Strummer come through anyway and save the day? Suffice to say it's as predictable as it is unlikely.

Where *Kathy Burke's Little Cracker* was an unlikely but nevertheless true story, *London Town* is an urban fairy tale that stretches implausibility way beyond breaking point, but then that, says Borte, is the point: 'If Shay were telling his story today, this is the way he would tell it, but who knows what the reality of the situation was. At the same time, I heard over and over again from people as I was making the film that in London in 1979, Joe was my next-door neighbour, or Joe lived next door to my grandmother. Back then, you could have these random encounters in a way that's quite different from today. There's a possibility that in London at that time, you could have had a brush with one of your heroes that was real.'

Before release, the director suggested his film, 'is going to have a wide audience... I hope that people... that have some sort of experience with The Clash will see something that reminds them of their own history or maybe their own history of music changing their lives, whether that is The Clash or something else.' Later however, reacting to some critics not buying into the film's version of Strummer, he said, 'I wish the film was marketed as a kids film, for 13 to 15-year-olds, because that's what it is.' This is more in keeping with Sondervan's view of the film as 'a *Billy Elliot* style film set in the music world.'

It's hard to know who the target audience was for *London Town*. Anyone approaching the film from a nostalgic viewpoint will have to turn a blind eye to an array of factual inconsistencies and may find themselves unable to run with the implausible series of events on which the story hinges, whilst caring little for the coming-of-age drama at its heart which plays out with the genres usual conventions - a love scene in which the outwardly knowing Vivian admits that she too is an innocent, a falling out when it is revealed she is from a rich family (the horror) and the eventual reconciliation as a Mickey Rooney and Judy Garland for the Punk generation in order to 'put the show on right here' and save dad's business. The age-old fantasy of having one's idol coming to your rescue or becoming your friend will doubtless be as valid to current teenagers as it ever was, though I imagine the number of today's teens who would choose Joe Strummer as their fairy godmother is negligible.

Nell Williams and Daniel Huttlestone in *London Town*

Punk soon began to have an influence in the theatre via works by emerging playwrights like Barrie Keeffe and Tony Marchant. Keeffe had been in his early twenties during the birth of the Hippie movement but did not feel the need to adapt those times into drama: 'The Vietnam experience had an effect, of course, the feeling of horror and the rude awakening to the adult world. But I thought Paris in 1968 was totally unrelated to England. I could see no similarity at all. The different thing about England to most other countries in the world is the class structure. I could never see the students and the working class uniting in England - ever.'

In the early 1970s Keeffe was working as a journalist in the East End and it was the small battles faced by the local population that interested him most, in particular its dispossessed youth which he first addressed in *Gimme Shelter* a trio of one-act plays staged between 1975 and 1977 that did much to further the career of a young Phil Davis. **BARBARIANS** is a trilogy of similar length productions – *Killing Time*, *Abide With Me* and *In The City* – about three working-class youths, two of whom, Paul and Jan, are white, and one, Louis, who is black. Set against a backdrop of youth unemployment, football violence, troubles in Belfast and the Notting Hill Carnival, they were first performed as a trilogy at the Greenwich Theatre, London on 29th September 1977. The role of Jan was played by Karl Johnson, though it had been originated by Phil Davis, in *Abide With Me* at the Soho Poly Theatre Club in 1976 (with Johnson playing Paul), and Robert Glenister, in *Killing Time* at the National Youth Theatre in August 1977. The original Louis had been Elvis Payne, who had played Otis in *Sunshine On Brixton* (1976) and Joe in *Pressure* (1976), with the role taken a year later in *Killing Time* by Dotun Adebayo, now better known as a BBC Radio 5 Live presenter.

Notably, all six of these short plays begin and end with music. For *Gimme Shelter*, this is provided by Suzi Quatro, Showaddywaddy, Gary Glitter, Thunderclap Newman, The Beatles and the Stones. In *Barbarians* we get the music of The Clash, the Pistols and The Jam to signify three summers in the lives of the three young friends who are first seen, in *Killing Time*, as unemployed school leavers, desperate to avoid the sort of factory jobs they consider 'bint work'. The three youths spend an evening attempting to steal a left-hand drive Rover 3500 to order for Jan's infamous Uncle Harold, but eventually settle for nicking a large quantity of booze and some legs of ham. Louis is the only one of the three with any ambition, having taken a course in refrigeration, to the derision of Paul, who tells him, 'Trained for what? They just got you out of the way for a year, you prick.' At the end, Jan owns up to having taken a job at the tin factory after meeting his school careers officer in the dole queue.

By *Abide With Me*, all three have succumbed to the monotony of work at the tin factory, spending their wages on following Manchester United home and away which, being from Lewisham, means away. 'Twenty odd times I've been to Manchester this year,' moans one. But this loyalty still can't get them Wembley tickets. Louis, still looking for a way out, has joined the army cadets and is encouraging Jan to do likewise. The play takes place outside Wembley Stadium on the afternoon of the 1977 FA Cup Final between Manchester United and Southampton, where the trio wait hopefully for Uncle Harold to turn up with tickets he has promised.

The wait allows for the lads to ponder the lot of the football fan: 'Standing in the train, five hours.. eight hours... standing in wet clothes, no fucking food on the train. Standing up in the rain on the terraces, like cattle. No roof to keep the rain off... Lavatories stinking like cesspits. Warm beer in paper cups... no food at the grounds... herded about by the cops. No wonder they call us animals. That's how they fucking treat us.'

And why they put up with it: 'There was this boy I used to know... a student at the factory one summer... Junkie... Said it happened at the Black Lion... Lots of pushers there... They pumped him with the stuff. Held him down and shot it into him and then, later, after he'd got hooked, they wouldn't always sell him it, 'cause they kept putting up the price. And he said, "Cunts, they got me hooked an' then said no." Bloody football clubs. Get you hooked. Get you boiling, get the fever rushing through you - all of them, build it up, get a head of steam and then when it explodes, wash their hands with you, call you animals, say piss off we don't want you. An' they know they've got you hooked. That you can't do without them. That seems more of a crime to me than the crimes we're supposed to do.'

The tickets, unsurprisingly, never materialise and their team lose, but for the increasingly angry Paul all is not lost: 'They'll barricade the windows, the pubs'll lock their doors, the lights will go off in the shops and the police will line the pavements white with fear... Cops hats'll bobble like decorations on a windy promenade. The air will be heavy with shouts and yells and the smashing of glass... No one will ignore us. We will not be ignored. They'll talk about us, write about us, hate us.'

Elvis Payne, Phil Davis and Karl Johnson are *Barbarians*

In *In The City*, Louis has got a job in refrigeration that comes with his own van and he's been out of touch with his old friends until he bumps into them at the Notting Hill Carnival, where Paul and Jan have arranged to meet two girls from an ad Paul has placed in the Time Out classified section. For Jan, it's also the last night before a posting to Belfast with the army. Paul has been running security for the National Front, and his racism boils over when Louis laughs at the fact they've used a lonely hearts service.

'He was one of us a year ago. Now pissed off, all niggers together. Piss off white men. That's nice isn't it, after all I've done for him. There's two kinds of Spades I hate. Spades who act like they ain't Spades and Spades who are cocky because they are Spades,' he says before giving his old friend a severe kicking and some even stronger racial abuse. 'Black shit. Flash nigger, you've made it boy, flash nigger,' he yells as he encourages a reluctant Jan to join in and get arrested, thereby getting him out of going to Northern Ireland.

Abide With Me was dramatised by Granada in 1978, with Karl Johnson, Michael Deeks and Ashley Barker. This comprised the recording of a specially staged performance of the play at the University Theatre in Manchester after the television company had failed to agree terms with The Royal Exchange, produced by Michael Cox and directed by Derek Lister. The TV drama proved surprisingly controversial and had to face a preview screening for regulatory body the IBA who passed it by a majority verdict. The programme even made the front page of the Daily Mirror with the headline 'FOUL! The soccer scenes that scared off ITV,' where the then Manchester United chairman, Louis Edwards, was amongst those quoted venting their disapproval.

Says Keeffe: 'On the same front page was a photo of The Sex Pistols Johnny Rotten accompanying some story about his sore throat infection. On the bus going to get her perm for Christmas my mum saw my story and photo of Johnny Rotten making a V-sign, thought it was me and got off the bus.' Re-titled *Champions* to avoid being mistaken for a religious programme (yes really!), it went out at 11 p.m. on the 12th of March. A poll of 1000 adults taken the next day found 79% in favour of its screening but 45% condemned the bad language. Surprisingly, or not depending on one's outlook, the role of Louis, though written as black, was cast with a white actor. Whilst the race of the character was not specified in this section of Keeffe's trilogy, given the paucity of decent roles for black actors the decision by the production seems somewhat suspect.

Losing much of its impact on the small screen, and divorced from the beginning and end, the TV version was not well received with the Birmingham Post saying *Champions* 'was not shocking, violent or even likely to make Bobby Robson reach for his flame-thrower. It was just boring,' adding that the story was 'extremely thin' and that 'some points were more entertainingly made ten years ago by *Zigger Zagger*.'

Barbarians has been accused of being pessimistic but Keeffe 'thought it was very optimistic. The wall was there, but there was a way to get through it. Next time they would find a more devious way of getting through to the other side. That is the lesson they learned from that brutality. They didn't accept anything, they challenged those who rejected them, and that's very optimistic I think.'

Overall, reviews were excellent with the Spectator saying: 'Except for the absence of religion, *Barbarians* is like a living demonstration of Wilhelm Reich's analysis of the conditions that breed fascism, in his 1933 pamphlet 'What Is Class Consciousness?' It's all there — the poverty, the unemployment, the sex repression and fierce puritanism, the machismo, the sentimental camaraderie, the appeal of the uniform, and the view of football as a political opium'. Though finding Keeffe 'perhaps too keen to hammer his points home,' they concluded that 'his real achievement has been to write a political parable in concrete detail, all the more forceful for being confined to the limited consciousness of his characters.'

In 2006 Keeffe revisited his three characters with Ciaran Owens, Joseph Stamp and Robert Bertrand in the roles of Paul, Jan and Louis for the 50th anniversary of the National Youth Theatre with a new play, *Still Killing Time*, where on the eve of the Queen's Silver Jubilee in 1977 they head to Buckingham Palace to partake in some bearskin baiting. *Barbarians* itself was revived for Royal Jubilee year at the Tooting Arts Club in 2012, fittingly staged in a defunct Wandsworth Youth Enterprise Centre, and again by the same company in 2015 at the former Central St Martins College of Art, venue for the first Sex Pistols performance to an audience of about twenty in November 1975. Later that same year a completely different production was staged at the Young Vic which the Guardian called '*A Clockwork Orange* in a more desperate key; *Waiting for Godot* recomposed to a soundtrack of furious Punk' but the Telegraph thought 'never quite cuts through the play's many culturally specific pillars to make it universal. What made Louis, Jan and Paul angry then, isn't necessarily what is making young people angry today. It feels very much rooted – strikes, race riots, racist comedians – in 1977.' Interestingly, both revivals had the three protagonists as Skinheads whereas the original production, with costume design by Voytek, best known for Roman Polanski's *Cul-de-Sac* (1966), had a more Punk look.

The misfortunes of three unemployed school leavers with little in the way of prospects was also the subject of two short plays, *London Calling* and *Dealt With*, written by a then 21-year-old Tony Marchant. They are Saf (John Fowler), Chris (Jamie Foreman) and Pimple (Martin Murphy) and the two plays were first presented together as **THICK AS THIEVES** at the Theatre Royal in November 1981, directed by Adrian Shergold.

In *London Calling*, which had appeared at the same venue in June, Saff and Paul are hiding out on a piece of waste ground, walled in by sheets of corrugated iron. It's 'the sort of place', says Saff, 'where The Clash used to have their picture taken'. They have with them a stolen briefcase, taken from a parked car. Unfortunately, the duo was interrupted in the act by a policeman who had been left unconscious on the pavement, 'or fucking dead' worries Paul, who had delivered the blow.

Tense and brooding with a fondness for the Jam, Paul takes everything seriously but Saff is more matter-of-fact and sees everything as a bit of a laugh: 'First offence – for you, anyway. Probation Officer with big tits, hairdo, and a trench mac. About 40 – one of the middle-class women with a guilty conscience... We can tell her how deprived we are. Never been shown no affection or nothing... They don't put you away no more – they got these new ideas. You have to spend so many hours doing something for the community – like decorating old people's homes, doing gardening, sweeping up leaves in the park... Better than doing cross-country runs around some Borstal in Slough or wanking yourself silly in a remand centre for two months.'

Containing plans for a new Dockland development, comprising an art gallery, a hotel, and shops, it's hardly the crime of the century. 'Can't understand why they wanna build a hotel there, can you? Bit like having a wine bar in the middle of a cemetery' says Saff. 'Might be some jobs going there though' he adds hopefully.

They are joined by Pimple. Where Saff and Paul are thieves, Pimple is thick, describing himself as 'a Skinhead but I ain't had me hair cut yet. I'm going to try and get a pair of Dr Martens for me birthday.' He's also a racist, having recently been recruited for the British

Michael Kelly and Robert Glenister are just *Killing Time*

Movement by a bloke who has been going door-to-door around the flats where the boys live: 'He was saying how we ain't a pure race no more, this country's getting swamped by Pakis and spades... He give us a badge each with a Union Jack and a dragon on it. He says the blacks have got all the white people's jobs. Ought to make 'em sorry they ever came here. Our duty, he reckons.'

Saff and Paul are initially mocking, but Saff changes his tune when Pimple suggests 'Bloke says he might be able to pay us - that won't be dumb. And we're all out of work ain't we - look at all the coons that got jobs on London Transport. That's proof innit?'

Dealt With opens with Pimple painting a wall as part of a youth training scheme, adding 'Wogs Out' as a personal touch as Saff appears out of nowhere, initially startling him. 'At the moment I'm learning how to paint walls. Getting training like. I'm becoming sort of qualified in painting walls. At the end of it all I'm going to get a certificate - to say I've got experience' he says with a sense of pride. He's supposed to be learning how to drive a forklift, 'so the Jobcentre said, anyway. Ain't happened yet though... Last two months, I've just been sweeping up in the yard and breaking up tea chests.' When Saff suggests it's a 'bit of a wank, innit?', he replies, 'It is when I have to clean the bloke's car, run round to the shops and get sandwiches for everybody. Jobcentre didn't say I'd be doing that when I came here.'

Saff is wearing Borstal clothes, having left without permission, and he's also brought along fellow escapee Roy, who happens to be black. They're looking for Paul, who Saff is hoping can help them out with a change of clothes and somewhere to lie low for a while. When Paul arrives he is suited up, having come straight from an unsuccessful job interview and suggests they might be able to get some quick cash by robbing the office he's just come from: 'Where I got shit on but couldn't smell nothing - cos it's all done with smiles and hints.'

Ned Chailett at the Times liked the play but was cautious with his praise, saying: 'Marchant is young and still feeling his way... he is excessively verbal... they talk too much about too many selected subjects.' In the Guardian Nicholas de Jongh suggested that despite being 'less concerned with any dramatic development than character sketches' for the 21-year-old Wapping writer it 'could be the beginning of a useful theatrical career.' Instead, Marchant found his home on the small screen but not before penning *The Lucky Ones*, performed at the Theatre Royal by a cast including Phil Daniels and Perry Benson. Set in the basement of a City stockbroker, this time Marchant dealt with the pressure to conform on four of the 'lucky ones' who manage to find a job. The leather jacketed Daniels leads a mini revolt when the four are press ganged into acting as waiters at their firm's anniversary party. Marchant returned to the subject of Punk in the television movie *Different For Girls* (1996), a romance between a 34-year-old man who still lives like the Punk obsessed teenager he was back in 1976 and a post-operative transsexual.

Another up-and-coming playwright, Stephen Poliakoff wrote a couple of plays about youth, *Hitting Town* and *City Sugar* in 1975 just before the Punk explosion, both of which were adapted for television. 'Punk' says Poliakoff, 'was just around the corner, it was literally about a year later when Punk exploded... the world was still serenely worshipping the sound of the Bay City Rollers. The mood was in the air, this nervy anger and nihilism.'

His **BLOODY KIDS (1979)** was written purely for TV and features a group of Punks led by Gary Holton. Directed by Stephen Frears, the film opens after dark in Southend where parka clad 11-year-old Leo Turner (Richard Thomas) wanders across the scene of a serious road traffic accident where the crowds and the media are out in force. With the police busy keeping order, Leo helps himself to an Inspector's hat from an unattended police car, taking it to school the next day to show his friend Mike (Peter Clark). Mike would like the hat and Leo offers him the chance to own it: 'Mike, how would you like to kill me at the match on Saturday? I don't mean really kill me, of course. As a joke. You and me, outside the match, have a fight, it'll look like we're tearing each other to bits like you're trying to kill me. And they'll all believe it, get really worked up. But you won't touch me at all; like the wrestling on the telly. I'll give you the hat if you do it... You drop the penknife and run. The police will come and question me, and then they'll find out it's all a joke.' 'Won't they be angry, asks Mike?' 'They haven't got the time,' Leo reassures him, adding, 'We're too young, you see. We can do anything.'

Come the big day, Leo pushes the knife into himself and is whisked off to the hospital where he wastes no time in giving Mike's name to the police. 'He's a bit weird... aggressive. He can frighten you sometimes. He suddenly changes, his eyes sort of change colour. He talks about attacking people, how he likes the idea of being on the run. Sometimes he talks about killing people. You should also look under his bed, he's got some very weird things there.'

Hippies, Skinheads, Rastas, Punks & Disco Dancing Bowie Boot Boys

Mike meanwhile bumps into some older youths - borderline Punks led by Ken (Holton) who take him to a disco run by Mel Smith. When the police arrive, looking for 'an 11-year-old child', they sneak him out, proceeding to rampage through a shopping centre where Ken throws a bin through a TV shop window. Much of what follows is largely against Mike's wishes. He's taken for a joyride in a stolen car and then into a restaurant where Ken tells him 'I'm gonna get everything I want here for a quid.' Acting like a loud, brash rock star he orders and then leaves Mike alone until he too eventually sneaks out. When Mike jumps onto a night bus full of unruly Punks, Ken follows in a car. When the bus stops and the driver orders everyone off, Ken climbs onto the roof before jumping off and landing with an awkward thud from which he presumably cannot get up. We next see him being wheeled into the hospital on a trolley when Mike finally meets back up with Leo in hospital.

The joke has worn somewhat thin for Mike, who is assured by his 'friend' that 'You'll never forget this night. The most important night of your life.' He has one more grand gesture to make, setting off the fire alarm as they both do a runner. In the lift going down, they get into a fight before exiting in the foyer to the chaos they've created - lighting up a couple of cigarettes as they stare blankly into the distance.

In the film's lead roles, both youngsters perfectly convey the detached listlessness of their characters with Thomas especially unsettling, hinting that there might be something disturbing lying not too far beneath the surface. Despite this Clark went on to just a handful of small TV roles and *Bloody Kids* remained the only credit on Thomas's CV. In a stand-out performance, it's hard to ignore Gary Holton, who died of an overdose in 1985 at just 33, who makes Ken mercurial and menacing in equal measure. After spending two years with a touring company of *Hair*, Holton fronted the heavy metal/Glam/proto-Punk band The Heavy Metal Kids from 1974 to 1977. His Punk credentials include standing in for Dave Vanian on The Damned's tour of Scotland in December 1978, and teaming with The Boys' Casino Steel (another hard drinker) to Punk up and have hits with, in Norway at least, country tunes such as Kenny Rogers 'Ruby' - releasing three albums. His fast-living attitude sometimes got in the way of career progression. When AC/DC's Bon Scott died from alcohol abuse, Holton was considered a shoo-in as a replacement until he arrived at the audition with a crate of whiskey. Not surprisingly the surviving members weren't looking for another alcoholic to front their band.

Derrick O'Connor as Detective Ritchie, tasked with taking a statement from Ken in hospital, was not first actor cast in the role, but just a few days into filming, first choice, Richard Beckinsale died from heart failure. Some footage remains and appeared in the TV tribute *The Unforgettable Richard Beckinsale* (2000), whilst the actor, unrecognisable, appears in some long shots.

The production has pedigree running through it like a stick of Southend rock. As well as a first screenplay from Stephen Poliakoff, there's director Frears, producer Barry Hanson, and cinematographer

Chris Menges. Amongst the smaller roles, Daniel Peacock, Jesse Birdsall, Gary Olsen and Gwyneth Strong are amongst the Punks, whilst other soon-to-be-famous faces include Brenda Fricker and Roger Lloyd Pack.

The film was not particularly well received with the Daily Mirror saying: 'Everyone... seems confused as to what they should be doing. And I'm not surprised, because this disjointed tale... has a sorry bunch of characters spouting stupid lines and wrestling with a ridiculous plot. Avoid this shockingly bad '70s film at all costs'. Clive James suggested: 'Youths with boiled-potato faces looked even worse for having their features bleached out by lights aimed from the floor. "I jest remembered sunning," they mumbled, stabbing each other. A nice boy was tempted into trouble by a nasty boy. Large themes might or might not have been touched upon it was too dark to tell.'

There were exceptions though. Sight & Sound called it: 'quite simply the best television movie I've seen,' and for the Guardian, it was: 'a marvellous helter-

Leo Turner and Peter Clark are *Bloody Kids*

skelter down the seven circles of Saturday Night Hell.' The Observer, when the film finally received a cinema outing, called it: 'a deeply disturbing portrait of modern urban life and a generation of morally numbed youth fed on the TV images of violence that are constantly to be seen in the background all the way through the picture.' Best of all, Frears told the Guardian: 'You know what really pleased me? The fact that Johnny Rotten liked one of my television things. I got an enormous kick out of doing *Bloody Kids*. It was cocky, noisy, aggressive and energetic. I often get offered material that is more fragile and complex than I might wish.'

Poliakoff also passed comment on the remnants of Punk in that same year's **AMERICAN DAYS** which premiered on the stage of the ICA with Phil Daniels, Toyah Wilcox and Caroline Embling as three would be recording artistes hoping to impress Jack Elliot, Antony Sher and Mel Smith in the listening room of a multinational record company's London offices.

Poliakoff's chief memory of writing the play was of Thatcher winning the election in the middle of the first act: 'In hindsight the play seems to encapsulate some of the values of the eighties. The hard-faced kids staring into the future with shrewd commercial eyes, the increasingly ephemeral nature of nearly everything, the importance of fashion and style, of hype, of surfaces and image.' With its three-man panel of two studio executives and a past-his-best rock star the set-up also predicts the *Pop Idol* type TV talent show with Sherman (Anthony Sher) as a prototype Simon Cowell.

Orange haired Tallulah (Toyah) is a Toyah/Hazel O'Connor type and Gary (Phil Daniels) could well be the same mercurial character that Gary Holton played in *Bloody Kids*. Tallulah's Punk credentials run no deeper than her hair dye, but Gary has the knowing swagger and the arrogance to go with it. If there was anything of substance behind this front, he wouldn't be in this situation in the first place.

He also wants to perform his own material but Sherman (Sher) has other ideas for whoever becomes his next protege: 'You want to sing songs that are "relevant"... the social angle... the lay of the Blacks category. That is what you want to do. I saw a group somewhere, in some city, singing an anti-fascist song, and in the middle they completely forgot what they were singing about and started strutting around on stage masturbating with their microphones, thrusting their pelvis out. That's how much they were concentrating. Two lots of twins they were, with very pale baby-like faces. They were almost interesting.'

'There isn't a market, can't you realise that. One song about the rights of the blacks may sell, or about being a happy gay, but look at the sales of the next one! - even by the very same artist, we have to throw millions away, fill pot holes with them, give them to the Salvation Army! The kids don't want it. There's no public demand for protest material.' Sadly, the villain of the piece, who goes for the less interesting, less talented but more flexible Lorraine (Embling), is right.

Phil Daniels, Caroline Embling and Toyah in *American Days*

That Daniels as Gary should mark his rejection by running amok and vandalising the room almost went without saying having become the go to young actor for a spot of vandalism after roles in *Class Enemy* and the TV adaptation of Graham Greene's *The Destructors* (1975). He had by this time become quite adept and according to lighting technician John Schwiller: 'Phil did something different each night. I jokingly suggested he tip Tony Sher's coffee in to the large fish tank. To my horror, he actually did that. I think the fish were okay.'

*

As well as unemployment, in 1979 the country was also at the mercy of rampant inflation and wage packets were struggling to keep pace with steeply rising prices, forcing increasingly militant action from the Unions which had led to the Winter of Discontent and helped Margaret Thatcher into Downing Street. Picket lines outside hospitals and piles of rubbish in the street because of strikes by refuse workers were one thing but the prospect of that also including corpses when gravediggers went on unofficial strike in the north-west was another. With the early months of 1979 also hit by blizzards, which blanketed the country in deep snow, there really was a feeling of despondency permeating the nation.

All of which made it the ideal time for a television adaptation of John Rowe Townsend's 1975 novel 'Noah's Castle' which was skilfully adapted by Nick McCarty, writer of the much-loved *The Siege of Golden Hill* (1975). The book envisages a near future where the Punk look seems to have become the standard dress of the packs of rioting youths who raid government supplies in a country where a combination of unemployment and hyperinflation has brought about almost total economic collapse. This is no place for brightly coloured Mohawks or Vivienne Westwood pirate outfits.

In the seven-part series **NOAH'S CASTLE (1980)**, ex-soldier Mr Mortimer looks after number one, moving his family to a large mansion in the countryside where, away from prying eyes, he can stockpile enough food to ride out the economic storm. As an old-school patriarch, the rest of the Mortimer family, put upon wife, daughter and two sons, are given little or no say in the proceedings. Younger son, the Generation X t-shirt wearing Geoff (Marcus Francis), is happy to serve as his father's number 2, but Barrie (Simon Gipps Kent) and Nessie (Annette Ekblom) are torn by their compassion for those having to go without.

Nessie is also the subject of romantic interest for two very different 'activists', the altruistic Cliff (Christopher Fairbank) who runs a distribution warehouse delivering food to the needy, and Terry (Alun Lewis) who believes in a more radical, revolutionary means of opposing the status quo and leads raids on government warehouses.

There's also Mr Mortimer's boss, the lecherous Mr Gerald who moves in and more or less expects the wife and daughter to be his slaves – sex slave in the case of Nessie despite being old enough to be her grandfather. Far more dangerous however is black marketeer Vince Holloway (Mike Reed) who with the aid of his young son (a pre *Grange Hill* Lee MacDonald) has his sights set on Noah's Castle.

Hippies, Skinheads, Rastas, Punks & Disco Dancing Bowie Boot Boys

I Am A Poseur
(Styrene)

These latter-day not-quite-Punks were the intended audience for **BREAKING GLASS (1980)**. Released into cinemas on August Bank Holiday 1980, in between *Rude Boy* and *The Great Rock 'n' Roll Swindle*, the press material promised 'a dramatic street-level look at modern youth... inspired by the current and volatile explosive trend in rock music.' Unfortunately, by the time of the film's release, the 'volatile and explosive trend' had largely passed by; late, like the film's star Hazel O'Connor herself, to the party, having spent much of her teenage years on a globe-trotting adventure through Paris, Amsterdam, Morocco and even Beirut that had taken in a teen marriage to a Polish cellist, erotic dancing and cabaret, soft porn movie acting and a terrifying rape in Marrakesh.

Back in the UK her brother Neil's band The Flys had by late 1977 issued a self-released EP, 'Bunch Of Five', and been snapped up by EMI in the major label Punk signing frenzy. O'Connor began acquainting herself with what remained of the scene's 'faces' who congregated around places like the James Street quasi-squat in Covent Garden, conveniently situated opposite the offices of Sounds music paper. These included future Pretender Chrissie Hynde, occasional Sounds writer Stephen Lavers, credited alongside the likes of the Pistols, The Clash, Andy Czezowski, Caroline Coon and other better-known movers and shakers in Sniffing Glue's Christmas 1976 list of 'good things'. It was Lavers, credited in *Breaking Glass* as a consultant, who suggested O'Connor should be tried out for a part in the film.

The writer and director was the 35-year-old Brian Gibson who had made a huge impact with the ground-breaking drama-documentary *Joey* (1974), broadcast as part of BBCs *Horizon*, the story of an intelligent young man with Cerebral Palsy who had been abandoned by the authorities into a mental hospital following the death of his mother because no one could understand him. A further drama-documentary for the *Horizon* series, *The Billion Dollar Bubble* (1978) about a 2 billion dollar insurance fraud and starring James Wood was followed by two highly regarded BBC *Play For Today*'s, Dennis Potter's *Blue Remembered Hills* (1979) and *Dinner At The Sporting Club* (1978) starring John Thaw. This, and doubtless the success of Howard Schulman's television series *Rock Follies* (1976), had helped land the director a £1.5 million budget for a big screen 'new wave' musical from producers Davina Belling and Clive Parsons with backing from Goldcrest's Jake Eberts, at the time flush with the success of their cinema version of *Scum* (1979). The concept of the rise and fall of a rock singer was hardly groundbreaking, having been done with David Essex in *Stardust* (1973) and, even more recently, Bette Midler in the fictionalised Janis Joplin story *The Rose* (1979), though the success of the latter would have done no harm with securing the funding from United Artists for a British version.

Initially, *Breaking Glass* was to star a male protagonist and the producers were searching for a singer with sufficient acting chops to pull it off. O'Connor had by that time signed a £1, one single contract with the small-time Albion Records. When standing in for the company's receptionist she answered a call about the possibility of her trying out for a small role in the film; soon after finding herself seated alongside Toyah Wilcox in the waiting room for auditions. O'Connor read for three parts and, like most people, thought the script was nothing to get excited about but, with a recording career that looked like it was going nowhere fast, she was grateful for the work and any exposure it might bring her.

Breaking Glass is generally dismissed, such as by Chris Barber in the book on Punk cinema 'No Focus', who calls it a 'shabby and silly British youth-sploitation movie' and suggests it was a pity the film's Nazi Skinheads 'didn't destroy the entire film set,' The film nevertheless provides an interesting insight into the late 1970s London music scene and some of its less well known behind-the-scenes protagonists.

O'Connor had approached the Albion Agency, run by co-directors Dai Davies and Derek Savage, early in 1978 to secure a live work and management deal. Davies had worked as a publicist for David Bowie during his 'Ziggy Stardust' period and, looking to move into management, had taken on Ducks Deluxe, largely thought of as one of the originators of 'Pub Rock' before the circuit was properly in place and began the process of taking progressive rock back to its roots in the years preceding Punk. Albion had started life as a booking agency and publisher in 1975 when, realising that by controlling a group of venues in the capital, they could cut out the need for up-and-

Phil Daniels & Hazel O'Connor join forces

coming bands to travel up and down the country to hone their craft. The oil crisis was causing petrol prices to spiral out of control and with the press being based in London anyway, bands could get the exposure they were seeking and make an at least meagre living by playing regularly around the various small venues. Starting with the Nashville, the Agency gradually increased its reach by taking over the contracts for other pub venues such as the Red Cow in Hammersmith, Islington's Hope & Anchor, the Newland Tavern in Putney and the Rock Garden in Covent Garden.

Though both the business and the scene it helped create grew, it was far from a cash cow, with Monday to Wednesday gigs being mainly free admission and those on Thursday to Saturday only being able to charge about 75p. But by the time Punk arrived, Albion was high on the calling list of every band, having as they did a monopoly on many smaller venues. One such band was The Stranglers who signed a management and publishing deal with the company on the promise of an almost continual run of gigs at the agency's venues which the band believed would enable them to build up a following and secure a major record deal - which eventually happened via United Artists. A similar opportunity was afforded 999 who likewise landed a UA contract.

The success of Stiff Records brought about a change in policy. Stiff owner Dave Robinson had managed the band Brinsley Schwarz at the same time Davies had managed Ducks Deluxe and the two had worked together in the past and aware of his friends success in the record business, a deal was made with United Artists which provided Albion with their own label and a recording and publicity budget in return for a percentage of the profits. A solo album from Brinsley Schwarz's Ian Gomm, 'Summer Holiday' had spawned a top twenty single in the US but little else and with Hazel O'Connor picking up a couple of promising live reviews in Sounds and Melody Maker and the prospect of additional publicity from a small part in a high profile film, Albion were finally persuaded to give the singer the longer-term publishing contract she had been pushing for, along with a £2,080 advance, paid at £40 a week. The record contract they offered her contained no advance and a payment of £2000 on delivery of her first album. Against her lawyer's advice, with royalty rates at less than half of what she might expect, she signed on the dotted line. The publishing deal was equally poor.

The enormity of her actions would soon become clear when just weeks later she received the news that the *Breaking Glass* producers had switched the gender of its lead and the role was to be decided between her and Lene Lovich, the final choice ultimately depending on their live abilities. O'Connor won and was soon given full soundtrack duties. Howard Schulman's original script was also jettisoned for a new one by Gibson. The change in screenwriter was probably a godsend on the evidence of the third episode of the second series of **ROCK FOLLIES OF 1977: THE HYPE**, where Punk - or at least a very broad caricature - inevitably reared its head. With a new single out, and on tour in Birmingham, the Little Ladies discover that their gig is at a Punk venue called the Aggro Club, more suited to their support band Zero who the promoter Charlie Chime (Karl Johnson) says are 'gonna be monster. They're absolutely amazing, they destroy audiences.' He was especially impressed the previous week in Sheffield when the band had been chatted up by a posh bird and one of them peed on her leg. The band's lyrics, 'We don't believe in queers/We don't believe in wogs', prove otherwise. Penny Borden (Gillian Rind), a (fictitious) writer for the NME, after seeing Zero, doesn't even bother with the Little Ladies, thus the NME review the band was counting on is instead all about Zero's 'metaphysical Punk.'

They also discover that their single is not in the shops, which brings about the following excruciating exchange:

Borden: 'This is your problem, your words and music aren't basic enough.'

Little Ladies manager Harry Moon (Derek Thompson): 'What's wrong with interesting words and intelligent harmonies?'

Borden: 'Intelligence is a cop-out… Rock should be basic like the sound of a football terrace'

Anna (Charlotte Cornwell): 'But rock can also analyse what the sound's about, deprivation, frustration. What I mean is the difference between being nihilistic and analysing nihilism.'

Borden: 'Ah, analysis isn't from the terraces.'

Gibson, having little insight into the workings of the music industry himself, crafted his new *Breaking Glass* script from O'Connor's own experiences. One important facet of this was that when in need of management, O'Connor turned to another of the crowd from the Covent Garden Punk scene, Alan Edwards who had started his own PR business in 1977 from his Covent Garden squat doing work for Albion on behalf of The Stranglers, and who is the basis for the character of Danny (Phil Daniels, top-billed ahead of the unknown O'Connor).

At the time of filming Daniels had just released his own album on RCA, 'Phil Daniels + The Cross', with a line-up that included fellow *Breaking Glass* actor Peter Hugo Daley on drums. Only it wasn't exactly setting the music world alight, and he admits to being: 'A bit resentful of the fact that Hazel O'Connor's music was getting all the attention. Everybody was singing her praises and not mine, and there I was playing the manager in the film. Don't get me wrong, I enjoyed doing the film, and it was a very good part, but at that point, it felt quite strange for me to be working in a fictional setting where I was surrounded by the music industry when all I wanted to be was a performer.' The film helped put the actor in the musical spotlight when Edwards became his co-manager and got him a gig standing in for Hugh Cornwell with The Stranglers when the singer was jailed on drugs charges. With two concerts booked at Finsbury Park's Rainbow at the beginning of April 1980, he became one of a number of guest vocalists along with Toyah, Ian Dury, and Hazel O'Connor, performing two songs - 'Dead Los Angeles' and 'Toiler on the Sea' - with the band.

Breaking Glass opens with Kate (O'Connor) on a tube train liberally placing stickers throughout the carriages before being seen in a back street near London's Rainbow Theatre, putting up posters for an upcoming gig. Inside the Rainbow for a concert is Danny who is on the bottom rung of the business, buying for the aptly named Overlord Records hundreds of copies of their singles from chart return shops in order to boost their chart positions. His attempts at networking backstage get him thrown out by security. Striking up a conversation with Kate outside he goes along to her next gig and gradually begins managing her, the first act of which is to sack her guitarists, replacing the bass player with Dave (Gary Tibbs - Adam & the Ants, Roxy Music, Vibrators), but retaining the 'mental' Mick (Peter-Hugo Daly) on drums. The replacement of lead guitarist Gary Holton with *Quadrophenia*'s Mark Wingett as Tony and the addition the drug-addicted and partially deaf Ken (Jonathan Pryce) seem less inspired.

It is in this period, the first two-thirds, that the film excels as the band hone their act in front of a hundred half pissed and often disinterested punters in numerous public bars, a circuit where only the strong survive. This section culminates with the band, newly signed to Overlord Records after Danny uses his knowledge of the company's chart rigging for leverage, playing a Rock Against 1984 free festival under the Westway which is invaded by a couple of hundred neo-Nazi boneheads, resulting in a youth being stabbed, screaming out just inches from Kate's face and sending the already troubled chanteuse into a downward spiral.

Gary's Holton and Tibbs, Peter Hugo Daley, Jim Carver from *The Bill*, Rat Scabies (over), and a whole lot more in *Breaking Glass*

The band begin with a Punk aesthetic that is gradually lost, first via the introduction of 'better' musicians and then by drugs and record company manipulation that take the music in a different and, ultimately, more commercial direction with tracks like 'Will You', complete with OTT music video - 'I want a forest of neon tubes' demands creepy producer Woods (Jon Finch) - and 'Eighth Day', both of which also propelled the real Hazel O'Connor into the top ten. With Danny elbowed out by the record company executives and Mick and Ken leaving, 'Eighth Day' provides the movie's final musical moment as the bands latest incarnation, with Kate needing to be forcibly injected with amphetamines to be able to perform, showcase their new direction at a huge concert filmed at the Rainbow in front of 2,000 extras. A glimpse into the audience which includes Robert Elms, Boy George and Marilyn, unwittingly suggests that Kate's, and therefore O'Connor's, days were already numbered with the development of a new scene of even brighter young things, too young to have made their mark during Punk's heyday that was developing around the Blitz night club and who, rather than confront newly elected premier Margaret Thatcher with anger, instead opted to party their way through the new decade. When O'Connor headed off on a tour to promote the soundtrack, the record company of a then-unknown band from Birmingham, Duran Duran, paid to be the support act. For the US release, the film ends with the song, cutting out a scene of Kate fleeing the stage into the London Underground, where, in full costume, she hallucinates people dressed as her and her former bandmates, and has a nervous breakdown before a final pointless scene shows her being visited by Danny in a hospital bed.

In the film, with the rest of the band eager to be signed, although eventually succumbing, Kate had declared: 'We're not into record contracts; sign a record contract become part of the machinery. I'm not into that.' It is one of *Breaking Glass*'s most unbelievable moments - a 'Punk' gesture in a scene that was always every bit as money dominated as those that came before and after it. It was also, sadly, a major digression from O'Connor's own back story which had seen her all too eager to sign the deal with Albion that, before filming, had become even worse when a major change was made to the movie's financing. United Artists were forced to back out when the *Heaven's Gate* disaster severely dented their finances and a new company, Allied Stars set up by the 26-year-old Dodi Fayed, rescued the film. With no major stars on board, the new company saw the soundtrack as an important revenue stream and with Arista, now Albion's backers, not taking up their chance of the first refusal, the album went instead to A&M with Albion allowing them to have the singer for the one album - in return for a cut of the profits. This effectively cut O'Connor's royalties to just 2.5% of retail.

The film was well-received at Cannes where O'Connor received countless publicity and the film was picked up for distribution by GTO who spent £150,000 on the UK rights and a further £600,000 on promotion only for its owner, former Rolling Stones accountant Laurence Myers, to conclude 'Hazel went to see it, her mum went to see it, my kids and about seven other people went - that was it.' In fact, it opened in seven West End cinemas and grossed £18,000 in its first week, average rather than appalling, but it did not find a significant audience when rolled out into the provinces.

The Tony Visconti produced album did, however, take off and within three months had shifted some 300,000 copies, enough to have grossed its star £100,000 with a decent contract but less than £35,000 under Albion's which after expenses left her with about £5000. The record eventually went Gold, peaking at number 5 and remaining in the charts for 28 weeks. Despite spawning two top ten singles, O'Connor's career was effectively over in battles over copyright and ownership. Like in *Breaking Glass*, O'Connor also fell out with manager Edwards who, also like in the movie, soon moved on to bigger and better things, representing The Roling Stones, The Who, Blondie, David Bowie, Paul McCartney, Prince, The Spice Girls, P. Diddy and Posh & Becks.

Hippies, Skinheads, Rastas, Punks & Disco Dancing Bowie Boot Boys

By the close of the decade the Punks we see in *Bloody Kids* can barely be termed that any more with hair creeping onto the shoulders like their hero Mick Jones who one imagines always felt somehow naked shorn of his Keith Richards pre-Punk locks. The first wave of Punk bands had already moved on, like John Lydon who revisited his love of free festival bands like Hawkwind and Can via Public Image, or widened out like The Clash whose 'London Calling' was released in time for Christmas 1979 and featured reggae, rockabilly, ska, r&b as well as Punk (or should that be new wave?). But Punk wasn't dead, it was splintering into factions - anarcho-Punks, street Punks, crust Punks - that would soon split into factions of their own. Bands like Madness and the Specials were mixing Punk and ska to create what would become 2-Tone, whilst others even combined Punk with its supposed arch enemies to create psychobilly.

By October 1983 Time magazine had made these new youth cults the focus of a cover feature, 'The Tribes of Britain', which said that mass youth unemployment and the nation's decaying towns and cities had combined to 'produce a generation of alienated youths who have turned to tribalism to give their lives meaning.'

It was they said 'a symbolic throwback to the original tribes of Britain. Seven centuries before Christ, the Damninii, Dutrotriges, Brigantes, Dobuni and Coritani dominated the yet unsceptered isle. They stained their tunics purple and scarlet. They wore Skins, gold ornaments, and long moustaches. Their bodies were covered in tattoos. So bizarre was the effect that the Roman legionnaires who later invaded the island were frightened of them.'

Guardian writer Alex Petridis described the 5th and 6th form, where uniform rules were more relaxed, at his own secondary school in the mid-80s 'a mass of different tribes, all of them defined by the music they liked, all of them more or less wearing their tastes on their sleeves. There were goths. There were metallers. There were Punks. There were soulboys, at least one of whom had made the fateful decision to try and complete his look by growing a moustache, the bum fluff result pathetic in the extreme. There were Morrissey acolytes, and even a couple of ersatz Hippies, one of whom had decorated his Adidas holdall with a drawing of the complex front cover of Gong's 1971 album 'Camembert Electrique': a pretty ballsy move, given the derision that Hippies had suffered during Punk, and at the hands of the scriptwriters of *The Young Ones*.'

By the end of the seventies synthesisers had become a prominent feature of the music of David Bowie via his collaborations with Brian Eno on the Berlin trilogy of albums that had begun with 'Low' in 1977 and ended with 'Lodger' in 1979. That they should therefore hold great influence for a large section of the more posey end of Punk went without saying. By 1978, Ultravox! had already released three albums with original vocalist John Foxx, fusing Punk with synths to great effect but negligible sales. A fan of both Bowie and Ultravox!, Gary Numan topped the UK singles chart in the summer of 1979 after discovering a mini-moog in the studio when recording Tubeway Army's debut album and in the words of Numan, turned 'Punk songs into electronic songs.' That same year Japan followed a couple of disappointing Glam albums with a Giorgio Moroder collaboration on the single 'Life In Tokyo' and a career high point with the electronic, Berlin influenced album 'Quiet Life'.

The divide between the 'loutish' Punks and a futurist new order was dramatised in the 24 minute short film, **KNIGHTS ELECTRIC (1980)**. Writer/producer/director Barney Broom (actually Geoffrey) was schooled in Norwich before attending University in Brighton after which, following a brief foray into publishing his own magazine in London, he headed to South Africa until ill health led to a re-assessment of his life. Enrolling in film school in Los Angeles, after graduation he returned to London where he started his film career at the bottom, as a tea boy on the Robert Powell remake of *The 39 Steps* (1978), an experience he found 'amazing'.

Broom subsequently made in excess of 350 pop videos, commercials and documentaries, including an ambitious reconstruction of the 8th century migration across the Indian Ocean, *Braving The Cape* (2003) for the Discovery Channel. But it's for the music driven *Knights Electric* that he will probably be best remembered. The film played in cinemas as the opening short to films such as *Inseminoid* (1981) and *Brimstone & Treacle* (1982) where, says Broom: 'It was quite a wow... people actually preferring it to the main picture it went out with.'

Dialogue free apart from occasional moments of voiceover, *Knights Electric* follows four Punks, led by Pete Lee Wilson and including a young Daniel Peacock, as they pursue four teenage girls around Great Yarmouth Pleasure Beach, only to find their, unwanted, advances thwarted by the quartet of *Knights Electric* of the title, spectral youths sporting a look somewhere between Kraftwerk and Numan. What the film lacks in plot it more than makes up for in exquisite photography from DOP David S Percy (who also shot *Discomania*), but its real draw is its soundtrack of the times that, alongside Numan's 'Down In The Park' also features four tracks from 'Metamatic'

Daniel Peacock (centre) in *Knights Electric*

era Foxx - 'Underpass', 'Film 1', 'No One Driving' and 'Mr No'; opening with the first and closing with the last. In between are tracks from the likes of The Ruts, The Pretenders, Blondie, and Madness.

Some of Punk's more flamboyant followers took Poly Styrene's cry of 'I Am A Poseur and I Don't Care,' and made it their watchword. This new movement was, according to one of their number, Marilyn, 'an extension of Punk... I always thought of them as Punks that had developed their style into what it developed into.' Another, DJ Jeremy Healy, formerly of Haysi Fantayzee, says 'We got very snobby about the people who were becoming Punks, because you forgot that in 77, most people said "Urgh!" but then in a couple of years started becoming a Punk, so we actually said "You have it then, and we'll move on." We were elitist really.'

These new poseurs soon found a guiding light in Steve Harrington (Strange) who would borrow Toyah Wilcox's then home, a large industrial warehouse in Battersea called Mayhem, and hold four day parties that would be attended by the likes of Boy George and Rusty Egan. These morphed into a club night at Billy's, Club For Heroes – essentially a Bowie night, which quickly gained momentum over the next couple of months before moving to the Blitz, bigger premises in a more salubrious part of the capital. As DJ, Egan mixed Bowie, Bolan and Roxy Music with Krautrock and the developing UK electronic scene with new releases such as The Normal's 'TVOD' and the Human League's 'Being Boiled'.

A trip to Düsseldorf in search of Kraftwerk put Egan on to the music of Neu, Cluster, and Moebius. Says Egan: 'Standing in the club listening was John McGeoch, Barry Adamson, Dave Formula, Midge Ure... members of Culture Club, all the people in bands.' Another important development came when theatrical costumier Burnham & Nathans decided they would sell off their old stock, including the uniform worn by David Hemmings in *The Charge of the Light Brigade* (1968) that would soon be worn by Adam Ant. Such items could be seen adorning many of the Blitz Kids as what would become New Romantic was born and the Kings Road trouser peddlers had a new tribe to dress. In 1981 the Observer's fashion writer Ann Boyd welcomed in the new year declaring: 'Punk is out, pirates and swashbuckling romance are in' and pointed them in the direction of the new lines at Vivienne Westwood and Acme Attractions and Boy's Helen Robinson's new shops, World's End and PX.

The club would soon spawn many stars but none who would shine as brightly as cloakroom attendant Boy George, for whom it all began in 1975 when he says, 'Honesty broke out.' He was talking about a television screening of *The Naked Civil Servant*: 'I thought it all started with Bowie and suddenly I see this man from the 1930s with hennaed hair and make-up, outwardly homosexual. It was a true story, and it just blew my mind. I just couldn't believe it. As a kid I thought Bowie was really brave, but then you look at what Quentin Crisp did, that's beyond brave... the other thing about Quentin Crisp was that he was apologetic, we were part of a new breed of gay people, and we were not apologetic. We weren't gonna apologise for being gay.'

These days are captured in writer Tony Basgallop and director Julian Jarrold's made for TV Boy George biopic **WORRIED ABOUT THE BOY (2010)** which opens with the young George O'Dowd (Douglas Booth) in front of his school careers officer who tells him 'You need a skill. What can you do better than others?' His response of 'make-up' is not considered a serious career choice. Next seen in a police cell having been arrested for stealing a dress, his father tells him 'You're not going to achieve anything in life looking like that.'

Soon after, he leaves the Eltham family home to the strains of 'Hong Kong Garden', suitcase in one hand and a mannequin tucked under the other arm, for life in a far from salubrious London squat. In studded leather jacket and jet black hair he more resembles Marilyn Manson than Boy George, or the other Marilyn he meets there, who asks: 'What are you exactly? You're not a Punk. Too much make-up, even for a Mod and I think we can rule out Skinhead or Hippie. Glam perhaps?' George: 'I'm nothing, which is why I can look good in anything.' Before long he's one of the faces at the Blitz and enjoying being a celebrity for nothing more than looking good, snapped by photographers as he leaves. He also learns about the perils of wandering around the city's dark alleyways at night dressed as a heavily made-up nun.

Says George: 'I remember going to a Punk gig, it was Gang of Four. I was doing this kind of Siouxsie Sioux look. I had the frilly shirt, heavy make-up and the spikey hair but it wasn't really Punk. It was something more than Punk and I remember someone throwing a beer over me and ruining my hair and I suddenly thought this is a not a scene I want to be part of. This is not for me... it became very studenty, violent, spitting, pogoing, all of that, and we departed over here.'

To Billy Bragg the New Romantics were 'the antithesis of Punk because what Punk had been about is there's no gap between you in the audience and the person performing on stage. We were all part of something together. There were no barriers. And Steve Strange came along on the door and says, "You can't come in 'cos you're wearing the wrong trousers". That to me is the opposite of what I believe.'

Despite its revellers finding themselves pictured in fashion spreads in magazines and newspapers, the scene around the Blitz was a remarkably small one, the club itself having a capacity of just 350. It was amongst the club's own clientele that Egan next turned in his search for new music to play, teaming with his fellow ex-Rich Kid Midge Ure in Visage, a band fronted by Steve Strange – the only character portrayed with anything less than affection in the film, with even George saying 'You know what this means don't you? If Steve Strange can get on television anyone can.'

The Blitz and many of its attendees are visited in the opening act of **TABOO** a stage musical with book by Mark Davies Markham, lyrics by Boy George, and music by George, John Themis, Richie Stevens and Kevan Frost. The musical premiered in the West End at the Venue Theatre during January 2002. Though largely based around Leigh Bowery's legendary Taboo nightclub between 1985 and 1987, the opening act is set some time earlier where the story's young hero, Billy, leaves home after an argument with his abusive father and finds himself in a squat with Boy George and hanging out at a nightclub presided over by Steve Strange and attended by real life regulars such as Marilyn and Philip Salon. Strange again is portrayed less than flatteringly; seen premiering his new hit record 'Fade To Grey', but having the plug pulled halfway through his performance by a crowd sick of hearing it. A re-vamped US production included George himself in the cast and opened in 2003, running for just 100 performances and losing backer Rosie O'Donnell $10 million in the process.

Steve Strange's nights at Billy's and Blitz weren't the only ones mining the

Douglas Booth as George and Richard Madden as Kirk Brandon in *Worried About The Boy*

electronic underground in search of new music. Another Steve, Pearce and known as Stevo, was running Stevo's Electro Tunes at the Clarendon Hotel in Hammersmith where acts such as Fad Gadget, Naked Lunch and DAF played. By 1980 he was compiling an electronic chart for Record Mirror and a futurist one for Sounds as well as the 'Some Bizarre Album' featuring early Soft Cell and Blancmange recordings and the very first studio outing for Depeche Mode on his own Some Bizarre label.

As that year came to a close both Strange with his 'supergroup' Visage and Blitz house band Spandau Ballet had hit the UK charts with 'Fade To Gray' and 'To Cut A Long Story Short'. Duran Duran weren't far behind with 'Planet Earth' in February 1981. Another label made-to-measure for this new electronic music was Mute, run by Daniel Miller to release his own 'TVOD/Warm Leatherette' single under the name of The Normal. By the end of 1981, Mute would be behind a string of hit singles for Depeche Mode and their debut 'Speak & Spell' album. In July that year Some Bizarre would take Soft Cell to the number one spot at home and number 8 in the US and make its influential and unpredictable owner one of the most influential movers and shakers in the business, getting major label deals for such seemingly unlikely recipients as Psychic TV and Cabaret Voltaire. By now the lid was well and truly off the bottle and New Romantic was in the mainstream and spawning a plethora of bands not unlike the fictional Venus Hunters.

Neither *Taboo* nor *Worried About the Boy* were the first tribute to the New Romantic era; that title belongs to ITV's **HUNTING VENUS** (1999), an affectionate look back at the era directed by and starring Martin Clunes as Simon Delancey, former bass player with one-hit wonders the Venus Hunters who has since made his living preying on lonely pensioners. That is until he checks into a guest house run by Cassandra (Jane Horrocks) and Jacqui (Esther Coles), two obsessive fans from the 80s who blackmail him into reforming the band – Ben Miller, Mark Williams and Clunes' Men Behaving Badly co-star Neil Morrissey as singer Charley, now Charlotte having undergone sex change surgery – for one last gig.

Along the way to a finale at the recording of a TV special with the Human League, Gary Numan, Simon Le Bon and Tony Hadley (all of whom appear in cameos), the script packs in references to the era, from an early shot of a flock of seagulls morphing into the band of the same name's only hit, 'Wishing (If I Had A Photograph Of You)', to a cocktail called an Enola Gay - 'Essence of Margaret Thatcher and fuel-injected Ford Capri' - and a song specially written for the band by Jools Holland, 'Starburst' - 'I launched my children skyward, I launched them into space, a Herculean effort, the strain shows on my face' - that is both catchy and masturbatory enough to be believable as a bona fide hit of the time.

The Venus Hunters are back for one last gig

In 1982 during the first episode of *The Young Ones*, Rick tunes in see Ben Elton's energetic introduction: 'Hi, my name's Baz and me and my mates thought that TV just wasn't now. Right. Like us. I expect you're not into all that stuff your old man's into. Right? So we just thought we'd have a programme for us. Right. And this is it. Nozin' Around… a programme for young adults, made by young adults and concentrating on all the subjects that young adults are interested in, like unemployment.'

The skit was aimed at programmes like *Something Else* (1978-1982), *The Oxford Road Show* (1981-1985) and *20th Century Box* (1980-1982). **JANGLES (1982)** stuck with its predecessors music and issues format but decided to add drama to the mix. The show was created at HTV's Bristol studios where a new director of programmes, Patrick Drongoole, had adopted the policy of a 'creative free-for-all'. He had recently come to the company with a host of new ideas and a desire to create drama, not an easy task in an environment where the major ITV companies like Granada, Central and London Weekend had carved the market between themselves. The only route for smaller companies to create network drama was via Children's Television.

Whatever happened to baby Hazel?

An early template was *The Dave Cash Radio Show* (1972) which linked lots of music with segments of drama involving former Radio 1 DJ Cash and his assistant. Also important in creating the *Jangles* template was the use of Chromakey, which was just beginning to find its way into the mainstream, a decision that Alex King, who directed three episodes, says 'came out of the fact that we didn't have any money and I said, "Well, how are we going to build the set for the home scenes?" "Oh, we can't build sets." "Well, shall we shoot them on location?" "Oh, we can't afford to do that." Well how are we going to do this? So Chromakey was beginning to come in and I think we actually used blue screen… I went out to flats in Barton Hill in Bristol and took lots and lots of stills and we Chromakeyed all these black and white stills as the background to the set because we didn't have any sets. We had no money and it actually worked.'

In keeping with *The Young Ones* assertion that young adults are interested in unemployment, career opportunities are at the heart of *Jangles*, with Steve's (Jesse Birdsall) step mother particularly scathing of her son's employment status: 'Bone idle. Frightened of a little work.' On the contrary, Steve is unhappy to be unemployed and keen to get a job: 'Believe it or not, I don't get any pleasure from being out of work. After a while you feel like everyone's staring at you. Like you've just crawled out of a sewer or something.' Which is more than can be said for his roller-skating black mate Gary (Tony Britts) who receives similar contempt from his mother but is happy to sign on, considering himself a 'giro technician'.

According to Steve: 'No one's better because they've got a job. Listen, I go in the Job Centre every day of the week. It's about the one job I can do. You've got to be 25 and have experience. You put my age and experience in their computer, you've got sod all.' In the end Gary decides to go into business with his recently redundant dad.

Steve's girlfriend Joanne (Hazel O'Connor) is attending sixth form, or at least she should be, but has decided to set that aside to pursue her ambitions of being a singer. Gary's girlfriend Mary (Julia Gale) has marriage, house, and motherhood in mind. Between them, they provide a realistic amalgam of youths' perceived prospects at the time.

The series touched on other subjects deemed on the radar of its intended audience, like the police and the potential consequences of teenage sex, which rears its head when after an argument with her parents, Joanne moves into a flat with Steve. After the act takes place, Joanne delivers a direct-to-camera lecture on responsibility in such matters: 'Steve never takes things seriously. Didn't even ask if I'd taken the pill. He didn't bother to use anything, for all he cares I could be pregnant. He doesn't have to worry about a thing. The number of girls in school who become pregnant is amazing; they all come back with the same old story. Of course everyone knows they've attended the mother and baby clinic. Well, I've made sure it's not going to happen to me. We should have talked about it first. Making sure I don't get pregnant is a joint responsibility. His as much as mine.'

It's sound enough advice but not the sort of thing likely to revitalise a career in rock, which I imagine is what O'Connor persuaded herself was the case on deciding to take on the role of a schoolgirl. This was always going to be a hard sell with the singer being 27 at the time, and the scenes in which she wears a school uniform are St Trinians meets *Whatever Happened to Baby Jane*. The role also required O'Connor to perform two numbers at the end of each episode. The first of these would be a cover of a 1940s standard, the synth pop arrangements of which did neither singer nor song any favours. The best that can be said of the original material is that it only confirms O'Connor's sudden decline in popularity.

Like *20th Century Box*, the series itself provides an amalgam of the various youth tribes dominant at the time, with certain episodes catering for a particular youth tribe and playing records and featuring a related live act such as the synth pop of New York's Our Daughter's Wedding in the opening episode, and rockabilly band The Fantoms in episode 4.

Episode 2 features the new wave of heavy metal and in the third, which opens with Sugar Minott's 'Good Thing Going', it's the turn of reggae represented on the club's stage by Bristol's multi-racial Talisman who never reached the heights of some of their contemporaries but toured with Burning Spear, The Roling Stones, and The Clash and released the memorable roots single 'Dole Age'. Reggae night also gives the programme a chance to introduce a couple of racist Skinheads.

The high point of the series comes in episode 6 where football hooliganism rubs shoulders with 2-Tone and the Mod revival and there's a live performance of 'It Ain't What You Do' by Fun Boy 3 and Bananarama. The episode begins with Steve and Gary at a football match where violence breaks out. None of your 80s casuals here though as men in 'Saxon' emblazoned denim jackets battle alongside men in National Coal Board donkey jackets, pounding a black policeman into the snow for good measure. When said policeman follows Steve and Gary into a deserted Jangles, the pursuit turns into a lengthy slapstick routine with roller skating policemen and the two youths arrested and fined.

Joanne attacks the police as prejudiced: 'Come on Mary, they don't like kids anyway and if you're a kid and black and in trouble you've had it… That's the way I see it. The police don't understand the kids, and the kids don't understand the police. And that's the way it is. It's a recipe for mutual hate. Right?' It's like *The Young Ones* Rick was actually there.

To the sound of a Native American drumbeat, the police raid the club and a detective takes to the stage to make a speech: 'Laws are there to make society work. They may not be perfect but they exist. At the moment there's a law against taking drugs and another about drinking underage. Now in time these laws may go, while they exist we're going to enforce them. We in the police are just human beings like yourselves, some good, some bad, some vicious, bent, straight, gay, some fat, some thin…' 'Some racist' a voice cries out from the crowd. 'Of course, just like those in your fraternity, the Nazi element,' he continues, pointing out a youth in the sort of Nazi armband not seen since 1977.

'What about you?' asks Joanne. 'You've still got a down on us. You're looking at a new society, one that's been taught to question. You lot want to keep things the way they used to be and you can't. This is a new generation. It's free thinking, fast moving, and multi-racial. It's a revolution!' By revolution she means dancing to Madness's 'My Girl'.

The final word goes to Herald (David Deeks), an other-worldly presence who acts as a sort of ringmaster, commenting on the proceedings, and occasionally providing a voice of reason when something deemed controversial requires a balanced response. 'The police may be rancid butter but they're on our side of the bread. True or false?' he asks as the credits roll to 'You Need Wheels' by the Merton Parkas. The part was conceived as being the DJ, an actual presence in the club, but after Deeks had been cast and found he couldn't make the recording dates, rather than recast it was decided to use Chromakey. This allowed all Herald's scenes to be shot in one day and, says King, 'we actually shot that after the narrative drama so that we could spin off what we'd already recorded.' This, what he refers to as 'necessity being the mother of invention' also serves to give the show an extra dynamic.

Bob Baker, another writer on the show, best known for his work with Wallace and Gromit and for 38 episodes of *Dr Who* in the 1970s, looks back favourably on *Jangles* as 'a most amazing effort, really great.' His recollection of having 'big well-known groups each week - I mean big names' is stretching reality somewhat. Despite being nominated for the Children's Television Award, Prix Jeunese, *Jangles* disappeared after one seven episode series, having failed to find an audience or a regular place in the schedule. LWT broadcast it in the weekend lunchtime slot vacated by *20th Century Box*, but other regions opted for various post 5.15 pm tea time slots.

The likely reason for this is that despite Dromgoole telling the IBA Children's Sub Committee that the programme was created 'for kids: twelve and up,' that dynamic was something of a Holy Grail. Says King: 'We all made it for a teenage audience. Of course we all knew a teenage audience doesn't exist. It didn't exist then, and it doesn't exist now. Teenagers are abandoned. Children's television, I think in the days we were making that, it was five to twelve [year-olds]: that was children's television, twelve being the upper limit. We were pushing the boat out I think, with *Jangles*, and pretending it was for thirteen-year-olds. It was still technically a children's programme... But we felt that it was for teenagers...'

Another regular in the cast was Lowri Ann Richards, who had featured alongside O'Connor in the supporting role of Jane in *Breaking Glass*. Richards was a recent graduate of the Webber Douglas Academy of Dramatic Art who had earned her Equity card by working as a professional disco dancer, touring Mecca nightclubs up and down the country with her boyfriend and dancing partner Robert Pereno.

Lowri Ann Richards (right) in *Jangles*

When she joined a crowd watching robotic mime dancers Tim Dry and Barbie Wilde in the window of the trendy King's Road store Liberated Lady in 1979, it convinced her that disco had had its day and, forming a connection with the robotic dancers, the dance/mime/music group Shock was born. Says Richards: 'We met and thought we would do a show together, us dancing and them doing mime and robotics. Our look was sort of disco bondage. We wore Liberated Lady, all suspenders, corsets, short skirts, thigh boots. The boys would wear clothes from Johnson's, pointy shoes, spangly trousers. And we'd get bondage stuff from a sex shop nearby in The Great Gear Market. The act was very sexual, but we'd go home and have a cup of tea. We were very middle class, it was all an act.'

Shock were soon a regular fixture at Blitz and gained support slots for the likes of Adam and the Ants, Depeche Mode, Ultravox and, biggest of all, Gary Numan at Wembley Arena, with an act in which, dressed in costumes designed by Duran Duran favourites Kahn & Bell, they mimed to music from Fad Gadget, Landscape, and Kate Bush. 'They were' Richards says, 'exciting times. One minute we'd be at mime artist Lindsay Kemp's beautiful house and the next backstage at an Elton John gig. I was just part of a decadent Chelsea set. There was no calculation. I just fell into it and became part of it.'

They were also awarded a recording contract with RCA, releasing a single that made an impact in the clubs but not in the shops, a cover of the Glitter Band's 'Angel Face' which was produced by Rusty Egan and Richard James Burgess of Landscape. A second Shock single, 'Dynamo Beat', did not feature Richards, but did future 'fashion consultant' to Cherie Blair, Carole Caplin, and Barbie Wilde, the female Cenobite from *Hellraiser II*. Instead, she and Pereno had a second crack of the whip as the synth pop duo Pleasure & the Beast who also released two singles, 1983s 'Dr Sex' and 'God's Empty Chair', both of which quickly vanished, though Richards did make it on to *Top of the Pops*, miming to the debut Tight Fit single 'Back To The Sixties', a medley in the vein of 'Stars on 45', actually recorded by a group of session musicians.

Richards returned to this period of her life in the first half of a 2013 one-woman cabaret show, *Whatever Happened To Lala Shockette*, belting out her renditions of Soft Cell's 'Say Hello Wave Goodbye', Tubeway Army's 'Are Friends Electric?', the Velvet Underground's 'Candy Says', Blondie's 'One Way Or Another' and even 'Wuthering Heights'.

Though LaLa is a thinly disguised reference to her 80s self, Richards calls her 'a version of me,' and that events are not necessarily true: 'I'm revisiting parts of my life. I wanted to find a vehicle to put over my story and the easiest thing was to create a character who had done some off centre things like I had, but why let the truth get in the way of a good story.' The thing is, Richards life had been such a roller-coaster that even the unlikeliest of events might be true - these include having been in an abusive relationship with notorious gangster-cum-actor Johnny Bindon, and, whilst spread-eagled on the alter, conceived a child with the deacon who presided over Danny LaRue's funeral, having worked with the drag queen on P&O cruise ships.

Richards continued to pick up bits of television work here and there for a few years, including a memorable role as a juvenile delinquent in an episode *The Gentle Touch* in 1982 and a chance to work with Paul McCartney as a dancer in *Give My Regards To Broad Street* (1984). Unfortunately, her years of nightclubbing had begun to catch up with her, admitting: 'At the end of Pleasure and the Beast I couldn't work as an actress anymore. I would turn up at film sets and they'd find me in wardrobes, I'd be asleep. I was thrown off sets.'

Richards is absent from episode 1 of *Jangles* which instead features Honey Bane as Michelle's (Saiward Green) friend Jane, before being replaced for the remainder of the series with a slight name change to Jenny. Bane had hit the top 40 the previous year with 'Turn Me On Turn Me Off', a collaboration with Jimmy Pursey. The singer, real name Donna Tracy Howse, had released a split single with anarcho Punks The Poison Girls in 1978 when just 14, as vocalist for The Fatal Microbes. In 1979, after a stint in a juvenile detention facility and on the run from the Social Services, she released a single backed by Crass as Donna and The Kebabs.

Bane followed her appearance in *Jangles* with a role as Molly in *Scrubbers* (1982) but perhaps her most impressive piece of acting was for an audience of one and is available on audio only. It takes the form of an interview with Gary Bushell recorded in a Covent Garden pub, near to the Sounds office with what the journalist believes is Bane and an EMI publicist but is in fact Crass guitarist Andy Palmer. Bushell, seen as an easy target for anarcho-Punks, is left in the role of almost silent observer as the two spend over an hour bickering about EMI involvement in weapons and their attempts to make her a pop commodity.

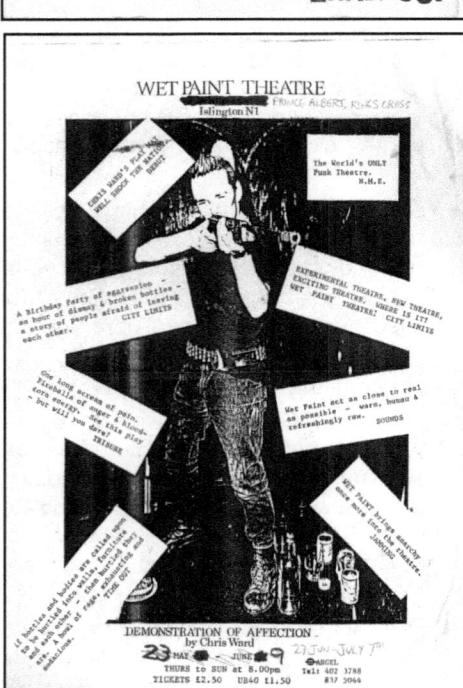

Bane made her acting debut in Chris Ward's 'visceral exploration of love and hate among the Punk generation', **DEMONSTRATION OF AFFECTION**, which premiered at London's Cockpit Theatre in April 1981 before moving to the West End at the Arts Theatre where it was redirected by Jonathan Moore with Bane added to the cast as Cressida, alongside Jennifer Landor as Eden, Jonathan Stratton as Devereaux, and Skids frontman Richard Jobson as Tarquin.

Devereaux is a bayonet toting manic depressive who fantasises about mass murder. It ends with him going berserk and killing Tarquin and Cressida. Along the way Eden makes Dev eat birthday cake out of a dog bowl and Tarquin slashes his wrists with a broken bottle.

The Guardian hated it, saying 'two thirds of the way through this 90 minutes "Punk tragedy"... not even self abuse or extreme unction could have saved' it. The reviewer nevertheless thought Bane and Jobson 'manage to be authentic contemporary zombies despite the ludicrous dialogue imposed on them'. The Telegraph wanted to know why these people were so fucked up, saying 'unmotivated violence is as good a basis as any for drama but is not the thing itself.'

Chris Ward started the Wet Paint Theatre Company 'after being thoroughly pissed off with the theatre and how it was being run'. Theatre, he thought, was 'determined to keep itself an elitist entertainment, not interested in the ordinary people in the street. A cosy snug make believe world of snobbery. Go to any theatre, watch any TV programme, and if there is a character who happens to be a Punk, he's made out to be stupid, mindless and nearly always violent... the traditional stereotype the media likes to see, because that's safe, that's something to laugh at. A figure of fun. But show a Punk like the majority of us are, in our real light, articulate, intelligent, for peace, not war, let them talk some sense, speak the truth and immediately we become a threat. We are dangerous! And capable of bringing their whole rotten system crashing down'.

Punk as fuck! Honey Bane in *Crown Court: A Sword in the Hand of David*

The system withstood the playwright's assault, but Ward continues to produce and direct his own plays via Wet Paint. Among those who have trod the boards in his productions are Beki Bondage, Max Splodge, Jenny Runacre, Hagar the Womb's Ruth Radish and George Cheex of !Action Pact!

Bane reunited with Jonathan Moore, this time in his guise as a writer, in **CROWN COURT: A SWORD IN THE HAND OF DAVID (1983)**. In the episode, 19-year-old Steve O'Reilly (Pete Lee Wilson) is accused of stabbing his mother's boyfriend to death whilst on the run from borstal. He had been convicted of joyriding at 17, had subsequently escaped twice and was not popular with the other inmates. A prison officer says he was something of a loner: 'I thought the other inmates thought he was a bit weird... Well he never spoke to anybody unless he was reading out his poems.' Though clearly a sensitive kid in a very insensitive environment, he is pegged by prosecution witnesses as a troublemaker.

Steve was into Punk and the other lads didn't share his taste in music. He had the Buzzcocks 'blaring out in the common room and he was annoying the other lads. Reading out his poems on top of the music. If you can call it that.' The judge has to be told what 'playing the Buzzcocks' means and is told: 'Oh that racket m'Lord. I believe they are popular Punk musicians.' One such poem, said to be about his unwanted stepfather, is read out: 'No light. No fun. No future. On the run. Never showed nothing. Never showed me nothing. No fun. I'll show him. I'll show him how I feel.'

He does on occasion lose his temper with the prosecuting barrister but expresses his anger with words. 'I despise you. You should be here instead of me you privileged bastard' are words that many a defendant might have wish they had said. 'My name is Steve and I can write, your name is Golding and you're full of shite' puts him somewhere on the Autistic spectrum.

In an echo of Bane's own past, during his time on the run Steve had joined a Punk band, using his poems as lyrics but calling it a day when discovering 'most of the crowds we played to were morons who didn't want to listen anyway.' Having also decided to leave the band, bass player Joey (Honey Bane) travels with him to his home because he wanted his parents to meet her. This he seemed to think would show them he could succeed in life but in 1983 he would have needed some very liberal minded parents to share this view, which his most certainly aren't. Joey, along with his mother, was an eyewitness to the subsequent fracas in which the stepfather had died and appears as a witness for the defence.

The singer returned to acting and to juvenile detention facilities in *Boys Behind Bars 2* (2014) for LGBT filmmakers Jason Impey and Wade Radford where as Governess Ms Muncher she got to stick the barrel of a gun up a boy's bottom. Calling the role 'risky' she says she 'had to really not give a fuck to play that role, literally about anything,' but 'was more fun to make than *Scrubbers*' which had a punishing schedule.

6. Where Have All The Bootboys Gone?
(Barrett, Rossi, Bates, Grantham)

Watching the Mods and rockers running wild on beaches along the south coast during the early 1960s, an early incarnation of the British National Party detected what it called 'a strong feeling of protest against coloured immigration' and was scheming how it might harness such 'healthy' instincts to their cause. Fortunately, the BNP hierarchy's intention to point young people's attentions towards such groups as The Bachelors, whose music they considered 'western and tuneful, in contrast to the scruffy twitching of The Rolling Stones type' would give them little chance of making any impact.

Like The Bachelors, that party's days were numbered and in 1967 they merged with AK Chesterton's League of Empire Loyalists to form the National Front and were soon after joined by the Greater Britain Movement, led by John Tyndall who would become the major player in the new organisation. The National Front combined fascism with the populist racial politics that was making Enoch Powell the nation's favourite politician. Where in the 1930s Oswald Mosley's British Union of Fascists had failed to convince the wider public of their perceived threat from Jewish financiers, AK Chesterton had more success in scapegoating New Commonwealth immigrants, all too visible by their skin colour. In 1970, with 'Paki bashing' making the headlines, writing in Spearhead, Tyndall likened Skinheads to 'lost sheep wandering in the city wilderness, desperately seeking some kind of leadership that they can look up to and some kind of cause in which they can believe.'

Following the murder in April 1970 of Tausir Ali, a detective supplied the Sun newspaper with an insight into what little effort was put into finding the perpetrator: 'This could escalate to a civil war in the East End we don't want. We're not even sure we could handle it. Regrettably, it's safer in the long run if the occasional coloured man gets beaten up than to have two sides facing each other with all sorts of weapons.' Ali, a Wimpy Bar worker, was attacked by two Skinheads who slit his throat and left him to die. Days earlier, the Observer had told its readers: 'Any Asian careless enough to be walking the streets alone at night is a fool.' In government, Home Secretary Reginald Maudling admitted that the Pakistanis had been the victims of some very serious crimes but insisted that was the norm for that part of the capital, not just Pakistanis, and that 'the situation as a whole had been greatly exaggerated.' No wonder then that the Sun should say 'Tonight, the boys will be out again. Along Brick Lane, Stepney and at nearby Mile End underground station, when the Skinheads team up to plan the "Sport" for the evening.'

According to the Times, one East London mosque had documented thirty-eight attacks in the previous few months, with on one occasion the Imam being hospitalised after having been beaten with an iron bar and kicked in the face. In July, there were press reports of 150 white youths running amok through Brick Lane. A combination of the bloody civil war in Bangladesh meaning that from 1971 there would be a significant rise in migrants arriving from the region and the indifference to racial attacks by both the police and politicians meant that the incidence of such skirmishes would continue to rise. By the time John Tyndall became the National Front's Chairman in 1972, the original Skinheads were already merging into new youth cults and he felt anyway that 'no group of people could be less politically or ideologically motivated than Britain's Skinheads.'

By the close of 1976, in the East End alone, five Bengalis had died that year as victims of racial violence. The National Front was on the rise and had amassed some 14,000 paying members, winning almost 20% of the vote in Leicester's local elections. 1976 also saw the birth of Punk, which provided a new home for a re-emerging Skinhead scene. Says Gary Bushell: 'Skinheads were in a very funny place when they started coming back, from 1976 onwards, but they were very small at the time and… the only places these kids could go were to Punk clubs and they didn't really like Punk because to them a lot of the Punks were middle-class, a lot of the Punks were poseurs. They didn't like the scruffiness.'

When in 1977 Slaughter & the Dogs asked 'Where Have All the Bootboys Gone?', they need have looked no further for the answer than at gigs of the likes of Sham 69, the Cockney Rejects and the Angelic Upstarts whose rejection of the art school pretensions and commercialisation of Punk was attracting a large Skinhead following. Martin Webster did not share Tyndall's distaste for the Skinhead, and as each new chart success from Jimmy Pursey's boys saw the numbers of the 'Sham Army' swell and amongst them the number cropping their hair, the National Front's Activities Organiser saw the basis for a youthful working-class army that might instead serve the far-right.

Speaking to the weekly music paper Sounds, Sham 69 frontman Jimmy Pursey cut to the nitty-gritty: 'A Skinhead

is not acceptable, but a Punk became acceptable because Punk to the parents was a joke. Half these fucking posers would walk around saying "Anarchy" – if they saw the law running down the street with a fucking riot going on they'd be the first to run down the road. These Skinheads who came from the Punks were actual Punks. They were the ones who believed in everything that was going on, so when they saw everything was going wrong they thought "Fuck this, let's do something that's not acceptable."'

Formed in Hersham in 1976, and named from a fading piece of graffiti painted when Walton & Hersham F.C. had won the Athenian League title in 1969, the band had moderate success with their debut single, 'I Don't Wanna', for the independent Step Forward label in 1977 and this secured them a contract with Polydor. As the band's popularity grew so too did a new Skinhead movement who were being targeted by the newly formed Young National Front, restricted to 14 to 25-year-olds and headed by Joe Pearce, himself a teenager. In September 1978 Pearce also launched the newsletter Bulldog, sold at football grounds, gigs and even outside school gates and featuring articles on music, sport and local NF activism alongside crude cartoons. Says Pursey: 'They saw a way of recruitment at our gigs. The lost souls of whoever they were in the weakness of whoever they were, could far more easily be contained and brought about in their party through a Sham 69 gig than probably any other gig they could go to.'

Unfortunately, while the original Skinheads had a shared identity with the county's young West Indian immigrants through a mutual love of blue beat and ska, the musical roots of this second generation were decidedly white. The look, stripped of its rude boy cool and replaced by the shock value of Punk, was taken by many to new and ugly extremes – military surplus MA-I jackets replaced the Levi or the Harrington, boots became higher, hair was shorn to complete baldness and tattoos crept way above the neckline. With the new look came a new, disparaging name – the bonehead. Telling the press that 'I'd rather have an NF Skinhead come to my gigs so I can turn round and say "I'm an anti-Nazi, what do you fucking think of that?" than a robot,' Pursey believed he could tame them adding, 'Skinheads aren't acceptable because they represent violence. But you can channel that violence, that energy, and excitement into something good, showing you can be a rebel with a cause. That's what I'm trying to do..' The boneheads, however, had other ideas.

Sounds, reporting on Sham 69s farewell gig at The Rainbow in the summer of 1979, said: 'The pub opposite the Rainbow appeared to be a meeting point for the British Movement. And not just little kids calling themselves that either, there were real evil characters, including some of the BM Leader Guard with their swastika tattoos, "This time the world" and the like. Passing black kids were assaulted and gig-goers subjected to "Seig Heils" and songs about the showers of Belsen...in between sets a gang of Skinheads numbering about 200 ran riot through the unseated venue, pushing, shoving or just plain assaulting everyone else. The main instigators were about 40 BM hardcore head-cases who assembled the hangers-on... the gig eventually had to be called off.'

Sham 69 may have been late to the party but when they arrived, they took it over with a string of powerful singles, beginning with 'Borstal Breakout' in January 1978 and quickly followed by the chart hits 'Angels With Dirty Faces', 'If The Kids Are United', 'Hurry Up Harry', 'Questions & Answers' and 'Hersham Boys' before the bands fortunes declined as 1979 came to a close. The band were less successful on the album front, their first two creeping into the top thirty before sliding quickly away - though their third, 'The Adventures of the Hersham

Boys', reached #8, but would be the last time Pursey's boys would make the top forty with any format until the 2006 World Cup cash-in 'Hurry Up England'. Part of the problem was the speed with which they released the albums, three in less than two years, meant there was a lot of filler included despite one of them being 50% live.

'That's Life', their second album of 1978, was no different, though it was unique for a Punk band in that it was a concept album, an area usually associated with everything the genre was said to be railing against. In reality, Punk musicians were far more ambitious than the three-chord, two-and-a-half minute blasts of fury that many would have restrained them to. Indeed, The Who, masters of the rock opea were an influence of most everyone. Sadly, 'That's Life' was no 'Quadrophenia' despite including keyboards and acoustic guitars that belied the belief that Sham was a one-trick pony. Nevertheless, it is the rabble-rousing anthems like 'Hurry Up Harry', 'Angels With Dirty Faces' and 'Sunday Morning Nightmare' that stand head and shoulders above the rest.

Despite its shortcomings, the album was dramatised for an episode of the TV arts series *Arena*. In **ARENA: TELL US THE TRUTH (1979)**, Jimmy Pursey pops up occasionally to offer a few words of 'wisdom' on the plight of youth today: 'They're all moving down the same conveyor belt. They're all being subjected to "you do this son; you come from there son, so you have to do that." If you come from a tower block in the East End, you are subjected to either working at the docks or so and so and so, "No, you mustn't go out; no you mustn't leave London and be something else, 'cos that's wrong; you're not born to do that."' Says director Jeff Perks: 'The whole Punk thing has been interesting because essentially anyone can do it, and Sham 69 are perfect examples of that.' That doesn't run to acting. Pursey doesn't appear because adds Perks, 'he's too big and would have hammed it up so much he'd have ruined it.'

It's 7.35 a.m. and in the kitchen mum is ranting about her son Grant (Grant Fleming) in bed upstairs: 'That kid's late again; every day I put the alarm on for 7 o'clock, half-past seven the kid's still not up.' When he finally stirs, his sister's in the bathroom and equally damning, telling him 'You're just a lazy bastard, ain't ya!' So it's out without breakfast and as the lift doesn't seem to want to come, it's down the stairs, across the walkways and down into the tube station just as the train pulls out.

The 'drama' is interspersed with footage from a Sham 69 gig, where there's no one looking remotely like the Bromley Contingent. What there are plenty of though are young working-class kids who seem to know every word to every song. That suits Jimmy Pursey, who told Sniffin' Glue in September 1977: 'D'you know what a 'real Punk' is? A real Punk today is the bloke with a belt joining the legs of his trousers together or a girl in fishnet stockings. And they're the first people to shout wanker at my band. Cos they're in their little smug groups of fashion and they look just like the Sunday Times has told them to look. They'll tell ya bands are selling out to business too. Fuckin' snobs. What was it last year? Bryan Ferry, Glenn Miller?'

Grant is late for work and receives his cards - the gaffer doesn't think much of his excuse that 'It's my mum's fault,' as the music cuts to 'The Cockney Kids Are Innocent'. Instead he meets a mate in a cafe, telling him he isn't going on the dole, he will instead go into the bookies and win some money; 'You never know, do ya?' He's given a cert and minutes later he's tossing his losing ticket to the floor. Cue, 'What have we got, Fuck all!' From there it's off to see another mate, Harry, who he persuades to leave his porn mags and help him do in his last fiver down the pub; several pubs. Cue, 'Hurry Up Harry'. At the pub he chats up a girl called Julie, getting on well until her boyfriend turns up - or at least he thinks he is, she's not so sure. A punch up ensues as the film switches back to the Sham 69 gig, where it's more of the same from the audience. Cue, 'If The Kids Are United'.

Grant Fleming, like *Rude Boy*'s Ray Gange, had been a Punk fan, following bands around - in particular, The Clash, The Jam and Sham 69. At 18 he was offered a job as 'personal assistant' to Jimmy Pursey, soon afterward becoming the band's tour manager as well as being bought a bass guitar and given a spot in Pursey's brother's band The Kidz Next Door. Says Fleming: 'At the tender age of 18, that was a baptism of fire as every one of those gigs, in those days, were pandemonium... I was used to riots and violence from being a football hooligan... we may just as well have been billed as RiotsRUs.'

In 1988, Fleming headed off to Central America to photograph the revolutionary upheaval of the late 1970s (inspired by Joe Strummer and Sandinista). Since then he's photographed the likes of Oasis (and was even mooted as a possible replacement for Guigsy in the band), David Beckham, Ronaldo, The Stone Roses, Nelson Mandela, and Fidel Castro. As the official Primal Scream photographer, he was also responsible for the iconic 'Screamadelica' logo.

Ain't Gonna Take It
(Robinson, Kustow)

An area of continuity between the boneheads and the 1969 Skinheads was their shared antagonism towards the Asian community, seen as something of an easy target. That was about to change. Writer Farrukh Dhondy began as an activist come journalist for the Brixton based magazine Race Today. He and a few others would travel to Brick Lane he says, to 'assist in the organisation of the first of the vigilante committees and then from that we heard that the main problem... was housing.' That knowledge led to the formation of Bengali Housing Action, which despite its more mainstream sounding title Dhondy calls an 'anti-racist vigilante movement.'

Instrumental in this was Terry Fitzpatrick of the Squatters Union who in the 1970s had combined his skills as a builder with his belief in the politics of self-help to assist the Bengali community who were being moved out of Spitalfields by the council to re-enter and squat the empty houses. Says Dhondy: 'He said that this was one of the ways of making grass-roots politics. Squatting homes and then forcing the council to make them legal. Terry was the mover and shaker, he was a twenty-four-hour worker.'

In the 32 minute documentary *Defending A Way of Life* (1980) Paul Beesley, the Labour leader of the local council, says: 'Walk along Brick Lane and look at the old houses there, the old shops. It's an area where people can come, they can get a job very cheaply at the beginning. Casual employment, maybe work in a restaurant, maybe they can work in a clothing factory. They can perhaps hide a little bit, find their feet, get to know an area. There's cheap accommodation, they can live somewhere and as time goes on, they can gradually move from there and move out. And once they do that they start to enrich the society in which they're living because they add something to it and contribute to it, exactly the way the Jews did. Jews settled here and they're now, in the main, living in other parts of London.'

This idyllic outcome did not tally with the experiences of the Bengali community when the GLC started to remove them from their homes and began housing them further afield into areas where they were very much a visible and vulnerable minority and, afraid to leave their new homes to the physical and verbal abuse they would face, they soon wanted to return. Says Dhondy: 'In Race Today and in our leaflets we propagated the idea that if... Bangladeshi's live together, they wouldn't get attacked, because there'd be strength in numbers.' The GLC, however, was having none of it. 'We went and talked to them... he said, "You want to ghettoise these people, we want to spread them out so that multiculturalism can thrive in Britain." We said that's a great Liberal idea... but we're getting thrashed, we're getting beaten when we're isolated.' And so, Dhondy, Fitzpatrick, and a few other members of the community did something about it.

Playing a character based on Fitzpatrick, Tim Roth sported a Skinhead haircut for the third time of his brief career in the opening episode of **KING OF THE GHETTO (1986)**, the seventies set four part drama from the BBC, written by Dhondy and directed by Roy Battersby. When producer W Stephen Gilbert took charge the drama had already begun the casting process under original director Franco Rosso who, as well as Roth, cast singer Ian Dury, whom he had studied alongside at the Royal College of Art and more recently worked with on the documentary *Ian Dury* (1983), in an important supporting role. Sadly, much of the singer's contribution ended up on the cutting room floor because of time considerations. It soon became clear that Gilbert and Rosso were a mismatch, the producer finding his director 'a disorganised field commander' with the two finding little they could agree upon. During auditions for the yet-to-be-cast leading lady, Gilbert says Rosso was 'random and incoherent' and thought 'he had clearly lost interest in the whole project and he walked.' Relieved the decision had been taken, but with deadlines looming he needed to find a replacement fast.

On the second page of the BBC's list of 'acceptable' directors Gilbert came across the name of Roy Battersby, a legend for his time working alongside the likes of Ken Loach on the early *Play For Today*'s, and who had more recently been pursuing political causes, standing in Parliamentary elections as a candidate for the Worker's Revolutionary Party and making a documentary *The Palestinian* (1977) with Vanessa Redgrave, a subject contentious enough that when showing at the Doheny Plaza theatre in Los Angeles the venue was bombed.

Within 24 hours of Rosso's walkout, Battersby had read the script and accepted Gilbert's offer to direct only for the BBC's Head of Drama to break the news that, due to his political affiliations, the director had been blacklisted

Tim Roth is not quite what he seems in *King Of The Ghetto*

and could not be hired. Says Gilbert: 'Back in my office, I found Roy smiling broadly. He gave me a history of his own dealings with the BBC and his political activism outside the business, to which he had only just returned. We noted that the BBC's failure to exclude him from the approved list had ensured that he could not be denied work there if a producer wanted him without lawyers being brought in. Game to us.'

Like in Roth's better remembered close-cropped appearance in *Made In Britain* (1982), episode one opens on a close cropped Tim Roth, though now the music is not The Exploited but an old blues tune. He's sitting silently on a train as it arrives in London. As he emerges from under a railway arch, another Skinhead runs past from the direction he is heading with a car in close pursuit. As it passes out of shot we hear the screech of brakes and the car reverses back into view and a young Pakistani opens the door and hurls a bottle at the startled young man. Now the car, reversing, is in pursuit and he heads through the terraced streets until he forced to leap onto it to avoid being mowed down. Braking violently, it throws him hard against a doorway of a house and the car's four occupants alight and work him over until an Asian man comes to his aid, saying he knows him. He's Matthew, and the reason for this is he's been inside. But the local youths don't like Skinheads and nor does his girlfriend, Sadie (Gwyneth Strong), who has moved on and so he finds himself a place to squat.

The story goes back eighteen months to where two Bengali youths of school age, Saliq (Dinesh Shukia) and Riaz (Aftab Sachak), are handing out leaflets to the various houses and business around Brick Lane. One occupant of a squat is Matthew (Tim Roth, now with hair), an ex-squaddie, and the leaflet is about a protest meeting to stop the GLC closing their school. He says he'll attend and before long he's teaching the Bengali community all about squatters' rights and the houses that were boarded up by the GLC are being used to re-house the community.

After several houses are wrecked by a gang, Matthew and some youths attack a group of National Front magazine sellers and are arrested. Once bailed they are soon making Molotov cocktails but the National Front and their ilk are not the major threat to harmony in the newly squatted community, that comes from the local businessman and would-be Labour councillor Timur (Zia Mohyeddin).

The series was well-received, with the Times calling it a 'lesson in cultural strife, character development and intelligent dialogue' although the production was not without its dissenters. Because some characters were based on loosely fictionalised versions of real people, the production caused a degree of consternation and before the entire series had completed its broadcast, a formal complaint was lodged with the BBC. When a small demonstration took place by members of the Bengali community outside Television Centre, the producer, director and writer were summoned to a meeting with the demonstrators representatives in the offices of the Controller of BBC2, Graeme McDonald. Gilbert says: 'I knew nothing of the background to his fiction and - call me irresponsible if you like - I was happy not to know. After all the BBC had committed to the production long before it was my sense of responsibility. My first duty was to get the thing done in time for the booked slots.'

'The Bengali's - clearly articulate young men with a particular axe to grind and no conceivable right to speak for 'the whole' Bengali community were angry and dismissive... I remember one young chap declaring "you have raped my language and culture" and I decided he would be a local councillor before too long.' That, however, was the end of the matter, though the producer found offers of future work from the Corporation to be not forthcoming.

Says Fitzpatrick: 'Little did a small group of housing activists know that a meeting at the Montefiore Centre in January 1976 would shape both the Bangladeshi East End and the first generation of Bangladeshi activists. What began as a small movement with white squatters helping homeless Bangladeshi families had, in two years, grown to fifty families with many more wanting to squat. Through the windows in the room where the meeting was held could be seen the almost empty Pelham Buildings. The meeting decided to do two things. Form the Bengali Housing Action Group, and occupy Pelham Buildings. On Easter Sunday a few weeks later, the first few families helped by myself and Farrukh Dhondy broke into the building and within a month sixty were in occupation.'

'Both the Greater London Council and the London Borough of Tower Hamlets were opposed to any negotiations with squatters and the official policy was to evict but in May 1977 the GLC became Conservative-run and they had an entirely different approach. They told the Bengali Housing Action Group that if it nominated what were considered safe estates, the GLC would re-house all of its members on them. A list was drawn up and gradually over several months, Pelham was emptied of its Bangladeshis. Tower Hamlets was then forced to follow the same policy and for the first time, a community had forced the British state to house them where they were safe from racial attacks. Through this, and the physical defence of the community against racial attacks, the first generation of young Bangladeshi activists learned about direct action and that has shaped the community making it what it is today.'

That direct action is visible at the close of *King of the Ghetto*, where the area's youth organise a protest independent of Matthew and barricade a street. Timur asks Matthew to help by speaking to Saliq, but the youths only response is to throw a petrol bomb at his feet. It was a beginning, but there was still a long way to go.

On 13th August 1977, Lewisham was chosen for a show of strength by the National Front via a march through the southeast London borough. In the 1976 council by-election, the National Front and the National Party had achieved a combined vote of 44.5% but this had fallen to 14% in the following year's council elections and the Front was looking to regain some momentum.

Opposing the National Front marchers was a huge counter-demonstration attended by, according to some reports, 9,000. The demonstration didn't halt the march but meant that instead of addressing the public in the town centre.It forced the Front to give their speeches to the massed ranks of the police in a car park. The day ended in battles between the protesters and, not the Front, the police who deployed riot shields for the first time on the British mainland. There were 214 arrests and 111 injured, 56 of them police officers.

The events were captured in a documentary, *Aug 13: What Happened?* (1977), recently re-discovered after gathering dust on a shelf for 40 years. It was shot by members of the Albany Video Project in Deptford, founded by BAFTA-winning producer John White in 1974, using then new to the market video cameras.

Speaking to Granada's *World in Action* during January 1978, Margaret Thatcher told interviewer Gordon Burns: 'Well now, look, let us try and start with a few figures as far as we know them... if we went on as we are then by the end of the century there would be four million people of the new Commonwealth or Pakistan here. Now, that is an awful lot and I think it means that people are really rather afraid that this country might be rather swamped by people with a different culture and, you know, the British character has done so much for democracy, for law and done so much throughout the world that if there is any fear that it might be swamped people are going to react and be rather hostile to those coming in.'

Thatcher insisted she would not make immigration a major election issue but said that not talking about it was driving some people to the National Front. After all, where votes are concerned what matter a little racial hatred? 'They do not agree with the objectives of the National Front, but they say that at least they are talking about some of the problems' she said, '... we ourselves must talk about this problem and we must show that we are prepared to deal with it. We are a British nation with British characteristics. Every country can take some small minorities and in many ways, they add to the richness and variety of this country. The moment the minority threatens to become a big one, people get frightened.'

Pressed further she said she hoped that recent converts to the National Front, which she thought were previously largely Labour voters might be won over by the Tory party: 'very much... never be afraid to tackle something which people are worried about. We are not in politics to ignore peoples' worries: we are in politics to deal with them.'

Like it had done for Enoch Powell in the past, making the interview about tackling immigration saw her popularity within the party soar. Though it was ten years since his 'Rivers of Blood' speech had seen Ted Heath expel him from the party and he was now an Ulster Unionist, Powell was still an influential voice when it came to Conservative party immigration policy, invited to address Tory branches on the subject.

The following year Mrs Thatcher would be Prime Minister and the National Front, having fielded 303 candidates, up from 90 at the previous election in anticipation of finally making a breakthrough, watched on as every single one lost their deposit with the party attracting just 0.6 percent of the vote. It was the beginning of the end for a party that at its peak in 1972 could boast of some 17,500 paid-up members but by the mid-eighties had seen this dwindle to between 1 and 2 thousand. This was probably the result of a combination of left-wing opposition, the Tory party's courting of racists, and tensions between John Tyndall and Martin Webster. Whilst no longer an immediate political threat, the National Front and other right-wing parties, such as the British National Party and the British Movement, remained very much a physical threat to the minorities that, with less to lose, they became increasingly vocal in their hatred of.

Whilst she would have known that her 'swamping' rhetoric would win her votes, Thatcher must have also been aware it would embolden the racists and that there would also be consequences. Sure enough, during April 10-year-old Kennith Singh was killed in Plaistow and his body dumped on a rubbish tip; in May Altab Ali was murdered in Adler Street, Whitechapel and during June 45-year-old Ishaque Ali was stabbed and killed after an attack by youths. As well as three murders in three months, the detectives investigating the Singh killing were also investigating a knife attack on a nine-year-old Rainham boy who had been grabbed by five youths in an alley leading to Rainham Junior School, who then slashed the boy's face with a flick knife, narrowly missing an eye.

The murder in May 1978 of 24-year-old Bangladeshi machinist Altab Ali as he made his way home from work was a particular turning point, leading to over 5,000 Asians marching from St Mary's Churchyard off Whitechapel Road, where he had been repeatedly stabbed, via Hyde Park to 10 Downing Street where a petition was handed in. The youths declared their intentions on the placards they held: 'Self-defence is no offence' and 'Here to stay, here to fight'. Ali had been attacked on local election day and the National Front had a candidate in every Tower Hamlets ward that year, gaining almost 10 percent of the vote. His assailants were three teenagers, the 17-year-olds Roy Arnold and Carl Ludlow and another boy of just 16. None of the boys cared nor knew who Ali was. They attacked him, said the 16-year-old, for 'No reason at all,' adding 'If we saw a Paki we used to have a go at them... We would ask for money and beat them up. I've beaten up Paki's on at least five occasions.'

Following Ali's murder, two youth organisations formed in the area, initially unknown to each other, the Bangladeshi Youth Movement and the Bangladeshi Youth Front, separated by Commercial Road, the main route between the City and the traditional East End. Director Simon Heaven's half-hour documentary **DEFENDING A WAY OF LIFE (1980)** looks at the Bangladeshi Youth Movement's attempts to balance their cultural identity with life in London's East End as we see them providing the children with after-school education in the Bengali language and culture. Tellingly we also witness them participating in self-defence classes.

Still happy to help Mrs Thatcher stir the pot, on the 10th June 1978 Enoch Powell told supporters in Billericay, Essex: 'Violence does not break upon such a scene because it is willed or contrived... but because it lies in the inevitable course of events... those who foresaw and feared they would be swamped will be driven by... strong impulses and interests to resist and prevent it.' The very next day, 150 National Front-supporting white youths, mainly Skinheads, translated these words into action. They rampaged down Brick Lane chanting race-hate slogans, throwing bottles, bricks, and rubble through shop windows. Bengali youths resisted and managed to kettle 20 of the perpetrators and hold them until the police, belatedly, made a few arrests. Says Sunawhar Ali, one of the founders of the Bangladeshi Youth Front: '[for the] first half hour police didn't do anything at all when they were smashing all the windows of the Bengali shops. We had hand to hand fights with them. We thought, this is Brick Lane, this is our home and if we don't defend Brick Lane, then we can't live in the country. We had to, we didn't have any choice.'

*

The East End wasn't the only part of London that was having to organise itself against racial attacks. On a 4th June

1976 edition of Granada's What The Papers Say, left-wing journalist Paul Foot put forward the argument 'race hate and race violence does not rise and fall according to the numbers of immigrants coming into Britain. It rises and falls to the extent to which people's prejudices are inflamed and made respectable by politicians and newspapers.' Race and Class, the periodical of the Race Relations Board had been monitoring press reports showing hostility to immigration over the previous months and subsequent acts of racial violence. They found that whilst it would be impossible to prove a direct correlation between the headlines and any subsequent crimes, the tone being used in the press was inflammatory. A headline in The Sun for the 2nd of May warned its readers that 'One slips by on every boat' whilst 4 days later they warned of 'Another 20,000 Asians... on the way.' The following day, the same paper was up in arms as '4-star Asians run-up £4,000 bill'. By the middle of the month, the Daily Express had issued an 'Asian flood warning' and the Sun, 18th May, alerted its readers to 'New Asian invaders'. Even the supposedly left-wing Daily Mirror was printing articles about 'Our Asian burden'.

During the evening following the Granada broadcast, an 18-year-old Sikh student, Gurdip Singh Chaggar, was stabbed to death outside the Dominion cinema in Southall. A few days later at a meeting held to discuss race relations in the area a group of young Asians, unhappy with the more conciliatory nature of their elders, walked out and assembled outside the cinema from where they marched in protest to the local police station. Noisy but relatively peaceful, with just two arrests, this protest would mark the birth of the Southall Youth Movement (SYM) and a time for the Asian community to stand their ground and fight back. The sit-down protest was abandoned when the crowd was told the two youths would be released without charge, only for this promise to be broken a few hours later. It was seen as a betrayal too far for youths who had suffered discrimination since they were young children, not just from their white neighbours but also from Government, who in response to complaints from parents of white children at the area's school began 'busing' the children to schools in other areas where, very much a minority, racist attacks and discrimination were a daily occurrence in the playground.

That it would be an uphill struggle soon became clear in remarks made by the former chairman of the Blackburn Young Conservatives John Kingsley Read, Chairman of the National Front between 1974 and 1976 who had recently quit to form his own National Party. Perhaps even more unsettling was the response to those remarks from the authorities. Kingsley Reid had told a meeting: 'Fellow racialists, fellow Britons, and fellow Whites, I have been told I cannot refer to coloured immigrants. So you can forgive me if I refer to niggers, wogs, and coons.' Of Chaggar's murder, he simply said, 'One down, a million to go.' Charged with incitement to racial hatred he found himself in front of a Judge, Neil McKinnon, who thought the defendant had used 'reasoned argument in favour of immigration control or even repatriation' which was not covered by the law against incitement to racial hatred. 'It was,' he said to the jury, 'difficult to say what it is that this defendant is alleged to have done' and ensured they would arrive at a not guilty verdict upon which he told Reid 'By all means propagate the views you have... I wish you well.'

A retrospective look at this period in Southall history, in particular the origins of the youth movement, is captured in the documentary **YOUNG REBELS (2014)**, which was made by the Asian Health Agency in partnership with digital:works and is available to view online. The documentary features interviews with many of those involved at the movement's birth, who all speak frankly about their experiences of coming-of-age in Southall at a time where racist abuse was an everyday occurrence. Whilst fighting back against the 'Skinheads' and the National Front was an important part of their activities, the Southall Youth Movement, we're told, 'wasn't like the Panthers' with an overt political agenda but instead was focused on issues reflecting the community. An early campaign, for instance, brought about a reduction in admission prices for the areas overpriced cinemas.

The film's high points though are in the recollections of the first major test of the Southall

Southall on the march in *Young Rebels*

Youth Movements resolve in April 1979 when, with a General Election imminent, the National Front made known its intention to hold a public meeting at Southall Town Hall on St. George's Day. One such youth, now an elder, recounts the exact moment he knew that this was the time to stand their ground once and for all: 'I remember sitting in my front room with many colleagues and my father came in... We all went silent, everybody respected the parent. All he said was, "Are you just going to talk or are you going to do something?" I think for a couple of seconds we were just looking at each other and I remember one of my friends said, "This is what they all think. There is no way that we are not going to do what we are going to do. We have to do something."'

On the 18th April, a delegation of Southall residents met with Labour Home Secretary Merlyn Rees hoping he could be persuaded to ban the meeting but was instead informed that he would instruct the Metropolitan Police that they should ensure the meeting could go ahead and be open to those who wished to attend. This the police did with much gusto and the specialist 'tactics' of the Special Patrol Group (SPG).

On the day of the meeting, the community began a planned sit down protest outside the Town Hall: 'Our leaders had decided we were going to do it peaceful, Gandhi style, sitting. And you could see their plan was never going to work because they thought they were somehow going to be allowed to sit in front of [the Town Hall] in the middle of a road... And you could see the police were not going to let us anywhere near the building.'

The protesters instead found themselves forced by the police into side streets with organisers and stewards arrested. Despite this, by 3.00 p.m a considerable crowd had assembled and, with the police sealing off all access to the Town Hall, numerous attempts to push through were met by charges using horses and SPG snatch squads. On one such occasion at around 5.30 protesters were chased into Southall Park and a nearby cul-de-sac Park View Road, which was home to the People's Unite Education and Creative Arts Centre, which was being used for the day as a makeshift centre for emergency legal advice and medical treatment and where many took refuge. The Centre was also home to the musicians co-operative to which Southall based bands such as The Ruts, The Enchanters and Misty in Roots belonged. By the time the SPG had finished, the building had been so badly damaged by the police that afterwards it had to be demolished.

Misty vocalist Poko recalls the incident in *Young Rebels*: 'They came inside... and they destroyed most of the building and arrested a lot of people. A lot of the band members and everybody was taken out of the building and were falsely accused of things that they never did. The manager of our band was coshed inside 6 Park View by the SPG... when I say cosh, they were beating people with heavy truncheons... he nearly died, he had fluid on the brain and fortunately he recovered.' Clarence Baker was in hospital for a month with serious head injuries and once discharged suffered the ignominy of being amongst the 342 who were charged by the police.

Blair Peach wasn't so lucky. Peach was a 30-year-old New Zealander working as a teacher in Bow who was struck on the head and suffered a fractured skull, one of three that day with such injuries. Peach never regained consciousness but despite numerous eyewitnesses, no police officer was ever disciplined, let alone charged, with the murder. An investigation concluded that Peach was almost certainly killed by an officer from the SPG, and narrowed it down to the six officers on the SPG carrier U11, and noted an 'indication' that one police officer in particular, who had been the first out of the van, was responsible for the fatal blow. That officer resigned from the force soon after and became a lecturer in corporate responsibility at the University of Winchester. There would never have been charges brought against Murray regardless of the evidence against him because the killing was deemed to be legal. As the report pointed out in its terms of reference: 'In case of riot or riotous assembly the officers endeavouring to disperse the riot are justified in killing them at common law if the riot cannot otherwise be suppressed.'

A raid on the lockers of the SPG officers uncovered several unauthorised weapons including knives, crowbars, a whip, home-made truncheons, and a lead-weighted leather cosh. One officer's locker contained his collection of Nazi regalia. The investigation recommended that several officers who had lied in order to cover up the actions of colleagues be charged with conspiring to pervert the course of justice but no officer was ever the subject of disciplinary procedures.

Whilst Linton Kwesi Johnson paid tribute to the murdered schoolteacher in 'Reggae Fi Peach', the Park View incident was immortalised by Misty in Roots former label mates The Ruts in 'Jah War', a track from their acclaimed debut (and only) long player 'The Crack', an album steeped in the streets of Southall. It was also released as the band's third single.

Hippies, Skinheads, Rastas, Punks & Disco Dancing Bowie Boot Boys

*

Despite unsuccessful attempts to mobilize a mass street presence, the National Front set their sights on Lewisham again in April 1980. By then their support consisted largely of young racist Skinheads and several hundred marched from Forest Hill to Catford, again protected by two thousand police who battled with the counter protesters. It is this march that is referenced in the playwright Hanif Kureishi's first screenplay, **MY BEAUTIFUL LAUNDERETTE (1985)** where a now reformed ex-Skinhead is reminded by an old friend of he and his Skinhead friends' past activities: 'What were they doing on marches through Lewisham? It was bricks and bottles and Union Jacks. It was immigrants out. It was kill us. And it was you.'

My Beautiful Laundrette tells the story of Omar (Gordon Warnecke), not long out of school and like so many others on the dole. Omar lives at home with his alcoholic father, once a famous journalist in Pakistan but on a steep and sorry decline since the death of his wife. Despite Omar's reluctance, his father wants him to go to college but in the meantime arranges for him to wash cars in his Uncle Nasser's car showroom. Omar quickly shows enough acumen and ambition to be offered the managership of his uncle's dilapidated, 'constant boil on the bum' laundrette, an offer he readily accepts.

Giving a lift home one evening to his uncle's business partner Salim and his wife, Omar is forced to a stop at a set of lights by a railway viaduct where the car is quickly surrounded by a bunch of Skinheads and Punks, the largest of whom presses his bare arse against the window while the rest bang on the car roof and hurl insults. To everyone's surprise, Omar climbs out of the car and walks towards a youth stood in the shadows, a few yards farther away than the rest. Any sense that Omar is walking into danger is dissipated by the broad grin that is spread across his face. 'It's me!' he says. 'I know who it is,' says the youth.

The youth is Johnny (Daniel Day Lewis), an old school-friend of Omar's until he one day cropped his hair and joined the National Front. Kureishi describes the transformation, based on a personal incident from his youth, in the introduction to the script: 'He was dressed in jeans so tough they almost stood up by themselves. They were suspended above his boots by Union Jack braces of 'hangman strength', revealing a stretch of milk bottle white leg. He seemed to have sprung up several inches because of his Doctor Marten's boots, which had steel caps and soles as thick as cheese sandwiches. His

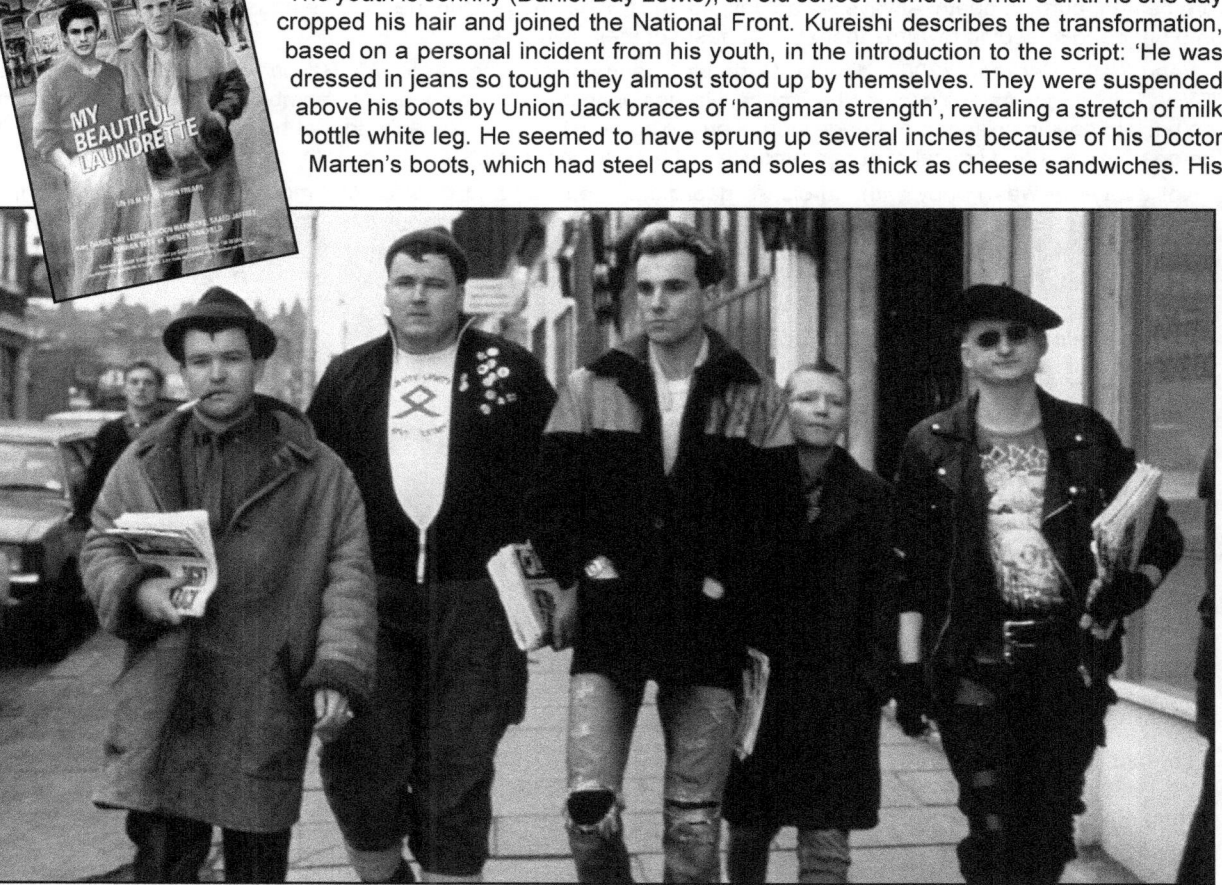

Ben Sherman shirt with a pleat down the back was essential. And his hair, which was only a quarter of an inch long all over, stuck out of his head like little nails. This unmoving creation he concentratedly touched up every hour with a sharpened steel comb that also served as a dagger... where before he was an angel-boy with a blond quiff flattened down by his mother's loving spit, a clean handkerchief always in his pocket, as well as being a keen cornet player for the Air Cadets he'd now gained a brand new truculent demeanour.'

The idea for the film, he says, 'came out of all the... boys I'd grown up with since I was four or five who became Skinheads... The Daniel Day Lewis character came out of all those boys. And the fact that being a young Asian kid, I knew those kids. I grew up with them, they were part of me. The gang that would hang around the launderette, that was like all those boys.' Such incidents helped drive Kureishi towards writing: 'When people insult you, when friends of yours become Skinheads and go out Paki-bashing and you don't have anyone to talk to about your feelings and you're far too nervous to confront your friends directly, you have to express yourself somehow.'

In the film, Omar and Johnny rekindle their friendship and, as Johnny is unemployed, Omar offers him a job running and renovating the run-down launderette. Johnny quickly agrees, seeing a way to make a new start. Also becoming lovers, they do truly make the launderette beautiful, but not without agreeing to pick up some drugs for Salim which they keep and sell themselves to help with the financing.

Johnny's friends are unimpressed by this turn of events and Genghis (Richard Graham) demands to know: 'Why are you working for them? For these people? You were with us once. For England... I'm angry. I don't like to see one of our men grovelling to Pakis. They came here to work for us. That's why we brought them over. OK?'

Salim has no better opinion of Genghis' boys than they do of him: 'These people. What a waste of life. They're filthy and ignorant. They're just nothing. But they abuse people. Our people. All over England, Asians, you call us, are beaten, burnt to death. Always we are intimidated.' 'What these scum need...' he adds whilst slamming his car into gear and speeding towards them '... is a taste of their own piss.'

Bend It Like Beckham (2002) director Gurinder Chadha says 'When I saw *My Beautiful Launderette* I was like, "Wow!" Hanif took Asians into another space. He was bringing us up to speed. I remember thinking that we'll never go back to having arranged-marriage stories on the screen. Ha! We invariably do. But he showed us that we could be open, honest and critical of our communities. It was so liberating.'

Not everyone was happy with Kureishi's depiction. Producer and director Mahmoud Jamal thought the film reinforced stereotypes 'for a few cheap laughs... what is surprising about the film is that it expresses all the prejudices that this society has felt about Asians and Jews - that they are money-grabbing, scheming, sex-crazed people.' Defending such accusations on *The Late Show* Kureishi said: 'I cannot do PR for special groups of people... I suppose I'm a chronicler of British society of the 1970s and 1980s, and my job as a writer is to tell the truth as I see it, not to tell lies in order to appease special interest groups.'

Kureishi's focus on sex, in particular Omar's relationship with someone who was not only not his fiancé, but a man, and a neo-Nazi former Skinhead, also ruffled more than a few feathers. In New York, screenings of the film were met with protesters from the Pakistan Action Committee holding banners that declared the film to be 'the product of a vile and perverted mind.'

With hindsight, that *My Beautiful Launderette* should make such an impact is a no-brainer. Prior to Kureishi and director Stephen Frears film, British Asians were almost invisible when it came to popular culture. There were no footballers, pop stars, and no homegrown film stars. Well, in the case of the latter two - almost. In April 1982 Monsoon, fronted by 16-year-old Sheila Chandra, appeared on *Top of the Pops* with 'Ever So Lonely', making history as the first Asian singer to perform on the programme. It would be the next decade before the feat was matched by the likes of Cornershop (whose first single in 1993 featured a B side called 'Hanif Kureishi Scene' and who would hit the top spot in 1997 with 'Brimful of Asha'), Talvin Singh, Asian Dub Foundation and Black Star Liner. Art Malik was becoming a star via Raj Revival television epics *The Far Pavilions* (1984) and *The Jewel In The Crown* (1984) and the film *A Passage To India* (1984). Ben Kingsley picked up an Oscar for *Gandhi* (1982) after a career spent playing anything but Asians despite his Gujarati Indian descent. In football, it would take until 2004 for a British Asian to appear in the Premier League when Birmingham born Zeshan Rehman, of Pakistani origin, turned out for Fulham.

Hippies, Skinheads, Rastas, Punks & Disco Dancing Bowie Boot Boys

Oi! Oi! Oi!
(Cockney Rejects)

Along with the National Front, by the close of the 1970s Sham 69 were also finished but the raw stripped-down version of Punk they had popularised was flourishing and soon had a name – Oi!, which according to Punk poet Garry Johnson was 'about real life, the concrete jungle, the old bill, being on the dole, and about fighting back and having pride in your class and background, Oi! is anti-politics cos they're all the same liars and cheats, but we know Labour are the real traitors they let us down. Oi! is about rock 'n' roll, football, beer, sex, going to gigs, having a laugh, fighting back, it's our life, our show, our world, it's a way of life.' Others had a less favourable view; like broadcaster Stuart Maconie who called Oi! 'Punk's stunted idiot half-brother, musically primitive and politically unsavoury, with its close links to far-right groups.'

The Oi! bands provided a belated soundtrack to Richard Allen's 'Skinhead' novels, with The Oppressed celebrating their eponymous hero in 'Joe Hawkins': 'See him walking down the street / Doctor Martens on his feet / Levi jeans, Ben Sherman shirt / Fuck with him and you'll get hurt / He's a Skinhead he don't care / Marten boots and short cropped hair'. Elsewhere songs such as 'Teenage Slag' by Condemned '84 could have been penned by Hawkins himself: 'She's a teenage slag / After she's had a good time / She'll probably pass you by / And then all your mates and everybody / In the street will have a try / Passing round all the pubs / Get as many as she can / And when she's been round them all once / She'll go back round again.'

With an example like that, it's hard to argue with Maconie's generalisation. But generalisation it is and while Max Splodge's 'Two Pints of Lager & A Packet of Crisps Please' is unquestionably awful despite making the top ten, the Angelic Upstarts, Marxists from South Shields, 'Murder of Liddle Towers' is a recognised classic and The Business were indeed the business (and still are). For most bands, the connection with right-wing politics was both unearned and unwanted, but because of the questionable judgement/ignorance shown by the Sounds and future Sun journalist Gary Bushell's combination of the title 'Strength Thru Oi' with a cover photo of British Movement activist Nicky Crane (Bushell says he 'thought it was a still from *The Wanderers*') for a compilation album it was inevitable.

It was Bushell's courting of East End Skinhead band the 4 Skins, who he included on the compilations 'Oi! The Album', 'Strength Thru Oi!' and 'Carry On Oi!' during the movements 1980-81 heyday that would forever seal Oi!'s reputation. Ostensibly non-political, references such as that to Enoch Powell's infamous speech in 'One Law For Them, One Law For Us' on the group's debut single on their own Clockwork Fun Label in 1981 hinted otherwise: 'We've been warned of rivers of blood / See the trickle before the flood / Pretend nothing happened, make no fuss / One law for them, One for us'. Or the reference to one symbol used by the British Movement, and the name of its newspaper, on the B side 'Brave New World': 'So rise up from the ashes / a Phoenix in the sky / birth of a new breed / the old one has to die'. According to British Movement literature of the time, it was considered 'vital that the slogans and symbols of our Movement become lodged in the public mind so that when they see the Sunwheel or the Phoenix and Sunwheel emblem, they register immediately 'British Movement' and they automatically know what BM stands for.'

When their manager, Gary Hitchcock, put the band on alongside The Business and Last Resort in Southall, the arrival of coach loads of Skinheads meant there was always going to be trouble from a local population still smarting over the killing of Blair Peach some two years previous. Although no Oi! band had ever directly aligned itself with the right, the event resulted in a riot in which 110 people were hospitalised and the venue, the Hambrough Tavern, was burned out after being petrol bombed. Says Bushell: 'the acres of hysterical newsprint that ensued drowned out... any chance of Oi! getting a fair hearing, for good.'.

Where the blame lies for starting the trouble that erupted is contested. The consensus, or at least that adopted by the media, was that the blame lay firmly at the Doctor Marten clad feet of the bands and their followers. There had been reports of incidents of racial abuse and harassment by some Skinheads prior to the concert beginning.

Some media coverage was, as Bushell suggests, 'hysterical' such as the Daily Mail's attack on Bushell and Sounds which they described as 'The Skinhead Bible of Hate from an Establishment Stable', and 'not merely a

pop paper but a vehicle for viciously extremist and fascist views.' Bible of hate? Something of a pot and kettle scenario there, surely. If it wasn't for the mention of 'pop' one might be mistaken for thinking the Mail was talking about itself.

There were also definite attempts to stitch up bands, who sometimes seemed all too willing to offer their accusers a helping hand. A television news report on the 4 Skins broadcast in 1981 as part of the BBC's *Nationwide* programme begins with the voice-over: 'These musicians are outcasts, the lepers of the music industry, they've been banned by the radio stations, boycotted by the record shops, blacklisted by promoters. The last time they played a concert was in July this year and tonight they're playing in secret in the back room of a pub in Kent in an attempt to clear their name. The landlord thinks he's booked a country and western band.'

Presenter Tom Wilkinson continues his voice-over outside the shell of the Hambrough Tavern: 'the last place that band played in.' After pointing out that even today the 4 Skins insist they are not racist, Wilkinson then shows a clip of singer Gary Hodges saying: 'Pakis just went a bit mad, didn't they. Just went over the top.' To further illustrate the programmes view of Oi! he reads out a few snatches of lyrics, including the first verse of Criminal Class's 'Blood on the Streets': 'Black youths standing in the lights / Crowding together they're ready to fight / The army's in, shooting is the rage / They wanna lock them up / Put them in a cage / There's blood on the street.' The impression given is that the song is racist, which it isn't.

Mick Geggus of the Cockney Rejects says the band were approached, and agreed, to appear on *TV Eye*, ITV's successor to *This Week*, in an episode ostensibly about football hooliganism. The production obtained permission to film on Saturday morning in the Bridge House pub in Canning Town and asked the band to bring along a load of their mates, which they duly did. After performing a couple of numbers it was time for an interview but it soon became clear that it was politics the programme was interested in and, says Geggus, 'we went... no politics... try again. But she kept forcing it and we said "end of, we're not here to talk about that". So she changed her tack. We thought we had it all sewn up, and this thing screened... and they called it a recruitment breeding ground for the far right. Not long after the band were banned by GLC, and lost a tour they were about to embark on for the 'Power & the Glory' album.'

In *Young Rebels* one of the Southall Youth Movement founder members suggests that what happened in 1981 was the preferred tactic of some Asian youth two years previous: 'Some of the other guys, their plan was simple, if we burn down the Town Hall there will be no meeting, there will be no problem.' This time their voice was the loudest: 'Every one of us wanted to and were going to burn the Hambrough Tavern down... the next day it was a shrine of celebration. The number of people that met there, proud of what had happened.'

To Bushell: 'the whole idea that the bands had gone into Middlesex to provoke a race riot was absurd,' and for the band members themselves that may well be true, but in the case of Gary Hitchcock that argument looks less solid. Talking about Trevor Griffiths television play *Oi! For England* (1982), which he found 'far fetched', Bushell says that what 'Griffiths seemed to be saying... was that in any group of Skins, you'd have one susceptible to the lure of race and nation, one drawn to class struggles, and two who couldn't give a toss about politics.' Not so the 4 Skins. When the notorious Charlie Sargent, the now-convicted murderer and onetime leader of Combat 18, joined the British Movement in 1976 there were supposedly only 3 Skinheads who had joined before him... 3/4 of the band's original line-up; Gary Hodges, Gary Hitchcock, and Steve Hamer. All could soon be found amongst the Skinheads of the so-called Sham Army. Gary Hitchcock told Garry Bushell at Sounds: 'Sham 69 was the first band we followed... But he [Pursey] used us. He dressed like us and encouraged us to come but as soon as he started getting famous he didn't wanna know. He started slagging us off in the music press.' He also touched on his right-wing affiliations: 'When we started it was really extreme to be NF. There was only a few of us who were BM. I used to think it was great' but was keen to point out 'I'm not political anymore.'

But he was at Skrewdriver's White Xmas gig on December 22nd, 1984 at Commerce Hall, Newham. A fellow gig-goer reminisces: 'Tufty, a Skinhead from Northern Ireland who was a real nasty cunt, stabbed four people in the audience. He was taking liberties. Because Skrewdriver Security was doing nothing about it, Gary Hitchcock pulled him on stage and started to hit him with a cosh. Scotch Eddie, a British Movement Skinhead, joined in. They kicked the fuck out of him on stage.'

According to Bushell: 'Johnny Rotten used to say "I want to destroy passers-by", with the 4 Skins you believed they were going to do it.' Back in the real world what the band managed to destroy was what little was left of the reputation of Oi! and the careers of bands who had unwittingly become associated with it. With shops refusing to stock the new album from the Cockney Rejects, frontman Stinky Turner was left to reflect ruefully that 'this awful, awful shit happened in Southall, we were never there, and we got the rug pulled out from under our feet. I went from the TV screen to the labour exchange in 18 months.' Regardless, 'The Good, The Bad & The 4-Skins', the 4 Skins first album, was released during June 1982 on Secret Records, topping the UK independent and Punk charts, and entering the Top 100 of the UK Albums Chart, which begs the question how well might it have done had they been able to properly promote it?

While an openly white power Punk movement existed, it was a distinct entity from Oi! and was fronted by Screwdriver who had released three singles and an album on Chiswick in the late seventies before singer Ian Stuart Donaldson resurrected the band with a new line-up and an up-front National Front affiliation in 1982. None of the associated bands would ever leave the confines of their self-imposed niche.

Despite Bushell's assertion that 'it was totally distinct from us, we had no overlap other than a mutual dislike for each other,' it should perhaps be noted that Paul Swain who played guitar with the 4 Skins during 1983-84 would later join Skrewdriver, and a later incarnation of the 4 Skins included original vocalist Gary Hodges, alongside three members of the Rock Against Communism band Indecent Exposure. Bushell refers to the frontman as simply 'a cynic' but lest anyone else might think Hodges politics had mellowed with age, more recent songs like 'Take no More' suggest otherwise: 'Illegal immigrants overrun our land. Benefits office with an outstretched hand/Competing for our homes and jobs. Begging in their gypsy mobs /Our country is full, fear the worst. Shouldn't we put our own people first?'

The events in Southall seemed to do little to improve Oi!'s quality control department. 'The Back on the Streets' EP which was compiled by Garry Bushell and released on Secret Records in 1982 includes a track by Tilbury Skinheads house band Angela Rippon's Bum whose guitarist and songwriter Dave Strickson had a history of right-wing affiliation and by his own admission 'used to go Paki bashing down Brick Lane and queer-bashing around Leicester Square.' As recently as 2010, Strickson stood for election in Thurrock, Essex, as a candidate for the BNP, along with no less than 4 other family members. Also included on the EP were a bunch of lads from Burnley calling themselves Skin Disease, but, unbeknown to Bushell, really the nucleus of agitprop legends Chumbawamba, whose obviously joke track 'I'm Thick', which apart from the introductory declaration that 'This is for Gary Bushell' contains the words 'I'm thick' repeated 64 times, was a little too subtle for the subject of their accolade.

In 1980 BBC Radio dedicated an episode of its *Checkpoint* series to a bunch of Skinheads from Tilbury, a deepwater port on the north bank of the River Thames in Essex. Presenter Roger Cook opens the programme with the statement: 'This is Tilbury, a grey desolate place with an evil stench of violence where local Skinheads roam the docklands like cropped rats.' Not his words but those of the Sun newspaper for the August Bank Holiday as part of a 'report' under the headline 'Aggro Britain'.

According to the local police spokesman: 'It was necessary at about quarter to three on the afternoon of the 27th

Hippies, Skinheads, Rastas, Punks & Disco Dancing Bowie Boot Boys

July to despatch three police cars to the bridge near Tilbury town railway station. The staff on the station had heard a commotion and disturbance and fearing that some violence might be in the offing they had reported the matter to the local police station and my officers attended. When they got there, they found a number of Skinhead persons, some of them stripped to the waist and some of them waving a Union Jack. They found another person who they later found was a Sun newspaper reporter, and they did in fact find that he had provided the Union Jack and had invited those of the crowd present who had tattoos to reveal those tattoos and to make a row or a disturbance so that they could be photographed in that position.'

According to one of the Skinheads they had arranged to meet a reporter at the local youth club where they would 'give them a story and they'd make it alright for us.' They were told to 'put your fist out... look evil... growl at the camera' and provided with a few drinks beforehand to get them in the mood. In uncovering this put-up job (and a tactic that the tabloids would continue to use throughout the decade - especially in relation to football hooliganism) the *Checkpoint* programme paints the boys as far from angels but not bad lads really - which is where it loses credibility.

Dave Strickson paints a different picture: 'The reason why the Tilbury Skins were so well known was because we put ourselves about especially, with the girls. Most of us were involved in football violence mainly West Ham and Chelsea, and we totally outnumbered any other Skinhead firm on the day. We used to go Paki bashing down Brick Lane and queer-bashing around Leicester Square. Can't say too much about this though'. Tilbury, he says 'is environmentally the best place for Skinheads to come from because it has atmosphere and it is like the East End without the immigrants.'

As well as the news media, the reputation of the Tilbury Skins had for a couple of years in the early eighties brought them to the attention of the film industry, resulting in several film appearances. In the Lewis Collins starring SAS action movie *Who Dares Wins* (1982) they appear at a Rock Against Nukes concert where they have been paid to cause a ruck. In *Take It Or Leave It* (1981) they chase the Nutty Boys from the venue after a 1978 gig at Acklam Hall. Says Madness guitarist Chrissy Boy Foreman: 'When we were filming what was supposed to be the gig at Acklam Hall, there was meant to be some trouble in the toilets, but instead of acting, you got the feeling they thought it was for real!'

Their most famous appearance was in Alan Parker's film version of Pink Floyd's **THE WALL (1982)** where they made sure their presence on set did not go unnoticed, leaving an indelible impression on the film's other extras before they even arrived on set. According to Richard Toller who as a Pink Floyd fan was excited to be among the 380 extras travelling to London's New Horticultural Hall for the shooting of a violent fascist rally: 'We set out

Bob Geldof gets acquainted with the Tilbury Skins on the set of *The Wall*

from Stanford-Le-hope, at 8 a.m. along with several hundred other teenagers. Worryingly, the recruits included a number of Tilbury Skinheads. As our buses pulled away, the kids in the back seat of the bus ahead kicked out the rear window and hung a swastika from it. I turned to my mates, exclaiming, "Oh shit, what have we let ourselves in for".'

Once on set director Alan Parker, himself from a North London council estate, was initially enamoured with the youths but soon ran into difficulties: 'I really loved them because they were my people. In between shots they used to make me laugh. Until they started to laugh about how they'd seen this Pakistani kid and had tried to throw him off a moving train... How could we make them behave in a civilised and safe manner? Stop them from being bored; stop them from kicking everybody's head in. It wasn't easy teaching them to understand the difference between reality and the filmed illusion.' Parker diffused the threat by promoting them to the more prestigious role of Pink's (Bob Geldof) 'Hammer Guard,' and to 'use this bunch of amiable loonies as the kernel of the recreated violence that was to follow. Our stunt coordinator had been working with them for a month previously at Pinewood, showing them the rudiments of film stunting, the ability to punch someone without the need for breaking their jaw, and we'd arrived at a sort of disciplined logic to their behaviour. Well, sort of.'

For the rally scene, the Skinheads were able to carry out the director's instructions with 'a zombie-like precision, perfected on the terraces of West Ham and Millwall.' Their next scenes, compiled into a brutal two minute sequence, involve the Hammer Guard brutally destroying a cafe, evicting a Pakistani family from their home and breaking up a liaison between a black youth and a white girl in a parked car, beating him senseless and raping her. Says Parker: 'They started to think it was real, so it was kind of difficult to control them in some of the more excessive, uglier scenes that I filmed. You always wonder as a film director if you might be crossing a line when you actually get people to do things that are not very pleasant... On the final cut, we kept the scene down to a minimum, as some of the shots were a little too much for us to take in the rushes, let alone an audience in a cinema.'

Skinheads from Tilbury it seems aren't the only ones who have trouble separating fiction from reality. Cartoonist and illustrator Gerald Scarfe who invented the Hammer Guard Skinhead militia and their insignia of two crossed hammers says: 'My worst moment in the entire film was when one Skinhead turned up with his hair shaved into the hammer design. I have nightmares about meeting people in the street who've taken up the Hammer look.' He would have been advised to stay away from the USA then, where groups of young Skinheads began to call themselves Hammerskins, with groups spreading across the USA and Canada and becoming the Hammerskin Nation, the most violent and well-organised neo-Nazi Skinhead group on the continent, spreading racist rock music and racially motivated violence under a banner bearing two red, white and black crossed hammers.

*

Dave Strickson has said of his home town: 'I think there is also an unknown evil that surrounds the town and if anyone is thinking about making a movie about Skins Tilbury is an ideal location.' That film would arrive in 2018 from an unexpected source.

It was whilst starring as the very frightening Adebisi in the hit US TV series *Oz* and finding himself unable to sleep at night that Adewale Akinnouye-Agbaje began working on what would become the script of **FARMING (2018)**, finding that writing five or ten pages a night would enable him to nod off. What had started as 'just a sleeping pill for me at the time' soon became a 500 page manuscript and, persuaded by friends that he should do something with it, the actor approached *Oz* writer and producer Tom Fontaine who put him in touch with the Sundance Writer's Lab which he attended in 2006 to turn his words into a screenplay. The following year he attended the Director's Lab and then the Producer's Lab, where he met Michael London, who would become the film's producer.

In 2008, with finance in place and the project all ready to go, the recession suddenly hit and the money he was promised disappeared, putting the film on hold. It would take another ten years for the completed film to premiere at the Toronto Film Festival, the project having received a much-needed shot in the arm when he received a £10,000 award at the London Sundance Festival 2012 where the script was read for investors by Minnie Driver, Ashley Walters, David Harewood and Mark Warren. A further six years on and Akinnouye-Agbaje's story would finally reach the big screen. All of which begs the question why did a famous US based actor of Nigerian descent go to such lengths to make a film about Skinheads in an Essex dock town?

In 1967 and just weeks old Akinnouye-Agbaje, who cemented his stardom by moving from the 1997 HBO prison drama to play Mr Eko in the even more successful *Lost* (2005), was fostered by his Nigerian parents into a white

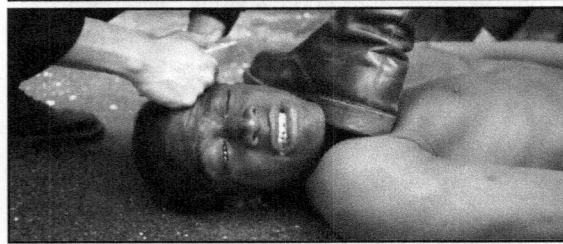

Teenage mutant Boneheads in *Farming*

working class family in Tilbury via a process known as farming. Not surprising then that when aged 8 his parents suddenly appeared and took him with them to Nigeria, he says the experience rendered him mute for about eight months: 'I couldn't speak the language, and if I spoke English I was abused for it. It was quite a culture shock; brutal. I was so traumatised and afraid that I stopped speaking and my parents thought there was something wrong with me., thought I was possessed. They tried various indigenous ways to deal with it, and when they didn't work they sent me home, back to Tilbury.'

The events are captured during the opening thirty minutes of Akinnouye-Agbaje's debut outing behind the camera, but it is after the young Akinnouye-Agbaje, depicted in the film as Enitan, returned from Nigeria and entered his teens that the youngster's problems really started as he began to come across racism with a more violent edge. A town whose dockers had led a strike in support of Enoch Powell, Tilbury's children had, encouraged by their parents, nurtured a violent fear of blacks. This was a feeling, despite his origins, shared by the young Akinnuoye-Agbaje himself, who was petrified of the black sailors who would arrive at the docks: 'It was as if they were the bogeyman to us. Fish and chips and corned beef, that's what I knew.'

The director offers a birdseye view of how some younger members of this almost entirely white town greeted its black visitors in the film's powerful 1983 set opening sequence in which a black sailor, bloodied and limping somewhere near the docks, is followed by his assailants, identifiable only by the 18 holes of their Doctor Marten boots visible below the turn-ups of their short, narrow Levis jeans and their calls of 'You fucking coon'. As they come slowly but surely to the spot where the man cowers and pleads for mercy and step out of the shadows we see that one of the group, 16-year-old Enitan (Damson Idris), is markedly different from his associates.

The action then steps back to 1967 where the six week old Enitan's parents Femi (Akinnuoye-Agbaje) and Tolu (Genevieve Nnaji) hand him over to a foster family along with a wad of pound notes. From there we learn that despite his siblings and foster siblings all managing to adjust to this strange environment where casual racism is ever present, as a more sensitive child Enitan had struggled, preferring the imaginary world he can escape to at the back of the settee. This is much to the annoyance of his stepmother and the two other ever present women of her extended family, each beautifully played by Kate Beckinsale, Ann Mitchell and Jaime Winston. This sensitive nature also does not sit well with the rough and racist kids he has to go to school with every day. Especially when, after being hit by a rock hurled by one of a group of local kids, his largely absent stepfather insists he goes back out and takes them on or face a worse beating at home.

Naturally this means that the young Enitan (Zephan Amissah) would soon learn how to both take a beating and hand one out, a far more useful qualification that a few CSE's in 1980s Tilbury. By the time he is sixteen, Enton's willingness to strike out when he is provoked leads to his suspension from school, a fact that he keeps from his stepmother by spending each day hanging round the perimeter. As do the local racist Skinhead gang.

Of his first-hand experience Akinnuoye-Agbaje says: 'They went to my secondary school; some of them were sixth formers, or were finished but would loiter outside and they would also hijack the bus that carried us to school.' This was a not uncommon phenomenon in a time when the only thing awaiting such school leavers was a place in the dole queue and long boring days without the money to finance what little passed for entertainment - usually alcohol. A similar scenario plays an important role in the explosive finale of the David Leland scripted *Birth Of A Nation* (1983), part of the *Tales Out Of School* quadrology of education-related TV plays that concluded with *Made In Britain* - filmed the same year in which *Farming* is set.

Having heard so much about it for such a long time, *Farming* was a movie I had been looking forward to. It's writer director's close association to the infamous Tilbury Skins of the 80s would surely offer an insight into a notorious place and time. Of Nigerian heritage, Akinnuoye-Agbaje's own early life would surely be a story worth telling even without its main character's eventual transition into a major Hollywood actor.

The problem is that the Skinheads that *Farming* presents us with are cartoon characters who have been nowhere near a school for decades. In fact, as their leader Levi, John Dalgleish was already 37 at the time of filming and as Jack, his sidekick, Lee Ross was not far behind. It's an unusual choice, despite it helping to shave a few years off the 26-year-old Damson Idris, to cast actors with such a disparity, more so when depicting real events.

Most of the Skinhead actors interpret their roles as close relatives of Warren Clarke's portrayal of *A Clockwork Orange*'s Dim, though Dagleish himself is more Charles Gray Bond villain than Malcom McDowell's Alex. These strokes are broad enough that could have only come at the behest of the director. This might be a deliberate slight at his former tormentors, or they could be how they appeared in his nightmares but it's probably more simply that as a director he wanted they scenes to look great, which they do.

Stanley Kubrick's depictions of gang violence are clearly a big influence and with the help of cinematographer Kit Stevens, Akinnuoye-Agbaje creates several haunting images that linger long after the film is over, but these do little for any sense of reality and jar with the earlier kitchen sink drama where his quest for reality had gone to lengths great enough to use the very same house he grew up in as a location. Also jarring is the hurried denouement in which Enitan turns his life around, gaining a Law degree and a Masters - an impossibility if we were to believe that his last on screen activities were plunging a five inch knife blade into one Skinhead and making a human fireball out of another (to say nothing of clobbering the odd copper).

Much of Akinnuoye-Agbaje's story remains untold. Likely it can be found in that 500 page manuscript, and so the true story of Tilbury's Skinheads remains somewhere amongst the mythology to which this adds another chapter. Presumably the internet will at some point come up with someone who remembers the young Akinnuoye-Agbaje but until then there's just Dave Strickson who says: 'As the founder member of the Tilbury Skinhead rock band Angela Rippon's Bum, would it surprise anybody if I said that up until this movie had been made, I'd never heard of, met or even clapped eyes on the inventor of this story before.'

A Nigerian Skinhead is also at the heart of Arinze Kene's 2013 play **GOD'S PROPERTY**, set in Deptford in 1982 and staged at London's Soho Theatre. The play concerns the return of Chima to the family home after a lengthy period at Her Majesty's pleasure to find his sixteen-year-old brother, Onochie, has rejected his heritage, taken a white girlfriend, Holly, and become a Skinhead. It has been an absence long enough that in the play's opening scene in their kitchen, Onochie believes that Chima is a burglar.

CHIMA. You're dressed like that for what?

ONOCHIE: Like 'ow?

CHIMA: Like a racist.

ONOCHIE: A Skinhead. It's a way of life.

CHIMA: I know what a Skinhead is. Ten years ago, this was me.

ONOCHIE. Dressed like a racist, as yer so put it.

CHIMA. Didn't know it at the time. Wore stuff like what you're wearing right now. Bought mine... on the high street there. Passed it by yesterday on my way to the market... Somehow you're dressed exactly like the mannequin in the shop window there.

ONOCHIE. What yer getting to?

CHIMA. The desire to camouflage. Just saying I wore that too. Thought it'd relieve some of the pressure with living round here. Wanted to fit in. Camouflage into my surroundings. Called myself a Skinhead.

Chima believes Onochie, who he is appalled to learn did not take part in the recent Brixton riot, should embrace his Nigerian heritage and join the struggle against the police and the racist system that, because he is only 'half' white, will always try to keep him down.

The reason for Chima's lengthy prison sentence is that he had murdered his white girlfriend, Poppy, and it is for this reason and the likelihood of her family seeking retribution that he would like his return kept secret. Unfortunately, Holly happens to be Poppy's godsister and exposes him. Soon Poppy's brother Liam arrives with his father and plenty of back-up waiting outside, should it be needed. In the ensuing scene it is discovered that it was Poppy's father who had been responsible for the killing after discovering she was expecting a black man's baby. Liam is aware of this but tells Chima that this won't stop his father and the gathering crowd outside, from burning them out. The play ends with the two brothers re-united as a family, drinking, smoking and listening to reggae as they await the seemingly inevitable violence that confronts them.

*

In **THE GENTLE TOUCH: AFFRAY (1982)**, a series of arrests are made during a scuffle between students and Skinheads at a protest about cuts to grants for overseas students. Those taken to the police station for questioning were all in the immediate vicinity of a WPC who had been stabbed. They include four students, two girls, a black youth, Roy (Larry Hodges) and a white one, John Douglas (James Simmons) who is not happy: 'I've got something to say to you, Sergeant. Who do you think you are? I demand to be able to telephone my father.' It seems he's the son of the Parliamentary Secretary to the Home Office, Sir James Douglas, and every bit as obnoxious as his father doubtless is. Once in the interview room, he asks the detectives, 'Are you thinking of roughing me up? Well, I box for my college and I wouldn't.'

There's also a middle-aged Iranian man, two Skinheads, and an older neo-Nazi, Mervin Tewson (Benny Young), who refers to having seen 'a blackie' commit the crime, though his description of the weapon does match the facts. 'I object to these people mollycoddling all these blacks and coloured foreigners... I want to see my country cleansed of this alien filth.' Kate (Jane Booker), the more assured of the two female students, the other being a complete wreck, is equally unhelpful and almost as racist - though being at the opposite end of the political spectrum she doesn't seem to realise it. She calls the Skinheads: 'mass-produced fascist nasties. Line them up and I couldn't tell one from the other' and 'They're like Chinamen to me. They all look the same.' 'They're not Chinamen' says DI Forbes helpfully, 'They're young Englishmen with short hair.' It's 1982 so to the police the Iranian is an 'Arab'.

A casual approach to the Skinhead look in *The Gentle Touch*

DI Forbes gets the job of interviewing Mick (Julian Jones) the main 'Skinhead,' though his haircut certainly isn't, and she succinctly sums up his appearance as 'like a hick country boy out of an American musical,' and asks him, 'Why is it a big boy like you... spends his time looking for aggro and punch-ups?' The

Musical differences come to the fore in the stage version of Oi For England

answer it seems is that he sees himself as the hero of Richard Allen's unwritten classic 'Ninja Skinhead': 'Better than telly. I mean, you're doing it and watching it. That's what it's all about these days - participation. I enjoy a punch up, it's exciting. But you don't enjoy it if you get hurt all the time. And do you know how you don't get hurt? You keep your eyes open. Your eyes are going everywhere. Who's tooled up. Who's got a shiv on them. Who's got boots that could kick your head in. Your eyes are taking it in like lightning. Your brain-box is flashing away like a computer, sussing it all in an instant so you don't get hurt. It's magic... better than sex.' His superpowers, however, don't stop one of the PCs giving him a kicking, busting his lip and loosening a tooth. He doesn't want to complain though.

The police methods are somewhat unorthodox, with the DI suggesting: 'After we've seen 'em why don't we bang 'em all in the big cell. I mean, if we can't soften 'em up maybe they'll do it themselves.' 'Why not?' says the Chief, and so they do just that. Instead of kicking off there's a sense of newfound commonality with John telling his father: 'You don't listen to anybody, that's the trouble. Nobody listens to us. Nobody listens to those poor bastards of Skinheads to find out what's bothering them. I've more sympathy for them, even though they attack us, than I have for you. We're all angry and frustrated because no one listens.'

Writer James Doran was responsible for 37 episodes of *Z Cars* and an episode apiece of spin-offs *Softly Softly Task Force* and *Barlow*, but also co-wrote *The Ipcress File* (1965). It's fair to say this isn't one of his finest moments, though the year's other Skinhead dramas would more than make up for it. The fallout from the Southall riot had shone a spotlight on the Skinhead subculture and 1982 saw three well-received dramatisations, a BBC documentary and the first published introduction to the Skinhead culture in Nick Knight's 'Skinhead', providing an overview of the origins, an illustrated fashion section, a music guide and a series of black-and-white photos.

The roots of **OI! FOR ENGLAND (1982)** lay in playwright Trevor Griffiths involvement with the Anti-Nazi League and in particular a conference he had chaired for the Leeds branch of the National Union of Teachers on race in the classroom which focused on the recruitment by extreme right-wing parties of youths in school playgrounds. Attended by about 140 people, Griffiths says: 'It quickly became clear from what was being said that yet another wave of Fascist recruitment was under way. What shocked me was the way the National Front and British Movement at this time were recruiting so successfully amongst kids in schools, especially third and fourth year pupils.'

Following the meeting, he began to investigate fighting against this via a play, visiting schools in Leeds, Manchester and Salford, and talking to pupils. Wanting to 'say something about schools as prisons' he originally decided to set the play in a 5th year detention until the outbreak of rioting throughout the country in 1981 led to him reconceiving the play around a group of Skinheads. Griffiths makes it clear that 'the play's message is definitely not that Skinheads are racists, and that is the problem. The problem is white society, and more specifically the society that is post-Imperial Britain. The whole society is saturated with racism, at every level... I wanted to argue that Skinheads, and Paki bashing represented just a rather more extreme version of a much more general, everyday level of racist exchange, which you can see going on all over the place. So the play does attempt to locate the issue of racism more broadly than just Skinheads.'

Beginning with an announcement that the 'language and atmosphere will be disturbing to some people', *Oi For England!* is set entirely in a Victorian basement in Manchester's Moss Side and focuses on Ammunition, a Skinhead Oi! band comprising the violent bigot Napper (Neil Pearson), his knucklehead lapdog Swells (Gary Mercer), the quiet one Landry (Richard Platt) and the band's singer/songwriter Finn (Adam Kotz) who is gradually revealed to be deeper than the others. Like most of the Oi! bands, Ammunition's lyrics are concerned with a strong sense of class conciousness rather than race or politics such as 'Keep the light on, you in charge / You with the butter, us with marge. / Take extra precautions before you retire / This time a song, next time the fire!' As a social statement it's not exactly up there with The Clash but their second song parodies a patriotic song from WW2, 'Praise the Lord & Pass the Ammunition', written in 1942. Where in the original, the final words go: 'Praise the Lord we're on a mighty mission! / All aboard! We're not a goin' fishin', / Praise the Lord, and pass the ammunition / And we'll all stay free', Ammunition's version goes: 'Law and order, up your arse! / The orders are yours and the law's a farce! / Watch out for the crash, the course is collision. / Sod the Lord - pass the ammunition!'

Napper is missing when we are first introduced to the band at a rehearsal but present is Gloria (Lisa Lewis) a fifteen-year-old girl in school uniform who also happens to be Jamaican, the daughter of the owner of the basement they're in who has come to collect the rent they owe. Swells is the first to speak: 'Piss off chocolate drop!' She laughs, and Finn smiles and pleads poverty but promises they'll pay. Swells becomes aggressive again but is calmed down by Landry. She asks what she should tell her father but at this point Napper arrives behind her, saying 'What'll you tell who, Topsy?' - his racism only slightly more subtle than Swells. Pulling out several pound notes from a brown envelope he sends her on her way, 'Bye Topsy. Say hello to Kunta Kinte, won't you?'

As she leaves, she passes The Man (Gavin Richards) who has arrived with a proposition. He's putting on a festival and has been let down by a London band and has offered the slot to them: 'On the night of May 6th - local election night... Moss Side will see its biggest concert ever. Half a dozen bands, twenty thousand kids from all over the area, bussed and trucked.... Doleboys like yourselves, school over years back, job not yet begun. Sicker bein' kicked around, ignored, shat on, pushed to the bottom of the midden, up to their necks in brown scum, the diarrhoea their rulers have seen fit to flood this England with.' Landry is non-committal, saying he 'don't really understand politics 'n' that. Never really bothered. Look after me own business. 'Cos no bugger else will' but Finn is adamant that he 'don't wear a swastika for nobody' and is unhappy that the band are now suddenly to be billed as White Ammunition. Napper and Swells are keen, with the former saying 'I'll play in a long white frock if I 'ave ter.'

In the streets outside there's a race riot already brewing, and it transpires that the brown envelope from which Napper paid the rent was the spark that lit the fuse, having mugged an Indian man of his wage packet, an action he has no problem justifying: 'I'm eighteen and I've never 'ad a job in me fuckin' life! So I blobbed 'im one an' took the lot. Fifty-eight quid. Serves the fucker right.' In the end the band splits and alone in the basement with Gloria, she and Finn form an uneasy alliance and he smashes the groups equipment before the two step out into the chaos on the streets outside.

Though most of Griffiths' work started life in the theatre, *Oi For England!* was written for television because he felt it was important that it should reach a large audience which the writer says it did: 'About five million people did actually get to see it.' The Guardian's Nancy Banks Smith said 'on a weekend when BBC 1 and ITV were apathetically banging each other over the head with old films, it was like finding a window open in a lunatic asylum. Under Margaret Matheson Central's drama department is now, in its 'Up Yours' way, as grittily good as any in television.'

Even more importantly for Griffiths, a lot of young people liked it: 'That was what gave us the idea of mounting some small scale touring productions, to transfer the play into live performances in youth clubs, community centres, and so on… Anybody who wanted to do it had to meet one condition, which was in turn for my 10% of the box office takings, which I left with the company concerned, they had to use that money to organise at least 30 minutes of discussion. I think it's probably the best theatre production of a play I've ever had.'

'The situations were often dangerous, particularly on the London tour. A lot of Skins would follow it around initially very hostile to the ideas in it, eventually becoming a sort of protection guard, and actually illustrating the point I was trying to make in the writing, that youth is a terrain of struggle. In a very tiny way, a discourse did take place. There was argument, some of it very fierce, but one got the sense that here for the first time, in open adult discussion kids could actually say what they felt and not get clouted or marginalised for it.'

'The reaction of Skinhead audiences generally was that the play knew quite a bit about their culture, and they respected it for that. But at the same time they thought the play was deeply wrong-headed in its central political message of 'Black and white, unite and fight'. Yet the significant thing for me was the way that, given the respect, and given the space, white Skins were eager to engage with the play, and talk about their experiences very concretely. After the performance, the actors and director would stay behind and hold a formal or informal discussion with the audience. That was a central feature of the whole exercise.'

Both television and theatre productions were not without their share of controversy, the former finding problems with the IBA, who objected to the strong language though Griffiths believed their objections ran a little deeper: 'They were a lot more concerned that people would be shocked by a few swear words than by the real obscenity of racism itself. In fact, it was the politics of the play they were really opposed to - the connections it tried to make between rising unemployment and the growth of fascism.' In 1992 the Doncaster Arts Co-op, which had started three years earlier with Manpower Services Commission money, proposed to tour the stage version of *Oi For England* but met opposition from Labour councillors who deemed the potential audience needed their protection. The Chairman of South Yorkshire Recreation Committee was worried that the young might be influenced in favour of the National Front rather than by the obvious message of anti-racism finding it, according to Griffiths, 'so explicit, so powerful, that it swamps the anti-racist position articulated by Finn. The charge is that I have given the devil all the best tunes!' The Chairman declared that the councillors were intelligent enough to make their own artistic judgement and he would insist they had prior access to scripts.

The stage version with Antonia Bird directing Paul McGann as Finn, supported by Peter Lovstrom, Dorian Healy and Robin Hayter, is explored in Robin Hayter's 44 minute documentary, *Oi For England's Green & Pleasant Land* (2018), which looks back at the extensive tour of Inner London community centres before a sell-out run at the Royal Court Theatre Upstairs and features interviews with Griffiths, musical director Andy Roberts, and Micky Geggus.

An insight into Oi!'s intended audience was provided by **40 MINUTES – Skinheads (1982)**. 'Most Skinheads stick together, know what I mean? It's something to identify with, and that's why a lot of people don't like Skinheads. Because they're frightened, because they realise they're a force, know what I mean? They all stick together... I'd say it's the music first, then girls, football and all that. Going out with your mates. Violence doesn't really come into it, you know. Nobody talks about it, papers play up the violence thing too much.' So says one of the four Skinheads, John, Brownie, Eddie and Chubby, six and a half minutes into director Ted Clisby's contribution to the BBC's documentary strand, *40 Minutes*, which, recorded without commentary, is intended to let the viewer experience what it's like to be a Skinhead. Which if this programme is anything to go by, despite the aforementioned protestations, means violent and racist.

Opening at a Punk gig in a pub, the camera follows the boys to the dole queue, on a tube ride, an afternoon in the launderette, a rehearsal for the band Combat 84 before ending up at another gig where rival factions of Skinheads end up in a mass brawl, wrecking the venue. So much for togetherness.

The Guardian said 'the style and quality of the film were so confused as to border on the incomprehensible,' but admitted it was 'certainly frightening in an impressionistic way... the camera caught enough foul language, alcoholic mind-blowing, and ritual violence to make most other citizens fear for tomorrow.' All in all though it was thought to be a 'lost opportunity.'

The year also provided one of the greatest ever made for television movies, British or otherwise, in **MADE IN BRITAIN (1982)**, the climactic film in the series *Tales Out of School*, about Trevor, a young Skinhead who had not so much fallen through cracks in the system as kicked his way out screaming a torrent of expletives. This would

Tim Roth debates the finer points of the criminal justice system in *Made In Britain*

cause problems further down the line, but first the project would need a director and a young lead actor capable of portraying Trevor's anger. The choices for both would prove vital in taking *Made In Britain* to almost unprecedented heights.

Alan Clarke was initially reluctant to take the helm, but the series producer Margaret Matheson persisted and the director and writer David Leland eventually began to talk over the project. It was in a cutting room in Soho Square where Stephen Frears was editing his 1982 TV movie *Walter* that Clarke had his eureka moment and knew how he wanted to shoot it - always a criterion for taking on a film.

Says Leland: 'Chris Menges had shot *Walter* using a Steadicam which was a very rare piece of technology back then - it had been used a little bit but it hadn't really caught on at all... What appealed to Alan was that Chris really liked shooting with what he called available light. When he walked into a location... he would look to see how the place was lit, so if there was overhead lighting such as one might find in an office suite, he would enhance that lighting, make it brighter by putting in more powerful bulbs... in order to boost the available light. The innovation of faster, more sensitive film stock also helped to make this happen. It created a very particular quality, almost anti-digital camera work. Everybody wants crystal clarity all the time, but this had a real lived in texture and depth to it... So eventually Alan said, "If I do this film... this is how I want to do it." Alan kept asking me questions about the piece and about Trevor and what he was like. I described him as a restless kid, always on the move and Alan said, "Yeah, right, right..." and he became very passionate about it.'

To subsidise his early acting career, Tim Roth was working in telephone sales when his car had a flat and he ventured into a West End theatre in search of a pump where, as it happened, auditions were being held for a TV movie and he was asked if he would like to audition. Getting a call back in front of the director, producer, and writer, Roth says, 'I turned up early on purpose. I came in and I told 'em, "When you need me I'll be in the park across the way," knowing full well they'd be watching me through the window. And I did some... character work in the park. And luckily a friend of mine turned up who was in a band called King Kurt. And he had this fucking huge Mohawk and I'm bald and we started mock-fighting and he's making a peacock noise -and then the police turned up and got involved - and Alan and his lot are watching me out of the window. And then I went in and did a reading. But by then it was more of a formality than anything else. Alan said, "Oh. we saw you through the window," and I'm like, "I know..."'

Hippies, Skinheads, Rastas, Punks & Disco Dancing Bowie Boot Boys

'I DON'T Know why I LiKE BEINg a SKIN But I do. But I don't SEE Why people grope us together as holigans 'cos we ain't alright you get troble makers in every facktion But they don't publish it if a niggeR does a old Biddy do they give us a faiR will someone as for stop being a SKIN I don't think I will'

In 1981, whilst undertaking research, writer and academic Dick Hebdige met a sixteen-year-old Skinhead in East London and asked him to write down why he enjoyed being a Skinhead and the statement above is what he quickly jotted down. It was, Hebdige thought, 'a genuine statement of Skin' that ranked alongside 'a graffiti slogan on a council estate wall, or a boot planted through an Asian's shop window or a gallon of petrol poured through the letterbox of a Bengali family's home.'

Hebdige called him the 'quintessential Skin,' embodying what is broadly seen to be typical of the subculture at the time. 'He isn't grateful or contrite. He isn't even heroically rebellious. Instead, he is as incomprehensible as the blurred tattoos which decorate his skinny arms, as jumbled as his own words... He is himself unreadable and hence ungovernable - a walking accusation levelled at the sympathetic, educated sensibility which seeks simultaneously to understand him and set him on the straight and narrow.'

His name was Harry the Duck, and he was, thought Hebdige, a 'social worker's nightmare.' In *Made in Britain*, Harry becomes Trevor (Tim Roth) and the social worker whose nightmare he is currently at the fore of is a different Harry (Eric Richards). As the film opens, Trevor is brought into court to the sound of The Exploited's 'UK '82'. It's a perfect choice that has with the passage of time taken on a significance beyond anything director Alan Clarke might have imagined. By 1982 Punk, as well as The Exploited themselves, was considered something of a joke amongst the British music press. After turning their rebellion into money, The Clash and the Pistols had moved on, but after three years of life under Margaret Thatcher youth unemployment had reached heights unimaginable when Chelsea sang about the 'Right to Work' and thousands of discontented youths in regions of the country that didn't appear on the radar of London based journalists decided to remake Punk rock in their own image. As the music became faster and more aggressive, there was no room for part-time poseurs as the new force of the music was perfectly complemented by studded leather jackets and mohawks that decreed their unemployed wearers virtually unemployable. Nearly forty years on UK '82 has become a sub-genre in its own right and bands like the Anti-Nowhere League, Discharge, Disorder and GBH with their Motorhead inspired sound went on in turn to influence the likes of Metallica as well as, for better or worse, forming the foundation stones for new genres like thrash metal and grindcore.

Trevor has been brought before the magistrate for, as well as nicking cassette tapes from Harrods, throwing a brick through an Asian man's lounge window. His attitude is hardly remorseful and when he is told, 'You don't invite leniency do you,' he curtly replies 'No.' It is far from being his first offence with a lengthy record already cataloguing instances of joyriding, shoplifting and violent behaviour and so his next port-of-call is for assessment at a residential centre. Harry, his caseworker, questions his choice of venue to go shoplifting and Trevor looks puzzled. 'Was Harrods full of Skinheads that day you went, was it?' he asks. 'No, it was full of wogs.' Oh, yes, Trevor is also a racist, the swastika tattooed on the centre of his forehead being something of a give-away - though not it would seem to the attendance centre who not are not expecting him, but also deem it good practice to put him in a double room with a black youth, though the pair happily head off to the job centre together. Trevor has been given money for bus fares which immediately goes on twenty fags and a pot of glue, so they attend the job centre in a stolen car, Trevor leaving a parting gift in the form of a slab of concrete through the window. His destructive form of protest continues back at the residential centre when, too late for lunch, he kicks the doors in before being restrained, though not before putting the boot into one of the care workers.

It is the second act that remains unforgettable, a twenty-minute two-hander between Trevor and a cynical Superintendent who maps out the young offender's future on a chalkboard: 'You start off here at HOME... there's your mum, your dad and the rest of 'em. Just like any other mum and dad all they ask you to do; all you have to do, is go to school. Now that's not too much to ask, is it? You're clever. You're bright. Everybody wants you to succeed; nobody wants a failure on their hands... but you didn't want to go to school did you? You knew best...'

'But you weren't just bunking off. You had to do something with all that time so you did a bit of thieving. First 2 or 3 times you get taken down the nick, and some policeman tells you off, shouts at you. Next time you get a caution; this time a Sergeant in full uniform shouts at you. That don't make any damn difference because you're apparently deaf to any kind of reason. They're getting used to you now, so you get fined or taken to the local police attendance centre, kept off the streets all day Saturday. Made to scrub floors by another loud policeman when you could be watching West Ham lose at home.'

'The magistrate doesn't know what to do with you... so they send you here to us for assessment... CHE, detention centre, borstal. Shame about CHE, community home and education... what used to be called an approved school... lots of lick me arse power trips around 15-year-olds but you've just turned 16. Bad luck. Not much left to bring you in line is there? Short sharp shock at the local detention centre or borstal...'

When he comes out, he is told, his path will take him from no job, to the dole, to prison and 'round and round you go.' For as long as it lasts, Trevor remains silent for the first time, but if they think he will tow the line, they have another thing coming as they discover when it his turn to speak: 'I'm British. You know what that means do ya? You proud to be British, are you? Don't you know? I'm proud. That's because you spend too much time locked in here with all these niggers. I'm more British than you are fuck face. You hate the blacks as much as I do only you don't admit it. You hate the blacks more than I do because they frighten you. That's why you lock them up. You lock up anything that frightens you. In here it's just the same as school. Do what we tell you, think what we tell you, say what we tell you. Squawk. Be a fucking parrot. I hate you for putting me in here. You're bullshitters. You swallow your own bollocks, you expect me to swallow it too.'

'... If I spend my life watching my p's and q's cos some mingy fucker like you is gonna write it all down on a piece of paper. "Your case conference is coming up, watch your step". Bollocks, I'll say what I want to say. You got decisions to make about my life then get on with it, it's got bugger all to do with me. I hate you for putting me in here. One day you'll pay for it.'

Trevor does agree to behave on the proviso that he can drive at the stock car racing but uses the trip to help himself to the centre's keys which give him access to the personal files he had raged against earlier. With Errol in tow, who we discover can't read in keeping with Trevor's earlier stereotype, they piss and shit on them before stealing the centre's mini bus. Visiting an Asian neighbourhood, they both hurl racist abuse and bricks through windows. 'Black nigger bastards' and 'You baboons get back to the jungle' shouts Errol without the slightest hint of irony. Trevor then deliberately rams the mini bus into a police car parked outside a police station, leaving an unconscious Errol inside, and, confirming another stereotype, when the first officer on the scene arrives and declares 'You little black bastard.'

Trevor stops briefly in front of a department store and stares at a window display of a family living room with a mother carrying a tray, the dad on the sofa watching TV and a young boy in a cubs uniform, before after walking down Rotherhithe tunnel shouting abuse at the traffic he visits Harry at his home. A final scene sees him in a cell at the police station with head pressed on the buzzer, all but demanding the beating he soon receives.

Gary Oldman and Phil Daniels in *Meantime*

The Stage had its reservations, finding the production: 'didn't so much present its ideas to you as club you with them... Hearing the same two swear words in virtually every line of dialogue from the lead character... became so tedious that we left the room for ten minutes only to return to hear the same words, seemingly the same lines, and the plot hardly advanced... Can Central really believe it engaged viewers and made them eager to watch with a script that was made of of repeated incoherence and incidents such as a man being violently kneed in the groin, and then kicked, whilst screaming, on the ground?' Thankfully, no one else seemed to agree.

Towards the end of the shoot, Clarke asked Roth if he wanted to continue to work in film and who he would like to work with. Roth said Mike Leigh and Clarke set up a meeting. The result was Leigh's **MEANTIME (1984)** where Gary Oldman got the chance to play a Skinhead, a tenure which, says the director, ended up with 'Gary's shaven head erupt[ing] into a thousand red blotches; in the film you can see the stitch marks.' Oldman and Tim Roth had been throwing a milk bottle around. Leigh, who rushed the actor to hospital in his car, says: 'As I drove him there, all done up in his Skinhead stuff, covered in blood, Gary said to me, "for fuck's sake, tell 'em I'm an actor." He could easily have lost his eye sight in the accident and I do not know to this day what I would have done if that had happened.'

Leigh got the idea for the film whilst sitting in the bath early one morning and listening to the radio when 'this story came on about two unemployed kids in Warrington or St Helens or somewhere who had committed suicide. And I thought - I always go through something like this - what we're doing is irrelevant. That's what we should be doing. Something about unemployment. We were two or three years into Thatcher. It was already an issue, and it lingered at the back of my mind.' It became a Film on Four made by Central, produced by Graham Benson and shot on 16mm. A few months later, and it would have been 35mm as Film Four looked towards getting cinema distribution for its productions.

Coxy (Oldman) is on the margins of a story about the Pollock family; Mavis, Frank and their two sons Colin (Roth) and Mark (Phil Daniels). The men are all unemployed. Coxy is a friend of Mark's: 'You're thick, I'm hard' he tells Mark, though he's actually both. The role got Phil Daniels the 'Parklife' gig, because he says: 'they're all *Meantime* freaks. Ditto Suede... Kids who play bass guitars don't like all that American *Teen Wolf* shit. They like something a bit more sort of bleak, a bit blacker.'

Of his character, Oldman told Blitz magazine: 'Coxy was such a kid. He has that childish idea that through behaving aggressively in front of a girl you can find deep love or emotion... That's how I felt, myself, doing wheelies as a kid - that "somehow" it would get a girl into bed.'

Writer and actor Jonathan Moore, who has gone on to a 30 year career as an in demand character actor, started out treading the boards in a one man show, *I Die For None of Them*, as doomed pre-romantic poet Thomas Chatterton; 'I remember when I first started on the Edinburgh Fringe with those shows, with my Punk theatre company, and saying things like, "Anybody on the official festival should be lined up against a wall and shot." Really ridiculous. Then four years later, there I was on the official festival with *Greek!* Then you start thinking, "Well, okay, anyone who gets an award should be put in a chain gang.' Then there you are saying, 'I'd like to accept this award on behalf of..."'

The following year, 1982, he returned with his play *Treatment*, the tale of a priest confronted by a Skinhead which having picked up a Fringe First Award transferred to London, where it was described as 'one of the most disturbing and exhilarating plays.' Moore himself was called the 'Johnny Rotten of the theatre' and a 50 minute dramatisation was broadcast by the BBC in 1984.

In **TREATMENT (1984)** a young man, Liam (Jonathan Moore), lies in a hospital bed, his face covered in gel, presumably the result of having been badly burnt. Into the room walks a priest with a black eye and cuts and bruises to his face. He says simply, 'What should I have said?' The story moves back in time as two Skinheads, one the invalided youth, walk along an underpass. They are discussing a ruck between two sets of football supporters: 'I bet he won't come down Stamford Bridge for a while.' They're not too fond of Tottenham and the reason has little to do with football. 'I think they're all the same these north London geezers... You can spot 'em a mile off. I think it's the smell... They should have passport checkpoints on Waterloo Bridge.'

Cutting back to the hospital, a girl, Julia (Suzan Crowley), with whom Liam was in a relationship speaks: 'He seemed so strong and aggressive but he had no real strength. I towered above him. I hate myself for that. I despised his ignorance, loved his body.' Moving back again to a pub where a Punk band plays, the other Skinhead, Liam's older brother, Rory (Peter McNamara), tries to chat up a girl wearing a Siouxsie and the Banshees t-shirt but his aggressive, cocky approach is resolutely ignored. Instead, she strikes up a conversation with Liam and the two go back to her flat where they have sex, though as soon as the act is over he's immediately thinking about Stamford Bridge in the morning.

The girl sums up Liam's appeal. 'Women are supposed to be so much more. More patient, more peace keeping, more understanding. Crap. The amazing thing about Liam was that he didn't expect that of me... not like the so-called Liberal thinkers. Emotional fascists most of them.' At uni she had been amongst 'all those patronising public

Hippies, Skinheads, Rastas, Punks & Disco Dancing Bowie Boot Boys

Top: Jonathan Moore & Peter McNamara; Below: Peter McNamara confronts Gabriel Byrne in *Treatment*

schoolboys with their please, thank you and screw you. Their utter fear of women. They're roughing it at Cambridge on enormous gifts from their parents. Sitting round on the floor and smoking joints and passing round red wine and being real with each other in assumed regional accents. Then Liam stormed into my life... he reminded me what a bunch of arseholes I'd mixed with most of my life. First thing in the morning I can love his innocence, his remarkable silence. He refreshed me.'

Liam visits the church he had attended regularly as a child, telling the priest, Mike (Gabriel Byrne), who looks somewhat alarmed to have a Skinhead in his vicinity, that he wants someone to talk to. His demeanour is alternatively nice and menacing, one minute threatening to steal the collection, the next remorseful. The visits to the church continue and the priest gives Liam a passion for reading, telling him, 'With that strength there must come love, understanding, compassion with a passion. Root out the real enemy that's inside you... cut away the hatred. Cultivate love, because if you don't you're dead.'

Liam offers an insight that the priest could never fully appreciate: 'You don't know what it's like though... it's exciting... we're ten handed. We're walking down Fulham Road, me and Rory in front. There's twenty of them at least. Getting closer. I can feel the energy rising. Closer. You can see their faces now. What they look like. They look heavy. Hard... No one says nothing. It's like slow motion. All of us lot are secretly shitting it. Even my brother. I can sense he's scared but he won't turn back. My throat feels like sandpaper, my legs are water. They aren't turning back; we aren't turning back. It's like a bleedin' western or something. *High Noon*. People on the other side of the street are stopping what they're doing. Shoppers.. standing in doorways. Model birds and geezers in Porche's stare... Closer. I ain't scared now. I'm excited. People leaning out of windows. Everyone looking at US... it's like the Albert bleedin' Hall or Madison Square Garden... star attraction. There ain't no sound. Just blink and you're there. I'm General bleedin' Custer. I felt proud... I did. I felt so bleedin' proud.'

Despite this his relationship flourishes and asked if he's going to Chelsea on Saturday he tells her he reckons he doesn't need it anymore. 'You'll be telling me next you've got a job' she says. 'I'm cutting away the hatred,' he tells her, 'Cultivating the love.' Rory has other ideas and when he discovers he's been visiting the church, he pays a visit of his own. He's got a lot to say but first simply nuts the priest.

Says Rory: 'Look at me... I ain't dead. What don't kill me makes me better. I'm hard, I'm strong and I don't fall easily for lies, not like my brother. I can see through their lies. Oxford and Cambridge, you're poison. Arsenic that eats my guts. Charles and Di, you're privileged poison with your ignorant empty smiles. Youth opportunity schemes, you're poison. Making me work for peanuts instead of a decent slab for my graft. Probation officers, you're poison.You pretend you're so interested but you're all there for the money, what you can get. And the church, you're double poison. You aren't speaking for Jesus. You lie, you cheat, you turn people into well-behaved tossers. Well, sod it, I don't need that. If you ain't thick and you don't swallow all that crap, then they try the other way. Fill your head with lies and posh books written by lazy prats with rich parents and too much time on their hands and then when it's too late you realise what you've done. They've turned you into an unthinking git. They've cut your balls off. Well, they ain't doin' that to me. I ain't gonna be soft soaped and I ain't gonna be lied to. They've offered me their poison and I ain't drinking it. They've tried to castrate me but I'll get the knife first and I'll be in there on me own, cos that is the only way I know.'

The Guardian said: '*Treatment* is meant to hit you in the face the way bar brawlers knock the top of a bottle and jab... The play certainly has energy, a certain boldness of form, but fails in the end to hit us in the way it promised.'

Hippies, Skinheads, Rastas, Punks & Disco Dancing Bowie Boot Boys

Young Savage
(Foxx, Shears, Currie)

The younger brothers of those Punks whose favourite band was The Jam and who thought the best Pistols song was 'Stepping Stone' smartened up and became Mods only to discover that those new Mod revival bands weren't The Small Faces or The Who, or even The Lower Third. Many of these would take the casual approach to what was acceptable dress in Mod circles such as yachting shoes, Farrah slacks, Lacoste polos and lambswool v necks. This look would eventually become even more casual as trainers, tracksuits and kagoules became popular - a proviso being that they were the most expensive - especially amongst young football fans. This new tribe would have no allegiance to any specific type of music and, dress aside, had little in common with their eventual title as football casuals. The full story is nowhere near so simple.

Football violence had continued to make headlines and would soon become the nation's number one preoccupation. The Daily Mirror ushered in the 1978-79 football season with an article headlined 'Saturday Afternoon Thugs' and the news that a declaration by a Judge the previous week that the courts would come done heavy on offenders had done little to dampen the thirst for violence, quoting one lad for whom it is 'better than going to the pictures' whilst another demonstrated how to turn a discarded newspaper into a 'Millwall brick'.

The report followed an opening weekend battle between Chelsea and Everton supporters in Kensington High Street underground station where the paper reported: 'Three hundred Chelsea fans lay in wait for home-going Everton supporters. Trains were stopped for more than an hour and the station was closed as fans fought a pitched battle' with similar incidents between Millwall and Newcastle supporters on New Cross Road.

But this wasn't just a case of business as usual. Out of sight of the London media a new breed of Bowie Boot Boys appeared in Liverpool where a David Bowie album cover had become a major reference point for the first 'Scallies' who emerged on the city's Scotland Road estate. Spreading first to north-west neighbour Manchester and then across the Pennines to Leeds, for once the capital was a few years late to the party. When Kevin Sampson wrote an article on this new breed for Face in 1983, the cat was finally out of the bag: 'Taking the cover of Bowie's 'Low' as a point of reference, they mixed the Bohemian cool of Bowie with Punk's snazzier trappings. The result was at once aggressive, effeminate, and extremely attractive. Mohairs worn with straights and plastic sandals, complemented by camel duffel coats. But it was the distinctive hairstyle that stamped Scally all over them, the unique and wonderful lopsided wedge - a haircut popular in the last great depression, ridiculously 'claimed' by hairstylist Trevor Sorbie at Vidal Sassoon.'

In 1996 the debut novel of John King, 'The Football Factory', was issued with only little expectation by publisher Jonathan Cape but had soon notched up sales figures over 140,000, sending a clear message to the industry that there was a ready audience for tales of hooliganism in and around the nations football stadia. Cape's next foray into the genre came two years later in the form of another debut novel, this time from Sampson. A Liverpudlian who prior to his spell as a freelance writer was famously fired from Sounds for submitting a review of a Sex Gang Children gig that had been cancelled when the venue burnt down, he had been 'a very unsuccessful football hooligan.'

Sampson had submitted an earlier manuscript of the story, then much shorter, to Penguin in 1982 and, inspired by the success of Irvine Welsh's 'Trainspotting', had dug it out and reworked it, finding interest from several publishers, helped one suspects by the success of King's novel. Sampson's 'Awaydays' was similarly successful, going into a reprint even before its official publication date, with positive reviews from the quality press driving sales further, and turning the author's mind to the possibility that, like 'Trainspotting', it might too be adapted for the cinema. Receiving a postcard from *Get Carter* (1971) director Mike Hodges shortly after publication, saying how much he had enjoyed it, would have done his confidence no harm whatsoever.

'Awaydays' covers an era in football and fashion that would come to be known as 'Casual', though that moniker would be still a few years away. It was a move away from boots and braces and donkey jackets, and into Fred Perry and Lacoste polo shirts, Farah and Lois slacks and Adidas Samba trainers. Says Sampson: 'At most of the away games I went to up north and in the Midlands in the 1970s you came across the same type of boot boys; guys with Bee Gees centre-parts, wide trousers and Doctor Marten boots. They were basically cavemen. Then you had this strangely androgynous Liverpool lot who had girls haircuts and wore very tight Lois jeans and training shoes. It's hard to imagine how subversive that look was.'

It was also an era where, on the football pitch, Liverpool ruled the roost, with legend pinning the birth of the new subculture to a European Cup semi-final tie against Saint Etienne in Loire in March 1977 where the visiting supporters were much taken by their opposing fans continental sportswear, unavailable in the UK, with the Scallies, as they would be called, stocking up on subsequent European jaunts using methods they had honed in a then deeply depressed Merseyside landscape.

Farm vocalist Peter Hooton described one such 'shopping' trip in an article in the Face to mark 10 years of the Casual. In May 1981, Liverpool faced Real Madrid in the European Cup Final in Paris and the contingent of Liverpool supporters to which he belonged arrived in the city on the Sunday ahead of the midweek match. The next three days were spent 'not looking at the buildings and architecture of gay Paree' but instead for the Holy Grail of a so-called Adidas Centre that had been heard described in hushed tones in the corner of a Liverpool snug. 'Naive teenagers we may have been' says Hooton, 'but if we had found it, we would have been heroes.'

'The newspaper Paris Soir reported the antics of Liverpool supporters with some confusion. They had been drinking, but they didn't seem to want to fight anybody. They were too busy shoplifting, with the main targets being clothes and trainers. By the morning of the game, the sports shops of Paris were locked, with staff supervising the doors, allowing only two people at a time into the shop.'

Wherever and whenever it started, it was a style, says Sampson, that spread quickly amongst the Anfield club's fans: 'You look back at Souness's debut away at West Brom in January 78 and Liverpool must have had 15,000 there. The season before maybe the look was a cult thing, 30 or 40 lads in the Road End wearing mohair jumpers, straights, and Samba. But by that West Brom game, everyone had a flick, everyone had a duffel coat, everyone looked the part.'

Forward to 1998, having turned his mind to seeing 'Awaydays' on the cinema screen, by the summer Sampson had been contacted by representatives of Muriel Gray's Glasgow-based indie, Ideal World, who duly snapped up an option on the rights for £4,000 and, more importantly to Sampson, he could begin work on the script. A few weeks after that deal was inked, interest also emerged from another source, one Matthew Vaughan, who had been handed a copy of the novel by Dave Hughes, a friend of the author from Liverpool's post Punk scene, who was then working on a soundtrack for a film by Vaughan, *Lock, Stock & Two Smoking Barrels (1998)*. With that film not yet released, Sampson says he was not too worried believing it a 'stupid fucking name for a gangster film' and asking 'is Norman Wisdom in it?'

After five years and countless drafts the required funding was still not forthcoming, and the rights reverted to the author in 2003 who vowed not to relinquish control again and with Hughes as producer, put forward a new script, taking into account a micro-budget in the region of £300,000. It was, Sampson believed, 'the best version yet - taut and punchy, but poetic too.' But £300,000 was still a lot of money and after another three years of chasing finance their major hope, North West Vision, ended in rejection with the author calling the detailed script report he received from that funding body, 'insulting'.

Far from defeated, Sampson declared 'What started as a vague desire to make a good film out of a good book has become a mission to prove the Industry wrong. It became a class war.' In 2007 the war was won. Sampson and Hughes newly formed production company, Red Union, had £400,000 in the coffers courtesy of a government investment scheme, a director who shared their vision in Pat Holden, with whom Hughes had previously worked on *The Last Weekend* (2005), and its Carty and Elvis courtesy of *This Is England* (2006) casting director Michelle Smith.

AWAYDAYS (2009) sets up Carty's (Nicky Bell) back story with a pre-titles opening scene set three months before the story begins by showing him with his father and sister Molly (Holly Grainger) as they attend the cemetery on the anniversary of their mother's death. In real life, Sampson's father had died the year he started going to the football which, he says, 'made me harder to control.' When it's time to leave, Carty stays behind, saying he'll catch them up, but as they wander into the distance he checks his watch, whispers 'sorry, mum', and to the frantic aural assault of Ultravox's 'Young Savage' he makes a run to where has stashed a holdall containing a change of clothes. In his new outfit he makes his way at speed across the dock front to the railway station where he makes it just in time to catch the train for an awayday - his first.

Three months earlier Carty is at a Tranmere Rovers home match with his dad where he watches a brief outbreak of violence on the largely empty Prenton Park terrace - Sampson's team is Liverpool but although the old Third Division setting would have helped keep the films budget in check, this is also the setting of the novel, the author feeling that 'Somehow the open terraces of Tranmere and the Northern wastelands of Crewe, Doncaster, Halifax etc. lend themselves better to that kind of narrative than the packed stadia of the old First Division' and also 'If Carty and Elvis followed Liverpool they'd have been two lads in an away following of thousands. They'd have never met!'. One young lad uses a Stanley knife on an opposition fan before quickly palming the weapon off. Soon after he has adopted the required look of a Peter Storm green smock cagoule, Lois straights and Adidas Forest Hill trainers, telling his bewildered sister 'it's what they wear'. They being the Pack, one of whom, Baby Millan (Oliver Lee), takes an instant dislike to him that will have repercussions later on.

Another member of the Pack, Elvis (Liam Boyle), meets Carty at a gig and is impressed that he was not only on the guest list but had also attended art school with members of the band, having been turned down himself. Elvis, as he admits, wanted 'to be a divvy in a raincoat.' Carty is more interested in running with the Pack, but, as Elvis points out, he is wearing the wrong trainers and that 'take it from me, a nice boy like you doesn't want to be playing out with naughty boys like that.' At the next home match, despite now having an 'in', his new friend won't let him stand with them, instead meeting him in the week at Probe, the cities famous indie record shop, where he even buys him a Bowie bootleg: 'Bowie Live in Santa Monica! It's like the only existing recording of him doing 'My Death''. Carty in return shows his hooligan potential by head butting the shop assistant for carrying on with his conversation rather than serving them straight away.

Elvis finally relents, and the story picks back up with Carty boarding the train for his awayday debut. When they exit the station at their destination, it's like two worlds colliding as they finally bump into the opposition supporters - a combination of Skinhead and latter day greaser haircuts, donkey and lumberjack jackets and scarves tied round the wrists. It is, says Sampson, who deliberately cast the Pack young to emphasise the contrast between how they look and how they act, 'how it was... I was one of the 90 on the Ordinary to Middlesbrough, August 1977 and the look on those men's faces was a treat. They obviously fancied their chances - they were men with moustaches and tattoos - we probably looked like rent boys... but you could see real unease with them. They were looking round at each other, obviously dead confused... who are these puftas. The Liverpool lads of that era were mainly all small, and the wedge haircuts made us look easy. Then you'd run at them and they were genuinely flummoxed.'

This use of youthful protagonists is a key, but far from the only element in *Awaydays* that makes it stand out in an ever-crowded market place of hooligan movies. In John S Baird's short film It's *A Casual Life* (2003), Alex Driscoll talks of the buzz you get that means 'suddenly you're not 35 with two kids and a mortgage' and in most hooligan movies there are far too many characters for whom 35 is likewise a low estimate and for some a more accurate measure of their waistlines or IQ. The Pack has just one, in the form of Godden (Stephen Graham), and Elvis is under no illusions regarding their would be camel-coated commander: 'Do you know how old that cunt is? He's fucking 30, I'm serious, the cunt's got about six kids and he's organising the pack like he's still in the army.'

There's also the unusual relationship at the heart of the drama. Both Elvis and Carty have been drawn to the violence as an outlet for what they feel is missing from their respective lives. For Carty it's the loss of his mother and for Elvis, who dreams of escaping to a better life in bohemian Berlin, it's a perceived failure from having stumbled or been rejected from his chosen path. He is far from at home with the Pack, who he refers to as 'a bunch of pricks', and having failed to find his fix in violence has turned instead to heroin. He's also into Carty, who is 100% heterosexual. When they pick up two proto-goth girls on a night bus and take them back to the 'Bat cave', it is left to Carty to attend to the needs of both girls while Elvis gets wasted.

Then there's the post-Punk milieu, be it in settings such as Elvis & Carty's meeting at an Echo & the Bunnymen gig where they sit under a Big In Japan poster and smoke a joint, or the music from the likes of Joy Division, the Cure, Cabaret Voltaire, Elvis Costello, Dalek I Love You, and Magazine, that cleverly avoids going for the big hits in favour of fitting the films themes. Then there's the delightful and unexpected choice of John Foxx-era Ultravox! who provide three tracks and provide a tantalising glimpse of where the Glam/Punk crossover might have gone instead of New Romantic.

Unsurprisingly, it doesn't end well as Carty gradually realises that Elvis might have been right after all when, after letting his enthusiasm get the better of him and trying to lead a charge, he's taken down a peg or two by Godden, whose own days are numbered when he objects to Baby's heroin dealing. This leaves the increasingly unreliable Elvis as all that stands between Carty and the clearly psychotic youth, whose grudge has continued to simmer below the surface.

Reviews were generally middling with The Guardian complaining of 'an almost hysterical level of romanticisation' but admitting that 'it sort of works - especially when all the impossibly yearning post-Punk music on the soundtrack really gets going'. The Daily Express thought: 'A meagre budget and a lack of clear-cut character motivations blunts the impact of what might have been a powerful *Mean Streets*-style study of male

friendship'.

The Telegraph, giving it four out of five, was more positive: 'What's convincing here is the pervasive unhappiness - the movie really understands violence as a drug, a way out of a void.' At the other end of the spectrum and clearly not impressed at all with the violence was Ali Catterall for Film4 who called it 'a pretentious, grubbily voyeuristic paean to football hooliganism, kitted out with ubiquitous slo-mo violence, tactical post-Punk hits and retro fashions.'

Jonathan Moore returned to his play *Treatment* at the Donmar Warehouse in 1986, directing himself in the central role of Liam, now an East End casual. It was a piece of cultural updating that the Observer said 'lessen[s] the dramatic impact - a Skinhead is a more effective icon of violence than someone in a Lacoste t-shirt and trainers.' Not everyone agrees, amongst them *Green Street* (2005) screenwriter Dougie Brimson who addressed the south east casual in the 12 minute short film **IT'S A CASUAL LIFE (2003)**, in which Alex Driscoll delivers a direct-to-camera soliloquy on the joys of being a football casual: 'You should have seen this geezer, geared up to fuck and dripping arrogance he was. Diamond Pringle jumper, Lois cords, Adidas trainers and a proper wedge haircut, layered. Not that stupid mushroom style like the Scousers used to have. This geezer was the absolute bollocks, and he knew it… straight away I knew I wanted to be like that, and by the time I was fifteen I was. A casual. A fully paid-up member of the Saturday scene.'

He longs for the good old days when: 'Back in the eighties we respected lads for their gear. Not just 'cos it looks good, but we know a bit of effort went into getting it. Now they just stick a Long Island jumper and a Prada cap on a Barclay card and all of a sudden they think they're fucking Supermen. It's bollocks… it's not what you wear it's how [you] wear it. You can't buy that. It's up here. You gotta learn it. This is why all these silly fuckers have ended up looking the same. Gear isn't a statement for them; it's a fucking uniform.'

There's no David Bowie in Nick Love's remake of **THE FIRM (2009)**, though they do like to strut their stuff down the local disco. What there is amongst the West Ham United and Millwall supporting casuals are more than a fair share of those who are old enough to know better but the film does at least elevate the character of 18-year-old Dom from Alan Clarke's original into his film's major role. It's one of several very smart choices by the director who was in little doubt of what he was up against in taking on re-making such a loved film, the announcement of which released a collective groan that might have been heard on the moon: '… with my track record of making immoral violence, you've got the odds stacked against you, so in a sense - what I tried to do was diffuse the situation as much as possible.' This rebalancing of the story had the added advantage of not having to find an actor to fill Gary Oldman's shoes. Love comes up trumps again with the casting of the unknown Paul Anderson in the role of Bex, rather than one of the usual suspects such as, the by then well over-used, Danny Dyer. Anderson is a convincing and believable hard man, a persona he would develop to even greater effect as Arthur Shelby in the TV series *Peaky Blinders* (2013) - with an equally deranged hair cut.

Love had originally intended to transfer the plot of the original to the present day, making Bex a more modern estate agent 'gadding about in town in his Foxton's mini, then going off for these secret violent kicks, a kind of British *Fight Club*.' Instead, he made another significant change that serves to make his *The Firm* its own animal, as opposed to a flashier, geezer version of Clarke's 1989 original. By setting the story earlier in the decade, he was able to explore London's equivalent of *Awaydays* scallies and the Perry boys of Manchester, who were briefly known as 'chaps' before all three groups were bundled together as casuals.

Confirmation that the film was still relevant in a modern setting came when West Ham and Millwall were drawn together for a second round League Cup tie in August 2009, less than a month before it was due its cinema release. It was, says Love, 'terrible timing' as both he and his film came under attack in the press, who also made much at his inclusion in a new book, 'Fifty People Who Fouled Up Football', though this 'humorous throwaway' also included World Cup winning manager Alf Ramsey, and the late Queen singer Freddie Mercury amongst his 49 co-defendants. Love was nevertheless forced to go onto news programmes to defend what he considered to be 'a pretty moral film and a positive film as well.'

At the heart of Love's film, as with *Awaydays*, is the relationship between its two main protagonists. In *Awaydays*, Elvis feelings for Carty are clearly romantic, though none of the film's characters, even Carty himself, seem able or willing to pick up on this. The longing looks from Dom (Calum MacNab) to Bex, first across the floor of a branch of JD Sports and then down the aisle of the train carriage on the return from Portsmouth, are likewise seeped in a homo-erotic subtext that Love is more than aware of, saying: 'of course the erotic subtext is undeniable - their obsession with clothes, the dandyism of it. They love each other but they can't fuck, so they fight.' It's also clear to Bex's Lieutenant, Trigger (Doug Allen), who, when Dom turns up at the pub in an identical red tracksuit to Bex, lays it on the line, much to the youngsters embarrassment: 'Funny thing about you, Dom. When you first came round here, you was dressed like a right div. Yet here you are and you're all dressed up like him. What's that about? There's a word for that isn't there?... Infatuation. But to us lot it just means you want to get stuck up him.'

In his book 'Perry Boys: The Casual Gangs of Manchester & Salford', Ian Hough refers to some time in 1983 as the point when: 'Journalists finally began to report on this movement, by now ironically constrained to the auspices of the local sporting goods shop and the stadium of his favourite football team. The thrill of the hunt had gone, replaced by an unadventurous ramble down the local high street…' which is the source of Bex's extensive wardrobe of brightly coloured tracksuits. It is telling that in *The Firm*'s creaky recreation of 1984 that the West Ham boys do their shopping in a branch of JD Sports (forgetting for a minute that the chain's stores were in the north and it would be another five years before they opened their first London outlet on Oxford Street. Their major competitor, the Maidenhead based Sports Direct had opened its first store in the capital in 1984, itself a clear signifier that the like of Fila, and Ellesse were entering the mainstream, the death knell for any youth subculture. As Hough points out, 'sometime in 1983, the individuals responsible for the creation of this movement grew jaded and bored, even as the rest of the country was set alight by the 'new' styles.'

The film opens with Bex selecting a blue Ellesse tracksuit from a rail of similar sportswear and lacing up his Adidas Forest Hills, with their gold stripes adoringly shown in closeup. It's 8.30 a.m. and there's an 'early kick off'. From the call box on the corner he telephones the Yeti (Daniel Mays) to arrange an 'early meet' at which he promises he will 'slit you open like an envelope' before strutting his way through the streets to the accompaniment of Kool & the Gang until reaching the Lord Nelson where 50 or so others are congregated outside, many similarly

adorned in continental sports wear.

Elsewhere, on a balcony overlooking the estate, 18-year-old Dom is looking for something more from his life, telling his friend Terry (Billy Seymour) 'I can't be dealing with break dancing and fingering your little sister. There must be something more.' All things considered though it's not such a bad life. He's working as an apprentice to his dad's one man building business but thinks nothing of failing to turn up until the middle of the afternoon - in this instance purely to cadge £20 to go out that night to a club where Terry makes the mistake of picking a fight with Bex, on a night out with his wife, and gets a head-but for his trouble.

The next morning Terry, having discovered just who it was he had had a run in with, tells Dom that they have to go to the Lord Nelson and apologise, 'otherwise it's on us'. At the pub Dom does all the talking and Bex takes a bit of a shine to the lad, telling him 'You ain't half got some bottle walking in here like that.' Given a 'pardon', after visiting Bex at his estate agent's office, Dom finds himself invited to make up the numbers at 5-a-side as long as he wears 'some sensible clobber'. This means another sub from dad, this time £38 - having been told 'there is only one trainer' - for a pair of Adidas Munchen as recently purchased by Bex, immediately scuffed up so they look like he's had them a while. At 5-a-side he's put in goal and when a penalty is awarded he's told, 'save this, and you'll be a legend'. Well not quite, but it means he's now one of the chaps and invited along to that weekends away day to Portsmouth.

As a first foray into organised football violence, it's clearly exhilarating for Dom but it's all downhill from there. When the Yeti turns the tables on the West Ham mob's attempt to catch their Millwall counterparts off guard by arriving tooled-up, their clubs, hammers and Stanley knives making short work of the Upton Park boys. Bex's subsequent reckless obsession with revenge at any cost alienates many of the crew. This includes Dom, who soon realises that his new lifestyle may be harder to get out of that it was to get in, told that: 'You ain't like Snowy and that mob, they live miles off the plot. They can run and hide and keep their nuts down. But you? You live on the fuckin' manor. You'll have to bump into me every day, and I can't stand seeing people who let me down, it fuckin' drives me mad. So you're in, champ. Right to the fuckin' end.'

Dom's background is fleshed out in a number of scenes of his home life where we see that, far from being a product of urban deprivation and neglect, his parents are loving and hardworking, the positive side of the Thatcherite dream as opposed to Bex's negative. Unfortunately, this leaves little time to learn very much about Bex, never more clear than in two key scenes transposed from Clarke's original, where his toddler gets hold of a Stanley knife and when he visits his family home to retrieve a collection of weapons, that lose much of their original impact when shoe-horned in to the proceedings with little forewarning.

It is often pointed out that the so-called casual movement is unique in not having a specific genre of music which those associated with it could call their own as the Teddy Boy's did with rock n roll and the Mods did with soul and R&B. When film producer and former hooligan Cass Pennant suggests 'jazz funk' in answer to this he is merely addressing his own preference because by the time Londoners cottoned on to what had been happening for a few years in the northwest, and christened themselves casuals, the look was not a subculture but mainstream culture.

Love's choice of music lacks the impact of that in *Awaydays* but is in keeping with that which would have soundtracked the lives of the protagonists themselves. There's a mixed bag of early 80s funk and pop, from Soft Cell's 'Tainted Love' over the opening credits, to Tears For Fears, ABC, Yarborough People's ' Don't Stop The Music', more Kool & the Gang and almost inevitably The Jam with 'Town Called Malice'. In *Awaydays* Elvis and Carty might have been at home with the likes of Dalek I at Eric's but Sampson himself admits 'the band that most of the football lads identified with was The Jam. If The Jam was playing up here, it was like a football match.'

Most of the broadsheet press was positive if somewhat begrudging. The Guardian's Peter Bradshaw said 'Love's films have, in the past, brought me out in a rash - but this one is watchable' and the Times thought: 'While it doesn't exactly break new ground thematically, this is Love's most accomplished film to date. Like the terrace heroes who are its subjects, it's as good-looking and stylish as it is dangerously seductive'. The tabloids were less impressed. The Daily Mirror thought it 'supplies yet further proof that hooligan movies have gone about as far as they can' and for the Daily Mail it was simply 'a redundant compendium of blokeish cliches'.

Stand Down Margaret
(Morton, Cox, Wakeling, Charley, Steele)

The first of the 'other useful things' mooted by the Chairman of the Merseyside Job Creation Programme in *Starting On The Dole* was the introduction of training schemes. 1978 saw the introduction of the YOP (Youth Opportunities Programme) which ran for five years and was generally seen as akin to a sticking plaster on a gaping wound. Writing in the Guardian, Penny Woolcock suggested the main beneficiaries of youth training had been not the youths but the adults in charge: 'Each step has involved a considerably larger adult bureaucracy which has incidentally turned youth unemployment into one of the few growth industries for amateur ideologues, administrators and supervisors.'

'Technically, trainees still occupy the same anomalous position. They are neither employed, unemployed nor students. All the punitive trappings of employment are there without any legislative protection. They are paid an allowance of £25 for a 40-hour week, which can be docked for bad behaviour or poor timekeeping. They can be suspended or sacked without redress, and at the end of a year they are unceremoniously thrown back on the dole.'

'Apparently the most imaginative response we can make to massive youth unemployment is to a) offer them the shoddy alternative of doing routine work for £25 per week, b) pretend that actually this training is necessary in order for bizarrely inadequate youngsters to be able to carry out the most simple tasks on the extraordinary assumption that this will help them get jobs and, c) invent a vast increase in paperwork, a lot more jargon and call the old cheap labour system Quality Improved. We tell them that having failed through school in preparation for mindless employment, the jobs are not there after all and in any case they need more practice pressing buttons, cleaning chamber pots and shovelling mud before they are quite ready for... what?'

Time Out reported on documents drafted by a Cabinet Office think tank, one of which stated that 'the prospects for young school leavers are bleak. By the end of 1983 between 50 and 70 percent of the labour force under 18 might never have had a proper job.' In response to this problem, the government announced the creation of YTS (Youth Training Scheme) 'to provide young people with a bridge between school and work through broad-based foundation training.'

YTS began in September 1983 as an £870 million scheme to provide a year's training for every 16-year-old who wanted a place. Whilst seen in most quarters as an improvement on what had gone before, with long-term unemployment statistics showing there was over 300,000 18 to 24-year-olds out-of-work for longer than a year, the scheme merely hid the underlying crisis by 'massaging' the monthly total of registered unemployed. The scheme was originally conceived with far fewer young unemployed in mind, intending to tackle the scarcity of basic industrial training for young school leavers - in the hands of government the opportunity to use it to dress up the jobless figures was never going to be ignored.

The leaked documents published in Time Out suggested the scheme was created to reduce the unemployment figures and cut training wage levels. The report said, 'The essence of the proposal is to reduce the size of the labour force by raising to 17 the age of entry to the national labour market. We estimate that the training year would reduce the level of registered unemployment by about 200,000.'

The YOP started by getting about 60% of young people into a job. In the summer of 1984, after a year in operation, YTS achieved a high of 62% school leavers in full-time work and an average between July and September of 59%. As soon as the traditional summer recruitment stopped by October, the unemployment rate increased by the same amount as the employment rate had decreased, meaning there was so significant rise in those going back to education. After two years of operation, 38% went straight back to the dole queue.

In the autumn of 1981, 200,000 plus school leavers were registered as out of work. In 1983, the Manpower Services Commission estimated that were it not for the YTS, the number of 16-and 17-year-olds unemployed would pass half a million. The YTS kept this unwelcome figure out of the headlines but there was now an even greater problem - that of one and a quarter million unemployed under 25s, more than half a million of them for over 6 months. This figure of 22% was roughly equal to that of overall unemployment in the thirties.

Before *This Is England* there was **JOHNNY JARVIS (1983)** which began life as a young adult novel by Nigel Williams, published in 1983 and hurriedly adapted by the author for the BBC who had it filmed and into the television schedules that same year, beginning its six-week run on November 12th in a 9.25 p.m. time slot. That the BBC should be so eager to get *Johnny Jarvis* onto the screen can partly be explained by the success of Williams' stage play, *Class Enemy*, a shoo-in for a *Play For Today* slot but for the production's strong use of language that, even if toned down to 'frigging' and 'arseholes', would, in the quantity required, have been problematic for 1970s television.

For *Johnny Jarvis* Nigel Williams takes his children out of the classroom and plonks them down in the real world, that by then was a place with three million already signing on the dole, saying: 'It's criminal, what's being done. The unemployment figures are terrifying. My central tenet is not to tell people what to think. It is presumptuous, insolent. Besides, you can shout your principles from the house-tops; but if people won't listen, the only person you've helped is yourself. To influence people about society, you should present them with real characters and real situations. You have to leave them to tell you what they take out of your plays.'

Beginning in 1977, over six episodes the series follows the lives of a group of classmates up to 1983 which is where we first meet some of the main characters' including the titular Johnny (Mark Farmer) who is seen with his girlfriend and baby on the concrete steps that lead to a block of council flats. Also present is his friend Alan Lipton (Ian Sears) whose offer to take them for a drink is turned down and who informs us in voice-over that this was the last time he saw Johnny Jarvis.

The story of how they reached that point begins six years earlier during the last term at school with Johnny arriving at school on his bike, watched closely by two teachers. 'I worry about Jarvis' says one. 'Jarvis'll be okay' says the other, 'someone up there likes Jarvis.' It's a feeling shared by fellow pupil Lipton for whom Jarvis has been 'exactly the sort of kid I'd always wanted to be. In our last year of school he looked like he could do anything he wanted.' What Jarvis wants though is to be a Skinhead like Manning (Jamie Foreman) and so at the barbers after school he asks for 'all off'. 'Want to be like your mates?' the barber asks, but is assured by Jarvis that he doesn't have any. 'Well, you'd better acquire a few then, son. You'll need 'em with this haircut.'

The fact that when he arrives home, his new haircut concealed by a hat until he retires to his room, he settles down to relax and prepare mentally for the day ahead by listening to Queen's 'News of the World' album suggests this new look is not really the right fit. This is confirmed when he arrives at school the next day to find Manning and his gang of Skins less than complementary of his change of image. 'Well, well, well. Look who's hard eh... Takes more than a haircut y'know.' He's pointed toward a middle-aged black woman crossing the road with her shopping and told 'Bring us back a fiver Jarvis, off our black friend if you're so hard.' He doesn't and what he gets instead is a hard time at school and so decides not to bother going in again, much to the annoyance of his usually calm father who tells him, 'You're gonna be out on the streets in a few months and what you want is some qualifications cos they ain't giving jobs away today, or ain't you noticed?'

Johnny and the rest of his class are all CSE students and employment prospects are bleak, Jarvis being the only member of 5C to get a job, having lined up one himself at a small engineering factory. For his friend Paul Turner (Alrick Riley), who is black, it is harder than most. In the second episode it's 1978 and we see him applying for a job at a car showroom where the interviewer mentions that they need a 'neat appearance' and an 'ability to work hard'. 'What's under that hat?' he's asked. Told it's his hair, he's then asked what his hair is like as they're 'looking for someone with a smart appearance'. 'I thought you wanted someone to clean cars; sounds like you're looking for a male model or something' he replies sarcastically before cutting to the chase. 'This is the fifth job I've been for this week. You know, sometimes I'd get there, and they'd heard me on the phone and they think I'm something different and then when they get sight of me, suddenly it's gone.' He eventually gets a YOP placement in the building trade upon completion of which there is, predictably, no job. He also has Manning's gang of Skinheads to contend with, who whilst an annoyance for Jarvis, for him constitutes a clear and present danger. The two finally catch up with each other midway through the series in a young offenders institute courtesy of a thriller-esque sub-plot involving a mysterious drug dealer/gangster called The Colonel who is involved with Lipton's 'father' and turns out to be a bent copper who frames both Manning (for business reasons) and Turner (because he can). The introduction of the Colonel's storyline otherwise seems somewhat contrived and makes little impact on the eventual outcomes of the two main characters, despite at one point holding Lipton prisoner in his mother's flat.

Johnny throws himself wholeheartedly into his new job, persuading his employer to allow him to do day release for his City & Guilds. Lipton, in contrast, is happy to sign on and at first cover any shortfall by sponging off his single-parent mum, before then sharing a squat with the spiky purple haired Stella (Johanna Hargreaves) who he and

Johnny meet in a cafe. She is officially neither boy's girlfriend, yet flits in and out and back in of relationships with both of them. She's also, despite an appearance that might suggest otherwise, not a Punk rocker, telling them 'It'd take too long to explain.'

It is in the complexity and depth that Williams gives to the characters of Johnny and Lipton and the equally complex and unusual relationships they form that sets *Johnny Jarvis* apart. Initially, it seems to be the story of the unpopular kid, all spectacles and nerves, who wants to be friends with the popular kid, but it soon becomes apparent that behind the smile and chirpy demeanour, the popular kid is riddled with his own insecurities. Whilst both boys quite clearly fall in love with Stella, it is obvious that it is with Lipton who she hoped it would work out. That may be a touch of childhood wish fulfilment for Williams: 'I was the bloke in the glasses, a bit like Lipton, and my abiding memory is of wanting to be friends with people who didn't want to be friends with me.' The real Lipton however, seems incapable of creating that strong a bond, even with his mother. Affected by his father leaving home at an early age, what has always been a hang up becomes an obsession when he discovers his father had written but his mother had not passed the letter on.

In the aftermath of the 1981 riots in Handsworth and Brixton, Employment Secretary Norman Tebbit responded to a suggestion that rioting was the natural reaction to unemployment: 'I grew up in the '30s with an unemployed father. He didn't riot. He got on his bike and looked for work, and he kept looking till he found it.' He would have found a kindred spirit in Johnny Jarvis who not only got on his bike to look for work but stayed on it for twenty miles every day to get him to his new job. By now even his optimism is faltering: 'It's twenty miles a day on that bike, two days of college and for what?... Apprentices, they're just cheap labour. And I'll be elbowed as soon as I get my exams, 'cos they'd have to pay me the rate wouldn't they.' He never gets the chance to find out as, with Stella in the family way he takes a couple of days off after the birth and returns to find the factory empty and that everyone has been made redundant.

Lipton had previously fallen out with Stella after learning she had slept with Johnny and left the squat. Temporarily homeless, he ends up in a hostel run by a kindly and hip gay vicar where he meets Guy Raines (Gary Shail) with whom he forms the houses post-Punk protest band, The New Wastrels. Shail, who already knew Williams having appeared in *Class Enemy* at the Oxford Playhouse, had originally auditioned for the part of Manning for which he was deemed unsuitable. Instead, having seen Shail's band (which also included Joe McGann who also has a role in the series) play at a private function, Williams suggested he read for Guy. Once cast Shail found himself adding music for the New Wastrels songs to lyrics written by the author and also the series incredibly catch title tune the memory of which, having never been repeated or released on video or DVD until 2017, was all fans of the series had to hang on to for 35 years.

Lipton's commitment issues means he leaves the band just before they make it, but he instead becomes a successful songwriter which provides a large flat and a healthy cheque book courtesy of a stream of songs for the band, all of which are about Johnny's downwards spiral. By 1983 Johnny, Stella and child have moved in with him but Johnny is still determined to find a new job 'even if it means washing dishes.' This arrangement doesn't last long and after six months out of work Johnny and Stella are both back living with his mother. Says Stella: 'They didn't do right by you Johnny, nobody did. They give you all these promises, all this training, you go to the end of the earth to

find something suitable, then at the end of the day they wash their hands with you and say, "No, we're sorry mate, that's you finished"'. I mean, you're twenty-one years old Johnny, why should you take it? Why should you lie down and take it? I don't know whether I want somebody that beaten.'

And there it ends, with little hope for the future despite the message being broadcast down below from a Conservative Party election vehicle's loudspeaker: 'In the last four years Britain has recovered her confidence and self respect. We have regained the regard and admiration of other nations. We are seen today as people with integrity, resolve, and the will to succeed. Britain is once more a force to be reckoned with. Formidable difficulties remain to be overcome but after four years of Conservative government, national recovery has begun. We have returned to free enterprise... we have cut income tax rates, we have strengthened the police and armed forces and the Crown. The bravery, skill and determination with which Britain's Task Force recaptured The Falkland's reverberated around the world.'

It's June 1983, the eve of a general election and it seems unlikely that Stella, the strongest and most self-assured character in the series, will stay with Johnny as long as the electorate did with Mrs Thatcher. Johnny has followed the 'rules' almost without question, steadfast in his belief that an apprenticeship will open the door to a prosperous future and his descent into depression as doors are continually shut in his face is completely heartbreaking - one amongst millions of victims of Margaret Thatcher's pursuit of monetarism whatever the cost.

That same summer the challenges that had faced Johnny Jarvis were facing Tucker Jenkins and his friends Tommy and Alan, part of the initial intake of pupils created by writer and producer Phil Redmond for his groundbreaking series *Grange Hill* who hit the nation's television screens in 1978 but were now, five years on, out of the school gates for the final time and into the real world.

The series **TUCKER'S LUCK (1983)** opens with Tucker (Todd Carty) being woken by his mum at ten o'clock. He tells her he is having a day off, but she says he has been doing that since he left school. He's due to sign on and he's got a massive hangover and sick all down his jacket from the night before. The sick belongs to Tommy (Paul McCarthy) one half of his two best friends, the other being Alan (George Armstrong). They too have to sign on.

Tucker is running late but doesn't seem too bothered; 'We're the unmotivated unemployed, full of despair at our hopeless plight.' It says so, he says, in the morning paper he's reading. He isn't confident of ever getting a job: 'There's millions in the queue ahead of us isn't there, some of them have even got their O Levels. You need three O Levels to deliver a paper these days.' College isn't an option he will consider: 'Why should I? I've just spent eleven years being educated... they fix it so you need exams, then teach 'em to you so that they're almost impossible to pass. Then they wonder why we get so cheesed off.'

In the second episode, it's Alan's turn to get grief for lying in. 'Finally managed to struggle out of your pit have you' says his dad. 'You know, it's got to the stage where I begin to wonder how tall you are... you're never vertical long enough for me to hazard a guess.' Tucker meanwhile almost explodes with rage when he's sent for a job, all trussed up in a suit and tie, that when he gets there doesn't exist, the post having already been filled. He marches straight back to the job centre to complain. 'The next time you take a look outside that door, have a close look at the people out there and even you might start to realise what it takes out of them to come in here and join all these pathetic no-hopers... Have you ever worked in any of these jobs? Because they offer even less self respect than

Todd Carty and George Armstrong in *Tucker's Luck*

they do wages. No one is expecting you to wave a magic wand just don't send people along for jobs that don't exist.'

For the first two series the nearest the trio get to a job is doing casual work for Alan's dad, but are careful to earn so little that it doesn't affect their ability to sign on (they're good lads but this is stretching credibility to breaking point) whilst they simultaneously juggle attempts at a love life and run-ins with their arch enemy, Skinhead Passmore (Peter McNamara). By series three, Tommy is working on a market stall which trades in jeans of somewhat questionable origin. Tucker is also standing in as a motorcycle courier for a friend whilst he is on crutches. Passmore, now with hair and a suit, answers an ad for a moneymaking opportunity which promises the chance to earn £400 a week, 'absolutely no selling involved' - which turns out to be 'demonstrating' for 'market research purposes' a magnifying screen that fits over a conventional TV. It is, of course, a scam targeting the vulnerable residents of low-income households. Tucker's temporary job is little better, with a schedule that disregards safety and almost results in him running over a child. Other avenues of earning a crust explored include the daily ritual humiliation of day work on a construction site where the foreman chooses the 'lucky' ones from the line of desperate would-be labourers – for work that, due to its 'unofficial' status, also has scant regard for health and safety.

Tommy's career as a market trader also looks dodgy when he gets involved in plans to rob a lorry containing 16 gross of Shetland sweaters, despite Tucker's protestations. 'Just go and bang your tambourine somewhere else, I can't stand you do-gooders you think you're so much better than everyone else... the whole world's bent and you know it, or have I heard wrong about you doing a bit of labouring on the side, no questions asked... It's all thieving Tucker, just a matter of how you look at it... [the lorry driver's] in on it, he gets a few bob. The people down the market get cheap clothes, the company claims insurance and nobody gets hurt. It's not like mugging.' Tucker, though, overhears the plan and, taking the proceedings into Children's Film Foundation territory, hatches a plan to scupper the robbery.

The third and final series introduces an old friend of Tucker's who is now a self-employed painter and decorator on Enterprise Allowance, the government scheme piloted in 1982 and rolled out nationwide the following year, paying £40 a week for 52 weeks. Tucker is unimpressed though, pointing out that it's the 53rd week you have to worry about. Instead, he spends the series pursuing a printing technology course. 'Two blokes have had a go at me today,' he tells his friends, 'one says as far as proper jobs go blokes like us don't exist; the other said all that we ever do is sit round and talk... we've all been piddling about for months doing jobs on the side that give us no identity and a few bob in our hand as long as we keep our heads down and mind our p's and q's... I listen to talk from you lot night after night about what a rip off it all is and how something ought to be done about it, yet... every fortnight you all turn out at the dole office and sign on the dotted line. If that's not being well drilled then I don't know what is.' First though, he first needs to gain O Levels in English and maths - causing problems with the dole who, taking into account a certain amount of homework, deem him to be breaking the 20 hour rule, making him 'unavailable for work'. We never did find out if Tucker got on his printing course but if he did, times might have still proved hard at the end of it with the industry going through massive upheaval due to changes in print technology.

The same year as his best known work, *Tom & Viv* (1984), about the troubled relationship between poet TS Eliot and Vivienne Haigh, playwright Michael Hastings visited another troubled couple, Carly (Perry Benson) and Paulette (Cathy Murphy) in the very different **STARS OF THE ROLLER STATE DISCO (1984)**, in which youth unemployment had become a bleak enough prospect that this Alan Clarke directed *Black Mirror*-esque vision seemed nowhere near as far fetched as it might do today.

In an undisclosed near future, the nation's young unemployed spend their days, and nights, at the roller state disco where they can, theoretically at least, learn new skills or hone existing ones, in areas like construction, carpentry or office work, whilst waiting for their number to be called should a suitable placement be found for them. In between there's banks of arcade video machines to pass the time or endless circuits of the roller rink.

Some, like Carly who has been there for three months, are there voluntarily, having parents who would be willing to support them in the family home. Those whose parents are unwilling or unable to support their unemployed offspring, are sent to the sealed-off concrete government run bunker from which gainful employment, or a YTS placement, is their only chance of escape.

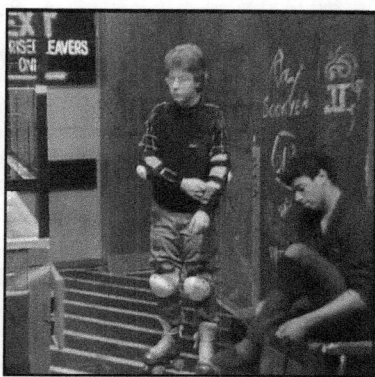

The newest arrival at the 'disco' is Carly's girlfriend Paulette who hopes to persuade him to leave - his parents having tried and failed. He's been offered jobs in his chosen field of carpentry but is holding out for something better: 'I'm not chopping out bits of boxwood. I'm a cabinetmaker... I've got qualifications, I've got a certificate... Any day now there's going to be this fantastic job, something to do with carving. That's what I am, I'm a furniture maker, I do it really well. Something like, this big cruise liner needs a refit and there's all this wood – walnut and mahogany.'

It soon becomes clear that Carly's reluctance is largely because he has become completely institutionalised, and when his dream job does, somewhat surprisingly, materialise it's no surprise that he finds a reason to dismiss it. Which is more than Paulette can take, saying her farewells and signing herself out.

Carly is not the only 'inmate' struggling to hold it together. There's Kate Hardie as a young mum who has had her baby taken away and is left with a rolled-up blanket as a replacement and a youth who seems to have entered into a romantic relationship with the disembodied head on the establishments many 'Voicespeak' monitors. Holding them together, after a fashion, is a somewhat suspect doctor who dishes out their weekly supplies of pills.

Half an hour before everyone has to be off the floor for the evening, a young Scouse lad arrives, declaring 'We don't get all this lark in Liverpool. What is it?' Carly offers to show him the ropes. 'Food's free,' he tells him, 'There's room for keeping up with your skills, play those machines all day if you want... You hang about here and they call you when they've got your job for you. They really get down to it in here you know.'

The newcomer seems unconvinced: 'I dunno. I don't think I'll ever work again. Even if I do like, all I do is learn a skill and get paid rubbish. I mean, if I get a job it'll only be a couple of quid more than supplementary. I mean, I can only do one more training scheme and then I'm eighteen. Then I'm past it. I mean, there's all these kids, younger than me, coming up. What do I do then?'

Carly is quick to reassure him: 'You mustn't think like that. You see it all makes sense. The governors, they know what they're doing. They want you to learn and then they want you to have a good time... it's tough outside... so you've got to be warm and comfortable, keep your skills up to date. Take up a sport, see films like. There's plenty of girls. You want girls? No problem. You want a job? It's a cert in the end... in the meantime it's like a pleasure palace. It's like one of those piers at Blackpool. Believe me, this is the life. You've got to stay here and enjoy it. There's all these things they give you and that's what's great about it.... The whole system is specially designed, and it's fantastic.'

Naturally it doesn't end well.

Not all latter day Skins were of the bonehead variety. Running parallel with Oi! was the so-called Two Tone movement, based around the Coventry band The Specials and their record label 2 Tone Records. Starting life in 1977 as The Automatics and then The Coventry Automatics, the band formed by songwriter and keyboard player Jerry Dammers would next become The Special AKA and, after Joe Strummer attended one of their gigs, were soon supporting The Clash on their 'On Parole' tour. The multi-racial band would record their debut single 'Gangsters', a re-working of the Prince Buster classic 'Al Capone', and release it on their own label in 1979, becoming a summer top ten hit.

Now simply The Specials the bands next single was a version of Dandy Livingstone's 'Rudy, A Message To You' which similarly reached the top ten later that year before they kicked off 1980 with a number one, 'Too Much Too Young'. Meanwhile, in North London another band, the North London Invaders, were treading a similar musical path, and in 1979 after a brief flirtation with the name Morris and the Minors, became Madness and quickly attracted a loyal following in the capital and the attention of Dammers. Their debut single, an homage to ska legend Prince Buster, named 'The Prince' became the 2 Tone label's second single release, reaching number 16. Though the band moved to Stiff for their subsequent releases, they would continue to be associated with the label and its other acts such as The Beat who had two 1979 top ten hits with 'Tears of a Clown' and 'Hands Off... She's Mine' and the Selector who reached number 8 with 'On My Radio' the same year. Two Tone was on its way to becoming a bona fide youth movement.

Opening in a Coventry swimming baths, **THREE MINUTE HEROES (1982)** was the BBCs *Play For Today*'s late-in-the-day take on the 2 Tone phenomenon, directed by Michael Custance from a script by Leslie Stewart, which also takes in the various other youth tribes of the time, from British Movement supporting boneheads to rockabilly kids, mohawk'd second generation Punks, New Romantics, Mods and Teds.

The wafer thin plot in which various youths hang out and attempt to cop off, is padded out with two fantasy musical pieces where high kicking Skinheads dance to The Specials '(Dawning Of A) New Era' and post-nuclear zombies stumbling through a subway to the Fun Boy Three's 'The Lunatics Have Taken Over The Asylum'. The most engaging of the stories that unfold is that of mixed race 2-Tone kid, Billy and his burgeoning friendship with the polio-stricken Adrian, despite the latter's insistence that '2-Tone is dead'. When, as proceedings draw to a close, Adrian is beaten up by Skinheads outside a chip shop, Billy carries him back to the swimming pool where the two first crossed paths. Not shown since its initial broadcast, nor released on DVD, a copy is held by the BFI and is occasionally screened at ska and Two Tone related events.

The same title was used for a jukebox musical, **THREE MINUTE HEROES**, by Bob Eaton, the artistic director of Coventry's Belgrade Theatre between 1996 and 2006. Originally staged at the Belgrade in 2000 before returning in 2014, the play focuses on a group of young people who form a ska band and achieve some early success supporting The Specials and The Selector before things takes a darker turn in the second act with the rise of the National Front. The play takes in real events from the city's past such as the murder of Satnam Gill a student at Henley College, who was beaten, kicked and stabbed to death by a group of Skinheads in broad daylight in 1981 and a march by the Anti-Nazi League and the Indian Workers Association, before the band reunite for one last Rock Against Racism gig at which point the play takes the form of a party as the audience bobs along to a live band that included original Selecter drummer Aitch Bembridge.

Before that, Catherine Johnson of *Mamma Mia* fame penned a musical, **TOO MUCH TOO YOUNG**, for the Bristol Old Vic in 1992 which she described as 'like a gig going off every night'. Featuring live versions of Punk, new wave and 2 Tone numbers, the play then toured various venues between February and March 1995, including Albany Theatre, Deptford, The Bridge, Harrow, Union Chapel Studio, Highbury, Waltham Forest Theatre and The Bottom Line, Shepherd's Bush.

Though *Too Much Too Young* disappeared soon after, it got her the gig for *Mamma Mia* when producer Judy Craymer was looking for someone to weave the Abba back-catalogue into a story. Despite Johnson not being much of a fan of the band: 'The Punk ska era was where I was musically most inclined but I always loved music and worked in a record shop for a few years where you needed to listen to everything. That's where my ABBA experience came from.'

The complex dynamics of being a ska-loving Skinhead during these times was finally given the treatment it deserved with **THIS IS ENGLAND (2006)**. Director Shane Meadows, who via *Twenty Four Seven* (1997) and *A*

Room For Romeo Brass (1999) had already shown an understanding of how vulnerable young men can compensate for their perceived weakness by resorting to violence, had become a Skinhead as an eleven-year-old growing up in Uttoxeter during the early eighties: 'My sister, who was older than me, was going out with a Skinhead who was older than her. I was 11, she was 14, and he was 16 – and all of his mates were older than him. So I was always the youngest person.'

Despite having his own experiences to draw on, revisiting the period for a screenplay had previously never crossed Meadows mind: 'Why I don't know because it's obviously so visceral,' he says. 'It's only as an adult... you look back at your life and... there's things you really didn't realise had had an impact on you and that was the first thing that I ever wanted to become a part of. I was very much like Shaun in the film, wearing a jumper with reindeers on. I was not a geek but a kind of nobody and so going to school you get shoved in the dinner queue, you've got shaggy hair and all that and the transformation to seeing these Skinheads one day in the shopping centre, walking through the precinct, and thinking they looked almost like marines to me. So smart, yet so aggressive and the crack that they had and the fact that they had this "F the state" attitude.'

The director remained hesitant: 'I looked at making this film and I actually went out [to] find a film about Skinheads that had been made... so that I didn't have to make one. When I went out there, with *Romper Stomper* (1992), *American History X* (1998), and *Made in Britain*, which obviously was more of a television film, you've only kind of really got that one side. And if I really wanted to go and pitch a film, it would probably be much easier to get a *Romper Stomper* British version made than it would be making *This Is England*, with piano music in it, and something far more sensitive to it. But I realised there was a huge gap there.'

The Skinheads in Meadows gang were a million miles removed from a Russell Crowe or an Ed Norton: 'I didn't want it to be... *Romper Stomper* style [with] alpha males, mistreated girls, all of that kind of thing. I remember the girls being as hard as the guys in that situation and as frightening as the guys if not more so and I wanted the gang to be all shapes and sizes as my gang was, because Uttoxeter wasn't big enough to have a really cool gang of Skinheads. It had a fat one, a thin one, a long one, a small one.'

Central to *This Is England*'s success would be in the casting of the 'small one', a character based on the director's own formative experiences. The role, the last to be filled, went to 13-year-old Thomas Turgoose who was found by Des Hamilton, a specialist street caster who had previously found the young kid in *Ratcatcher* (1999), on a project called Open Space in Grimsby for kids with irregular attendance at school. With no acting experience to call upon, Turgoose had a more valuable weapon in his armoury, he was the real thing. The character needed to be both tough and vulnerable and in Turgoose Meadows find someone who was already both. There's an occasional awkwardness in his performance, the result of being at the centre of an alien world of filming, that suits the character perfectly but which a trained actor of that age would have found difficult to fake.

This Is England opens with a montage of popular images of the time - Roland Rat, Maggie Thatcher, Space Invaders, *Night Rider*, the Falklands, BMX, Duran Duran, Charles & Diana, Greenham Common, Aerobics, CDs, Striking Miners, the National Front. It's July 1983, just a month after Margaret Thatcher had ridden the upsurge in patriotic fervour brought on by the Falklands War to her second election victory despite overseeing a 43% rise to, 2.6 million, in the number of people living on or below the level of supplementary benefit since taking office in 1979. With over 11% out of work, unemployment was at levels not seen since the Great Depression.

At 7.45 a.m. an alarm rings to herald in the last day of term for 12-year-old Shaun who having slipped uneasily into his flares, heads off to school for a non-uniform day. 'I never knew Keith Chegwin had a son... Woodstock's that way pal' taunts Harvey (Michael Socha), an older two tone kid. His next 'joke' oversteps the mark: 'How many people can you fit in a mini? Two in the front, three in the back and your dad in the ashtray.' What Shaun lacks in cool, height, and brawn he makes up for in bottle, charging at the much bigger kid, sending him flying into a flower bed to the delight of the watching Skins, Mods, 2-Tone kids and Boy George lookalikes that comprised an early eighties playground. Thankfully Shaun is rescued by the intervention of teachers before the bigger lads strength leads to a severe beating. Clearly marking the film as a period piece, the teacher whacks Harvey across the face when he gets mouthy (Try doing that today sir!) as both boys are frogmarched to the headmaster's office for that other staple of eighties school discipline the cane.

This is the year that, inside a cover featuring a threatening Mohawk adorned Punk, the international edition of Time magazine ran a seven-page cover feature on the UK's warring youth called 'The Tribes of Britain': 'Noone knows exactly how many tribes there are. The most visible and visually outrageous are the neon-dyed, ripped-jeans-clad, truculently anarchic Punks who have claimed Kings Road as their capital and parade ground. But there are also Skinheads, stalking mean city streets from London's East End to Belfast's Corn Market. In nightspots from Glasgow to Portsmouth, Trendies seek the next new wave of fashion. Teddy Boys, meanwhile, are content to jive on the last wave. Rock-a-Billies rock around the clock to a bygone beat they know only from old movies. On weekends, grungy Bikers in black leather roar over the open road, while stylish Mods in surplus military olive-drab parkas putter around Brighton on their Lambrettas. Sloane Rangers, comfortable and privileged, prowl London's Sloane Square in their pinstripes and Hermes scarves or tramp the countryside in their tweeds and green wellies. Fearsome elements of the Soccer Tribes do battle with one another on stadium terraces in Chelsea and Manchester. Each tribe boasts its own war paint, totems and idols, its own music, even its own language.'

This proliferation of youth tribes is prominent in Meadows's memories of the time; 'I look around now any shopping centre and it's boring, you can just about spot a skateboard kid and you can spot a chav but there isn't the same separation amongst kids anymore. It's all been a bit sanitised and sterilised and you look back at where you were... from the real super geeks who were wearing deely boppers, one pink sock, one green sock, through your New Romantics, Rockers, Gothics, Punks still around, Mods second generation and in a place like Uttoxeter where there isn't enough people... the rockers were all mixed with the Skinheads, you know, everyone was all together at the discos... a really incredible time.'

On the way home Shaun has to pass a bunch of Skinheads led by the charismatic Woody (Joe Gilgun) but rather than receiving the expected grief they are friendly towards him, at least until Gadget (Andrew Ellis) returns from the shop with the beers, having waited an hour for someone to go in and buy them for him. The chubby youngster, the usual target for the gangs playful bullying, sensing a promotion in the pecking order gives Shaun a hard time and so he leaves. 'I've been picked on three times today, all because of my trousers,' he tells his mum, 'look at the fucking size of 'em!' We also learn that Sean's earlier angry reaction was because his father had died in the Falkland's.

Thomas Turgoos, Joseph Gilgun, Jack O'Connell in *This Is England*

Out shopping with his mum, Shaun has his heart set on a pair of Dr Martens but he's only a size 4 and they only have adult sizes so he has to settle for 'Tomkins' – 'they're from London' offers the sales assistant by way of comfort. Before long though Shaun is befriended by the Skins and sporting the requisite cropped hair, Ben Sherman shirt and braces, singing along to Toots & the Maytals' 'Pressure Drop'. A montage sequence to 'Louie Louie' challenges perceived notions of Skinhead culture better than either of the documentaries covered earlier by showing the apolitical world of the gang which involves hanging about, playing footy, going swimming - the sort of things kids of that age do during the summer holidays –and the coolest slo-mo walking sequence since *Reservoir Dogs*. 'The best day of my life' says an ecstatic Shaun arriving home with his new look two hours late.

'Oh my God!' is all mum can say.

The good times come to an abrupt end when a firm knock on the door as the gang hang out at Gadget's house turns out not to be, as was feared, the police but Banjo (George Newton), a giant of a bald tattooed geezer of about thirty odd, waving a machete and scaring the shit out of everyone. Then, in bursts Combo (Stephen Graham) an old pal of Woody who is fresh out of prison, as we learn is Banjo. 'Three and a half years with this fucker!' he declares. Woody owes him for keeping shtum about whatever his part in Combos indiscretion was. Most of the group don't know him as they would have been too young but all are soon aware that Combo is a full-on racist, presumably politicised whilst doing time; a situation bound to cause problems for Milky (Andrew Shim), a Skinhead of West Indian heritage.

Combo wastes no time in putting Milky on the spot, asking the youngster if he considers himself English or Jamaican. The answer of 'English' affords a little breathing space but a speech blaming 'fucking Pakis' for all the country's ills doesn't bode well: '50 or 60 to a fucking flat… 3 ½ million of us who can't find fucking work cos they're taking 'em all cos of cheap fucking labour, cheap and easy labour, fucking cheap and easy which makes us cheap and easy… and that fucking Thatcher sits there in her ivory tower and sends us on a phoney war. The Falklands. Fucking Falklands. What the fuck's the Falklands. Fucking innocent men. Fucking good strong men. Good soldiers. Real people losing their lives, going over there thinking they're fighting for a cause, and what are they fighting for? What are they fighting against? Fucking shepherds. Shepherds with rocks and little rifles.'

At that final part, Sean jumps to his feet and starts throwing punches at the startled Combo, who rather than retaliating instead appears deeply impressed. 'Fucking hell, that little whipper snapper has set the standard' he declares, learning of Shaun's situation and apologising. Following this he spits and marks a line on the floor. They're either with him or they leave. Woody, Lol (Vicky McClure), Milky and Kes (Kieran Hardcastle) head for the door, the rest including Sean stay. The gang is split in two. 'Woody's not like me and he's certainly not like you,' Combo tells Shaun. 'No one's fucking ever took a swing at me like that… it's like looking in the mirror, twenty years ago when I was fucking 12, taking swings at the big men.' Shaun, in need of a father figure, is under his spell, continuing the theme of vulnerable youngsters being taken under the wing of older, flawed man visited by Meadows previously in *Dead Man's Shoes* (2004) and *A Room for Romeo Brass*.

Though Combo is the villain of the piece, and thanks to Stephen Graham's powerful performance, a very effective one at that, Meadows qualifies him with emotions and motivations that make him a much more fully rounded character. His paternal relationship with Shaun is genuine, heartfelt, and informed it seems by deficiencies in his own upbringing: 'I know what it's like' he tells the youngster, 'people walking out on you, people leaving you.' Interestingly, Stephen Graham has a mixed-race heritage. Says Meadows: 'He has a Swedish grandmother, a fully Jamaican grandfather and brothers who look black, but Stephen himself is just very fair skinned. So when I offered him the part, he rang me one night at one o'clock in the morning, and he was beside himself. He said, "You've asked me to play this extreme right wing character. But I need to tell you that my Dad's black." And I didn't have a clue.'

A second slo-mo walking sequence with Combo, Shaun, Gadget, Banjo and Meggy (Perry Benson) is, in stark contrast with its predecessor, less than cool. Spray painting 'Paki Bastards' in the underpass is more uncool. Nicking a football of three young Asian kids is even more so. Their behaviour hits an all-time low when they rob an Asian shop at machete point during which Meggy even tries to take a shit on the floor but can't.

Worse is to come when Combo's already fractured mental state is given a severe blow when he declares his love for Lol, presenting her with a box he made for her in prison, and is knocked back. They had spent a night together before he went inside. To Combo it was 'the best night of my life.' To Lol, 'it was the worst night of my life. I've done nothing but try to forget about that night.' 'But it was beautiful' pleads Combo. 'I was 16; I was pissed off my head. It wasn't beautiful,' he's told.

Combo buys some cannabis from Milky and the youngster reluctantly agrees to smoking it with him. This goes smoothly enough at first: 'What you've got to remember is I'm an original Skinhead. 69. It was people like your uncle that introduced [black music] to me. The soul of that music just resonated with us, you know. It was unity. It was black and white together. You know what I mean.' The unity doesn't last long. When Milky eulogises about his extended family it strikes a raw nerve in Combo who finally snaps, leaving Shaun to look on in horror as he beats the absolute shit out of Milky; taking time out to bottle Banjo and threaten Meggy with more of the same for good measure. When Combo finally breaks down in tears at what he's done, Shaun helps him get the seriously injured youth to hospital.

According to the director Graham's own racial heritage is at play during this scene, though there's little visible on the screen to back this up for an audience without this prior knowledge: '...because he wasn't as dark-skinned as his brothers, he was never quite sure if he fitted in. And I thought it was very brave of him to bring it forward and use that complication for his character. So if you watch that scene with him and Milky at the end, knowing that, that that's what he was thinking, you can see jealousy in his eyes - he's jealous the guy is black.'

Johnny Vaughan in the Sun called it 'the best of British... UNMISSABLE' and the Daily Mirror said 'in short, this is, mostly, bloody brilliant'. Empire thought it was: 'Deeply impressive, as both a recreation of 80s working-class England and an intimate tale of one childhood's brutal end' whilst Peter Bradshaw at the Guardian said simply: 'This is English cinema'. The industry agreed, and it wasn't just *Small Faces* director Gillies MacKinnon who rated it the best of the year with Meadows and producer Mark Herbert picking up the Alexander Korda Award for Best British Film at the 2007 British Academy Film Awards as well as Best Film at the 2006 British Independent Film Awards, and Turgoose collecting an award for Most Promising Newcomer. The characters were reintroduced by Channel 4 for a four-part mini-series, *This Is England '86* (2010), which was successful enough to be followed by two celebrated sequels, *This Is England '88* (2011), and *This Is England '90* (2015).

Meadows inclusion of strong female characters who were their male counterparts equals rather than the usual accoutrements had a major impact on filmmaker Sharon Woodward, who directed, produced and edited a documentary, **THANK YOU, SKINHEAD GIRL (2009)**. The film primarily focuses on the experiences of the director herself, a Skinhead in her youth, but she also chats to two other women, each a Skinhead girl in different time periods. Ali Palmer Smith was a Skinhead in the early days from 1969 to 1972, Woodward herself in the 2-Tone days from 1979 to 1983, and finally Bridget Faller was a Skinhead between 1984 and 1987.

After watching *This Is England*, says Woodward: 'I couldn't stop thinking about it; it was the first time I had ever seen in a drama - Skinhead girls.' Having started making films when she was 18 or 19, working with community groups to make films about local issues, she originally intended to make a film about her old gang but quickly discovered that not everyone was as keen to talk about their youth as she was.

Stephen Graham amd Vicky McClure in *This Is England*

Despite broadening out the scope, the film does not pretend to provide a complete history of the subculture but succeeds in offering a snapshot of a localised scene. All three women speak of feeling equal to their male counterparts, one of whom is also interviewed, in an era where equality was in short supply. Woodward says that having her head shaved allowed her to escape unwanted male sexual attention in a period where having found herself in care to escape an impossible home life, she found a replacement family in the Skinhead scene. Faller mentions getting a spider's web tattoo and finding that, without her permission, the artist had added a flower to the middle to make it more feminine – the last thing she wanted.

Gaining the occasional screening at ska gigs, **BEVERLEY (2015)** is a short film loosely based on events in the life of Beverley Thompson who first came to the attention of producer Cass Pennant when he was putting together his first film, *Casuals* (2011), a documentary on the 80s football hooligans. Says Pennant: 'The football casual didn't come from music so I wanted to make the definitive documentary on the fashion behind the violence, and I didn't believe there were female football casuals. It left women out. What would be the point of it? They don't do the violence. But there were a few; we tracked them down and one was Bev Thompson.'

But Thompson's dalliance with football violence was brief, and she defined her persona in those times as a rude girl and as Pennant had 'always wanted to do a film that gives a legacy to the Two-Tone era,' he saw the potential in Thompson's experiences to bring that ambition to fruition. Revisiting these times with writer/director Alexander Thomas to get her story down on tape, the result is the 24 minute crowd-funded *Beverley*, shot in and around the actual locations of Beverley's life in Leicester.

Laya Lewis and Kieran Hardcastle in *Beverley*

The film opens in the home that the mixed race Beverley (Laya Lewis) shares with her white mother (Vicky McClure) and black father (Winston Ellis). When her father comes into a large sum of money, the family escape the racist Skinheads that create menace in their working class area for middle class suburbia, only to discover that the natives are equally unfriendly – from the curtain twitching of their new neighbours to the new gang of Skinheads who, armed with BB guns, make a nuisance of themselves on the waste ground near their new home.

Beverley finds common ground with the Skinheads through a shared love of ska and the new 2-Tone bands, and develops a relationship with one of them, Wilson (Kieran Hardcastle). Unfortunately the less savoury aspects of the scene soon rear their ugly head when a gig by fictional 2-Tone band The Mixtones descends into violence, orchestrated by another of the gang, Dean (Tom Cowling) who has National Front affiliations.

Though writer and director Thomas recognises 2-Tone's power as 'an amazing cultural force that swept across the nation' and the positive effect it had on lives in Britain at the time, the film provides a twist that denies the story a happy ending, the director insistent that 'From issues of race to high unemployment my film certainly isn't about how 2-Tone "won" that political fight... It was all very crazy at that time and also culturally conflicted. It was chaotic, and it's complex and that's the reality of it.'

When embarking on the project, Pennant says that 'What '*Quadrophenia*' did for Mod I wanted a film to do the same for Two-Tone'. The chance of that particular dream ever coming true will depend on whether the creative team's hopes of expanding *Beverley* to feature length ever see fruition.

*

In September 1986 a two year YTS began, promising that they would improve the quality as well as the quantity, the necessity of such a promise speaking volumes of the quality in the previous three years.

The numbers of volunteers to the scheme had always fallen far short of expectations; children, their parents and teachers feeling that that YTS was just the old Youth Opportunities Programme, which provided little in the way of opportunity for the youths, but an excellent source of cheap labour for unscrupulous employers.

After years of threats, the 'actively seeking work' component of the 1989 Social Security Act removed the entitlement to Income Support for under 18s – a process that had begun with the introduction of Restart interviews in 1986. During these periods of increasing work-related welfare conditionality, the Labour Party, in opposition, were vehemently opposed to compulsory training initiatives, with the party's National Executive signing a Charter Against Welfare stating that all initiatives to encourage people back into work should be voluntary, calling it 'a recipe for lower standards, resentment and disruption. It could drive the unemployed into the shadow economy or into even greater poverty.'

Margaret finally stood down and in 1998 and finally in power, New Labour under Tony Blair went even further than the Tories with their New Deal programme for young people and the long-term unemployed, targeting previously exempt groups like single parents and the disabled.

Index

20th Century Box (1980-1982) 267-269
40 Minutes: The Outlaws (1985) 113

A

Abide With Me 252-253
A Bigger Splash (1975) 249
Acme Attractions 217, 247, 264
Adam Ant 33, 225-227, 229, 264
Adam Kotz 294
Adewale Akinnouye-Agbaje 289-290
Adrienne Posta 199
Adventures of a Plumber's Mate (1978) 199
Adventures of a Private Eye (1976) 199
Aftab Sachak 278
A Hard Day's Night (1964) 69
Alan Clarke 248, 296-297, 305, 312
Alan Edwards 261
Alan Fountain 186, 187
Alan Gibson 106
Alan Gorrie 72
Alan Parker 22, 31, 288-289
Alecky Blythe 179
Aleister Crowley 99, 101-102
Alex Cox 237, 239
Alex Driscoll 304, 305
Alex Harvey 143, 201
Alexis Kanner 86
Alex Sanders 99-100
Alex Sharp 240
Alex Wheatle 182
Alfie Fagon 161
Allan Prior 120, 135
All You Need Is Love (1977) 210
Alrick Riley 309
Altab Ali 219, 280
Alton Ellis 125
Alun Lewis 258
Alvin Stardust 197
American History X (1998) 315
Andrew Ellis 316
Andrew Marr 230
Andrew Schofield 239
Andrew Sinclair 36
Andy Ellison 202
Angela Rippon's Bum 287, 291
Anita Pallenberg 16, 21, 102
Anna Cropper 73-74
Ann Holloway 96
Anthony Burgess 136, 140, 144

Anthony Sher 257
Anthony Welsh 190
Antonia Bird 295
Anton La Vey 101
A Passage To India (1984) 284
Archie Pool 175
Are You Being Served 233
Arinze Kene 291
Armchair Theatre 82, 90
A Room for Romeo Brass (1999) 317
A Room For Romeo Brass (1999) 314
Arthur Blessitt 94
Ashley Barker 253
Ashley Kozak 71
Ashley Walters 289
Aswad 170, 175, 187
A Taste of Honey 59
Audrey Erskine Elliot 85
Aug 13: What Happened? (1977) 279
Au Pair Girls (1972) 65

B

Babymother (1998) 169
Bananarama 268
Bangladeshi Youth Front 280
Bangladeshi Youth Movement 280
Bank Holiday (1971) 113
Barney Broom 263
Barrie Keeffe 179, 252
Barrie K Sharpe 217
Barry McGuire 93
Basil Kirchin 84
Bed Peace (1969) 171
Being Blacker (2017) 182
Bend It Like Beckham (2002) 284
Benjamin Zephania 184
Bernie Rhodes 247-248
Billy Bragg 265
Billy Hamon 244
Billy Seymour 307
Black Audio Film Collective 185
Black Dwarf 17, 32, 40, 42, 53-54
Black Slate 170
Blair Peach 282, 285
Blue Remembered Hills (1979) 259
Bob Baker 268
Bob Geldof 288, 289
Bob Harris 98
Boy George 262, 264-265, 315
Boys Behind Bars 2 (2014) 271
Braving The Cape (2003) 263
Bread (1971) 24

Brennan Reece 212
Brian Bovell 175-176
Brian Eno 194-195, 263
Brian James 247
Brian Pettifer 121
Brim Fuentes 186
Brimstone & Treacle (1976) 168
Brinsley Forde 175, 177
Brinsley Schwarz 260
Britain's Black Legacy (1991) 156
Broadwater Farm 183, 184, 186-188, 190, 229
Bromley Contingent 217, 220-222, 224, 238, 276
Bruce Beresford 198
Bryan Marshall 84
Buju Banton 219
Burning An Illusion (1981) 180

C

Cabaret Voltaire 186, 266, 304
Cadillac Records (2008) 250
Calum MacNab 306
Caroline Coon 19, 20, 56, 61, 220, 222, 247, 259
Caroline Embling 257-258
Caroline Munro 104-106
Cash Money 186
Casino Steel 202, 256
Cass Pennant 307, 318
Catherine Johnson 314
Catherine Kessler 160
Cathy Murphy 312
Ceddo 159, 185-186
Chaguaramas 216-217
Champions (1978) 253
Charles Manson 16, 99, 105, 140
Chas Chandler 197
Checkpoint 287
Cherry Groce 186-188, 190
Cherry Vanilla 193
Cheryl Hall 48, 199
Children of God 95
Chloe Webb 237-238
Chris Menges 257, 296
Chrissie Hynde 226, 240, 259
Chrissy Boy Foreman 288
Christopher Assante 155-156
Christopher Eccleston 45
Christopher Fairbank 258
Christopher Lee 104-106
Christopher Mitchell 92
Christopher Neame 104
Christopher Stagg 203
Chris Ward 270-271

Church of Satan 99, 101
Ciaran Owens 254
Cinderella - The Truth 233
Citizen Smith (1977-1980) 47
Clarence Baker 170, 282
Class Enemy 258, 309-310
Cliff Richard 34, 40, 95-96, 109, 214
Clive Olive 111, 113
Clive Parsons 259
Clocking Off (2000-2003) 212
Cockney Rebel 195
Cockney Rejects 274, 285-287
Colin Roach 184, 217
Colin Welland 113
Come Back Peter (1969) 21
Conor McCarron 151
Cool It Carol (1970) 63
Coronation Street 65-66, 121, 128
Cosey Fanni Tutti 66
Crackers 216-217
Craig Parkinson 212
Crass 270
Crown Court 46, 57, 60, 155, 173, 231, 271
Crown Court: A Difference In Style (1974) 57
Crown Court: An Evil Influence (1975) 60
Crown Court: Conspiracy (1972) 46
Cutting It (2002-2004) 212

D

Damson Idris 291
Dandy Livingstone 126, 314
Danger: Diabolik (1968) 62
Daniel Day Lewis 283-284
Daniel Huttlestone 250
Daniel Kaluuya 190
Danny Boyle 51, 142, 149
Danny Dyer 305
Danny John-Jules 216
Danny Opatoshu 235
Darcus Howe 166, 170, 172, 182
Dateline Diamonds (1965) 199
Dave Grodin 209
Dave Humphries 203
Dave Strickson 287, 289, 291
David Bowie 23, 44, 102, 192-194, 196, 216-217, 221, 227, 259, 262-263, 301, 305
David Cooper 76
David Deeks 268
David Dimbleby 56
David Easter 206
David Farrant 103, 106
David Grant 66

David Halliwell 48
David Harewood 289
David Hayman 238
David Hemmings 89, 137, 199, 264
David Mingay 248
David N Haynes 175
David Sherwin 26, 30
David Vorhaus 105
David Warner 51
Davina Belling 259
Deadly Strangers (1974) 85
Dead Man's Shoes (2004) 317
Dealt With 254
Debbie Horsfield 211
Demonstration of Affection (1981) 270
Dennis Potter 82, 259
Dennis Waterman 65, 89, 109, 200
Dennis Wheatley 99, 101, 105
Derek Ford 68, 70
Derek Jarman 224, 229
Derek Lister 253
Derek Long 100
Derek Thompson 261
Derrick Borte 250
Derrick Morgan 125-126
Desmond Dekker 124-125, 143, 198
Diana Dors 197, 200
Diane Abbott 178
Dick Fontaine 186
Diddy David Hamilton 205
Dinesh Shukia 278
Dinner At The Sporting Club (1978) 259
Disco Pigs (2001) 250
Divide & Rule - Never (1978) 223
Dixon of Dock Green: Baubles, Bangles & Beads (1975) 91
Dodi Fayed 262
Donald Cammell 21, 70, 102
Don Boyd 234
Don Houghton 106
Don Kirshner 33
Don Letts 127-128, 217, 224
Donna Summer 198, 203
Donovan Winter 20
Don't Be Like Brenda (1973) 54
Don Warrington 173
Dora Bryan 96
Doreen Valiente 99
Dotun Adebayo 130, 252
Doug Allen 306
Doug Aubrey 127
Dougie Brimson 305
Douglas Booth 264-265

Doug Lucie 181, 233
Dracula AD 1972 (1972) 103
Dread Beat and Blood (1979) 172, 174
Dressing For Pleasure (1977) 237
Ducks Deluxe 259, 260
Duke Reid 125, 169, 175
Duran Duran 238, 262, 266, 269, 315

E

Eamonn Walker 218
Eastenders 78, 181
East Of Elephant Rock (1978) 234
Eddie Grant 126
Edward Bond 97-98
Elaine Constantine 208, 214-215
Elastica 195
Eleanor Bone 99
Eleanor Crooks 181
Eleventh Hour 186-187
Elle Fanning 241
Elliot James Langridge 214
Elton John 194, 201-202, 269
Elvis Payne 252-253
Emerson, Lake & Palmer 23, 223
Emma Lundy 124
Empire of the Ants (1977) 203
Empire Road 168, 175
Enoch Powell 128, 154, 179, 213, 274, 280, 285, 290
Equus (1977) 78
Eric Clapton 41, 68
Eric Richards 297
Esme Johns 70-71
Ester Anderson 68
Ethan Lawrence 240
Eurovision Song Contest 227
Ewan McGregor 51, 195
Expresso Bongo (1959) 65

F

Family Life (1971) 76
Farrukh Dhondy 166, 277, 279
Felicity Jones 212
Festival (1967) 23
Festival of Light 95
Fiona Richmond 207
Flame In The Streets (1961) 159
Fragile Things 240
Frances Gallymore 231
Franco Rosso 171, 174, 177-178, 277
Fran Franklin 215
Frankie Miller 152
Frankie Vaughan 134, 145, 147, 149

Frank Thornton 198, 233
Frank Windsor 118
Free For All Truce 130
Fun Boy 3 268

G

Games That Lovers Play (1971) 100
Gandhi (1982) 284
Gary Bushell 128, 270, 274, 285, 287
Gary Glitter 162, 193, 195-198, 202, 252
Gary Hitchcock 285-286
Gary Hodges 286
Gary Holton 201, 255-257, 261
Gary Kemp 217
Gary McDonald 188
Gary Mercer 294
Gary Oldman 237-239, 298-299, 305
Gary Olsen 257
Gary Shail 206, 310
Gary Tibbs 261
Gavin Richards 294
Gavin Watson 127
Gavrik Losey 173
Gene October 226, 245
Generation X 192, 247, 258
Genesis P Orridge 66, 105
Geordie 201
George Gently: Son of a Gun (2015) 123
George Harrison 16, 39, 49, 53, 68-69
George Newton 317
Georgie Fame 70, 125, 169
Gerald Scarfe 289
Gerry O'Hara 204
Gerry Sundquist 205-206, 244
Get Carter (1971) 301
Getting it Straight in Notting Hill Gate (1970) 19
Gillian Hills 137
Gillian Slovo 179
Gillies MacKinnon 147, 149, 318
Gimme Shelter 252
Give My Regards To Broad Street (1984) 270
Glastonbury Fayre (1971) 23
Glitter (1975) 224
Godspell 56, 93
Golden Hill (1976) 244
Goldie 186
Goodbye Gemini (1970) 85
Graham Benson 166, 299
Graham Bonnet 199-200
Grange Hill 258, 311
Grant Fleming 276
Green Street (2005) 305
Gregory Munroe 155-157

Groupie Girl (1970) 70
GTO 197-198, 262
Gurdip Sing Chaggar 281
Gurinder Chadha 284
Gwyneth Strong 257, 278

H

Hagar the Womb 271
Hair 21, 56, 93
Hammerhead (1968) 15
Hammersmith Gorillas 202
Hanif Kureishi 190, 219, 220, 283, 284
Hardcore (1977) 207
Harry Nilsson 49, 68
Hawkwind 19-20, 23, 25, 113, 208, 222, 263
Hayley Mills 62, 82, 83, 85, 199
Hazel O'Connor 206, 257, 259-262, 267
Heavy Metal Kids 201, 256
Hedwig and the Angry Inch 240
Hedwig And The Angry Inch 241
Helen Mirren 62
Hells Angel (1971) 114
Help (1965) 69
Here We Go Round The Mulberry Bush (1968) 86
Her Private Hell (1968) 62
Holly Grainger 303
Honey Bane 270, 271
Horace Ové 161, 165-166, 171
Horizon 259
Hornsey College of Art 32-33
Howard Barker 97
Howard Brenton 51, 166
Howard Shapman 199
Hugo Charteris 114
Human Punk 249
Hywel Bennett 82

I

Ian Charleson 224, 226
Ian Dury 238, 261, 277
Ian Gillan 93
Ian Gomm 260
Ian La Frenais 70
Ian Reddington 181
Ian Sears 309
I Die For None of Them 299
If... (1968) 26
Iggy Pop 192-193, 195, 223, 237
In The City 252-253
In Two Minds (1967) 73
Invocation Of My Demon Brother (1969) 101
Isaac Julien 184, 217

I Start Counting (1969) 84
It's Trad Dad 199
It's Trad Dad (1962) 199

J

Jack Hazan 248
Jackie Collins 203-204
Jack Rosenthal 187
Jack Wild 31
James Bolam 90, 199
James Doran 293
James Fox 21, 94, 102
James Moffat 117
James Patrick 150
Jamie Foreman 254, 309
Jane Asher 21, 86
Jangles (1982) 267-270
Jason Durr 219
Jennifer Guy 198
Jennifer Landor 270
Jenny Agutter 62, 80, 84
Jenny Runacre 160, 224, 226, 228-229, 271
Jerry Dammers 314
Jess Conrad 64
Jesse Birdsall 257, 267
Jesus Christ Superstar 44, 56, 93, 199
Jim Hawkins 166
Jimmy Page 98, 102, 192
Jimmy Pursey 270, 274, 276
Jim Sheridan 121
Joan Collins 90, 203, 205
Joanna (1968) 62, 105
Joanna Lumley 37-38
Jody Latham 124
Joe Mansano 126
Joe McGann 310
Joe Strummer 223, 239, 241, 248,-251
Joe Strummer: The Future Is Unwritten (2007) 250
John Bird 37
John Cameron Mitchell 240-241
John Dalgleish 291
John Foxx 263
John Hewlett 202
John Hurt 49, 50, 234
John King 301
John Kingsley Read 281
John Lennon 14-15, 18, 39, 40, 44, 97, 171, 194
John Lydon 192, 230, 232, 237, 239, 247, 263
John Mackenzie 97, 151
John MacKenzie 118
John McEnery 50
Johnny Green 249
Johnny & the Self Abusers 152

John Peel 56, 240, 242
John Pilger 165
John Rowe Townsend 258
John Samson 237
John S Baird 304
John's Children 193, 202
John Sichel 244
John Tyndall 274, 280
John White 279
Jonathan Moore 270-271, 299-300, 305
Jonathan Pryce 261
Jonathan Rhys Meyers 194, 251
Jon Savage 202, 229
Jook 202
Jordan 220, 224-226, 228, 229
Joseph Stamp 254
Joseph & The Technicolour Dreamcoat 93
Joshua Whitehouse 215
Judy Geeson 15, 68, 85-86, 90
Judy Huxtable 68
Juicy Lucy 24-25, 71
Julia Gale 267
Julian Henriques 169
Julian Jarrold 264
Julian Jones 292
Julian Temple 235-236, 250
Julie Burchill 220
Juliet Mills 79

K

Karen Berlinski 244
Karl Howman 175
Karl Johnson 224, 226, 252-253, 260
Kate Beckinsale 290
Kathy Burke 249-251
Keep Your Eyes Down 246
Keith Allen 233
Keith Moon 202
Keith Richards 86, 92, 102, 263
Ken Loach 73, 76, 151, 277
Kenneth Colley 49, 197
Kenneth Cranham 52
Kennith Singh 280
Kes (1968) 171
Kevin McKidd 143, 148-149
Kevin Sampson 301
Kieran Hardcastle 319
Killing Time 252, 254
King Carnival (1973) 172
Kirk Brandon 237, 265
Kirsten Sheridan 250
Kylie Minogue 142

L

Landscape 269
Larry Hodges 292
Laura Fraser 144, 149
Laya Lewis 319
Led Zeppelin 98, 102
Lee Drysdale 238
Lee MacDonald 258
Legend of the Witches (1970) 100
Leigh Bowery 265
Lene Lovich 260
Lenora Crichlow 214
Leo Marks 81
Leon Vitali 91
Leslie North 199
Leslie Stewart 314
Let It Rock 192, 216-217
Let's Get Laid (1978) 207
Liberated Lady 269
Linda Marlowe 160
Lindsay Anderson 26, 28
Lindsay Kemp 193, 269
Lindsay Shonteff 63, 72
Linton Kwesi Johnson 170-172, 174, 282
Little Buddha (1993) 91
Little Malcolm & His Struggle Against the Eunuchs (1974) 48
Little Nell 224, 226
Live It Up (1963) 199
Lock, Stock & Two Smoking Barrels (1998) 302
London Calling 254
Looking For Langston (1987) 217
Lost (2005) 289
Lou Reed 22, 192-193, 195
Love Unlimited Orchestra 203
Loving Feeling (1968) 72
Lowri Ann Richards 269
Lucifer Rising (1972) 102
Lust For A Vampire (1971) 199
Lynda La Plante 245

M

Made (1972) 97
Madeleine Smith 21
Madonna 142, 238
Maggie Pinhorn 160
Maggie Stride 72
Magical Mystery Tour (1967) 173
Magnificence (1973) 51
Mahler (1972) 224
Malcolm McDowell 27-30, 104, 137, 139, 142
Malcolm McLaren 192, 220, 225, 230, 232, 234, 238-239, 247
Mamoun Hassan 173
Man Alive 67-68, 94-95, 111, 122, 127-130
Man Alive: The Jesus Trip (1971) 94
Man Alive: WHat's The Truth About Hells Angels and Skinheads (1969) 111
Mandy Perryment 206
Marc Bolan 98, 104, 192-194
Marcus Francis 258
Marcus Lipton 232
Margaret Matheson 238, 294, 296
Margaret Thatcher 46, 154, 185, 190, 229, 245-246, 258, 262, 266, 279, 297, 311, 315
Marianne Faithfull 86, 101, 102, 137
Mark Farmer 309
Mark Lester 31
Mark P 222, 223
Mark Warren 289
Mark Wingett 261
Marsha Hunt 104
Martin Compston 212
Martin Potter 85
Martin Stellman 172
Martin Tomlinson 240
Martin Webster 280
Mary Whitehouse 54, 99, 140-141, 205, 228
Massive Attack 186
Matthew Vaughan 302
Matumbi 174, 175
Max Romeo 125
McVicar (1980) 172
Melody (1971) 31
Mel Smith 256, 257
Menelik Shabazz 159, 180, 186
Message To Love (1997) 23
Michael Custance 314
Michael Deeks 253
Michael Feast 195, 206
Michael Kitchen 52, 104, 106, 114
Michael Klinger 65
Michael Powell 81
Michael Winner 186
Michele Breton 21, 102
Mick Farren 25, 42
Mick Jagger 16, 21, 39, 41, 53, 71, 86, 104, 137, 195, 207, 234
Mick Jones 192, 223, 247-248, 250, 263
Mick Norman 107
Midge Ure 198, 264-265
Mike Dupree 67
Mike Hodges 301
Mike Leigh 48, 299
Mike Reed 258
Minder 168, 189
Misty in Roots 170, 282
Mods and Rockers (1965) 70

Molly Dineen 182
Monica Ringwald 68
Mo Sesay 216, 218
Mott the Hoople 144, 192, 193, 250
Mud 197, 198, 202, 212
Mudhoney 195
Mumsy, Nanny, Sonny & Girly (1970) 44
Muriel Gray 302
Mustapha Matura 161

N

Nancy Spungen 68, 237
Natalie Ford 211
Nat Cohen 38, 76
Naveen Andrews 220-221
Neil Gaiman 240
Neil Pearson 294
Nellee Hooper 219
Nell Williams 250
Network (1976) 227
New Horizons: The Alternative Society (1971) 19
Nick Kent 239
Nick Love 305
Nick McCarty 244, 258
Nicky Bell 303
Nicole Kidman 240
Nic Roeg 21, 70, 137
Nigel Planer 14, 56
Nigel Williams 308-309
Nightmares in a Damaged Brain (1981) 66
Noddy Holder 196-197, 201-202
Norman Jay 217
Norman J Warren 62-63, 72
Norman Tebbit 310
Northern Soul: Keeping the Faith (2003) 215
Notting Hill 16, 18-19, 54, 100, 156, 159, 162, 164-165, 168,
    171, 183, 221, 252-253
Notting Hill (1999) 221

O

Obi Egbuna 77
Oi For England's Green & Pleasant Land (2018) 295
Oliver Lee 304
Oliver Tobias 203-204
Olivia Newton John 34
Omnibus 50, 172
Once Upon a Time In Wigan (2003) 208
Onnie McIntyre 72
Operation Julie (1985) 22
Oscar Riesel 205
Oswald Mosley 274
Our Daughter's Wedding 268

Our Friends In The North 45-46, 55, 123
Our Friends in the North (1996) 45
Our Live Experiment Is Worth More Than 3000 Text Books
    (1969) 32
Oz 20, 26, 53-57, 104

P

Paddy Considine 214
Pamela Franklin 92
Panorama 78, 129, 201
Passion of Remembrance (1987) 217
Patrick Drongoole 267
Patti Boulaye 205-206
Paul Anderson 305
Paul Burnley 127
Paul Cook 232, 238
Paul McCartney 53, 69, 72, 86, 262, 270
Paul McGann 295
Paul Nicholas 43, 93, 199-200, 205
Paul Simonon 239, 247
Paul Tickell 236
Peeping Tom (1960) 81
Penny Woolcock 308
Performance 16, 21, 70
Performance (1970) 21
Permissive (1970) 72
Perry Benson 255, 312, 317
Pete Cave 107
Pete Doherty 240
Pete Howitt 211
Peter Blake 137
Peter Buckman 57
Peter Collinson 89
Peter Cushing 90, 104
Peter Denyer 91, 198
Peter Firth 78-80
Peter Flannery 45, 123
Peter Hall 55
Peter Hooton 250, 302
Peter Hugo Daley 121, 261
Peter Kay 223
Peter Lee Wilson 238
Peter MacDougall 151
Peter McNamara 299, 312
Peter Mullen 149, 151
Peter Shaffer 78
Peter Walker 63, 78, 236
Pete Townshend 33, 40, 42, 44, 116
Phil Daniels 224, 245, 255, 257-258, 260-261, 298-299
Phil Davis 252, 253
Phil Redmond 245, 311
Pink Fairies 19, 20, 23, 25, 208
Pink Floyd 15, 23, 68-69, 98, 223, 288

Play For Today 60, 151, 161, 166, 168, 173, 181, 246, 259, 277, 309, 314
Playground 246
Poly Styrene 192, 264
Pool of London (1951) 159
Pork 193
Pretty Things 23, 33
Prince Buster 125, 160, 169, 314
Psychomania (1973) 107
Public Eye: The Fatted Calf (1975) 47
Pulp 195
Punk in London (1978) 224
Punk In London (1978) 248
Puppet On A Chain (1971) 108

Q

Quadrophenia 42, 172, 203, 224, 261, 276, 319
Quadrophenia (1979) 172
Quentin Crisp 264
Quentin Masters 204

R

Race Today 165, 170, 172, 218, 277
Radio Caroline 15, 197
Radiohead 91, 195
Rat Scabies 247
Ray Burdis 163, 245
Ray Gange 223, 247-248, 276
RD Laing 73-74, 76, 165
Reach for Glory (1962) 86
Reece Dinsdale 211
Reefer Madness 54, 61, 210
Rene Daalder 234
Rex Obano 180
Richard Allen 117, 127, 129-130, 201, 285
Richard Beckinsale 200, 256
Richard Dormer 241-242
Richard E Grant 142
Richard James Burgess 269
Richard Jobson 138, 143, 239, 270
Richard Lester 36, 69, 199
Richard Neville 20, 55-56
Richard O'Brien 225
Richard Platt 294
Richard Warwick 28, 36-37
Ricky Alleyne 121
Rikki Brown 146
Ringo Starr 49, 194
Rita Tushingham 89
Robert Bertrand 254
Robert Elms 129, 262
Robert Glenister 252, 254

Robert Lindsay 47-48, 199
Robert Pereno 269
Robert Stigwood 70, 93
Robin Asquith 64
Robin Hayter 295
Roddy Moreno 127
Rodney Bewes 49
Rod Stewart 41, 68, 204, 207
Roger Daltrey 41, 202
Roger Dean 223
Roger Eagle 208
Roger Ebert 79, 140, 197, 234, 238
Roger Michell 221
Romper Stomper 315
Romper Stomper (1992) 315
Rosalind Ayers 51
Rosemary's Baby (1968) 101
Roxy Music 192-193, 195, 204, 220, 240, 261, 264
Roy Battersby 277
Roy Boulting 81
Roy Harper 98
Roy Williams 190
Rumpole and the Alternative Society (1978) 21
Rupert Everett 238
Russ Meyer 234-235
Russ Winstanley 208
Rusty Egan 264, 269

S

Salman Rushdie 185, 221
Sammy Abu 168
Sam O'Shanker 246
Sam Palladio 249
Samuel Selvon 161, 163, 167
Sandy Lieberson 234
Sankofa Film and Video Collective 185
Sapphire (1959) 159
Sara Clee 46, 244
Satyricon (1969) 86
School for Sex (1969) 63
Screaming Lord Sutch 192, 197
Scum (1977) 168
Second City First 224
Secret Rites (1971) 100
Secret World (1969) 69
Seditionaries 225-226
Selfish Cunt 240
Sepultra 142
Sex Education, No. 1 (1971) 54
Sex Pistols 217, 235
Sham 69 274-276, 285, 287
Shane Briant 89
Shane Connaughton 121

Shane Meadows 314
Sharon Woodward 318
Sheila Chandra 284
Shoestring: I'm A Believer (1979) 94
Showaddywaddy 197, 199, 252
Sid Vicious 192, 224, 233, 235, 237, 246
Simon Brent 72
Simon Driver 246
Simon Gipps Kent 258
Simon Heaven 280
Simple Minds 152
Sinead O'Connor 184
Six Days of Justice: We'll Support You Evermore (1973) 121
SkinFlicker (1972) 52
Skinhead (2018) 128
Skinhead Farewell (1996) 117
Slaughter and the Dogs 192
Smack and Thistle (1991) 161
Snow Patrol 241
Softly Softly Task Force: Kick Off (1971) 119
Softly Softly Task Force: Sunday Sweet Sunday (1970) 122
Softly Softly Task Force: The Aggro Boy (1970) 119
Softly Softly Task Force: Trouble Maker (1973) 156
Soldier & Me (1974) 207
Something Else (1978-1982) 267
Songs of Praise 229
Soo Catwoman 220, 226
Sophie Okonedo 218
Southall Youth Movement 281, 286
South Park 142
Spaghetti House siege 156, 166-168
Spandau Ballet 207, 217, 266
Stanley Kubrick 28, 136, 138, 141-142, 291
Stanley Long 24, 25, 65, 70, 100
Stardust (1974) 31, 44, 173
Steel Pulse 170, 187
Stephanie Beacham 104
Stephen Graham 317, 318
Steve Jones 197, 201, 224, 233, 234, 236, 238, 247
Steven Mackintosh 221
Steve Strange 265
Still Killing Time (2006) 254
Stoneground 104
Straight On Til Morning (1972) 89
Stratford Johns 118, 199
Stuart MacKenzie 205
Sucker Punch (2010) 190
Sue Bond 62
Sue Lloyd 204
Sunawhar Ali 280
Sunshine On Brixton (1976) 252
Susan George 34, 89
Suzan Crowley 299

Suzanne Mercer 24, 70
Sydney Newman 75
Sylvestra Le Touzel 231
Symarip 124, 126
Symond Lawes 127

T

Take It Or Leave It (1981) 288
Tales Out of School (1985) 295
Tales Out Of School (1985) 291
Tales Out Of School (2005) 291
Ted Clisby 295
Teenage Fanclub 195
Terri Hooley 241
Territories (1985) 217
Terry Fitzpatrick 277
Terry Southern 137
That Kind of Girl (1963) 160, 204
That'll Be the Day (1973) 173
That'll Be The Day (1973) 199
The 4 Skins 285-286, 287
The 39 Steps (1978) 263
The Avengers 44, 69, 81
The Beatles 33, 39-40, 49, 51, 67, 69, 71, 91-93, 97, 101, 116, 137, 140, 195, 252
The Billion Dollar Bubble (1978) 259
The Black People's Day of Action 180-181
The Blitz 262, 264-265
The Boys 256
The Boys From The Blackstuff (1982) 246
The Boy With the Transistor Radio (1980) 246
The Breaking of Bumbo (1970) 36
The Business 285
The Canterbury Tales (1972) 224
The Cuban Heels 152
The Damned 192, 222, 240, 247, 256
The Dave Cash Radio Show (1972) 267
The Day the Earth Caught Fire (1961) 65
The Death of A Teddy Bear (1967) 82
The Destructors (1975) 258
The Devils (1971) 224
The English Programme 246
The Exploited 278, 297
The Family Way (1966) 82
The Farm 250
The Far Pavilions (1984) 284
The Football Factory 301
The Gentle Touch 157, 270, 292
The Girl Who Knew Too Much (1963) 62
The Goodies 205, 233
The Greyhound 216
The Hollywood Brats 202
The Hornsey Film (1970) 32

The Ipcress File (1965) 293
The Jewel In The Crown (1984) 284
The Knack (And How To Get It) (1965) 62
The Loneliness of the Long Distance Runner (1962) 73
The Mangrove Nine (1973) 171
The Mini Affair (1968) 70
The Naked Civil Servant (1975) 264
The Oxford Road Show 267
The Oz Trial 55
The Oz Trial (1972) 55
The Palestinian (1977) 277
The Power of the Witch: Real Or Imaginary (1971) 99
The Process Church of the Final Judgement 105
The Punk Rock Movie (1978) 224
The Ramones 202, 220
The Ravers (1967) 67
The Rose (1979) 259
The Rubettes 198
the Ruts 264
The Ruts 170, 264, 282
The Saliva Milkshake (1975) 52
The Satanic Rites of Dracula (1974) 106
These Dangerous Years (1957) 146
The Simpsons 142
The Slits 226
the Specials 263
The Specials 314
The Strange Report 92
The Strange Report: Murder Shrieks Out (1969) 92
The Stranglers 240, 260, 261
The Sweet 192, 200, 202
The Touchables (1968) 68
The Trials of Oz (1991) 56
The Twisted Wheel 208
The Undertones 242
The Vampire Lovers (1968) 199
The Wall (1982) 288
The Who 14, 40, 41, 42, 134, 169, 262, 276, 301
The Wife Swappers (1970) 24, 100
The Wild One (1953) 111, 140
The Yellow Teddybears (1963) 59
The Yes Girls (1971) 62
The Young Ones 14, 56, 263, 267-268
The Young Ones (1961) 109
This England 210
This Is Not An Aids Advert (1987) 217
This Week 61, 146, 158, 286
Thomas Turgoose 315
Thom Yorke 91, 195
Three Piece Suite (1977) 225
Three Smart Girls (1936) 200
Thunderclap Newman 40, 252
Thurston Moore 195

Tim Brooke Taylor 205, 233
Time and Judgement (1988) 187
Timothy Leary 14, 74, 91
Tim Roth 277-278, 296-297, 299
Tobi Bakare 181
Today 129, 171, 222
Todd Carty 311-312
Todd Haynes 194, 201
Tom Bell 89
Tom Brown's Schooldays (1971) 54
Tom Conti 197
Tom Courtenay 27, 73
Tommy (1975) 44
Tom & Viv (1984) 312
Tonite Lets All Make Love in London (1968) 15
Tony Britts 267
Tony Garnett 73, 75-76
Tony James 247
Tony Marchant 252, 254
Tony Palmer 210
Tony Parsons 136, 220, 248
Tony Tenser 65
Tony Visconti 193, 262
Toomorrow 33-37
Toomorrow (1970) 33
Top of the Pops 192-194, 198, 209-210, 224, 242, 269, 284
Topsy Jane 73
Toyah Wilcox 224, 226, 229, 257, 259, 264
Tracy Hyde 31
Trainspotting 51, 142, 149, 301
Trevor Griffiths 55, 181, 286, 293
Trevor Laird 175, 177
Trojan 125, 126
Tudor Gates 199
Twins of Evil (1971) 199
Twisted Nerve (1968) 81
Two A Penny (1967) 96

U

Ultravox 263, 269, 303, 304
United Coloured People's Association 77
Up The Junction (1965) 73, 151
Up The Junction (1968) 59

V

Valentine Nonyela 216, 218
Valerie Solanas 228
Val Guest 34, 65
Vanessa Howard 43
Van McCoy 203, 205
Vicky McClure 317-319
Victoria Gillick 60

Victor Romero Evans 175, 181
Vinyl (1965) 136
Vivienne Westwood 192, 225, 229, 240, 249, 258, 264

W

Wah Wah (2006) 142
Walter (1982) 296
Wayne County 193, 227, 247
Wet Paint Theatre Company 271
What Became Of Jack & Jill (1971) 43
Whatever Happened To Baby Jane (1962) 43
What The Papers Say 281
Where The Buffalo Roam (1966) 82
Whistle Down The Wind (1961) 109
Who Dares Wins (1982) 288
Wigan Casino 208, 210-212, 215
Windrush Square (2018) 184
Windsor Davies 120, 123
Wolfgang Buld 224
World of Skinhead (1994) 127
W Stephen Gilbert 277

Y

YOP 308-309
YTS 308, 313, 319

Z

Zandra Rhodes 234
Z Cars 118, 293
Zephan Amissah 291

www.ingramcontent.com/pod-product-compliance
Lightning Source LLC
Chambersburg PA
CBHW060418010526
44118CB00017B/2262